D1209505

WHO'S WHO
OF THE
COLORED RACE

WHO'S WHO

OF THE

COLORED RACE

A GENERAL BIOGRAPHICAL DICTIONARY OF
MEN AND WOMEN OF AFRICAN DESCENT

VOLUME ONE
1915

EDITED BY

FRANK LINCOLN MATHER

MEMENTO EDITION
HALF–CENTURY ANNIVERSARY OF
NEGRO FREEDOM IN U. S.
CHICAGO, 1915

Republished by Gale Research Company, Book Tower, Detroit, 1976

Library of Congress
Cataloging in Publication Data

Main entry under title:

Who's who of the colored race.

No More published.
Reprint of the ed. published in Chicago.
1. Negroes--Biography. I. Mather, Frank Lincoln.
E185.96.W6   1976   920'.0092'96073 79-178669
ISBN 0-8103-4247-2

CONTENTS

PREFACE

SUCCESS is a favorable or prosperous result or termination of anything attempted, and the claim of success on the part of its author in presenting the first edition of Who's Who of the Colored Race is justified by the fact that it appears at all. Quite a few people withhold their confidence; but doubt lies altogether in the mind and has no force, while success is the result of a firm and fixed purpose and a constant grind to the end. Therefore there is a certain pleasure in presenting the first volume with the confidence that the book merits approval and meets the needs of the American people in general.

BIOGRAPHY is properly a department of history, and this book records sufficient evidence of progress in the 50th year of freedom to prove that the Negro of America "has a place in the Sun"; therefore this work seems timely, and, it is believed, will be THE standard biographial dictionary of the colored people. No other biographical work extant, or extinct, has covered the field in such an authentic way, tho it is far from complete, of course.

NAMES which should have been included will be missed, but in practically all cases the omission is not in the least due to the lack of effort of those having the preparation of the book in hand. By mailed request hundreds who were regarded as eligible were solicited, in a respectful way, to furnish personal data. The majority of those whose names appear in this volume furnished the data freely and in a courteous manner, and to them thanks is hereby extended. A few gave information with evident reluctance and others showed complete indifference and let the requests for data go unnoticed, due largely to the fact that the work was not understood.

NOTWITHSTANDING the reasons named, which have prevented the inclusion of persons whose life-sketches it had been intended to give, the publication may make just claim to a greater degree of accuracy and a more dependable and authoritive record in regard to the leaders in business, professional, industrial, official and intellectual life of men and women of African descent than has ever been collected before.

BISHOPS, as well as names of all general officers of the various churches, will be found in this edition, tho some of the sketches are not as complete records of their lives as is desired. The attempt was also made to include all the officers, professors, instructors, principals and teachers of the leading educational institutions. Requests for data were sent to principals of all the colored high schools; extra effort was made to give full recognition to the Anna T. Jeanes Fund by mention of all the supervising industrial teachers in the various states, whose work

vii

is aided by that fund; the list is not complete, yet there is a creditable representation of the supervising industrial teachers.

THE JEWISH religion is represented by one subject in this volume. The only clergyman of the Movarian Church in the United States is mentioned herein, also the only Greek Orthodox Catholic colored priest in the world. There are three of the Roman Catholic priests, and a considerable number of persons of the Catholic faith, as well as clergymen and laymen of practically all denominations. The sketch of the only Negro silk manufacturer will be found in the book, one proctor in admiralty, one municipal judge, the King of Uganda, President of Liberia, legislators, city councilmen, and persons filling various offices and positions in city, county, state and nation. In the professions and different lines of trade the representation is quite general. If the reader will think of twenty persons of prominence throughout the country it is safe to say he will find more than three-fourths of them represented in this book; furthermore, it may be mentioned that, the now famous book—Who's Who in America—began with 827 pages in its first edition, with a field of 80,000,000 people, therefore this volume is certainly a fairly good showing for the first attempt to produce a biographical dictionary exclusively of colored people.

THE WAR in Europe made the collection of data from foreign countries almost impossible. Letters sent to Germany were all returned, tho the addresses had been furnished from responsible sources. For some time we abandoned all hope of any representation from Abroad, but it will be found that some interesting sketches appear. The number of sketches secured from Africa will suggest what may be looked for in future editions; it will be the aim to present sufficient information in the second volume to make a special section of foreign subjects.

TO INFORM those who may not be familiar with the book and its purposes, the following statement is presented. It aims to give a brief, crisp, personal sketch of men and women of African descent in all parts of the world who are most prominent in all branches of effort, also persons who are identified with work of every description which tends to the advancement of colored people. Some of these may not be particularly prominent, in their own eyes, even if others do so regard them; it should be understood that all "must creep before they walk," and it seems a duty to recognize those who are making an effort in creditable lines. The book tells the things every intelligent person wants to know about those who are making progress in every reputable walk in life—birthplace, age, parentage, education, degrees, position and achievements, politics, religion, societies, clubs, business, profession, occupation, marriage, children; in fact the chief features of each career without any puffery of eulogy, praise or criticism (except that a word intended for information is regarded as such).

FREE INSERTION of all sketches is the rule. Not a line in this book has been paid for. Not a single sketch can be paid for in future editions. Not even a subscription for a copy of the book is obligatory, tho the hope for orders from all sources is frankly admitted. When a person pays a price for inserting business of personal matter he naturally exacts that "copy" be followed to the letter. On the other hand, when money will not buy the space, the editor exercises his right to reduce the data to pure facts. Therefore the information this book possesses may be relied upon in its use for all purposes. Portraits are not admitted in these pages, principally because there is a suggestion of charge; in fact we have been offered pay for their insertion surely a score of times. Plain language can not too strongly emphasize the fact that there are no "trade secrets" used in the preparation of this work, and no "book agent tricks" connected with its sale. Merit alone counts; men and women making an effort for self improvement and the advancement of the colored people are entitled to sketches in the book without other consideration, and the book is sold strictly on its merit. Those who on first thought might wish to criticise the price per copy, will, on second thought, admit they know nothing of the labor and expense required to produce it. The printer may estimate the mechanical cost, but no author can estimate by his own works the time, labor and expense of producing this one. The fact that fifteen months were required to produce it will answer the critics.

TWENTIETH CENTURY BIOGRAPHY: Tho the term "biography" is modern, the kind of literature it represents is ancient. In the book of Genesis there are biographies, or at least memoirs, of Adam, Noah, Abraham, Isaac, Jacob, Joseph and others. Homer's "Odyssey" may be considered to be an extended biography of Ulyssus, limited, however, to the most interesting periods of his life—that of his wanderings. Tho the "Ilaid" may be loosely called a history of the Trojan war, yet, more accurately, it is a chapter from biography of Achilles, describing calamities brought upon the Greeks by the revenge which he took on Agamemnon for carrying off his female captive Briseis. The most elaborate ancient Greek biography was Plutrach's Parallel Lives, consisting of 45 memoirs of Greek, Roman and other celebrities; it was published about A.D. 80. In B.C. 44, Cornelius Nepos had sent forth a biographical work, his Vitoe Imperatorum, Lives of Commanders.

Biographical dictionaries (much like Who's Who of the Colored Race) date from the Eleucidarius Carminum et Historiarum (Holland, 1498). But the nineteenth century was, as the twentieth is and promises to be, a flourishing period for them. Among the best general dictionaries are the Biographie Universelle, ancienne et moderne (new ed., 45 vols., Paris, 1843-65); and the Nouvelle Biographie Generale (46 vols., Paris, 1852-77). One of the best works of the kind published in the United States is Lippincott's Pronouncing Biographical Dictionary, by Dr. Joseph Thomas, often re-edited; others include Appleton's Cyclopaedia of American Biography (6 vols., New York, 1887-89), a seventh volume appearing as a supplement, and Lamb's Biographical Dictionary of the United States.

For contemporary biography we have Men and Women of the Time, Who's Who (London); Who's Who in America (Chicago); Who's Who in New York (New York). These are revised annually or biennially. They contain only the biographies of living persons, tho reference is made to preceding volumes in the case of distinguished men and women who have died.

Aspiring to the high standard and a place in all public and private libraries beside the famous works mentioned above, Who's Who of the Colored Race asks the co-operation and support of men and women of African descent throughout the world.

SUCCEEDING GENERATIONS will regard the Negro of the nineteenth and twentieth centuries with similar honor and respect that descendents of the Pilgrim Fathers regard their ancestors. Even at this early date in the advancement of the colored people the Bustill Family Association exists in Philadelphia, and there are several sketches in this book in which the ancestry is mentioned. Coming generations will value accurate records of the Negro of today more than any other one thing that the men and women of the twentieth century can hand down to posterity. This fact should move every person to aid in making these records of progress complete by furnishing date for insertion in WHO'S WHO OF THE COLORED RACE.

Chicago, August 6, 1915.

————

HOW TO HELP

Additional names, suggestions for improvement of the work in future editions, changes in biographical data, notices of death, and announcements of changes of address as they occur, are invited. The counsels and cautions of critical friends of the work will doubtless aid in the future development of Who's Who of the Colored Race.—Editor.

ABBREVIATIONS

A.B. (also **B.A.**) Bachelor of Arts.
A.C.........Analytical Chemist.
Acad........Academy.
Adj.........Adjutant.
Agr.........Agriculture.
Agrl........Agricultural.
A.M. (also **M.A.**) Master of Arts.
A.M.E.......African Methodist Episcopal.
Appmt.......Appointment.
Apptd.......Appointed.
Arty........Artillery.
Assn........Association.
Asst........Assistant.
Atty........Attorney.
B.A. (also **A.B.**) Bachelor of Arts.
B.Agr.......Bachelor of Agriculture.
B.Chir......Bachelor of Surgery.
B.C.E.......Bachelor of Civil Engineering.
B.D.........Bachelor of Divinity.
B.F.A.......Bachelor of Fine Arts.
B.L. (also **Litt.B.**) Bachelor of Letters.
B.Pd. (or **Pd.B.**) Bachelor of Pedagogy.
B.S. (also **S.B.** or **Sc.B.**) Bachelor of Science.
Capt........Captain.
Cav.........Cavalry.
C.E.........Civil Engineer.
Ch..........Church.
Chem........Chemical.
Chmn........Chairman.
C.M.........Master of Surgery.
Co..........Company; county.
Col.........Colonel.
Coll........College.
Com.........Committee.
Comd........Commanded.
Comdr.......Commander.
Commd.......Commissioned.
Conf........Conference.
Congl.......Congregational.
Contr.......Contributor.
Conv........Convention.
Corpn.......Corporation.
Corr........Corresponding.
C.P.A.......Certified Public Accountant.
Ct..........Court.
D.Agr.......Doctor of Agriculture.
D.C.L.......Doctor of Civil Law.
D.D.........Doctor of Divinity.
D.D.S.......Doctor of Dental Surgery.
D.Eng.......Doctor of Engineering.
Dept........Department.
Dist........District.
D.Litt. (or **L.H.D.**) Doctor of Literature.
D.M.D.......Doctor of Mental Medicine.
D.Sc. (or **Sc.D.**) Doctor of Science.
D.V.S.......Doctor of Veterinary Surgery
Ed..........Educated.
Edn.........Education.
E.E. and **M.P.**, Envoy extraordinary and minister plenipotentiary.
Engr........Engineer.
Exam........Examination.
Exec........Executive.
Expn........Exposition.
Gen.........General.
Gov.........Governor.
Govt........Government.
Grad........Graduate.
Hist........Historical.
Hon.........Honorably; honorary.
Ho. of Rep., House of Representatives.
Hosp........Hospital.
Inf.........Infantry.
Ins.........Insurance.

Inst........Institute.
Instn.......Institution.
Instr.......Instructor.
K.T.........Knight Templar.
L.H.D.......Doctor of Literature.
Litt.B. (or **B.L.**) Doctor of Letters.
LL.B........Bachelor of Laws.
LL.D........Doctor of Laws.
Lieut.......Lieutenant.
M.A. (or **A.M.**) Master of Arts.
M.Agr.......Master of Agriculture.
Maj.........Major.
M.A.L.......Master of Ancient Literature
M.B.........Bachelor of Medicine.
M.D.........Doctor of Medicine.
M.E.........Mechanical Engineer.
M.M.Sc......Master of Mechanical Science
M.E.Ch......Methodist Episcopal.
Mfg.........Manufacturing.
Mfr.........Manufacturer.
Mgr.........Manager.
Mil.........Military.
M.L.........Master of Laws.
M.Pd........Master of Pedagogy.
M.S. (or **M.Sc.**) Master of Science.
Mus.B.......Bachelor of Music.
Mus.D. (or **Mus.Doc.**) Doctor of Music.
Pd.B. (or **B.Pd.**) Bachelor of Pedagogy.
Pd.D........Doctor of Pedagogy.
Pd.M........Master of Pedagogy.
P.E.........Protestant Episcopal.
Pharm.......Pharmaceutical.
Pharm.D.....Doctor of Pharmacy.
Pharm.M.....Master of Pharmacy.
Ph.B........Bachelor of Philosophy.
Ph.C........Pharmaceutical Chemist.
Ph.D........Doctor of Philosophy.
Ph.G........Graduate in Pharmacy.
Phys........Physician.
P.I.........Philippine Islands.
Prep........Preparatory.
Pres........President.
Presbyn.....Presbyterian.
Prin........Principal.
Prof........Professor.
Prof.Sc.....Professor of Science.
Propr.......Proprietor.
Pub.........Publisher; publishing.
Q.-M........Quartermaster.
Regt........Regiment.
Rep.........Republican; representative.
R.P.D.......Doctor of Political Science.
S.B. (also **B.S.**, **Sc.B.**) Bachelor of Science
Sc.D. (or **D.Sc.**) Doctor of Science.
Sec.........Secretary.
Sem.........Seminary.
Sergt.......Sergeant.
Soc.........Society.
S.S.........Sunday School.
S.S.B.......Social Science degree.
S.T.B.......Bachelor of Sacred Theology.
S.T.D.......Doctor of Sacred Theology.
S.T.L.......Licentiate in Sacred Theology.
Supt........Superintendent.
Surg........Surgical.
Tech........Technology; technical.
Th.D........Doctor of Theology.
Th.M........Master of Theology.
T.P.........Teacher of Principles.
Treas.......Treasurer.
Univ........University.
U.S.C.T.....U. S. Colored Troops.
U.S.V.......United States Volunteers.
Vol.........Volunteer; volume.
V.-P........Vice-President.

ABRAHAM LINCOLN
1809–1865

I do the very best I know how the very best I can; and I mean to keep doing so until the end. If the end brings me out all right, what is said against me won't amount to anything. If the end brings me out wrong, ten angels swearing I was right would make no difference.

EMANCIPATION PROCLAMATION

Now, therefore, I, ABRAHAM LINCOLN, President of the United States, by virtue of the power in me vested as Commander-in-Chief of the Army and Navy of the United States in time of actual armed rebellion against the authority and Government of the United States, and as a fit and necessary war measure for suppressing said rebellion, do, on this first day of January, in the year of our Lord one thousand eight hundred and sixty-three, and in accordance with my purpose so to do, publicly proclaimed for the full period of one hundred days from the day first above mentioned, order and designate as the States and parts of States, wherein the people thereof respectively are this day in rebellion against the United States, the following, to-wit:

"Arkansas, Texas, Louisiana (except the parishes of St. Bernard, Plaquemine, Jefferson, St. John, St. Charles, Ascension, Assumption, Terre Bonne, Lafourche, St. Mary, St. Martin, and Orleans, including the city of New Orleans) Mississippi, Alabama, Florida ,Georgia ,South Carolina, North Carolina, and Virginia (except the forty-eight countries designated as West Virginia, and also the counties of Berkley, Accomac, Northampton, Elizabeth City, York, Princess Anne, and Norfolk, including the cities of Norfolk and Portsmouth), and which excepted parts are, for the present, left precisely as if this proclamation were not issued.

"And by virtue of the power and for the purpose aforesaid, I do order and declare that all persons held as slaves within said designated States and parts of States, are and henceforward shall be free; and that the Executive Government of the United States, including the military and naval authorities thereof, will recognize and maintain the freedom of said persons.

"And I hereby enjoin upon the people so declared to be free, to abstain from all violence, unless in necessary self-defense; and I recommend to them that, in all cases when allowed, they labor faithfully for reasonable wages.

"And I further declare and make known that such persons, of suitable conditions, will be received into the armed service of the United States to garrison forts, positions, stations, and other places, and to man vessels of all sorts in said service.

"And upon this act, sincerely believed to be an act of justice, warranted by the Constitution upon military necessity, I invoke the considerate judgment of mankind, and the gracious favor of Almighty God.

"In testimony whereof, I have hereunto set my name and caused the seal of the United States to be affixed.

"Done at the City of Washington, this 1st day of January, in the year of our Lord, 1863, and of the independence of the United States the 87th.

"By the President: ABRAHAM LINCOLN.

"WILLIAM H. SEWARD, Secretary of State."

13th AMENDMENT TO CONSTITUTION

Sec. 1. Neither slavery nor involuntary servitude, except as a punishment for crime whereof the party shall have been duly convicted, shall exist within the United States, or any place subject to their jurisdiction.

Sec. 2. Congress shall have power to enforce this article by appropriate legislation.

Adopted December 18, 1865.

NATIONAL
Half-Century Anniversary of Negro Freedom Exhibition and The Lincoln Jubilee

Chicago, Illinois, Aug. 22 to Sept. 16, 1915
In Charge of the Illinois Commission.

[Appointed by Governor Edward F. Dunne, July 1st, 1913, to arrange Half Century Anniversary of Negro Freedom, under Act passed by 48th General Assembly.]

OFFICERS

President Ex-Officio—Hon. Edward F. Dunne, Governor of Illinois (W)

Rt. Rev. Samuel Fallows, D.D., LL.D., President (W)

Hon. John Daily, V.-President (W) Maj. Geo. W. Ford, Treasurer (C)

Rev. A. J. Carey, Ph. D., D.D. (C) Hon. W. Duff Piercy (W)

Hon. R. R. Jackson (C) Hon. Medill McCormick (W)

Dr. May Fitzbutler Waring, M.D.(C) Thomas Wallace Swann, Sec'y. (C)

(The white and colored members are shown by the W and C affixed to names).

HOUSE BILL No. 919

A BILL.

For an Act providing for an exhibition and celebration to commemorate the fiftieth anniversary of the emancipation of the Negro, creating a commission to conduct same and making an appropriation therefor.

Section 1. Be it enacted by the People of the State of Illinois, represented in the General Assembly: That there is hereby created a commission to consist of the Governor and eight persons, residents of the State of Illinois, two of whom shall be members of the Senate and two of the House of Representatives in the State of Illinois, all of whom shall be appointed by the Governor, to arrange for and conduct during the year 1915 at a place to be selected by said commission, an exhibition and celebration to commemorate the fiftieth anniversary of the freeing of the Negro from slavery. Such exhibition and celebration shall be so conducted as to show the industrial, educational and religious progress of the Negro inhabitants of this commonwealth. The commission shall serve without compensation, but shall be allowed such expenses for traveling, clerical help, stenographers and necessary employees as shall be actually and necessarily incurred in the performance of its duty: Provided however, that the secretary of said commission, who shall be elected by said commission, and who may or may not be a member of said commission, shall receive such reasonable compensation as shall be determined upon and fixed by said commission. Said commission shall have full power and authority to collect, maintain and properly house said exhibit, and pay the expenses thereof.

Sec. 2. To carry out the purposes of this Act the sum of twenty-five thousand dollars, or so much thereof as may be necessary, is hereby appropriated. . . All payments shall be made on warrants of the Auditor of Public Accounts on vouchers of the commission approved by him.

Sec. 3. As soon after the organization of the commission, notice shall be filed with the State Treasurer and State Auditor of Public Accounts, of the election of the officers of said commission who from time to time, shall be authorized through the president and secretary of said commission, to draw warrants on the State Auditor of Public Accounts for such salaries or expenses incurred by the State Commission. such warrants, however, to be subject to approval of the Governor of the State of Illinois, and the Treasurer of the State of Illinois is hereby directed and empowered to pay the same.

Sec. 4. The Commission shall annually make a report to the Governor, and within 60 days after the close of its exhibition, the commission shall make a complete report and statement of all its doings, which shall include all exhibits and representations made, and the awards made on such exhibits, if any, and such other matters as the commission may deem of value to the State of Illinois, together with a list of all receipts and disbursements, with complete vouchers therefor. The commission shall keep a strict account of its receipts and disbursements.

Sec. 5. The commission shall in no manner create or incur any indebtedness or obligation in behalf of the State of Illinois in excess of any appropriation herein made.

Approved June 27, 1913.   Edward F. Dunne, Governor.

HOUSE BILL No. 132

Passed by House, June 10, 1915   Passed by Senate June 18, 1915

"That the sum of twenty-five thousand ($25,000) dollars be and hereby is appropriated under the terms of this Act to be expended as herein provided by the commission authorized and appointed under the Act entitled, "An Act providing for an exhibition and celebration to commemorate the fiftieth anniversary of the emancipation o fthe Negro, creating a commission to conduct same, and making an appropriation therefor," approved June 27, 1913.

Sec. 2. "Only so much of the said appropriation of $25,000 to the Negro Emancipation Celebration Commission shall be paid from the State treasury as shall equal the sum raised by subscriptions, leases, concessions and from other sources, and paid in cash to the treasurer of the commission by said commission up to August 15, 1915, and the question as to the amount so raised shall be determined and certified by the Governor. And the commission shall in no manner create or incur an indebtedness or obligation on behalf of the State of Illinois, nor expend any fund of the State other than in the manner provided herein."

Approved June 30, 1915.   Edward F. Dunne, Governor.

PERCENTAGE NEGRO IN TOTAL POPULATION, BY STATES: 1910.

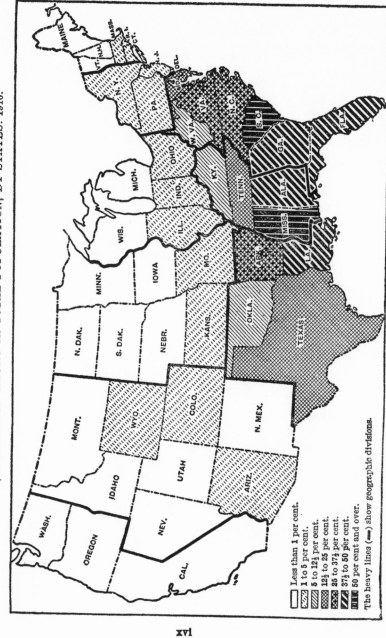

Less than 1 per cent.
1 to 5 per cent.
5 to 12½ per cent.
12½ to 25 per cent.
25 to 37½ per cent.
37½ to 50 per cent.
50 per cent and over.

The heavy lines (━) show geographic divisions.

STATISTICS OF NEGRO POPULATION

(United States Census, 1910)

	Total	Urban	Rural	Black	Mulatto
UNITED STATES	9,827,763	2,689,229	7,138,534	7,777,077	2,050,686
GEOGRAPHIC DIVISIONS:					
New England	66,306	60,877	5,429	44,156	22,150
Middle Atlantic	417,870	339,246	78,624	335,901	81,969
East North Central	300,836	230,542	70,294	201,027	99,809
West North Central	242,662	164,301	78,361	173,031	69,631
South Atlantic	4,112,488	909,520	3,202,968	3,256,669	855,819
East South Central	2,652,513	509,097	2,143,416	2,145,458	507,055
West South Central	1,984,426	435,838	1,548,588	1,586,440	397,986
Mountain	21,467	15,446	6,021	15,332	6,135
Pacific	29,195	24,362	4,833	19,063	10,132
NEW ENGLAND:					
Maine	1,363	924	439	737	626
New Hampshire	564	356	208	356	208
Vermont	1,621	1,341	280	1,185	436
Massachusetts	38,055	35,243	2,812	24,100	13,955
Rhode Island	9,529	9,055	474	6,350	3,179
Connecticut	15,174	13,958	1,216	11,428	3,746
MIDDLE ATLANTIC:					
New York	134,191	117,486	16,705	103,583	30,608
New Jersey	89,760	65,427	24,333	75,533	14,207
Pennsylvania	193,919	156,333	37,586	156,765	37,154
EAST NORTH CENTRAL:					
Ohio	111,452	82,282	29,170	72,203	39,249
Indiana	60,320	48,425	11,895	45,767	14,553
Illinois	109,049	85,538	23,511	72,221	36,828
Michigan	17,115	12,156	4,959	9,079	8,036
Wisconsin	2,900	2,141	759	1,757	1,143
WEST NORTH CENTRAL:					
Minnesota	7,084	6,518	566	4,468	2,616
Iowa	14,973	9,786	5,187	11,329	3,644
Missouri	157,452	104,462	52,990	112,762	44,690
North Dakota	617	306	311	460	157
South Dakota	817	412	405	521	296
Nebraska	7,689	6,621	1,068	5,602	2,087
Kansas	54,030	36,196	17,834	37,889	16,141
SOUTH ATLANTIC:					
Delaware	31,181	11,157	20,024	27,475	3,706
Maryland	232,250	99,230	133,020	189,098	43,152
District of Columbia	94,446	94,446	....	61,494	32,952
Virginia	671,096	158,218	512,878	448,186	222,910
West Virginia	64,173	15,380	48,793	43,294	20,879
North Carolina	697,843	115,975	581,868	533,720	144,123
South Carolina	835,843	101,702	734,141	701,462	134,381
Georgia	1,176,987	224,826	952,161	972,782	204,205
Florida	308,669	88,586	220,083	259,158	49,511
EAST SOUTH CENTRAL:					
Kentucky	261,656	106,631	155,025	195,713	65,943
Tennessee	473,088	150,506	322,582	354,391	118,697
Alabama	908,282	156,603	751,679	756,872	151,410
Mississippi	1,009,487	95,357	914,130	838,482	171,005
WEST SOUTH CENTRAL:					
Arkansas	442,891	59,147	383,744	361,520	81,371
Louisiana	713,874	160,845	533,029	561,297	152,577
Oklahoma	137,612	36,982	100,630	98,269	39,343
Texas	690,049	178,864	511,185	565,354	124,695
MOUNTAIN:					
Montana	1,834	1,455	379	1,223	611
Idaho	651	426	225	425	226
Wyoming	2,235	1,041	1,194	1,942	293
Colorado	11,453	9,359	2,094	7,815	3,638
New Mexico	1,628	795	833	1,189	439
Arizona	2,009	1,310	699	1,561	448
Utah	1,144	959	185	854	290
Nevada	513	101	412	323	190
PACIFIC:					
Washington	6,058	4,699	1,359	4,218	1,840
Oregon	1,492	1,264	228	1,058	434
California	21,645	18,399	3,246	13,787	7,858

POPULATION IN CITIES HAVING OVER 5,000 NEGROES

(United States Census, 1910)

City	Total popu'l'n	Negro popu'l'n
ALABAMA		
Bessemer	10,864	6,210
Birmingham	132,685	52,305
Mobile	51,521	22,763
Montgomery	38,136	19,322
Selma	13,649	7,863
ARKANSAS		
Helena	8,772	5,596
Little Rock	45,941	14,539
Pine Bluff	15,102	6,124
Texarkana	5,655	2,101
CALIFORNIA		
Los Angeles	319,198	7,599
COLORADO		
Denver	213,381	5,426
DELAWARE		
Wilmington	87,411	9,081
DIST. COLUMBIA		
Washington	331,069	94,446
FLORIDA		
Jacksonville	57,699	29,293
Key West	19,945	5,515
Pensacola	22,982	10,214
Tampa	37,782	8,951
GEORGIA		
Athens	14,913	6,316
Atlanta	154,839	51,902
Augusta	41,040	18,344
Brunswick	10,182	5,567
Columbus	20,554	7,644
Macon	40,665	18,150
Savannah	65,064	33,246
Waycross	14,485	6,729
ILLINOIS		
Cairo	14,548	5,434
Chicago	2,185,283	44,103
East St. Louis	58,547	5,882
INDIANA		
Evansville	69,647	6,266
Indianapolis	233,650	21,816
KANSAS		
Kansas City	82,331	9,286
KENTUCKY		
Lexington	35,099	11,011
Louisville	223,928	40,522
Paducah	22,760	6,047
LOUISIANA		
Alexandria	11,213	5,854
Baton Rouge	14,897	7,899
Monroe	10,209	5,320
New Orleans	339,075	89,262
Shreveport	28,015	13,896
MARYLAND		
Baltimore	558,485	84,749
MASSACHUSETTS		
Boston	670,585	13,564
MICHIGAN		
Detroit	465,766	5,741
MISSISSIPPI		
Greenville	9,610	6,010
Jackson	21,262	10,554
Meridian	23,285	9,321
Natchez	11,791	6,700
Vicksburg	20,814	12,053
MISSOURI		
Kansas City	248,381	23,566
St. Louis	687,029	43,960
NEW JERSEY		
Atlantic City	46,150	9,834
Camden	94,538	6,076
Jersey City	267,779	5,960
Newark	347,469	9,475
NEW YORK		
New York	4,766,883	91,709
Manhattan Borough	2,331,542	60,534
Bronx Borough	430,980	4,117
Brooklyn Borough	1,634,351	22,708
Queens Borough	284,041	3,198
Richmond Borough	85,969	1,152
N. CAROLINA		
Asheville	18,762	5,359
Charlotte	34,014	11,752
Durham	18,241	6,869
Greensboro	15,895	5,710
Newbern	9,961	5,649
Raleigh	19,218	7,372
Wilmington	25,748	12,107
Winston	17,167	7,828
OHIO		
Cincinnati	363,591	19,637
Cleveland	560,663	8,448
Columbus	181,511	12,739
OKLAHOMA		
Muskogee	25,278	7,831
Oklahoma City	64,205	6,546
PENNSYLVANIA		
Philadelphia	1,549,008	84,459
Pittsburgh	533,905	25,623
RHODE ISLAND		
Providence	224,326	5,316
S. CAROLINA		
Charleston	58,833	31,056
Columbia	26,319	11,546
Greenville	15,741	6,319
Spartanburg	17,517	6,873
TENNESSEE		
Chattanooga	44,604	17,942
Jackson	15,779	5,719
Knoxville	36,346	7,638
Memphis	131,105	52,441
Nashville	110,364	36,523
TEXAS		
Austin	29,860	7,478
Beaumont	20,640	6,896
Dallas	92,104	18,024
Fort Worth	73,312	13,280
Galveston	36,981	8,036
Houston	78,800	23,929
San Antonio	96,614	10,716
Texarkana	9,790	3,218
Waco	26,425	6,067
VIRGINIA		
Danville	19,020	6,207
Lynchburg	29,494	9,466
Newport News	20,205	7,259
Norfolk	67,452	25,039
Petersburg	24,127	11,014
Portsmouth	33,190	11,617
Richmond	127,628	46,733
Roanoke	34,874	7,924

MARITAL CONDITION.

The United States census for 1910 shows that the Negro population 15 years of age and over, 64 per cent of the males and 73.1 per cent of the females had married. The percentage is larger for females than for males because females marry at a younger age. The fact that the percentage who have married is larger for the Negroes than for either of those termed by the census bureau as "the two classes of native whites" is likewise to be explained as indicating that in general Negroes marry at a younger age than whites.

The total difference is not so great, however, as statistics show that of the total population in the United States 60.8 per cent of the males and 70 per cent of the females had married, while 64. per cent of the males (Negroes) and 73.1 of the females had married.

DIVORCED.

The number of divorced persons reported by the census necessarily falls short of the number of persons who have been divorced, since many divorced persons have remarried, and the census reports simply the marital condition of the population at the date of the enumeration. Moreover, it is practically certain that census returns as to the number divorced persons not remarried are below the true total, some divorced persons having reported themselves as single, some as married, and some as widowed. The number of Negro males reported as divorced was 20,146, female 33,-286. The proportion is 0.7 per cent for the males and 1.1 per cent for the females, both of these percentages being higher than the corresponding ones for any other classes of the population, the differences being pronounced in case of the females. The reports show that of the males of all classes, 0.5 per cent were divorced, females 0.6 per cent. It should be kept in mind in this connection that a greater proportion of divorced persons is a natural result of earlier marriage on the part of the Negroes.

SCHOOL ATTENDANCE.

There were 1,670,650 Negroes reported as attending school in the school year 1909-10, this number forming 9.3 per cent of the total number of persons attending school in the United States. The census tables give a comparison of the percentages attending school, for the Negroes and the native whites, by age groups, and show that the proportion is lower for the Negroes in every group. The difference appears to be most pronounced in the youngest group, 6 to 9 years, and is less in the age groups 10 to 14, and 15 to 17. The proportion also shows that more Negro females than males in each age group were attending school.

OWNERSHIP OF HOMES.

The aggregate number of all homes occupied by Negro families in the Southern states in 1910 was 1,917,391, of which 430,449, or 22.4 per cent, were reported as owned, including 314,340 reported as owned free from incumbrance, the owned-free homes constituting 16.4 per cent of all homes. The 98,987 encumbered homes formed 23 per cent of the owned homes.

AGRICULTURE.

There were 893,370 Negro farm operators in 1910, and 5,440,619 white farm operators, the Negro operators forming 14 per cent of the total number, a considerable greater proportion than the proportion of the Negro population to the total population of the United States which was 10.7 per cent.

The total acreage of farms operated by Negroes was 42,279,510 in 1910, the average per farm being 47.3 acres, as compared with an average of 153 for the farms operated by whites. The average improved acreage of Negro farms was 31.2, as compared with 82.6 for farms operated by whites.

The total value of farm prpoerty operated by Negroes in 1910 was $1,-141,792,526; in 1900 the same item was $499,941,234, so that there was an increase of 128.4 per cent during the decade, while the farm property operated by whites increased 99.6 per cent.

The value of implements and machinery on farms operated by Negroes increased 81.2 per cent during the 10 years 1900-10, the value of live stock increased 117.7 per cent, the value of buildings 131.6 per cent, and that of land 133.2 per cent.

The difference in the rate of growth between farms operated by Negroes and by whites is greatest when value of live stock is considered, the rate of increase being only 58.6 per cent on farms operated by whites, as compared with 117.7 per cent on those operated by Negroes.

The average value of farms operated by Negroes in 1910 was $1,280.75, as compared with an average of $669.52 for 1900, and of $299.21 for farms operated by whites in 1910; the average value of farm property per acre was $27.01 on farms operated by Negroes in 1910, as compared with $13.08 for 1900, and $47.72 for farms operated by whites in 1910.

Three-fourths of the Negro farmers in 1910 were tenants and one-fourth owners, the number of managers being small. The proportion of owners decreased slightly and that of tenants increased slightly between 1900 and 1910. Among whites about two-thirds of the farms are operated by owners.

It occurs that the census reports contain the term "colored" which includes, besides Negroes, Indians, Chinese, and Japanese, but of the total of 678,118 farms operated by colored tenants, 672,964, or 99.2 per cent, were operated by Negro tenants, and therefore the figures for colored tenants approximate closely to those for Negro tenants alone.

RELIGIOUS BODIES.

The last report of Negro churches was a special census of religious bodies in 1906 based upon returns received direct from the local organizations. While the report shows 36,770 organizations consisting in whole or in part of Negro organizations, it is deemed best to confine this to Negro organizations exclusively. The denominations consisting exclusively of Negro organizations numbered 31,393; the number of communicants or members, 3,207,307; church edifices, 30,-053; value of church property, $44,-473,049. The Baptists (National Baptist Convention) led with 18,534 bodies, 2,261,607 members, 17,913 edifies, and value of church property at $24,437,272; the African Methodist Episcopal Church second with 6,647 bodies, 494,777 members, 6538 edifices, property value, $11,303,489. There were 2,381 bodies of the Colored Methodist Episcopal Chrch, 172,996 members, 2,327 edifices, property value, $3,017,849. African Methodist Episcopal Zion Church had 2,204 bodies, 184,542 members, 2,131 edifices, property value, $4,833,207. Colored Cumberland Presbyterian Church 196 bodies, 18,066 members, 195 edifices, and property valued at $203,778. There were 3,750 Negro organizations in the Methodist Episcopal Church, 156 Congregationalists, 198 in Protestant Episcopal Church, 38 Reformed Episcopal Church, 36 organizations in the Roman Catholic Church with 38,235 members, and 2 bodies in the Moravian Church (Unitas Fratrium).

Only brief mention of the churches is given here because more detailed reports will be found in the Negro Year Book.

OCCUPATIONS.

Of the total number of 7,317,922 Negroes 10 years of age and over enumerated at the 13th ensus, 5,192,-535, or 71 per cent, were reported as gainfully employed. As they are identified with practically every line of industry, trade and profession, much of which is understood and known to the general public, we will simply mention some of the more important ones, and those in special lines.

Agriculture, Forestry, and
   Animal Husbandry (total)..2,893,380
Extraction of Minerals 62,129
    Among these: Managers.   17

Officials	3	Lighthouse keepers	36
Operators	126	Professional Service (Total)..	67,245
Manufacturing and Mechan-		Actors	1,279
ical Industries (Total)	631,421	Architects	59
Goldsmiths	37	Artists and Sculptors....	
Jewelers (factory)	19	Authors	27
Watchmakers	101	Editors and reporters....	220
Loom Fixers	8	Chemists, etc.	123
Manufacturers	1,727	Civil Engineers	217
Officials	44	Mining Engineers	20
Transportation (Total)	255,969	Clergymen	17,495
Officials: Steam Railroads	37	College (pres. and prof.)	242
Street Railroad	2	Dentists	478
Tel. and Telephone	5	Designers	30
Trade (Total)	119,491	Draftsmen	47
Bankers and officials	135	Inventors	19
Loan Brokers	76	Lawyers	798
Pawnbrokers	11	Musicians and teachers..	5,606
Stockbrokers	36	Photographers	404
Auctioneers	14	Physicians, Surgeons	3,077
Public Service (Total)	22,282	School Teachers	29,432
Detectives	72	Trained Nurses	2,433
Marshalls, constables ...	121	Veterinary Surgeons	122
Life-savers	12	Theatrical Owners	93

GREEK-LETTER FRATERNITIES.

Societies of students are found in nearly all the colleges and universities in the United States. In general they are secret in character; but this secrecy is largely nominal, consisting chiefly of extreme care in protecting their constitutions, mottoes, and grips from outside knowledge and in holding secret meetings. Aside from this they do not cultivate mystery in their methods of work.

The first Greek-letter society, Phi Beta Kappa, was organized at the College of William and Mary in England, 1776. The Yale chapter was established in 1780 and that of Harvard, 1781. In 1787 these two chapters united to found a chapter at Dartmouth College.

Quite a number of colored men are members of chapters of the older American universities. The first society organized in a colored college, however, is said to be Alpha Phi Alpha. The Boule fraternity seems to have been adopted from the ancient Greece advisory council. The boule

of the Homemic times was composed of princes and leading men and was purely a consultive body, and is traced to an age of more than 500 years B.C. More complete information will be collected for the second volume of Who's Who of the Colored Race, but at this time it was simply intended to name the following fraternities most often mentioned in the sketches in this volume.

Alpha Phi Alpha.
Alpha Zeta.
Boule, The
Chi Delta Mu.
Chi Delta Nu.
Delta Eta Sigma.
Delta Sigma Rho.
Kappa Alpha Nu.
Kappa Eta Chi Kappa.
Phi Beta Kappa.
Phi Psi.
Sigma Chi.
Sigma Pi Phi.
Tau Delta Sigma.
(Local Society)
Skull and Dagger,
(Univ. of So. Calif.)

NATIONAL ORGANIZATIONS

(Educational)

The names of these organizations may be found in some of the sketches occasionally without the word Negro attached, the short method being used in the belief that this explanation would make it commonly understood.

The American Negro Academy.

The American Negro Historical Society.

National Association of Teachers' in Colored Schools.

Negro National Education Congress.

Association of Secondary and Industrial Schools.

The Negro Society for Historical Research.

(For Economic Advancement)

National Negro Business League.

National Negro Bankers' Assn.

National Association of Funeral Directors.

National Marine Cooks', Stewards', Head and Side Waiters' Assn.

National Alliance of Postal Employes.

(For Professional Advancement)

National Medical Assn.

National Association of Colored Graduate Nurses.

National Negro Bar Assn.

National Negro Press Assn.

Western Negro Press Assn.

National Association of Colored Musical and Art Clubs.

(For Political Advancement)

National Independent Equal Rights League.

The National Civil Rights Protection Assn.

(In the Interest of Women)

National Asociation of Colored Women.

National League for the Protection of Colored Women.

(For the General Advancement of Negroes)

National Sentiment Moulding Bureau.

National Association for the Advancement of the Colored People.

(Branches in all important cities)

Committee of Twelve for the Advancement of the Interests of the Negro.

(For Improving Social Conditions)

National League on Urban Conditions Among Negroes.

Social Settlements for Negroes.

For improving social conditions among Negroes, social settlements exist in various cities, and a few rural districts, including those under various Woman's Federations, Church Missions, Day Nurseries, and Music Settlements, the address of these will be furnished upon request addressed to the editor, return postage to be enclosed, always.

NEGRO YEAR BOOK.

An annual encyclopedia of the Negro is published at Tuskegee Institute which is planned to meet the demand for accurate and concise information concerning the history and progress of the Negro race. It is based to a large extent on the inquiries that have come to the Tuskegee Institute and turned over to Monroe N. Work, the author and in charge the division of records and research. It is a record of current events, a directory of persons and a bibliographical guide to the literature of the subjects discussed. The book has been enlarged each year, and in addition to its interest to the general reader, it is adapted for use in schools of every description. Sold at a very low price. Address: The Negro Year Book Publishing Co., Tuskegee Institute, Ala.

FRATERNAL ORGANIZATIONS

In this volume we have given the short name of all organizations under this class, always, such as Mason; member Odd Fellows, Knights of Pythias, etc., yet it should be made plain that these organizations usually bear names that distinguish them from the white organizations with names almost similar. There are instances where persons have joined the Masons in foreign countries, and there are sketches of a few persons who are members of the Independent Order of Odd Fellows, but the membership in white organizations is always plainly stated; otherwise they belong to the colored fraternities.

Masonic Bodies.

Grand United Order of Odd Fellows.

Knights of Pythias of Europe, Asia, Africa, North and South America.

Knights of Pythias (Eastern and Western Hemisphere).

Improved Benevolent and Protective Order of Elks.

National Ideal Benefit Assn.

United Order of True Reformers.

Grand United Order of Galilean Fishermen.

United Brothers of Friendship and Sisters of the Mysterious Ten.

Grand United Order of Wise Men and Women.

United Order of Good Shepherds.

Grand United Order of Tents of the J. R. Giddings and Jollifee Union.

Independent Benevolent Order.

National Order of Mosaic Templars of America.

Knights and Daughters of Tabor.

Independent Order of St. Luke.

Grand United Order of Brothers and Sisters and Daughters of Moses.

Grand United Order Sons and Daughters of Peace.

Royal Circle of Friends of the World.

General Grand United Order of Brothers and Sisters of Love and Charity.

NOTICE TO SUBSCRIBERS

This work will be thoroughly revised, brought down, and issued biennially. The second volume, however, will appear as soon as conditions warrant.

Corrections and additional information respectfully invited from those whose names appear in this volume, to aid in their perfection in Volume 2.

New material will be prepared and published in "Preliminary Issues" to the second volume, each neatly bound, and mailed to old and new subscribers without extra cost to them.

New names to aid in enlarging the work are respectfully invited, and persons who fail to receive the data blank are urged to make request for copies. Aid from all sources will be appreciated.

PUBLIC HIGH SCHOOLS (Negro)

Furnished from the United States Bureau of Education, but is not given as a complete list. For a complete list of all educational institutions, except high schools, see the Negro Year Book.

ALABAMA:

Industrial High School, Birmingham
New Canaan High School, Camp Hill.
Colored High School, Decatur.
Colored High School, Huntsville.
Colored Graded School, Phoenix.
Colored High School, Tuscaloosa.

ARKANSAS:

Langston High School, Hot Springs.
M. W. Gibbs High School, Little Rock.
Missouri Street High School, Pine Bluff.

DELAWARE:

Howard High School, Wilmington.

DISTRICT OF COLUMBIA:

Armstrong Manual Training School, Washington.
M Street High School, Washington.

FLORIDA:

Colored High School, Fernandina.
Union Academy, Gainesville.
Colored High School, Green Cove.
Stanton High School, Jacksonville.
Washington Graded and High School, Miami.
Howard Academy, Ocala.
Lincoln High School, Tallahassee.

GEORGIA:

North Georgia Industrial High School, Atlanta.
Colored High School, Elberton.
Burney Street High School, Madison.
Eddy High School, Milledgeville.
Colored High School, Moultrie.
Colored High School, Rome.
Clay Street High School, Thomasville.

ILLINOIS:

Sumner High School, Cairo.
Colored School, DuQuoin.
Lincoln High School, E. St. Louis.
Dunbar High School, Metropolis.
Lovejoy High School, Mound City.

INDIANA:

Clark Street High School, Evansville.
Broadway High School, Madison.
Booker T. Washington High School, Mount Vernon.
Scribner High School, New Albany.
Lincoln High School, Princeton.
Colored High School, Vincennes.

KANSAS:

Sumner High School, Kansas City.

KENTUCKY:

State Street High School, Bowling Green.
Clinton Street High School, Frankfort.
Colored High School, Hopkinsville.
Central High School, Louisville.
Colored Graded School, Murray.
Western High School, Owensboro.
Lincoln High School, Paducah.
Western High School, Paris.
Colored High School, Richmond.

LOUISIANA:

Southern University and A. and M.
Colored High School, New Orleans.

MARYLAND:

Colored High School, Baltimore.

MISSISSIPPI:

Union Academy, Columbus.
Colored Graded School, Grenada.
Graded and High School No. 2, Macon.
Welchsler Graded School, Meridian.
Union High School, Natchez.
Colored High School, Port Gibson.

MISSOURI:

Sumner High School, Boonville.
Washington High School, Bowling Green.
Garrison High School, Chillicothe.
North High School, Fulton.
Evans High School, Glasgow.
Douglass High School, Hannibal.
Lincoln High School, Kansas City.
Lincoln High School, Louisiana.
Dumas High School, Macon.
Lincoln High School, Moberly.
Washington High School, Plattsville.
Sumner High School, St. Louis.
Lincoln High School, Springfield.

NORTH CAROLINA:

Colored Graded School, Ashboro.

OHIO:

Lincoln High School, Gallipolis.

OKLAHOMA:

Logan County High School, Guthrie.
Douglass, High School, Kingfisher.
Manual Training High School, Muskogee:
Douglass High School, Oklahoma City.
Dunbar High School, Okmulgee.

PENNSYLVANIA:

Lincoln High School, Carlisle.

SOUTH CAROLINA:

Colored High School, Anderson.
Colored High School, Central.
Howard High School, Columbus.
Howard High School, Georgetown.
Colored Graded School, Greenwood.
Colored High School, Lancaster.
McBeth Street High School, Union.

TENNESSEE:

Colored High School, Brownville.
Colored High School, Clarksville.
Colored High School, Columbia.
Bruce High School, Dyersburg.
South Jackson High School, Jackson.
Austin High School, Knoxville.
Kortrecht High School, Memphis.
Pearl High School, Nashville.

TEXAS:

Emile High School, Bastrop.
Colored High School, Beaumont.
West Belton High School, Belton.
Booker T. Washington High School, Bonham.
East End High School, Brenham.
Colored High School, Bryan.
Colored High School, Caldwell.
Colored High School, Chapel Hill.
Booker Washington High School, Cleburne.
Fred Douglass High School, Corsicana.
Colored High School, Cuero.
Colored High School, Dallas.
Anderson High School, Denison.
Fred Douglass High School, Denton.
Colored High School, Edna.
Douglass High School, El Paso.
Colored High School, Fort Worth.
Central High School, Galveston.
Colored High School, Gonzales.
Ross High School, Greenville.
Colored High School, Hempstead.
Peabody High School, Hillsboro.
Colored High School, Houston.
Colored High School, Jefferson.
Colored High School, La Grange.
Colored High School, Lampasas.
Colored High School, Lovelady.
Central High School, Marshall.
Anderson High School, Mart.
Colored High School, Nacogdoches.
Colored High School, Navasota.
Lincoln High School, Palestine.
Gibbons High School, Paris.
Colored High School, Rockdale.
Douglass High School, San Antonio.
Fred Douglass High School, Sherman.
Colored High School, Temple.
Colored High School, Victoria.
A. J. Moore High School, Waco.

VIRGINIA:

Jackson High School, Lynchburg.
Peabody High School, Petersburg.
Armstrong High School, Richmond.

WEST VIRGINIA:

Garnett High School, Charleston.
Water Street High School, Clarksburg.
Douglass High School, Huntington.
Sumner High School, Parkersburg.

ADDENDA

Received too late for insertion in the regular order in the body of the book.

ALSTON, Charles Henry, lawyer; born at Raleigh, N. C., Sept. 16, 1873; son of Deaton and Lydia Alston; B.S., Shaw Univ., Raleigh, 1891, LL.B., 1894; married Inez T. Lewenthal, of Darlington, S. C., Feb. 14, 1895; 1 child: Clara T. Admitted to Florida bar, 1894; practiced in Sanford 1year; associated with Hon. I. L. Purcell at Palatka, 1895-7; now in practice in Tampa; attorney for City Negro Board of Trade, also Afro-American Civic League; identified in more than 11,000 criminal cases, including 2 of rape, 31 murder, and death sentence was never executed on single case handled; raised constitutional question of Negroes being excluded from juries in Florida courts, and won. County supervisor of Negro Schools of Hillsboro County; vice-president Florida Negro Business League; owns stock in number Florida corporations. Delegate to Republican National Convention, Chicago, Ill., 1912; has served as chairman county and congressional committees, also as secretary Republican State Central Committee. Episcopalian. Grand master of ceremonies Grand Lodge F. & A. M.; temple commissioner of Grand Lodge, assistant judge-advocate-general Uniform Rank, and supreme deputy grand chancellor of Cuba, Knights of Pythias; past grand attorney Grand Lodge of Odd Fellows; member Universal Brotherhood. Home: 1611 Lamar Ave. Office: Jefferson and Constant Sts., Tampa, Fla.

BLACKNALL, George B., contractor, builder; born at Kittrell, N. C., Feb. 4, 1860; son of Dr. Rufus P. and Malinda Blacknall; ed. Shaw Univ., Raleigh, and Shiloh Institute, Warrenton, N. C.; married Louise Davis, of Newberry, S. C., June 6, 1908. Began work in building trades near Port Cross Roads, Franklin Co., N. C., 1885; conducted largest contracting and building business of any colored man in North Carolina, 1894-1904; contractor and builder in Cambridge, Mass., since

1907; also real estate operator, and controls modern apartments that accommodate about 25 colored families. Was one of speakers at 16th annual convention National Negro Business League, Boston, Mass., 1915. Address: 18 Lopez St., Cambridge, Mass.

BUSH, William Herbert, teacher of organ. Was organist at Louisiana Purchase Exposition, St. Louis, Mo., 1904; organist for Second Congregational Church, New London, Conn., more than 30 years; when the new organ was purchased its selection was left almost entirely in his hands. Address: 751 Bank St., New London, Conn.

CAREY, Archibald James, pastor Institutional Church; publisher the Chicago Conservator; member executive committee Illinois Commission, National Half-Century Anniversary of Negro Freedom, 1915; appointed investigator in office of corporation counsel, City of Chicago, July, 1915. Home: 3428 Vernon Ave. Church: 3825 S. Dearborn St. Office: Law Department, City Hall, Chicago, Ill.

COVINGTON, Eugene Gray, physician, surgeon; born in Caroline Co., Va., Aug. 1, 1872; son of Joseph and Elizabeth (Holmes) Covington; attended public schools, Annapolis, Md.; A.B., Howard Univ., Washington, D. C., 1895, M.D., 1899; married Alice Allena Lewis, of Oswego, N. Y., Sept. 10, 1902; 3 children: Girard H., Eugene G., Jr., Joseph H. Assistant demonstrator in anatomy at Howard Univ. School of Medicine, 1899-1900; practiced in Bloomington, Ill., since Sept. 30, 1900; was assistant surgeon on regimental staff 8th Inf. Illinois National Guard, 1902. President, Lincoln Protective League of McLean Co., Ill., Physical Culture Club, Bloomington; district supt. Loyal Legion Cooperative Educational System in Bloomington; secretary State Medical Assn., and elected delegate to national convention of National Medical Assn., Chicago, 1915; was delegate to

Negro National Educational Congress at Kansas City, Mo., also to 50th Anniversary Celebration of Emancipation at Philadelphia, Pa., 1913; member advisory board Illinois Commission in charge National Half-Century Anniversary of Negro Freedom, Chicago, 1915. Candidate for city commissioner in Bloomington's first campaign under the "Commission Plan" of government, 1915, and only colored man among 50 candidates; received letter from person who claimed to be "president of a newly organized Colored Black Hand Society" warning him to withdraw with the threat that "if you don't you and your family will be killed like dogs;" replied through the public press, "I am still in the race," and he was defeated in the election only by a small majority. Financial secretary board of trustees A. M. E. Church. Member National Negro Business League. Mason; surgeon with rank of colonel, uniform rank, Knights of Pythias. Home: 410 E. Market St. Office: 313 N. Main St., Bloomington, Ill.

DARBY, Nathaniel, lumber merchant, contractor and builder; born at Troy, Ala., June 24, 1863; son of Robert and Tabitha (Gibson) Darby; public school edn.; married in 1887; 3 children: Minnie Lee, Leona, Edgar; 2d marriage, Frances Skinner, of Arkansas City, Ark., Mar. 15, 1898. Began as a farmer and still owns the property; removed to Cotton Plant, Ark., and established as contractor and builder; now proprietor N. Darby Lumber Co. Trustee Philander Smith College, Little Rock, Ark. Republican. Methodist. Mason. Address: Box 237, Cotton Plant, Ark.

GREEN, Edward D., real estate, former legislator; born at St. Louis, Mo., Feb. 25, 1867; son of Jonathan and Maudline Green; ed. Sumner High School, St. Louis; unmarried. Organized the national commercial department Knights of Pythias, 1904, and since served as secretary; also secretary Pythian Temple Sanitarium Commission; in real estate business, Chicago, since 1911; secretary North-

ern Assets Realization Co. Republican; member Illinois House of Representatives, 1905-7, 1911-13; introduced bills resulting in the Anti-Mob Law, the law against the policy gambling game, and the law prohibiting discrimination in the price of burial lots in cemetaries. Methodist. Club: Appomatox. Home: 2641 Federal St. Office: 3613 State St., Chicago, Ill.

HAMILTON, "Mme. Estelle" Brown, hairdresser, teacher of beauty culture; born at Savannah, Ga., Nov. 28, 1883; daughter of Abraham and Marion (Marshall) Brown; grad. public school, Savannah, 1896; finished course in Rohrer's College of Beauty Culture, New York, 1910; married William Henry Hamilton, of Savannah, Dec. 4, 1902 (died 1909). Began as hair culturist in New York, 1910; now conducts Mme. Estelle's Beautifying Parlors, School of Hairdressing and Beauty Culture; introduced "Nu-Life for the Hair," a preparation to promote the growth. Baptist. Member Business Women League of Greater New York, Young Ladies Independent Circle, Court of Calanthe. Address: 72 W. 133d St., New York.

HOLLOWAY, Richard Jones, clergyman, teacher; A.B., Fisk Univ., Nashville, Tenn., 1885. Dean of theology and vice-pres. Edward Waters College. Address: 1603 4th St., DeLyons Block, Jacksonville, Fla.

HUDSON, Oscar, lawyer; admitted to membership San Francisco Bar Assn., July 15, 1915, and is first colored member of any bar association in California (see full sketch in regular alphabetical order, as this data was received after that section had been printed).

JACKSON, George Henry, lawyer, real estate; born in Ontario, Can., Oct. 4, 1847; son of George and Julia (Burke) Jackson; public school edn., Cincinnati, Ohio; married Virginia A. Gordon, of Cincinnati, Apr. 24, 1879; 2 children: Gordon (M.D.), Helen (Mrs. Thorne). Began practice in Cincinnati, 1884; was member House of Representatives, from Hamilton County, Ohio, 1891-3; attorney-at-law and in real estate business in Chicago several years. Was trustee New Orphan Asylum for Colored Children, Crawford Old Men's Home, and Sallie McCall Industrial School of Cincinnati; president Liberal Culture Club of Chicago 2 terms. Active in Republican politics. Member Appomatox Club. Home: 3416 Vernon Ave. Office: 3437 S. Wabash Ave., Chicago, Illinois.

JACKSON, Giles B., president the Negro Historical and Industrial Association in charge the National Negro Exhibition held at Richmond, Va., July 4-27, 1915. Address: 511 N. 2d St., Richmond, Va.

JOHNSON, J. Rosamond, musician; born at Jacksonville, Fla., 1873; son of James and Helen Louise (Dillette) Johnson; studied at New England Conservatory of Music; developed new and distinct style of Negro music; now supervisor Music School Settlement for Colored People, New York. Composer: Under the Bamboo Tree; Since You Went Away; The Awakening; Morning, Noon and Night; I Sold My Love to the Roses; Southland; Lazy Moon; The Congo Love Song. Has written light operas for Klaw & Erlander, theatrical managers, and songs for May Irvin, Lillian Russell, and Anna Held; while director of music at London Opera House, England, 1912-13, composed the music to the successful "Come Over Here." Address: Music School Settlement, 6 W. 131st St., New York.

JOHNSON, James Weldon, writer, ex-consul; born at Jacksonville, Fla., June 17, 1871; son of James and Helen Louise (Dillette) Johnson; ed. public schools, Jacksonville, to 1887; A.B., Atlanta (Ga.) Univ., 1894, A.M., 1904; studied at Columbia Univ., New York, 1904, 5, 6; married Grace Elizabeth Nail, of New York, Feb. 3, 1910. Began as principal Colored High School, Jacksonville, 1894, continuing to 1901; admitted to Florida bar, 1899; removed to New York, 1901; collaborated with brother, J. Rosamond Johnson, in writing light opera for New York stage. Co-author: "Humpty Dumpty," "In Newport"; first was produced at New Amsterdam Theatre, 1904, the other at Liberty Theatre, 1906, in New York; has collaborated on many musical plays, and written words for number classic, semi-classic and popular songs. Author: The Autobiography of an ex-Colored Man, 1912. Contributed poems to the Century, Independent, and other magazines; now contributing editor New York Age. Was United States consul to Puerto Cabello, Venezeula, 1906-9, Corinto, Nicaragua, 1909-12, to The Azores, 1912-13; resigned. Member Sigma Pi Phi. 32d degree Mason. Home: 2311 7th Ave. Office: Care G. Ricordi & Co., New York.

LANE, Charles Franklin, publisher, law student; born at Savannah, Ga., Aug. 15, 1893; son of Charles Lawrence and Josephine (DeLyons) Lane; grad. West Broad Street Grammar School, Savannah; attended Beach Normal Institute, Savannah, and Boston (Mass.) Latin School; private tuition 4 years under Prof. Edward Pierce of Harvard; studied at Suffolk Law School; student Boston Law School, 1915; unmarried. Publisher of The Citizen, (a purely literary magazine), since Aug., 1915; the contributing editors, William Stanley Braithwaite of Boston, George W. Ellis and Elizabeth Lindsay Davis, Chicago, T. Montgomery Gregory, Washington, Mrs. Mary Talbert, Buffalo, are writers of national reputation. Address: 105 Kendall St., Boston, Mass.

LEE, M. D., general secretary A. M. E., Zion Church, Rock Hill, S. C.

LUCAS, W. W., clergyman; assistant general secretary Epworth League, M. E. Church, S., Atlanta, Ga.

MASON, James Edward, college professor, clergyman, lecturer; born at Wilkes-Barre, Pa., Mar. 30, 1859; son of Sylvester L. and Elizabeth (Huff) Mason; grad. public schools, Wilkes-Barre, 1876; private tuition in theology under Revs. I. Stewart, E. White, Dr. Russell, Wilkes-Barre, Prof. Brown and Dr. Curtis, Syracuse Univ.; took Chautauqua Literary and

Scientific course, 1880-4; attended lectures at Cornell Univ., 1885-6; (D.D., Livingstone College, 1898); married Abbie Kelly Keene, of Syracuse, N. Y., Oct., 1887 (died 1908). Licensed to preach in A. M. E. Zion Church, 1876, at age of 17, and was soon known as the "Boy Preacher and Orator"; joined Genesee (now Western N. Y.) Conference, 1877; ordained deacon, 1879, elder, 1880; pastored at Binghamton, Syracuse, Elmira, Ithaca, and Rochester; secretary and compiler, Genesee Conference, 1882-97; leading evangelist of the conference several years, and called into service of many white churches; music director Onondaga County Sunday School Convention (white), 2 years; delegate to General Conference A. M. E. Zion Church since 1884; fraternal delegate to M. E. General Conference, Chicago, Ill., 1900; delegate to Ecumenical Conference on Methodism, Toronto, Can., and delivered addresses in leading churches there, 1911; first colored guest of Empire Club, Toronto, and one of banquet speakers. Resigned as presiding elder, 1897; since professor of political economy, and financial secretary, Livingstone College, Salisbury, N. C.; has addressed many leading white churches, conferences and educational associations in U. S.; for years has been a lecturer for Y. M. C. A.; was in same lecture course with Bishop Henry C. Potter in New England, and his guest during centenary celebration of Cooperstown, N. Y.; was twice called to open Senate and General Assembly with prayer at Albany, during administration of Gov. Theodore Roosevelt; occupied carriage with him and spoke from same platform at fair grounds, Elmira, N. Y. Republican. Member American Academy Political and Social Science, National Educational Assn. Mason, K. T.; member Independent Order of Odd Fellows. Lectures: Darkest Africa and the Way Out; The New Negro; Lincoln and the Negro; Objections Answered; The First Century Hero; Woman and Matrimony; The Brother in Black; Negro Pathfinders; Living Issues; Big Blunders. Home:

249 Columbia Ave., Rochester, N. Y. Offices: Livingstone College, Salisbury, N. C.

McCLENDON, Caesar P., physician; A.B., Lincoln Univ., Pa., 1899; M.D., Univ. of Mich. In practice in New Rochelle, and conducts sanitarium. Officer in grand lodge Knights of Pythias of N. Y. Home: 10 Winthrop Ave., New Rochelle, N. Y.

MITCHELL, Z. W. William, founder Loyal Legion Co-operative Eduational System; born in Vigo County, Ind., June 26, 1867; son of Lambert A. and Susanna Mitchell, and Curtiss College, Minneapolis, Minn.; married Lorena C. Connor, of Springfield, Ohio, Mar. 5, 1895; 1 child: Beulah E. Was writer more than 2 years on regular staff of Minneapolis Tribune; began study of conditions among colored people, 1892, and experimental work along the lines of race co-operation for mutual helpfulness, 1897; studied the conditions as they exist between the races in England and Europe, 1910; actual work of organizing "Council Boards" with purpose of extending the Loyal Legion Co-operative Educational System began in 1912; held mass meetings in western cities and lectured on the "American Race Problem" before bodies of representative citizens; has educational quarters in Quincy, Ill., where expenditures for 1914 was $5,-400; established Social Center in Bloomington, Ill., 1915, and had spent about $2,000 there in few months ending Aug. 1; the purpose set forth as incorporated under the laws of Illinois state: "To improve the living conditions of colored people; to encourage closer co-operation between the white and colored races; to promote thrift, economy and enterprise among Afro-Americans. Address: 1103 N. 5th St., Quincy; 322 S. Main St., Bloomington, Illinois.

PRATT, Thomas William, teacher; A.B., Fisk Univ., Nashville, Tenn., 1900. Now principal Ross High School, Greenville. Address: 888 Gordon St., Greenville, Texas.

RAGLAND, Fountain Washington,

druggist; son of Rev. Fountain G. and Addie Washington (Stevens) Ragland; B.S., Talladega (Ala.) College, 1903; Pharm.D., Northwestern Univ. School of Pharmacy, Chicago, Ill., 1908. Proprietor of Ragland's Pharmacy, Birmingham, Ala.

ROSS, Isaac Nelson, clergyman; born in Hawkins County, Tennessee, Jan. 22, 1856; son of Isam N. and America Jane (Colie) Ross; educated in schools of Ohio at Bigwoods, Maxwell, Grassy Branch, Bowersville, and private instruction under Pres. James A. Fairchilds of Oberlin College; (D.D., Wilberforce Univ., 1903); married Mamie Robinson Fletcher, of Elizabethtown, Ky., Jan. 1, 1879; children: William O. H. (M.D.), Martha H., Isaac N., Jr., Mamie E., and 2 deceased. Joined Ohio Conference A. M. E. Church, 1880, and was in the 3d Episcopal District 25 years; pastored Oberlin (O.) Mission, St. Paul's at Washington, Pa., Oil City and Titusville Circuit, Brown's Chapel at Allegheny City, Wiley Avenue Church in Pittsburgh, Warren Chapel, Toledo, and St. Paul's at Columbus, Ohio; joined General Conference, 1900; pastor, Allen Temple, Cincinnati, 5 years, Big Bethel Church, Atlanta, Ga., 1905-8, Metropolitan Church, Washington, D. C., 1908-13, Ebenezar Church, Baltimore, Md., since 1913; his entire career has been one of building, remodelling, paying off and reducing church debts, leaving general improved conditions for successors, always; installed steam heating plant in the Metropolitan Church at Washington, made interior and exterior improvements, reduced the bonded debt $2,000, and after five years service left the church on self-supporting basis. Was president Colored Clergymen's Home at Cincinnati; life trustee Wilberforce Univ.; conference trustee Kittrell (N. C.) College. Republican. Member National Association for Advancement of Colored People, Washington Ministerial Assn., Baltimore Ministers' Alliance. Royal Arch Mason; chaplain Order Eastern Star; member Odd Fellows, Veteran Association of Odd Fellows, Knights of Pythias, Knights of Daughters of Tabor. Club: Monday (Atlanta). Address: 18 W. Montgomery St., Baltimore, Md.

SMITH, Franklin Gatewood, principal high school; A.B., Fisk Univ., Nashville, Tenn., 1887; M.D., Meharry Medical College (Walden Univ.), 1892. Principal Pearl High School. Home: 142 14th Ave. N., Nashville, Tenn.

STRONG, John Wesley, college president; grad. Theological Dept. Talladega (Ala.) College, 1880; (D.D., Guadaloupe College, Seguin, Tex., 1903). President Central Texas College, Waco, Texas.

SWANN, Thomas Wallace, newspaper man; secretary Illinois Commission, National Half-Century Aniversary of Negro Freedom; was the principal organizer of the movement to celebrate the event in Chicago, 1915, and was appointed secretary after the commission was created by the act passed by the 48th General Assembly; has been identified with number colored newspapers and magazines in different parts of U. S. Address: Wabash Avenue Dept. Y. M. C. A., Chicago, Ill.

THOMAS, I. L., clergyman; field secretary Board of Home Missions and Church Extension, M. E. Church, 2111 Druid Hill Ave., Baltimore, Md.

TRIMBLE, James Guinne, physician; A.B., Fisk Univ., Nashville, Tenn., 1902; M.D., Harvard Medical School, 1906. Practiced in Brooklyn, N. Y., since 1906. Address: 503 Vanderbilt Ave., Brooklyn, N. Y.

WESTBROOKS, Richard Edward, lawyer; born at Waco, Tex., Oct. 13, 1886; son of Charles P. and Laura A. (Moore) Westbrooks; ed. public schools of Waco, Victoria, Bastrop, Cuero, Dallas, Ft. Worth, San Antonio; Columbus High and Normal School, all in Texas; LL.B., John Marshall Law School, Chicago, Ill., 1911; married Alice Solomon, of Boston, Mass., July 14, 1911. Began as principal Moody (Tex.) High School,

WHO'S WHO OF THE COLORED RACE

A

ABBOTT, Ebenezer Augustus, Jr., writer, lecturer; born at Basseterre St. Kitts, British West Indes, Aug. 27, 1890; son of E. Augustus and Phoebe Ann (Woods) Abbott; grad. Ebenezer Wesleyan Grade School, St. Kitts, 1907; unmarried. Began as writer for St. Christopher Advertiser and staff correspondent of St. Kitts Daily Express; writer and lecturer in New York since 1909. Republican. Deacon Rush Memoral A. M. E. Zion Church; superintendent Sunday School. Member Odd Fellows, Fishermen of Galilee. Club: Spartan Field. Address: 546 Lenox Ave., New York.

ABINGTON, George Sexton, principal public school; born at Foristell, Mo., Jan. 5, 1861; son of Jerry N. and Rhoda Ann (Phillips) Abington; attended public schools, Foristell; B.S.D., Lincoln Institute, Jefferson City, Mo., 1887; married Amelia J. Price, of Tipton, Mo., Dec. 4, 1890; 3 children. Began teaching school, 1881; principal Grant School, Clarksville, Mo., since 1892; during same period conducted Colored Teachers' Institute. Republican. Baptist. Member State Teachers' Assn. of Mo.; was president Central Teachers' Assn. 10 years. Mason; members United Brothers of Friendship, Knights of Tabor. Address: Box 44, Clarksville, Mo.

ABNER, David, college president; born at Gilmer, Tex., Nov. 25, 1860; son of David and Louise (Brown) Abner; studied at Wiley Univ., Marshall, Tex., Straight Univ., New Orleans, La., Fisk Univ., Nashville, Tenn.; A.B., Bishop College, Marshall, 1884, A.M., later; (D.D., Ph.D., Virginia Theological Seminary and College); married Ella Mae Wheeler, of Brenham, Tex., Sept. 24, 1891; 2 children: Ewart G., Eulalia L. Professor of Latin at Bishop College, 1884-94; president Guadalupe College, Seguin,

Tex., 15 years; president Conroe College since 1909; vice-president Orgen Banking Co., Houston, Tex.; director Orgen Realty Co. Delegate to Republican National Convention, Chicago, 1888, 1892, St. Louis, 1896, Philadelphia, 1900, Chicago, 1904, 1908. Grand Master, Odd Fellows of Texas; member Household of Ruth. Wrote number pamphlets on moral subjects. Translations: Caesar; Cicero; Virgil. Home: 3310 McKinney Ave. Office: Conroe College, Conroe, Texas.

ADAMS, Lucien, druggist; born at Point Coupee, La., 1856; son of Lucien and Louisa (Dickerson) Adams; studied law at Straight Univ., New Orleans, La., 1884-5; grad. Fisk Univ., Nashville, Tenn., 1894; B.S., Roger Williams Unv., 1897; M.S., Bishop College, Marshall, Tex., 1903; pharmacy course International Correspondence School, 1908; married Delia Duncan, of Mobile, Ala., June 15, 1886; 2 children: Nellie, Geneva. In drug business in Fort Worth, Texas, since 1906; proprietor Citizen's Drug Co. Republican. Baptist. Mason. Address: 309 E. 9th St., Fort Worth, Texas.

ADAMS, Moses Samuel, insurance; born at Greenville, Madison Co., Fla., Dec. 18, 1882; son of Anthony and Susie (Fielder) Adams; attended public school at Monticello, Fla.; grad. Florida Baptist College, 1904; married Annie Lee Corthran, of Jacksonville, Fla., Sept. 28, 1904; 1 child: Russell Nathanial. Taught in public schools of Fla., 10 years; secretary Union Mutual Insurance Co.; began as bookkeeper for company, 1906. Missionary Baptist. Home: 2216 Mars Ave. Office: 534 W. Church St., Jacksonville, Fla.

ADGER, Julian Francis, pipe organ instructor; born at Philadelphia, Pa., Oct. 6, 1876; son of Robert and Lucy A. (Davidson) Adger; ed. public schools and Institute for Colored

Youth, Philadelphia; married Loretta M. V. Scott, of Atlantc Cty, N. J., Oct. 18, 1905; 1 child: Julian F., Jr. Has been organist and choirmaster St. Augustine's P. E. Chapel, Crucifixion P. E. Church, Philadelphia, Pa., St. Phillip's Church, New York; assistant organist St. James P. E. Church, Milwaukee, Wis., St. Simon the Cyrenene, St. Thomas Church, Philadelphia, St. Barnabas P. E. Church (Germantown), Philadelphia; published number hymn tunes and part songs for male and female voices. Member American Organ Players' Club, Music Teachers' Assn., Philadelphia Organist Alliance (president). Republican. Episcopalian. Home: 1521 Catherine St. Office: 110 W. Rittenhouse St., Philadelphia (Germantown), Pa.

AGGREY, James Emman Kwegyir, registrar, college prof.; born at Anamabu, Gold Coast, West Africa, Oct. 18, 1875; son of Kodwa Kwegyir Aggrey and Abina (Araba Andua; descended from Royal families or ruling kings of Edwumaku and of Dankyira, also ruling chiefs of Ashanti; graduated, ranking first, from Wesleyan Mission School, 1889, and Minsterial Training School, 1895, at Cape Coast, Gold Coast W. Africa; ordained in the A. M. E. Zion ministry; trained for Cambridge University (England) Higher Local; came to America, 1898; A.B., Livingstone College, Salisbury, N. C., 1902, A.M., later; won S. C. Fuller Prize English (gold medal), also Bishop C. R. Harris Gold prize for best scholarship and deportment; made highest average in the whole college; post-graduate in French, German and metaphysics, 1904, also took course in Spanish besides emphasizing in educational psychology, diagnosis and treatment of atypical children, sociology and economies, 1914, at Columbia Univ., New York; married Rose Rudolph Douglass, of Portsmouth, Va., Nov. 8, 1905; 3 children: Abina Andua Azales, James E. K. Jr., Rosebud Douglass. Was chief secretary executive and general committee Gold Coast Aborigines Rights Protection Society;

now captain in Anamabu Army; linguist and aid in the Court of King Amonu IV. and V.; teacher, 1889-98, school master, 1895-8, at Wesleyan Centenary Memorial schools, Cape Coast, Gold Coast, W. Africa; won first honor of the colony as teacher; awarded prizes and honorary mention by Gold Coast Legislative Council with Her Majesty Queen Victoria's governor presiding. Registrar and secretary since 1900, professor of English language and literature since 1902, at Livnigstone College, Salisbury, N. C.; delivered third Latin salutatory since Livingstone College was founded; wrote first Latin poem and delivered first Greek oration in that college, 1902; secretary-treas. Rowan Realty Co.; director Salisbury-Spencer Building & Loan Assn. Fellow North British Academy of Arts, Ltd.; member Hellenic Society, Roman Society, Royal Society of Arts (London); elected member National Geographical Society, Washington, D. C., 1914; also member American Negro Academy, Negro Society of Historical Research. 33d degree Mason; member Rechabites, Foresters (English lodges), Odd Fellows, Knights of Pythias, True Reformers. Clubs: Royal Societies (London). Home: 700 W. Monroe St. Office: Livingstone College, Salisbury, N. C.

ALDREDGE, Amanda Ira ("Montague Ring") musician, composer; great-granddaughter of a ruling prince in the Senegal country of Africa; grandfather escaped when rest of family was murdered during an uprising, and was educated for ministry in America; daughter of Ira Aldridge, most famous of Negro actors, who had few equals as Othello; he was presented with Prussian gold medal of first class for art and science. received grand Cross of the Order of Leopold from Emperor of Austria, given Maltese Cross with medal of merit by City of Berne, received Royal Saxe-Ernest House Order, higher title than Sir in England. She has made remarkable success in rendering own compositions; is regarded as worthy successor to Samuel Coleridge-Taylor, the distinguished Negro composer who died in London, Sept. 1, 1912; she is known in the profession as "Montague Ring." Home: 2 Bedford Gds., London, England.

ALEXANDER, Archie Alphonso, civil engineer, contractor; born at Ottumwa, Iowa, May 14, 1888; son of Price and Mary (Hamilton) Alexander; grad. Oak Park High School, 1905; Cummings School of Art, Des Moines, Iowa, 1906; student Highland Park College, Des Moines, 1907-8; C.E., State Univ., of Iowa, 1912; married Audra Linzy, of Denver, Colo., June 25, 1913. Began as designing engineer with Marsh Engineering Co., Des Moines, 1912; after 1 year was given charge bridge construction work in Iowa and Minn.; general contractor for self since 1914. Was member track and football teams, also active in general sports while at university. Vice-president, Des Moines Branch, National Association for Advancenent of Colored People. Republican. African Methodist. Member Kappa Alpha Nu. Club: Compass (Iowa City). Address: 1911 Des Moines St., Des Moines, Iowa.

ALEXANDER, Charles, author, lecturer; born at Natchez, Miss., Mar. 7, 1868; son of James and Angerline (Thompson) Alexander; public school edn., New London, Conn.; studied literature under private teachers; finished Chautauqua course, 1893; married Fannie Worthington, of Washington, D. C., Aug. 1, 1897. Teacher in Agricultural and Mechanical College, Normal, Ala., 3 years, Tuskegee Normal and Industrial Institute 1 year, Wilberforce (O.) Univ., 4 years; publisher Monthly Review, Boston, Mass., 1893-6, Boston Colored Citizen, 1906, Alexander's Magazine, 1906-10; organized Enterprise Collection Agency, Los Angeles, Calif, 1914. Trustee Harriet Tubman Home of Boston. Republican candidate for Mass. House of Representatives and twice defeated in strong Democratic ward. African Methodist. Mason; member Odd Fellows. Author: Evidences of Progress Among Colored People, 1896; One Hundred Distinguished Leaders,

1897; Under Fire With the 10th U. S. Cavalry, 1898; Making Printers in Tuskegee, 1900; Battles and Victories of Allen Allensworth, 1910. Home: 1584 W. 37th St. Office: 501 Thorpe Bldg., Los Angeles, Calif.

ALEXANDER, Ethel Vivian, teacher; born at Marshall, Texas, Feb. 11, 1888; daughter of Thomas and Ellen (Armstrong) Alexander; grad. Wiley Univ., Marshall, from normal dept., 1909, millinery, 1910, printing, 1911. Assistant forewoman in printing dept., Wiley Univ., 1908-10; teacher in rural schools of Harrison County, Tex., since 1910. Methodist. Member Texas State Teachers' Assn., East Texas Teachers' Assn., Knights and Daughters of Tabor, Young Ladies' Reading Circle. Home: 316 Carter St., Marshall, Texas.

ALEXANDER, Walter Gilbert, physician; born at Lynchburg, Va., Dec. 3, 1880; son of Royall and Amalia (Terry) Alexander; grad. public schools, Lynchburg; A.B., Lincoln (Pa.) Univ., 1899; M.D., College of Physicians and Surgeons, Boston, Mass., 1903; married Elizabeth B. Hemmings, of Boston, May 3, 1904. Practiced in Kimball, W. Va., 1903-4, in Orange, N. J., since 1904; director Progressive Building and Loan Assn. First colored man to receive nomination for N. J. House of Representatives; was Progressive party candidate, 1912; candidate for office of City Commissioner, Orange, N. J., 1914; received 11th highest vote of 53 primary candidates. Presbyterian. Secretary National Medical Assn.; member New Jersey State Medical Society, Odd Fellows, Knights of Pythias, Elks, Sons and Daughters of Moses. Address: 14 Webster Place, Orange, N. J.

ALLEN, Alfred James, clergyman; born on Singleton Allen's plantation in Elbert County, Ga., Sept. 11,1859; son of David and Frances Allen slaves; attended public schools of Elbert County; grad. Atlanta (Ga.) Baptist College, normal dept., 1885, theological dept., 1887; married Rebecca A. Lane, of LaGrange, Ga., Dec 12, 1889 (died 1912); 2d marriage

Louise Miles, of Arlington, Ga., Mar 8, 1914. Taught in public schools in 7 different counties of Georgia to 1888; ordained Baptist ministry at Cuthbert, Ga., Feb. 24, 1888; state missionary and colporteur for Georgia Sunday School Convention and American Baptist Publication Society of Philadelphia since 1890; vice-president General State Baptist Convention; clerk for Southwest Georgia Baptist Assn., since 1906; board manager of Reformatory institution founded by Dr. W. G. Johnson of Macon, Ga.; was principal Benevolence Institute, Shellman, Ga., 1910-14. Republican. Mason. Address: Box 43, Cuthbert, Ga.

ALLEN, Benjamin Franklin, college president; born at Savannah, Ga., Sept. 8, 1872; son of Albert Kelly and Elizabeth (Proctor) Allen; A.B., Atlanta (Ga.) Univ., 1894, A.M., later; A.M., National Univ., Chicago, Ill., 1896; (Ph.D., Morris Brown Univ., Atlanta, Ga., 1904; LL.D., Wilberforce Univ., 1904); married Mayme Lee Williams, of Macon, Ga., June 27, 1907; 2 children: Julia Elizabeth, Ruth Louise. Began as teacher public schools in Ga., 1888; later taught in Atlanta Univ.; was elected, 1894, princpal of manual department and professor of science at State Univ., Louisville, Ky., principal Risby Public School, Brunswick, Ga., teacher with principal's rank Florida Baptist Academy, Jacksonville; professor, Greek and Latin, 1894-9, English and pedagogy, 1899-1901, at Lincoln Institute, Jefferson City, Mo.; professor English and pedagogy Georgia State College, Savannah, 1901-2; president Lincoln Institute since 1902. African Methodist. Member American Academy Political and Social Science, American Economic Assn., American Humane Assn., National Negro Educational Assn., State Historical Association of Mo., State Teachers' Association of Mo. (president). Mason; member Odd Fellows, Knights of Pythias. Address: Lincoln Institute, Jefferson City, Mo.

ALLEN, Charles Emery, clergyman; born at Indianapolis, Ind., June 2, 1863; son of Emery and Eliza Jane Allen; attended McCoy and Central High schools, Indianapolis; grad. Morris Brown Univ., Atlanta, Ga.; (D.D., Wilberforce Univ., 1911); married Ida May Hammons, of Noblesville, Ind., July 22, 1888; 1 child, Mrs. Beulah Allen Johnson. Licensed to preach in A. M. E. Church, Noblesville, 1887; pastor at Anderson 3 years, Seymour 2 years, Lafayette, Ind., 2 years, Ebenezer Church, Detroit, Mich., 6 years; presiding elder Michigan Conference 5 years; pastor at South Bend since 1912; member financial board A. M. E. Church; was delegate to general conference at Kansas City, Mo., 1912. Trustee Wilberforce Univ.; director Payne Theological Seminary. Delegate from Indiana to National Half-Century Anniversary Celebration of Negro Freedom at Chicago, 1915. Republican. 32 degree Mason. Home: 420 S. Main St., South Bend, Ind.

ALLEN, George Wesley, clergyman, editor; born in Russell County, Ala., Aug. 10, 1854; son of George and Margaret Allen; while servant to students of Agricultural and Mechanical College at Auburn, Ala., they assisted him in primary studies; studied while servant to principles of white high schools at Opelika, Enon, Phoenix, Girard, Ala.; also studied 12 years under various professors; (D.D., Payne Univ., Selma, Ala., 1902); married Phoebe C. Harvey, of Barbour County, Ala., Mar. 2, 1876; 8 children: Griffin A. (M.D.) William W., James L., John S., Alexander J., Nimrod B., Marion A., Bertha Lee. Taught in district schools of Ala., 1869-1900; principal colored schools at Gerard, 1884-1900; examiner of colored teachers in Russell County 2 years. Licensed to preach, A. M. E. Church, 1880; presiding elder, 1897-1904; editor and manager Southern Christian Recorder since 1904. Trustee Wilberforce Univ., Morris Brown Univ., Payne College. Republican; member Alabama House of Representatives, 1875-7. Mason. Home: 1315 Fifth Ave. Office: 1033 First Ave., Columbus, Ga.

ALLEN, William Frederick, contractor, builder; born at Baltimore, Md., 1856; son of George Washington and Eliza (Brown) Allen; educated in Freedman's School, Baltimore; married Emma Ridgeway, of Baltimore, Nov. 10, 1889; 2 children: Mary R., George S. Served apprenticeship in carpentry and cabinet making; contractor and builder in Baltimore since 1874; was officer in Court of Common Pleas, 1898-1904. President, St. Paul Lyceum; trustee Christian Church (Disciples of Christ). Progressive party candidate for City Council from 5th Ward, Baltimore, 1915. Member East Baltimore Improvement Assn. Mason; member Odd Fellows, Order of Moses, Nazerites. Address: 508 Somersett St., Baltimore, Md.

ALLISON, Guy William, physician, surgeon; born at Fort Scott, Kan., Oct. 19, 1885; son of Robert C. and Martha (Ray) Allison; grad. high school, of Fort Scott; student Univ. of Kan. 2 years; M. D., Meharry Medical College (Walden Univ.), Nashville, Tenn., 1908; married Eunice Reeves, of Fort Scott, Dec. 26, 1909. Practiced in Hutchinson since 1908, largely among white people; examining physician for local lodges of Masons, Odd Fellows, Knights of Pythias, Order of Eastern Star, Household of Ruth; representative Grand Lodge K. of P. of Kan. Republican. Methodist. Member Reno County Medical Society, Hutchinson Negro Business League (president). Address: 25 1-2 E. Sherman St., Hutchinson, Kan.

ALLISON, John McIntosh, deputy sheriff; born at Vincennes, Ind., 1856; son of William H. and Johanna (McIntosh) Allison; public school edu., Beloit, Wis.; prepared for college; married Jennie Stafford, of Atlantic City, N. J., July 2, 1911; 1 child: Florence. In government service at Washington 2 years; deputy sheriff in Hennepin County, Minn., since 1892; has served as acting bailiff under 14 different judges and executed every kind of process that comes within duty of sheriff. Republican. Baptist. Mason; member Knights of Pythias. Home: 2925 Tenth Ave. Office: Sheriff's Office, Minneapolis, Minn.

ALLSTON, James Henderson, salesman; born at Edenton, N. C., Feb. 26, 1862; son of Joseph S. and Emily (Page) Allston; public school edn., Boston, Mass.; married Gertrude Hawley, of Bridgeport, Conn., July 9, 1895; 1 child: Emily Elizabeth. Began as errand boy, 1875, with Samuel Stephens printers supply house, Boston; worked through various departments to that of salesman. Was member Boston Common Council, 1894-5; 1908-9, and president pro tem, 1909; Republican. Methodist. Secretary Boston Negro Business League, also Greater Boston Club. Home: 5 Watson St. Office: Care of Samuel Stephens, 174 High St., Boston, Mass.

ALLSTON, Philip J., manufacturing druggist; born at Edenton, N. C., Aug. 12, 1860; son of Joseph S. and Emily (Page) Allston; brother of James H. Allston; ed. public school of Edenton; English High School, Boston, 8 years; King Drawing School, 5 years; Y. M. C. A. Bible School, 3 years; Massachusetts College of Pharmacy, 3 years; married Margaret A. Whiting, of Portsmouth, Va., Sept. 21, 1892; 2 children: Philip R., Clifford W. Manufacturing druggist with Potter Drug & Chemical Corpn., Boston, since 1878; director Suffolk Investment Assn. African Methodist. Member Boston Historical and Literary Assn., Cosmopolitan Equal Rights Assn. (president); friendly visitor Associated Charities. Clubs: Lincoln Republican; Wendell Phillips; Crispus Attucks (secretary). Home: 227 W. Canton St. Office: 135 Columbus Ave. (care Potter Drug & Chemical Corpn.), Boston, Mass.

ALSTON, Alice Manolia, supervising industrial teacher; born at Seaboard, N. C., Feb. 10, 1890; daughter of Taylor and Fannie Agnes (Philips) Alston; grad. North Carolina State Colored Normal School, 1910. Teacher in graded schools Elizabeth City, N. C., 2 years; supervisor Negro Rural Schools in Pasquotank County since Oct. 6, 1913; this branch of education is under the State Superintendent of Public Instruction; aided by the Anna T. Jeanes Fund it reaches the most remote schools and homes in the state. Baptist. Home: Seaboard. Office: Elizabeth City, N. C.

ALSTON, Caesar Jony, farmer, preacher; born in Alamance County, N. C., June 10, 1855; son of Caesar and Chesny Alston; common school education; married, Dec. 21, 1882; General farmer and successful cotton planter since 1882; owns 205-acre farm; was rural mail carrier, 1901-9; pastor Christian Church, Chatham County, N. C. Republican. Address: Route 4, Siler City, N. C.

ALSTON, Nellie V. Landry, missionary; born at Donaldsonville, La., May 10, 1875; daughter of Rev. Pierre and Amanda (Grisby) Landry; A.B., New Orleans Univ., La., 1896; married Rev. J. W. Alston, of Paris, Tex., June 9, 1911. Began teaching in La., 1895; now missionary in Africa; dean of Cape Palmas Seminary. Methodist. Address: Cape Palmas, Liberia, West Africa.

ALSTORK, John Wesley, bishop; born at Talladega, Ala., Sept. 1 1852; son of Rev. Frank and Mary Jane Alstork; educated in Talladega College; (D.D., Livingstone College; 1892; LL.D., Princeton (Ind.) Normal and Industrial Univ., 1908); married Mamie M. Lawson, of Talladega, May 26, 1872. Ordained in ministry, 1882; financial secretary, Alabama Conference, 1884-92, connection property, 1892-1900, of A. M. E. Zion Church; presiding elder, 1889-1900; elected bishop, May 14, 1900. Delegate to Ecumenical Conference on Methodism, London, Eng., 1901, Toronto, Canada, 1911. Trustee Livingstone College, Lomax-Hannon High and Industrial School, Greenville, Ala., Langridge Academy, Montgomery, Ala., Atkinson College, Madisonville, Ky., Censor Medical College, Louisville, Ky. Address: 261 Cleveland Ave., Montgomery, Ala.

AMES, James Webb, physician, former legislator; born at New Orleans, La., Oct. 12, 1864; son of Wil-

liam Q. and Mary (Washington) Ames; grad. Straight Univ., New Orleans, 1888; M.D., Howard Univ., Washington, 1894; married Florence F. Cole, of Detroit, Mich., Sept. 23, 1897 (deceased); children: Chester C., William E., Marion C., Florence F.; 2nd marriage, Norma Almbe, of Springfield, O., Oct. 23, 1908. Apprentice to coopers trade, 1876-81; teacher in public schools of La., summers, 1882-9; clerk in record and pension div. War Department, Washington, 1890-4. Practiced medicine in Detroit since June 5, 1894; was physician to United States prisoners, 1899-1900; only colored man ever held that position; diagnostician of contagious diseases for Detroit Board of Health since 1901; no other colored physician holding similar municipal position in America; physician in Home for Aged Colored Women; secretary and treasurer Almo Amusement Co., Villa Amusement Co., Zeloh Amusement Co.; secretary Cole Realty Co.; trustee Phyllis Wheatley Home for Aged Colored Women. Was member Mich. House of Representatives, 1901-2; alternate delegate Republican National Convention, Chicago, Ill., 1908; delegate to number of state and county conventions. Presbyterian. Member Mich. State Medical Society, Wayne County Medical Society; associate mem. Alumni Assn. of Detroit College of Medicine. Mason; member Knights of Pythias, Independent Order Forresters. Clubs: Union League Republican. Osceola. Home: 331 Frederick Ave. Office: 155 Gratiot Ave., Detroit, Mich.

AMIGER, William Thomas, university president, clergyman; born at Culpeper, Va., July 16, 1870; son of Howland and Margaret (Alexander) Amiger; preparatory edn. State Normal School, Geneseo, N. Y.; A.B., Lincoln (Pa.) Univ., 1899, A.M., 1902, S. T.B., 1902; special work in Newton (Mass.) Theological Seminary, 1903; (hon. D.D., Lincoln Univ., 1909; LL.D., Central Law School, Louisville, Ky., 1912); married Eleanor Green, of Castleton, Va., Nov. 30, 1892; 5 children: Virginia, Naomi, Rowland Kittridge, Ruth, Eleanor. Ordained Baptist ministery, 1903; pastor 3d Baptist Church, Springfield, Mass., 1903-8; president State Univ., Louisville, Ky., since 1908. Member National Geographic Society, National Teachers' Assn., Religious Education Assn. Address: 722 W. Kentucky St., Louisville, Ky.

ANDERSON, Charles Harry, banker, merchant; born at Jacksonville, Fla., July 25, 1879; son of John and Charlotte (Lewis) Anderson; ed. Florida Baptist College, Jacksonville, and business college at Philadelphia, Pa.; married Margaret H. Myatt, of Jacksonville, Sept. 18, 1907. 4 children: Hodgie, Seattle, Charles. H. Jr., Joseph M. Began in fish and oyster business, 1902; now proprietor Charles H. Anderson Fish & Oyster Co.; cashier Anderson & Co., Bankers. African Methodist. Member Odd Fellows, Knights of Pythias. Home: 8th and Centre Sts. Office: 402 Broad St., Jacksonville, Fla.

ANDERSON, Charles William, former internal revenue collector; born at Oxford, Ohio, Apr. 28, 1866; son of Charles W. and Serena Anderson; ed. public schools, Oxford; high school, Middleton, O.; took course in Spencerian Business College, Cleveland, O., and Berlitz School of Languages, Worcester, Mass.; married Emma Lee Bonaparte, of Hampton, Va. United States gauger in 2d Dist. New York, 1890-3; private secretary to state treasurer of N. Y., 1893-5; chief clerk in State Treasury, 1895-8; supervisor of accounts for New York State Racing Commission, 1898-1905; collector of internal revenue in 2d Dist. New York, 1905-15; (when removed from office under administration of President Woodrow Wilson, Apr. 4, 1915, The World (New York) published an editorial quoted as follows: "Charles W. Anderson goes out of office to-day after holding for ten years this responsible post under the Treasury. Many millions of dollars have passed through his hands. His dealings have been practically all with white men of the keenest intellect and of substantial business standing. Capacity and courtesy have been the qualities most remarked in his conduct of an office maintained always in the highest efficiency. In Collector Anderson's time, three complicated and important new revenue measures, the income tax, the corporation tax and the war revenue tax, have made this office the most difficult, as it is the most important, ever held by a colored man under the Government. He has stood the test. No race is fairly judged by holding up as types for reprobation its most degraded specimens. Every race has the right to be judged by its patient, toiling, useful average, and by its best.") He was president New York Commission to Tennessee Centennial Exposition at Nashville, 1897, appointed by Gov. Levi P. Morton; one of speakers at banquet tendered by Columbia Post, G. A. R., to President William McKinley, at Buffalo, N. Y., Aug. 24, 1897; member Hudson-Fulton Celebration Committee, citizens committee to welcome Admiral George Dewey and the fleet on return from Phillipine Islands, citizens committee to welcome Admirals William T. Sampson and Winfield S. Schley when fleet returned from Cuba, committee to welcome Col. Theodore Roosevelt on return from Africa; honorary pall bearer at funeral of Mayor William J. Gaynor of New York; one of speakers at Peace Banquet of citizens representing 50 foreign nations at Hotel Astor, New York, Jan. 4, 1914; member committee on unemployed appointed by Mayor John P. Mitchel, 1914; member citizens committee to receive bodies of U. S. marines killed at Vera Cruz, Mex., 1914; permanent member New York City Independence Day Commission. Was alternate delegate at-large to Republican National Convention, Chicago, Ill., 1908, 1912; served on Republican State Committee 16 years. Member National Geographical Society, Metropolitan Museum of Art, Institute of Art and Sciences of Columbia Univ., Academy of Political Science, New York Peace Society, Japanese Franchise League. Home: 156 W. 132d St., New York.

ANDERSON, Chester A., clergyman; first colored preacher to organize colored church in Los Angeles; was moderator Western Baptist Assn., 1912-14, and is oldest member; pastor Hope Baptist Church, Paloma Ave., near 16th St., Los Angeles, Calif.

ANDERSON, Dennis Henry, college president; born on farm at Claybrook, Tenn., Feb. 14, 1868; son of William and Lucinda Anderson; never attended elementary school, yet he began teaching at age of 15, studying at same time for 5 years following; grad. Lane College, Jackson, Tenn., 1893; (D.D., M.S., Princeton Normal and Industrial Univ., Ind., 1914); married Artelia Harris, of Va., July 14, 1897. Began teaching school in Madison County, Tenn., 1883; organized educational leagues at Palistine, Fulton, and Mayfield, Ky.; erected school houses at these places before the state began building schools for colored children; founded, 1910, since president, West Kentucky Industrial College at Paducah. Republican. Mason; member Knights of Pythias. Author (pamphlets): Fire Side Talks, 1907; The Guide, 1910; published Syllabus for State of Tenn., 1906. Address: Paducah, Ky.

ANDERSON, Florence Gray, supervising industrial teacher; born at Louisville, Ky., Oct. 28, 1890; daughter of Charles William (M. D.) and Mildred English (Saunders) Anderson; grad. Central High School, Louisville, 1907; Hampton Institute, Va., 1911; unmarried. Taught in Kindergarten at Tuskegee Institute, Ala., 1912; teacher in Summer School for Teachers, Hopkinsville, Ky., 1912, 1913; supervising industrial teacher of colored schools under the Department of Education, Commonwealth of Kentucky, since 1913; member Kentucky State Teachers' Assn., Hospital Club in Winchester, and Church Aid Club in Frankfort. Episcopalian. Home: 609 High St., Frankfort. Address: 36 S. Highland St., Winchester, Ky.

ANDERSON, James Harvey, clergyman, statistician; born at Frederick City, Md., June 30, 1848; son of James Harvey and Minerva Ann (Key) Anderson; self-educated; (hon. D.D., Livingstone College, Salisbury, N. C., 1896; Ph.D., Eastern North Carolina Industrial Academy, 1908); married Julia Ann Moore, of Paterson, N. J., Mar. 10, 1870; 9 children. Began work for white family when 7 years old, continuing to 1863; was with 13th N. J. Vol. Inf., in the service of an officer who was severely wounded at Chancellorsville and with whom he returned to Paterson, 1863; enlisted in Co. G. 39th Regt. Colored Vols., Sept. 10, 1864; engaged in battles of Petersburg and Stone Fort, Va., also Fort Fisher, N. C.; discharged, Oct. 10, 1865. Worked on farm and at other labor for a time; traveled with minstrel troupe 1 yr.; joined A. M. E. Zion Church at Lodi, N. J., 1870; licensed to preach, 1871; ordained deacon, 1874, elder, 1876; pastored in New York and New England states, Philadelphia, Baltimore, New Jersey, Allegheny and North Carolina conferences; was fraternal delegate to Centennial Conference of Methodism, Baltimore, 1884; elected delegate to Ecumenicial Conference, London, Eng., but could not attend; delegate to 8 general conferences during period, 1884-1912; statistician for A. M. E. Zion church in America 28 years; now presiding elder Harrisburg District. Correspondent more than 30 years for Star of Zion under caption of "Searchlight Scenes"; founder and editor A. M. E. Zion Church Year Book; wrote history of the church for National Encyclopaedia of American Biography; wrote and published biographies of 300 clergymen. Trustee Eastern North Carolina Industrial Academy. While pastor at Providence, 1881, was instrumental in securing repeal of law prohibiting intermarriage between white and colored persons in R. I.; led Republican party revolt, 1882, which nominated for governor ex-Gov. William Sprague; was himself nominated for state legislator and declined to run. Member Post No. 19, G. A. R., Baltimore, Md., 32 degree mason; member Odd Fellows, Knights of Pythias. Home: 430 Herr St., Harrisburg, Pa.

ANDERSON, James Henry, editor, publisher; born at Columbia, S. C., Dec. 15, 1868; son of Alexander and Martha (Barnes) Anderson; public school education. Began in bill posting business, 1905, continuing to 1908; founded in 1909, and since managing editor, Amsterdam News, of New York. Served in navy, 1897-9; organized Monitor League; commissioner Boy Scouts; member Emancipation Celebration Committee of New York, 1913. Republican candidate for alderman from 31st Dist., New York, 1913; ex-member Republican County Committee. Episcopalian. Member American Academy Political and Social Science, New Amsterdam Medical Assn., William J. Gayner Memorial Assn., Excelsior Military Band. Mason; member Odd Fellows. Home: 59 W. 139th St. Office: 17 W. 135th St., New York.

ANDERSON, James Wayman, station master; born in Sparta Co., Tenn., Apr. 8, 1863; son of David M. and Mary (Rickman) Anderson; attended school in Harvey Co., Kan.; married Winnie Hubble, of Toledo, Ohio, Dec. 22, 1886; 3 children: Zola M., Chester D., James W., Jr. During war between the states the family moved North and lived at Bethel, O., 1864-71; father acquired homestead and removed to Harvey Co., Kan., 1871; worked on farm to age of 20 yrs.; opened first laundry in Hutchinson, Kan., 1883; sold to a Chinaman, 1886; worked on father's farm following 2 yrs.; was platform man 2 yrs., and station master since 1900, for A. T. & S. Fe R. R. Co., at Newton, Kan. Republican. Methodist. Mason. Home: 618 E. 7th St. Address: Santa Fe Ticket Office, Newton, Kan.

ANDERSON, Jefferson Charles, physician; born at Monticello, Fla., July 20, 1868; son of Azor and Amelia (Cuyler) Anderson; grad. Wayland Seminary, 1887; A.B., Lincoln (Pa.) Univ., 1894; M.D., New York Homoeopathic Medical College and Flower Hospital, 1889; married Mary J. Fossett, of Baltimore, Md., 1899; 3 children: Zenaide, Loyse, Jesse. Practiced in Plainfield, N. J., since Feb. 9, 1900;

member National Medical Assn., New Jersey Homoeopathic Medical Assn., North Jersey Medical Assn. Republican. Episcopalian. Mason; member Odd Fellows. Address: 405 W. 4th St., Plainfield, N. J.

ANDERSON, Louis Bernard, lawyer; born at Petersburg, Va., Apr. 7, 1871; son of Moses E. and Elizabeth C. (Rooney) Anderson; ed. public schools, Petersburg; Virginia Normal Institute; grad. Kent College of Law, Chicago, 1897; married Julia E. Barr, of Mattoon, Ill., Nov. 17, 1897; 1 child: Jessica C. Admitted to Illinois bar, 1897; since practiced in Chicago; assistant county attorney, Cook County, 1898-1914; appointed assistant corporation council, City of Chicago, July, 1915. Served as captain and adjutant in 8th Inf. I. N. G. Republican. Mason; member Odd Fellows, Knights of Pythias, Elks. Club: Appomatox. Home: 2821 Wabash Ave. Office: 184 W. Weshington St., Chicago, Ill.

ANDERSON, Peyton Everett, supervising industrial teacher, clergyman; born in Prince Edward County, Va., Aug. 3, 1861; son of Paskal and Martha (Dupuy) Anderson; attended public schools and 3 terms in Richmond (Va.) Institute; grad. State Summer School at Petersburg, Va., 1909; studied theology at Princeton (Ind.) Normal and Industrial Univ., 1909; married Pattie E. Price, of Meharrin, Va., May 2, 1892; 9 children: Charles, Jesse, Mary, Geneva, Mattie, James, Rudolph, Roosevelt, Lucy. Began as teacher in public schools, Va., 1877; supervisor Negro Rural Schools, Prince Edward County, since 1909; supervisor of children for Virginia State Board of Charities; secretary Keystone Mission Industrial School. Ordaned Baptist ministry; pastor at Drakes Branch, Va. Republican. President Prince Edward County Teachers' Assn.; member Knights of Pythias, United Order of Moses, Order of St. Luke. Address: Meharrin, Va.

ANDERSON, Peyton Fortine, physician, surgeon; born at Aetna Mills,

King William County, Va., Nov. 5, 1890; son of Thomas L. and Ida Bell (Fortine) Anderson; grad. high school, Shelton, Conn., 1909; M.D., New York Homoeopathic Medical College and Flower Hosptial, 1913; postgraduate work in universities at Vienna and Berlin, 1913; unmarried. While in college took charge practice of Dr. E. P. Roberts (New York), who was traveling in Europe, 1912-13; practiced in Waterbury, Conn., since 1914; lecturer on hygiene and sanitation to colored people. Member American Institute of Homoeopathy, Connecticut Homoeopathy Society, New York Homoeopathic College and Flower Hospital Alumni Assn.; secretary Civic League of Waterbury. Mason. Address: 57 Center St., Waterbury, Conn.

ANDERSON, William Louis, printer; born at Dover, Ky., Aug. 31, 1868; son of Louis and Althaea (Foley) Anderson; public school edn.; married Sara E. Porter, of Cincinnati, Ohio, Oct. 13, 1900. Editor the American Reformer, Cincinnati, 1892-4, Rostrum, 1897-1902, Cincinnati Pilot, 1911-12; book and job printer. Secretary board of trustees Cincinnati Colored Industrial school. Was alternate delegate at-large to Republican National Convention, Chicago, 1912. Baptist. Grand Chancellor Knights of Pythias of Ohio. Home: 313 Stone St. Office: 226 W. 8th St., Cincinnati, Ohio.

ANDERSON, William T., clergyman; born at Wilkesboro, N. C., Mar. 1, 1863; son of William and Nancy Anderson; public school edn., Abingdon and Glade Springs, Va.; studied dentistry 2 years under Dr. William Farmer at Wytheville, Va.; (D.D., Princeton (Ind.) Normal and Industrial Univ., 1914); married Rosa Finley, of Columbus, Ohio, 1910. Teacher in public schools, Dublin, Va., 1884, Newburn, 1885, Graham, 1887; licensed as local preacher A. M. E. Church, Abingdon, Va., 1885; ordained élder, 1901; pastor at Columbus, Ind., 1911, Princeton, 1912-13, Mt. Vernon since 1913; was editor for a time of Knoxville (Tenn.) Gleaner. Republican; speaker for party during campaigns in Tennessee. Member Methodist Ministerial Alliance, Knoxville. Mason; member Odd Fellows, Knights of Pythias. Home: 221 W. 6th St., Mt. Vernon, Ind.

ANDREWS, Albert Anson, lawyer; born at Clarksville, Tenn., Sept. 17, 1882; son of George Thomas and Susan (Watkins) Andrews; ed. Clarksville Normal Academy; Business High School, Washington, D. C.; LL.B., Howard Univ. School of Law, 1912; married Marion E. Freeman, of Washington, June 24, 1914. Began as shipping clerk with Luckett-Wake Tobacco Co., Clarksville, 1902; in biochemical laboratories, bureau of animal industry, Department of Agriculture, Washington, 1907-13; work included cattle inspection for glanders and tuberculosis. Admitted to Kentucky bar, 1913; since practiced in Louisville; attorney for Louisville Branch, National Association for Advancement of Colored People in suit testing segregation ordinance, 1914; director Louisville Conservatory of Music; special correspondent for Lexington News, and Washington Bee; contributing editor Louisville News. Republican. Congregationalist. Member Howard Univ. Alumni Assn., Bethel Literary and Historical Society (Washington); also member Odd Fellows. Home: 2929 S. 6th St. Office: 422 S. 6th St., Louisville, Ky.

ANDREWS, William Trent, lawyer, real estate operator; born at Sumter, S. C., Mar. 25, 1864; son of Robert M. and Martha E. (Burroughs) Andrews; was cadet at U. S. Military Academy, West Point, N. Y., 1885; B.S., Fisk Univ., Nashville, Tenn., 1890; LL.B., Howard Univ. School of Law, Washington, D. C., 1892; married Anna Virginia Lee, of Washington, 1896; 2 children: William, Jr., Norman P. Admitted to South Carolina bar, 1894; since in practice at Sumter and operated in real estate; owns 60 houses, 4 brick business buildings, and part interest in 9 store buildings; president Sumter Investment Co.; director Negro Development Co. Delegate to all Republican conventions in state since 1894, and to natianal convention at Chicago, 1908; delegate at-large to Republican National Convention at Chicago, 1912. Methodist. Mason; member Odd Fellows, Knights of Pythias. Home: 116 Manning Ave. Office: 26 1-2 W. Liberty St., Sumter, S. C.

ANTHONY, Isham Henry, physician, surgeon; born at Brownsville, Tenn., Dec. 25, 1868; son of Jerry and Matilda (Robinson) Anthony; attended schools in Haywood County, Tenn., to 1882; A.B., Fisk Univ., Nashville, 1892; M.D., Univ. of Pa., 1895; married Theresa E. Reed, of Brownsville, Nov. 29, 1899; 2 children: Vivian Beatrice, Eula Eunice. Began practice in Brownsville, 1895; physician and surgeon to Aid and Relief Society, also Sisters of Charity; was often called to patients within 40 mile radius; practiced in Kansas City, Kan., since 1901; physician and lecturer Douglass Hospital and Training School. Trustee 1st Baptist Church. Republican. Member Kansas State Medical Assn., Wyandotte County Medical Assn. Mason; member Knights of Pythias. Home: 2020 N. 3d St. Office: 1514 N. 5th St., Kansas City, Kan.

ANTHONY, Robert Lincoln, principal high school, penman, lecturer; born at Lancaster, O., Nov. 28, 1866; son of Mark and Malissa Anthony; grad. high school, Gibson City, Ill., 1885; Iowa State Normal School later; LL.B., Wilberforce (O.) Univ. Law Dept., 1888; A.B., Cornell Univ., 1891; A.M., Eastman College, N. Y., 1892; (LL.D., Campbell College, Jackson, Miss., 1900); married Carrie B. Gaddie, of Louisville, Ky., June 28, 1893; 7 children: Frank, Julia, Esther, Naomi, Robert, Helen, Minnie. Began as principal colored school at Olmsted, Ill., 1885; head master St. Michaels Academy (Episcopal), Cairo, Ill., 1886; teacher elocution and penmanship at Wilberforce (O.) Univ., 1887-8; principal of school at Indianapolis, Ind., 1889, business dept. State Univ., Louisville, Ky., 1890-3, colored school DuQuoin, Ill., 1895-9, Colored High School, Carmi, Ill., 1899-1901, Colored High School, Vin-

cennes, Ind., 1901-6; while at Du-Quoin, began giving instruction by correspondence which finally resulted in regular institutions; founded, 1906, president to 1908, since director, McKinley Memorial Univ., Vincennes; president, 1908-13, and president board of trustees, Princeton (Ind.) Normal and Industrial Univ., since 1913; principal Booker T. Washington High School, Mt. Vernon, Ind., 1913-15; founder and president Tri-State Orphanage for Colored Children, Mt. Vernon. Has remarkable gift as artist-penman; awarded medals and deplomas for art and penmanship exhibits at World's Fair, New Orleans, La., 1885, Negro Exposition at Nashville, Tenn., Columbian Exposition, Chicago, Portland (Ore.) Exposition, Cotton States Exposition, Atlanta, Ga., Louisiana Purchase Exposition, St. Louis, Mo.; designed and published Historical-Pictorial Record of M. E. Church (20x32 inches), and similar design for other churches; has contracts for deplomas from 16 or more counties in Indiana, also patrons in many parts of U. S. for his designing, engrossing and engravings; editor and publisher The Orphan; ex-secretary and owns interest in Church Publishing Co., at Vincennes. Lecturer on educational and reform movements; was delegate to National Negro Educational Congress, Denver, Colo., 1911. Republican; speaker for party during campaigns in Ind., Ill., Ohio; was enrolling and engrossing clerk 34th and 35th General Assemblies in Illinois. Baptist. Member National Penman and Business Educators' Assn., Western Penmans' Assn., National Teachers' Assn., Indiana State Teachers' Assn., Tri-State Association for Advancement of Colored Orphans, Civic League of Mt. Vernon (secretary). Mason; member Knights of Pythias. Author: How to Teach Writing, 1896; Elementary Mechanical Drawing, 1899; Manual of Penmanship, 1900; University Extension Publications, 1900; How to Read Character from Handwriting, 1901; How to Succeed in Literature, 1902; Household Arts, 1913; Quotation

Gems, 1913; Afro-American Literary Readers, 1915. Home: 133 Sawmill St., Mt. Vernon, Ind.

ARBUCKLE, John Milton, reader, impersonator, music publisher; born at Keokuk, Iowa, Mar. 24, 1865; son of Samuel and Caroline (Johnson) Arbuckle; ed. Sumner High School, St. Louis, Mo., Lincoln Institute, Jefferson City, Mo.; New England Conservatory of Music; married Mary V. Turner, of St. Louis, 1888; children: Lillie May (Mrs. E. L. Evans), Birdie (Mrs. W. E. Price); 2d marriage, Minnie E. Kenney, of Cambrdge, Mass., 1906. Shipping clerk for 12 years with Methodist Book Concern at St. Louis; helped in founding Cambridge (Mass.) Advocate, and now advertising manager; member music publishing firm of Burkes & Arbuckle, Boston, since 1910; director W. O. P. Realty Co.; reader and impersonator; choir and concert soloist; superintendent 4th M. E. Church, Boston. Republican. Member St. Mark's Musical and Literary Society, Boston Historical and Literary Society, Boston Negro Business League, Advertisers League of Boston; also member Knights of Pythias. Home: 1556 Cambridge, St., Cambridge. Office: 800 Tremont St., Boston, Mass.

ARCHER, Samuel Howard, teacher; born in Chesterfield Co., Va., Dec. 23, 1870; son of Nelson and Keziah (Howe) Archer; attended Peabody public school, Petersburg, Va.; preparatory edn. Wayland Normal School, Washington; A.B., Colgate Univ., Hamilton, N. Y., 1902; took course in pedegogy, Colgate Univ.; married Annie Courtney Johnson, of Millwood, Va., Sept. 7, 1905; 4 children: Samuel Howard, Rosalind E., Nelson Thomas, Leonard Courtney A. Began as teacher in rural schools, Va., 1887; teacher of mathematics Roger Williams Univ., Nashville, Tenn., 1902-5; instructor in theology, 1905-6, teacher in mathematics since 1906, in Morehouse College, Atlanta, Ga. Republican. Baptist. Club: Monday. Address: Morehouse College, Atlanta, Ga.

ARMISTEAD, Henry Watson, physician; born at Nashville, Tenn., June 15, 1868; son of Henry and Agnes (Watson) Armistead; grad. Fisk Univ., Nashville, 1888; Ph.D., Meharry Medical College (Walden Univ.), 1894, M.D., 1895; post-graduate work Chicago Polyclinic, 1902; married Catherine H. Baughman of Indianapolis, Ind., June 17, 1899; 1 child: Emma L. Began practice in Nashville, 1896; now physician on staff of Lincoln Hospital, and Sisters of Charity Hospital, Indianapolis, Ind.; medical inspector public schools; medical register Knights of Pythias, Odd Fellows, United Brothers of Friendship; president Royal Mfg. Co. Republican. African Methodist. Former president Aesculapian Society of Indianapolis; secretary-treasury Tri-State Medical Assn. of Ind., Ky. and Ohio. Mason. Club: Dumas. Home 1116 Cornell Ave. Office:605 N. West St., Indianapolis, Ind.

ARMSTRONG, Reuben Hanson, clergyman; born at Fishing Creek, Lancaster Co., Pa., Nov. 28, 1854; son of Jerome and Mary Jane (Underhill) Armstrong; A.D., Lincoln (Pa.) Univ., 1877, S.T.B., 1880 (D.D. 1899); married Louisa Shepard, of Philadelphia, Apr. 15, 1880. 5 children: Lillian L., Gertrude J., David I., William D., Florence V. Ordained Presbyterian ministry, 1880; pastored at Lynchburg, Va., 1 year, and principal graded school in Liberty; supply minister, and principal public school, Louisburg, N. C., 1881-5; supplied at Chestnut Street Church, Wilmington, N. C., 1885-6; pastor Capitol Street Church, Harrisburg, Pa., 1886-98, Madison Street Church, Baltimore, Md., 1898-1904, Beran Church, 1905-7; missionary, stated supply, and pastor Faith Church, Germantown, Pa., since 1907; secretary Afro-American Presbyterian Council. Was clerk in recorder of deeds office at Harrisburg 1 year. Republican. Mason; Odd Fellow. Home: 220 W. Coulter St., Philadelphia, Pa.

ARNETT, Charles Henry, clergyman, contractor; born at Henderson, Ky., Nov. 15, 1858; son of James and Arnett; public school edn., Henderson; correspondence course from Princeton (Ind.) Normal and Industrial Univ.; married Anna Brooks, of Dixon, Ky., Feb. 8, 1876; 1 child: Louis; 2d marriage, Charlotte Watkins, of Henderson, July 9, 1880; child: Callie Z. Learned carpenter trade and worked 4 years for wages; in contracting business since 1880; erected 2 churches at Sebree, Ky., 1880, 1902, and one church each in 5 other towns in Ky., also built many homes. Ordained in Baptist ministry at Union, Ky., 1887; pastor at Robard 13 years, Henderson, 1900, Bellfield, 1900-9, Lick Creek, Ky., since 1909; moderator Young Men's Baptist Assn. of Western Ky. Trustee I. & N. College, Hopkinsville. Republican. Missionary Baptist. Mason; member Odd Fellows. Home: 110 Holloway St., Henderson, Ky.

ARNOLD, A. Sherley, embalmer; born at Newburg, Ind., Oct. 28, 1892; son of Perry and Cora (Williams) Arnold; ed. public schools, Evansville, Ind.; student Hampton (Va.) Normal and Agricultural Institute, 1911-12; grad. Askins Training School of Embalming, Indianapolis, Ind., 1914; unmarried. Began with undertaking firm of Shelton & Co., Indianapolis, 1913; embalmer and manager for W. A. Gaines Co., funeral directors, Henderson, Ky., since 1914; licensed in Ind. and Ky. Republican. African Methodist. Member Kentucky State Undertakers' Assn., Knights of Pythias. Home: 828 Powell St. Office: 132 2d St., Henderson, Ky.

ARTER, Jared Mawrice, clergyman, college president; born at Harper's Ferry, W. Va., Jan. 27, 1850; son of Jeremiah and Hannah Frances (Williams) Arter; ed. public schools, Newfield and Ithica, N. Y.; student Storer College, Harper's Ferry, State College, Bellefonte, Pa., Hillsdale College, Mich., Univ. of Chicago Theological Seminary; married Emily Carter, of Rippon, W. Va., June 1, 1890 (d.1907); 4 children: Charles, Rose, Julia, Jared; 2d marriage, Maggie May Wall, of Washington, D. C., Dec. 29, 1910. Worked on farm, in paper mills, steel mills, hotels and restaurants; served

as nurse, sold maps and books; principal public school, Hagerstown, Md., 1892-4; teacher in Storer College, 1894-7, Lynchburg Theological Seminary, 1897-1900, Manning Theological Seminary, Cairo, Ill., 1900-9; president and financial agent W. Va. Industrial Seminary and College, Hill Top, W. Va., since 1909. Republican. Missionary Baptist. Mason; member Knights of Pythias, True Reformers. Club: Seminary Industrial. Home: Hill Top. Office: Red Star, W. Va.

ARTIS, Dillard, municipal contractor; born in Howard Co., Ind., Dec. 24, 1868; son of Thomas and Ester (Hall) Artis; public school education; married Manerva Ward, of Indianapolis, June 22, 1910. Began as janitor of court house, Marion, Ind., 1900; later accepted private contracts trimming trees, laying sod and making lawns, this work led to contracts for digging cellars, sewer and cement work, street building, and finally municipal contracting; had cement contract connected with $100,000 residence of J. W. Wilson, the First Baptist Church and number others; finished contracts on tarvia roads amounting to $40,000 in 1914; president Grant Security & Loan Co., Gill Coal & Supply Co., Marion. Was vice-president Grant County Republican Central Committee, 1904. African Methodist. Former president Marion Negro Business League; member Odd Fellows, Knights of Pythias, Knights of Tabor. Address: 1813 S. Boots St., Marion, Ind.

ATKINS, S. G., clergyman; secretary of education and general officer African Methodist Episcopal Church. Address: Winston-Salem, N. C.

ATKINS, Thomas V. Dolivia, clergyman; born at Manchester (now S. Richmond), Va., May 28, 1877; son of Job and Mary Ann (Jonathan) Atkins; grad. Manchester High School, 1895; theological training Richmond Theological Seminary (now Va. Union Univ.), and in Indiana; (A.M., Friendship College, Rockhill, S. C., April, 1911; D.D., Guadalupe College, Seguin, Tex., May, 1911); married Willette R. Jones, of Charlotte, N. C., Aug. 7, 1901. Ordained Baptist ministry, 1897; pastored at Charlotte and Greensboro, N. C., Charlottsville, Va., Steelton, Pa.; now pastor Mt. Carmel Baptist Church, Philadelphia; built 3 churches. Founded in 1908, and editor to 1912, the Charlottsville Messenger; literary editor Christian Banner, 1908-14; associate editor Christian Review, Philadelphia; was principal organizer Charlottsville Fair Assn., Albermarle Co., Va., 1910. Secretary Eastern Baptist Assn. of Pa., Colored Relief Protective Assn. of Pa., Afro-American Protective League of Pa. Mason. Author: Religious Romance, 1909. Home: 143 N. 58 Place, Philadelphia, Pa.

ATWOOD, Louis K., banker; A.B., Lincoln (Pa.) Univ., 1874. Served 2 terms in Miss. House of Representatives. President, Southern Bank, Jackson, Miss.

AUTEN, Theodore Augustus, clergyman, born at Somerville, N. J., June 25, 1870; son of James Albert and Eliza (Schenck) Auten; public school edn., Somerville and Plainfield, N. J.; A.B., Lincoln (Pa.) Univ., 1896, A.M., later, S.T.B., 1899; married Florence Alverteen Storey, of Bath, N. Y., Sept. 26, 1900. Licensed to preach, A. M. E. church, 1898; ordained deacon, 1898, elder, 1899; pastor at Bath, N. Y., 1899-1900, Amsterdam and Jamestown Circuits, 1900-3, Ithica, 1903-8; presiding elder Western New York Conference 4 years; pastor at Cambridge, Mass., since 1912; burned parsonage mortgage at Ithica and church mortgage at Bath; founded Rush Zion Brotherhood at Cambridge. Delegate to general conferences, St. Louis, Mo., 1904, Philadelphia, 1908, Ecumenical Conference on Methodism, Toronto, Can., 1911, general conference at Charlotte, N. C., 1912; president Interdenominational Ministers' Union of Boston, 1912-14; served 9 years as trustee Harriett Tubman Home for Aged and Infirm Colored People, Auburn, N. Y. Member publicity committee National Association for Advancement of Colored People; also member Wendell Phillips Memorial

Assn., Boston. Address: 148 River St., Cambridge, Mass.

AVERY, John Moses, insurance; born near Morganton, N. C., Oct. 10, 1876; son of Thomas and Harriett Elizabeth (Kincaid) Avery; grad. Kittrell (N. C.) College, 1900; married Lulu L. Aiken, of Reidsville, N. C., Apr. 8, 1903; 2 children: Jannette E., Vivian B. Began as local agent for North Carolina Mutual and Provident Assn., 1900; now assistant manager in home office at Durham, N. C.; was principal school at Hickory, N. C., 1900-1, and at Monganton, 1901-6; resigned to devote full time to insurance business. Trustee and treasurer Lincoln Hospital; trustee Kittrell College; superintendent St. Joseph's Sunday School; was lay delegate to General Conference A. M. E. Church at Chicago, 1904, also at Norfolk, Va., 1908. Progressive. President, Durham Negro Business League. 32 degree Mason; director Royal Knights of King David; member Knights of Pythias. Home: 306 Unstead St. Office: Mutual and Provident Assn., Durham, N. C.

AYERS, Mary Lizzie, secretary secret society; born at Baxley, Ga., Feb. 20, 1877; daughter of Samuel S. and Louise (Hall) Sellers; ed. Atlanta (Ga.) Univ., 1890-3; Spellman Seminary 4 years; married William Judson Ayers, of Milledgeville, Ga., Oct. 20, 1904; 2 children: Willie Mae, Samuel J. Teacher in schools of Ga., 10 years; in millinery business, 1908-9; secretary Order of Eastern Star of Ga., since 1909. Missionary Baptist. Member Court of Calanthe. Address: Box 21, Ashburn, Ga.

AYERS, William Judson, contractor; born at Milledgeville, Ga., Feb. 6, 1875; son of Judson and Annie Ayers; ed. Eddy High School, Milledgeville; Connecticut Industrial School, Thomasville, Ga.; married Mary Lizzie Sellers, of Baxley, Ga., Oct. 20, 1904; 2 children: Willie Mae, Samuel J. Began business career in general merchandise store; was president Stanley & Ayers Co., 10 years; brick, cement and plastering contractor at Ashburn, Ga., since 1900.

Trustee Evergreen Academy. Baptist. Member Odd Fellows, Knights of Pythias. Address: Box 21, Ashburn, Ga.

B

BACOTE, Samuel William, clergyman, lecturer, author; born at Society Hill, S. C., Feb. 1, 1866; son of Bembo and Harriett Bacote; attended public schools at Society Hill; prep. edn. Benedict College, Columbia, S. C., 1883-8; student in Shaw Univ., Raleigh, 1 year: B.D., Richmond Theol. Sem., 1892; A.B., Kansas City Univ., Kan., 1898, A.M., 1900, D.D., 1904; married Lucy Jeannette Bledsoe, of Topeka, Kan., Aug. 22, 1902; children: Samuel and Geraldine (deceased); Clarence and Lucille. Ordained Baptist ministry, Marion, Ala., 1892; same year was member advisory council World Parliament of Religion; pastor Second Baptist Church, and president Marion Baptist College, 1892-5; pastor Second Baptist Church, Kansas City, Mo., since 1895; erected $100,000 church edifice; elected statistican National Baptist Convention, 1902, continuing without opposition to 1914; organized the department so thoroughly that statistical information of achievements by that convention each year are made clear at a glance; personally contributes over $500 annually to denominational enterprises. Prohibitionist. 32 degree Mason. Author: Who's Who Among the Colored Baptist of the United States, first volume, 1913; compiled the National Baptist Year Book, 1905. Home: 2210 Kansas Ave., Kansas City, Mo.

BAGNALL, Robert Wellington, clergyman; born at Norfolk, Va., Oct. 14, 1883; son of Rev. Robert and Sophronia (Harrison) Bagnall; attended public schools and Mission College, Norfolk; grad. Bishop Payne Divinity School, 1903, (B.D., 1911); studied at Temple Univ., Philadelphia, Pa.; married Lillian Anderson, of Baltimore, Md., July 11, 1906. Ordained in Episcopal ministry, 1903; minister in charge Epiphany Church, Blackstone, Pa., 1903-4; prin. Croom

Normal and Industrial School, and rector St. Simon's Church, Croom, Md., 1904-6; rector St. Andrew's Church, Cleveland, O., 1906-10; removed mortgage, remodeled edifice and doubled congregation; rector St. Matthews Church, Detroit, Mich., since 1911; doubled membership and income. Was speaker at opening of Bethel Historical and Literary Assn.; sec. Detroit branch National Assn. for Advancement of Colored People and principal speaker at opening its first session at Baltimore, 1914. Mem. Michigan Clerical Union, Diocesan Sunday School Commission of Mich., Detroit Institute of Religious Education (mem. exec. com.), Detroit Society of Prophylaxis; also mem. Wayne County Committee on Equitable Legislation; was instrumental in defeating anti-intermarriage bill in Mich., 1913. Author: What Every Churchman should Know (a manual), 1915. Home: 329 Antoine St., Detroit, Mich.

BAILEY, Edward Walter, teacher; born at Brownsville, Tenn.; son of Edward and Peggie (Alsbrooks) Bailey; A.B., Fisk Univ., 1887; married Fannie Virginia Perdue, of Ripley, Tenn., 1894; 4 children. Principal Bruce High School, Dyersburg, Tenn., 1887-9, Lane College, Jackson, Tenn., 1889-91; again prin. Bruce High School, 1891-7; prin. Covington Grammar School, Tenn., 1897-1900, Gibbons High School, Paris, Tex., since 1900; sec. Citizens Undertaking Co.; prop. Bailey's Airdome Theater. Colored Methodist. Hon. member National Teachers' Educatonal Assn., member Tenn. Teachers' Assn. Mason; member Odd Fellows, Knights of Pythias, Mosaic Templars, Knights of Tabor. Club: Progressive. Address: 191 N. 21st St., Paris, Texas.

BAILEY, Isaac, sergeant U. S. A., retired. Enlisted in 9th Cav., July 10, 1883; assigned to scout duty near Rio Grande river in Mexico, 1884; in campaign against Geronimo's Apache Indians, 1885-6; recommended for bravery by Lieut. J. B. McDonald in report of Aug. 28, 1886, also for special service in Arizona, 1887; discharged July 9, and re-enlisted July

10, 1888; on scout duty with Gen. Corbin settling Moqui Indian troubles; enlisted for 3d time, 1893; was in engagement at Las Guasimas, June 24, 1898; went to rescue of Rough Riders during siege of Santiago, Cuba, July 1-17, 1898; received medal of honor for gallantry in Cuba; discharged July 9, 1898; retired. Home: Omaha, Neb.

BAILEY, Neill Alexander, farm demonstrator for U. S.; born in Harnett Co., N. C., Nov. 10, 1861; son of Edward and Phillis (McLean Bailey; student Fayetteville (N. C.) State Normal School, 1880-3; degree B.Agr., Agrl. and Mech. College, Greensboro, 1908; married Lucy Minon, of Guilford Co., N. C., Sept. 18, 1913; 2 children: Florence, Victoria. Teacher in public schools, N. C., 1884-1904; farmer during same yrs.; U. S. farm demonstrator in Agrl. and Mech. College, Greensboro, since 1910; writer of scientific farming articles. Republican. African Methodist. Member Royal Knights of King David. Home: Pittsboro, N. C. (R. F. D. No. 2). Office: Agricultural and Technical College, Greensboro, N. C.

BAILEY, Robert Lieutenant, lawyer; born near Florence, Ala., June 29, 1885; son of Robert and Mary Ann (White) Bailey; grad. Talladega (Ala.) College, 1903, B.S., 1906; LL.B., Indiana Law School (Univ. of Indianapolis), 1912; married Mary Constance Stokes, of Atlanta, Ga., Jan. 27, 1909. Was railway mail clerk number of years; admitted to Indiana bar, 1912, U. S. Distrct Court, later; was attorney for founders, now director, Supreme Royal Circle of Friends of Indiana; counsel for incorporators of National Alliance of Postal Employes. Won second Whiton prize and Oratorical prize at Talladega, Senior Law School prize at Indianapolis, also prize of $25 for best contributed article to Colored People's Magazine. Republican. Congregationalist. Mason; Shriner; Elk. Author (pamphlet) The Vexing Question as to What Constitutes an Accident Within the Terms of an Accident Policy, 1913. Home:

1760 N. Senate Ave. Office: 46 N. Pennsylvania St., Indianapolis, Ind.

BAILEY, Walter Thomas, architect; born at Kewanee, Ill., Jan. 11, 1882; son of Emanuel and Lucy (Reynolds) Bailey; grad. Kewanee High School; B.S., Univ. of Illinois, 1904, A.M., 1910; married Josephine L. McCurdy, of Champaign, Ill., Oct. 31, 1903; 2 children: Edyth, Hazel. Draftsman for Henry Eckland, Kewanee, and Spencer & Temple, Champaign, 1905; head architectural department at Tuskegee Normal and Industrial Institute, 1905-14; architect in Memphis, Tenn., since 1914. African Methodist. Member Alabama Teachers' Assn. Clubs: Seminar, Twentieth Century. Office: 358 Beale Ave., Memphis, Tenn.

BAKER, David, inventor; born at Louisville, Ky., Apr. 2, 1881; son of John B.; ed. Meda Night School, New Orleans, La.; took course from National Correspondence School, Washington, D. C.; married Celena Le-'Cleac, of New Orleans, Apr. 18, 1903; 1 child: Hilda Katherine. In charge elevator service Board of Trade Building, New Orleans, 10 yrs.; in stationary dept. Morgan State Bank, 2 yrs.; removed to Los Angeles, Cal., 1910; invented scales for use in elevators to prevent overloading, also sanitary cuspidor; with Prof. T. V. Baquet, of New Orleans, invented street-car transon opener; inventor of railway signal apparatus for installation adjacent to railway bridges over streams; special deputy constable and director of elevator service at Hall of Records. Methodist. Member Knights of Pythias. Address: 2425 Lenord St., Los Angeles, Cal.

BAKER, Oscar William, lawyer; born at Bay City, Mich., Aug. 30, 1879; son of James H. and Mary (Edwoods) Baker; grad. high school, Bay City, 1898; Bay City Business College, 1899; LL.B., Univ. of Mich., 1902; married Ida Mae Harrison, of Lima, O., June 6, 1910; 3 children: Oscar W. Jr., Albert H., Dorothy F. Employed in office of lieutenant-governor at Lansing, Mich., 1899-1901; admitted to Michigan bar, 1902; since practiced in Bay City. Active in Republican politics; appointed commissioner in Circuit Court of Bay County by Gov. Fred M. Warner. Baptist. Member Bay County University of Michigan Alumni Assn.; hon. member Alpha Phi Alpha. When 7 years old, lost leg below the knee in railroad accident. Home: 223 N. Van Buren St. Office: 305 Shearer Brothers Bldg., Bay City, Mich.

BALDWIN, Manuel Liston, clergyman, teacher; born at Troy, N. C., Dec. 18, 1862; son of Dudley and Sylvia Baldwin; preparatory edn. Peabody Academy, at Troy; grad. Talladega (Ala) College, 1896; married, Dec. 25, 1912. Ordained Congregational ministry, 1896; pastor at Bethania, N. C., 1903, Greensboro, 1903-9, Wilmington, N. C., 1909-11, Dudley since 1914; was principal Bethania Normal and Industrial School, 1897-1903, city schools at Wilmington, 1911-13, public school, Dudley, since 1913; owns 200-acre farm, also photographing business. Address: Dudley, N. C.

BALLARD, Claudius, physician; born at Los Angeles, Cal., June 14, 1890; son of William L. and Mary (Tibbs) Ballard; grad. Los Angeles High School, 1909; student Polytechnic High School, 1 yr.; M.D., Univ. of Cal., 1913; unmarried. Practiced in Los Angeles since Mar. 15, 1914; secretary Baily Mfg. Co. Republican. Catholic. Mem. Physicians, Dentists and Druggists Association of Southern Cal. Forresters, United Brothers of Friendship. Address: 1201 1-2 Central Ave., Los Angeles, Cal.

BALLARD, William Henry, Sr., druggist; born in Franklin Co., Ky., Oct. 31, 1862; son of Dowan and Matilda (Bartlett) Ballard; attended public schools, Louisville, Ky.; took special course at Roger William Univ., Nashville, Tenn.; grad in pharmacy, Northwestern Univ., Chicago, Ill., 1892; married Bessie H. Brady, of Nashville, Dec. 28, 1892; 4 children: William H. Jr., Orville L., Edward H. Vivian E. Proprietor Ballard's Pharmacy, Lexington, Ky., established 1893; first colored man to open drug store in state; secretary and treas. Greenwood Cemetery Co.; assistant sec. Agricultural and Mechanical Assn.; director Lexington News Co., Greenwood Realty Co. Republican. African Methodist. Member National Medical Assn., National Negro Business League. 32d degree Mason; grand master United Brothers of Friendship in Ky.; past deputy state grand chancellor Knights of Pythias. Home: 551 Maryland Ave. Office: 148 N. Limestone St., Lexington, Ky.

BALLOU, John Henry, lawyer; born at Providence, R. I., June 9, 1853, which date shows his parents, David N. and Anna R. (Uchee) Ballou, were free; ed. public schools, Schofield's Commercial College, and took special course under Prof. C. W. Tarleton at Brown Univ., Providence; (LL.D., Selma Univ., Ala., 1892); married Carrie B. Sampson, of Jacksonville, Fla., Oct. 23, 1883 (died 1909); 4 children: Ella E., (Mrs. Butler); Dr. Edgar S.; Mamie A. (deceased); Serena D. Was first colored man admitted to Rhode Island bar, 1874; began practice in Providence; was instrumental with George T. Downing in securing repeal of law prohibiting inter-marriage of colored and white people in Rhode Island; delegate from R. I. to Civil Rights Convention; editor Eastern Review, 1874-5. Professor of physics and mathematics at Cookman Institute, Jacksonville, Fla., 1883-4; elected judge of Justice Court, 11th Dist. in Duval Co., Fla., 1888, continuing to 1892; attorney for Alabama Penny Savings Bank, Birmingham, 1892; same year founded Co-operative grocery Co., Birmingham; now practicing law in Jacksonville. He edited number race newspapers, including Daily Promotor, Jacksonville, 1912; now associate editor The Standard; as public speaker has addressed important meetings and lectured in many parts of the U. S. Was secretary Lincoln League, auxiliary to the Union Republican organization in Baltimore, Md., 1903, and prominent in city and state politics. Baptist. Mason; member Grand Lodge of Fla.; supreme commander Royal Lions of America; supreme pres. Good Samaritan Benefit Society; supreme vice-pres. Afro-American Union; secretary Florida Citizens Protective League. Author (with P. H. Thompson and I. W. Crawford) Multum in Parvo, 1912; wrote pamphlet: The National Publishing Board From a Denominational Standpoint, 1902; compiled and published Dictionary of the Colored People of Jacksonville, Fla., 1912. Office: Masonic Temple, Jacksonville, Fla.

BANKS, Alida Priscilla, supervising industrial teacher; born at Bacon's Castle, Va., June 1, 1887; daughter William Ruffin and Rebecca Victoria (Barlow) Banks; attended public school to 1904; student Hampton Normal and Agricultural Institute, 1904-9; unmarried. Worked during summers in northern states to meet expenses while at Hampton; taught school in Middlesex Co., Va., 1909-10; supervisor of Negro public schools, Cumberland, Co., Va., 1910-12; supervising industrial teacher, Surry Co., since Nov., 1913, this branch of modern public instruction is under the State Board of Education; it reaches most remote schools and homes of colored children through the aid of the Anna T. Jeanes Fund, the Negro Organization Society (Tuskegee), and Virginia Negro Teachers' Assn.; they teach sewing, shuck work, wood work, basketry, cord work, etc.; in the summer months gardening and canning is included in the instruction at homes of the children. Baptist. Member Virginia Negro State Teachers' Assn., Negro Organization Society of Va., School Improvement League, Home Makers' Club of Surry County. Home: Beacon's Castle. Office: Barco, Va.

BANKS, Charles, banker, planter; born at Clarksdale, Miss., 1873; son of Danial A. and Sallie Ann B.; ed Rust College, Holly Springs, Miss.; married, Trenma O. Booze, of Natchez, Miss., 1893. Senior member firm of Banks & Bro., general merchandise, Clarkesdale, 1891-1903; organized Bank of Mound Bayou, 1903, cashier to 1914; organized and is gen. mgr. Mound Bayou Oil Mill & Mfg. Co.,

$100,000 corpn.; director Union Guaranty Co., Jackson, also Miss. Beneficial Ins. Co., Indianola; among foremost citizens in Negro town of Mound Bayou. Trustee Wilberforce Univ., Campbell College. Delegate to Republican National Convention, 1904, 1908, delegate at-large, 1912. African Methodist. Mason; member Odd Fellows, Knights of Pythias. Address: Mound Bayou, Miss.

BANKS, William Webb, newspaper correspondent; born at Winchester, Ky., July 4, 1862; son of Patrick and Catherine (Martin) Banks; father was prominent man in town, and funeral was attended by mayor, circuit judge and other representative white citizens; grad. State Univ., Louisville, Ky., 1886; married Anna B. Simms, of Louisville, July 10, 1906. Taught school at Winchester 2 years; in mercantile business 27 years; editor National Chronical since 1891; correspondent for number white and colored newspapers; active in racial betterment movements, political and religious work. Was president Baptist Sunday School Convention 2 years; recording secretary Consolidated Baptist Assn., 5 years; massenger to Baptist General Assn., several times. Issued first call for organization of Negro business men and women in Ky.; made protest before state legislature on anti-separate coach movement; was Republican party candidate for recorder in United States Land Office at Washington, 1891; declined number political nominations. Was commissioner at Inter-State Exposition, Raleigh, N. C., and custodian of Kentucky building at Jamestown Tri-Centennial Exposition, Norfolk, Va., 1908; commissioner to Emancipation Exposition at New York, 1913; delegate to Half-Century Anniversary Celebration of Negro Freedom, Chicago, Ill., 1915. Address: 122 W. Broadway, Winchester, Ky.

BANTON, Conwell, physician; born at Philadelphia, Pa., June 10, 1875; son of Edward Washington and Laura Belle (Scott) Banton; public school edn., Philadelphia; grad. Institute for

Colored Youth, 1892; student Lincoln Univ., Pa., 1892-3; A.B., Univ. of Pa., 1897; M.D., Univ. of Pa., 1900; two jears post-graduate work at Phipps Institute for Treatment of Tuberculosis; married Elizabeth Davis, of Baltimore, Md., Nov. 11, 1903; 1 child: Alice Lucretia. Practiced in Wilmington since 1900; visiting physician of dispensary for treatment of tuberculosis; medical director Delaware State Tuberculosis Sanitarium for Colored People; member firm of Hopkins & Banton, druggists; director Royal Mutual Aid Benefit Assn. Republican. Episcopalian. Member National Medical Assn. Mason; member Odd Fellows. Club: Monday. Address: 924 French St., Wilmington, Del.

BARABIN, Joseph Hercules, physician; born at Jeanerette, La., Mar. 19, 1874; son of Joseph and Madaline (Cerf) Barabin; prep. edn. Gilbert Academy, Baldwin, La.; A.B., Fisk Univ., 1900; M.D., Illinois Medical College, 1905; married Lulu M. Benson, Dec. 28, 1905; 3 children: Jennie M., Joseph B., William S. Practiced in Marianna, Ark., since 1905; president and fiscal agent Negro National Life Ins. Co.; director and land agent Progressive Investment Co.; director Mound Bayou Oil Mill & Mfg. Co.; a founder the Negro town of Thomasville, Ark. Progressive. Congregationalist. Was president 4 yrs. Arkansas Medical Assn.; chairman commission of Negro Medical, Dentist and Pharmacy Assn. for study of tuberculosis. Member Odd Fellows, Knights of Pythias, Mosaic Templars, Royal Circle of Friends. Home: 314 Lousisiana St. Office: Alpha Bldg., Marianna, Ark.

BARBER, J. Max, dentist; born at Blackstock, S. C., July 5, 1878; son of Jesse and Susan (Crawford) Barber; grad. Friendship Institute, Rock Hill, S. C., 1887; teachers' course Benedict College, Columbia, S. C., 1901; A.B., Virginia Union Univ., Richmond, 1903; D.D.S., Philadelphia Dental College, 1912; married Hattie B. Taylor, of Philadelphia, Nov. 9, 1912. Founded magazine called Voice of the Negro, Atlanta, Ga., 1904, continuing until driven from the city during race riots, 1907; published again at Chicago, Ill., 1907-8; paper was sold to T. Thomas Fortune; practiced dentistry in Philadelphia since 1912. Baptist. Member executive committee and vice-pres. Philadelphia Branch, National Association for Advencement of Colored People, Philadelphia Odontographic Society. Club: Negro Professional. Home and Office: 3223 Woodland Ave., Philadelphia, Pa.

BARCUS, Emma Mason, chiropodist; born at Gallipolis, Ohio; daughter of James and Eliza (Woodson) Mason; high school edn., Gillipolis; married Robert B. Barcus (lawyer), of Columbus, O., July 12, 1911. Chiropodist in Columbus since 1900; member National Association of Chiropodists. Episcopalian. Home: 1021 E. Rich St. Parlors: 903 Oak St., Columbus, Ohio.

BARCUS, Robert Barclay, lawyer; born at Charlottsville, Va., Mar. 6, 1878; son of William and Eliza (Walker) Barcus; A.B., Virginia Normal and Collegiate Institute, 1901; LL.B., Howard Univ., Washington, D. C., 1904; married Emma Mason, of Columbus, Ohio, July 12, 1911. Admitted to Ohio bar, 1905, United States Court, 1913; in practice in Columbus; attorney Grand Lodge, Knights of Pythias of Ohio; chairman board of managers Young Men's Christian Assn. Baptist. Member Franklin County Bar Assn., National Association for Advancement of Colored People; was first president People's Lyceum. Member Knights of Pythias. Home: 1021 E. Rich St. Office: 503 Eberly Bldg., Columbus, Ohio.

BARNES, Asa David Clifford, dentist; born at Albany, Ohio, Jan. 24, 1877; son of Samuel and Mary (Barnes) Barnes; student, Wilberforce Univ.; D.D.S., Chicago Dental Coll., 1901; married Lillian Goodson, of Little Rock, Ark., Oct. 24, 1906; 1 child: Asa, Jr. Practiced in Chicago since 1901; president Chicago Dental Club, 1913-14. Republican. Episcopalian. Club: Appomatox. Home: 3239 Vernon Ave. Office: 3431 State St., Chicago, Ill. (Died July 23, 1914.)

BARNES, Jeremiah, principal public school; born in Tuscaloosa County, Ala., Feb. 28, 1844; parantage unknown; educated in night school; married Dema Marks (slave), of Dallas County, Ala., 1865; 5 children. Taught in district schools, 1874-86; teacher in public schools at Tuscaloosa several years, now principal. Leads choir, also organist, A. M. E. Zion Church. Mason; member Order Eastern Star, Odd Fellows. Address: Box 45, Tuscaloosa, Ala.

BARNES, Robert Christopher, lawyer; born in Mercer Co., Ohio., Sept. 22, 1856; son of John and Julia Ann (Banks) Barnes; ed. Wilberforce Univ., O.; Liber College, Ind.; Ida (O.) Normal School; married Mabel Brown, of Mercer County, Dec. 25, 1877; 3 children: Florence R., Frances M., Gladys A. Admitted to Michigan bar, 1889; since practiced in Detroit; member law firm of Barnes & Stowers; attorney fos White Sewing Machine Co.; counsellor of Dorl-Wiley Top Co., Acme Repair & Tire Co., Almo Amusement Co., Zelah Amusement Co., Villa Amusement Co. Republican. African Methodist. Member Detroit Bar Assn. Mason. Home: 207 Josephine Ave. Office: 404 Chamber of Commerce Bldg., Detroit, Mich.

BARNHILL, Leonard Ellsworth, druggist; born at Bethel, Pitt County, N. C., July 16, 1889; son of Alexander and Lavinia Barnhill; Pharm.D., Howard Univ., Washington, 1911; unmarried. Worked way through university, the senior year being spent in the drug dispensary at Freedmen's Hospital, Washington; proprietor Barnhill Pharmacy, New Haven, Conn., since 1912. Mason; member Forresters. Club: Renaissance. Home: 68 Dixwell St. Pharmacy: 135 Goffe St., New Haven, Conn.

BARNETT, Ida B. Wells, probation officer, writer; born at Holly Springs, Miss.; daughter of James and Elizabeth (Bowling) Wells; ed. Rust Univ.,

Holly Springs; married, June 27, 1895, Ferdinand L. Barnett, assistant states attorney in Cook County for 14 years; 4 children: Aked, Herman, Ida, Alfred. Was editor newspaper called "Free Speach," Memphis, Tenn., 1889-92; connected with several newspapers since 1892; leader in agitation against lynching for many years; lectured on subject in England, 1893-4. Organized Ida B. Wells Woman's Club, Chicago, Ill., 1893; later organized Woman's Loyal Union, New York and Brooklyn, Woman's Era Club, Boston, Mass., first colored woman's clubs in New Bedford, Mass., Providence, R. I., New Haven, Conn., Louisville, Ky., and elsewhere; organized North Side Woman's Club, Douglas Center, and Ideal Club, in Chicago; served as president of several clubs, is honorary member others; organized Negro Fellowship league, 1908. Probation officer for City of Chicago since 1913; elected vice-president Chicago Branch, National Independent Equal Rights League, Jan. 3, 1915. Trustee Amanda Smith Industrial School for Girls. Active in politics among colored people. Presbyterian. Home: 3234 Rhodes Ave. Office: 3005 State St., Chicago, Ill.

BARRETT, Harold W., insurance; born at Baltimore, Md., Aug. 8, 1868; son of Robert and Ann Eliza (Williams) Barrett; public school édn., Baltimore. Began business career as caterer, 1888, continuing 2 years; general manager Metropolitan Mutual Benefit Assn. of N. J., at Newark, since 1900; founded Co-operatitve Benefit Association of New York; president New Jersey Home Assn. Was commissioner to Emancipation Exposition at New York, 1913. Progressive; active in Republican party several years. Methodist. Mason; member Knights of Pythias, Odd Fellows, Order of Moses, Elks. Home: 11 Webster Place, Orange, N. J. Office: 36 Clinton St., Newark, N. J.

BARRETT, James Richard, clergyman; born at Danville, Va., 1863; son of James and Mary Frances (Pinn) Barrett; attended Friends Mission

School of Danville; grad. Hampton Normal and Agricultural Institute, 1879; A.B., Lincoln (Pa.) Univ., 1887, A.M., 1891, S.T.B., 1894; married, May 22, 1888; 5 children. Taught school about 30 years in Va.; was ordained in Presbyterian ministry, 1894; pastor of church at Chula, Va. Member Knights of Pythias, True Reformers. Address: Chula, Va.

BARRETT, William Henry Ambrose, physician, surgeon; born at Jamacia, B. W. I., May 4, 1887; son of Ambrose and Floris Barrett; attended Home High School, 1900-3, Wolmer's High School, 1903-4, at Kingston, Jamaica; came to America, 1906; M.D., Howard Univ., Washington, D. C., 1910; unmarried. Reporter for Daily Gleanor (West Indian newspaper), 1904-5; clerk in office of secretary Jamaica Agricultural Society, 1905; interne at Freedmen's Hospital, Washington, D. C., 1910-11; practiced in Keystone, W. Va., since 1911; city health officer, 1913-15; had absolute direction of police and all public agencies when spread of smallpox threatened the city; head physician in anasthetis department at Lomax Hospital, Bluefield, W. Va., and at Harrison Hospital, Kimball; has written on subject of "Ether Anesthesia" for medical journals. Republican. Episcopalian. Member National Medical Assn., West Virginia Medical Society (president), Flap Top Medical Society (secretary), Wolmer's Old Boys Assn. (Jamaica); past chancellor local lodge Knights of Pythias. Address: Keystone, W. Va.

BARTON, John Pembroke, therapeutist, evangelist; born in Franklin Co., Ala., Nov. 27, 1845; left slave home, 1861; followed Union army until close of war between the states; during 1863 received instruction in studies under Dr. R. F. Dyer, surgeon in 104th Ill., Inf.; grad. from theological dept. Talladega College (Ala.), 1892; D.D., Guadalupe College, Seguin, Tex., 1900; finished course in suggestive theropeutics at Weltner Institute, Nevada, Mo., Mar. 20, 1900; married Ruth Ann Jacobs, Feb. 9, 1875. Purchased home in Johnsonville, Tenn, 1866; later farmed at birthplace in Ala., 3 years; clerk for Baptist association, 1872-9; organized first colored District Sunday School in U. S., at Tuscumbia, Ala., 1874; bought land and established first colored city school in Tuscumbia, 1876; taught there 4 years; entered Ministerial Institute and taught among colored Baptists in Montgomery to Dec., 1876; ordained in ministry, 1877; pastor Mt. Canaan Baptist Church, 1879-86; organized first Woman's Missionary State Convention in Ala., 1886; state evengelist, 1886-7; built $6,000 edifice in Talladga, 1886; resigned as its pastor, 1900; organized first State Sunday School Convention in U. S., at Union Springs, Ala., 1894; from this followed similar organizations in other states and the National Baptist S. S. Convention; was president Ala. Colored Baptist State Conv., 1893-9; evengelist since 1899; has united over 2,500 couples in marriage; baptized more than 3,000 persons. Practitioner in suggestive therapeutics since 1900; gives treatment at home or office, and by mail; patients number more than 10,000; has accumulated comfortable fortune. Author (pamphlets): Barton's Rules of Order; Barton's Sermons and Lecturs; Barton's Road to Health and Prosperity; Barton's Seven Seals and Seven Triumphs (14 sermons). Home: 355 W. B. St., Talladega, Ala.

BASS, Harry W., lawyer; A.B., Lincoln (Pa.) Univ., 1884; was member Penna. House of Representatives, 1910. Address: Philadelphia, Pa.

BATCHMAN, John M., amusement manager; born at Greenville, Tenn., Jan. 10, 1874; son of Alfred and Myra Caroline (Brown) Batchman; A.B., Fisk, Univ., Nashville, Tenn., 1898; married Scott Hancock, of Wheaton, Ill., May 24, 1904; 2 children: Alfred E., Clifford H. Began as professor of mathematics and Latin at Agricultural and Mechanical College, Normal, Ala., 1899; founded "The International," at Danville, Ill., 1902, first colored newspaper in eastern part of state; was street exhibitor, 1902-6; since in general amusement business;

proprietor Batchman's Amusement Palace, St. Louis, Mo.; president Queensberry Athletic Club; secretary Beaumont Social Club; conducts only place in America for colored people where roller skating, bowling, boxing exhibitions and club apartments are all combined. Was quarter-master sergeant in Co. K., Illinois National Guard, 1902. African Methodist. Mason; member Knights of Pythias. Home: 319 E. Madison St., Danville, Ill. Office: Beaumont & Morgan Sts., St. Louis, Mo.

BATE, John W., principal public school; born near Louisville, Ky., Dec. 22, 1857; son of John Bate (slave owner) and Nancy Dickerson (slave); attended public and Ely Normal schools at Louisville; A.B., Berea (Ky.) College, 1881, A.M., 1884; married Ida W. Lindsay, of Lexington, Ky., Oct. 1886; 2d marriage, Lettie J. Floyd, June 26, 1912; 5 children: William, Clarence, Langston, Helen, Vivian. Began as teacher in Berea College, 1880; principal city colored schools in Danville, Ky., since 1881; writer on subjects of food and education; lecturer. Secretary Boyle County Republican Committee since 1894. Congregationalist. President Danville Negro Business League. Mason. Address: 509 Russell St. Danville, Ky.

BATTLE, Augustus Allen, institute principal; grad. Theol. Dept. Talladega (Ala.) College, 1890. Principal of Spring Hill Normal Institute, Corinth, Miss.

BATTLE, Charles T., industrial teacher; born at Wilson, N. C., Oct. 20, 1888; son of Charles and Leeh (Hargrove) Battle; grad. public school, Wilson, 1902, and Brick Agricultural, Industrial and Normal School, N. C., 1910. Teacher in manual training dept. Fessenden Academy, Fla., 1910-11, 1911-12; instructor in iron work at Tougaloo Univ., Miss., since 1912. Presbyterian. Home: Fallis, Okla. Address: Tougaloo University, Tougaloo, Miss.

BATTLE, Samuel Jesse, policeman; born at Newbern, N. C., Jan. 16, 1883; son of Thomas C. and Annie V. (Delaman) Battle; ed. graded schools, Newbern; Boardman Manual Training School, New Haven, Conn.; Y. M. C. A. School (colored branch), New York; married Florence B. Larrington, of Newport News, Va., June 28, 1905; 3 children: Jesse E., Florence, Caroline E. Began as painter and paper hanger in Hartford, Conn., 1899, continuing 2 years; waiter in number New York hotels, 1902-5; attendant at Grand Central Terminal, 1905-11; member police force since 1911; was first colored policeman appointed after consolidation of Greater New York. Republican. Member A. M. E. Zion Church, St. Phillip's Young Men's Guild. Mason; member Odd Fellows, Elks, United Civic League. Home: 47 W. 139th St., New York.

BATTLE, Wallace Aaron, president industrial school; born at Hurtsboro, Ala., May 10, 1872; son of Augustus and Jennette Battle; grad. Talladega (Ala.) College, 1897; A.B., Berea (Ky.) College, 1901. A.M., 1908; married Effie Threat, of Okolona, Miss., Sept. 9, 1903; 3 children: Thelma E., Wallace A. Jr., Annie M. Founded Okolona Industrial School, 1902; since president of institution, which has 380 acres, 10 buildings, etc., valued at about $120,000. President Mississippi State Teachers' Assn. Address: Okolona, Miss.

BATUM, William Henry, custom house clerk; born at Providence, R. I., Dec. 18, 1876; son of William E. and Minnie (Lewis) Batum; grad. Phillips Grammar School, Boston, Mass., 1892, English High School, 1895, Cambridge High School, 1896; took course in Pernin Shorthand School, Boston, 1896-7; unmarried. Began as stenographer with wholesale produce house of Byram & Rogers, Boston, 1897; messenger for Museum of Fine Arts, 4 yrs.; civil employe in Boston Custom House since 1902; now entry clerk and acting deputy collector. Member athletic team of Boston Y. M. C. A., since 1904; won 3 championship tokens, also number medals and cups in contests. Was 2d lieut. Boston English High School Cadets, 1895, only colored commanding officer. Supt. A. M. E. Zion Sunday School. Republican. Mason; member Foresters. Club: Allston Culture (pres.). Address: 5 Amboy St., Allston, Mass.

BAUGH, Philander Valentine, printer; born at Richmond, Va., Feb. 14, 1882; son of John Gordon and Maria (Hemmons) Baugh; edn. in Boys' Grammar School, Germantown, Philadelphia, Pa.; unmarried. Was youngest member printing firm of Baugh Brothers; purchased full control, 1906; now doing business under own name. Episcopalian. Home: 103 W. Duval St. Office: Jefferson and Duval Sts., Germantown, Philadelphia, Pa.

BAUMANN, Albert, druggist; born at Kenner, La., June 2, 1881; son of James C. and Matilda (Johnson) Baumann; ed. Southern Univ., New Orleans; Tuskegee Normal and Industrial Institute, Ala.; Ph.C., Flint Medical College, New Orleans, 1908; married Rosetta Mason, of New Orleans, Aug. 1, 1903. Clerk in postoffice, New Orleans, 1900-10; member drug firm of LaBranch & Baumann, New Orleans, 1907-10; proprietor of drug store under own name since Sept., 1910; annual business exceeds $50,000. Episcopalian. Member burial and relief board of District Tabernacle No. 6, General Grand United Order Brothers and Sisters of Love and Charity; also member Knights of Pythias. Address: 3d and Howard Sts., New Orleans, La.

BEAM, Augustus Godfrey, physician, surgeon; born near Beardston, Nelson County, Ky., Jan. 16, 1882; son of Hines and Mirah (Porter) Beam; ed. public schools in Nelson County; Curry's College, Urbana, Ohio, 1902; grad. Louisville (Ky.) Normal School, 1905; M.D., Louisville National Medical College, 1906; interne Auxillary Hospital, Louisville, 1906; married Ida Grace Reed, of Lima, Ohio, July 4, 1904; 2 children: Arnett, Earl. Began with brother as Drs. Beam & Beam, Lima, O., 1906; practiced in Springfield, Ky., 1907-14, in Henderson since 1914. Republican.

African Zion Methodist. Member Kentucky State Medical Society. Mason; member Knights of Tabor. Home: 335 8th St. Office: 312 2d St., Henderson, Ky.

BEAMAN, Joseph N., evengelist; born in Prince Georges Co., Md., June 19, 1868; son of Mills and Lucy (Lyons) Beaman; public school edn., Md., and Washington, D. C.; took engineering course from International Correspondence Schools; grad. Howard Univ. School of Theology, 1905; married Margaret E. Mitchell, of Culpeper Co., Va., June 26, 1894. Employed in government printing office, Washington, since 1903; was pastor Union Baptist Church, Vienna, Va., 3 yrs. Trustee Interdenominational Bible College, Interstate Old Folks Home. Republican; was delegate to Prince Georges County Conv., 1910. 33d degree mason; member True Reformers. Address: 927 R. St., N.W., Weshington D. C.

BELL, Robert Benjamin, physician, surgeon; born, Homer, Claibourne Parish, La., Sept. 4, 1872; son of Richard Samuel and Anna (Hanson) Bell; public school edn., Homer; student Mt. Pisgar Academy, Blackburn, La., 1891-2; Sc.B., Central Tennessee College, 1900; A.M., Walden Univ., Nashville, Tenn., 1903; M.D., Meharry Medical College, Walden Univ., 1903; married Julia M. Stewart, of Nashville, Mar. 17, 1903; 3 children: Modestine Elnora, Bennie Venetta, Callisto Flodora. Began as teacher at Eddyville, Ky., 1896, continuing 4 yrs.; teacher in public schools, Nashville, 1900-3; practiced medicine and surgery in Russellville, Ky., 1903-8, Owensburg, Ky., since 1908; was city physician, 1909-13; makes specialty of gynecology and pediatrics; president Greenwood Stock Co.; part owner Owensboro Publishing Co. Trustee and recording steward Asbury M. E. Church, Owensboro. Republican. Member Owensboro Medical, Dental and Pharm. Assn., Owensboro Negro Business League (president. Mason; member Odd Fellows, Knights of Pythias, United Brothers Friendship,

Good Samaritans, Court of Calanthe. Home and office: 1208 W. 5th St., Owensboro, Ky.

BELL, William Augustus, teacher; born at Elberton, Ga., Feb. 16, 1882; son of Luther Henry Augustus and Mary Jane (Thompson) Bell; grad. Paine College, Augusta, Ga., 1906; later studied at Columbia Univ., New York; married Helen Matile Caffey, of Charleston, S. C., Sept. 3, 1913. Began as principal public school, Toccoa, Ga., 1902, continuing 2 yrs; was clerk at postoffice at New York, 1907-8; professor of mathematics, 1908-12, president, 1912-13, at Miles Memorial College, Birmingham, Ala.; professor of science and field agent, Paine College, since 1913. President board of control, Bethleham House which is supported by M. E. Church, South. Republican. Mason; member Odd Fellows. Address: 1276 Druid Park Ave. Augusta, Ga.

BELSAW, Edward Thomas, dentist; born at Madison, Ga.; son of Rev. John Thomas and Mary Francis (Chambers) Belsaw; attended public schools, Atlanta, G., 1884-9; prep. edn. Dickerson Institute, Pittsburgh, Pa.; D.D.S., Meharry Dental College (Walden Univ.), Nashville, Tenn., 1908; married Mrs. Marie V. Lovelle, of Chattanooga, Tenn., Aug. 25, 1901. Taught school in Georgia several yrs.; later in real estate business at Birmingham, Ala.; practiced dentistry in Mobile since May 25, 1908; dental inspector in Mobile public schools; member staff of John A. Andrew Memorial Hospital at Tuskegee Institute; the Negro member Mobile Tuberculosis Executive Committee; member executive committee Negro Board of Trade; chairman executive committee Mobile Negro Emancipation Assn.; member A. M. E. Zion Church. Treasurer Mobile County Republican Exec. Committee. Secretary executive board National Medical Assn.; former pres. Alabama Medical and Dental Assn., also Mobile Medical Assn. Mason, past master St. John Lodge No. 2; past chancellor Gulf City Lodge, No. 60, Knights of Pythias. Clubs: Bachelors and Benedicts,

Men's Volunteer Civic (pres.). Home: 255 N. Cedar St. Office: 500 Dauphin St., Mobile Ala.

BELT, Herbert F., constable; born at Lynn, Mass., July 14, 1858; son of Joseph and Josephine (Caple) Belt; public school edn., Lynn; unmarried. Policeman in Boston, Mass, 1883-93; was one of four colored members the department for several years, and first among them to serve in business section of city; constable since 1907. Republican. Mason; grand secretary Prince Hall Grand Lodge of Mass. Home: 15 Dundee St. Office: 15 Court Square, Boston, Mass.

BENNETT, Ambrose Allen, university professor; born at Nashville, Tenn., June 18, 1882; son of Charles C. and Mary F. (Allen) Bennett; grad. Pearl High School, Nashville, 1904; A.B., Roger Williams Univ., 1913; married Jennie Brady Smith, of Nashville, Dec. 29, 1909; 2 children: Geraldine, Ambrose, Jr. Professor of mathematics at Roger Williams Univ.; president the university Alumni Association. Baptist. Mason; member Knights of Pythias. Address: Roger Williams University, Nashville, Tenn.

BENNETT, Stephen Alexander, lawyer; born at Uniontown, Ala., Apr. 8, 1881; son of Frederick and Adeline (Smith) Bennett; A.B., Talladega (Ala.) College, 1900; A.B., Yale, 1904; LL.B., New York Law School, 1908; unmarried. Began as clerk in law office of Charles E. Toney, New York, 1908, continuing 3 years; admitted to N. Y. bar, 1911; since in practice at Yonkers; appealed first case defended in Yonkers City Court, and secured first reversed decision recorded against Judge Joseph H. Beall. Republican. Episcopalian. Secretary, Lawyers' Association of Greater New York City and Vicinity. Home: 21 Kellinger St. Office: 65 N. Broadway, Yonkers, N. Y.

BENSON, John Meade, physician, surgeon; born in Brunswick Co., Va., Jan. 1, 1872; son of James A. and Susan (Meade) Benson; B.S., Ph.G., Illinois College, 1891; instructor and student in Shaw Univ., 1892-5; M.D.,

Howard Univ. School of Medicine, 1907; married Nellie C. Forrester, of Richmond, Va., June 27, 1899; 2 children: Nellie Meade, John Forrester. First colored man to pass examination before the Virginia Board of Pharmacy, 1895; in drug business with George A. Thompson under firm name of Thompson & Benson, Richmond, Va., 1895-1910; practiced medicine in St. Louis, Mo., since 1910. Republican. Member American Pharmaceutical Assn., National Medical Assn., Missouri Medical Society, Mound City Medical Society, Sigma Pi Phi. Mason; member Odd Fellows. Club: Anniversary. Home: 1908 Goode Ave. Office: 2400 Pendleton Ave., St. Louis, Mo.

BENTON, Edward Walden, principal public school; born at Springfield, Tenn.; B.S., Roger Williams Univ., Nashville, Tenn., 1889, M.S., 1892, A.M., 1899; special course in science and sociology, at Univ. of Minn, 1901; studied anatomy, physiology, histology, chemistry, qualitative analysis embryology, toxicology and urinalysis at Meharry Medical College to 1907; B.S., Fisk Univ., 1908; married Lula Glass, of Hopkinsville, Ky., July 23, 1893. Began as principal public school, Hammond, Tex., 1889, continuing 2 years; principal Lane College, Jackson, Tenn., 1891-4, Lincoln High School, Paducah, Ky., 1893-1906; instructor in normal dept. Walden Univ., Nashville, 1906-7; principal Hadley Public School, Nashville, 1907-14; established first public night school for colored men and women in Nashville, 1908; instructor in State Institutes, Nashville and Jackson, 1911-13; principal Belleview Public School since 1914. Was president W. Kentucky Teachers' Assn., 1895-1906; pres. Associated Alumni of Roger Williams Univ., 1910-13, Colored Principals' Assn. of Nashville, 1912-13, and Sunday School Convention of Nashville District, 1913. Methodist; member Odd Fellows. Home: 1213 11th Ave. N., Nashville, Tenn.

BEST, William E. St. Clair, principal high school; born at Bridgetown, Barbodos, B. W. I., Apr. 12, 1885; son of William Edward and Evangeline (St. Clair) Best; came to America, 1898; grad. high school at Ellicottville, N. Y., 1905; student in Alfred (N. Y.) Univ., and Cornell, 3 years; A.B., Indiana State Normal School at Terre Haute, 1910; married Evaline Artis, of Rockville, Ind., Apr. 16, 1911; 1 child: Pauline L. Principal high school in Rockville, 1910-13, at Clark High School, Evansville, Ind., since 1913. Republican. African Methodist. Member Southern Indiana Teachers' Assn., Southwestern Teachers' Assn. of Ind. Mason; senior warden Pythagoras Lodge. Home: 1504 Walnut St., Evansville, Ind.

BETHUNE, Mary McLeod, principal private school; born at Mayesville, S. C., July 10, 1875; daughter of Samuel and Patsy (McIntosh) McLeod; grad. Scotia Seminary, 1904, Moody Bible School, 1906, at Chicago, Ill.; married, May 6, 1898 (widow); 1 child. Founded in 1904, and since principal, Daytona (Fla.) Educational and Industrial School for Girls; state organizer Florida Woman's Christian Union. Trustee Industrial School at Miami, Fla., and Rescue Home, Jacksonville. African Methodist. Member National Federation of Colored Women, Florida State Federation of Colored Women (vice-pres.), Amanda Smith Community, Married People's Council, Jennie Dean Hospital Club. Address: Daytona, Fla.

BIAS, John Henry, university professor; born at Palmyra, Marion Co., Mo., June 11, 1877; son of James William and Dinah (Arnold) Bias; attended graded schools at Palmyra; B.S.D., A.B., Lincoln Institute, Jefferson City, Mo., 1901; studied science at Univ. of Chicago 2 years, also attended 2 summer terms; married Frances Lenora Lane, of Baxter Springs, Kan., Aug. 31, 1907; 3 children: John Calvin, Frances Bernice, James Henry. Teacher of science 1 year in Lincoln Institute, mathematics and science at North Carolina State Colored Normal School, 4 years; professor in department of natural science, 1907-10, director in biology since 1910, at Shaw Univ., Raleigh, N.

C.; also head the department of chemistry in Leonard Medical School. Has collected and mounted large number of insects and reptiles; made report of trees near Raleigh to U. S. Department of Agriculture; studied and experimented with native plant known as Dionaea, which is commonly called "Venus' Fly Trap" and the "Eating Plant," because its leaves enclose any object, as a fly, which may light on them, and the food thus captured is digested by the action of its fluids. Republican. Methodist. Home: 228 E. Worth St., Raleigh, N. C.

BIBB, Merwyn R., physician, surgeon; born at Indianapolis, Ind., May 10, 1876; son of Mathew R. and Malissa E. (Burton) Bibb; grad. Hyde Park High School, Chicago, 1896; M.D., Harvey Medical College, Chicago, 1902; married Francenia V. Thomas, June 28, 1900; (divorced, 1911). Practiced in Chicago since 1903; state examiner Court of Calanthe; surgeon-in-chief and brigadier-general, uniform rank, Knights of Pythias. Member Odd Fellows, Elks, Foresters, Knights of Tabor, United Brothers of Friendship; member management committee, Physicians, Dentists and Pharmacists Association of Chicago, to entertain National Medical Assn., during convention, Aug. 24-26, 1915. Republican. Presbyterian. Club: Appomatox. Address: 2900 S. State St., Chicago, Ill.

BIBBS, Edmund, educator, clergyman; born in Columbia Co., Ga., July 31, 1866; son of Fred and Jane (Dozier) Bibbs; grad. Paine College, Augusta, Ga., 1892; finished course in vocal music under Prof. Charles A. Driscoll, of New England Conservatory of Music; married Mary F. Willis, of Atlanta, Ga., Nov. 9, 1892; 4 children. Entered Methodist ministry at Thomson, Ga., 1886; began teaching in 1890; pastored C. M. E. Churches in Ga., at Madison, Athens, Toccoa and Griffin; now president Unadilla High and Industrial School; traveling evangelist, educational agent, lecturer on eugenics; was originator the Colored Colony and Young People's Educational movements, also Negro University Jubilee Convocation; editor the Ensign, published in Atlanta. Mason; member Odd Fellows. Address: Box 26, Unadilla, Ga.

BIGHAM, John Alvin, teacher; born at McLemoresville, Tenn., Jan. 18, 1881; son of Robert and Penelope (Boyd) Bigham; grad. high school, Topeka, Kan., 1904; A.B., Univ. of Kan., 1908; A.M., Harvard, 1909; studied economics and sociology at Harvard, 1910, 11, 12; unmarried. Began as instructor in St. Augustine's School, Raleigh, N. C., 1909; associate professor of economics and sociology, Atlanta (Ga.) Univ., since 1913; director study of Negro crime, 1914-15, which study was published as 19th Atlanta University Conference Publication. Presbyterian. Member American Sociological Society. Address: Atlanta University, Atlanta, Ga.

BILLUPS, Henry Lee, teacher, lawyer; born at Goliad, Texas, Jan. 10, 1863; son of Washington and Matilda Billups; grad. Wiley Univ. (Acad. Dept.), 1888, B.S., 1892, M.S., 1897, Ph.B., 1905; student Univ. of Mich. Law School, 1911; LL.B., Carnegie Law School, Rogers, Ohio, 1914; married Hattie V. Goodby, of Marshall, Tex., May, 1893; 1 child: Homer M. Served 25 years in schools of Freedmen's Aid Society, as teacher, accountant, bursar, and teacher of law, 12 years at George R. Smith College, Sedalia, Mo., and 13 years in Wiley Univ.; now financial secretary $100,000 Endowment Fund for Wiley Univ.; was appointed to educational work in San Juan, Porto Rico, 1901. Admitted to Missouri bar, 1902; member law firm of Bouron & Billups, Kansas City, Mo. Member M. E. General Conference 3 times. Republican. Mason; member Knights of Pythias, Mosaic Templars. Address: Wiley University, Marshall, Texas.

BINFORD, Henry Connard, principal high school; born at Huntsville, Ala., Feb. 28, 1874; son of Henry C. and Frances Ann (Hendley) Binford; A.B., Howard Univ., Washington, D.

C., 1897; married Mary A. Woods, of Montgomery, Ala., Dec. 27, 1899; 5 children: Claxton P., Elmer C., Ruth P., Henry F., Dorothy C. Teacher district school Wathena, Kan., 1897-8; principal public school, Huntsville, Ala., 1898-1905; instructor in commercial law at Colored High School, Baltimore, Md., 1905-8; principal high school at Huntsville since 1908. Methodist; treasurer Lakeside Church. Republican. Mason. Home: 604 Pearl St., Huntsville, Ala.

BINGA, Anthony, J., clergyman; born at Amherstburg, Ontario, Can., June 1, 1843; son of Anthony and Rhoda (Story) Binga; attended King's Institute, Buxton, Can.; came to U. S., 1872; D.D., Shaw Univ., Raleigh, N. C., 1889; married Rebecca L. Bush, of Xenia, O., Dec. 2, 1869 (died 1907); 2d marriage, Mrs. Mary V. Young, of Richmond, Va., Dec. 2, 1909; 3 children: Jessie C., Ida May, Anthony J. Ordained in Baptist ministry, 1867; was president Albany (O.) Enterprise Academy, 1868-9; pastor 1st Baptist Church at S. Richmond, Va., since 1872; treasurer General Baptist Association of Va.; chairman Foreign Mission Board; member Lott Carey Foreign Missions. Trustee Virginia Union Univ. Address: 1306 Decatur St., S. Richmond, Va.

BISHOP, Hutchens C., clergyman. pastor St. Philip's Protestant Episcopal Church, New York; the land and building cost $225,000; the church owns apartment-houses worth $620,000; has distinction of being richest Negro church in the world. Address: St. Philip's P. E. Church, New York.

BLACK, Clyde Wigbert, principal public schools; born at Brunswick, Mo., Aug. 31, 1873; son of George W. and Lucy (McKinney) Black; public school edn., Salisbury, Mo.; A.B., Natchez (Miss.) College, 1891; married Eudora Clinkscale, of Chillicothe, Mo., Dec. 27, 1899. Taught school at Gaylesville, Miss.; bookkeeper for William Grocery Co., Greenville, Miss.; was mail carrier at Chillicothe, Mo., 6 years; principal of schools at Triplett, Dalton, and Brookfield, Mo.;

now principal Washington School, Plattsburg. Republican. Baptist. Mason; deputy grand master United Brothers of Friendship; member Knights of Tabor. Address: Plattsburg, Mo.

BLACKSHEAR, Edward Levocscer, principal state college; born at Montgomery, Ala., Sept. 8, 1863; son of Abram and Adline Blackshear; attended Swayne High School at Montgomery; A.B., Tabor (Ia.) College, 1881 (A.M., 1902; LL.D., Wilberforce Univ., 1902); married Rachel Verta Works, of Austin, Tex., Mar. 12, 1891; 3 children: William, Roosevelt, Eddie L. Began teaching school in Tex., 1882; principal Colored High School, Austin, 1883-96; principal Prairie View State Normal and Industrial College since 1896; public speaker and writer on educational work and racial subjects. Republican. Baptist. Fellow American Association for Advancement of Science; member Negro National Educational Congress. Mason; member Odd Fellows, Knights of Pythias. Author: Education of Childhood. Address: Prairie View, Texas.

BLACKWELL, Annie Walker, teacher, missionary worker; born in Chester, S. C., Aug. 21, 1862; daughter of Dublin Isaiah and Mathilda (Potts) Walker; grad. Scotia Seminary, Concord, N. C., 1876; attended Temple College, Philadelphia, Pa.; married Rt. Rev. George Lincoln Blackwell, D.D., bishop A. M. E. Zion Church, Dec. 7, 1887; 2 children, both died. Began in missionary work and teaching schools at Charlotte, N. C.; was recording secretary Woman's Christian Temperance Union of N. C., and editor W. C. T. U. Tidings, 4 years; corresponding sec. Woman's Home and Foreign Missions Society since 1901; president Staff Auxiliary of Douglass Hospital, Philadelphia, Pa.; associate editor Missionary Seer. Was delegate to Ecumenical Conference on Methodism, Toronto, Can., 1911; also delegate to National Civic Movement Convention, Kansas City, Mo., 1914, appointed by Gov. John K. Tener. Member Order of Eastern Star, Heroines of Jericho. Compiler (song-book):

Missionary Call, 1911. Home: 624 S. 16th St., Philadelphia, Pa.

BLACKWELL, George Lincoln, bishop; born at Henderson, N. C., July 3, 1861; son of Hailey and Catherine (Wyche) Blackwell, both slaves; A.B., Livingstone College, Salisbury, N. C., 1888, A.M., 1895; S.T.B., Boston Univ. School of Theol., 1892; (D.D. Kansas Wesleyan Univ., 1896); married Anne E. Walker, of Chester, S. C., Dec. 7, 1887. Entered A. M. E. Zion minstry, 1881; dean of theol. dept. Livingstone College, 1893-6; editor Sunday School Literature and general agent A. M. E. Zion Pub. House, Charlotte, N. C., 1896-1900; general secretary of same, 1900-4, missionary sec., 1904-8; consecrated bishop, 9th Episcopal Dist., May, 1908; editor "Missionary Seer," also "Discipline Delegate" to Ecumenicial Conference on Methodism, London, Eng., 1901, Toronto, Can., 1911; trustee Livingstone College. Author: The Model Homestead, 1893; Cloaks of Sin, 1904; A Man Wanted, 1907. Home: 624 S. 16th St. Office: 420 S. 11th St., Philadelphia, Pa.

BLACKWELL, Paul Julian, principal high school; born at Elberton, Ga., Feb. 16, 1882; son of Willis and Henretta (Henry) Blackwell; preparatory edn. Morris Brown Univ., Atlanta, Ga.; A.B., Paine College, Augusta, Ga., 1902; unmarried. Began teaching in schools of Ga., at Rayston, 1902; principal Elberton High School since 1908. Trustee and steward Colored M. E. Church. Member Georgia State Teachers' Assn., Knights of Pythias, Odd Fellows, Good Samaritans. Address: 339 Elbert St., Elberton, Ga.

BLEACH, Herny Augustus, educator; born at Charleston, S. C., Dec. 25, 1872; son of Edward and Rebecca (Edmunds) Bleach; A.B., Atlanta Baptist College, Ga., 1897, T.P., 1898; student Univ. of Chicago, 1901-3; (A.M., Morehouse College, Atlanta, 1914); married Frances M. Coleman, of Centralia, Ill., June 27, 1910; 1 child: Henry A. Jr. Professor of mathematics in Benedict College, Columbia, S. C., 1898-1901; founded

the practice school there; vice pres. Western College, Macon, Mo., 1901-3; associate founder, 1903, now president, Selden Institute, Brunswick, Ga. Presbyterian. Member Odd Fellows. Address: Selden Institute, Brunswick, Ga.

BLOUNT, George Wesley, banker; grad. Hampton Normal and Agricultural Institute; took business course at Boston, Mass. Accountant in treasurer's department at Hampton Institute, 6 years; assistant to Maj. R. R. Moton 4 years; teacher of bookkeeping and principal business department at Hampton 10 years; business manager and director Crown Savings Bank at Newport News since 1914. Member executive committee and corresponding secretary Negro Organization Society of Virginia; member Newport News Negro Business League, and Bachelors' Club. Address: Crown Savings Bank, Newport News, Va.

BLUE, Thomas Fountain, librarian, clergyman; born at Farmville, Va., Mar. 6, 1866; son of Noah H. and Henry Ann Blue; preparatory edn. Hampton Normal and Agricultural Institute; B.D., Richmond Theological Seminary, 1898; unmarried. First secretary to Colored Branch, Young Men's Christian Assn., Louisville, Ky.; 1899; served to 1905; since member committee on management and treasurer; appointed librarian at Western Colored Branch, Louisville Free Public Library, 1905; librarian at both Western and Eastern branches since 1914. Served as army secretary with 6th Va. Vols. during Spanish-American war. Baptist. Home: 1723 W. Chestnut St. Library: 10th and Chestnut St., Louisville, Ky.

BLUFORD, John Henry, chemist, college prof.; born in Gloucester Co., Va., May 16, 1876; son of John Wesley and Mary Ellen Bluford; grad. Gloucester Agricultural High School, 1894; B.S., Howard Univ., Washington, 1900, A.M., 1904; appointed "university scholar" in chemistry, Graduate School Univ. of Pa., 1900; graduate student in agriculture and chemistry, Cornell Univ., Ithaca, N.

Y., 1900-1; received certificate from Jefferson Laboratory of Physics, Harvard Univ., 1903; married Viola Christine Harris, of Salisbury, N. C., June 29, 1909; 2 children: John H. Jr., Lucile Harris B. Teacher in Sumner High School, St. Louis, Mo., 1901-2; professor of chemistry and director department of agriculture and chemistry, State Agricultural and Technical College, Greensboro, N. C., since 1903; official city chemist of Greensboro since 1904; teacher in State Normal School, Elizabeth City, N. C., summer sessions, 1904, 5; director summer school, Agri. and Mech. College. President Farmers' Educational Co-operative Union of America; director Pioneer Building and Loan Assn.; secretary Negro Section American Association Agricultural Colleges and Experiment Stations; member American Association Farmers' Institute Workers, North Carolina Forestry Assn. Baptist. Member Knights of Pythias. Author: Outline on Qualitative Chemical Analysis; contributed to Southern Workmen, and Cyclopedia of American Agriculture. Home: 901 Lindsay St., Greensboro, N. C.

BOARD, William Louis, druggist; born at Bedford City, Va., Sept. 7, 1876; son of Jackson and Diana (Lipscomb) Board; B.S., Wilberforce Univ., 1896, also grad. Military Dept.; Pharm.D., Howard Univ., Washington, 1903; unmarried. Began as railway mail clerk, 1897; detailed as clerk in office of the general supt., 1898; resigned from the postal service, 1910, to give full time to business; member firm of Board & McGuire, established 1906, now operating 2 drug stores in Washington; general mgr. W. L. Board Co.; president Health Culture Co. Republican. Member National Medical Assn., National Association of Retail Druggists; also member Odd Fellows Clubs: Short Story, Mu-So-Lit, Wilberforce. Home: 944 T St., N. W. Office: 1912 1-2 14th St., N. W., Washington, D. C.

BODDY, James Mamaduke, clergyman; born at Wrightsville, Pa., Sept. 2, 1866; son of James and Cassandra Boddy; attended Roberts Vaux Grammar School, Philadelphia; A.B., Lincoln Univ., Pa., 1890, A.M., later; grad. Princeton Theol. Seminary, N. J., 1895; M.D., Albany Medical College, N. Y., 1906; married Elizabeth G. Davis, of Troy, N. Y., Oct. 8, 1906. Ordained Presbyterian ministry, 1895; pastored Siloam Presbyterian Church, Elizabeth, N. J., Liberty Street Church, Troy, N. Y., the Allison Chapel, Little Rock, Ark., Zion Presbyterian Church, St. Paul, Minn. Contributor to various publications; in his article "The Ethnic Unity of the Negro and the Anglo-Saxon Race," it presents a positive opinion that European peoples are of an African and Negro origin (The Colored American Magazine, of March, 1905); in same magazine, July, 1905, his article entitled "Brain Weight" attempts to show, if any exists, why the physical variation of white and colored races; and in the October number, 1905, "The Ethnology of the Japanese Race" is an attempt to show that the Japanese are Asian Negroes. Address: Minneapolis, Minn.

BOLDEN, Richard Manuel, clergyman; born at Marion Station, Somerset Co., Md., Mar. 1, 1878; son of Charles and Adline (Potter) Bolden; attended district school in Somerset Co., high school, Providence, R. I., Livingstone College, Salisbury, N. C.; grad. Bible Teachers' Training School, New York, 1907; married Medora Richardson, of New York, June 5, 1899. Licensed to preach in A. M. E. Zion Church, 1897; pastor of number important churches to 1913; founded the Emmanuel Church in the World; delegate World's Sunday School Convention, Zurich, Switzerland, 1913; visited England, France, Italy, Austria, Germany, Belgium, Holland, Canada. Republican. Mason; member Odd Fellows, Elks, St. Luke's Ethiopian Council, Order of Moses. Author: Emmanuel Creed and Covenent; contributor to New York Age. Address: 105 W. 130th St., New York.

BONNER, Frederick Douglass, school supervisor, lecturer; born at

New Haven, Conn., Jan. 26, 1878; son of Willis Method and Elizabeth (Young) Bonner; grad. grammar school, 1892, New Haven ·High School, 1896, (class orator in each); A.B., Yale, 1901(won college prize in elocution); married Charlotte Drucila Stokes, New Haven, Nov. 1, 1897; children: Daisy, Gwendolyn, Frederick and Walter (3) born in the Phillipine Islands. Began as teacher in the Phillipine Islands, 1901; member board of education, also board of health, Subic, Zambales, P. I., 1901-11; appointed postmaster, Subic, 1902, school supervisor in Phillipine service, 1904, chairman Civil Service Examining Board for district of Masbate, 1912; resigned from all service in the Phillipine's in June, 1914; now giving illustrated lectures on the Phillipine Islands; has traveled around the world twice. Republican; was recommended as E. E. and M. P. to Haiti, 1911, at time Henry W. Furniss tendered his resignation, later withdrew and no change was made at that post. Member National Geographical Society, Phillipine Society of New York, Alumni Assn. of Manila. Mason. Home: 246 Dixwell Ave., New Haven, Conn.

BOOKER, Joseph Albert, college president, clergyman; born at Portland, Ashley Co., Ark., Dec. 26, 1859; son of Albert Clark and Mary (Punsard) Booker; student Normal School, Pine Bluff, Ark., 1878-81; A.B., Roger Williams Univ., Nashville, Tenn., 1886, A.M., 1889; (D.D., State Univ., Louisville, Ky., May 26, 1901); married Mary Jane Caver, of Helena, Ark., June 28, 1887; 8 children: Mattie, Albert, Carrie, Joseph, Helen, William, Sarah, Walter, James. Missionary Baptist minister since 1878; taught schools in Ark., 1879-1914; pres Arkansas Baptist College, Little Rock, since Oct. 4, 1887; director Douglass Industrial Assn., Negro National Life Ins. Co. Republican. Member Southern Sociological Congress, Knights of Pythias, Mosaic Templars, International Order of Twelve. Clubs: Searchlight, Owl, Lotus. Home: 1600 Bishop St. Office: Arkansas Baptist College, Little Rock, Ark.

BOONE, Charles Henry Mantelle, clergyman, teacher; born in Franklin Co., Ohio, Feb. 28, 1870; son of William and Elizabeth Boone; grad. grammar school, Springfield, O., 1888; B.S., Wilberforce Univ., 1896, A.B., 1898, B.D., 1900; married Mary A. Alexander, of Georgetown, Ky., Aug. 26, 1902 (died Mar. 19, 1907); 2d marriage, Willie B. Nichols, of Nashville, Tenn., Nov., 1908; 1 child: Willie Mantelle B. Licensed to preach in A. M. E. church, 1889; principal Turner Normal and Industrial Institute, Shelbyville, Tenn., 1902-5; pastor, Nashville, Tenn., 1905-8, Clarksville, 1908-11, Colorado Springs, Colo., 1911-13; prin. Wayman Institute, Harrodsburg, Ky., since 1913. Was chosen by colored citizens of Colorado Springs to protest to legislature against proposed act to segregate colored children in public schools; candidate for election to board of education at Colorado Springs. Member Knights of Pythias. Address: Wayman Institute, Harrodsburg, Ky.

BORDEN, Edwin Howard, clergyman, professor; born at Truro, Nova Scotia, Dominion of Canada; son of James Ivory and Susie Marie (Prevost) Borden; A.B., Acadia Univ., Wolfville, Nova Scotia, 1892, A.M., 1895; B.D., Univ. of Chicago, 1897; grad. student in Old and New Testment theology, Univ. of Chicago; grad. student in economics, German literature, and Biblical theology, Univ. of Goettingen, 1904, Univ. of Berlin, 1905, 1 semester each; (D.D., Conroe College, Texas, U. S. A., 1911); unmarried. Was principal public school, Greenville, Nova Scotia, 1886; came to U. S., 1892; ordained Baptist ministry, 1895; pastor at Bay City, Mich., 1895-7, Oak Park and Macomb, Ill., 1897, 98; organized 2d Baptist Church at Wanlock, Ill., 1899; professor of ancient and modern languages, and mathematics, 1898-1905, at Western College, Macon Mo., and at Central City College, Macon, Ga., 1905-9; pastor at Paris, Ill., 1909-12; organized Beth Eden Institutional Baptist

Church, E. St. Louis, Ill., Sept., 1912, was pastor to April, 1913; now pastor Mt. Olive Church, St. Louis, Mo.; president Wood River Baptist Sunday School Convention; corr. secretary Illinois General Baptist Convention; supt. Baptist Missions of Illinois; founded the "Tidings," 1912, and editor to 1914; associate editor the Home Guard. Member the Odd Fellows, Knights of Pythias, United Brothers of Friendship. Author: Are the Baptists Waning? Home: 1917 Converse Ave., E. St. Louis, Ill.

BOUCHET, Edward Alexander, teacher; born at New Haven, Conn., Sept. 15, 1852; son of William Francis and Susan (Cooley) Bouchet; ed. New Haven High School, 1866-8; grad. Hopkins Grammar School, 1870; A.B., Yale, 1874, Ph.D., 1876; one of the two colored men who have earned the Doctor of Philosophy degree at Yale Univ.; unmarried. Began as teacher of science in Institute for Colored Youth, Philadelphia, Pa., 1876, continuing to 1902; teacher in Sumner High School, St. Louis, Mo., 1902-3; director of academics St. Paul School, Lawrenceville, Va., 1905-8; principal Lincoln High School, Gallipolis, Ohio, since 1908. Republican. Episcopalian. Member Yale Chapter, Phi Beta Kappa. Home: 837 Third Ave. Office: Lincoln High School, Gallipolis, Ohio.

BOUEY, Forrest Lee, clergyman; born a: Lexington, S. C., Jan. 8, 1870; son of Augustus and Leah (Coleman) Bouey; preparatory edn. Western College, Macon, Mo.; D.D., Morris Brown Univ., Atlanta, Ga.; married S. Aldrich Gardner, of Allendale, S. C., Apr. 7, 1895. Licensed to preach in C. M. E. Church, 1893; member Washington and Philadelphia Annual Conference, 1902-10, Alabama Conf., 1910-11, Central and Southwest Georgia Conf., since 1911; pastor Colored M. E. Church, Americus, Ga.; was circulating mgr. "Daily Christian Index," published during the General Conference at St. Louis, Mo., 1914; compiled work entitled "My Autobiography and Sermons." Republican. Mason; member Odd Fellows. Home: 409 Anchrom St., Americus, Ga.

BOURGES, Arthur, painting contractor; born at Lafayette, La., Nov. 29, 1877; son of Francis and Laura (Guidry) Bourges; private tuition under the late Mrs. William Campbell, wife of Judge Campbell, while in her employ as yard boy; attended night school under Prof. P. L. Breaux, 1892; married Louise Mouton, of Lafayette, Dec. 3, 1901; 4 children. In grocery business for self, 1897-9; recording secretary for Society of St. Joseph number yrs.; secretary People's Co-operative Mercantile Co., 1913-14; now painting contractor; also has local trucking business. Recording secretary for Young Men's Progressive Benovolent Assn.; secretary and mgr. Building Fund Committee of St. Paul Catholic Church, also usher. Grand Knight of the Knights of Peter Claver. Address: Lafayette, La.

BOUSFIELD, Midian Othello, physician; born at Tipton, Mo., Aug. 22, 1885; son of Willard H. and Cornelia C. (Gilbert) Bousfield; grad. high school at Kansas City, Kan., 1903; A.B., Univ. of Kan., 1907; M.D., Northwestern Univ., Chicago, Ill., 1909; married Mandelle Tanner Brown, of St. Louis, Mo., Sept. 9, 1914. Was interne in Freedmen's Hospital, Washington, D. C., 1909-10; made trip with intention to settle at Brazil, 1911, and visited West Indes, Bahia, and Rio de Janeiro; visiting physician on staff of Old General Hospital at Kansas City, 1912-14; practiced in Chicago since 1914. Episcopalian. Member Physicians, Dentists and Pharmacists Club of Chicago, Knights of Pythias. Contributor to National Medical Journal. Home: 4630 Evans Ave. Office: 3401 S. State St., Chicago, Ill.

BOUTTE, Matthew Virgil, teacher of chemistry; B.S., Fisk Univ., Nashville, Tenn., 1908; Ph.G., Univ. of Illinois, School of Pharmacy, 1914. Teacher of chemistry at Meharry Medical College, Walden Univ., Nashville. Address: 639 Wetmore St., Nashville, Tenn.

BOWEN, Cornelia, teacher; born at

Tuskegee, Ala., Sept. 24, 1870; daughter of Henry Clay and Sophia (Carroll) Bowan; grad. Tuskegee Normal and Industrial Institute, 1885; student Teachers' College, New York, 1893, Glasgow Univ. (Annex Queen Margaret College), Scotland, 1898-1900; unmarried. Principal Mt. Meigs Institute, Waugh, Ala., since 1890; also in real estate business; has sold many farms to colored people. President State Federation of Wom-ans' Clubs. Address: Waugh, Ala.

BOWEN, John Wesley Edward, theologian; born at New Orleans, La., Dec. 3, 1855; son of Edward and Rose Bowen; A.B., Univ. of New Orleans, 1878, A.M., 1886; B.D., Boston Univ., 1885, Ph.D., 1887; (D.D., Gammon Theological Seminary); married Ariel S. Hedges, of Baltimore, Md., Sept. 14, 1886. Professor of ancient languages at Central Tennessee College, Nash-ville, 1878-82; pastor at Boston, Mass., 1882-5, Newark, N. J., 1885-8, Balti-more and Washington, 1888-92; pro-fessor of church history and syste-matic theology at Morgan College, Baltimore, 1888-92; professor of He-brew in Howard Univ., Washington, 1891-2 professor of theology since 1893, and now president Gammon Theological Seminary, Atlanta, Ga. Member and examiner American In-stitute of Sacred literature, 1889-93; was editor The Voice for some time, also The Negro, and the Stewart Mis-sionary Magazine. Field secretary for missionary society, 1892-3; librarian and secretary Stewart Missionary Foundation for Africa; member Gen-eral Conferences, 1896, 1900, 1904, voted for bishop in each; secretary of standing committee on the Episco-pacy in General Conference, 1900-4; member board of control of Epworth League of church, 1892-1900; served on staff of United Editors' Eycyclopedia and Dictionary. Member American Negro Academy, Philosophical and Literary Society, American Historical Assn. Author: National Sermons; Africa and the American People; The United Negro; The Religious History of the Negro; The Educational His-tory of the Negro, etc. Address: Gam-mon Theological Seminary, Atlanta, Ga.

BOWLES, Benjamin Franklin, man-ager teachers' agency; born on farm near Cooperville, O., Apr. 3, 1869; son of John H. and Delia (Nash) Bowles; student Wilberforce (O.) Univ., 1889-92 (A.M., 1905); married Annie R. Anderson, of Abingdon, Va., Aug. 11, 1896; 2d marriage, Carrie K. Johnson, of Selma, O., July 8, 1902; 5 children: Frank E., Ernelle, Alice L., Ruth E., Isabele. Worked on farm, learned engineering, and jewelers re-pairing trade; taught school in Ohio 6 years; principal grammar school at DuQuoin, Ill., 1893-5, Metropolis, Ill., 1 term, at Lincoln High School, E. St. Louis, Ill., 1896-1914, resigned; manager National Teachers' Agency since 1914. Plays all brass instru-ments from cornet to tuba; composer of music. Life member National Association Teachers' in Colored Schools; member St. Clair County Teachers' Assn., E. St. Louis Teach-ers' Assn.; honorary member The Forum (St. Louis); chairman board of directors University Club of St. Louis. Author: The Musician's Man-ual; Technics of the Brass Instru-ment. Address: 2739 Converse Ave., E. St. Louis, Ill.

Bowles, George W., physician, born at York, Pa., July 23, 1882; son of Adolphus and Harriett (Bowie) Bowles; grad. York High School, 1898; A.B., Livingstone College, Salis-bury, N. C., 1902; M.D., Howard Univ. School of Medicine, Washington, D. C., 1906; unmarried. Practiced in York since 1906; has large num ber of patients among Italian popu-lation, and other white people, as well as colored; president Negro Savings Fund. Methodist. Member National Medical Assn., American Medical Assn., York County Medical Society, Na-tional Association for Advancement of Colored People, Odd Fellows. Club: People's Forum (pres.). Home: 127 W. Princess St. Office: 112 W. King St., York, Pa.

BOWLING, Alonzo Jesse, editor, moving picturer censor; born at Lin-coln, Ill., Aug. 25, 1879; son of

Thomas and Jane (Simmons) Bowling; grad. Kansas State Normal College, 1902; A.B., Albion (Mich) College, 1906; A.M., Ohio State Univ., 1908; student Harvard (Graduate School of Arts and Sciences), 1909-10, 1911-12, A. M., later; graduate work in education, sociology, philosophy and theology, Northwestern, Univ., 1906-7, Boston Univ., 1909, Univ. of Chicago, 1912-13; student Chicago School of Civics and Philanthropy, 1914-15; unmarried. Editor Chicago Conservator; contributing editor to Broad Ax, also Northwestern Christian Recorder; member Board of Moving Picture Censors, City of Chicago; director Dearborn Social Center; director of education Wabash Ave. Dept. Y. M. C. A. African Methodist. Member American Association for Advancement of Sciences, National Geographical Society, Royal Society Clubs of London. Mason; member Odd Fellows, Knights of Pythias, Elks. Club: Economic (Boston). Author: Negro Education, 1912. Phamphlets: Industrial Education vs. High Education, 1907; Retardation and Elimination of Negro Children in Public Schools, Columbus, O., 1908; Comparison of Brookline, Mass. and Kansas City, Kan. Public School Systems, 1912; Education of the American Negro, 1912. Home: 3223 S. Park Ave. Office: 3825 S. Dearborn St., Chicago, Ill.

BOYD, Charles Wesley, supervisor colored schools; born at Mt. Sterling, Ky., Aug. 19, 1865; son of John and Ella (Steel) Boyd; grad Wilberforce (O.) Univ., 1891; student Ohio State Univ., 1904-5; married Kate Jarrison, of Georgetown, O., Nov. 9, 1891; 5 children: Kanawha Valley, Nokomis, Rheba, John, Hyte. Began as teacher in first grade school, Charleston, W. Va., 1893; gradually advanced to 8th grade; was principal Garnett High School several years; supervisor colored schools in Charleston since 1904. Secretary board of directors, Pythian Mutual Investment Assn.; member Knights of Pythias. Baptist. Address: 927 Morris St., Charleston, W. Va.

BOYD, Henry Allen, clergyman, editor. Publisher the Nashville Globe and several periodicals; corresponding secretary the National Negro Press Assn.; assistant secretary National Baptist Publishing Board. Address: 523 Second Ave.N., Nashville, Tenn.

BOYD, Richard H., clergyman, pub.; (D.D., LL.D.). Ordained Baptist ministry; established in 1896 and since secretary National Baptist Publishing House, Nashville, Tenn.; director Nashville Institute for Negro Christian worker; president National Negro Doll Co. Address: 523 Second Ave. N., Nashville, Tenn.

BOYD, Robert James, barber; born in N. C., July 15, 1860; son of Robert and Francis Boyd; public school edn., Morgantown, W. Va., to 1876, Uniontown, Pa., to 1880; married Emma P. Barrett, of Corsicana, Texas, June 7, 1903; 4 children: Robert Barrett, Willis Gordon, Helen Nela, Edward Francis. Began business at Morgantown, W. Va.; was in Toledo, Ohio, number years; now has large business at Riverside, Calif. Home: 373 E. 10th St. Shop: 202 E. 12th St., Riverside, Calif.

BOYDEN, John Allen, clergyman; born at Lexington, N. C., 1862; son of John and Mary Boyden; A.B., Lincoln (Pa.) Univ., 1884, S.T.B., 1887, A.M., 1887 (D.D., 1903); attended lectures Western Theological Seminary, Pittsburgh, Pa., 1890-3; married Mary J. Clawson, of Baltimore, Md., May 3, 1887 (died 1902) 2d marriage, Octavia Feimster, of Charlotte, N. C., May 16, 1907; 4 children: John A. Jr., Edna I., Mary A., Wilmer C. Ordained Presbyterian ministry, 1889; pastor, Wilkes-Barre, Pa., 1889-90; Pittsburgh, 1890-3, Danville, Ky., 1893-1903; pres. Fee Memorial Institute, Camp Nelson, Ky., 1903-14; pastor Concord Church, Danville, since Aug. 1, 1914; secretary and trustee Lincoln Cemetery, Camp Nelson. Republican. Member American Academy Political and Social Science. Home: Danville, Ky.

BOYER, Charles Henry, professor

of Greek; born at Elkton, Cecil Co., Md., Nov. 12, 1869; son of Edward and Indiana Clinton (Caldwell) Boyer; attended public schools, Elkton; grad. Institute for Colored Youth, Philadelphia, Pa., 1886; preparatory edn. Hopkins Grammar School, New Haven, Conn., 1890-2; A.B., Yale, 1896, A.M., 1915; married Alethea Amelia Chase, of New Haven, Sept. 22, 1897; 7 children: Harriet Stewart, Clinton Caldwell, Adelaide Alverda Louise, Charles Edward, Daniel Chase, James Alexander, William Henry. Taught school at Charlotte Hall, Md., 1886-90; began teaching in St. Augustine's School, Raleigh, N. C., 1896; now dean of Collegiate Dept., and professor of Greek and mathematics; as a reward for 15 years service, the school management and friends gave him a trip to Europe where he traveled during the summer of 1911. Episcopalian; secretary Colored Convocation, diocese of N. C. Member American Negro Academy. Royal Arch Mason, Shriner, K. T. Address: St. Augustine's School, Raleigh, N. C.

BRABOY, Joseph Albert, music and musical instruments; born at Kingston, Ind., Dec. 9, 1846; son of Steven and Mariah (Freeman) Braboy; common school edn., Franklin County, Ind.; married Alice McCoy, of Indianapolis, Jan. 7, 1879; 2 children: Otis B. G., Etelka F. Began in musical instrument business, 1879; sold fully 3,000 pianos in northern part of Indiana; now has only regular music store conducted by a colored man in state; carries stock of pianos, player pianos, organs, music, etc. Served in 28th U. S. Colored Vols., 1863-5; was in Battle of the Wilderness, Chickhomney Swamps, Va., in charges on Petersburg and Richmond; on one of guard boats that escorted President Abraham Lincoln from Richmond to Washington, Apr. 12, 1865. Charter member T. J. Harrison Post No. 30, G. A. R. Dept. of Ind. Republican; was City Commissioner of Kokomo, 1885-9. State delegate from Indiana to Half-Century Celebration of Negro Freedom, Chicago, Ill., 1915. Royal

Arch Mason. Address: 213 E. Superior St., Kokomo, Ind.

BRADDAN, William S., clergyman; born at Fort McKavett, Tex., Mar. 15, 1871; son of Alfred and Elizabeth (Noal) Braddan; attended Cutler Academy, Colorado Springs, Col., 1891-2; student Newton Theol. Seminary, Mass., 1893-95; (hon. D.D.); married Loula Primstead, of Colorado Springs, June 30, 1902; 8 children: Durwood, DeVere, Julia, Elizabeth, William, Jr., Mary, Love, Joy. Pastor of Salem Baptist Church, New Bedford, Mass., 1892, while studying at Newton; ordained, 1895; pastor at Ann Arbor, Mich., 1895-6, Detroit, Mich., 1896-1901; pastor Berean Baptist Church, Chicago, since 1901. Served as private in Troop L. 10th U. S. Cav.; enlisted as private 8th Regt. I. N. G., Chicago, 1904, promoted to corporal, later sergt.; commissioned captain and chaplain, 1912. Republican. Member Knights of Pythias., Forresters. Home: 5008 Fifth Ave., Chicago, Ill.

BRAGG, George Freeman, Jr., clergyman, editor; born at Warrenton, N. C., Jan. 25, 1863; son of George F. and Mary Bragg; attended St. Stephen Normal School, Petersburg, Va.; theological course at Bishop Payne Divinity School; (D.D., Wilberforce (O.) Univ., 1902); married Nellie G. Hill, of Petersburg, Sept. 20, 1887; 4 children: Harry G., Mary H., Arthur M., Nellie G. Has followed newspaper work since 1872; founded The Lancet at Petersburg when 19 years old; now editor and publisher the Church Advocate; also editor Afro-American Ledger, Baltimore, Md. Was ordained in Protestant Episcopal ministry, 1887; rector St. James Church in Baltimore since 1891, and now president the corporation; only colored member Episcopal Diocesan Convention of Maryland. President and chaplain Maryland Home for Friendless Colored Children; member board of managers House of Reformatory for Colored Boys; (Baltimore is also represented in the management of this state institution by City Councilman Harry

S. Cummings, colored). Member Odd Fellows, St. James Beneficial Society. Author and publisher: Colored Harvest in the Old Undivided Diocese of Virginia, 1901; Afro-American Work and Workers, 1904; Old St. Stephens of Petersburg, Va., 1906; Negro Ordinations from 1795 to 1906; The First Negro Priest on Southern Soil, 1909; A Bond Slave of Christ, 1912; Birth and History of the Missionary District Plan, 1913; Men of Maryland, 1914; Richard Allen and Absalom Jones. 1915. Address: 1133 Park Ave., Baltimore, Md.

BRAGG, Jubie Barton, teacher; born in Twiggs Co., Ga., Feb. 17, 1876; son of Andrew and Rebecca (Smith) Bragg; attended Ballard's Normal School, Macon, Ga.; grad. Tuskegee Institute, Ala., 1900; B.S., Talladega College, 1910; married Anna Mariah Smith, of Orangeburg, S. C., Sept. 15, 1904; 4 children. Teacher at Florida Agricultural and Mechanical College, Tallahassee, 5 yrs., and W. Va. Colored Institute, 1 yr.; instructor of manual training and professor of science Jackson (Miss.) College since 1911. Episcopalian. Progressive. Home: 1406 Lynch St., Jackson, Miss.

BRAITHWAITE, John Alexander, physician; born, Barbados ,B. W. I., Dec. 17, 1877; son of Dr. James Alleyne and Ann. Elizabeth (Favey) Braithwaite; attended Combermere School to 1891, Harrison College, 1892-6, Codrington College, 1897-1900, at Barbados; A.B., Univ. of Durham, England, 1901; M.D., College of Physicians and Surgeons, Boston, Mass., 1912; married Nettie Alvena Swan, of Somerset, Bermuda, July 30, 1903. Was assistant master Combermere School, Barnados, 1900; principal Sandys High School, Bermuda, 1901-3; came to America, 1903; private tutor in classics and mathematics at Cambridge, Mass, 1903-8; practiced medicine since 1912. Episcopalian. Member New England Medical, Dental and Pharm. Assn. Mason; member Odd Fellows, Knights of Pythias, Brothers and Sisters of Love and Charity. Ad-

dress: 75 Brookline St., Cambridge, Mass.

BRAITHWAITE, William Stanley Beaumont, author; born at Boston, Mass., Dec. 6, 1878; son of William S. and Emma (DeWolfe) Braithwaite; self-educated; married Emma Kelly, of Montrose, Va., June 30, 1903; 4 children: Fiona, Katherine, William Edith. Author: Lyrics of Life and Love, 1904; The Book of Elizabethan Verse, 1906; The House of Falling Leaves, 1908; The Book of Georgian Verse, 1908; The Book of Restoration Verse, 1909. Contemporary Reviews: Essays in Literary Opinion, 1914; New England Poems and Lyrics, 1914. Contributor of literary criticisms for Boston Transcript; also contributor of verse and essays to The Forum, Lippincott's, Scribner's and Century magazines. Published the Poetic Journal in Boston, 1912-14. Home: 27 Ellsworth Ave., Cambridge. Office: With Boston Transcript, Boston, Mass.

BRANCH, Clement Tazewell, Jr., physician; born at Farmville, Va., Jan. 21, 1869; son of Clement T. and Harriett (Lacy) Branch; A.B., Virginia Normal and Collegiate Institute, 1896; student Leonard Medical College (Shaw Univ.), and Cornell Medical College; M.D., Howard Univ., Washington, D. C., 1900; married Bessie D. Avery, of Petersburg, Va., June 10, 1903. Practiced in Jersey City, N. J., 1900-2, in Camden since 1902. Was commissioner of New Jersey Negro Emancipation Proclamation Exposition at Atlantic City, 1913. Delegate to Progressive National Convention, Chicago, Ill., 1912. Episcopalian. Member National Medical Association, Philadelphia Academy of Medicine and Allied Sciences. Mason; member Odd Fellows. Club: Professional (Phila.). Address: 727 Walnut St., Camden, N. J.

BRANCH, Mary Elizabeth, teacher; born at Farmville, Va., 1880; daughter of Clement Tazewell and Harriett (Lacy) Branch; sister of Dr. Clement T. Branch; grad. Virginia State Normal School at Ettrick, 1897; student Hampton Summer School, 1901-5, Univ. of Pa., summer school, 1911, 14; unmarried. Taught school at Overly P. O., Va., 1897-1900; teacher in Virginia Normal and Industrial Institute since 1900. African Methodist. Address: 506 Chambers St., Farmville, Va.

BRASEY, S. B., clergyman, planter; born on Williams Maderson's plantation, Clarke Co., Ala., 1852; self-educated. Entered Baptist ministry, 1887; pastor at New Hope, Macedonia, Mt. Gilead, Oak Grove, Magnolia, and Union, Ala.; moderator Eastern Shore Baptist Association since organized; owns and operates 116-acre farm at Bromley, Baldwin County, Ala.; dealer in cattle and horses. Chairman board of trustees Baptist College, Daphne, Ala. Member Odd Fellows; past chancellor Knights of Pythias. Address: Battles Wharf, Ala.

BRASWELL, William Edward, dentist; born at Macon, Ga., July 22, 1875; son of Willis and Josephine (Troutman) Braswell; grad. Ballard Normal School, Macon, 1891, Meharry Dental College, Walden Univ., Nashville, Tenn., 1900; married Aneuretta B. Matthews, of Washington, D. C., Apr. 26, 1905. Practiced at Macon, Ga., 1900-13, in Atlantic City, N. J., since 1913. Republican. Presbyterian. Member National Medical Assn. Mason; member Knights of Pythias, Elks. Clubs: Ivy, University of Atlantic City. Home: 34 N. Indiana Ave. Office: 1407 Arctic Ave., Atlantic City, N. J.

BRAWLEY, Benjamin Griffith, college dean; born at Columbia, S. C., Apr. 22, 1882; son of Edward McKnight and Margaret S. (Dickerson) Brawley; A.B., Atlanta (Ga.) Baptist College, 1901 (now Morehouse College); A.B., Univ. of Chicago, 1906; A.M., Harvard, 1908; married Hilda Damaris Prowd, of Kingston, Jamaica, B. W. I., July 20, 1912. Instructor in English language at Atlanta Baptist College, 1902-6, professor, 1906-10; professor of English, Howard Univ., Washington, D. C., 1910-12; dean of Morehouse College, Atlanta, since 1912. Baptist. Member American Historical Assn., American Geographical Society. Club: Monday. Author: The Negro in Literature and Art,

1910; Short History of the American Negro, 1913; also number booklets of verse. Address: Morehouse College, Atlanta, Ga.

BRAY, James Albert, clergyman; born at Carnesville, Ga., Aug. 23, 1870; son of Andrew Jackson and Mary Frances (Webster) Bray; A.B., Atlanta Univ., 1893, A. M., 1904; attended summer school at Harvard, 1906; (LL.D.), Wilberforce Univ., 1909); married Mattie B. Davis, of Athens, Ga., Apr. 23, 1902; 1 child: Ella C.; 2d marriage, Martha Freeman Childs, of Marion, Ala., Dec. 28, 1910; 1 child: Martha Frances. Principal W. Broad High School at Athens, Ga., 1902-3; represented Colored M. E. Church at Negro Congress in Atlanta, 1902; pastor Trinity Church, Augusta, Ga., 1902-3; president Lane College, Jackson, Tenn., 1903-7, Miles Memorial College, Birmingham, Ala., 1907-12 presiding elder North Alabama Conference, 1912-14; general secretary of education for Colored M. E. Church in America since 1914; delegate to World's Ecumenical Conference on Methodism at Toronto, Can., 1911. Editor the Voice of the People. Member National Geographical Society, National Economic League, Southern Sociological Congress, Negro Business League of Greater Birmingham. Mason; Knights of Pythias. Address: Alabama Penny Savings Bank Bldg., Birmingham, Ala.

BRAY, Paul Henry, government clerk; born at Bellefontaine, Ohio, Oct. 19, 1868; son of Tapley D., and Susan (Boyd) Bray; ed. public schools in Ohio and Kan.; grad. high school, Leavenworth; took course in Pond's Commercial College, Topeka, Kan.,; LL.B., Howard Univ. School of Law, 1899, LL.M., 1900; married, June 26, 1901, Sarah Eleanor Dorsey, teacher of public schools, Washington. Began active career as newspaper man and served several years with Indianapolis Freeman, Ind., Leavenworth Advocate, and Topeka Plaindealer in Kan.; was attache U. S. Consulate at Tamatave, Madagascar, 1892-5; appointed clerk in Congressional, Postoffice, Washington, 1897; editor Yonkers Standard, 1907-11 (first Negro newspaper in Westchester Co., N. Y.); founded, 1908, since president Westchester County Negro League, which has 12 clubs; clerk in customhouse, New York. Republican. Member Howard University Alumni Assn. 32d degree Mason; past grand chancellor and special deputy Knights of Pythias; exalted ruler Westchester Lodge No. 116, Terrytown, Elks of the World, and traveling deputy in New York state. Home: 6 Locust Hill Ave., Yonkers, N. Y.

BRAZELTON, James Henry Augustus, supervisor colored schools; born at New Market, Tenn., 1875; son of Anderson and Leaner (Branner) Brazelton; attended county and Parochial schools., Tenn., to 1886, Austin High School, Knoxville, 1 year; grad. Freedman's Normal Institute, Maryville, Tenn., 1894; student Maryville College, 1894-1901; A.B., Knoxville College, 1902; was one of 3 colored students in Maryville when an Act passed by the legislature excluded Afro-Americans from white schools; that college, however, conferred the degree of Master of Arts in 1910; married Victoria M. Carson, of Jefferson City, Tenn., 1902; 2 children: Zethel A., Mable. Began as principal grammar school at White Pine, Tenn., 1896, continuing during fall terms for 3 yrs.; instructor in Latin and Greek, Freedman's Normal Institute, Maryville, 1899-1901; principal Douglas High School, also serving as supervisor of Afro-American schools of Oklahoma City, Okla., since 1903. Delivered address at convention of National Association Teachers' of Colored Schools, 1912, under title "Negro Ideals and Negro Textbooks," in which he proposed a change in primary readers, geographies and histories, as a means of teaching race ideals in colored schools, and solving the so-called "race problem." Republican. Presbyterian. 32d degree Mason; past illustrious potentate Great Western Temple No. 20, Knights of Pythias. Home: 906 E. 7th St., Oklahoma City, Okla.

BRAZIER, J. Sidney, pharmacist; born at Hahnville, La., Dec. 19, 1886; son of Aaron and Antoinette (Rombeau) Brazier; Ph.G., New Orleans Univ., 1910; married Evelyn H. Lowery, of Donaldsonville, La., Nov. 23, 1914. Began with the Capital City Drug Store, Jackson, Miss., 1909; later manager the Astoria Pharmacy, Franklin, La.; in drug business for self at New Orleans, 1912-14; now manager for father-in-law, Dr. J. H. Lowery, at Donaldsonville, La. Methodist. Member the Odd Fellows, Knights of Pythias, Independent Order Tabernacle. Home: 412 Charles St. Office: 806 Railroad Ave., Donaldsonville, La.

BRICE, Carrie Elizabeth, editor, manufacturer toilet goods; born at Philadelphia, Pa., Apr. 30, 1890; daughter of Rev. Henson and Leah A. (Price) Brice; public school edn., and private business course; unmarried. Began as bookkeeper in law office of E. Spencer Miller (white), 1907, continuing 7 years; resigned and later assumed charge property interests bequeathed on death of parents, at Darby, Pa.; proprietor of mail order business under name of Necessary Specialties Co.; editor woman's column Philadelphia Tribune; corresponding secretary Business Clerks' Assn. of Phila. Episcopalian. Home: 912 Cedar Ave., Darby, Pa.

BRIDGEFORTH, George Ruffin, teacher of agriculture; born at Athens, Limestone Co., Ala., Oct. 5, 1873; son of George and Jennie (Andrews) Bridgeforth; grad. Trinity School, Athens, 1894; prep. edu. Talladega College, 1897; grad. Massachusetts Agricultural College, Amherst, 1901; married Datie Miller, of Athens, June 15, 1905; 3 children: George M., Elna V., Datie Mae. Teacher of agriculture at Tuskegee Normal and Industrial Institute since 1902; now director its agricultural department; president Southern Small Farm Land Co.; vice-pres. Tuskegee Farm & Improvement Co. Congregationalist. Mason. Club: Delphi. Address: Tuskegee Institute, Ala.

BRIGGS, Cyril V., editor; born at Chester's Park, Nevis, B. W. I., May 28, 1888; son of Louis and Marion (Huggins) Briggs; grad. Wesleyan Parochial School, Basseterre, St. Kitts, B. W. I., 1904; married Bertha Florence Johnson, of Talcott, W. Va., (U. S. A.), Jan 7, 1914. Began as sub-reporter with Basseterre Advertiser and Daily Express in British West Indies, 1904; came to America, 1905; society reporter, 1912-13, now sporting editor and editorial writer, Amsterdam News, New York; writing book under title of "Arizona." Episcopalian. Home: 2107 Madison Ave. Office: Amsterdam News, 17 W. 135th St., New York.

BRIGHT, Mme. Lida Thomas, church organist, teacher; born at Princeton, N. J.; daughter of Rev. Dr. William Henry and Christiana (Hasbrouck) Thomas; ed. public schools, Newport, R. I.; high schools Brooklyn and Buffalo, N. Y.; State Normal School, Albany, N. Y.; grad. Gregory Normal School, Wilmington, Del., 1890, New England Conservatory of Music, Boston, 1904; studied under Prof. Henry Dunham, 3 yrs.; married William H. Bright, of Boston, Nov. 8, 1910. Teacher of piano and organ in Boston since 1903; organist at Ebenezer Baptist Church, 1899-1907, and Charles Street A. M. E. Church, Boston, since Nov. 1907. African Methodist. Member the Beneficial Society, also Alumni Assn., of N. E. Conservatory of Music; member Brothers and Sisters of Love and Charity. Studio: 19 Harwick St., Boston, Mass.

BRIGHT, Ruth Bean, masseur; born at Canton, Mo., Feb. 4, 1865; daughter of Henry C. and Maria Bean; public school edn., Burlington, Ia.; grad. Teachers' Training School, Davenport, Ia.; married Benjamin Bright, of Kansas City, Mo., Sept., 1900; 2 children. Grand Matron the Order of Eastern Star, State of Iowa; manicure and facial massage specialist. Member Iowa Commission National Half-Century Anniversary of Negro Freedom. African Methodist. Home: 1106 Ripley St., Davenport, Iowa.

BROOKS, Edward Ulysses Anderson, clergyman, former lawyer; born at Elmira, N. Y., Oct. 7, 1872; son of George and Fannie E. (Olden) Brooks; grad. Grammar School, Elmira, 1886; prep. edn. Elmira Free Acad., 1886-89, post-grad. studies 1 yr.; LL.B., Cornell Univ., 1892, LL.M., 1893, post-grad. in history and political science 1 yr.; grad. Auburn Theol. Seminary, 1911; married at Waverly, N. Y., Marie E. Millberry, of Passaic, N. J., Jan. 31, 1901. Admitted to N. Y. bar at Syracuse, 1893; practiced in Elmira, 1894-1901. Organized the colored branch Y. M. C. A., at Elmira, 1895, and general secretary 6 yrs.; was pastor at Hope Chapel, Utica, N. Y., 1895; pastor at Waverly, N. Y., 1896-8; ordained deacon, 1897, elder 1899; pastor at Utica, 1901-8, Auburn, N. Y., 1908-13, and Dyer Phelps Memorial A. M. E. Zion Church, Saratoga Springs, N. Y., since 1913; built and paid for $2,500 parsonage, 1910; member General Confs., A. M. E. Zion Church, Mobile, Ala., 1896, Washington, D. C., 1900, St. Louis, Mo., 1904, Philadelphia, Pa., 1908, Charlotte, N. C., 1912; was assistant sec. General Conf., 1900-4; compiler and sec. Western N. Y. Conf., 1905-14; now member board of finance A. M. E. Zion Church of America. Trustee, general supt. and editor the "Bulletin" of Harriet Tubman Home for Aged Colored Persons, Auburn; trustee Walter's Institute, Warren, Ark. Republican; was census enumerator for U. S., 1900; member city and county conventions, 1901. Member Alpha Phi Alpha; was member Utica Ministerial Assn., 1901-8, president, 1903; member Auburn Minestrial Assn., 1908-13, secretary and treas., 1910-13. Royal Arch Mason, Knights Templar. Wrote poems: Zion Centennial Hymn, 1896; Zion Rally Song, 1904. Parsonage: 21 High Rock Ave., Saratoga Springs, N. Y.

BROOKS, George Wesley, artist; born in Matagorda County, Texas, Feb. 14, 1880; son of George and Martha Ann (Bellows) Brooks; attended school at Victoria, Tex.; studied art under Prof. F. Burr, St. Louis, Mo.

Painter of natural scenery; exhibited oil paintings of California Natural Scenery, and other pictures, at National Half-Century Anniversary of Negro Freedom Exposition at Chicago, Ill., 1915. Address: 811 Agatha* St., Los Angeles, California.

BROOKS, Reuben, Benjamin, clergyman; born at Greenville, Madison Co., Fla., Dec. 18, 1860; son of Daniel and Hanna Brooks; public school edn., Fla.; student Turner Theological Seminary (Morris Brown Univ.), Atlanta, Ga., (D.D., 1903); married Jennie L. Dinkins, of Ocala, Fla., May 28, 1885; 6 children. Taught school in Fla., 1879-84; clerk and bookkeeper in general merchandise store of F. P. Gadson, Ocala, 1884-6; member firm and manager store of Brooks & Chandler, 1886-8; was inspector of customs Port of Key West, 1892; published Ocala Ledger, 1892-3. Licensed to preach in A. M. E. Church, 1893; presiding elder East Florida Conference since 1902. Trustee Wilberforce (O.) Univ., Edward Waters College, Jacksonville, Fla., was treas., 1903-10. Republican; was nominated as candidate for Fla. House of Representatives, 1888, but counted out by the opposing party. Member Religious Education Assn., Jacksonville Negro Business League. Mason, grand sec. Grand Lodge of Fla.; member Odd Fellows, Knights of Pythias. Home: 1501 Tyler St. Office: Room 407, Masonic Temple, Broad St., Jacksonville, Fla.

BROOKS, Thomas L., contractor; born in Va.; public school edn.; resided in Frankfort, Ky., since 1881. Contractor and builder of many costly buildings in Frankfort and eastern Ky.; fully 85 per cent. of his work has been done for white people; over half the residences in the exclusive section called Watson Court were built by him; the colored Odd Fellows building, $10,000, the Paptist Church, $25,000, and the Columbia Theater, $15,000, are to his credit; employed Negro labor exclusively in the erection of the Ky. Normal and Industrial Institute building, costing $30,000. Baptist; trustee of his church 16 yrs.

Mason; secretary Capital City Lodge, Odd Fellows, since 1895; frequently delegate to B. M. C.; member Knights of Pythias, United Brothers of Friendship, Union Benovelent Coc., Masaic Templars. Address: Frankfort, Ky.

BROOKS, Walter Henderson, clergyman; born at Richmond, Va., Aug. 30, 1861; son of Albert Royal and Lucy (Goode) Brooks; mother with six children sold as slaves to settle an estate, 1858; his father was owned by another man, but for a stated annual payment was granted his own time and permitted to engage in business for self; through a white friend he purchased his wife and 2 youngest children and set them free; during the war between the states the father also purchased freedom of oldest son, but oldest daughter was sold to traders, taken to Tenn., and died in bondage: by request of his mother Walter and his brother David were purchased by the tobacco firm of Turbin & Yarbrough, who placed them with their mother as borders; later she hired them from the owners and paid stipulated amount quarterly until the close of the war. The subject of this sketch attended private school in Richmond about 2 months, and Wilberforce Institute, Carolina Mills, R. I., about 1 yr.; A.B., Lincoln Univ., Pa., 1872; student in theol. dept., Lincoln, 1872-3; A.M., Lincoln, 1886; (D.D., Roger Williams Univ.; D.D., State Univ., Louisville, Ky.; D.D., Howard Univ., Washington, D. C., 1912); married Eva Holmes, of Richmond, Va., Apr. 21, 1874; 6 children: Warren R., Ottie B. (married Dr. R. L. Jones), Alberta G. (Tellell), Julia E., Antornette A. (Mitchell), Albert. Postoffice clerk at Richmond, 1873-4; served under the American Publishing Society of Philadelphia as Sunday School missionary in Va., 1874-7; ordained African Baptist ministry, 1876; pastor 2d Baptist Church, Richmond, 1877-80; Sunday School missionary, New Orleans, La., 1880-2; pastor 19th Street Baptist Church, Washington, D. C., since 1882; delegate to International Sunday School Convention, London, Eng., 1889; one of the most widely known clergymen in U. S. Trustee, National Training School for Women and Girls, also Stoddard Baptist Home. Wrote: (pamplet) Silver Bluff Church, 1910. Home: 1769 Tea St., N. W. Study: 19th Street Baptist Church, Washington, D. C.

BROOKS, William Henry, clergyman; born in Calvert Co., Md., Sept. 6, 1859; son of John I. and Sarah (Brown) Brooks; preparatory edn., Morgan College, Baltimore, Md.; student Howard Univ., 1878-95, Union Seminary, New York, 1897-9; (D.D., Wiley Univ., 1897); student, New York Univ., 1903-6; special student at Dijon, France, 1910; married Sarah C. Corroll, of Washington, D. C., Nov. 2, 1882; 5 children: Arthur E., Mamie V., Ashbie C., Estella B., N. Cannon. Pastor Greenbrier Co., W. Va., 1879-81, at Talcott, 1881-2, Harpers Ferry, 1882-4; ordained M. E. ministry, 1884; pastor at Hartford, Md., 1884-7, Frederick Co., Md., 1887-8, Washington, D. C., 1888-90, Wheeling, W. Va., 1890-2; presiding elder Washington Dist., 1892-7; pastor St. Mark's Church, New York, since 1897. Trustee Whitte Rose Home, Union Rescue Mission, Brooklyn Orphan Asylum. Member National League on Urban Conditions Among Negroes, National Assn. Protection Colored People, and Civic League. Home: 316 W. 53d St., New York.

BROWN, Aaron, religious worker; born at Montgomery, Ala., May 9, 1872; son of Rev. Simon and Antnette W. (Rogers) Brown; ed. public schools, Fla., and Ala.; student Teachers' Institute of W. Fla., 1889-91; took special course of instructions for U. S. government service, Atlanta, Ga., 1899; married Alice Lowe, of Calhoun, Ala., Feb. 17, 1893; 6 children. Simon, Aaron, ohn, Alice, Wesley, Antnette. Teacher in public schools, W. Fla., 1891-9; began service in U. S. Custom House, Pencacola, 1899; inspector of customs, 1906-12; general secretary Varick Christian Endeavor Union of A. M. E. Zion Church since May 20, 1912; editor Varick Christian Endeavor; also edits and publishes literature for 740 Christian Endeavor societies of A. M. E. Zion Church; supervisor Public School No. 31, Pencaloca. Trustee Lomax-Hannon Institute, Greenville, Ala. Republican. Address: P. O. Box 439, Pencacola, Fla.

BROWN, Arthur McKimmon, physician, surgeon; born at Raleigh, N. C., Nov. 9, 1867; son of Winfield Scott and Jane Minnie (Curtis) Brown; preparatory edn. Shaw Univ., Raleigh; A.B., Lincoln (Pa.) Univ., 1888; M.D., Univ. of Mich., 1891; married Minnie Lou Coleman, of Atlanta, Ga., June 5, 1895; 2d marriage, Mamie Nellie Adams, of Birmingham, Ala., Sept. 27, 1905; 4 children: Arthur, Harold, Walter, Marjorie. Practiced in Bessemer, Ala., 1891-3, Cleveland, O., 1893-4, Birmingham, 1894-1902, Chicago, 1902-4, Birmingham since 1904; was interested in Peoples Drug Store, Birmingham, 1895-1902; surgeon in Provident and George C. Hall Hospitals; chairman Convict Improvement Board; director Ala. Penny Savings Bank; was asst. surgeon 10th Cav. U. S. Army, 1898-9. Progressive. Baptist. Pres. of National Medical Assn., also Tri-State Medical, Dental and Pharm. Assn. (Ala., Ga., Fla.). Mason; member Odd Fellows, Elks, Knights of Honor. Clubs: Owl, Whist, Advance. One of Composers (history): Tenth Cavalry Under Fire; contr. to National Medical Journal. Home: 519 Fifth Ave. Office: 310 N. 18th St., Birmingham, Ala.

BROWN, Calvin Scott, clergyman, teacher; born at Salisbury, N. C., Mar. 23, 1859; son of Henry and Flora (Hackett) Brown; grad. high school, Salisbury; A.B., Shaw Univ., Raleigh, N. C., 1886, A.M. later (D.D.); married Amoza J. Drummond, of Lexington, Va., Dec. 8, 1886; 9 children: William D., Flora B., Julia, Calvin, Purcell, Marie, Schley, Eunice, Christine (dead). Pastor number of rural churches to 1885; founded in 1886, and since principal Walters Normal Institute, Winton, N. C.; president Lott Carey Foreign Mission Convention; corresponding secretary Baptist Educational and Missionary Convention; director Chowan Educational

Assn. Republican. Mason; grand sec. Grand Lodge of N. C.; grand auditor Dist. Grand Lodge, No. 7, Odd Fellows of N. C. Address: Waters Normal Institute, Winton, N. C.

BROWN, Charlotte Hawkins, principal private school; born at Henderson, N. C., June 11, 1883; grad. high and normal schools in Mass.; studied at Harvard, and Univ. of Chicago; married Edward S. Brown, June 14, 1911. Taught in rural school under Congregationalist society, where conceived idea of the farm-life school; raised first hundred dollars by giving jubilee selections and recitations from Dunbar at summer resorts in Mass.; among those interested was Alice Freeman Palmer (wife of Prof. George Herbert Palmer, of Harvard Univ.) in whose honor Palmer Memorial Institute was named, when founded by Miss Hawkins, 1901; from small beginning the institution has acquired 330 acres of land valued at $35,000; has served as principal since school opened. Member National Association of Woman's Clubs, State Federation Woman's Clubs (sec), Greensboro, (N. C.) Woman's Club (pres.). Baptist. Home: Cambridge, Mass. Address: Palmer Memorial Institute, Sedalia, N. C.

BROWN, Cleon Whitemarch, lawyer, real estate dealer; born at Elizabeth City, N. C., Oct. 26, 1884; son of Jesse R. and Araminta (Harvey) Brown; ed. Normal and Industrial Institute, State Colored Normal School, both Elizabeth City, and Shaw Univ., Raleigh, N. C.; married Catherine Wilson Whitehurst, of Elizabeth City, Oct. 26, 1911. In real estate business for self in Elizabeth City since 1903; editor Industrial Advocate, 1912-14; began practice of law in 1915. Member A. M. E. Zion Church. Mason; member Odd Fellows, Knights of Pythias. Home: 107 E. Church St. Office: 2 S. Poindexter St., Elizabeth City, N. C.

BROWN, Edward G., banker; born at Philadelphia, Pa., 1877; son of Robert and Annie Brown; ed. public schools and Spencerian Business College, Philadelphia; unmarried. President Crown Savings Bank, Newport News, Va., Brown Savings & Banking Co., Norfolk, Va., Beneficial Insurance Co., Norfolk; real estate operator in Philadelphia. Home: 1519 Chestnut St. Office: 427 S. Broad St., Philadelphia, Pa.

BROWN, Edward Hall, blacksmith; born in Henderson County, Ky., May 8, 1861; son of Michael and Susan (Watson) Brown; public school edu; married Emma B. Coleman, of Louisville, Ky., Sept. 5, 1883; 5 children: Michael E., Rosa E., Lelia M., Susan E., Andrew. Worked number years for father, who for 30 years was leading blacksmith in Henderson, Ky.; in business for self since 1898; owns number of homes, his home and shop, also stock in mercantile interests and organizations. Has served as jurorman in U. S. District Court, and on other juries. Episcopalian. Member National Horseshoers' Assn., Henderson Blacksmiths' Assn. Home: 935 Clay St. Shop: 422 First St., Henderson, Ky.

BROWN, Frank James, court messenger; born at Helena, Ark., Mar. 17, 1868; son of Nicholas Von Straubburg and Ellen Elvira Randalls; Brown was his step-father's name; attended public school, Helena, 21 months, and Sumner High School, St. Louis, Mo., 4 months; married Mary Jones, of Springfield, O., Feb. 23, 1887 (died Jan. 28, 1888); 1 child: Frank Jones B.; 2d marriage, Martha Louisa Few, of Graham, Tenn., Feb. 21, 1890 (died Oct. 20, 1903); 3d marriage, Tennessee Carter, of Allville, Mo., Mar. 2, 1904; 4 children: Allamae, Helen, Sadie Ester, Frank J. Jr. Was obliged to leave school, as well as to give up grocery business twice, on account of eye-sight, which troubled him from infancy; was totally blind 2 years; on recovering sight, 1884, became cashier for Robert O. Smith & Bros., St. Louis; was president Bell Boys' Assn., 1885-6; borrowed $1,000 from a banker, 1886, and invested $1,500 of the $3,000 capital in the grocery firm of Brown & Williams, Helena, Ark.; sold interest about 2 years later; was attached to the secret service, 1888-92; worked in tobacco trade 3 years; messenger in Circuit Court, St. Louis, Mo., since 1895; director St. Louis Grocery & Supply Co., 1901-3; appointed supt., 1903, but resigned on account of court duties; president Negro Masonic Hall Assn., $50,000 corporation; secretary-treas. Dunbar Realty Co., a $50,000 coproation. Was president Local Branch No. 10, National Tobacco Workers' Union of America, and delegate to first 4 annual conventions of National and Industrial Wrappers' Union, 1892-5; delegate to World's Congress of Labor, Berne, Switzerland, 1895, to International Congress of Labor, Montreal, Can., 1895; a representative of St. Louis Labor Council at the reception of England's noted labor leader, John Burns, M. P., in New York, 1895; a vice-president of the committee to welcome President Roosevelt during the dedication exercises at Louisiana Purchase Exposition, St. Louis, 1903. Was delegate to each bi-ennial Republican State Convention, 1892-1904; vice-president Sound Money League, 1896; delegate to 11th Congressional Convention, 1906. Baptist. 32d degree Mason; deputy grand master Missouri and jurisdiction; recorder Medinah Temple No. 39, Mystic Shrine; supreme representative Supreme Lodge, Knights of Pythias. Clubs: Dumas, Dramatic, Forum, Lyceum. Home: 5475 St. Louis Ave., St. Louis, Mo. Office: 310 Municipal Court Bldg.

BROWN, Geogre Henry, teacher; born at Corydon, Ind., Aug. 19, 1877; son of William Henry and Margarett (Lawes) Brown; grad. Corydon High School, 1897, State Normal School, Terre Haute, 1904; student Ind. Univ., summers, 1906, 7, 8, 10, 13, 14; married Emma P. Terrell, of Mitchell, Ind., June 1, 1905; 2 children: Leland G., Louis C., Teacher public schools at Corydon, 1897, 1904-8; principal Lincoln High School in Princeton, Ind., since 1908. African Methodist; member choir. Mason. Club: Progressive Literary. Address: 703 Harrison St., Princeton, Ind.

BROWN, Gideon Washington, phy-

sician, surgeon; born at Mecca, Mo., Apr. 8, 1877; son of William H. and Laura (Esters) Brown; attended public school of Mecca; grad. Western College, Macon, Mo., 1900; grad. Howard Univ. School of Medicine, Washington, 1907; married, Edmonia Hubbell, of Kansas City, Mo., June 1, 1910. Began practice of medicine, Apr. 8, 1908; asst. surg. in Perry Sanitarium, Kansas City, Mo., since 1911. Trustee St. Stephen Baptist Church. Republican. Member Kansas City Medical Society (pres. 1912-14); also member Knights of Pythias, United Brothers of Friendship. Club: Ivanhoe Social. Home: 2630 Highland St. Office: 800 Indianapolis Ave., Kansas City, Mo.

BROWN, Grant Gratz, physician, surgeon; born at Linneus, Linn Co., Mo., July 4, 1875; son of Rice and Marie (Seamon) Brown; grad. Atchison High School, Kan., 1891; took minor course at Univ. of Kan. School of Fine Arts; M.D., Howard Univ., Washington, 1899; interne at Freedmen's Hospital, Washington; married Practiced in Kansas since graduation; was health officer for Atchison County, 1905-6; now physician to Phillis Wheatley Orphans Home, Wichita. Progressive. Baptist. Mason, Knights Templar, Shriner; held nearly all important offices; member Odd Fellows, United Brothers of Friendship. Address: 601 N. Main St., Wichita, Kan.

BROWN, Hallie Quinn, lecturer, reciter; born at Pittsburgh, Pa., daughter of Thomas A. and Frances Jane (Scroggins) Brown; B.S., Wilberforce Univ., 1883, M.S., 1890; unmarried. Began lyceum work in New York, 1874; was teacher on Sonora Plantation, Miss., Yazoo City, Miss., and Dayton, O., 4 years; dean, Allen Univ., Columbia, S. C., 1885-7, Tuskegee Institute, Ala., 1892-3; lectured in Great Britain, Germany and Switzerland, 1894-1900; lectured at Grindewald Conference, Switzerland, 1895; one of seven members that formed first British Chautauqua, North Wales, 1895; was entertainer at dinner given to London poor children by the Princess of Wales, 1897; appeared before Queen Victoria, 1899; professor of elocution at Wilberforce Univ., O., 1900-3, teacher of English and public speaking since 1903. Lectures: The Progress of Negro Education and Advencement in America Since Emancipation; The Status of the Afro-American Woman Before and Since the War; Songs and Sorrows of the Negro Race; The Life-Work of Frederick Douglass, Slave, Freedman, Orator, Editor and Emancipator; Negro Folk-Lore and Folk-Song; My Visit to Queen Victoria and Windsor Castle; also lectures on Woman Suffrage of which is strong advocate. Reciter of miscellaneous selections. As lecturer was also member British Womna's Temperance Assn.; member Royal Geog. Soc., and International Woman's Congress, 1899; pres. Ohio State Federation of Woman's Clubs, 1912. Address: Wilberforce, O.

BROWN, James Walter, clergyman; born at Elizabeth City, N. C., July 19, 1872; son of Jesse R. and Araminta (Griffin) Brown; A. B., Shaw Univ., Raleigh, N. C., 1893; A.M., S.T.B., Lincoln (Pa.) Univ., 1903; (D.D., Livingstone College, Salisbury, N. C., 1912); married Martha Hill, of Alexandria, Va., Oct., 1903. Was assistant principal North Carolina State Colored Normal School, at Elizabeth City, 1893-1907; licensed to preach in A. M. E. Zion Church, Bethleham, Pa., 1903; pastor at Rochester, N. Y., 8 years; built $25,000 church edifice and acquired other property; pastor Mother A. M. E. Zion Church, New York, since 1913; president Ministerial Union of the New York Conference; member board of control Varick Christian Endeavor Society of the church; member board of management Colored Branch Y. M. C. A., New York. Member National Association for Advancement of Colored People, National League on Urban Conditions Among Negroes. National Negro Business League. Mason; member Odd Fellows. Home: 110 W. 139th St. Study: 151 W. 136th St., New York.

BROWN, John Henry, clergyman, institute pres.; born in Dooly County, Ga., Nov. 25, 1859; son of Mary Ann Brown; A.M., Morehouse College at Atlanta, Ga., 1885; married Bettie L. Newberry, of Hawkinsville, Ga., Jan. 27, 1887; 6 children: Carrie A., Charles H., Virginia H., Herman N., Perry McK., Virgil R. President the Jeruel Baptist Institute, Athens, Ga., since graduation in 1885; began with 40 pupils in Laudrum Baptist Church; president County Educational Institute in Ga.; trustee Hartwell High School, Ga. Missionary Baptist minister; secretary General State Baptist Convention for 17 years. President Athens Historical and Literary Society. Republican. Member the Odd Fellows, Knights of Pythias. Address: Jeruel Baptist Institute, Athens, Ga.

BROWN, Lee Lowell, newspaper correspondent; born at Springs Station, Ky., June 29, 1879; son of Edward D. and Lucy A. (Gaines) Brown; A.B., Eckstein-Norton Institute, 1901, A.M., 1905; unmarried. Teacher in Eckstein-Norton Institute, Ky., 1902-8; assistant principal high school, Henderson, Ky., 2 years; now owner school of stenography in Louisville; correspondent for Dobson's News Service; editor Louisville News. Republican; was candidate for state legislature, 1913. Baptist. Member National Negro Press Assn., Alpha Phi Alpha, and Knights of Pythias. Address: 1006 W. Chestnut St., Louisville, Ky.

BROWN, Lewis Jenks, lawyer; born at Little Rock, Ark., Jan. 16, 1855; son of Jenks and Caroline Frances (Parker) Brown; atttended public schools in Cincinnati and Little Rock, 1874; took special courses in stenography, typewriting and modern languages, 1878; LL.B., Howard Univ., Washnigton, D. C., 1886; married Victoria E. O. Caroline, of Lake City, Fla., Jan. 14, 1892 (deceased); 3 children: Gertrude F. (Mrs. Henry Cullins), Walter L., Carolina F. Taught schools in Ark., 1875-87; president Institute of Science and Mental Improvement, 1880-4; editor Arkansas Mansion, 1881-4; was vice-president and editor the People's Herald,

1900. Admitted to Ark. bar, 1887, to U. S. District Courts, 1889; attorney Interior Department, Washington, 1889, Treasury Dept., 1890; admitted to Mo. bar, and practiced in St. Louis, 1898; now in practice in Little Rock; legal advisor Little Rock Commercial League. Delegate to several Republican County Conventions; was vice-pres. Ark. Republican League, 1895. Methodist. Secretary of State Colored Bar Assn.; was president 4 terms; president Pulaski County Teachers' Assn., 1887; secretary Arkansas Colored Teachers' Assn., 1890; member Little Rock Commercial League. Mason; member Odd Fellows, Ancient Order of Craftmen. Club: Search-light (pres. 4 terms.) Home: 122 W. 25th St. Office: 703 1-2 Main St., Little Rock, Ark.

BROWN, Mack Clinton, physician; born at Bethony, Tex., Dec. 7, 1856; son of Irving and Easter Brown; grad. LeMoyne . College, Memphis, Tenn., 1880; M.D., Meharry Medical College, Walden Univ., Nashville, Tenn., 1894; married Isola Mary Elizabeth Snead, of Huntington, Tenn., Feb. 4, 1903; 2 children. Practiced in Alexandria, La., since 1894. Member Medical Association of La. Republican. Baptist. Address: 824 Beauregard St., Alexandria, La.

BROWN, Maudelle Tanner ,teacher; born at St. Louis, Mo., June 1, 1885; son of Charles Hugh and Arrena Isabella (Tanner) Brown; grad. Sumner High School, St. Louis, 1903; A.B., Univ. of Illinois, 1906; unmarried. Teacher in E. St. Louis, Ill., 1906-7, in Colored High School, Baltimore, Md., 1907-14; teacher of mathematics at Sumner High School, St. Louis, Mo., since 1914. Episcopalian. Home: 1287 Sutter Ave., St. Louis, Mo.

BROWN, Robert Elmer, Sr., teacher natural science; born at Houston, Texas, Sept. 29, 1874; son of William Harrison and Lucy (Martin) Brown; A.B., Wiley Univ., 1900, A.M., 1906; studied chemistry, physics and zoology at Univ. of Chicago, 1903; correspondence course in chemistry from International Correspondence Schools, 1904; finished course in Nyles Bryant Piana Tuning School; married Sallie Bertha Donegan, of Huntsville, Ala., July 29, 1903; 5 children: Robert E. Jr., Elias W. (deceased), Frederic Marion, Richard Shepard, Lyman Donegan. Began as teacher at Philander Smith College, Little Rock, Ark., 1900; head instructor in department of natural science at Wiley Univ., since 1901; without any appropriation to aid, he worked for years to build up this department to its present high standerd, in which instruction is now given in chemistry and zoology; instructor in physics and psychology as applied to teaching in Tex., 5 years; taught physiology in Nurse Training Dept. of Shepherd Sanatarium, 1913-14. Organized the choir, the band, orchestra, quartette, and the first Willing Workers' of Wiley Univ.; toured Texas and Arkansas as baratone soloist with the Wiley Jubilee Singers, 1897, with Male Quartette, 1910; modernized many jubilee songs for quartettes, and wrote "The Busy Bees' operatta. Was drummer boy in Co. D., Texas State Militia, colored, stationed at Bryan, 1889-90. Republican; collector of data on migratory birds for U. S. Department of Agriculture, 1903-4. Methodist. Member National Association for Advancement of Colored People. Club: Searchlight (Little Rock, Ark.). Author (pamphlets): Look Ere You Leap, 1900; Souvenir History of the Science Department of Wiley University, 1910. Address: Wiley Universitty, Marshall, Texas.

BROWN, Robert Sirrelle, physician, surgeon; born at Staunton, Va., Dec. 8, 1863; son of Richard H. and Margaret (Miller) Brown; grad. high school, Staunton; M.D., Bennett Medical College, Chicago, Ill., 1895; married Julia A. Perrin, of Goshen, Va., Apr. 25, 1882; 2d marriage, Anna L. Webb, of Berryville, Va., Aug. 22, 1892; 7 children: Minnie B., Richard L., Emery R., Margaret A., Robert S. Jr., R. Corrol, W. Donald. Practiced in Oskaloosa, Iowa, 1895-8, Minneapolis, Minn., since 1898; medical examiner for number societies. Republican. Episcopalian. Member National Medical Assn., American Medical Assn., Minnesota State Medical Society, Hennepin County Medical Society. 32 degree Mason; member Odd Fellows, Knights of Pythias, Elks, Civic and Commercial Assn. Home: 608 E. 14th St. Office: Tribune Annex Bldg., Minneapolis, Minn.

BROWN, Roscoe Conklin, dentist; born at Washington, D. C., Oct. 14, 1884; son of John R. and Blanche (Maguire) Brown; grad. M Street High School, Washington, 1903; D.D.S., Howard Univ. Dental College, 1906; unmarried. Practiced in Richmond, Va., since 1907; visiting dentist to St. Francis De Sales Institute at Rock Castle, Va.; member faculty, hygiene and sanation, Richmond Hospital and Training School for Nurses; associate editor Journal of National Medcal Association. Elected as delegate to International Hygiene Congress, Lyons, France, 1914, which was abandoned on account of European war. Republican. Baptist. Member National Medical Society, Richmond Medical Society, Old Dominion State Dental Assn., Tri-State Dental Assn. of N. C., Md., Va., Robert T. Freeman Dental Society of D. C.; secretary George Mason School Improvement League; member Kappa Eta Chi Kappa, also Order of St. Luke. Address: 604 N. 29th St., Richmond, Va.

BROWN, Samuel Joe, lawyer; born at Keosauqua, Iowa, July 6, 1875; son of Lewis and Elizabeth (Henderson) Brown; grad. high school at Ottumwa, Iowa, 1894; A.B., State Univ. of Iowa, 1898, LL.B., 1901, A.M., 1902; married Sue M. Wilson, of Buxton, Iowa, Dec. 31, 1902. Principal public school at Muchakinock, Ia., 1898-9; professor of ancient languages at Bishop College, Marshall, Tex., 1899-1900. Admitted to Iowa bar, 1901; since practiced in Des Moines and Buxton; member firm of Woodson & Brown. Was member committee of 300 citizens that drafted Commission Plan of government for City of Des Moines, 1908; candidate for Councilman, 1910; secretary Des Moines Negro Business League; founder and honorary president Des Moines Negro Lyceum Assn.; former president Inter-State Literary Association of Kansas and West; commissioner from Iowa to National Half-Century Anniversary of Negro Freedom, Chicago, Ill., 1915. African Methodist. Member Iowa State Bar Assn., Polk County Bar Assn.; ex-president Iowa Negro Bar Assn., Iowa Afro-American Council; member Phi Beta Kappa, Kappa Alpha Nu. Mason; past grand patron Order of Eastern Star. Author: A Constitutional View of the Abridgement of the Rights of Negro Citizens by Certain States of the Union, 1902. Home: 1058 Fifth St. Office: 507 Mulburry St., Des Moines, Iowa.

BROWN, Sterling Nelson, .clergyman, university prof.; born in Roane Co., Tenn., Nov. 21, 1858; A.B., Fisk Univ., Nashville, Tenn., 1885; B.D., Oberlin Theological Seminary, 1888; (A.M., Fisk Univ., 1891; D.D., Howard Univ., 1906); married; 6 children. Ordained in Congregational ministry, 1885; pastor at Cleveland, Ohio, 4 years; Plymouth Congregational Church and Lincoln Congregational Temple, Washington, D. C., 1889-1913; resigned. Professor in Howard Univ. School of Theology since 1892; now professor of English Bible, director of extension work and correspondence study; was member board of trustees public schools; D. C., 3 years; president Oak Park Realty Co.; owns 100-acre farm in Maryland, operated by his family. Author: Bible Mastery, 1907. Lectures: The Problems in the Negro Church; The Negro Ministry; The Forces that Win; The Coming Man, and I'm Dead Broke; has written number of treatices on Bible Study, and Christian Work. Home: 2464 6th St. N. W. Office: Howard University, Washington, D. C.

BROWN, Sue M., social worker; born at Staunton, Va., Sept. 8, 1877; daughter of Jacob and Maria (Harris) Wilson; high school edn., Oskaloosa, Iowa; married S. Joe Brown, of Des Moines, Ia., Dec. 31, 1902. Director and chairman educational committee of Iowa Federation Colored Woman's Clubs, also editor its official publication, "Iowa Colored Woman"; superintendent social science dept. National Association Colored Women; organized Mothers' Congress of Des Moines, High School Girls' Club, Boys' Social Center, Interlectual Improvement Club; founded and now president Richard Allen Aid Society of A. M. E. Church; former supt. A. M. E. Sunday Schools of Iowa; historian of Inter-State Literary Association of Middle West. Member Order Eastern Star; grand lecturer Grand Chapter of Iowa. Author: (pamphlets): American Social Science, 1911; Social Science Bulletin, 1914. Home: 1058 Fifth St., Des Moines, Iowa.

BROWN, Walter, physician; born at Richmond, Va., Nov. 8, 1872; son of Alexander and Pauline (Ellis) Brown; grad. Richmond High and Normal School, 1889; M.D., Shaw Univ., Rauleigh, N. C., 1905; married Mary Spencer McDougald, of Whiteville, N. C., June 3, 1908; 1 child: Emma Corinne. Began as hotel employe, 1889; worked on steamboat and railroad for 4 years; in mercantile business, 1893-1901; studied medicine, 1901-5; practiced in Richmond since June, 1905; lecturer on obstetrical nursing at Richmond Hospital and Nurse Training School. Republican. Baptist. Member National Medical Assn., Old Dominion Medical Society, Richmond Medical Society (pres.); also member Odd Fellows. Home: 621 N. 29th St., Richmond, Va.

BROWN, W. David, undertaker; born at Wilmington, Del., Oct. 24, 1865; son of Jeffrey J. and Mary A. (Williams) Brown; grad. Howard High School, Wilmington, 1883; only colored person in class of 30 graduates of Renouard's Embalming College, New York, 1903; married Henrietta Thompson, of New York, Apr. 28, 1891. In undertaking business in New York since Nov. 12, 1902. Republican. Methodist. Member New York Undertakers' Assn. Mason, Shriner; national grand treasurer S. C. M., and grand master jurisdiction of New York in Grand United Order of Odd Fellows. Owns property in Wilmington, Del., Philadelphia, Pa., Newark, N. J., New York, Brooklyn, and Long Island City, N. Y. Home: 2315 Seventh Ave. Office: 146 W. 53rd St., New York.

BROWNE, Alexander Cecil, dentist; born in Savannah, Ga., Oct. 1, 1880; son of Horace and Hariet Elizabeth (Delegall) Browne; public and private school edn. at Savannah; A.B., Fisk Univ. Nashville, Tenn., 1906; D.D.S., Univ. of Illinois, 1910; unmarried. Practiced in Chicago since Jan. 1, 1911. Episcopalian. Member Chicago Dental Society, also Alpha Phi Alphha. Clubs: Extempo (Fisk U.), Astra. Office: 3613 State St., Chicago, Ill.

BROWNE, Robert Tecumtha, record clerk in War Dept.; born at Lagrange, Texas, July 16, 1882; son of James and Mary Elizabeth (Dowell) Browne; attended public schools, Lagrange; preparatory edn., 1902, graduated, 1903, at Samuel Huston College, Austin, Tex.; studied experimental chemistry and literature at College of the City of New York; married Mylie De Pre Adams, of Corsiciana, Tex., Dec. 29, 1904 (died July 3, 1911); 1 child: Robert T. Jr. Taught schools in Texas 11 years; was assistant teacher in Samuel Huston College, 1900-3; instructor in high school at Fort Worth to 1908; entered service in U. S. Army, at San Antonio, Tex., Dec. 10, 1908; now record clerk, Q. M. Corps, War Dept., at 39 Whitehall St., New York; was president Supplementary News Bureau; founded and now president Methodist Brotherhood in St. Mark's Church (Rev. Dr. William H. Brooks, pastor); has about 450 members; also founded Brooks Library of Negro Literature; editor-in Chief Saint Mark's Church Life; member board of management Colored Y. M. C. A., New York. Served as commissioner for State of Texas at Young People's Religious and Educational Congress, Atlanta, Ga., 1902; was vice-pres. Texas State Teachers' Assn., 1903-4; delegate to National Convention of Methodist Men, Indianapolis, Ind., 1913. Republican; delegate to several county and district conventions in Texas; was chairman Platform Committee, 1903; one of speakers in the campaign favoring "poll tax amendment" to constitution of Texas. Fellow World's Theosophical Society (Madras, India); member Negro Civic League of Greater New York, and Equity Congress (wrote its constitution). Author: Hyperspace and Evolution of New Psychic Faculties. Home: 223 W. 133rd St., New York.

BRUCE, John Edward ("Grit"), newspaper correspondent, historian; born at Piscataway, Md., Feb. 22, 1856; son of Robert and Martha Allen (Clark) Bruce; self-educated; married Florence A. Bishop, of Cleveland, O., Sept. 10, 1895. Established The Argus (weekly newspaper) at Washington, D. C., 1879, the Sunday Item, 1880; editor The Republican, of Norfolk, Va., 1882; associate editor and business manager the "Commonwealth," Baltimore, Md., 1884; established Grit, Washington, 1884; under name of "Bruce Grit," paid contributor to Boston Transcript, Albany Argus, Buffalo Express, Sunday Gazette and Sunday Republic of Washinton; member literary bureau of Republican National Committee, 1900; established Yonkers (N. Y.) Weekly Standard, 1908; American correspondent to African Times and Orient Review, London, Eng.; probation officer in Yonkers since 1910; a founder and president Negro Society for Historical Research. Republican. Methodist. Mason; member Order of African Redemption (Liberia) African Society (London). Author (children's book): Biography of Eminent Negroes, 1910; wrote (pamphlets) The Blood Red Record (a history of lynching in the South), 1905; The Blot of the Scutcheon; The Nation, the Law, the Citizen—Their Relation Each to the Other; Concentration of Energy; No Heaven for the Black Man. Address: 146 Warburton Ave., Yonkers, N. Y.

BRUCE, Nathanial C., educator; born in Virginia, 1869; son of Edmund and Jane (Farmer) Bruce; preparatory edn. Shaw Univ., Raleigh, N. C.; A.B., Bates College, Lewiston, Me., 1893, A.M., later; studied history and literature at Harvard; took technical courses, Hampton Normal and Agricultural Institute, Tuskegee Normal and Industrial Institute; (A.M., Shaw Univ., 1913); married Mary J. Tinsley, of Bedford City, Va., 1894; 4 children. Dean of College at Shaw Univ., 1893-1902; introduced inter-college debating contests, football and regular system of athletic exercises, also organized jail missions and Y. M. C. A. at Shaw Univ.; principal Colored High School, St. Joseph, Mo., 1902-7; introduced vocational system there which so interested the citizens that $800,000 was appropriated for similar system in public schools; founded, 1907, since president Bartlett Agricultural and Industrial School, Dalton, Mo.; the institution, which has 180 acres under scientific cultivation, was first counttry-life school for colored people in state. Baptist. Member National Educational Assn., National Association of Teachers' in Colored Schools, Missouri State Teachers' Assn. Address: Bartlett Agricultural and Industrial School, Dalton, Mo.

BRICE, R. B., clergyman; editor Sunday School literature A. M. E. Zion Church. Address: 2d and Brevard Sts., Charlotte, N. C.

BRUCE, Roscoe Conklin, educator; born at Washington, D. C., Apr. 21, 1879; son of Blanch Kelso and Josephine (Beall) Bruce; A.B., Harvard, 1902; married Clara Washington Burrill, of Washington, June 3, 1903. Began as director in academic department of Tuskegee Normal and Industrial Institute, Ala., 1902, continuing to 1906; supervising principal in 10th Division of public schools in Washington, 1906-7; assistant superintendent of instruction in colored schools since 1907. Has written and lectured extensively in interest of Negro education. Republican. Member Phi Beta Kappa, Sigma Pi Phi. Clubs: Mu-So-Lit. Address: 1327 Columbia Road N. W., Washington, D. C.

BRUNNER, John William, supervisor county colored schools; born at Burkittsville, Md., Aug. 7, 1880; son of Noah Washington and Emma

Augusta (Jones) Brunner; grad. Storer College, Harper's Ferry, W. Va., 1898; took correspondence course for A.B. degree from University of Chicago, business course from International Correspondence Schools of Scranton, Pa.; married Jeanette C. Offutt, of Frederick City, Md., Apr. 18, 1906; 6 children: Mildren O., Kermit E., Drexel F., Margaret I., Gladys J., and Geraldine, twins. Teacher in public schools at Frederick City, 1899-1910; clerk in bureau of the census Department of Agriculture, Washington, 1910, resigned; supervisor of colored schools in Frederick County, Md., since Feb. 1, 1911, also assistant examiner of colored applicants for teachers certificates; organized first Colored Anti-Saloon League in county. Republican. African Methodist. Member Maryland State Teachers' Assn. Wrote (pamphlet): Hints and Suggestions on Teaching Reading in First and Second Grades, adopted by school board for use in colored schools in county. Address: 109 E. 5th St., Frederick City, Md.

BRYAN, Felix Angus, physician, surgeon; A.B., Fisk Univ., Nashville, Tenn., 1895; M.D., Meharry Medical College (Walden Univ.), 1902. Address: 304 N.Central Ave., Dallas, Texas.

BRYANT, Alonzo William, clergyman, editor; born at Sparta, Ga., Dec. 25, 1874; son of Isaac and Lettie (Moody) Bryant; ed. public schools, Sparta, and high school, Dublin, Ga.; student Atlanta Baptist College; B.D., Central City College, Macon, Ga., 1906; (D.D., Princeton Normal and Industrial Univ., Indiana, 1909); married Katie L. Flewellen, of Sparta, Mar. 27, 1901; 1 child: Josephine Alice. Ordained Baptist ministry, Savannah, Ga., Jan. 6, 1900; pastor Union Church, Mayfield; West Hunter Street Church, Atlanta; Macedonia Church, Grantville; Macedonia Church, Valdosta; Union Church, Moultrie; 1st Baptist Church, Valdosta; Mt. Olive Church, Pearson; Mt. Moriah Church, Alapaha; now pastor St. James Church, Valdosta, Ga.; corresponding secretary Missionary Baptist Conv. of Ga., under joint appmt. of the State Missionary Board of Ga., Home Missionary Board of National Baptist Convention of America, and Home Missionary Board of Southern Baptist Convention, white; pres. State Baptist Young Peoples' Union; member National Baptist Young Peoples' Union Board; was principal Forrest City High and Industrial School at Savannah, Ga., former editor and mgr. Baptist Truth; now editor Valdosta Recorder; pres. Record Pub. Co. Trustee Central City College. Served with 9th U. S. Cav. during Spanish-American war; was postmaster at Thunderbolt, Ga.. 1900. Member Ga. State Central Republican Committee; delegate to Republican National Convention, Chicago, 1912. Mason; grand prelate Grand Lodge Knights of Pythias, jurisdiction of Ga.; member Odd Fellows. Address: 705 Johnson St., or Box 603, Valdosta, Ga.

BRYANT, Henry Clay, Jr., physiciancian; A.B., Fisk Univ., Nashville, Tenn., 1906; M.D., Northwestern Univ. Medical School, Ill., 1910. Practiced in Birmingham since graduation. Address: Birmingham, Ala.

BRYANT, Ira T., secretary of missions, editor; born at Selma, Ala., Oct. 14, 1877; son of Mansfield E. and Alice A. (Choice) Bryant. Began as monotype operator in U. S. printing office, Washington, D. C.; secretary and treasurer publishing house of A. M. E. Sunday School Union, Nashville, Tenn., since 1908; business manager Southern Christian Recorder; editor Young Allenite Monthly; director People's Saving Bank & Trust Co. Trustee Wilberforce Univ., Payne Univ., Turner Normal College. Progressive. Mason; member Odd Fellows. Club: Ving-it-Cing. Home 1205 2d Ave. Office: 8th Ave. and Lee St., Nashville, Tenn.

BRYANT, Mildred, music teacher; born at Macon, Ga.; grad. Fisk Univ., normal, 1897, music, 1898; studied at New England Conservatory of Music, Boston, Mass.; grad. American Institute of Normal Methods (Northwestern Univ.), Evanston, Ill., 1913. Assistant superintendent of music, in charge of work in 14 colored schools, Louisville, Ky., since 1909. Home: 1514 W. Chestnut St., Louisville, Ky.

BUCHANAN, Charles Andrew, clergyman, editor; born at Brookville, Miss., Feb. 22, 1860; son of John R. and Ann Buchanan; public school edn.; married Alice Dupree, of Macon, Miss., April, 1880; 4 children. Ordained in Baptist ministry, 1884; elected president Central Mississippi College, 1893; now educational secretary Baptist College of the Baptist State Convention, Okla; began newspaper work as editor "Preacher Safeguard," Kasciusko, Miss, 1894; an article appearing in that paper caused a mob to order him from the state, 1905; removed to Okla., and since published the Oklahoma Safeguard at Guthrie. Republican. Mason; member Odd Fellows, Knights of Pythias. Address: The Oklahoma Safeguard, Guthrie, Okla.

BUCHANAN, Walter Solomon, educator; born at Troy, Ala., Feb. 8, 1882; son of Frederick and Harriet (Segars) Buchanan; ed. public schools, Troy, Ala., 1889-96; grad. Tuskegee Normal and Industrial Institute, 1899; finished course in Sloyd Training School, 1902, Y. M. C. A. Night School, 1903, at Boston, Mass.; B.A.S., Bussey Institution, Harvard Univ., 1906; (A.M., Selma Univ., Ala, 1910); married Ida Councill, of Normal, Ala., Aug. 24, 1909; 2 children: Councill, Walter S. Jr. Began as teacher in Schofield Normal and Industrial School, Aiken, S. C.; president State Agricultural and Mechanical College for Negroes, Normal, Ala., since 1909; director Standard Life Insurance Co., Atlanta, Ga. Missionary Baptist. Member National Geographical Assn., American Academy Political and Social Science. Mason; member Knights of Pythias, Independent Order of Immaculates. Address: State A. and M. College, Normal, Ala.

BUCHANAN, William, physician, surgeon; A.B., Fisk Univ., Nashville, Tenn., 1899; M.D., Rush Medical College, Univ. of Chicago. Practiced in Chicago since graduation. Address: 3611 State St., Chicago, Ill.

BUCKNER, George Washington, consul-general; born in Green Co., Ky., Dec. 1, 1855; attended Freemen School, Ky., public schools, Ind., State Normal School, Terre Haute, M.D., Indiana Eclectic Medical College, 1890. Taught school in Kentucky and Indiana for 17 years; practiced medicine in Evansville, Ind., 1890-1913. Minister resident and consul-general to Liberia since Sept. 10, 1913. Home: 710 Oak St., Evansville, Ind. Address: American Legation, Monrovia, Liberia, West Africa.

BULLOCK, Charles Harmon, secretary Y. M. C. A.; born at Charlottsville, Va., Mar. 5, 1875; son of Burkley and Mary (Washington) Bullock; ed. in public schools at Charlottsville to 1892; married Lottie D. Lewis, of Charlottsville, Apr. 4, 1901; 6 children: Robert K., Charles H. Jr., Mary O., Virginia L., Lewis M., Louise L. When a boy worked in Union Station Restaurant operated by his father, Charlottsville; was secretary Land Improvement Co., 4 years; teacher in public schools of Charlottsville, 6 years; during same time acted as correspondent for local daily papers (white) and colored weeklies; was identified with civic and religious movements at Charlottsville; organized the Colored Y. M. C. A., Brooklyn, N. Y., was secretary, 1902-6; secretary Colored Y. M. C. A., Louisville, Ky., since 1906. Baptist. Mason. Address: Y. M. C. A., 920 W. Chestnut St., Louisville, Ky.

BULLOCK, Matthew Washington, lawyer; born at Dabney, N. C., Sept. 11, 1881; son of Jesse and Amanda (Sneed) Bullock; A.B., Dartmouth, 1904; LL.B., Harvard, 1907; grad. work at Cornell, summer, 1909; married Katherine Wright, of Boston, Mass., Sept. 21, 1910. Admitted to Illinois bar, 1908; with school book house of Ginn & Co., Chicago, 1908; professor of science at Atlanta Baptist College, Ga., 1908-12; admitted to Georgia bar, 1912; since practiced in Atlanta; special counsel for Grand District Lodge No. 18, Odd Fellows;

counsel for Standard Life Insurance Co.; director West Side Mercantile Co. Republican. Baptist. Member Southern Sociological Congress, Young Men's Christian Assn. (dir.). Mason; member Odd Fellows. Club: Monday.: Home: 342 Queensferry Ave. Office: 209 Odd Fellows Auditorium, Atlanta, Ga.

BUMPASS, James, lawyer; born at Aberdeen, Miss., Oct. 10, 1867; son of James and Julia (Saddler) Bumpass; high school edn., Aberdeen; student for while at Roger Williams Univ. Nashville, Tenn.; grad. Walden Univ. Law School, 1903; married Cassie Johnson, of Nashville, July 30, 1893; adopted child: James Johnson Bumpass. Practiced in Nashville since 1899; supreme attorney for Knights of Peter Claver, and Independent Order of Imaculates; attorney and director People's Saving Bank & Trust Co., also Star Realty & Investment Co. Republican. Catholic. Member Nashville Negro Board of Trade. Home: 1308 14th Ave. N., Office 411 4th Ave. N., Nashville, Tenn.

BUNDY, James F., lawyer, university secretary; born at Washington, Va., Sept. 25, 1862; son of Armstead and Annie (Strothers) Bundy; preparatory edn. Oberlin (O.) College; A.B., Howard Univ., Washington, D. C., 1884, A.M., later, LL.B., 1886, LL.M., 1887; married Delia Freeman, of Rappahannock Co., Va., June 6, 1884. Admitted to bar in Washington, 1897; examiner in chancery, Supreme Court of D. C.; secretary treasury Howard Univ., 1890 to time of death. Was trustee public schools, 1900-6. Baptist. Home: 403 O St. N. W., Washington, D. C. (Died Dec. 14, 1914).

BUNDY, Richard C.; born in Ohio; appointed, Mar. 31, 1910, Secretary of American Legation, Monrovia, Liberia, W. Africa.

BURGAN, Isaac Medford, college president, clergyman; born in McDowell County, N. C., Oct. 6, 1848; son of Sylvia Burgan; attended public schools at Evansville, Ind., 1870-3; State Normal School, Terre Haute, 1873-5; B.D., Wilberforce (O.) Univ.,

1883; D.D., Philander Smith College, Ark., 1884; (LL.D., Wilberforce, 1911); married Cora L. Moore, of Detroit, Mich., Sept. 4, 1889. Licensed to preach in A. M. E. Church, 1878; pastored churches in Ohio 2 years, Calif., 2 years, Indiana 3 years, Arkansas 7 years; pastor at Waco, Tex., since 1911; president Paul Quinn College. Trustee Wilberforce Univ. Republican. Member National Association Teachers in Colored Schools, Texas State Teachers' Association. (president). Mason; member Knights of Pythias, United Brothers of Friendship. Club: Good Government. Home: 218 Maple St., Detroit, Mich. Office: Paul Quinn College, Waco, Texas.

BURGESS, Abel Monroe, caterer; born at Baltimore, Md., Aug. 20, 1866; son of Albert J. and Mary Ann (Jones) Burgess; attended public school and took course in Biblical Institute, Baltimore; married D. Gertrude Anderson, of Baltimore, Aug. 26, 1900; 4 children: Albert A., Lillian R., Abel Monroe, Jr., Marian Gertrude. Began as clerk for uncle in catering business, Baltimore, 1887, continuing until house failed, 1905; with cousin, J. Henry Hammond, bought up the assets, 1906; incorporated, 1908; since president and manager Burgess-Hammond Co. Republican; served as clerk and judge of elections 4 years. Member National Association for Advancement of Colored People, St. James Protestant Episcopal Beneficial Society, Odd Fellows. Home: 546 Dolphin St. Office: 510 St. Paul St., Baltimore, Md.

BURGESS, Albert, lawyer, ex-assistant city attorney; born at Detroit, Mich., Oct. 14, 1856; son of Amos and Sarah Ann (Monroe) Burgess; grad. high school, Detroit, 1874; A.B., Univ. of Mich., 1877; married Mary Thomas, of Pike County, Ill., Sept. 10, 1885; 3 children: Wilmot A., Myrtle A., Elmer A. Admitted to Michigan bar, 1877; first colored lawyer admitted to bar in St. Louis, 1877; was assistant city attorney 2 terms, and only Negro to occupy that position. Republican. Episcopalian. Home: 218

Elwood St. Office: 1101 Clark Ave., St. Louis, Mo.

BURKETT, Hugh Mason, lawyer, real estate; born in Howard Co., Md., May 16, 1874; son of Richard H. and Sarah J. (Jones) Burkett; public school edn., Baltimore, Md.; A.B., Lincoln Univ., Pa., 1896, A.M., 1898; LL.B., Howard Univ., Washington, 1898; unmarried. Admitted to Ind. bar, 1898; practiced in Indianapolis 1 year; real estate operator in Baltimore, Md., since 1899; was first colored man licensed as real estate broker in the city, and only one now (1915) a member Fire Underwriters Assn.; organized Exchange Building and Loan Assn., 1904, and Profit-Sharing Building & Loan Assn., 1914. Presbyterian. Home: Govans, Md. Office: 307 St. Paul St., Baltimore, Md.

BURKS, James Hampton, clergyman; born at Boonsboro, Va., Dec. 7, 1873; son of Johnson and Jane (Moorman) Burks; grad. College Dept., 1896, Theol. Dept., 1900, at Virginia Theological Seminary and College, Lynchburg (D.D., 1910); married Rosa A. Davis, of Lynchburg, Jan. 2, 1901; 2 children: Theresa Hayes, Tyrrell Davis. Ordained Baptist ministry, 1900; pastor at Manchester, Va., 2 years; now pastor High Street Church, Roanoke, Va.; moderator Valley Baptist Assn.; president Midway Cemetery Co. Chairman trustee board Virginia Theological Seminary and College. Mason; member Knights of Pythias, St. Lukes. Home: 19 High St., Roanoke, Va.

BURLEY, Mack Primus, teacher; born at Macon, Ga., July 20, 1880; son of Hilliard and Lydia (Lambright) Burley; grad. Ballard Normal School, Macon, 1902; A.B., Atlanta Univ., 1908; unmarried. Taught school in Tattnall Co., Ga., 1 term, before entering the university; also teacher in public schools and worked as photographer during vacations; teacher of science, English and Latin at Homer (La.) College since 1909; work at Homer caused a laboratory to be installed for which he made part of the scientific apparatus. Republican. Baptist. Member National Associa-

tion for Advancement of Colored People. Address: Homer College, Homer, La. Home (summers): 473 Chestnut St., Macon, Ga.

BURNETT, Junius Battish, dentist; born at Paris, Texas, Apr. 17, 1892; son of Outrey B. and Sallie (Stovall) Burnett; public school edn., Paris, Tex.; grad. Bishop College, Marshall, Tex., 1911; D.D.S., Howard Univ. Dental College, 1914; unmarried. Practiced in Dallas, Tex., since Aug. 24, 1914. Baptist. Member Lone Star Medical, Dental and Pharm. Assn.; charter member Chi Delta Mu. Clubs: Fortnightly, Bachelors, Upper Classmen's (Howard Univ.), all of Washington, D. C. Home: 2818 State St. Office: 1027 Boll St., Dallas, Tex.

BURNS, Fannie Kay, hair culturist, manicure; born at Cincinnati, Ohio, Apr. 9, 1866; daughter of James and Priscilla (Stewart) Gilbert; grad. Gaines High School, Cincinnati; married John Burns, of Cooperstown, N. Y., Apr. 24, 1883; 4 children: William A., Henrietta P. (Mrs. Henry Cachemaille), Ida E. (Mrs. James E .Starks), Gilbert John. In hairdressing, facial massage, manicuring and allied lines of business in Syracuse, N. Y., since 1904; has one of the most thoroughly equipped establishments of kind in the state; patrons include people of wealth in Syracuse and vicinity; serves as hairdresser to ladies in Buffalo, Rochester, Utica, Albany and New York when attending important social events. Baptist. Member Order Eastern Star. Home: 606 Harrison St. Parlors: 126 E. Fayette St., Syracuse, N. Y.

BURNS, James Albert, lawyer; born at New Orleans, La.; son of James R. and Sarah (Hynes) Burns; preparatory edn. Southern Univ., New Orleans; A.B., Columbia Univ., New York, 1887; married Clara Gaines, of Mobile, Ala., 1905; 4 children: Isam A., Geraldine A., Frederick D., Euchariste C. Admitted to Mississippi bar, 1902; since practiced in Biloxi. Served several years with Orleans Light Guard, last of various colored military organizations abolished by law in southern states. Progressive. Baptist. Member Knights of Pythias. Address: Biloxi, Miss.

BURROUGHS, Edward Butler, clergyman, editor; born at Alexandria, La., Sept. 3, 1863; son of Edward and Charlotte (Aldrich) Burroughs; attended Emerson Institute, Mobile, Ala., to 1876; grad. Claflin Univ., Orangeburg, S. C., 1887; LL.B., Allen Univ., Columbia, S. C., 1897; (A.M., Bennett College, Greensboro, S. C., 1898; D.D., Claflin Univ., 1902); studied Chautauqua Literary and Scientific Circle; married Emma B. Belton, of Camden, S. C., Oct. 3, 1883; 7 children: Minnie J., Geneva B., Hattie M., Edward B. Jr., Gordon W., Elizabeth V., Mary A. Licensed to preach Nov. 3, 1883, Camden, S. C.; district supt. Orangeburg District, M. E. Church, 1910-15; delegate to General Conf. M. E. Church, Minneapolis, Minn., 1912. Was editor Sunday School department of Southwestern Christian Advocate, New Orleans, 8 years; editor Methodist Messenger, 1887-9, Plain Speaker, 1889-90; now editor Southern Reporter, Charleston, S. C.; president South Carolina Methodist Pub. Co. Trustee Charleston Industrial Institute, Claflin Univ. Was assistant postmaster at Camden, 1881; delegate to Republican National Convention, Chicago, Ill., 1912. Member American Historical Assn., American Geographical Soc., American Academy Political Science, Young Men's Charitable Assn. of Charleston. 32d degree Mason; grand master, and trustee Grand Lodge, A. F. M. of S. C.; supreme vice-chancellor Knights of Pythias, E. & W. H.; member Odd Fellows. Address: 65 Nassau St., Charleston, S. C.

BURROUGHS, Nannie Helen, president training school; born at Culpepper, Va., May 2, 1879; daughter of John and Jennie (Poindexter) Burroughs; grad. M St. High School, Washington, D. C., 1896; took course in business college, 1902; A.M., Elkstein-Norton Univ., Ky., 1907; unmarried. Bookkeeper and stenographer with Foreign Mission Board of National Baptist Conventions, Washington, 1898-1908; president National Training School for Women and Girls since 1909; sec. Douglass Improvement Co.; cor. sec. Woman's Auxiliary of National Baptist Conv.; department secretary Young Woman's Dept., National Association Colored Woman's Clubs; editor The Worker; contributor to leading Negro papers. Member Ladies' Union Band, Louisville, Ky.; also member St. Luke's. Clubs: Saturday Evening, Daughters of the Round Table. Address: Lincoln Heights, Washington, D. C.

BURROWS, William, contractor; vice-president Fraternal Savings & Trust Co. Methodist; general officer C. E. M. Church in America. Address: 1272 Keel St., Memphis, Tenn.

BURRUS, James Dallas, druggist; A.B., Fisk Univ., Nashville, Tenn., 1875; A.M., Dartmouth, 1879. Address: 815 Cedar St., Nashville, Tenn.

BURRUS, Preston Robert, physician, college professor; A.B., Fisk Univ., Nashville, Tenn., 1879, A.M., 1885; M.D., Meharry Medical College (Walden Univ.), 1889. Practiced in Nashville since 1889; partner with brother in drug business; professor of anatomy in Meharry Medical College. Address: 815 Cedar St., Nashville, Tenn.

BURT, Robert Tecumseh, physician, surgeon; born at Kosciusko, Miss., Nov. 25, 1873; son of Robert and Silvia Ann (Sanders) Burt; attended public school, Attala Co., Miss.; preparatory edn. Jackson College; was student Walden Univ., Nashville, Tenn., 3 years; B.S., Central Mississippi College, 1893; M.D., Meharry Medical College, Walden Univ., 1897; took course in surgery at Harvard, 1899-1902; married Emma E. Williams, of Clarkesville, Tenn., June 11, 1913. Began practive at McMinnville, Tenn., 1897; was also principal of high school, McMinnville; removed to Clarksville, Tenn., 1902; now owner and surgeon-in-charge the Home Infirmary; has performed hundreds of operations with success exceeding 99 per cent.; member Clarksville Board of Health; president Mutual Trust &

Loan Co. Trustee A. M. E. Church. Republican. Member National Medical Assn.; former pres. Tenn. State Medical Assn.; pres. Clarksville Negro Business League. Home: 20 Current St. Office: 122 N. 3rd St., Clarksville, Tenn.

BURTON, Cherles Wesley; clergyman, social worker; born at Meridian, Miss., Apr. 19, 1884; son of James William and Mary Ellen (Shumate) Burton; attended Lincoln School, Meridian, 1900-5; B.S., Talladega College, Ala., 1910; A.M., S.T.B., Yale, 1913; specialized in sociology and religious education; won prize in sermonic elocution; also had 3-year scholarship at Yale; married Emma Mae Walker, of Atlanta, Ga., June 1, 1914. Ordained Congregational ministry, 1914; pastor First Church of Macon, Ga.; instructor of sociology at Ballard Normal School, Macon, Ga., 1913-14; president Organized Charities and Social Betterment League. Member Alpha Phi Alpha, Ministers' Evangelical Union of Macon, General Conventional Congregational Churches of Ga. (secretary). Author: Living Conditions Among Negroes in the Ninth Ward, New Haven, 1913, a social study in pamphlet form. Home: 209 Calhoun St., Macon, Ga.

BURTON, George Samuel, clergyman, music teacher; born at Marietta, Lancaster Co., Pa., Oct. 31, 1879; son of George E. and Annie E. (Johnson) Burton; grad York (Pa.) High School, 1898; A.B., Lincoln Univ., Pa., 1902; S.T.B., 1905; unmarried. Assistant pastor Faith Presbyterian Church, York, Pa., since 1909; private tutor in music to 1913; instructor in Burton's Musical School; in the early part of 1915 there was enrolled 41 pupils studying piano, organ, violin, cornet, other instruments and vocal music; recitals are given each Spring. Secretary the Colored Ministers' Interdenominational Assn., and Negro Protective League, both of York. Republican. Address: 31 E. Jackson St., York, Pa.

BUSCH, Oliver Roy, physician, surgeon; born at Independence, Mo., Oct. 14, 1886; son of Charles and Annie (Hickox) Busch; grad. Independence High School, 1901; prep. edn. Lincoln Institute, Jefferson City, Mo., 1903-5; student violin dept., Michigan Conservatory of Music, at Detroit, 1906; M.D., Meharry Medical College (Waldon Univ.), Nashville, Tenn., 1911; unmarried. Secretary of clinics in George W. Hubbard Hospital, Nashville, 1911-12; resident physician and surgeon Kansas City (Mo.) General Hospital, 1912; supt. Morgan-Busch Sanatarium at Dallas, Texas, since 1914; secretary Mecca Sanatarium; grand medical examiner Grand United Order Wise Men and Women of the World. African Methodist. Member Lone Star Medical, Dental and Pharm. Assn., Dallas Medical Society (vice-pres.), Negro Citizens League, Business and Laboring Men's League, Knights of Tabor. Home: 2921 Thomas Ave. Office: Boll and Central Aves., Dallas, Tex.

BUSH, John E., secretary fraternal order; born at Moscow, Tenn., Oct. 14, 1858; son of Mary Cobb; public school education in Little Rock, Ark.; married Cora W. Winfray, of Little Rock, June 19, 1879; 3 children: Stella E., Chester E., Aldridge E. Postal clerk in Little Rock, 1875-82; with C. W. Keatts organized National Order of Mosaic Templars of America, 1882; since served as national grand secretary; has lodges in 13 states and in Central America; assets about $164,000. Was receiver of public money in U. S. Land Office, Little Rock, 1898-1913. Baptist. Member Odd Fellows, Knights of Pythias. Home: 1600 Chester St. Address: Box 36, Little Rock, Ark.

BUTLER, Henry Pierce, college professor, clergyman; born at Charleston, S. C., Mar. 1, 1872; son of Nelson Pierce and Annie Marie (Snirley) Butler; ed. Schofield Normal and Industrial School, Aiken, S. C., 1879-80; grad. Manual Training High School, Aiken, 1890; A.B., Lincoln (Pa.) Univ., 1895, A.M., later, S.T.B., 1898; married Iva D. James, of Aiken, Dec. 17, 1902; 3 children: Ella Marie, Ivy D., Henry P.Jr. Principal Manual Training High School, Aiken, and pastor

St. Luke's Presbyterian Church at Orangeburg, S. C., 1898-1900; director department of natural science, State Agricultural and Mechanical College, Tallahassee, Fla., 1900-2; pastor Moore's Chapel (Presby.), also vice-principal Albany Bible and Manual Training Institute, Albany, Ga., 1902-5; professor of Latin and English since 1905, and now vice-president, State Agricultural and Mechanical College, Orangeburg, S. C. Colonel supreme staff U. R., and past supreme representative, Knights of Pythias. Home: Aiken. Office: State Agri. and Mech. College, Orangeburg, S. C.

BUTLER, Henry Rutherford, physician, surgeon; born in Cumberland Co., N. C., Apr. 11, 1862; son of William T. and Caroline (Noyes) Butler; A.B., Lincoln (Pa.) Univ., 1887, A.M., 1890; M.D., Meharry Medical College (Walden Univ.), Nashville, Tenn., 1890; married Salena May Sloan, of Atlanta, Ga., May 2, 1893; 1 child: Henry R. Jr. Practiced in Atlanta since 1890; was member of Butler, Slater & Co., owners first drug store established by colored men in Ga., 1890; organizer, first president and now dir. Atlanta State Savings Bank. President Masonic Relief Assn.; president board of trustees Masonic Industrial School and Orphans Home; sec.-treas. Fair Haven Infirmary; trustee Carrie Steele Orphanage. African Methodist. Was surgeon with rank of 1st lieu. Ga. Battalion Colored Vols., 1890-8. Member National Medical Assn.; was organizer and first pres. Ga. Medical Dental and Pharm. Assn. 33d degree Scotish Rite Mason; member Knights of Pythias, and surgeon on staff of maj.-gen.; member Odd Fellows, Order Eastern Star, Court of Calanthe. Author: History of Masonry in Georgia Among Colored Men, 1911; Acute Gastro-Infestion of Infants and Children, 1912. Was first colored man on regular contributing staff of Atlanta Constitution. Address: 200 Auburn Ave., Atlanta, Ga.

BUTLER, Pinkney Ernest, principal graded schools; born at Easley, S. C., Mar. 1879; son of Abraham and Rebecca (Bowen) Butler; grad. Colored Normal, Industrial and Mechanical College, Orangeburg, S. C., 1904; A.B., Lincoln (Pa.) Univ., 1909, A.M., later, S.T.B., 1912; married Olivia Jane Peters, of Bangor, Me., June 3, 1914. Taught schools in Pickens County, S. C., 5 years; assistant principal Dowingtown (Pa.) Industrial and Agricultural College, 1912-14; principal graded schools at Bristol, Tenn., since 1914. Republican. Baptist. Member Odd Fellows. Home: R. F. D. No. 2, Easley, S. C. Address: 520 College Ave., Bristol, Tenn.

BUTLER, Robert Henry, sewing machine dealer; born in St. Marys County, Md., Apr. 8, 1869; son of Henry A. and Emely (Magee) Butler; common school edn.; married Columbia Lovins, of Essex Co., Va., Apr. 8, 1900. Began as repairer of sewing machines for M. S. Faust, Baltimore, Md., 1894; prop. Singer-Machine Sales Co., since 1896. Catholic. Republican. Member Baltimore Negro Business Men's Assn.; also member Elks. Office: 1211 Druid Hill Ave., Baltimore, Md.

BUTLER, Solomon ("Sol"), athlete; born 7 miles from Kingfisher, Okla., Mar. 3, 1895; attended public schools at Kingfisher, and Wichita, Kan.; Hutchinson (Kan.) High School 1911-14, Rock Island High School in Illinois, 1915-16. Began athletic contests with football team of Hutchinson High School, 1911, continuing 3 seasons during which period the team lost only 2 games and won championship of Kansas; gained name of "whirlwind half-back"; in spring of 1912 he joined the school track team; at 7th District meet in Stafford, Kan., won 100 yard dash in 10 2-5 seconds, 220 yard dash in 26 seconds, the 220 hurdle race in 29 seconds, and the broad jump by leap of over 19 feet; awarded gold medal for highest number of points of any athlete on the field; won 100 yard dash against 35 entries at Hutchinson in 10 2-5 seconds, 50 yards at Lawrence, Kan., in 5 3-5 seconds, and 100 yards in 10 1-5; awarded loving cup for breaking record; won 100 and 220 yard dashes during Interscholastic meet at Wichita and 2 more medals. In 1913 his successes were continuous in 100 and 220 yard dashes, 220 yard hurdles, and the broad jump; won the individual cup at Manhattan, Kan., under the auspices of State Agricultural College, and broke all previous records at that school. During the indoor meet at Northwesterrn Univ., Evanston, Ill., Mar. 26, 27, 1914, won 60 yard dash in 6 3-5 seconds, later reducing that to 6 2-5 seconds, equalling the world's record; in 7th District meet, Pratt, Kan., won 100 yard dash in 9 4-5 seconds, 50 yards in 5 2-5, equalling world's record, the 220 hurdles, broad jump, and the put-shot with mark of 46 feet 2 inches; won five first places and the individual cup at Wichita that season; won cups during Amos A. Stagg's meet at Chicago, June, 1914, defeated Carter, the representative of the Univ. of Chicago High School, in 10 seconds, and won high jump with leap of 21 feet 11 1-2 inches; ran against Joe Loomis at Grant Park, under auspices of the Chicago Athletic Club, Aug., 1914, and was defeated by few inches. Running under the colors of Rock Island High School (Illinois), during the northwestern indoor interscholastic meet in Evanston, Ill., Mar. 27, 1915, he won 60 yard dash in 6 2-5 seconds, 60 yard high hurdles in 8 seconds, equalling world's record, and the put-shot with mark of 45 feet, the broad jump with a leap of 21 feet 11 inches and broke the interscholastic record; he led with 20 points for the individual trophy and won 4 gold medals, in a field of over 200 athletes representing 37 schools. Author (with his brother and trainer, Ben Butler): Three Years in High School, 1915; this booklet gives a narrative of his athletic experiences. Address: Rock Island, Ill.

BUTT, Israel La Fayette, clergyman; born in Norfolk Co., Va., May 3, 1846; son of John W. and Adaline (Grimes) Butt; attended Richmond Institute, 2 years; grad. Hampton Theological Institute, 1881; (D.D., Wilberforce Univ., 1903); theol. grad.,

correspondence course, Payne Univ., Selma, Ala., 1905; married Marie Church, of Eastville, Va., May 29, 1912. Principal public and private schools, Martinsville, Va., 2 years; licensed to exhort in A. M. E. Church, 1874, local preacher St. John's Church, Norfolk, 1876; joined Va. Annual Conference, 1877; ordained elder, 1881; pastored Norfolk Mission, Chesterfield Circuit, Henry Circuit, Hampton, Staunton, Brighton, Capeville, Trinity, Berkley; presiding elder Danville, Portsmouth and Norfolk dists.; now pastor Allen Chapel, Franktown, Va. Served 3 years with Co. A. 38th Regt. U. S. Army, in war between the states. Mason; member Good Samaritans. Wrote: History of African Methodism in Virginia, or Four Decades in the Old Dominion. Address: Nassawadox, Va.

BUTTEESE, Shearman, inventor; born at Richmond, Texas, May 15, 1870; son of Louia and Lizzie (Crowder) Butteese; attended public schools, Richmond and Harrisburg, Tex.; also a Methodist seminary at Houston, 1885; married Annie Williams, of Richmond, Tex., Sept. 25, 1895; 2 children: Faure Mercedes, Orleans Maderic. Inventor of the E. Z. Adjustable Sides, a simple device intended for use on wheelbarrows, express, baggage, motor trucks, etc. Address: 1511 Corcoran St. N. W., Washington, D. C.

BUSTER, Harry Crindlon, physician; A.B., Fisk Univ., Nashville, Tenn., 1905; M.D., Northwestern Univ. Medical School, Chicago, Ill., 1910. Address: 432 S. Broadway, Decatur, Ill.

BYRD, William Paul Quinn, clergyman; born at Cedar City, Calloway Co., Mo.; son of Samuel William and Sarah Ann (Dunica) Byrd; attended public schools of Mo., Neb., and Wyo.; Centennial High School, Pueblo, Colo., 2 years; student Wilberforce Univ., Ohio; B.D., Payne Theological Seminary at Wilberforce, 1901; (D.D., Morris Brown Univ., Atlantta, Ga., 1908); married Elizabeth V. P. Jones, of Wilberforce, O., Oct. 3, 1901; 1 child: Sarah E. J. Converted in Shorter's

Chapel, A. M. E. Church, Denver, Col., and licensed to preach, 1896; ordained deacon, 1901, elder, 1903; received first appointment to Cripple Creek, Colo., 1901; later assigned to Mission Church, Pueblo; transferred to Mich., March, 1902; pastor one year each at Whittaker and Adrian; St. Joseph 2 years., Lansing 3 years, Ann Arbor, 1 year; transferred to Miss., 1909; pastor at Mound Bayou about 4 years; appointed to Clarksdale, 1912; presiding elder Moorhead District since 1913. Was selected in Michigan to open State Constitutional Convention with religious service; raised brick church edifice and constructed stone foundation at Lansing; paid church dept in Mound Bayou; delegate to A. M. E. General Conference, Kansas City, Mo., 1912; associated with Rev. Drs. C. M. Tanner of Atlanta, Ga., and P. H. Polk of Natchez, Miss., in movement to established permanent pension department for superannuated missions preachers, widows and orphans of ministers all ranks; lecturer and finacial agent Campbell College, Jackson, Miss. Trustee Wilberforce Univ. Home: 198 Fifth St., Clarksdale, Miss.

C

CABELL, Aaron Hall, merchant, born at Henderson, Ky., Mar. 4, 1855; son of James Banks and Harriett (Jones) Cabell, slaves; public school education, Henderson; married Amanda Rucker, of Henderson, Mar. 11, 1874; 1 child: Viola (Mrs. C. Gowdy). Began in grocery business in Henderson, 1874, and conducted one of the leading mercantile stores in city to 1915; retired to care for real estate interests; owns 2 brick store buildings, number houses, stocks in corporations, and regarded among most substantial colored men in state; president Fraternal Hall Assn., Cemetary & Burial Co. Was delegate to Republican Convention, Chicago, 1888, to Progressive National Convention, 1912. Republican. Missionary Baptist. State officer in Sons of Veterans; member Knights of Pythias. Home:

118 Alvania St. Office: 140 Holloway St., Henderson, Ky.

CABELL, George Clarence, grocer; born at Henderson, Ky., Mar. 16, 1860; son of James Banks and Harriett (Jones) Cabell, slaves; public school edn., Henderson; married Lavenia Dixon, of Henderson County, near Corydon, Ky., Mar. 2, 1909; 4 children by 1st marriage: Flora, Ida, Jackson, Georgia; 2d. Harriett, Martha D., Aaron Dixon. Began as driver of grocery wagon for brother (Aaron); in grocery and general merchandise business for self since 1895; director Cemetery and Burial Co. Republican. Missionary Baptist. Member Sons of Veterans. Address: 429-431 Plumb St., Henderson, Ky.

CALDWELL, George Overall, pharmacist; born at Columbia, Mo., Mar. 31, 1883; son of Moses H. and Mary (Moberly) Caldwell; A.B., Fisk Univ., 1906; Ph.G., State Univ. of Ia., 1909; unmarried. Began with Whetstone's Pharmacy, Iowa City, Ia., school year, 1908-9; manager Sherred Drug Co., Meridian, Miss., 1910; agent for Hopkins & Bethea, wholesale house of Meridian, had charge People's Drug Store, Hattiesburg, Miss., 1910; member firm of Caldwell & Holmes Drug Co., Columbia, Mo., 1910-12; prop. Caldwell's Pharmacy, since 1912; pres. Columbia Choral and Symphony Society; manager Caldwell's Band, also Caldwell's Orchestra. Republican. African Methodist. Mason; member Knights of Pythias; hon. mem. Extempo Club (Fisk Univ.); mem. Mortor and Pestle Club (Univ. of La.). Home: 401 N. 3d St. Office: 3d and Allen Sts., Columbia, Mo.

CALDWELL, Josiah Samuel, bishop; born at Charlotte, N. C., Aug. 2, 1862; son of Dice and Martha (Howie) Caldwell; public school edn., Charlotte; A.B., Livingstone College; Salisbury, N. C., 1888; (hon. D.D.); married Ella Melchor, of Concord, N. C., Jan., 1881. Entered A. M. E. Zion ministry, 1890; pastor, Elizabeth City, N. C., Petersburg, Va., New York, and Philadelphia, to 1904; financial sec. A. M. E. Zion Church, 1900-4; elected bishop, 1904; chairman board of bishops since 1911. Delegate to Ecumenical Conference on Methodism, London, Eng., 1901, Toronto, Can., 1911. Trustee Livingstone College, N. C., Atchinson College, Madisonville, Ky., Douglass Hospital, Phila., Pa., Author: Book of Sermons, 1908. Home: 763 S. 15th St. Office: 420 S. 11th St., Philadelphia, Pa.

CALDWELL, Julian Carr, clergyman; born at Chapel Hill, N. C., Nov. 1, 1870; son of John and Mary A. (Davis) Caldwell; ed. public schools, Manual Training School, and National School of Elocution and Oratory, Philadelphia, Pa.; A.B., Wilberforce Univ., O., 1893; B.D., Payne Theol. Seminary, Wilberforce, 1896, D.D., 1896; married Mattie B. Bell, of Louisville, Ky., Oct. 29, 1900. Licensed to preach A. M .E. Church, 1891; pastor, Jefferson City, Mo., 1898-1900, Lexington, 1900-2, Independence, 1902-3, St. Joseph, Mo., 1903-8; general officer A. M. E. Church, at Nashville, Tenn., since 1908; gen. sec. Alle'n Christian Endeavor League; sec. Christian Endeavor Society for Work Among Colored People; editor Allen Christian Endeavor. Trustee Wilberforce Univ., Turner Normal and Theol. Seminary, United Society Christian Endeavor. Mason; member Odd Fellows, Knights of Pythias, Mosiac Templars. Home: 172 Scovel St. Office: 206 Public Square, Nashville, Tenn.

CALHOUN, Albert Robert, clergyman, denominational secretary; born at Mansfield, La., Aug. 7, 1862; son of Thomes and Hannah (Howard) Calhoun; self-educated; took correspondence course from Texas College; married Norah Cobb, of Pine Bluff, Ark., Feb., 1909; 3 children. Joined Louisiana Conference, M. E. Church, 1883; pastor Northeast Homer Circuit, 1884-5, Oak Ridge, 1886-7, Collinsburg, 1888-90, Houghton, 1891; presiding elder, New Orleans District, 1892, Homer District, 1893-4; pastor at Mender, La., 1895; transferred to Texas Conference; pastor at Houston, 1896-8; transferred to Arkansas Conf.; pastor, Little Rock, 1899-1901, Prescott, 1902; presiding elder, Prescott Dist., 1903-7, Little Rock Dist., 1908-9; elected general secretary Epworth League of C. M. E. Church at Augusta, Ga., 1910, re-elected at St. Louis, Mo., 1912; publisher Epworth League Guide. Trustee Arkansas Industrial Institute. Republican. Member Knights of Pythias, Mosaic Templars. Home: 816 Kentucky St., Pine Bluff, Ark.

CALLIS, James Augustus Braxston, teacher; born at Baltimore, Md., Oct. 17, 1884; son of Rev. Augustas Braxston and Ella (Lively) Callis; grad. Colored High School, Baltimore, 1904, and Teachers' Training School, 1905; attended Hampton Institute, summer school, 1904, 06; unmarried. Teacher at Colored High School, Baltimore, since 1905; was chairman executive committee, 1908-11, and president, 1911-14, Alumni Association of Colored High School; president Inter-Scholistic Athletic Assn., Baltimore Athletic League; also president board of directors Y. M. C. A., and was executive chairman its campaign (1911) to secure $25,000 for the $100,-000 building fund; secretary board of governors Baltimore Assembly; assistant sec. Colored Public Health Assn. Republican. Presbyterian; president Men's Association of Madison Street Church. Member National Association for Advancement of Colored People, Baltimore Educational Assn., Baltimore Forum. Club: Schoolmaster's. Home: 2113 Druid Hill Ave., Baltimore, Md.

CALLOWAY, Charles Henry, lawborn at Cleveland, Tenn., June 16, 1878; son of John M. and Ann (Tibbs) Calloway; grad. Meigs High School, Nashville, Tenn., 1897; B.S., Fisk Univ., 1901; read law in office of William R. Morris, Minneapolis, Minn.; LL.B., Univ. of Minn., 1905; married Cora Jones, of Kansas City, Mo., Sept. 10, 1907. Admitted to Mo. bar, 1905; since practiced in Kansas City; grand attorney for United Brothers of Friendship of Mo.; director Wheatley Provident Hospital. African Methodist. Member Kansas

City Negro Business League. Home: 2546 Michigan St. Office: 601 Delaware St., Kansas City, Mo.

CALLOWAY, Thomas Junius, lawyer, real estate; born at Cleveland, Tenn., Aug. 12, 1866; son of George Washington and Elizabeth (Grant) Calloway; A.B., Fisk Univ., 1889; took course in Bryant and Stratton Business College, 1889; LL.B., Howard Univ., 1904; married Lettie Nolen, of Bellbuckle, Tenn., May 25, 1892; 3 children: Lettie Lucile, Coroline Clinton, George Nolan. Correspondence clerk office of adj.-gen. in War Dept., Washington, D. C., 1890-4; pres. Alcorn Agri. and Mech. College, Miss., 1894-7; vice prin. Tuskegee Institute, Ala., 1897-9; U. S. special agent to Paris Exposition, France, 1899-1901. Admitted to bar before Supreme Court, D. C., 1904, since practiced in Washington; vice-pres. and general manager Lincoln Land & Improvement Co.; was chairman Negro Dept., Jamestown Exposition, Norfolk, Va., 1907; director and general manager Lincoln Memorial Building Co., 1910. Contributor to New England Magazine, Harpers Weekly, World's Work. Home: Lincoln, Md. Office: 1335 T St. N. W., Washington, D. C.

CAMERON, Henry Alvin, teacher; born at Nashville, Tenn., Feb. 4, 1872; son of Walter J. and Jane Porterfield (Bently) Cameron; grad. high school, Nashville, 1892; A.B., Fisk Univ., 1896; LL.B., Walden Univ. Law School, 1898; married Louise S. Brien, of Nashville, June 7, 1899. Began teaching school in Sept., 1897; now head teacher of science at Pearl High School, Nashville. Republican. Presbyterian. President the Middle Tennessee Teachers' Assn.; member Nashville Teachers' Literary and Benefit Assn. 32d degree Mason; organic member Grand Lodge of Tenn., Knights of Pythias. Home: 1811 Heiman St., Nashville, Tenn.

CAMPHOR, Alexander P., college president; born in Orleans Parish, La., Aug. 9, 1865; son of Perry and Elizabeth Camphor; ed. Ned Orleans Univ., Columbia Univ. (New York), Univ. of Chicago; (D.D., Gammon

Theol. Seminary); married Mamie Weathers, of Woodville, Mo., Nov. 19, 1895. Teacher and preacher, New Orleans, number years; president College of W. Africa, 1898-1908; pres. Central College, Birmingham, Ala., since 1909. Author: Missionary Story, Sketches and Folklore of Africa, 1909. Address: West End Station, Birmingham, Ala.

CAMPHOR, Mamie Anna Rebecca, missionary, teacher; born at Woodville, Miss., Nov. 27, 1869; daughter of William Henry and Adelia Douglas (Turner) Weathers; grad. Natchez College, Miss., 1889; student New Orleans Univ., 1889-90; grad. nurse training, New York, 1896; post-graduate work Lincoln Hospital, New York, 1907; married Alexander P. Camphor, of NewOrleans, La., Nov. 19, 1895. Teacher in rural schools in Wilkerson County, Miss., 188493, city school at Woodville, 1893-5; missionary in Monrovia, Liberia, 1896-1907; teacher in Central Ala. College, Birmingham since 1907. Methodist. Matron and Associate Royal Grand Matron, Order Eastern Star; member Household of Ruth. Clubs: Sojourner South, Reading Circle. Contr. to Southwestern Christian Advocate. Address: West End Station, Birmingham, Ala.

CANN, John William, physician; born at Somerset Bridge, Bermuda, May 10, 1873; son of Robert James and Frances Harriet (Burrows) Cann; prep. edn. St. James Day School, Bermuda; came to America to study medicine, 1893; M.D., Meharry Medical College (Walden Univ.), Nashville, Tenn., 1897; post-graduate work, Harvard Medical School, Boston, Mass., 1897-8; married Isedore Susan Campbell, of Hamilton, Bermuda, 1898; 4 children: Eunice, Braxton, Eustace, Millard. Medical practitioner in Bermuda since 1898; elected as member Bermuda Chamber of Commerce, 1905, to Colonial Legislature, 1911; member joint committee House of Assembly and Legislative Council on Tuberculosis. Trustee Wilberforce Univ., O. African Methodist. Mason; member Independent Order of Odd Fellows. Address:

Mangrove Bay P. O., Sandys, Bermuda.

CANNADY, Beatrice Hulon Morrow, associate editor, public speaker; born at Littig, Texas, Jan. 9, 1890; daughter of George M. and Mary Francis (Carter) Morrow; public school edn., Houston, Texas; attended New Orleans Univ., 1905-6; grad. Wiley Univ., Marshall, Tex., 1908; specialized at Burton School of Domestic Science and Art, and studied voice culture in Kimball Hall, Univ. of Chicago, summers, 1908, 09; married, June 27, 1912, Edward Daniel Cannady, founder of the Advocate, Portland, Ore.; 1 child: George Edward Morrow C. Teacher, 1908-12, in literary and domestic depts., Gilbert College, Baldwin, La., and High School, Guthrie, Okla.; associate editor and business partner with husband since Aug., 1913; speaker on race problems at clubs and before audiences of white people; took active part in campaign, 1914, and speaker for candidates in campaign of 1915; Republican. Methodist. Secretary of Portland branch National Association for Advancement of Colored People; also secretary Wanauma Chapter No. 29, Order Eastern Star. Club: Swastika. Address: 520 E. 26th St. N., Portland, Ore.

CANNADY, Edward Daniel, editor; born at Jefferson City, Mo., Nov. 27, 1877; son of George and Caroline (Wilkins) Cannady; ed. public schools, Jefferson City, high school, St. Louis; married Beatrice H. Morrow, of Littig, Tex., June 27, 1912; 1 child: George Edward. In money broker business, Portland, Ore., 1904-12; also real estate dealer; editor and pub. The Advocate since 1903. Methodist. 32d degree Mason; member Order Eastern Star, Odd Fellows. Home: 520 E. 26th St. N. Office: 703 Rothchild Bldg., Portland, Ore.

CANNON, George Epps, physician; born at Carlisle, S. C., July 7, 1869; son of Barnett G. and Mary (Tucker) Cannon; A.B., Lincoln (Pa.) Univ., 1893 (hon. LL.D., 1914); M.D., New York Homoeopathic Medical College and Flower Hospital, 1900; married Genevieve Wilkinson, of Washington,

D. C., Apr. 10, 1901; 2 children: George D., Gladys W. Practiced in Jersey City, N. J., since July 1, 1900; large practice among both races; president John Brown Building & Loan Assn.; also president Committee of One Hundred of Jersey City; devotes much time and labor to betterment movements; has magnificent home. Republican. Presbyterian. Chairman executive board National Medical Assn.; member North Jersey Medical Assn., Academy of Medicine of Northern N. J., Lincoln University Alumni Assn. (president). Mason; member Odd Fellows, Elks. Club: Lincoln Association, organized in 1865; only colored member ever enrolled. Home and Office: 354 Pacific Ave., Jersey City, N. J.

CANNON, William Sherman, former postmaster, farmer, fraternal insurance; born at Cross Hill, S. C., July 11, 1869; son of Mercer and Annie (Young) Cannon; ed. Claflin Univ., Orangeburg, S. C.; Knoxville College, Tenn.; Morris Brown Univ., Atlanta, Ga.; did not grad.; married Lula Bell Latham, of Marietta, Ga., Mar. 5, 1895; 3 children: William S. Jr., M. Ethel, A. Lorena. Founded in 1896, and now sec.-treas. Independent benevolent Order, which has 30,000 members and Atlanta property exceeding $50,000 in value; supreme grand master of the Order; founded town of Cannonville, Ga.; postmaster there, 1901-3, in grocery business 4 years; in coal business, Atlanta, 1905-10; owner of 1,155-acre farm in Troup Co., Ga., valued at $10,000, and Atlanta property worth about $35,000; pres. Standerd Pressing Club; sec-treas. Eagle Laundry Co.; dir. Atlanta State Savings Bank; stockholder Standard Life Ins. Co.; editor The Truth, a semi-monthly publ. Republican. African Methodist. Home: 336 Richardson St. Office: 161 Bell St., Atlanta, Ga.

CARDOZO, F. Henry, horticulturist, landscape gardener; born at Topeka, Kan., Mar. 22, 1879; son of Isaac Nunez and Elizabeth (Williamson) Cardozo; ed. Biddle Univ., Charlotte, N. C.; Colored Normal, Industrial and

Mechanical College, Orangeburg, S. C.; Tuskegee Normal and Industrial Institute, 1901; special 2-year course Cornell Univ., Ithaca, N. Y., took full summer course and received certificate, Oxford Univ., England, 1909; married Flora L. Garbon, of Summerville, S. C., June 27, 1906; 2 children: Dorothy E., Inez G. Teacher of horticulture at Tuskegee Institute, Ala., 4 years; instructor in dairying Georgia State Industrial College, winter, 1902; professor and director of agriculture Florida Agricultural and Mechanical College, Tallahassee, since 1907; chairman board of editors and quarterly Bulletin issued by the college. Member American Association of Agricultural Colleges and Experiment Stations. Episcopalian. Address: Agricultural and Mechanical College, Tallahassee, Fla.

CARDOZO, Francis Nunez, physician; born at Cincinnati, Ohio, Feb. 14, 1882; son of Rev. Isaac N. and Elizabeth (Williamson) Cardozo; preparatory edn. Colored Normal, Industrial and Mechanical College, Orangeburg, S. C.; student Biddle Univ., Charlotte, N. C., 1898-9; A.B., Lincoln (Pa.) Univ., 1903; M.D., Howard Univ. School of Medicine, Washington, D. C., 1907; married Fannie B. Alexander, of Baltimore, Md., Dec. 25, 1909; 1 child: Edith A. Began practice in 1907, under Dr. C. W. Birnie, Sumter, S. C.; practiced in Manning, S. C., 1907-9, in Baltimore since 1909. Trustee Sharon Baptist Church. President Baltimore Branch and director National Association for Advancement of Colored People; secretary Maryland Medical, Dental and Pharm. Assn. Home and Office: 1524 Druid Hill Ave., Baltimore, Md.

CORROLL, C. H., physician; born at Tazewell, Va., May 10, 1877; son of Charles and Billie Elizabeth (Jones) Carroll; A.B., Va. Union and Collegiate Institute, 1900; M.D., Univ. of Pittsburgh, Pa., 1906; unmarried. Principal of school at Fredericksburg, Va., 1900-2; practiced in Pittsburgh, Pa., since 1906; examining physician for I. B. P. O. Elks. African Methodist. Member American Medical Assn., Allegheny County Medical Society. Address: 1109 Federal St. N. S., Pittsburgh, Pa.

CARTER, Edward Albert, physician, surgeon; born at Charlottsville, Va., Apr. 11, 1881; son of Charles Nelson and Patsy (Flannagan) Carter; grad. Oskaloosa High School, Iowa, 1899; B.Ph., State Univ. of Ia.; M.D., 1907; only colored M.D., from State Univ. of Ia.; married Rose E. Warren, of Columbus, O., Jnne 30, 1908; 1 child: Marion. Began practice for salary of $50.00 per month with Dr. L. S. Henderson, Buxton, Ia., 1907, later with Dr. C. B. Powell (both white); was partner with Dr. R. O. Early (white), 1912; bought his interest, May 1, 1913; employs white assistant; health physician for Bluff Creek Township; local surgeon for C. & N. W. Ry., also for Consolidation Coal Co., Buxton. Baptist. Member National Medical Assn. (Ia. v.-p.), Iowa State Medical Society, Monroe County Medical Society (only Negro member). Mason; member Knights of Pythias. Home: 16 E. 2nd St. Office: 4 E. 1st St., Buxton, Ia.

CARTER, James G., U. S. Consul at Tamative, Madagascar, since Nov. 1, 1906. Address. American Consulate, Tamative, Madagascar.

CARTER, Randall Albert, bishop; born at Fort Valley, Ga., Jan. 1, 1867; son of Tobias and Grace (Chivers) Carter; prep. edn. Allen Univ., Columbia, S. C., 1880-4; A.B., Paine College, Augusta, Ga., 1891 (A.M., 1900, D.D., 1901); married Janie S. Hooks, of Macon, Ga., Apr. 22, 1891; 1 child: Grace. Joined South Carolina Conference, C. M. E. Church, 1887; transferred to Georgia Conf., 1888; pastored number leading charges of the church in Georgia; elected bishop in 1914; with largest vote any candidate ever received; was elected secretary Epworth League when organized by the C. M. E. Church, 1898, reelected, 1902; has served more than 20 years as member the Episcapacy Committee; was chairman 5 times of the Georgia delegation to General Conferences of his church; fraternal delegate to General Conference M. E. Church,

Chicago, Ill., 1900; member C. M. E. delegation to the Ecumenical Conference on Methodism, London, Eng., 1901. President board of trustees Texas College; member National Geographical Society. Republican. Mason; member Odd Fellows, Knights of Pythias. Home: 37 Howell St., Atlanta, Ga.

CARTER, William Justin, lawyer; born at Richmond, .Va., May 28, 1866; son of Edmund and Elizabeth (Reeves) Carter; grad. Howard Univ., Washington, D. C., 1898; LL.B., Howard Univ. School of Law, 1892; married Elizabeth M. Allen, of Baltimore, Md., Feb. 17, 1894; 3 children: Harlam A., Wm. Justin, Jr., Thaddeus S. Was first .assistant principal Staunton Public School, Annapolis, Md., 1892-4; admitted to Pa. bar, 1894; since practiced in Harrisburg; attorney for number large business houses; clientage mostly white people; held in high regard by bench and bar; orator of ability and often invited to address important meetings and lecture on various subjects. Republican. Presbyterian. Member American Academy of Political and Social Science, National Geographical Society. Mason. Home: 527 Maclay St. Office: 420 Market St., Harrisburg, Pa.

CARUTHERS, Sampel Sumner, physician, surgeon; A.B., Fisk Univ., Nashville, Tenn., 1897; M.D., Meharry Medical College (Walden Univ.), 1902. Practiced in Nashville since graduation. Address: 1824 Jefferson St., Nashville, Tenn.

CASH, William Levi, clergyman; born at Cowpens, S. C.; son of Rev. Calvin and Eliza (Hatchet) Cash; preparatory edn. Grant (Presby.) School, Spartanburg, S. C.; A.B., Fisk Univ., Nashville, Tenn., 1902; B.D., Oberlin (O.), Theological Seminary, 1905; married Clifford Sidoria Brown, of Savannah, Ga., Apr. 16, 1913; 1 child: Winifred Elizabeth. Ordained 1905; pastor First Congregational Church, Savannah, since Nov. 19, 1905; was moderator General Convention Churches of Ga., 1909-11; delegate to National Council of Congregational Churches, Kansas City, Mo., 1913. Republican. Home: 515 Huningdon St. E., Savannah, Ga.

CASTON, John Tolbert, clergyman, physician; born at Canonsburg, Pa., Nov. 11, 1860; son of Jonathan and Lucretia (Wasler) Caston; (in the war between the states father served in 54th Regt. Mass. Vols. to time of death on Folly Island, S. C., 1864); B.S.D.,. Western College and Industrial Institute, Macon, Mo., 1893, B.S., Th., 1895 (D.D., 1908; M.D., Meharry Medical College (Walden Univ.) Nashville, Tenn., 1899; married L. Leota Chandler, of Macon, Apr. 16, 1897; 6 children: Jessa A., John H., Jonathan L., Jasper C., Jewell J., Joseph T. Ordained Baptist ministry, 1887; president Mo. State Baptist Convention, 1889-96; reelected 1904. Began practice of medicine, St. Louis, Mo., 1899; chairman Negro Anti-Tuberculosis Commission, appointed by Gov. Herbert S. Hadley of Mo.; a organizer Pan-Missouri Medical Society; treas. Mound City Medical Society. President Provident Novelty Mfg. Co.; chairman board of mgrs. Searchlight Pub. Co., Sedalia, Mo.; succeeded the late Bishop Grant as president Mo. Negro Constitutional League; chairman trustees and managing board of Western College and Industrial Institute; director Moten's School of Expression, St. Louis. Has served as campaign speaker under Republican National and State committee. Grand master U. B. F., and S. M. T., Mo. and jurisdiction. Home: 4348 W. Belle Pl. Office: 100 N. Jefferson Ave., St. Louis, Mo.

CATER, James Tate, university professor; born at Atlanta, Ga., Aug. 2, 1889; son of Charles Columbus and Mary Olivia (Tate) Carter; A. B. Atlanta Univ., 1909, A.M., 1914; A.B., Harvard, 1912; unmarried. Instructor in Atlanta Univ., Ga., 1909-10; instructor, 1912-14, professor ofmathematics and science since 1914, at Straight Univ., New Orleans, La. Congregationalist. Home: 32 N. Jackson St., Atlanta, Ga. Address: Straight University, New Orleans, La.

CAUSLER, Charles Warner, teacher, rapid calculator, lawyer; born at Maryville, Tenn., May 15, 1871; son of Hugh Lawson and Laura Ann (Scott) Causler; grad. Freedmen's Normal Institute, Maryville, 1887; student Maryville College, 1887-90; at that time the college accepted white and colored students; married Lillian Clara Webber, of Tate Springs, Tenn., June 24, 1898; 1 child (girl): Willard Wilson C. Admitted to bar in Tenn., 1892; practiced in Knoxville, 1892-6; toured the U. S. giving exhibitions of "lightning calculations", 1896-7; has few equals at quickness in figures and adding columns; multiples large numbers of figures mentally, writing only a single product; an account of his feats was published in the Literary Digest; teacher, 1898-1910, principal since 1910, in Austin High School, Knoxville, Tenn.; contributing editor for the People's Advocate. Was party nominee for state legislator, 1894, though 75 per cent. the Republican voters in Knox County are white people. Congregationalist. Member Knoxville Bar Assn. Author: Causler's Short Methods in Arithmatic, 1894. Home: 1805 Brandon Ave. Address: Box 80, Knoxville, Tenn.

CEPHAS, Benjamin A., real estate; born at New York, Nov., 1875; son of Alexander and Ella (Calloway) Cephas; grad. high school, Richmond, Va., 1892; married Fannie B. Dixon, of Richmond, June, 1901; 7 children: Helen, Marion, Ruby, Thelma, Benjamin A. Jr., James, Adele. District superintendent for 12 years and since vice-president Southern Aid Society, Newport News, Va.; secretary Citizens Building & Loan Assn., Newport News, 2 years; in real estate business at Richmond since 1910; director Negro Historical and Industrial Assn., which was in charge of the 50th anniversary celebration of Negro freedom and exposition held in Virginia, 1915. Delegate to National Half-Century Exposition at Chicago, 1915. Home: 723 N. 5th St. Office: 2d and Leigh Sts., Richmond, Va.

CERUTI, Edward Burton, lawyer; born at Nassau, N. P., Bahamas, West Indies, Aug. 14, 1875; son of Edward Burton and Elizabeth (Anderson) Ceruti; brought to America, 1880; ed. St. Augustine (N. C.) Normal and Industrial Institute, Shaw Univ., Howard Univ., Brooklyn Law School; LL.B., St. Lawrence Univ., Canton, N. Y., 1911; married Elizabeth Wilkerson Jones, of Charleston, S. C., 1900. Admitted to Calif. bar, Jan. 17, 1912; since practiced in Los Angeles; attorney for Enterprise Collection Agency; attracted attention as pleader in defence of Burr L. Harris, charged with murder, winning equittal at first trial. Episcopalian. Member Faben Phi (vice-chief scribe). Mason; exalted ruler Golden West Lodge No. 86, Elks; grand representative Damon Lodge No. 6, Knights of Pythias. Home: 1540 W. 36th Place. Office: 500 Thorpe Bldg., Los Angeles, Calif.

CHANCE, William Claudius, institute president; born in Martin Co., N. C., Nov. 14, 1880; son of William V., reared by grandparents, Bryant and Pennie Chance; grad. Agri. & Mech. College, Greensboro, N. C., 1904; student Howard Univ., 1905-9; married Evelyn Darlin Payton, of Washington, N. C., May 28, 1914. Founded in 1909, since president Parmele Industrial Institute; bought 33 acres of land and erected building, 1914; has accommodations for 150 students; the community has special agent teaching scientific methods of cultivation to colored farmers. Republican. Presbyterian. Member Knights of Pythias. Address: Parmele, N. C.

CHANDLER, George William, fraternal order president; born at Talladega, Ala., Dec. 25, 1882; son of Hardie and Bettie (Williams) Chandler; ed. Talladega College; married Mary L. Redding, of Macon, Ga., Dec. 31, 1914; 1 child: Nettie Lena. Founded in 1905, and since pres. United Order of Good Shepherds of U. S. A.; founded Good Shepherds Home in Dallas Co., Ala., 1909; the tract of land contains 3,100 acres; 500 acres were set aside for the support of old and discrepit members, widows, and orphan children; a half mile square was provided for a Negro town, which is chartered and more than 250 people were there Jan. 1, 1915. Trustee Miles Memorial College, Birmingham, Ala. Colored Methodist. Editor the Good Shepherd Magazine. Home: 1109 E. Grove St. Office: 825 E. Grove St., Montgomery, Ala.

CHAPMAN, Valcour, clergyman; born in St. Charles Parish, La., July 4, 1856; son of Robert and Emily (Hawkins) Chapman; ed. New Orleans Univ; (D.D., Gammon Theological Seminary, Atlanta, Ga., 1892; Ph.C., Flint Medical College, New Orleans, 1907); married Margaret Lee Yarbrough, of Natchitoches, La., Apr. 21, 1884; 5 children: Deborah, Emily L., S. Harold, Valcour, Jr., Gammon W. Ordained M. E. ministry, 1883; member Louisiana Conference and taught school 10 years; presiding elder New Orleans South District of Louisiana Conference, 1897-9, and district superintendent since 1910; teacher of pharmacy, Flint Medical College, 1907-11. Trustee New Orleans Univ. Member Knights of Pythias. Contributor to Southwestern Christian Advocate. Address: 7320 Elm St., New Orleans, La.

CHAPPELLE, Charles Ward, dealer in African merchandise; born in Putnam Co., Ga., July 11, 1874; son of George W. and Annie (Dickerson) Chappelle; ed. public schools of Ga.; took engring. course from International Correspondence School of Scranton, Pa.; unmarried. Brick and stone mason, 1886-90; practically forced out by labor unions and was not permitted to join on account of color; was painter with Albert Williamson, Cincinnati, O., 1890-4; carpenter for United States Leather Co., Chattanooga, Tenn., 3 years; in electric department Park Steel Works, Pittsburgh, Pa., 1902-5; member contracting firm of Gray & Chappelle, 1906-10; contractor, builder and architect at Brooklyn, N. Y., 1910-12; invented Multiplane Aeroplane; vice-pres. Meteoric Aeroplane Co.; went to Gold Coast, West Africa, 1912; made close observations of conditions and found natives earnest in desire for co-operation of Americans; returned to New York to plan for extensive operations in Africa; second trip to Gold Coast resulted in actual beginning of operations; organized African Union Co., in New York, Dec. 3. 1913; president since 1914; also pres. Chas. W. Chappelle & Co., mahogany merchants. Republican. Methodist. Member U. S. Aeronautical Reserve, and Odd Fellows. Home: 3314 Camp St., Pittsburgh, Pa. Main Office: 1821 Dean St., Brooklyn, N. Y. Foreign Office: Seccondee, Gold Coast, West Africa.

CHAPPELLE, William David, bishop; born at Winnsboro, S. C., Nov. 16, 1857; son of Henry and Patsie (McCrory) Chappelle; prep. edn. Fairfield Normal Institute; A.B., Allen Univ., Columbia, S. C., 1881; (hon. D.D., Campbell College, 1896, LL.D., 1913); married Eliza A. Ayers; 3 children; 2d marriage, Rosina C. Palmer, of Columbia, S. C., Apr. 26, 1900; 2 children. Licensed to preach in A. M. E. Church, Winnsboro, 1881; presiding elder 11 years; editor of Sunday School literature for his church 8 years; was president Allen Univ., first for 2 years, later served 4 years; elected bishop, 1912; now presiding over 12th Episcopal District, A. M. E. Church, including states of Ala. and Okla.; much of his work was published by the State Company, Columbia, S. C., under title of Sermons and Addresses; part owner the Ideal Pharmacy. Trustee Wilberforce Univ., and Allen Univ. Republican. Mason. Home: 1208 Hardin St., Columbia, S. C.

CHEEKS, Robert Roy, lawyer; born in Virginia, Nov. 1, 1881; son of James R. and Laura (Fowler) Cheeks; grad. high school, Washington, D. C.; took course in business college; studied commercial law 1 year in Cleveland Y. M. C. A.; grad. Cleveland Law School, 1906; married Miranda L. Skeene, of Cleveland, Ohio, July 21, 1909; 1 child: Louise M. Admitted to Ohio bar, 1906; practiced in Cleveland to 1908, also since 1910; in practice in McDowell County, W. Va., 1908-10; as attorney defending in man-damas case for Town of Kimball, was second colored lawyer to appear before Supreme Court of W. Va. Appointed on Citizen's Reception Committee to welcome Ambassador Myron T. Herrick on return from Paris; member advisory committee School Survey, Cleveland Foundation. Republican candidate for City Council from 18th Ward, 1915 (election Nov. 2). Vestryman at St. Andrew's Episcopal Church, 1915. Member Cleveland Association of Colored Men (president 2 terms). Home: 2338 E. 87th St. Office: 312-314 Superior Bldg., Cleveland, Ohio.

CHERRY, David King, teacher, drill-master; born near Powellsville, N. C., May 7, 1883; son of Wright and Malinda (Mitchell) Cherry; attended Bertie County public schools and Bertie Academy, Windson, N. C.; grad. North Carolina State Colored Normal School, 1904; A.B. and Cadet Captain, Wilberforce (O.) Univ., 1911; student Univ. of Chicago, summers, 1912, 14; unmarried. Began teaching in public schools of Bertie County at age of 16; drill-master and instructor in mathematics Negro Agricultural and Technical College of N. C. (formerly A. & M. College), at Greensboro, since Sept. 1, 1911. Republican. Baptist. Member Alpha Phi Alpha. Club: Negro Business and Professional Men's. Address: Agricultural and Technical College, Greensboro, N. C.

CHERRY, S. O., physician; born at Waynesboro, Ga., Aug. 24, 1882; son of Stark O. and Fannie (Walker) Cherry; preparatory edn. Haines Normal School, Augusta, Ga.; A.B., Lincoln (Pa.) Univ., 1905; M.D., Temple Univ., Philadelphia, Pa., 1909; unmarried. Practiced in Pittsburgh since 1905; medical director American Univ. Beneficial Ins. Co.; medical examiner for 2 lodges, Knights of Pythias, also Western Life Indemnity Co., of Chicago, Bankers Life Ins. Co., of Pittsburgh; treas. Sinot Drug Corpn. African Methodist. Mason; member Odd Fellows, Knights of Pythias. Address: 6217 Frankstown Ave., Pittsburgh, Pa.

CHESNUTT, Charles Waddell, lawyer, author; born at Cleveland, O., June 20, 1858; son of Andrew J. and Ann Marie (Sampson) Waddell; attended public schools, Cleveland, Fayetteville, N. C., and studied privately some years; married Susan Utley Perry, of Fayetteville, June 6, 1879; 4 children: Ethel, Helen, Edwin, Dorothy. Taught schools in N. C., 9 yrs.; principal State Normal School, Fayetteville, 3 years; newspaper writer in New York, 1884. Admitted to Ohio bar, 1887; since practiced law in Cleveland; served as court stenographer 25 years. Author: The Conjure Woman, 1899; The Wife of His Youth and Other Stories, 1899; Life of Frederick Douglass, in Beacon Biographies, 1899; The House Behind the Cedars, 1900; The Marrow of Tradition, 1901; The Colonel's Dream, 1905. Contributor to Atlantic Monthly, and Century Magazine. Republican. Episcopalian. Club: Rowfant. Home: 9719 Lamont Ave. Office: 1105 Williamson Bldg., Cleveland, Ohio.

CHINN, Alexander Roderick, teacher; born in Chariton County, Mo., June 3, 1857; son of Alfred and Emily (Chapman) Chinn; ed. public schools, Glasgow, Mo., and Lincoln Institute, Jefferson City; married Effie B. Fisher, of Independence, Mo., Dec. 31, 1904. Teacher in public schools at Glasgow since 1880. Was member board of regents, Lincoln Institute, 1880-7, and first colored man appointed by the governor; vice-president Home Protective Assn., since 1904. Delegate to Republican National Convention, Chicago, 1912; has been delegate to 9 state conventions, and served as member Howard County Republican Committee 16 years. Baptist. Member Missouri State Teachers' Assn.; was president 1905-7. Mason; past grand master; chief grand mentor Knights of Tabor; chief grand scribe International Order of Twelve; member Knights of Pythias, Forum Club of St. Louis. Address: Glasgow, Mo.

CHISUM, Melvin Jack, publisher; born at Tehuacana Hills, Tex., Jan. 12, 1873; son of John and Rachel (Henderson) Chisum; ed. public schools, Mexia, Tex.; high school, Chicago, Ill.; School of Technology, Boston, Mass.; business college, New York; married, Mae Montague, of Marshall, Tex., Nov. 5, 1896. In real estate business, New York, 1900-9; removed to Virginia and organized the Brickhouse Banking Co., Hare Valley, now member board of directors; editor The Tribune, Baltimore, Md., since 1910; sole owner Tribune Publishing Co.; elected pres. National Negro Press Assn., 1914. Home: Salisbury, Md. Office: 1022 Druid Hill Ave., Baltimore, Md.

CHRISTOPHE, Frank Eugene, physician; born at Oscar, La., Aug. 1, 1877; son of William and Amanda Christophe, preparatory edn. Straight Univ., New Orleans, grad., 1900; M.D., Univ. of West Tennessee, 1904; married Eva C. Loeffel, of Baton Rouge, La., June 29, 1904. Began practice in Augusta, Ark.. Mar. 2, 1904, continuing 3 years; now in practice at Newport, Ark.; partner with brother in drug store at Newport. Trustee St. Paul A. M. E. Church. Member the Odd Fellows. Mosaic Templars. Home: 621 Main St. Office: 618 Front St., Newport, Ark.

CHRISTOPHE, William Rodolph, druggist; born at Lakeland, La., Sept. 11, 1879; son of William and Amanda (Bradley) Christophe; ed. private school, Oscar, La., 1885-93; Straight Univ., New Orleans, 1894-1901; Ph.C., Flint Medical College, 1905; married Laura Marmillian, of Laplace, La., Feb. 3, 1904; 6 children: William E., LeRoy M., Aldrich C., Franklin, Frank. Member drug firm of Cason & Christophe, Gregory, Ark., 1905-6; removed to Newport, Ark., and organized the Standard Drug Co.; has acquired all but 2 shares of capital and stock and had full control since 1911. Baptist. Home: 1206 Second St. Store: 614 Front St., Newport, Ark.

CHURCH, Robert Reed, Jr., banker; born at Memphis, Tenn., Oct. 26, 1885; son of Robert R. and Anna (Wright) Church; father long recognized among representative men of Memphis; when city was in bankrupt condition, 1892, was first citizen to come forward with aid; purchased No. 1 of the city bonds at $2,000 which was considered magnanimous by white people; was only colored man recognized in 50th anniversary edition of Memphis Scimitar, 1894, with full page article, portrait of family and engraving of home; Robert, Jr., was educated in Protestant Episcopal Parochial School, Memphis, Tenn., and Oberlin (O.) College; married Sallie P. Johnson, of Washington, D. C., July 26, 1911; 1 child: Sarah Roberta. Began as cashier Solvent Savings Bank & Trust Co., Memphis, 1905, president since 1908; one of organizers and now director Standard Life Insurance Co., Atlanta, Ga. Delegate from 10th Congressional Dist. of Tenn. to Republican National Convention, Chicago, 1912; only colored member Tenn. State Republican Executive Committee; member Sherby County Republican Executive Committee. Mason. Club: The Frogs (New York). Home: 384 S. Lauderdale St. Office: 391 Beale Ave., Memphis Tenn.

CHURCHMAN, James E., clergyman; born in Laudoun Co., Va., Mar. 2, 1874; son of Thomas and Isabelle (Johnson) Churchman; ed. public schools, Prince William Co., Va.; grad. Champion College of Embalming, Springfield, O., 1898; student Institute for Colored Youth, Phila., Pa., 1899; finished course study for elder, N. J. Conf. A. M. E. Church, 1903; married Minnie Anna Brown, of Memphis, Tenn., Dec. 6, 1899; 3 children: Joseph Enoch, James Wormely Grant, Minnie Esabella. Licensed to preach in Baptist Church, Philadelphia, 1894; joined A. M. E. Church 1895; pastor St. Paul Mission, St. Luke's Church, Newark, and Sea Bright, N. J.; joined 19th Street Baptist Church (Rev. Walter E. Brooks is pastor), Washington, D. C., 1913; pastor 2d Baptist Church, S. Richmond, Va., since Feb. 1, 1914; member Afro-American State Convention of N. J., N. E. Convention, Va. State Convention; was in undertaking business, Orange, N. J., 1899-1914; president James E.

Churchman Co. Founder United People of America; director Negro Historical and Industrial Society of Va., Invincible Order Colored Cooperators of America; financial agent Brethern Baptist Univ. Republican; was delegate to Progressive National Convention, Chicago, Ill. 1912. Member Essex and Union County Funeral Directors Assn., Lincoln United Brotherhood of Newark. Mason; chaplain, with rank of col. U. R., Knights of Pythias; member Odd Fellows, Order of St. Luke, Order of Moses, True Reformers. Home: 78 Oakwood Ave., Orange, N. J. Address: 21 W. 19th St., S. Richmond, Va

CHWA, Daudi; His Highness the Kabaka (King) of Uganda; born at Mengo, Uganda, Aug. 8, 1896; son of Danieri Mwanga and Eva Ivini Kulabako; his father was King of Uganda, 1884-97; grandson of Mutesa, the King of Uganda when Speke (John Hanning), the Englishman and noted explorer, visited the country in 1861, and Sir Henry Morton Stanley in 1875. His Highness succeeded to the Throne, Aug. 16, 1897. then one year of age. Mr. J. C. R. Sturrock, of Oxford Univ., was his private tutor; served as Hon. Lieut. 4th Battalion of Kings African Rifles. Attained his majority, Aug. 8, 1914. married Airini Dulasira Namaganda Kaizi, Sept. 19, 1914. Uganda is a rich agricultural country with a mild and uniform climate; it is the seat of the Church Missionary Society, which is highly regarded in East Africa; the population is estimated at more than 5,000,000; the inhabitants are of a comparatively high type. Address: Mengo, Uganda, B. E. Africa (See also in this volume the sketches of Sir Apolo Kagwa, and Ham Mukasa.)

CLARK, John Thomas, social worker; born at Louisville, Ky., July 21, 1881; son of John Richard and Sallie Ann (Cutter) Clark; grad. Central High School, Louisville, 1899; A.B., Ohio State Univ., 1905; unmarried. Registered Pharmacist; in government service at Norfolk Navy Yard, Va., 1906-7; instructor Central High School, Louisville, 1907-13; secretary Housing Bureau National League on Urban Conditions Among Negroes, New York, since 1913; member faculty of the officers School of Instruction for the Provisional Regt. of New Y. Presbyterian. Member Alpha Phi Alpha, also Civic League of N. Y. Wrote (pamphlet): Study of the Housing Conditions of Negroes in New York City, 1914. Home: 15 W. 132d St. Office: 127 W. 135th St., New York.

CLARK, Lewis Sherman, teacher; born at St. Marys, Ga., Jan. 1, 1865; son of William Henry and Sarah (Hopkins) Clark; attended public schools at St. Marys; B.S., Atlanta Univ., 1887, A.M., 1894; student in Martha's Vineyard School at Cottage City, Mass., 1896; attended summer school, Hampton Institute, 1902, Columbia Univ., New York, 1904; married Rosa E. Low, of Savannah, Ga., Aug. 4, 1897; 3 children: Herbert L., Elias S., Robert L . Principal of Knox Institute and Industrial School, Athens, Ga., since 1887; this little school was first opened in 1868, and named in honor of Maj. John J. Knox; it passed to the control of American Missionary Assn., and was practically abandoned when Prof. Clark took possession; the institute now has 4 buildings, accommodates 400 students, the faculty and officers numbering 14; in 1903 he was manager the only summer school ever conducted for colored people in Georgia to that time. Republican. Congregationalist. Member Georgia State Teachers' Assn.; was president, 1898-9. Address: Knox Institute and Industrial School, Athens, Ga.

CLARK, Mary Frances, registered nurse; born in Chesterfield County, Va., Mar. 6,1873; daughter of Henry and Abbie (Mayo) Clark; attended public schools, Richmond, Va., grad. Nurse Training Dept. Freedmen's Hospital, Washington, D. C., 1900. Was bookkeeper for Grand Fountain True Reformers, Richmond, 1894-8; first colored registered nurse in Richmond, 1900; serves white people exclusively; called to cases by leading physicians of Virginia and Washington, D. C. Baptist. Honorary president National Association of Colored Graduate Nurses; member National Federation Colored Woman's Clubs, Virginia State Federation Colored Clubs, Council of Colored Women, Richmond, Order of St. Luke. Address: 1119 N. 5th St., Richmond, Va.

CLARKE, Edward Alexander, clergyman, teacher; born at Wilberforce, O., Mar. 28, 1861; son of John A. and Maria Louise (Kerr) Clarke; A.B., Wilberforce Univ., 1881, A.M., 1892; married Dovie King, of Cincinnati, O., June 24, 1891; 8 children: Edward K., Vashti E., Robert K., Phyllis W., Benjamin K., John L., Amanda C., Daniel P. Principal high school at Evansville, Ind., 1881-9; professor of sciences, Lincoln Institute, Jefferson City, Mo., 1889-93; was assistant examiner in patent office, Washington, D. C., 1893-6; professor of classics, sciences and English, 1896-1909; also pastor College Chapel; president Lincoln Institute, 1902-9; pastor St. Paul A. M. E. Church, Lexington, Ky., 1909-12, Quinn Church, Louisville, since 1912. Trustee Douglass Home, Anacostia, Md. Address: Y. M. C. A., 10th and Chestnut Sts., Louisville, Ky.

CLARKE, Richard Claybourne, chemist, bacteriologist; born at New Brunswick, N. J., Feb. 3, 1879; son of Samuel M. and Pauline (Moody) C.; ed. public and high schools, New Brunswick, and Cooper Union, New York; married Nellie V. Giles, of Savannah, Ga., June 1, 1904. Chemist and bacteriologist in the psyciological labratory of Dr. E. E. Smith, New York, since 1901. Baso soloist in St. Philip's Episcopal Church; member St. Philip's Men's Guild. Home: 117 W. 137th St. Office: care Dr. E. E. Smith, 50 E. 41 st St., New York.

CLARKE, Thomas Henry Reginald, real estate; born at Washington, D. C., Feb. 17, 1876; son of Cornelius and Emily (McCoy) Clarke; grad. M Street High School; LL.B., Howard Univ. School of Law, 1904; unmarried. Clerk in the U. S. Treasury, Washington, 14 years, and for 10 years was acting chief clerk under the register of the treasury; now president Clarke - Williams - Plummer Co., real estate operators. Served with 8th U. S. Vol. Inf. during Spanish-American war; was 2d lieut., 1st lieut., regimental adjutant, and judge advocate of two General Courts Martial. Republican. Member Spanish War Veterans, Odd Fellows. Club: Mu-so-lit. Office: 1346 You St. N. W., Washington, D. C.

CLAY, Boston, chef, inventor; born at Iowa City, Ia., Apr. 30, 1879; of African, Irish and Cherokee Indian descent; son of Boston and Mary Ann (Roberts) Clay; his grandfather, Judge Henry Clay, was an Irishman; ed. in the public schools, Muscatine, Ia.; widower. Began work at early age to help widowed mother, with 3 other children, and to gain education for self; has served as chef in different places for more than 20 years; worked under 18 landlords in Muscatine, 15 of them in the old Oglevie Hotel, later called the Commercial; was chef for the Andrews Opera Co., 2 years, traveling in the United States and Canada; 1st asst. chef (1915) at the Kahler, at Rochester, Minn. Was member of the first chef's union organized in Iowa; at Muscatine he served as constable and detective for a time, in charge a force of 5 men and 1 woman; handled the "Dynamite Cases" after 3 homes had been wrecked; caused 19 persons to be indicted, 1 was convicted. Invented a Button Cutting Machine; it cuts 3 blanks at once and 3 different sizes at one operation; holds controlling interest in the American patent; sold German patent and has patents pending in other foreign countries; now working on other useful inventions. Served with 10th U. S. Cav. during Spanish-American war. Republican. Mason; member Knights of Pythias. Permanent Address: Lock Box 362, Muscatine, Ia.

CLAYTON, Joseph Edward, teacher, lecturer; born at Fulshear, Fort Bend County, Tex., Feb. 8, 1879; son of Joseph E. and Elizabeth (Moore) Clayton; attended school on plantation of Clem Bassett, his employer, 1892; grad. high school at Houston, 1895; B.S., Guadalupe College, Sequin, Tex., 1899; attended summer school at Dearborn Univ., Chicago, and Conroe (Tex.) College; (B.Pd., Princeton Normal and Industrial Univ., Indiana, 1913); married Brittie White, of Manor, Tex., Dec. 27, 1900; 4 children: Joseph, Essie, Dicy, Elizabeth. Taught school at Bastrop, Tex., 1900-3; principal of Manor School since 1903; editor Manor Appeal (the school magazine). National lecturer for Negro National Educational Congress; moral lecturer National Congress Mother's and Parent-Teachers' Assn.; general superintendent college extension bureau of Princeton Normal and Industrial Univ.; president and general manager Texas Realty Co.; owns 2 farms of 100 acres each. Trustee Conroe College. Republican. Missionary Baptist. President Manor Negro Business League. Mason; member Odd Fellows. Address, Manor, Texas.

CLEAVES, Nelson Caldwell, bishop; born on farm at Oakland, Fayette Co., Tenn., Oct. 7, 1865; son of Lilbon and Ann Cleaves; attended public school in Fayette County; entered private school of William Penn Liston, who came into the county about 1883; took normal course at Lane College, Jackson, Tenn.; entered Fisk Univ., Nashville, Tenn., but left on physicians advice in senior preparatory year; (D.D., Benedict College, 1912); married Jennie E. Lane, of Jackson, Tenn., Aug. 27, 1889; 4 children: Frances N., Shellie B., Lane C., Florence E. Principal city schools, Minden, La., 2 years; founded Minden High School; principal department of English, Lane College, Jackson, 3 years; entered ministry at Dyersburg, Tenn., 1893; served South Jackson Circuit, C. M. E. Church, 1 year; stationed at Humboldt, Tenn., 2 years, Clarksville, 3 years, Collins Chapel, Memphis, 3 years, Israel Metropolitan Church, Washington, D. C., 8 years; elected bishop at General Conference, St. Louis, Mo., 1914; since presiding over 7th Episcopal Dist.;

was fraternal messenger of his church to General Conf. A. M. E. Church, Columbus, O., 1900; secretary General Board, 1898-1906, and of General Conf., 1914, C. M. E. Church; member Federal Council Churches of Christ in America; while in Washington was pres. Inter-denominational Ministers' Alliance; in 1909 preached Commencement sermon at Benedict College, addressed Y. M. C. Societies of Colored Normal, Industrial and Mechanical College, Orangeburg, S. C., and delivered literary address before the faculty and students at Allen Univ., Columbia, S. C. President board of Trustees Miles Memorial College, Birmingham, Ala., Mississippi Industrial College, Holly Springs. Republican. Member Southern Sociological Congress. Mason; member Odd Fellows, Knights of Pythias. Home: 422 Lacont St., Jackson, Tenn.

CLEM, Charles Douglass, decorator; born at Greeneville, Tenn., July 10, 1875; son of Henry C. and Melvina (Robinson) Clem; ed public schools, Tenn., Ky., and Okla.; grad. Greeneville College, Tenn., 1898; married Kittie Smothers, of Lawrence, Kan., Apr. 13, 1903; 3 children: Irene, Lawrence, Helen. Editor Western World, Oklahoma City, Okla., 1901-2, Vindicator, of Coffeeville, Kan., 1906; in decorating business Chanute, Kan., since 1909; best known as magazine writer, poet and orator; has given recitals throughout Kan., Okla., Colo., also lectures on metaphysical science, which includes psychic phenomena, hypnotism, suggestive and psycho therapeutics, telepathy. Author: Oklahoma, Her People and Professions. 1892; Rhymes of a Rhymster, 1896; A Little Souvenir (poems), 1908; Fourteen Years in Metaphysics, 1913; writer series of articles for Kansas City Post, 1912; special articles on economic and philosophical subjects have been published in leading papers and magazines; contributor to African Times and Orient Review, London, Eng. Socialist. Spiritualist. Mason. Club: Swastika Culture. Address: Chanute, Kan.

CLEMENT, George C., clergyman,

editor; born at Mocksville, N. C., Dec. 22, 1871; son of Albert Turner and Eveleand Clement; public school edn., Mocksville; A.B., Livingstone College, Salisbury, N. C., 1898 (A.M., 1904, D.D., 1906); married Emma C. Williams, of Providence, R. I., May 25, 1898; 7 children. Ordained Methodist ministry, 1893; pastor A. M. E. Zion churches at Charlotte and Salisbury, N. C., Louisville, Ky., and Washington, D. C.; editor Star of Zion since 1904; now also manager A. M. E. Zion Publishing House, Charlotte. Trustee Livingstone College; president board of directors Reform and Manual Training School for Colored Youth. Democrat. Mason; member Order Eastern Star. Home: 510 Myers St. Office: 2d and Brevard Sts., Charlotte, N. C.

CILFFORD, John Robert, lawyer, editor; born at Williamsport, W. Va., Sept. 13, 1848; son of Isaac and Satilpa (Kent) Clifford; was enabled to attend public and high schools, Chicago, Ill., thru friendly aid of John J. Healy, former clerk Superior Court; took course in Prof. D. A. White's Business and Writing School grad. Storer College, Harper's Ferry, W. Va., 1875; (LL.B., Shaw Univ., Univ., 1893); married Mary E. C. Franklin, of Harper's Ferry, Dec. 28, 1876; 11 children: Albert F., John P., Coralie L., Mary F., Helen H., John R., Jr.; 5 deceased. Teacher in schools of W. Va., 14 years; principal Martinsburg School, 1 year; editor The Pioneer Press, Martinsburg, since 1882; only printing plant in city conducted by colored man; practiced law since 1887. Served as corpl. 13th Regt. Heavy Arty., in war between the states. Republican; pres. National Independent Political League. Member American Negro Academy, W. Va., Editorial Assn. 33d degree Mason; ex-grand Master Grand Lodge of Odd Fellows. Address: 523 W. Martin St., Martinsburg, W. Va.

CLINTON, George Wylie, bishop; born, Cedar Creek Township, Lancaster Co., S. C., Mar. 28, 1859; son of Jonathan and Rachel Clinton, both slaves; grad. Brainerd Institute, Chester, S. C.; grad. junior classical course, Univ. S. C., 1878; took course in Chautauqua Scientific Lit. Circle; student in theol. dept. Livingstone College, Salisbury, N. C.; (A.M., Livingstone, 1893; D.D., Wilberforce Univ., 1894, LL.D., 1906); married Marie Louise Clay, Feb. 6, 1901. Teacher high school, Lancaster, S. C., 12 years; president Literary and Industrial School, 8 years; in ministry since 1879; founder A. M. E. Zion Quarterly Review, 1889; was its editor to 1891; elected bishop, 1896; was first mgr. A. M. E. Pub. House; pres. Negro Young People's Educational and Religious Congress; delegate to Ecumenical Conference of Methodism, London, England, 1901; editor Star of Zion, 1902-6; member executive committee Federal Council of Churches of Christ in America. Trustee Livingstone College. Author: The Negro in the Ecumenical Conference of 1901; The Three Alarm Cries, 1906; Tuskegee Lectures, 1907; Christianity Under the Searchlight, 1909. Address: 415 Myers St., Charlotte, N. C.

CLINTON, John, Jr., clergyman, editor, born at Richmond, Va., Jan. 2, 1867; son of John and Isabelle Clinton; public school edn., Richmond; studied composition and art of printing, Moore Street Industrial School, Richmond; married Rosa Bell Boisseau, at Washington, D. C., Aug. 8, 1889; 4 children: Clarence A.(deceased), Mildred O., Janie I., Charles B. Began active career as printer with Richmond Planet, and was foreman the composing room number of years; publisher of the Weekly Reporter, 1890-1, the Daily Reporter, an afternoon issue, 1891-2, which was the first colored daily newspaper in America. Admitted to the practice of law in courts of Va., Jan. 31, 1894; removed to Philadelphia, Pa., 1900; organized the First Colored Bank North, incorporated July 7, 1901, operated by Northern Co-operative Banking Assn. until liquidated and paid dollar for dollar, 1907; first colored member American Bankers' Assn., admitted in 1901; was only representative of a colored northern financial institution at the convention of National Negro Business League, Chicago, Ill., 1901; issued call for a National Negro Banker's Convention at Buffalo, N. Y., 1901, which was posponed on account of the death and out of respect to President William McKinley. Founded in 1908, now president and general mgr., Solid Rock Union, a national fraternal secret society; was editor and pub: Solid Rock Herald, 1908-14. Joined Ebenezer Baptist Church, Richmond, Va., 1889; transferred membership to Shiloh Baptist Church, Philadelphia, May, 1901; licensed as minister of the gospel, July 12, 1912; now pastor Antioch Baptist Church. Republican. Home: 5231 Arch St., Philadelphia, Pa.

COBB, Andrew Jackson, clergyman; born at Oakman, Ala., May 10, 1865; son of Rev. Erasmas May and Elizabeth Hall; public school edn., Walker Co., Ala.; A.B., Payne College, Augusta, Ga., 1895 (D.D., 1912); postgraduate studies Gammon Theological Seminary, Atlanta, Ga.; married Helena Maud Cobb, of Barnesville, Ga., Dec. 19, 1899. Licensed to preach in Colored M. E. Church, 1882; joined Ala. Conference; appointed to Detroit Circuit, 1886; ordained elder, 1895; transferred to Georgia Conference; pastor West Mitchell Street, Atlanta, 1896-7, Barnesville, 1898-9, Marshallville, 1900-2, Milledgeville, 1903; presiding elder Dublin District, Ga., 1904-7; served Milledgeville Dist., 1907-10; editor the Christian Index, 1910-14; took charge at time the church was threatened with split, but a conservative editorial policy resulted in a closer brotherly union and he gained the name of "Pacificator"; presiding elder Macon District since 1914; editor Washington Park Era. Trustee and treas. Helena B. Cobb Industrial Institute. Republican; was secretary state convention and speaker for campaign committee, 1893-4. Address: Barnesville, Ga.

COBB, Helen Maud Brown, educator; born near Smarrs, Monroe Co., Ga., Jan. 24, 1870; daughter of Jonah and Louvenia Brown; ed. public schools, Monroe and Pike counties;

grad. Storr School, Atlanta, Ga., 1883-5; Atlanta Univ., 1891; married Rev. Andrew J. Cobb, of Barnesville, Ga., Dec. 19, 1899. Began as teacher in schools of Ga., 1891; was principal in public schools, Milner, 6 years; assistant prin. public schools, Columbus, 1 year; teacher at Haines Normal and Industrial School, Augusta, 7 years, and Lamson Normal School, Marshallville, 3 years; president Helen B. Cobb Industrial Institute, Barnesville, since founded in 1908; it is the only girls' school in the Colored M. E. Church, also only school of the kind conducted exclusively by colored people in the southern states; it was named as an honor and recognition of achievement. Was unanimously elected president of the Woman's Home Missionary Society at first session of the Central Georgia Conference, C. M. E. Church, at Milledgeville, 1902; elected lecturer for Ga., and Fla., 1904, since president Inter-Conference movement; elected editress-in-chief the Woman's Missionary Age magazine, 1904, and the official publication of the Woman's Home Missionary Society, the Age, 1906. Author: (pamphlet): Our Women, a Sketch of Their Work. Address: Barnesville, Ga.

COBB, James A., assistant attorney District of Columbia; born at Arcadia, La., Jan. 29, 1876; ed. Straight Univ., New Orleans, Fisk Univ., Nashville, Tenn.; LL.B., Howard Univ., Washington, D. C., 1899, LL.M., 1900, Ph.B., 1902; unmarried. Ammitted to District of Columbia bar, 1901; special assistant United States attorney for D. C., since 1907. Republican. Congregationalist. Member Sigma Pi Phi. Mason. Home: 1925 13th St. N. W. Office: 609 F. St. N. W., Washington, D. C.

COCHRAN, Arthur Myron, training school supt.; born at Charleston, S. C., Sept. 27, 1878; son of Thomas Izzard and Coreline (Elfe) Cochran; grad. Avery Normal Institute, Charleston, 1896; A.B., Fisk Univ., Nashville, Tenn., 1901; grad. Music Dept. (Fisk), 1902; married Sarah Jane Bly, of Haverhill, Mass., Apr. 17, 1903; 4

children: Marion, Edward, Gwendolyn Elliott, Morris Bartlett, Thomas Oliver. Teacher in St. Michael Training and Industrial School, Charlotte, N. C., since Sept. 14, 1903; began as assistant principal; supt. and trustee since Nov. 16, 1910. Episcopalian. Home: 104 Martin St. Address: St. Michael Training and Industrial School, Charlotte, N. C.

COCHRAN, Sarah Jane Bly, teacher; born at Norfolk, Va., Sept. 24, 1878; daughter of Oliver and Prescilla (Morris) Bly; grad. Haverhill High School, Mass., 1894; A.B., Fisk Univ., Nashville, Tenn., 1901; married Arthur Myron Cochran, of Charleston, S. C., Apr. 17, 1903; 4 children: Myron Edward, Gwendolyn Elliott, Morris Bartlett, Thomas Oliver. Teacher in St. Michael's Training and Industrial School, Charlotte, N. C., since Sept. 20, 1903. Episcopalian. Address: R. F. D. 29, Box 3, Charlotte, N. C.

COFFIN, Alfred Oscar, contracting agent Blind Boone Concert Co.; born at Pontotoc, Miss., May 14, 1861; son of Samuel and Josephine Maria (Drake) Coffin; prep. edn. Rust Univ., Holly Springs, Miss.; A.B., Fisk Univ., 1885; A.M., Ill. Wesleyan Univ., 1888, Ph.D., 1889; 1 child: Lillian Viola. Professor in Alcorn Agricultural and Mechanical College, Miss., 1887-9; professor of mathematics and modern languages, Wiley Univ., Marshall, Tex., 1889-95; secretary and disbursing agent, Alcorn Agricultural and Mechanical College, 1895-8; principal public schools, San Antonio, Tex., 1898-1901, Kansas City, Mo., 1902-9; advance agent for Blind Boone Concert Co., since 1910. Methodist. 33d degree Scottish Rite Mason. Author: Origin of the Moundbuilders, 1889; Native Plants of Marshall, Texas, 1896; A Land Without Chimneys, or the Byways of Mexico, 1897. Address: 1704 E. 10th St., Kansas City, Mo.

COFFIN, Frank Barbour, druggist; born at Holly Springs, Miss., Jan. 12, 1871; son of Samuel and Josephine (Barton) Coffin; student Rust Univ., Miss., 1886-7; Fisk Univ., Tenn., 1887-90; Ph.G., Meharry Medical College

(Walden Unv.), 1893; married Lottie E. Woodford, of Lexington, Ky., Apr. 27, 1913. With two partners opened drug store at Little Rock, Ark., 1893, sole proprietor since 1898. Secretary Philander Smith College, treas. Wesley M. E. Church; trustee Wesley Chapel. Progressive. Author: Coffin's Poems, 1899; contr. to Southwestern Christian Advocate, Boston Guardian, Our Review. Home: 1118 Izard St. Office: 700 W. 9th St., Little Rock, Ark.

COGGIN, John Nelson Clark, clergyman, temperance worker, fraternal order secretary; born at Abbeville, Miss., May 8, 1870; son of Daniel and Martha (Blakly) Coggin; preparatory edn. Rust Univ., Holly Springs, Miss.; grad. Gammon Theological Seminary, Atlanta, Ga., 1896; A.B., Clark Univ., Atlanta, 1899; (B.D., Gammon, 1899; D.D., Rust Univ., 1907); married Jessie Gray Hill, of Holly Springs, Jan. 30, 1892. Taught school during vacations to pay way while in Rust Univ.; joined Upper Mississippi Conference M. E. Church, 1888; assigned to Holly Springs; pastor Fort Street Church, Atlanta, 1893-1906; was field secretary for Young People's Christian and Educational Congress, 1903-6, traveling throughout U. S., working among Negroes of all denominations; pastor Grace M. E. Church, Covington, Ga., 1906-14, also traveling evangelist; field secretary of Temperance Society, M. E. Church, since 1914; only colored man in U. S. holding similar position, the work being among all colored people without regard to affiliations. Founded the Independent Order of Woodmen, at Covington, Ga., 1908; since supreme banker and financial secretary; this order issues $500 and $1,000 policies to men and women at the 4 per cent. rate adopted by the Fraternal Congress of America. Address: Covington, Ga.

COLE, Ellis Calvin, clergyman; born at Macon, Miss., June 16, 1866; son of George Washington and Hannah (McMullen) Cole; ed. in public schools and Macon Academy, Miss.; student State Univ. of Iowa, 1894-5;

(D.D., Central Miss. College, 1904); married Zenia Miller, 1887 (died, 1890); 3 children; 2d marriage, Eugenia Blanche Chiles, of Starksville, Miss., Sept. 29, 1891. Teacher in schools of Miss., 1881-92; active in the Missionary Baptist ministry since 1892; while pastoring in Springfield, Ill., 1913, was elected president Illinois Protective League, an organization that gave material aid in securing the appropriation from the state for the Half-Century Anniversary Celebration of Negro Freedom, 1915; president Fidelity Beneficial and Protective League; vice-president National Federation Colored Men; director Home Protective Assn. (Hannibal, Mo.). Trustee National Training School for Women and Girls, Washington, D. C. Republican. Member United Brothers of Friendship, Knights and Daughters of Tabor. Home: 3121 Fair St., St. Louis, Mo. Office: 1223 Myrtle St., Cincinnati, O.

COLE, James Archibald Sterling, clergyman; born in Howard County, Md., Oct. 14, 1876; son of Thomas B. and Sarah C. (Chambers) Cole; attended public school, Baltimore, Md.; preparatory edn. Morgan College; S.T.B., Boston School of Theology, 1896; (D.D., State Univ., Louisville, Ky., 1899); married Margarite Alice McDowell, of Camden, S. C., Mar. 23, 1902; 3 children: Mary E., Henrietta H., George W. Licensed to preach, Baltimore, Md., 1889; taught school in Va., number years; presiding elder Philadelphia and Baltimore Conference, A. M. E. Zion Church, for some time; now pastor East King Street Church, York, Pa. Served as sergeant Troop B. 10th Cav. U. S. A., 1892-5. Republican. Mason; member Odd Fellows. Home: 221 E. King St., York, Pa.

COLEMAN James Harold, newspaper man, colonization agent; born at Richmond, Wa., Aug. 23, 1871; son of Spencer and Williana (Gay) Coleman; public school edn. at Washington, D. C.; married Julia P. Hughes, of Mebane, N. C., Feb. 16, 1900. Began active career as manager the Chat Publishing Co., Philadelphia,

Pa., 1895; managing editor Sunday Herald, 1897; manager Columbia Chemical Co., Newport News, Va., 1906-10; editor New Century at Norfolk, Va., 1908-9. Colonization agent for Blackdom, New Mexico, since 1912 (Blackdom is a Negro colony founded, 1909, on free government land by Francis M. Boyer); manager Blackdon Realty Co . Served on citizen's committee, G. A. R. Encampment, 1897, committee to welcome Spanish war veterans, 1898, at Philadelphia. New Mexico delegate to National Half-Century Celebration of Negro Freedom, Chicago, Ill., 1915. Democrat. Member Negro Historical Society, Hotel Brotherhood. Club: Citizens (Philadelphia). Address: Blackdom, New Mexico.

COLEMAN, John Wesley, real estate; born at Columbus, Tex., Mar. 12, 1865; son of Sam and Mattie (Green) Coleman; grad. Tilleston Institute, Austin, Tex., 1884; married Lydia Lee, of Austin, Jan. 15, 1885; 4 children. Active in Sunday School work, Texas, 1882-7; removed to Calif., 1887; was church clerk, 4 yrs.; later landscape and gardening contractor, and proprietor cafe; with Pullman Company, 12 years; proprietor Hotel Coleman, Los Angeles, 5 years; in furniture busines 2 years; traveling advance agent for Venice and Santa Monica Bay, Cal., 3 years; valet for Dr. Burner, and deputy superintendent his chain of sanitariums 2 years; agent Colored Insurance Co., 1 year; deputy constable, Los Angeles County Township, 9 years; in real estate and loan business since 1907; also conducts employment bureau; director J. J. Nemo Stock Co. Republican. Member Baptist Young Peoples' Union, Allen's Christian Endeavor League, Y. M. C. A., Business Men's League. 32d degree Mason; past noble father Odd Fellows; member Knights of Pythias, United Brothers of Friendship. Clubs: Political, Texas of Los Angeles. Home: 2916 New Jersey St. Office: 211 E. 2d St., Los Angeles, Cal.

COLEMAN, Julia P. H., pharmacist; born in North Carolina; daughter of John P. and Mary (Moore) Hughes; grad. Scotia Seminary, Concord, N. C.; Phar.D., Howard Univ., Washington, D. C., 1897; post-graduate work at Pennsylvania College of Pharmacy, Philadelphia; married James H. Coleman, Feb. 16, 1891. In drug business at Philadelphia 10 years; now president and manager Hair-Vim Chemical Co., Washington. Presbyterian. Address: 1234 You St. N. W., Washington, D. C.

COLEMAN, William, teacher; born in Georgia, Aug. 26, 1870; son of Bertha Jackson; attended Valdosta Academy, Ga., 1880-8; student Howard Univ., Washington, 1888-93; A.B., Brown Univ., Providence, R. I., 1897; married. Began in home county as clerk in dry goods store for William Jones, colored; professor of modern languages at Benedict College, Columbia, S. C., 1897-99; assistant principal in Colored High School, Fort Worth, Tex., 5 years; principal Douglass High School, El Paso, Tex., since 1907; vice-pres. International Investment Co. Was one of leading organizers of first bank conducted in Texas by colored men, now out of existence; assisted organizing the existing Fraternal Bank & Trust Co., of Fort Worth. Republican. Baptist. Member National Association for Advancement of Colored People, National Association Teachers' in Colored Schools, Texas Colored Teachers' Assn. 32d degree Royal Arch Mason, Knights Templar, Shriner; grand lecturer of Negro Masons in Texas; grand director Court of Heorines of Jericho; member Odd Fellows, Knights of Pythias. Address; 518 Tornillo St., El Paso, Texas.

COLEMAN, William Tyler, physician, clergyman; born at Uniontown, Ala., Oct. 20, 1867; son of John Granville and Mary (Glassco) Coleman; grad. Selma (Ala.) Univ., 1892; B.D., Richmond (Va.) Theological Seminary, 1895; M.D., Leonard Medical College (Shaw Unlv.), Raleigh, N. C., 1909; married Veola Guerrant, of Danville, Va., July 31, 1901; 2 children: Cecil Granville, Thelma Antionette. Ordained in Baptist ministry,

1895; pastor Berean Church and principal Marian Baptist Academy 1 year; teacher of mathematics, mental and moral philosophy, Selma Univ., 1897-9; pastor Selma, Ala., 1899-1903, Raleigh, N. C., 1903-12; erected church edifice at Raleigh; now pastor Union Grove Church, Youngsville, N. C. Practiced medicine in Raleigh, N. C., since 1909; also passed Maryland board of medical examiners and registered in Baltimore, 1909. Republican. Mason; member Knights of Pythias. Home: 739 Fayetteville St. Office: 125 E. Hargett St., Raleigh, N. C.

COLLIER, Nathaniel White, college president; born at Augusta, Ga., May 14, 1871; son of Madison Jordan and Frances (Tyler) Collier; public school edn. Augusta; A.B., Atlanta Univ., 1894 (A.M., 1906); unmarried. Began as one of 6 teachers in charge of 106 pupils at Florida Baptist College, Jacksonville, the year he graduated; served as assistant principal, 1894-6; president since 1896; the enrollment now exceeds 500 students, and 23 teachers; property is valued at about $100,000. Republican. Baptist. Member American Academy of Political and Social Science. Home: 1611 Harrison St. Office: Florida Baptist College, Jacksonville, Fla.

COLLINS, George Franklin, university secretary, lawyer; born at St. Louis, Mo., July 7, 1876; son of Albert and Eudora (Jackson) Collins; grad. Sumner High School, St. Louis, 1894, Southwestern Business College, 1897; LL.B., Howard Univ., 1901; married Bertha Grace Howard, of Washington, 1907. Admitted to bar in Washington, 1901; attorney for Provident Heights Industrial School in Alexandria County, Va., Baptist Ministers' and Layman's Union, Zion Baptist Church, Providence Baptist Church (Washington); attorney and director Lincoln Memorial Building Co.; director Columbia Benefit Assn.; elected as secretary Howard Univ. School of Law, 1914; secretary Howard University Alumni Assn.; was commissioner of deeds, State of New Jersey, 2 years. Delegate to Progressive National Convention, Chicago, Ill., 1912. Member Odd Fellows. Home: 132 S St. N. W. Office: Howard University, Washington, D. C.

COLLINS, John M., clergyman editor, publisher; born in South Carolina, Nov. 10, 1854; son of Toney Darlington and Sabina Beck, both slaves; never attended school; self educated; married Oneida G. Jones, of Sacramentto, Calif., Dec. 15, 1910. Taught school in Bullock Co., Ga., 1877; ordained Baptist ministry, 1881; began church work in Cal., 1902; was moderator General Baptist Assn. of Calif., 1903-4, secretary, 1905-9; withdrew from Baptist, 1909, and founded Unity Tabernacle (non-sectarian); editor and pub. Western Review. Author and publisher: Raising and Training of Children, 1905; A Negro Opinion on a Great Subject, 1910. Home: 1814 Sixth St. Address: P. O. Box 1127, Sacramento, Calif.

COLLINS, Victor Homer, teacher; born at Lexington, Mo., Mar. 24, 1888; son of Dennis and Anna Collins; high school edn., Lexington, Mo.; grad. Lincoln Institute, Jefferson City, Mo., 1908; married Lena Tucker, 1908; 1 child. Began as assistant in pedagogy at Lincoln Institute, 1908; teacher of geometery and arithmetic since 1910. Address: Lincoln Institute, Jefferson City, Mo.

COLSTON, Lillian Elizabeth, private secretary; born at Springfield, Ill., Mar. 13, 1893; daughter of Rev. Almstead and Lucy (Smith) Colston; ed. public schools, commercial college, and high school, Des Moines, Ia.; unmarried. Stenographer in Jesse Binga Bank, Chicago, Ill., 1910-11; with physician at Des Moines, 1911-12; in law office, Memphis, Tenn., 1912-13; private secretary to Dr. A. M. Townsend, president Roger Williams Univ., Nashville, Tenn., since 1913. Baptist. Club. Cosmopolitan. Address: 1011 Crocker St., Des Moines, Ia.

CONICK, Edward Gearing, private secretary; born at New York, Nov. 4, 1879; son of Charles E. and Kate V. (Gearing) Conick; attended public schools, New York; grad. high school, Yonkers, N. Y., 1900, Spencerian Business School, 1901; married Minnie Shanks Benjamin, of Boston, Mass., Dec. 3, 1911; 1 child: Edward G. Jr. Secretary and managing clerk in law office of G. N. Rigby, 1901-13; subsitute stenographer in City Court, Yonkers, 1913-14; served as official stenographer for several commissions, 1913, as stenographer for coroner of Westchester County, private secretary to W. A. Johnson, publisher, New York; now private secretary for V. Everit Macy, superintendent of poor in Westchester County. Member Y. M. C. A., Yonkers. Clubs: The Frogs, the Tempo (New York), Hollywood Inn (Yonkers). Home: 14 Lamartine Ave., Yonkers, N. Y.

CONNER, James M., bishop; born in Winston County, Ark., Mar. 9, 1865; son of William and Mariah Conner; ed. in Miss. and Ala.; (D.D., Shorters College, Little Rock, Ark., 1905); married Glovinia Stewart, of Forest City, Ark., Dec. 25, 1886; 4 children: William James, Wilberforce, Quintilla, Zola. Licensed to preach in A. M. E. Church, 1883; presiding bishop in 8th District, including Miss., and La. Trustee Wilberforce Univ., Shorters College. Progressive. Author: Outlines of Christian Theology and Doctrines of Christ. Address: 1519 Pulaski St., Little Rock, Ark.

CONNOR, Edward T., physician; born at Dublin, Va., May 20, 1869; son of Harry T. and Lauretta (Ingram) Connor; B.S., Virginia Collegiate and Industrial Institute, 1895; M.D., Leonard Medical College (Shaw Univ.), Raleigh, N. C., 1899; married Nannie E. McClauahan, of Abingdon, Va., June 20, 1901. Interne at Freedmen's Hospital, Washington, 1 year; practiced in Clifton Forge, Va., since 1900; owns 191-acre farm. Trustee Clifton Forge Normal and Industrial Institute. Republican. Methodist. Member Clifton Forge Negro Business League, Knights of Pythias. Address: 1 W. Main St., Clifton Forge, Va.

CONNOR, Miles Washington, teacher; born near Portsmouth, Norfolk

Co., Va., Jan. 16, 1886; son of Miles and Joanna (Watts) Connor; grad. Norfolk (Va.) Mission College, 1905; A.B., Virginia Union Univ., Richmond, 1909; A.M., Howard Univ., Washington, D. C., 1912; unmarried. Began as instructor in Selma Univ., 1909, continuing to 1910; assistant principal Corey Memorial Academy, Portsmouth, Va., 1911; instructor in pedagogy, Virginia Union Univ., summer sessions, 1912, 1913, and Christiansburg Institute, summer, 1914; head of department of education and director of training school at Virginia Normal and Industrial Institute, Petersburg, since 1912. Baptist. Member the Gamma Chapter, Alpha Phi Alpha. Mason. Club: Skull and Bones (Portsmouth). Home: 1005 Mt. Vernon Ave., Portsmouth. Address: Virginia Normal and Industrial Institute, Petersburg, Va.

CONRAD, George Washington Bryant, lawyer with Penn. R. R. System; born at Xenia, Ohio, June 22, 1867; son of Thomas A. and Elizabeth (Jackson) Conrad; attended public schools, Xenia; took course in business college at Richmond, Ind.; preparatory edn. Oberlin College, O.; LL.B., Univ. of Mich., 1902; married Beatrice A. Cox, of Walnut Hills, Cincinnati, O., June 8, 1910; 1 child: Elizabeth. Began with Pennsylvania Railroad System at Richmond, Ind., when 15 years of age; was stenographer and telegraph operator, 1882-95; private secretary to Col. J. F. Miller, vice-pres. Penn. R. R. and U. S. Commissioner at Louisiana Purchase Exposition, St. Louis, Mo., 1903-4; now with Claim Department and assistant in Law Dept. of the System at Richmond. Republican. Catholic. Member Crispus Attucks Loyal League. Home: 22 N. 22d St. Office: Union Station, Richmond, Ind.

COOK, Coralie Franklin; social worker; born at Lexington, Va.; daughter of Albert and Mary (Edmondson) Franklin; ed. Storer College, Harper's Ferry, W. Va.; studied at Shoemaker School of Elocution, Philadelphia, Pa., 1881; grad. Emerson College of Oratory, Boston, Mass., 1901; married, Aug. 31, 1898, George

William Cook, secretary of Howard Univ., Washington; 1 child: George Wm. Jr. Taught school 2 years in Maryland and Missouri; was teacher at Storer College some time; teacher of elocution and oratory at Howard Univ., 1896-1901, also in Washington Conservatory of Music. Superintendent of woman's work in the Industrial Home School, Blue Plains, D. C.; member board of education in District of Columbia; public speaker and active in uplift sork. Trustee Storer College. Free Baptist. Member Young Woman's Christian Assn.; honorary member Delta Sigma Theta of Howard Univ. Club: Book Lovers. Address: Howard University, Washington, D. C.

COOK, Frank Henry, clergyman, editor; born at Vidalia, La., Feb. 22, 1873; son of Pless and Patsy Cook; ed. Natchez College, Miss., and Southern Univ., New Orleans; (hon. B.D., D.D. Ph.D.); married Retta Barbery White, of Sibley, Miss., July 12, 1905; 4 children: Ordained Baptist ministry at Vidalia, Aug. 20, 1897; founded in 1901 and since editor the Natchez Herald; secretary Sons and Daughters of Charity of American Building & Loan Assn., and financial secretary of the Order. Mason; member Odd Fellows, Knights of Pythias, Knights of Tabor. Author: Can a Man Be Wholly Sanctified? Home: Vidalia, La. Office: Natchez Weekly Herald, Natchez, Miss.

COOK, George William, university secretary, college dean; born at Winchester, Va., Jan. 7, 1855; son of Payton and Eliza (Sperry) Cook; attended public school, Harrisburg, Pa., 1864-6, night school, New York, 1873; A.B., Howard Univ., 1877, A.M., 1881, LL.B., LL.M., 1897; married Coralia Franklin, of Harper's Ferry, W. Va., Aug. 31, 1898; 1 child: George William, Jr. Began as instructor in Howard Univ., Washington, D. C., 1881, secretary since 1908, and now dean of the Commercial College, professor of civics, commercial law, and international law. In building business to some extent since 1881; erected 10 houses for self, 3 as contractor, and remodeled others; owns shares in a syndicate for which has built 12 houses at average cost of $4,000. Appointed member board of charities in District of Columbia, by Presidents William McKinley, 1900, Theodore Roosevelt, 1904, William H. Taft, 1908; served 12 years. Treasurer an outing resort for working women and small children, supported by voltary contributions, called Camp Pleasant; director Lindsay Center, also Colored Social Settlement of D. C. Republican. Episcopalian. Member Association for Advancement of Colored People, Petworth Citizens Assn., Epsilon Chapter of Sigma Pi Phi. Mason. Club: Mu-So-Lit. Wrote "Early Discoveries of America," for A. M. E. Review; occasional contributor to other publications. Address: Howard University, Washington, D. C.

COOK, Will Marion, musician. Composer: Exhortation; The Rain Song; The Casino Girl; Bandana Land; Cruel Popupa, etc. Address: care Chef Club, 134 W. 53rd St., New York.

COOK, William Decanter, clergyman; born at Warrenton, N. C., Feb. 17, 1860; son of William B. and Fannie G. (Williams) Cook; grad. Johnson High School, Raleigh, N. C.; grad. Howard Univ. School of Theology, Washington, D. C., 1883; (hon. D.D., Wilberforce Univ.); married Bertha B. Wolfe, of Boston, Mass., Aug. 1886; 2 children: Edna H. Frances E. Began preaching at Warrenton, 1877; pastor in A. M. E. Churches at Norfolk, Va., Wilmington, Del., Philadelphia, Pa., Brooklyn, N. Y., New York, Atlantic City, N. J., St. Louis, Mo., Chicago, Ill.; presiding elder Chicago District A. M. E. Church. Life trusteé Wilberforce Univ.; charter member board of trustees Kittrell College, N. C. Republican. Home: 4732 Evans Ave., Chicago, Ill.

COOKE, James Dee, editor, publisher; born at Georgetown, Tex., June 19, 1880; son of James Henry and Elvina (McDonald) Cooke; high school edn; married Eva Hampton, of Boley, Okla., June 3, 1912; 1 child: Emma E. Representative of the American Publishing Co., Chicago,

Ill., Success Magazine, New York, Curtis Publishing Co., Philadelphia, Pa., at Milwaukee, Wis., 1904-6; editor and publisher Wisconsin Weekly Defender since 1906; has published number monographs on conditions among colored people. President, National Liberty League; secretary Western Negro Press Assn. Member Odd Fellows; advocate-general Lodge No. 9320. Home: 2436 Hadley Ave. Office: 714 Montgomery Bldg., Milwaukee, Wis.

COOPER, Anna Julia, teacher; born at Raleigh, N. C.; daughter of Hanna (Stanley) Haywood; entered St. Augustine's Normal and Collegiate Institute, Raleigh, when 6 years old; A.B., Oberlin (O.) College, 1884, AM., 1888; matriculated for Ph.D., at Columbia Univ., New York, 1915; married Rev. G. A. Cooper, while in the institute at Raleigh; widow at age of 20. Teacher of algebra while at Oberlin; head the department of modern languages at Wilberforce (O.) Univ.; teacher of Latin and Greek in St. Augustine's Normal and Collegiate Institute; teacher of mathematics, languages, science, and principal for 5 years at M Street High School, Washington, D. C.; professor of Greek and Latin, Lincoln Institute, Jefferson City, Mo., 1906-10; teacher of Latin at M Street High School, Washington, since 1911. Organizer and guardian of Camp Fire Girls for Colored Y. W. C. A.; supervisor Colored Social Settlement; has promoted several dramatic, literary and social science clubs, for improvement of young people . Author: A Voice From the South by a Black Woman of the South (poem), 1892; Christ's Church (a short story); Simon of Cyrene (poem). Home: 1630 Tenth St. N. W., Washington, D. C.

COOPER, John Benjamin, undertaker; born at Mobile, Ala., Apr. 1872; son of Benjamin and Elizabeth (Agee) Cooper; attended public schools and Emerson Institute of Mobile, high school in Cincinnati, O.; grad. Barnes School of Embalming Chicago, Ill.; married Lavinia Brady Watson, of Louisville, Ky., Aug. 19,

1907. Funeral director and embalmer in Louisville since 1907; director Falls City Realty Co. Methodist. Member National Funeral Directors Assn., Kentucky Funeral Directors Assn., Falls-Cities Undertaking Assn., National Negro Business League. 32d degree Mason; member Odd Fellows, Knights of Pythias, United Brothers of Friendship, Sisters and Brothers of Friendship, Sons and Daughters of Moses, Coopers Union. Address: 1001 W. Chestnut St., Louisville, Ky.

COPPIN, Levi J., bishop; born at Fredericktown, Md., Feb. 24, 1848; grad. Protestant Episcopal Divinity School, Philadelphia, Pa., 1887; (D.D., Wilberforce, O., 1889); married Fannie M. Jackson, of Philadelphia. Teacher in schools of Delaware number of years; ordained to ministry, 1877; pastor in Philadelphia city missions and later A. M. E. Churches in Philadelphia and Baltimore; was editor and manager A. M. E. Review for some time; now bishop A. M. E. Church. Author: The Relation of Baptized Children to the Church and Key to Scriptural Interpretation. Home: 1913 Bainbridge St., Philadelphia, Pa.

CORROTHERS, James David, clergyman, author; born at Calvin, Mich., July 2, 1869; son of James Richard and Maggie (Churchman) Corrothers; of Negro, Indian and Scotch-Irish blood; mother died when he was born; attended school at South Haven, Mich., 1874-83; worked in lumber camps, saw mills, hotels, sailed the lakes one season, bootblack in barber shop, and taught boxing; encouraged by Henry D. Lloyd, the author, and Frances E. Willard, who helped him, and by working to assist himself, attended Northwestern Univ., 1890-3; student Bennett College, Greenboro, N. C., 1 year; (hon. D.D.); married Fannie Clemens, of Chicago, Ill., 1894 (deceased); 2 children: Willard, Richard; 2d marriage, Rosina B. Harvey, of Washington, D. C., 1906; 1 child: Henry H. Ordained Baptist ministry, 1894. Author: The Black Cat, 1902; Selected Poems, 1907; A Man They Didn't Know (story), 1913;

The Dream and the Song (poem), 1914; At the End of the Controversy (article in American Magazine, Mar., 1914); wrote the sketch of Dr. C. Albert Tindley for Associated Sunday Magazines; two of his poems which appeared in New York Herald were illustrated by R. F. Outcault, the creator of "Buster Brown" in comic artists section of metropolitan newspapers. Address: 600 N. 39th St., Philadelphia, Pa.

COSEY, Auger Augustus, clergyman; born at Newellton, La., July 2, 1876; son of Elias and Jane (Emerson) Cosey; ed. at Natchez College, Miss.; married Ida Hope Carter, of Helena, Ark., July 10, 1901. Taught public school at Newellton 4 years; ordained Baptist ministry, 1896; pastor Metropolitan Church, Clarksdale, Miss., 1898-1905, First Baptist Church, Mound Bayou, Miss., since 1905; erected brick edifice costing $15,000; general officer National Baptist Convention serving as corresponding sec. National Baptist Benefit Assn., 1906-11; now moderator Bolivar County Baptist Assn.; treasurer Mound Bayou Ice, Coal & Power Co., a $15,-000 corporation. Trustee Natchez College. Republican. Address: Mound Bayou, Miss.

COTTRELL, Elias, bishop; born near Holly Springs, Miss., Jan. 31, 1853; son of Daniel and Ann (Mull) Cottrell; father was his first teacher; later improved his edn. while teaching in public schools; took theological course, Walden Univ., Nashville, Tenn., 1878-9; (D.D., Rust Univ., Holly Springs, 1895); married Catherine Davis, of Nashville, Jan. 1, 1880. Licensed to preach in Colored M. E. Church, 1875; ordained deacon, 1877, elder, 1878; member General Conference, 1882-94; fraternal messenger to general conference M. E. Church, Omaha, Neb., 1892; was educational commissioner, 1890-4; elected bishop, 1894. Trustee, gen. mgr. and treas. Miss. Industrial College, Holly Springs. Republican. Mason. Address: Holly Springs, Miss.

COTTRILL, Charles A., internal revenue collector; born at Findlay,

Ohio, Dec. 3, 1863; son of William and Martha Jane (Bass) Cottrill; public school edn., Toledo, O.; grad. Ohio State Business Univ., Toledo, 1884, studied evenings; read law in office of John F. Kumler, Toledo, spare time, 1894-1902; married Alma G. Clark, of Columbus, O., June 29, 1898; 2 children: Charles A. Jr., James Clark C. Began as clerk in internal revenue service, 1881; later advanced to deputy collector in which position he remained to June 1, 1887; bookkeeper in office of the treasurer of Lucas County, O., 1887-8; corporation clerk in Department of State (Ohio), 1888-93; chief deputy recorder of Lucas County, 1893-1910; collector of internal revenue for U. S., District of Hawaii, 1911-15; Republican. Member Central Union Church, Honolulu. Mason; past grand commander Knights Templar (Ohio); past grand chancellor Knights of Pythias of Ohio; member Odd Fellows; Ad Club of Honolulu. An editorial in the Pacific Commercial Advertiser, Hawaii, Feb. 15, 1915, said: "The Advertiser is in complete agreement with the general expressed regret that the administration at Washington has seen fit to terminate the official life of Charles A. Cottrill, as collector of internal revenue for Hawaii. On every point he has distinctly made good— as a courteous official, as an efficient public servant and as a respected and popular citizen; his dismissal can only have narrow political reasons as a justification." He was the first colored man ever appointed to Federal position in Hawaii. Home: 1246 Kinau St., Honolulu, Hawaii.

COVINGTON, Eugene Clay, physician, surgeon; born in Caroline Co., Va., Aug. 1, 1872; son of Joseph and Elizabeth (Holmes) Covington; ed. public schools, Annapolis, Md.; A.B., Howard Univ., 1895, M.D., 1899; married Alice Allena Lewis, of Oswego, N. Y., Sept. 10, 1902; 3 children: Girard Holmes, Eugene Gray, Jr., Joseph Howard. Assistant demonstrator in anatomy Howard Univ., Washington, D. C., 1899-1900; practiced in Bloomington, Ill., since Sept. 30,

1900; assistant surgeon on staff, 8th Inf. I. N. G., 1902; delegate to National Negro Educational Congress, Kansas City, Mo., July 15-19, 1913, Emancipation Celebration, Philadelphia, Pa., Sept., 1913; member advisory board National Half-Century Anniversary of Negro Freedom, 1915; president Lincoln Protective League of McLean Co., Physical Culture Club (Bloomington). Financial secretary board of trustees, Wayman A. M. E. Church. Member National Negro Business Men's League. Mason; surgeon with rank of colonel Uniform Rank Knights of Pythias. Home: 410 E. Market St. Office: 313 N. Main St., Bloomington, Ill.

COX, Ephraim Jackson, clergyman; born at Harrison, Tenn., Dec. 8, 1870; son of Ephraim and Maggie (Matthews) Cox; grad. high school in Hamilton County, Tenn., 1890; student Athens (Tenn.) Academy, 1892-3; grad. Gammon Theological Seminary, Atlanta, Ga., 1900; married Marie Barnwell, of James County, Tenn., July 28, 1891; 2 children: Fred, Albert. Ordained M. E. ministry, 1900; pastor at Morristown, Tenn., 1900-3, Marion, Va., 1903-5, Bristol, Va., 1905-7; presiding elder Chattanooga (Tenn.) District, 1907-12; pastor E. Vine Avenue Church, Knoxville, since 1912; secretary East Tennessee Conference, 1902-6; member General Conference at Baltimore, Md., 1908. Was active in movement that closed saloons in both Morristown and Bristol. Republican. Mason; member Knights of Pythias. Address: 508 Temperance St., Knoxville, Tenn.

COX, James Monroe, college president; born at Fredonia, Ala., Feb. 26, 1896; son of John Wesley and Martha Cox; A.B., Clark Univ., Atlanta, 1884; grad. Gammon Theological Seminary, Atlanta, 1886 (D.D., 1908); married Harrie W. Robinson, of Macon, Ga., Sept. 20, 1887. President Philander Smith College, Little Rock, Ala., since 1896. Represented Little Rock Conference in 4 General Conferences of M. E. Church; member University Senate of M. E. Church.

Republican. Address: 912 W. 11th St., Little Rock, Ark.

COX, Wayne Wellington, bank cashier, planter; born at Lexington, Miss., Aug. 8, 1864; son of Caroline Griffin; ed. at Alcorn Agricultural and Mechanical College, Miss.; married Minnie M. Geddings, of Lexington, Miss., Oct. 30, 1889; 1 child: Ethel C. (Mrs. Dr. Wayne Cox Howard). One of the largest colored planters in Mississippi; cashier Delta Penny Savings Bank, Indianola, since 1905; secretary-treas. Mississippi Beneficial Life Ins. Co.; supreme treas. Woodmen of Union. Trustee Campbell College, Jackson, Miss. Republican. African Methodist. Mason; member Odd Fellows, Knights of Pythias. Address: Delta Penny Savings Bank, Indianola, Miss.

COX, William Alexander, dentist, lawyer; born at Baltimore, Md., July 25, 1872; son of Thomas R. Cox (freeman) and Laura J. Fry (slave); attended public schools and Cambridge (Mass.) Manual Training School; student in Suffolk Evening Law School, 1907-10; married Cora Etta Parham, of Cambridge, Mar. 18, 1898; 3 children: William A. Jr., Oliver T., Doris S. Worked in dental office of Dr. A. J. Jones, Boston, Mass., 1892-7; with Bates Dental Co., 1897-1900; proprietor Cambridge Dental Parlors Co., since 1900; has large practice among white people; employs 4 colored assistants; was president school for tutoring unregistered dentists under State Board of Registration in Dentistry, 1901-8. Admitted to Mass. bar, 1911; practices law in addition to dental business; manager Harding, Cox & Martin real estate syndicate. Republican. Episcopalian. Member National Medical Assn. (ex-v-p.); secretary New England Medical, Dental and Pharm. Assn.; life member National Negro Business League; secretary Boston Negro Business League. Mason; member Odd Fellows, Elks, Foresters, Order of St. Luke. Home: 100 Ellery St. Dental Parlors: 586 Massachusetts Ave, Cambridge. Law Office: 121 Kendall St., Boston, Mass.

CRABB, Edward Joseph, electrician; born at Tuscaloosa, Ala., Dec. 24, 1865; son of Edward and Harriett (Walker) Crabb; attended the John Furman and Jeremiah Barnes private schools to 1882; student at Talladega College, 1883-5; took course in steam engineering and electricity with International Correspondence Schools, 1896; married Dorcas Mary White, of Talladega, Ala., Apr. 25, 1886; 11 children. Began as carpenter, Birmingham, Ala., 1886, continuing 4 years; was utility man in Birmingham shops of Louisville & Nashville Railroad, 1890-91; instructor in the handling of air brakes for Westinghouse Air Brake Co., Pittsburgh, Pa., traveling through U. S. and Canada, 1891-1901; air brake inspector, 1901-3, and foreman of electricians in the car lighting department since 1903, for the Erie Railroad at its shops in Jersey City, N. J. Republican. Congregationalist. Home: 128 Hamilton Ave., Richmond Hill, N. Y. Office: Erie R. R. Shops, Jersey City, N. J.

CRAIG, Arthur Ulysses, teacher, psychologist, vocational conselor; born at Weston, Mo., Dec. 1, 1871; son of Henry and Harriet (Talbert) Craig; attended public schools at Weston; grad. Atchison (Kan.) High School, 1890, completed 4 year course in 3 years; B.S., Univ. of Kan. School of Electrical Engineering, 1895; was first colored man to graduate as electrical engineer in U. S.; while at the university was third assistant in the physical laboratory; studied Sloyd at Naas Sloydlarareseminarium, Naas, Sweden, under Herr Otto Solomon, the founder of Sloyd; industrial edn. in London, Eng., Stockholm and Goteberg in Sweden, summer, 1899; psychology and manual training at Columbia Univ., New York, 1901; philosophy under Dr. W. T. Harris, 1904-8; ethics, psychology and philosophy at Catholic Univ. of America, 1909-10; married Luella C. G. Moore, Aug. 26, 1896; 3 children: Louise H., Walter L., Jason F. Began as teacher of physics and electricity, Industrial Dept. Tuskegee Institute, Ala., 1896, continuing to 1901; helped design the first automobile manufactured by the F. B. Stearns & Co., summer, 1900; elected but declined position as head the Industrial Department at Lincoln Institute, 1901; teacher in high school, Washington, since 1901; helped develope the vacation schools of D. C., 1902; practicing vocational counselor since 1904; principal Armstrong Manual Training Night School, 1904, 5, 6; now teacher in M Street High School; introduced mechanical and architectual drawing in colored schools of D. C.; has assisted in the formulation of manual training courses of study in a number of cities; originated the public playgrounds of Washington, and was supt. 3 years; visited principal playgrounds in the country as special representative the Playground Committee of Washington, D. C.; one of the originators of the Colored Social Settlement of Washington, and drew plans for its building; to a considerable extent was responsible for securing the building and grounds; introduced moving pictures in churches for religious and educational purposes in 1911; planned first public meeting with the aim to make home of the late Frederick Douglas a "Mount Vernon". Supertendent the Lincoln Temple Congregational Sunday School, 1909-15. Member National Association for Advancement of Colored People, National Educational Assn., American Negro Academy, Teachers' Assn. of D. C. 33d degree Mason. Address: Anocostia, D. C.

CRAWFORD, David Eugene, lawyer; born at Lynchburg, Va., Dec. 26, 1869; son of Joshua A. and Matilda (Conifax) Crawford; ed. at Lynchberg and Hampton, Va., Y. M. C. A., at Boston, Mass.; married Almira G. Lewis, of Chelsea, Mass., Dec, 23, 1894; 4 children: J. William A., Mildred L., Helen F., Mary V. Practiced law in Boston since 1907; founded Eureka Co-operative Bank, now secretary-treasurer; real estate agent. Republican. Baptist. Member Suffolk Bar Assn. 33d degree Mason; member Elks. Home: 14 Wellington St. Office: 930 Tremont St., Boston, Mass.

CRAWFORD, George Williamson, lawyer; born at Tuscaloosa, Ark., Oct. 21, 1877; son of William and Charlotte (Oliver) Crawford; grad. Tuskegee Normal and Industrial Institute, Ala., 1900; LL.B., Yale Univ. Law School, 1903; married Sadella M. Donalson, of Aberdeen, Miss., Sept. 2, 1911; 1 child: Charlotte Elizabeth. Admitted to bar in Conn., 1903; was clerk in Probate Court, District of New Haven, 1903-7; practiced law since 1907; director National Association for Advancement of Colored People. Trustee Talladega College. Republican. Congregationalist. Member Sigma Pi Phi. Mason; member Odd Fellows, Foresters. Author: Prince Hall and His Followers. Home: 580 Orchard St. Office: 42 Church St., New Haven, Conn.

CRAWFORD, Traverse Samuel, editor, bank teller; born at DeKalb, Miss., May 1, 1871; son of Samuel and Fannie (Rush) Crawford; ed. Lincoln School, Meridian, Miss.; A.B., Tougaloo Univ., 1901; took course in law from American Correspondence School of Law, Chicago, 1914; married Eva Cordelia Roberts, of Tougaloo, Miss., May 22, 1912; 1 child: Era Lydia. Principal of schools at Scooba, Miss., 1901-3; teacher in public schools, Austin, Tex., 1903-4; principal Baird, Miss., 1904-8; teacher in county schools, Sunflower County, summers, 1905-8; with Delta Penny Savings Bank, Indianola, Miss., since 1909; bookkeeper for Woodmen of Union, Miss and Ark.; editor New Era; director Miss. Beneficial Life Ins. Co.; member endowment fund com. Alumni Assn. Tougaloo Univ.; owns farm, cattle raiser. Progressive. African Methodist. Mason. Address: Indianola, Miss.

CREDITT, William Abraham, clergyman, teacher; born at Baltimore, Md., July 14, 1864; son of Bush Rod and Mary (Lindsey) Creditt; A.B., Lincoln (Pa.) Univ., 1885, A.M., 1891; S.T.B., Newton Theological Institute, Mass., 1889; A.M., State Univ., Louisville, Ky., 1890; (Ph.D., Guadaloupe College, Tex., 1898; D.D., Lincoln Univ., 1900, LL.D., 1901); married

Stella Vessells, of Washingtton, D. C., 1890; 3 children: Annice, Alvah, Addie. Ordained Baptist ministry, 1889; teacher in State Univ., Louisville, 1889-90, State Normal School, Frankfort, Ky., 1890-1; pastor in Frankfort, 1889-91, Washington, D. C., 1891-7, 1st African Baptist Church, Philadelphia, Pa., since 1897; built new edifice at cost of $100,000, 1905; pres. N. E. Convention, 1908-12; a founder and president Downingtown (Pa.) Industrial and Agricultural School; president Cherry Building and Loan Assn., vice-president Reliable Mutual Insurance Co. (organized both). Member Republican State Central Committee, 1911-12. Home: 628 S. 19th St. Church: 16th and Christian Sts., Philadelphia. Office: Downingtown, Pa.

CREWS, Nelson Caesar, editor, former clerk of court; born at Fayette, Howard Co., Mo., Oct. 15, 1866; son of Jacob and Joanna Crews; public school edn., Chillicothe, Mo.; married Margaret Bass, of Topeka, Kan., Oct. 21, 1914. Clerk in Municipal Court, Kansas City, Mo., 1900-8; assistant city clerk 2 years; special agent U. S. Department of Agriculture 1 year; editor and owner Kansas City Sun since 1911; director Afro-American Realty & Investment Co. Trustee Western Univ., Quindaro, Kan. Republican. African Methodist. Mason, grand master Grand Lodge of Mo.; member Knights of Pythias, United Brothers of Friendship. Office: 1803 E. 18th St., Kansas City, Mo.

CROGMAN, William Henry, Sr., university professor; born St. Martins, West Indies, May 5, 1841; son of William and Charlotte (Chippendale) Crogman; orphan at age of 12; A.B., Atlantic Univ., Ga., 1876, A.M., 1879 (Litt.D., 1901; LL.D., Clark Univ., Atlanta, 1901); married Lavinia C. Mott, of Charlotte, N. C., July 10, 1878. Began as professor of classics, Atlanta Univ., 1876, president 1903-10, professor of ancient languages since 1910. Member American Philological Assn., American Geographical Society. African Methodist. Address: Clark University, S. Atlanta, Ga.

CROMWELL, John Wesley, lawyer, teacher; born at Portsmouth, Va., Sept. 5, 1846; son of Willis Hodges and Elizabeth (Carney) Cromwell; prep. edn. Institute for Colored Youth, Philadelphia, Pa.; LL.B., Howard Univ., Washington, D. C., 1874: (hon. A.M., Wilberforce Univ., 1914); married Lucy A. McGuinn, of Richmond, Va., 1873; 7 children: Otelia, Mary E., Lucy A., Willis R., Martha, John W., Fannie; 2d marriage, Annie E. Conn, of Mechanicsburg, Pa., Oct. 20, 1892. Admitted to bar in District of Columbia, 1874; practiced in Washington to 1892; was first colored lawyer to appear before Interstate Commerce Commission; principal of Crummell School since 1908. Republican. African Methodist. Corresponding secretary the American Negro Academy. Mason. Author: The Negro in American History, 1914. Address: 1439 Swann St., Washington, D. C.

CROSBY. Robert Dewite, undertaker; born at Jackson, Mich., Dec. 2, 1880; son of John Alfred and Margaret (Dennis) Crosby; ed. in Detroit at Bishop School, the Detroit Business College, and Boston (Mass.) School of Embalming; married Caroline May, of Detroit, Dec. 5, 1901; children: Marion Berneice, Herald Dewite, Robert Donald. Undertaker and embalmer in Detroit since July 15, 1901. Methodist. Mason, Knight Templar; member Odd Fellows, Knights of Pythias. Club: Iroquois. Address: 530 St. Antoine St., Detroit, Mich.

CROSTHWAIT, David Nelson, Sr., teacher; born near Murfreesboro, Tenn., Apr. 8, 1856; son of Scott and Joyce Elizabeth (Thompson) Crosthwait; A.B., Fisk Univ., 1881, A.M., 1884; M.D., Meharry Medical College (Waldon Univ.), 1890; post-graduate work Armour Institute of Tech., Chicago, Ill., 1911; married Minnie Lee Harris, of Nashville, Tenn., Dec. 26, 1889; 3 children: Anne Elizabeth, David N. Jr., Paul V. Principal, 1881-95, first Colored High School opened in Nashville; teacher of chemistry and biology, Lincoln High School, Kansas City, Mo., since 1895. Republican. Congregationalist. Member National Negro Educational Congress, State Teachers' Assn. of Mo., Kansas City branch National Association for Advancement Colored People. Mason; member Knights of Pythias; charter member Pythian Temple Building Assn. Address: 1020 Virginia Ave., Kansas City, Mo.

CROSTHWAIT, Minnie Lou, university registrar, teacher; born at Nashville, Tenn., Aug. 20, 1860; daughter of Frances (McAlister) Scott; attended private school, 1865-7, public schools to 1874; A.B., Fisk Univ., Nashville, 1879; married Dr. Scott W. Crosthwait, of Nashville, June 12, 1884; 4 children: Holcombe Sinclair, George Scott, Scott W. Jr., Lenida Thomas. Instructor in school management and registrar at Fisk Univ. Congregationalist. Club: Fisk. Home: 1815 Morena St. Office: Fisk University, Nashville, Tenn.

CROSTHWAIT, Scott Washington, physician, clergyman; born near Murfreesboro, Rutherford Co., Tenn., Apr. or May, 8, 1856; son of Scott Taylor and Joyce Elizabeth (Keeble) Crosthwait; worked as 'shineboy" and barber, bellboy and waiter, to gain education; attended public schools of Nashville, Tenn.; grad. Meharry Medical College, 1889, Chicago Homoeopathic Medical College, 1891; B.D., Fisk Univ., Nashville, 1909; married Minnie Lou Scott, of Nashville, June 12, 1884; 4 children: Holcombe Sinclair, George S., Scott W. Jr., Lenida T. Began as teacher in country schools, summer, 1874, continuing part of each year to 1879; Dr. R. S. White, Minnie Lou Scott (now his wife), and self were elected, 1879, to demonstrate whether colored teachers could be successfully employed in the city schools of Nashville, and he was the first colored principal; there are now about 100 colored teachers in Nashville schools; practiced medicine in Nashville and Knoxville, 1891-96, with limited practice in Nashville in later years; in the ministry since 1909; was pastor Gay Street Christian Church, Nashville, 2 years; is not a sectarian; advocates that Christians unite on the essentials of religion; chairman Committee of Religious Education, for Middle Tennessee Colored Teachers' Assn., since 1914; the committee is made up of 12 different denominations, including Catholic, the purpose being to propose a course of Bible reading adapted to public schools; the idea is his own. Member Carnegie Library Committee, committee on sanitation Nashville Negro Board of Trade. Wrote "The Progress of the Negro in Nashville Since Emancipation," which was given one-half page in the Nashville Democrat (white newspaper), Dec. 1, 1912. Home and Office: 1815 Morena St., Nashville, Tenn.

CRUMBLY, Floyd Henry, ex-soldier, conveyancer, real estate agent; born at Rome, Ga., May 10, 1859; son of Robert and Mariah Crumbly; private primary tuition under Rev. George Standing at Lagrange, Ga.; while in army attended school at Fort Still, Ind. Ty., 1876-81; married Myrtle B. Carter, of Los Angeles, Calif., Sept. 8, 1904. Enlisted in Troop I., U. S. Cav., Nov. 16, 1876; appointed corporal, June, 1877, promoted to sergt., Jan., 1878, and sergt.-major at Fort Stockton, Texas, Dec. 1880; discharged, Nov. 16, 1881; was lieut.-colonel Georgia State Guard, 1892-8; served in Spanish-American war, July 1, 1898 to Mar. 8, 1899, as 1st lieut. 10th U. S. Inf.; captain 48th U. S. Inf., in the Phillipine Islands, Sept. 9, 1899 to June 30, 1901. Was in mercantile business, Atlanta, Ga., 1885-96; director Negro Dept., Cotton States Exposition, Atlanta, 1895; real estate operator and conveyancer, Los Angeles, Calif., since 1905; part owner People's Realty Co., R. C. Owens Investment Co. President, A. M. E. Church Brotherhood; director Y. M. C. A. Republican; director Spanish War Veterans Political Assn. Mason. Home: 1107 Dewey Ave. Office: 775 S. San Pedro St., Los Angeles, Calif.

CUFF, Harlan Austin, physician; born at Wilmington, Del., Aug. 22, 1888; son of Richard and Letitia (Wilson) Cuff; attended Howard

High and Manual Training School at Wilmington; grad. Teachers' School, Wilmington, 1906, where made special study of Greek, Latin and chemistry; M.D., Howard Univ. School of Medicine, Washington, 1911; unmarried. Practiced in Middletown, Del., since Feb., 1912; in charge the colored clinic with the Delaware Tuberculosis Society. Republican. Methodist. Member Knights of Pythias. Club: Counts (Wilmington). Home and Office: E. Lake St., Middletown, Del.

CUMMINGS, Harry Sythe, lawyer, city councilman; born at Baltimore, Md., May 19, 1866; son of Henry and Elizabeth Cummings; A.B., Lincoln (Pa.) Univ., 1886; LL.B., Univ. of Md., 1889; married Blanche T. Conklin, of Baltimore, Dec. 19, 1899; 2 children: Harry S. Jr., Louise. Admitted to Maryland bar, 1889; since practiced in Baltimore. Member Baltimore City Council since 1891; delegate to Republican National Convention, Minneapolis, 1892, Chicago, 1904; seconded nomination of Theodore Roosevelt; appointed by mayors of both parties as director House of Reformation for Colored Youth and served since 1904. Presbyterian. Mason; member Odd Fellows, Knights of Pythias. Home: 1318 Druid Hill Ave. Office: 219 Courtland St., Baltimore, Md.

CUMMINGS, Thomas James David, clergyman, publisher; born at Maxton, N. C., July 12, 1867; son of David R. and Amanda (Farrar) Cummings; A.B., Atlanta Univ., 1887; married Hettie Ellen Gilmore, of Albany, Ga., Sept. 12, 1897. Teacher in public schools of Fla., 1887-99; agent for insurance company 6 years; pastored A. M. E. churches in Fla., since 1896; built church edifices in San Antonio, Kissimee, and Leesburg, a parsonage in Brooksville; editor and pub. The Outlook since 1910; sales representative for The Cable Co. Trustee Edward Walters College. Republican. Mason, captain U. R., Knights of Pythias, Fla.; member Odd Fellows. Club: Progressive. Address: Main and Canal Sts., Leesburg, Fla.

CUNEY, Joseph, lawyer; born at Sunny Side, Tex., son of Col. Philip N. and Adeline (Stuart) Cuney; brother of the late Norris Wright Cuney; ed. in Wylie Institute, Pittsburgh., 1853-61 married Josephine Barbour, of Washington, D. C. (deceased); 2 children: Nisi (deceased), Charles E. Served in 63d Penn. Vols. in war between the states; was in Battle of the Wilderness. Appointed clerk in Freedman's Bureau, Washington, 1866; chief clerk in U. S. Custom service, Galveston, Tex., 1889-92; practiced law since 1893; active in public affairs and welfare of colored race. Republican. Office: 1925 Mechanic St., Galveston, Tex.

CUNNINGHAM, Isaac Summerville, physician, surgeon; born at Hillsboro, N. C., July 29, 1877; son of Zack and Elsie Cunningham; B.S., Agricultural and Mechanical College, Greensboro, N. C., 1899; M.D., Meharry Medical College (Walden Univ.), Nashville, Tenn., 1908; married Hattie B. Johnson, of Raleigh, N. C., Sept. 24, 1902; 3 children: Lewis Irving, Russell J., Isaac S. Jr. Began practice in Springfield, Tenn., June 6, 1908; removed to Owensboro, Ky., 1911; city physician among colored people of Owensboro; owns stock in Owensboro Record. Republican. Baptist. Secretary of Owensboro Medical Assn. Member Knights of Pythias. Home and Office: 524 Vine St., Owensboro, Ky.

CURTIS,, Arthur Leo, physician, surgeon; born at Chicago, Ill., July 26, 1889; son of Dr. Austin Maurice and Namah Gertrude (Sockum) Curtis; attended public school, Chicago; grad. M Street High School, Washington; preparatory edn. Williston Seminary, Easthampton, Mass.; M.D., Howard Univ. School of Medicine, Washington, D. C., 1912; unmarried. Practiced in Washington since 1913; appointed member visiting staff of Freedmen's Hospital, and instructor in minor surgery at Howard Univ., April, 1914; now visiting minor surgeon at the hospital, and associate professor of anaestheics in Howard Univ. Dental College. Republican. Presbyterian. Member National Medical Assn., Medico-Chirurgical Society of D. C., Freedmen's Hospital Medical Society. Odd Fellow. Home and Office: 1939 Thirteenth St., Washington, D. C.

CURTIS, Austin Maurice, surgeon; born at Raleigh, N. C., Jan. 15, 1868; son of Alexander W. and Elenora (Smith) Curtis; ed. public schools, Raleigh; A.B., Lincoln (Pa.) Univ., 1888, A.M., later; M.D., Northwestern Univ. Medical School, Chicago, Ill., 1891; married Namah G. Sockum, of Oakland, Calif., May 8, 1888; 4 children: Dr. Arthur Leo, Dr. Austin M. Jr., Merrill H., Gertrude E. Began practice in Chicago, 1891; attending surgeon Provident Hospital, Chicago, 1892-8; was first colored man on staff of Cook County Hospital, appointed as attending surgeon in 1896; surgeon-in-chief Freedmen's Hospital, Washington, D. C., 1898-1902, and now attending surgeon; consulting surgeon to Provident Hospital, Baltimore, Md., and Richmond (Va.) Hospital; professor clinical surgery Howard Univ. Medical Post-graduate School, and associate professor of surgery at Howard Univ. Medical School, Washington. Republican. Presbyterian. Member National Medical Assn., American Medical Assn., Medico-Chirurgical Society of D. C., Freedmen's Hospital Medical Society; Physicians Reading Club of D. C. Mason. Clubs: Mu-so-lit, Common Welfare. Address: 1939 13th St., Washington, D. C.

CURTIS, Austin Maurice, Jr., physician, surgeon; born at Chicago, Ill., June 21, 1890; son of Dr. Austin Maurice and Namah Gertrude (Sockum) Curtis; brother of Dr. Arthur Leo Curtis; these data record the only family mentioned in this volume in which father and two sons are practicing physicians and surgeons; primary school edn., Chicago; grad. M Street High School, Washington, D. C., 1908; student Univ. of Mich., 1909-10; M.D., Howard Univ. School of Medicine, 1914; unmarried. Practiced in Washington since July, 1914; attending physician and surgeon in Freedmen's Hospital. Was assistant

director of Howard Playground, 1911-13. Episcopalian. Member Alpha Chapter, Chi Delta Mu. Clubs: Gama Beta, Bachelors, Frogs, Pyrs. Home: 1939 Thirteenth St. N. W. Office: Freedmen's Hospital, Washington, D. C.

CURTIS, Austin Wingate, teacher of agriculture; born at Wilmington, N. C., May 17, 1872; son of Austin and Margaret Ann (Wingate) Curtis; ed. public schools to 1890, and St. Augustine School 3 years, at Raleigh, N. C.; worked at N. C. Experiment Station 4 years; B.Agr., Agricultural and Mechanical College, Greensboro, N. C., 1899, M.Agr., 1909; attended Summer School at Cornell Univ., 1900; married Dora T. Brown, of Institute, W. Va., 1905; 2 children: Alice C., Austin W. Jr. Professor of agriculture and director Agrl. Dept. at W. Va. Collegiate Institute since Sept. 1, 1899; taught agriculture and nature study in Summer School 5 years. African Methodist. Member Association of American Agricultural Colleges and Experiment Stations, W. Va. Horticultural Society, W. Va. Agricultural Society, W. Va. Teachers' Assn. Address: Institute, W. Va.

CURTRIGHT, Edward Eusebia, teacher; born in Greene Co., Ga., May 22, 1873; son of George Pierce and Savanah (Weaver) Curtright; A.B., Atlanta Univ., 1902; student Univ. of Chicago, summer, 1911; married Lola May Brooks, of High Point, N. C., June 27, 1906. Teacher, registrar and treas. High Point Normal and Industrial Institute, N. C., since 1902; secretary and treas. Ramsey Drug Co. Republican. Missionary Baptist. Mason. Home: 121 E. Broad St. Office: Box 292, High Point, N. C.

CURTRIGHT, Felix Alonzo, clergyman; born at Greensboro, Ga., May 10, 1869; son of George Pierce and Savannah (Weaver) Courtright; A.B., Atlanta Univ., 1896; married Juliet Gertrude Monroe, of Savannah, Ga., June 28, 1905; 5 children: Andrenaka, Martile Monroe, Felix Alonzo, Jr., Armobel Matilda, Essie Merika, Andrew Marshall. Teacher in public schools of Ga., 1887-96; principal N.

La. Industrial High School, 1896-7; instructor of sciences Haynes Industrial High School, Augusta, Ga., 1897-8; principal Ga. Normal and Industrial Institute, Greensboro, 1898-1906; ordained Baptist ministry, 1900; financial sec. General Baptist Convention of Ga., 1907-8; gen-sec. Y. M. C. A., Atlanta, 1909-10; pastor Second Church, Joliet, Ill., since 1910; membership doubled in 4 years, church property improved with social center and parsonage largely increasing valuation. Address: 502 S. Joliet St., Joliet, Ill.

CUTTS, Wen Galaway, physician; born in North Carolina; son of Andrew and Susan (Foard) Cutts; attended schools in Virginia and Washington, D. C.; A.B., Geneva College, Beaver Falls, Pa., 1905; studied medicine at Univ. of Pa., 2 years, Boston, Mass., 1 year; M.D., Detroit (Mich.) College of Medicine and Surgery, 1909; married Ada Graham Mahoney, of Pittsburgh, Pa., June 27, 1912; 1 child: Mary Josephine. Practiced in Pittsburgh since 1910. Won prize in oratorical contest at Geneva College, 1904; now public speaker of various subjects. Republican. Presbyterian. Member Allegheny County Medical Assn. Mason; member Odd Fellows, Knights of Pythias. Address: 2834 Wylie Ave., Pittsburgh, Pa.

D

DABNEY, Lillian Beatrice, supervising industrial teacher; born at LeGrand, Ala., Mar. 8, 1893; daughter of Harry Westley and Marah (Sharp) Dabney; grad. Montgomery Industrial School for Girls, 1906; State Normal School, Montgomery, Ala., 1911; took special course in elocution. Began as teacher in public schools, Enterprise, Ala., 1911, continuing 2 years; supervisor Negro Rural Schools, Coffee County, Ala., since 1913; one of 22 supervising industrial teachers under the State Department of Education; aided by the Anna T. Jeanes Fund, this branch of public instruction reaches the most remote schools and homes in the state; children are taught to mend, sew, cook, to be economical and self supporting. Congregationalist. Home. R. F. D. No. 1 Snowdoun. Address: Box 70, Enterprise, Ala.

DABNEY, Wendell Phillips, deputy city treasurer, musician, editor; born at Richmond, Va., Nov. 4, 1865; son of John and Elizabeth (Foster) Dabney; grad. Richmond Normal and High School, 1883; student Oberlin (O.) College, 1885-6; married Nellie Foster Jackson, of Madison, Ind., 1897; 1 child: Wendell P. Jr. (deceased); 2 stepsons: Leo, Maurice. Teacher in Richmond public schools, 1886-92; taught music in leading white families of Richmond, later in Cincinnati, Ohio; had studio in Wurlitzer's several years; wrote 6 books published by Rudolph Wurlitzer Co., including Dabney's Complete Method of Guitar, Dabney and Roach Mandolin and Guitar Method. Composer: You Will Miss the Colored Soldiers; God Our Father (songs); Fall Festival March (instrumental), adopted by the association in charge and played at opening the exposition in Cincinnati, 1900. Editor and owner The Union (weekly newspaper) since 1905; president Dabney Pub. Co., Royal Union Improvement Co.; speculator in real estate. Was licensed clerk in 1896; first colored man to serve in Cincinnati as assistant city paymaster, 1898-1900; reappointed, 1907, 09, 14. 33d degree Mason, Shriner. Club: Republican Union. Author: (pamphlet): The Wolf and the Lamb, 1903. Office: Dabney Building, 420 McAllister St., Cincinnati, Ohio.

DANCY, J. C., clergyman; secretary of Church Extension, A. M. E. Zion, 420 S. 11th St., Philadelphia, Pa.

DART, John Lewis, clergyman; born at Charleston, S. C., Mar. 10, 1854; son of William and Susan Dart; prep. edn., Avery Institute, Charleston; A.M., Atlanta Univ., Ga., 1879; B.D., Newton Theol. Institute, Mass., 1882; married Julia Pierre, of Washington, D. C., Nov. 27, 1887; 4 children: William A., John L. Jr., Anna P., Susie (Butler). Teacher in Washington, D. C., 2 years; ordained Baptist ministry, Newton Center, Mass., 1882; pastor, Providence, R. I., 1884-5, Augusta, Ga., 1885-6, Charleston, S. C., since 1886; prin. Charleston Industrial Institute since 1894; also in real estate business; was editor and owner Southern Reporter, 10 years. Progressive. Address: 112 Bogard St., Charleston, S. C.

DAUPHIN, W. J., physician; M.D., Flint Medical College, New Orleans, La., 1903. Practiced in Miss., 2 years; demonstrator of anatomy and professor of practical chemistry at Flint Medical College, 1905-6; practiced in Opelouses, La., 1906-10; now at Alexandria. Address: 619 Lee St., Alexandria, La.

DAVAGE, M. S., business manager Southwestern Christian Advocate, 631 Baronne St., New Orleans, La.

DAVIDSON, Shelby Jeames, lawyer, inventor; born at Lexington, Ky., May 10, 1868; son of Shelby J. and Amelia (Scott) Davidson; attended public, high and normal schools in Lexington; State Univ., Louisville, Ky.; A.B., Howard Univ., 1893; read law in office of Col. William A. Cook; married Leonora · Coates, of Massaponax, Va., Feb. 1, 1894; 2 children: Eugene L., Ophelia. Began as clerk in Post Office Dept., Washington, D. C., 1893; later commissioned by the Treasury Dept. to study the operation and uses of adding machines at Detroit, Mich.; prepared plan for auditing accounts in Post Office and Treasury departments; invented rewind device for tabulating and totalling accounts; also invented attachment to automatically total money order reports submitted to postmasters, a special copy holder, and coin machine counting attachment; his articles on "Adding Machines" were published in Burroughs Journal, and in System; resigned from government service, 1912. Admitted to Ky. bar at Lexington, and bar at Washington, D. C., 1900, to Court of Appeals, D. C., 1903, to Supreme Court of the U. S., 1912; Belva A. Lockwood, who in 1884 and 1888 was nominated by the Equal Rights Party as President of the U.

S., moved his admission to the Supreme Court; practices in Washington; also in real estate business. Trustee Burean Baptist Church .Republican. Member Colored Bar Assn. of D. C. Mason; member Odd Fellows. Club: Mu-So-Lit. Home: 1911 13th St. N. W. Office: 639 F St. N. W., Washington, D. C.

DAVIS, Benjamin O., lieutenant U. S. A. Served in Cuba during Spanish-American war, later in the Phillipine Islands; was detailed by the War Dept., 1905, as instructor in military science and tactics at Wilberforce (O.) Univ., continuing to 1909; now 1st lieut. 10th U. S. Cav. Address: War Department, Washington, D. C.

DAVIS, Edward Jackson, physician, health officer for Zuni Indians; born at Charleston, S. C., May 25, 1870; son of William Pinkney and Anna (Bradford) Davis; A.B., Fisk Univ., 1895; M.D., Harvard Univ., 1899; married Mary Louise Moseley, of St. Louis, Mo., June 1, 1905; 1 child: Pauline Alexandra. Began practice in St. Louis, 1900; resident physician Provident Hospital, 1901-3; school physician in U. S. Indian Service, Dept. of Interior, at Zuni, N. Mex., since 1903; also in private practice; examiner for N. Y. Life Ins. Co., Pacific Mutual Life Ins. Co., Western States Life Ins. Co., Kansas City Life Ins. Co., Occidental Life Ins. Co. Member A. M. E. Church; also member Knights of Pythias. Address: Zuni, N. Mex.

DAVIS, Edward Porter, university professor; born at Charleston, S. C., Jan. 24, 1879; son of Prince Nelson and Mary Ann (Fennick) Davis; prep. Avery Institute, Charleston, S. C.; A.B., Howard Univ., 1907; A.M., Univ. of Chicago, 1911; unmarried. Associate professor of Greek and Latin, Howard Univ., Washington, D. C., since 1912, African Methodist. Member Archaeological Institute of America, Classical Assn. of the Atlantic States. Mason. Author: The Conditional Sentence in Terence, 1911. Contributor: A Brief for the Classics to "Education", and other articles. Address: Howard University, Washington, D. C.

DAVIS, Henrietta Vinton, elecutionist, impersonator; born at Baltimore, Md.; daughter of Mansfield Vinton and Mary Ann (Johnson) Davis; father was a musician; public school edn., Washington, D. C.; studied elocution and dramatic art under Margarite E. Saxton, Washington, Prof. Edwin Lawrence, New York, and Rachel Noah, Boston, Mass; attended Boston School of Oratory. Began as teacher in public schools in Maryland at age of 15; later taught school in Louisiana; was copyist in recorder of deeds office, Washington, 4 yrs; made first appearance as dramatic reader in Washington, Apr. 25, 1883, and was introduced to the audience by Frederick Douglass; has since toured principal parts of U. S., West Indies, Central and South America; her recitals include Negro dialects from Paul Laurence Dunbar's works, classical, humorous and pathetic selections from Romeo and Juliet, As You Like It, Mary Queen of Scots, Cleopatra's Dying Speech, "The Battle," by Sciller, Mark Twain's "How Tom Sawyer Got His Fence Whitewashed," and others in variety; was first colored person to attempt Shakespearean delineations. African Methodist. Member Knights and Ladies of Malachites. Home: 1219 Linden St. N. E., Washington, D. C.

DAVIS, Highland Leonard, agricultural supervisor; born at Hendersonville, S. C., Nov. 28, 1889; son of James Edward and Fannie (Ruger) Davis; grad. Mather Industrial School, Beaufort, S. C., 1910; took course in printing at Laurinburg (N. C.) Normal School, printing and agriculture in Robert Hungerford School, Eatonville, Fla.; married Flarrie B. Hankerson, of Dunbarton, S. C., Nov. 26, 1914. Agricultural director of Mather Industrial School since 1913; this school was founded, 1868, by Rachel Cane (Rice) Mather, widow of Rev. Joseph H. Mather of Deep River, Conn.; students come mostly from the "Cotton Belt," where common schools are open only 3 months in duration. Republican. Colored Methodist. Member United Band of America. Address: Mather Industrial School, Beaufort, S. C.

DAVIS, Samuel Jacob, manufacturer; born at Petersburg, Va., Aug. 27, 1874; son of William and Maria (Goodwyn) Davis; ed. public schools, Petersburg; married Hattie B. Russell, of Richmond, Va., June 17, 1897; 3 children: Marie, Ella, Samuel, Jr. Sole owner S. J. Davis Mfg. Co., specialties for agents; prop. Cash Grocery Store; sec. and mgr. New Rochelle Co-operative Business League since 1905. Was secretary Colored Republican Club, 1905; sec. Westchester County Republican League, 1908-11, and editor its journal, 1911; member County Committee National Progressive Party, 1914. Baptist. Mason; member Order Eastern Star. Knights of Pythias, Southern Beneficial League. Home: 89 Horton Ave. Office: 24 Brook St., New Rochelle, N. Y.

DAVIS, Samuel Rosemond, physician; born at Allegheny, Pa., Oct. 5, 1888; son of Robert Jeremiah and Helen (Jennings) Davis; grad. Pittsburgh High School, 1907; M.D., Univ. of Pittsburgh, 1911; interne Freedmen's Hospital, Washington, D. C., 1911-12; unmarried. Practiced in Pittsburgh since Nov. 1, 1912. Baptist. Club: Loendi Literary and Social. Address: 6358 Frankstown Ave. E. E., Pittsburgh, Pa.

DAVIS, William Leonard, teacher; born at Hallettsville, Tex., Jan. 6, 1873; son of James Edward and Leatha Davis; ed. rural school, Lavaca County, Tex., public school, Lagrange; Paul Quinn College, Waco; Prairie View Normal and Industrial College; married Emma Sampson, of Carmine, Tex., July 7, 1906. Began teaching at Hallettsville, 1895; now principal Hempstead (Tex.) High School. Secretary Farmers' Improvement Society Bank, Farmers' Improvement Society Overall Factory. Trustee Boyds Industrial Institute, Dallas; sec. Texas Baptist Sunday School Convention. Leader among school teachers in state-wide prohibition movement; served as secretary executive committee Fayette County Republican party. Member board directors Grand Lodge, Knights of Pythias, Texas. Address: Box 36, Hempstead, Texas.

DAY, William Edward, teacher; born at Milford, Tex., Mar. 16, 1865; son of Samuel and Clara (Austin) Day; B.S., Paul Quinn College, Waco, Tex, 1889; married A. B. Banes, of Baton Rouge, La., June 28, 1898; 1 child: Nannie Clara. Teacher in various schools since 1889; has conducted normal for teachers in Tex. and Okla., since 1899; teacher of mathematics in Manual Training High School, Muskogee, Okla. Republican. African Methodist. Member executive committee National Negro Teachers' Assn.; pres. Okla. State Teachers' Assn. Mason. Address: 915 N. 9th St., Muskogee, Okla.

DEAN, William Henry, clergyman; born at Front Royal, Va., Sept. 21, 1877; son of Charles and Rachel (Brooks) Dean; grad. Harrisburg High School, Pa., 1898, Gammon Theological Seminary, Atlanta, Ga., 1903; freshman Howard Univ., 1904; married Ella C. Greene, of Baltimore, Md., June 27, 1903; 4 children: Elaine J., Thelma L., William H. Jr., Ruth E. Ordained M. E. ministry, 1903; teacher in Normal School, Baltimore, and pastor Oxon Hill, Md., 1903-5; pastor, Richmond, Va., 1905-9, Lynchburg, 1909-12, Ebenezer M. E. Church, Washington, D. C., since 1912; as evengelist has received over 2,000 converts, improved and built new church edifice and reduced church debts many thousands of dollars. Mason; member Odd Fellows, Order of St. Luke. Address: 332 Fourth St. S. E., Washington, D. C.

DEANS, David Crocket, clergyman, teacher; born near Murfreesboro, N. C., May 15, 1853; son of Adline Deans; grad. Hampton Normal and Agricultural Institute, Va., 1876, Wayland Theological Seminary, Washington, D. C., 1879; A.B., Howard Univ., 1883; teachers' training course at W. Va. Colored Institute, 1913; married Rosetta Munday, of Tappahannock,

Va., May 28, 1885; 6 children. Ordained Baptist ministry, Tappahonnock, 1883; now pastor and teacher at Montgomery, W. Va. Trusttee W. Va. College and Seminary. Republican. Member Odd Fellows, St. Lukes', great lecturer Improved Order of Red Men. Address: Montgomery, W. Va.

DeBERRY, William Caleb, clergyman, teacher; born at Mt. Gilead, N. C., May 31, 1873; son of Caleb and Parthenia (Ingram) DeBerry; prep. edn. Biddle Univ., Charlotte, N. C.; A.B., Livingstone College, Salisbury, N. C., 1905; B.D., Moody Bible School, Chicago, Ill., 1911; married Mrs. Laura P. Solomon, of Washington, D. C., 1906; 2 children: Hattie, William C. Began teaching in Montgomery Co., N. C., 1896; founded and now prin. Rockingham Normal and Industrial Training School for Colored Youth. Pastor in A. M. E. Zion Church since 1905. Member Knights of Pythias. Address: Box 273, Rockingham, N. C.

DeBERRY, William Nelson, clergyman, lecturer; born at Nashville, Tenn., Aug. 29, 1870; son of Caswell and Charlotte (Mayfield) DeBerrry; B.S., Fisk Univ., 1896; B.D., Oberlin College, 1899; (D.D., Lincoln Univ., 1914); married Amanda McKissack, of Pulaski, Tenn., Sept. 6, 1899; 2 children: Charlotte Pearl, Anna Mae. Ordained Congregational ministry, 1899; since pastor St. John's Church, Springfield, Mass., among leading instutional churches in northern states. Life member American Board of Commissioners for Foreign Missions, American Missionary Assn.; member Hampton Assn. of Congregational Ministers' of Mass. Trustee Mutual Housing Co. of Springfield. Lectures include: The Negro Problem in its Darker and Brighter Aspects; The New Negro and the Chance for Which He Pleads; The Negro in New England; The Social Effects of Race Amalgamation. Address: 643 Union St., Springfield, Mass.

DeBOW, Samuel P., editor; born at Leavenworth, Kan., Nov. 25, 1865; son of Larkin and Edith E. (Huston) De-

Bow; public school edn.; married Ida Duncan, of San Francisco, Calif., Jan-9, 1889. Editor the Seattle Search-light; president Searchlight Pub. Co. Republican. Home: 424 19th Ave. Office: 408 Marion St., Seattle, Wash.

DECATUR, William Jefferson, principal industrial school; born at Atlanta, Ga., Oct. 16, 1874; son of Isaac and Olivia (North) Decatur; A.B., Atlanta Univ., 1899; post course Univ. of Chicago; married Harriett Mae Ish, of Little Rock, Ark., Sept. 9, 1908. Began as assistant superintendent of industries at Tougaloo (Miss.) Univ., under American Missionary Assn., 1899, continuing 2 years; superintendent of industries, Talladega College, Ala., 1901-4; architect and builder, Atlanta, Ga., 1904-5;'instructor in School of Applied Sciences, Howard Univ., Washington, D. C., 1906-12; director of vocations at Wilberforce (O.) Univ., 1912; principal Manassas Industrial School since 1913. Address: Manassas, Va.

DePRIEST, Oscar, alderman, real estate dealer; born at Florence, Ala., Mar. 9, 1871; ed. in public schools and business college; married Jessie Williams, of Rockford, Ill.; 2 children: Lawrence, Stanton. Began as journeyman painter, 1887; later painting contractor in Chicago to 1912; member real estate firm of DePriest & DePriest since 1912. Was member Board of Cook County Commissioners, 2 terms, 1906-10; first colored man ever member Chicago City Council; elected for 2 year term from 2d Ward, Apr. 6, 1915; Republican. Presbyterian. Mason; member Odd Fellows. Club: Appomatox. Home: 3815 Vernon Ave. Office: 3439 S. State St., Chicago, Ill.

DeREEF, George Heriot, lawyer; born at Charleston, S. C., Sept. 5, 1869; son of Joseph Moulton Francis and Georgiana Oldfield (Heriot) De-Reef; attended public school, Charleston; prep. edn. Claflin Univ., Orangeburg, S. C.; A.B., Howard Univ., Washington, 1901, LL.B., 1905; unmarried. Admitted to District of Columbia bar, 1905, to Court of Appeals, D. C., 1907, Supreme Court of U. S.,

1912, to Wis. bar by state Supreme Court, 1913; began practice in Washington, 1905; was associated with Judge Robert H. Terrell, 1907-9; deputy clerk in Municipal Court of D. C., 1909-13, resigned; practiced in Milwaukee, Wis., since Oct. 7, 1913. Delegate form Wis. to the Emancipation Liberation Exposition, New York, 1913; chairman Wisconsin Commission to Half-Century Anniversary Celebration of Negro Freedom, Chicago, Ill., 1915. Republican. Episcopalian. Member Milwaukee County Bar Assn. Home: 708 Clarke St. Office: 217 Empire Bldg., Milwaukee, Wis.

DeTOSCANO, Bettie Elizabeth, society goods; born in Va., Aug. 13, 1867; daughter of Thornton Davis and Lydia G. (Ulivee) Hatchett; her mother was an Indian girl; ed. public schools in Va., and night school, New York; grad. in dressmaking, embroidery and designing from Trade School, New York; married at New York, Lucius A. de Toscano, of Havana, Cuba, Aug. 13, 1885 (died Aug. 25, 1893. Oldest society goods house conducted by colored people in New York; began business with husband, 1887, continuing under name of L. A. de Toscano Co., until after his death; now under name of Mrs. B. E. de Toscano; employes about 6 assistants on on average; has organized number of societies; presented plans for the Odd Fellows Home for Aged; was its first financial secretary; now president St. Luke Hall Committee; grand worthy recorder in America for Household of Ruth; member Order of Eastern Star, Order of Moses, Order of St. Luke. Episiopalian. Address: 222 W. 133d St., New York.

DETT, R. Nathaniel, composer, pianist; born at Drummondville, Ontario, Can., 1882; son of Robert Tue and Charlotte (Johnson) Dett; public school edn. Drummondville; grad. Niagara Falls (Ont.) Collegiate Institute, 1903; student Oliver Willis Halsted Conservatory of Music; Mus.B., Oberlin Conservatory of Music, 1908; unmarried. Organist of Liberty Church, Jackson, Tenn., 2 years; director of music, Lane College, Jackson, 1908-11, at Lincoln Institute, Jefferson City, Mo., 1911-13, and at Hampton Normal and Agricultural Institute, Hampton, Va., since 1913; director Hampton Choral Union; musical editor: The Hampton Student (magazine), Presbyterian. Member Musicians League of America; hon. member Sumner Literary Society (Hampton-Phoebus). Mason; member Knights of Pythias. Club: The Bachelors; hon. member Hampton Shakespeare and Dramatic, Sophoclean, and Hampton Institute Y. M. C. A. Author: The Album of a Heart (verse), 1911; composer: Magnolia Suite, part 1 and 2 for piano, 1912 (Clayton F. Summy Co., Chicago, Pubs.); In the Bottoms, suite for piano, 1913 (Summy Co.); Listen to the Lambs, a choral work (G. Schirmer, Inc., New York, pub.). Home: 362 Second St., Niagara Falls, N. Y. Address: Hampton Normal and Agricultural Institute, Hampton, Va.

DICKERSON, Earl Burrus, teacher; born at Canton, Miss., June 22, 1891; son of Edward and Emma Gertrude (Garrett) Dickerson; attended public schools, Canton; prep. edn. Evanston (Ill.) Academy (1909); student Northwestern Univ., 1909-10; A.B., Univ. of Illinois, Urbana, 1914; married Inez Camelia Moss, of Champaign, Ill., June 7, 1912. Began as teacher of English at Tuskegee, Ala., 1913, continuing 1 year; principal Colored High School, Vincennes, Ind., since 1914. Member Beta Chapter, Kappa Alpha Nu, at Univ. of Illinois. Home: 1227 Seminary St., Vincennes, Ind.

DICKERSON, John Henry, capitalist, clergyman; born at Madison, Fla., Sept. 14, 1864; son of George and Annie (Short) Dickerson; common school edn.; studied in Divinity Night School; (D.D., Wilberforce Univ., Ohio, 1906); married Fannie Sims, of Madison, Mar. 23, 1883; 1 child: Minnie Lee. Taught school in many of the important towns in Fla.; licensed to preach and was pastor in A. M. E. churches several years; pres. Central Building & Loan Assn.,

Jacksonville, since 1905; also pres. Negro Business League; vice-pres. State Negro Business League. Trustee Wilberforce Univ.; vice-pres. board of trustees Edward Walters College. Owns an orange orchard of 21 acres valued at $10,000; owner of other valuable property and is considered one of the most wealthy and substantial colored men in Jacksonville. Grand master of most worshipful Union Grand Lodge F. & A. M. of Florida since 1899; during his administration has given property to the order valued at $250,000, and built the Masonic Temple, costing above sum, which is the finest of the kind in the world owned by colored Masons. 33d degree Mason; member Knights of Pythias, Odd Fellows. Republican. Home: 706 De-witt St. Office: 410 Broad St., Jacksonville, Fla.

DICKERSON, Samuel Newton, druggist; born in Talladega Co., Ala., May 17, 1866; son of Samuel and Mattie (Montgomary) Dickerson; prep. edn. Talladega College; student, theol. dept., Talladega, 1897-1902; Ph.G., corr. course Ohio School of Pharmacy, 1910; married Alice Camp, of Talladega, Mar. 27, 1891. Began as painter Talladega, 1880, continuing employment to 1887; painting contractor 1887-1905; in drug business since Sept., 1905; pres. Highland Drug Co.; also pres. Farmers investment & Benevolent Co., Negro Business League. Trustee Colored Y. M. C. A. Republican. Baptist. Mason. Home: 160 Nolen St. Office 124 W. Battle St., Talladega, Ala.

DIGGS, Alberta Peck, teacher; born at Hinton, W. Va., Oct. 22, 1876; daughter of Erastus Garland and Anna Dora (Smithers) Peck; grad. Wayland Seminary, normal course, 1895; academic, Virginia Union Univ., Richmond, and State Univ., Louisville, Ky.; A.B., Selma Univ., Ala., 1912, A.M., 1914; married Prof. James R. L. Diggs, of Forrestville, Md., June 5, 1901; 5 children: Aurelia, Anna Garland, Lucile, Robert. Began teaching in public schools, Hinton, W. Va., 1895, continuing, with exception of

1897, to 1901; was teacher at Wayland Seminary, 1897, Washington, D. C.; assistant in Latin, State Univ., Louisville, Ky., 1907; substitute, and regular teacher of German, history and word-analysis, Selma Univ., Ala., 1913-14. Republican-Suffragette. Baptist. Member Selma Univ. Alumni Assn. President, Trinity Culture Club of Baltimore. Home: 713 Mosher St., Baltimore, Md.

DIGGS, Charles S., physician, surgeon; born at Tallula, Miss., Jan. 14, 1873; son of John and Ida Diggs; prep. edn. Natchez (Miss.) College; student Shaw Univ., Raleigh, N. C., 3 years; A.B., Lincoln (Pa.) Univ., 1898; M.D., Meharry Medical College (Walden Univ.) 1901; post-graduate work Post-Graduate Medical School and Hospital, Chicago, Ill.; married Lillie E. Alexander, of Nashville, Tenn., June 19, 1902; 2 children; Charles Herbert, Gwendolyn. Practiced in Waxahachie, Tex., since 1901; grand medical examiner Knights and Ladies of Harmony of the World; pres. Waxahachie Negro Business League. Republican. Missionary Baptist. Member Lone Star State Medical Assn., Knights of Pythias, American Woodmen, Ancient Order of Pilgrims. Address: 521 E. Main St., Waxahachie, Texas.

DIGGS, James Robert Lincoln, clergyman, university pres.; born at Upper Marlboro, Md., Nov. 7, 1866; son of John Henry and Mary Virginia (Clark) Diggs; grad. Wayland Seminary, Washington, D. C., normal dept., 1886, preparatory, 1894; also took theological course at Wayland; A.B., Bucknell Univ., Lewisburg, Pa., 1898, A.M., 1899; studied at Cornell Univ., 1902; Ph.D., Illinois Wesleyan Univ., Bloomington, 1906; is one of the 12 colored men that has earned degree of Doctor of Philosophy from a universitty in Northern states; one of the first honor men at Bucknell Univ.; was president Thata Alpha Literary Society in college, an editor of college publications, and twice represented Bucknell in successful inter-collegiate debates; won prize in Junior debate, 1907; married Alberta M.

Peck, of Hinton, W. Va., June 5, 1901; 5 children. Began as teacher in public schools of Md., 1889; elected professor of Latin and economics, Virginia Union Univ., 1890; professor of Latin and instructor in philosophy, 1903-6; president State Univ., Louisville, Ky., 1906-8, Virginia Seminary, 1908-11; dean of college and literary depts. Selma Univ., Ala., 1911-14; president Clayton-Williams Univ., Baltimore, Md., since 1914; pastor Trinity Baptist Church, Baltimore, since 1915. Republican. Member American Negro Academy, American Academy. Political and Social Science, American Geographical Society, National Association for Advancement of Colored People, Baltimore Association Advancement of Colored People, Bucknell College Alumni Assn., Virginia Union University Alumni Assn., Baltimore Forum. Home: 713 Mosher St., Baltimore, Md.

DILL, Augustus Granville, newspaper man.; born at Portsmouth, O., Nov. 30, 1881; son of John Jackson and Elizabeth (Stratton) Dill; A.B., Atlanta Univ., 1906, Harvard, 1908; A.M., Atlanta Univ., 1909; unmarried. Brothern secretary for Atlanta Univ., 1908-10, associate professor of sociology, 1910-13; business manager The Crisis, New York, since 1913. Joint editor following articles: The College Bred Negro American, 1911; The Common School and the Negro American, 1912; The Negro American Artisan, 1913; Morals and Manners Among Negro Americans, 1914. Address: 70 Fifth Ave., New York.

DILLARD, George T., clergyman; born in Fairfield Co., S. C., 1855; son of Thomas and Julia (Woodward) Dillard; normal school edn., Winnsboro, S. C.; B.D., Howard Univ. School of Theology, Washington, 1880; (hon. D.D., Biddle Univ., 1900); married Dora Eunice Russell, of Newberry, S. C., Feb. 8, 1912; 4 children: George E., W. L., Jennie V., Maud E. Ordained Presbyterian ministry, 1880; one of the two colored district superintendents of Sunday School work among Negroes in the South for the Presbyterian Church of the United

States of America; since that mission work began, 1890, more than 3,000 schools have been organized; out of them over 200 churches have grown. Address: 2019 Marion St., Columbia, S. C.

DIXON, Charles F., retired; born at Halifax, Nova Scotia, 1824; son of William A. and Annie (Taylor) Dixon; common school edn.; married Maria Ann Dilliver, of Nova Scotia, 1851; father of William, Charles, John, Henry, five girls, and George Dixon, noted as the most clever featherweight boxing champion in history. Worked at trade with largest cleavering concern in Nova Scotia for 40 years; was member the Victoria Rifles of Nova Scotia, which company once served as body guard to the Prince of Wales. Came to the U. S., 1888; was china and glassware packer with McKenna & Waterbury, Boston, Mass., for 19 years; retired. Baptist. Mason. Home: 20 Grove St., Boston, Mass.

(George Dixon is credited in the sporting annals with 145 battles of importance enough to record; the first of importance with Eugene Hornbacher in New York, Dec. 27, 1889, which he won easily in two rounds; others were as follows: "Cal" McCarthy, Feb. 7, 1890, draw after 70 rounds; "Nunc" Wallace, at Pelican Club, London, Eng., 1890; 40 rounds with John Murphy, Providence, R. I., Oct., 1890; defeated "Jack" Skelly 9 rounds, New Orleans, 1892; lost to Billy Plimmer, English bantamweight, in New York, Aug. 22, 1893; finally fell the victim of "Terrible Teddy" McGovern. His winnings were estimated at $100,000, but he was generous to a fault and immense sums of money melted away as fast as it came; when he died a leading newspaper in Boston said: "Those who knew the whitest little men with a black skin who ever drew on a boxing glove can record the passing of a favorite whose like will never be seen in the ring again; everybody swore by George Dixon.")

DODD, Jno. Horace, physician, surgeon; born at Dallas, Tex., Mar. 7,

1880; son of John Dodd; grad. Dallas High School, 1899; A.B., Howard Univ., Washington, D. C., 1905; M.D., Howard Univ. School of Medicine, 1909; married Mary Simmons, of Dallas, July 16, 1913. Practiced in Washington, 1909-10, at Dallas since 1910. Republican. Baptist. Member National Medical Assn., Lone Star Medical, Dental and Pharm. Assn. (sec. 2 years); also member Odd Fellows, Court of Calanthe, Knights of Pythias, Knights of Tabor. Home: 3109 State St. Office: 2604 Williams St., Dallas, Tex.

DODSON, Nathaniel Barnett, editor; born at Boydton, Va., Mar. 11, 1870; son of William A. and Lucy (Carnard) Dodson; grad. Boydton Institute, 1889, Wayland Seminary, Washington, D. C., 1891; continued studies in academic dept. Wayland, to 1892, and in Brooklyn, N. Y. to 1895; married Sarah Elizabeth Goode, of Boydton, May 4, 1898; 6 children: Lillian C., Nathaniel B. Jr., Evelyn L., Harold P., Edith K., Kenneth S. Teacher public schools, Shiloh, Va., 1886-7; elevator operator, old Pierrepont House, Brooklyn, summers, 1887, 9, and night clerk, 1891-3; manager grocery store, 1895-6; began as inside messenger and confidential man to pres. American Negro Press Assn., New York, 1897; for more than year urged officers of association to give illustrated weekly news service, which was finally inaugurated as Afro-American Page, 1909; since editor and manager of same; colored papers in 28 states receive this service. Contributor to Amsterdam News, New York Age. Chairman exec. com. National Negro Press Assn.; mem. exec. com. Brooklyn branch National Association for Advencement Colored People; secretary Northern Chapter, Alumni Assn. Virginia Union Univ., pres. N. E. Baptist Sunday School Convention; supt. Concord Baptist Sunday School, Brooklyn, since 1892; regarded authority on Sunday School problems and management; member com. of management Carlton Ave. branch of Brooklyn Y. M. C. A.; leader number movements in interest of young people. Member Society of Virginia (pres. 4 yeas). Home: 309 Berriman St., Brooklyn. Office: 225 W. 39th St., New York.

DOGAN, Matthew Winfred, university president; born at Pontotoc, Miss., Dec. 21, 1863; son of William and Jennie (Martin) Dogan; grad. Rust Univ., Miss., 1886 (Ph.D., 1904; D.D., New Orleans Univ., La., 1910); married Fannie Falkner, of Ripley, Miss., June 21, 1888; 5 children: Lucile, Clara, Ruth, Blanche, Matthew W. Jr. Teacher of mathematics, Walden Univ., Nashville, Tenn., 1890-6; pres. Wiley Univ., Marshall, Tex., since 1896. President Standard American Mutual Fire Ins. Co. Republican. Member board of education, M. E. Church; delegate to General Conference, 1904, 8, 12. President National Association Teachers' in Colored Schools, E. Tex. Colored Teachers' Assn; member Knights of Pythias. Address: Wiliy University, Marshall, Tex.

DONALDSON, John Isaiah, clergyman, superintendent blind institute; born in cabin at Clarksville, Tex., June 10, 1866; oldest of 10 children; son of Godfrey and Nancy Ann Donaldson; attended public schools of Paris, Tex., to 1885; student Talladega (Ala.) College, 1885-96, B.D., later; married Mrs. Katie Randolph Feaster, of Montgomery, Ala., Sept., 1890; 6 children: Allen F., Anna N., Ruth M., Mary B., Katie L., Isaiah T. Worked on farm, at carpentry, in iron furnace, brick yard, shoe making, house painting, upholstering, also teaching and preaching, to pay way through college; ordained Congregational ministry, 1896; pastor and teacher at Paris, Tex., 1896-9, Corpus Christi, 1899-1905; treasurer Tillotson College, Austin, Tex., 1908-13, also pastor there; superintendent Christi, 1899-1905; Dallas, 1905-8; treasurer Tillotson College, Austin, Tex., 1908-13, also pastor there; superintendent Texas Deaf and Dumb and Blind Institute for Colored Youth at Austin since Sept. 1, 1913. Moderator Texas Congregational Assn.; member

Texas State Teachers' Assn., also American Woodmen. Clubs: Talladega College; 20th Century (Austin). Address: Texas Deaf, Dumb and Blind Institute, Austin, Texas.

DONATTO, Dewey Benjamin, teacher; born at Opelousas, La.; son of Benjamin and Mary L. Donatto; ed. in public schools of Baton Rouge, La., and St. Joseph Institute, Opelousas; unmarried. Perfect of discipline at St. Joseph Institute for Colored Boys at Opelousas; manager St. Joseph Baseball Club. Member Knights of Peter Claver, an organization for Roman Catholic Men. Address: St. Joseph Institute, Opelousas, La.

DONES, Sidney Preston, real estate; born at Marshall, Texas, Feb. 18, 1889; son of Dr. Deltor and Lucy (Gray) Dones; ed. at Wiley Univ., Marshall; took course in law from LaSalle Extension Univ., Chicago; also course at National Business College, Los Angeles; married Bessie Williams, of Los Angeles, June 18, 1913; 1 child: Sidnetta. Resided in Los Angeles since 1900; was first colored man ever licensed as pawn broker in California; engaged in that business 2 years; real estate and insurance agent since 1907; president Sidney P. Dones Co.; has departments of real estate, law, fire and life insurance. Trustee 1st A. M. E. Church. Republican candidate for City Council, 1915. Member Dunbar Literary Society, Knights and Daughters of Africa. Clubs: Alhambra, Fred Douglass, Los Angeles Tennis. Home 1566 W. 37th St. Office: 411-415 Germain Bldg., Los Angeles, Calif.

DORSEY, Charles Marcellus, printer, publisher; born in Md., 1876; son of Daniel and Emily Dorsey; ed. public schools, Baltimore; married Mary Agnes Ireland, of Md., Sept. 12, 1900; 3 children: Irvin, Charles, John. Began as apprentice in printing business conducted by white people; learned the trade thoroughly and became foreman in composing room of the Baltimore Afro-American Ledger, later teacher of printing in St. Joseph's Industrial School, Clayton, Del., a Roman Catholic institution for colored boys; proprietor of printing house, Baltimore, since 1900; served as member the Grand Jury that investigated the most notorious election fraud in history of the state, Sept., 1911. Widely known in Roman Catholic Church circles; earnest and consistent agitator for the ordination of colored men to the priesthood. Republican. Address: 1310 N. Fremont Ave., Baltimore, Md.

DORSEY, Reverend Father John Henry, priest; born at Baltimore, Md., 1873; son of Daniel and Emmaline Dorsey; attended public schools, Baltimore; was baptised at St. Francis Xavier's, the oldest Catholic Church for colored people in Baltimore; his early desires to enter the priesthood were encouraged by the Very Reverend John R. Slattery who arranged for the first studies for the ministry; was under Most Rev. Archbishop John Ireland at St. Paul, Minn., 1888-9; grad. Epiphany College, under the Fathers of St. Joseph's Society for Colored Missions, Baltimore, 1893; in September, 1893, he matriculated for Colored Missions at St. Joseph's Seminary, Baltimore, but was forced to suspend studies on account of ill health; taught school at Richmond, Va., and Baltimore, 4 years; resumed studies in Sept., 1897; the students of St. Joseph's Seminary attended lectures at St. Mary's Sulpician Seminary, and there he made the course of philosophy and theology; received all degrees given by the seminary. Ordained to priesthood of the Roman Catholic Church at the Baltimore Cathedral by His Eminence James Cardinal Gibbons, June 21, 1902; was the second colored man ordained by the R. C. Church in the United States; celebrated his first Mass the next day, Sunday, June 22, at St. Francis Xavier's Church; was pastor of the Colored Catholic Church, Pine Bluff, Ark., 1 year; later perfect of studies at St. Joseph's College, Montgomery, Ala.; he is a Missionary Priest and now travels in the South visiting churches and schools; has preached in every southern city; director Knights of Peter Claver, a Roman Catholic society of colored people. Address: St. Joseph's Seminary, Baltimore, Md.

DORSEY, Joseph, editor; born at Baltimore, Md., May 30, 1863; son of Charles and Airy (Baker) Dorsey; public and normal school edn., Baltimore; married Mary Morris, of Frederick, Md., June 1, 1891; 4 children: Walter J., Charles M., Josephine, Margaret. Editor of The Crusader, a national weekly newspaper; has served in the capacity of publicity and newspaper man for number of candidates for office in various states; has wide acuaintance among public men in all parts of the country. Attended 7 Republican National Conventions. Methodist. Member number social and political clubs. Address: 1344 Stricker St., Baltimore, Md.

DOUGLASS, Joseph Henry, concert solist, violin instructor; born at Washington, D. C., July 3, 1871; son of Charles R. and Mary Elizabeth, and grandson of Frederick Douglass, the most notable American lecturer and journalist of African descent; ed. public schools, Washington and New York; grad. New England Conservatory of Music, Boston, Mass.; studied with European masters; married Fannie M. Howard, of Atlanta, Ga., 1907; 2 children: Blanche Elizabeth, Frederick III. Instructor on the violin at Howard Univ., Washington, number years; now concert soloist, making annual tours of the U. S.; regarded by leading newspaper musical critics as master of the violin; only colored violinist invited to make records for the Victor Talking Machine Co.; has composed number violin melodies including a romance "The Soul of the Violin." Home: 925 S Street, N. W., Washington, D. C.

DUMAS, Henry J., pharmacist; born at Houma, La., 1875; attended school in Terrebonne Parish; grad. Houma Academy, 1896; Pharm.B., Meharry Medical College (Walden Univ.), Nashville, Tenn., 1901. Soon after graduation joined his brother, Dr. A. W. Dumas, at Natchez, Miss., where he has since engaged in business. Address: Natchez, Miss.

DOWNING, Lilburn Liggins, clergyman; born at Lexington, Va., May 3, 1862; son of Lilburn and Ellen (Harvey) Downing; A.B., Lincoln Univ., Pa., 1885, S.T.B., A.M., 1894 (D.D., 1906); married Lottie J. Clinton, of Atlantic City, N. J., June, 1888. Instructor in Greek and Latin, prep. dept., Lincoln Univ., 2 years; ordained Presbyterian ministry, 1894; since pastored in Roanoke, Va.; chaplain, grand staff council, Odd Fellows; moderator Presbytery of Southern Va.; was commissioner to Gen. Assembly Presbyterian Church of America, 3 times; delegate to National Educational Assn., 3 times; director Viaduct Tailoring Co. Only colored member Roanoke City Republican Committee; delegate to state convention 4 times. Mason; deputy grand master Grand Lodge of Va.; district grand master District Grand Lodge No. 15, Odd Fellows. Club: Business Men's, of Roanoke (mem. exec. com.). Address: 236 Patton Ave. N. W., Roanoke, Va.

DOXEY, Freeman B., barber, owner theatre; born at Nashville, Tenn., Feb. 6, 1864; son of Louis and Amanda (Miller) Doxey; public school edn., Nashville; married Sallie P. Harvey, of Henderson, Ky., 1884; 1 child: Arthur; 2d marriage, Mary Snipes, of Henderson, May 24, 1907. Began business in Henderson, 1880, and has since conducted leading barber shop and bath room in city; proprietor Doxey Theatre; only moving picture house conducted by colored person in vicinity; owns house and other property. Trustee A. M. E. Zion Church. Mason; past master local lodge; delegate to Grand Lodge of Ky., several times; past chancellor Knights of Pythias. Home: 210 Elm St. Office: 105 Main St., Henderson, Ky.

DREW, Howard Porter, student, athlete; born at Lexington, Va., June 28, 1890; son of David Henry and May E. (Mackey) Drew; grad. Springfield (Mass.) High School, 1913; studied at Lincoln Univ., Pa., 1 year; student Univ. of Southern Calif. Law School, 1913—; married Ethel Hawkins, of Springfield, Mass., Apr. 2, 1908; 2 children: David Henry, Barbara Hope. Was captain High School Track Team, Springfield, Mass., 1912; member American Olympic Team at Stockholm, Sweden, 1912; won heats in race of 100 metres, but prevented from finishing thru injury; won 50 yard dash in 5 2-5 seconds, New York; 60 yards, 6 2-5 seconds, Patterson, N. J., 61 yards, 6 2-5, Elizabeth, N. J., 1913; these records were not allowed by A. A. officials; won 75 yard dash in 7 3-5 seconds, Madison Square Garden, 70 yards, 7 1-5 seconds. New York, 1913; won 100 yard dash in 9 3-5 seconds, Berkeley, Calif., 120 yards, 11 3-5, Providence, R. I., 220 yards, 21 1-5 seconds, Pomona, Calif., 1914; has won several national championships and equaled records for distances ranging from 50 to 220 yards; assistant manager of athletes Univ. of Southern California, 1915; sporting editor university paper. Republican. Baptist. Member Skull and Dagger Fraternity of Univ. of Southern Calif. Mason. Club: Los Angeles Athletic. Address: University of Southern California, College of Law, Los Angeles, Calif.

DRURY, Theodore, singer, music promoter; born in Kentucky. Teacher in Boston, Mass., for number of years; in addition to vocal and piano classes, he teaches elocution, French conversation, etc.; produced with a colored company Bizet most famous grand Opera Carmen, 1900; that has been followed each year by such operas at Faust, Aida, Pagliaccia and Cavalleria Rusticiana; filled 2 weeks engagements in New York City at first theaters giving such operas as Carmen and Aida. Address: 20 Kendall St., Boston, Mass.

DuBOIS, William Edward Burghardt, editor; born at Great Barrington, Mass., Feb. 23, 1868; son of Alfred and Mary (Burghardt) DuBois; A.B., Fisk Univ., 1888; A.B., Harvard, 1890, A.M., 1891, Ph.D., 1895; post grad work Univ. of Berlin, Germany; married Nina Gomer, of Cedar Rapids, Ia., May 12, 1896; 1 child: Yolande. Editor of the Atlanta University Studies (15 vol.), 1898-1914; editor The Crisis, New York, since 1910; director of publicity and research National Association for Advancement Colored . People. Fellow American Association Advancement of Science. Mason. Clubs: Liberal (New York), Royal Societies (London, Eng.). Author: The Slave Trade, 1896; The Philadelphia Negro, 1899; Souls of Black Folks, 1903; John Brown, 1909; The Quest of the Silver Fleece, 1914; History of the Negro Race, 1915. Address: 70 Fifth Ave., New York.

DUDLEY, James Benson, educator; born at Wilmington, N. C., Nov. 2, 1859; son of John Bishop and Annie (Hatch) Dudley; ed. public schools, Wilmington; Institute for Colored Youth, Philadelphia, Pa.; student Shaw Univ., Raleigh, N. C.; (A.M., Livingstone College, 1897; LL.D., Wilberforce Univ., 1900); married Susie W. Sampson, of Wilmington, Feb. 23, 1884; 2 children: Vivian, Inez. Principal Peabody Graded School, Wilmington, 1880-96; president Agrircultural and Mechanical College, Greensboro, N. C., since 1896; also pres. N. C. Association of Negro Teachers, Inter Church Association for Negroes; advisory mem. board of directors Inter Church Assn. for white people; chairman board of trustees National Religious Training School; sec-treas. Pioneer Building and Loan Assn.; was founder. Trustee several schools. Methodist. Mason; member Knights of Pythias, Odd Fellows. Home: 327 Dudley St. Office: Agricultural & Technical College, Greensboro, N. C.

DUNBAR, Alice Ruth Moore, teacher, author; born at New Orleans, La., July 19, 1875; daughter of Joseph and Patricia (Wright) Moore; prep. edn. Straight Univ., New Orleans; student: Univ. of Pa.; Cornell Univ.; Columbia Univ.; School of Industrial Art, Philadelphia; made special study of English, history, philosophy, drawing; married Paul Laurence Dunbar, of Dayton, O., Mar. 6, 1893 (died 1906); he was the most noted author born of Negro descent; his works include:

Oak and Ivy Poems, 1893; Majors and Minors, 1895; Lyrics of Lowly Life, 1896; Folks from Dixie, short stories, 1898; The Uncalled, novel, 1898; Lyrics of the Hearthside, 1899; Poems of Cabin and Field, 1899; The Strength of Gideon, short stories, 1900; The Love of Landry, novel, 1900; The Sport of the Gods, novel, 1901; The Fanatics, novel, 1901; Candle Lightin' Time, poems, 1902; Lyrics of Love and Laughter, poems, 1903; Heart of Happy Hollow, short stories, 1904; Li'l Gal, poems, 1904; Lyrics of Sunshine and Shadow, 1905; Howdy, Honey, Howdy, 1905. Mrs. Dunbar has taught in schools as follows: New Orleans, 1893-6; Brooklyn, N. Y., 1897-8; Hampton Institute, summer school, Va., 1903-4; State College, summer school, Dover, Del., 1908, 09, 10, 11, 13, 14; National Religious Training School, Durham, N. C., summer, 1912; teacher in Howard High School, Wilmington, Del., since 1912. Vice- pres. Douglass Publishing Co., Harrisburg, Pa., publs. Masterpieces of Negro Eloquence, of which she was editor. Author: Violets and Other Tales, 1895; Goodness of St. Rocque, 1899; The Negro in Louisiana, 1914. Contributor to London Academy, Lippincott's, McClures, Leslie's Weekly, Good Housekeeping, New York Mail, New York Sun, Boston Transcript, Chicago Herald, New York Age, the Crisis, and Education. Episcopalian. Member Negro Society for Historical Research, Woman's Auxiliary, Teachers' Beneficial Assn. Club: Suffrage Study. Address: 916 French St., Wilmington, Del.

DUNBAR, Reberta Johnson, club woman, organizer; born at Narragansett Pier, R. I.; daughter of John Daniel and Louisa (Cartwright) Dunbar; grad. English High School, Providence, R. I. Was president the North Eastern Federation of Woman's Clubs, 1902-5, organizer since 1905; makes annual tour through New England and Middle Atlantic states lecturing among women in interest of club work; her work in 10 years brought into the federation about 85 clubs and 3,000 members; president Woman's New Century Club of Providence, which founded a Home for Working Girls; 3d recording sec. National Association of Colored Women; member local council of Rhode Island Women, and Rhode Island Union of Colored Women. Dressmaker, manicure, masseur, and hair specialist. Free Baptist. Home: 58 Winter St., Providence, R. I.

DUNCAN, Sallie L., secretary, editor; born at Wetumpka, Ala., Mar. 18, 1877; daughter of Alexander and Caroline (Robinson) Gaston; public school edn; married J. Arthur Duncan, of Montgomery, Ala., July, 1900.' Taught in public schools, Ala., more than 20 years; secretary United Order of Good Shepherd's since 1906, also associate editor and business mgr. Good Shepherd's Magazine; secretary Woman's Spring Hill District Assn.; member Order Eastern Star. Missionary Baptist. Home: 132 Clay St. Office: 825 E. Grove St., Montgomery, Ala.

DUNGEE, John Riley, teacher; born in King William Co., Va., Apr. 16, 1860; son of Jesse and Mary James (Custello) Dungee; prep. edn. Hampton Normal and Agricultural Institute, Va.; LL.B., Howard Univ. Law School, 1888; (A.M., Kittrell College, 1914); married Flossie Bell Wingfield, of Lynchburg, Va., Aug. 27, 1896. Admitted to Va. bar, 1889; practiced in West Point, 1889-91; began as teacher, Roanoke, Va., 1893, continuing as principal to 1905; principal Abraham Lincoln School, Norfolk, since 1905. Presbyterian. Address: 1480 Dungee St., Norfolk, Va.

DUNSTON, Mary Alice Jackson, teacher, verse writer; born at Wilmington, N. C.; daughter of George H. and Frances Stanly (Sampson) Jackson; grand-daughter of Rev. John D. Sampson, contractor, advance thinker, and wealthy freedman; ed. in native city and Boston, Mass.; married Dr. Charles A. Dunston (dentist), Raleigh, N. C., Sept. 14, 1911. Taught in public school in Wilmington several years; teacher in Summer School for Teachers' at A. & M., Col-

lege, Greensboro, N. C.; teacher of speech State Institute for Deaf and Dumb and Blind, Raleigh, N. C., 1907-14; has written number peoms; was chairman Woman's Aid Dept. which assisted the N. C. Medical, Dental and Pharm. Assn. in entertaining delegates to convention of National Negro Medical Assn., at Raleigh, 1914. Address: 220 E. Davis St., Raleigh, N. C.

DUNWOOD, Presley, retired; born in Clark Co., Va., 1844; taken from his mother when 1 year old; was "hired out" at age of seven; never attended school. Worked for Isaac Gantz, 1851-2; hired to Henry Hose, Perrysville, Va., 1853-4, Henry Hess, Loudoun Co., 1856-7; fell to ownership of Judge Richard Parker, Winchester, Va., 1857, who had judicial charge courts of Jefferson and Frederick counties; here had opportunity to witness much that is now important history of the war between the states; drove Judge Parker to the court each day during the trial of John Brown and his men, 1859; following the hanging of Brown, slaves were sold rapidly until the election of Abraham Lincoln; he was pressed into the Confederate army at the beginning of the war and served with that army in first battle of Bull Run; captured by a company of the 46th Pa. Vols.; was in the battle at Cedar Mountain, in Union army, also 2d battle of Bull Run; saw much of the fight at Antietam; went to Pittsburgh, Pa., with Capt. Benjamin W. Morgan after the war and worked for him; brought mother to Pittsburgh, 1868, and cared for her during life; after her death removed to Lisbon, O.; resided in Alliance since 1912. Address: Alliance, Ohio.

DYSON, Walter, university professor; born at Paris, Ill., Sept., 1882; son of Nathaniel and Elvira (Mitchem) Dyson; A.B., Fisk Univ., 1903, Yale, 1905; A.M., Univ. of Chicago, 1913; grad. student in history and economics, Columbia Univ., New York, 1914-15; unmarried. Teacher in public schools, Paris, Ill., number years; associate professor of history, Howard Univ., Washington, D. C., since 1905. Member History Teachers' Assn. of the Middle States and Md.; also member National Association for Advancement of Colored People. Mason (past master Prince Hall Lodge No. 14, Washington, D. C.,). Author: Syllabus of United States History, 1908; History Textbook Review Chart, 1912; The District of Columbia in the Civil War, 1913. Address: Howard University, Washington, D. C.

E

EASTER, Benjamin Franklin, physician, surgeon; born at Waco, Texas, Dec. 17, 1875; son of Pope and Annie (McCrary) Easter; grad. high school at Waco, 1890; prep. edn. Bishop College, Marshall, Tex.; Ph.G., Meharry Medical College (Walden Univ.), Nashville, Tenn., 1896, M.D., 1903; married Evelyn Blanchet, of New Iberia, La., Apr. 19, 1899; 1 child: Benjamin F. Jr. Pharmacist in Louisiana and Texas, 1896-1901; first Negro to pass La. Board of Pharmacy; practiced medicine and surgery in New Iberia since 1903. Was representative from New Iberia during Dr. Booker T. Washington tour of state; treasurer local Negro Business League. Republican. Baptist. Mason; chairman railroad and transportation committee Grand Lodge, and past chancellor, Knights of Pythias; member Odd Fellows, Wise Men and Women of the World, also Tabernacle. Address: 514 Bank Ave., New Iberia, La.

EASTON, William Edgar, newspaper man; born, New York, Mar. 19, 1861; son of Charles F. and Maria (Legett) Easton; descended from Hosea Easton of the American revolution, or mother's side from Gen. Octave Oliviers of the Haitain revolution; ed. public schools, New Bedford, Mass., La Salle Academy, Providence, R. I., Seminary Trois Rivieres, Quebec, Canada., St. Cesaire College, Canada; married Mary Elizabeth Thornton, of Austin, Tex., Aug. 7, 1888; 4 children: Athenaise M. (Mrs. Geo. J. Talbot), Berenice L. (Mrs. Andrew F. Summers), William E. Jr., Dorothy I. Teacher in public schools of Tex., 1885; later followed newspaper and engaged in political work; secretary Republican State Central Committee, Austin, Tex., 12 years; first pres. Colored State Press Assn.; chairman Travis County Republican Committee 2 terms; editor Texas Blade, Austin, 1885-9; storekeeper U. S. Custom House, Galveston, Tex., 1889-93; clerk in police dept., San Antonio, 1894-9; removed to Los Angeles, Cal., 1901; cashier Green Chili Packing Co., 1903; accountant in tax collectors office during several collecting periods; first colored field deputy in city and county assessors office; prepares papers for public speakers; special newspaper correspondent; publicity man for The New Age (illustrated weekly journal) since 1911. Republican. Catholic. Qualified by birth and applicant for membership, 1914, Sons of American Revolution. Author: Dessalines (historical drama of Haiti), 1893; Christiphi (4-act tragedy), 1912; Is She a Lady in the Underworld, and Misery in Bohemia (1-act sketches). Home: 442 E. 30th St. Office: 829 San Pedro St., Los Angeles, Cal.

EDMISTON, Althea Maria Brown, missionary; A.B.., Fisk Univ., Nashville, Tenn., 1901; grad. Missionary Training School, Chicago, Ill., 1902; married Alonzo L. Edmiston; missionary under Southern Presbyterian Board of Missions. Address: Danj, Congo Belge, Africa, via Antwerp.

EDWARDS, Abner Beecher, supervising industrial teacher; born at Salem, Lee Co., Ala., June, 1870; son of Phillip and Mary Ann (Dawkins) Edwards; attended public schools near Salem and at Opelika, Ala.; grad. Tuskegee Normal and Industrial Institute, 1892; unmarried. Began as teacher in schools near Salem, 1889; taught in public schools, Russell Co., Ala., 6 years; principal Salem District School 14 years, Phoenix City School, Ala., 6 years; supervisor of Negro Rural Schools in Lee County since Oct. 1, 1914; there are 22 supervising industrial teachers in this branch of instruction under the State Board of Education; aided by the Anna T. Jeanes Fund the system reaches the most remote schools and homes in the state; children are taught to mend, sew, cook, to be economical and self-supporting. Methodist. Mason; member Odd Fellows. Address: Phoenix City, Ala.

EDWARDS, Samuel Lewis, dentist; born at Anderson, S. C., Jan. 9, 1877; son of John Lewis and Nancy (Jones) Edwards; public school edn., Anderson; grad. Knox Institute, Athens, Ga., 1902; D.D.S., Meharry Medical College (Walden Univ.), Nashville, Tenn, 1906; married Zadie M. Chancellor, of Anderson, Nov. 16, 1910. Began practice in McMinnville, Tenn., 1906; was demonstrator in mechanical dentistry, Meharry Dental College, 1907-8; practiced in Anderson since July, 1908. Republican. Baptist. Dental secretary National Medical Assn; member and former vice-pres. Palmetto Medical Assn, of S. C. Address: 206 W. Market St., Anderson, S. C.

EICHELBERGER, James W. Jr., educator, editor; born at Columbia, S. C., Aug. 30, 1886; son of James W. and Josephine (Myers) Eichelberger; grad. normal dept. Allen Univ., Columbia, 1900; A.B., Livingstone College, Salisbury, N. C., 1904; married Hattie B. Miller, of Warren, Ark., Aug. 30, 1911. Began as teacher in Clinton College, Rock Hill, S. C., 1904, continuing to 1907; editor Sunday School Headlight, Rock Hill, 1906-8; prin. Walters Institute, Warren, Ark., since 1909; editor and mgr. The School Herald; mgr. Herald Pub. Co. President Warren Reading Research Club; trustee Walters Institute, and Temperance Commission of the Federal Council of Churches in Christ in America; founded the Civic League in Warren. Delegate to World's Sunday School Convention at Rome, Italy, 1907, Washington, D. C., 1910, Zurich, Switzerland, 1913; delegate to International Sunday School Convention, Toronto, Ont., 1905, Louisville, Ky., 1908, and Chicago, Ill., 1914; as member A. M. E. Zion General Conference,

1908, inaugurated a reform movement in Sunday School Dept. of the church which has grown to larger proportions each year; member General Conference of A. M. E. Zion Church, 1912. Appointed by acting Gov. J. M. Futrell as member committee of 10 to represent Arkansas at the Pennsylvania Semi-Centennial Emancipation Celebration, 1913. Republican. Mason; member Knights of Pythias. Address: Walters Institute, Warren, Ark.

ELLIS, George Washington, lawyer, author; born at Weston, Platte Co., Mo., May 4, 1875; son of George and Amanda Jane (Drace) Ellis; grad. Atkinson (Kan.) High School, 1891; LL.B., Univ. of Kansas., 1893; while practicing law studied 4 years in collegiate dept. Univ. of Kan.; postgraduate studies, philosophy and psychology, 2 years, at Howard Univ., Washington; grad. Gunton's Institute of Economics and Sociology, New York, 1900; grad. from school of stenography and typewriting, 1902; married. Passed examination and appointed clerk in bureau of the census Dept. of Commerce, Washington, 1900; was secretary America legation to Republic of Liberia, 1902-10; practiced law in Chicago since 1910; contributing editor Journal of Race Development issued by Clark Univ.; has large collection of ethnological specimens loaned to the National Museum at Washington; elected pres. Chicago branch National Independent Equal Rights League, Jan. 3, 1915; campaign speaker and director colored western bureau of National Progressive Headquarters at Chicago, 1912. African Methodist. Fellow Royal Geographical Society, Great Britain; member African Society (London), American Academy Political and Social Science, American Political Science Assn., American Sociological Society, American Society of International Law, Cook County Bar Assn. (secretary); hon. member Luther Burbank Society. Decorated Knight Commander Order African Redemption. Author: Negro Culture in West Africa; Liberia in the Political Psychology of West Africa; Dynamic Factors in the Liberian Situation; Islam as a Factor in West African Culture; Political Institutions in Liberia; Education in Liberia; Justice in the West African Jungle; The Psychology of American Race Prejudice. Home: 3262 Vernon Ave. Office: 3000 State St., Chicago, Ill.

ELMORE, Cornelia Sylvester, supervising industrial teacher; born at Stockton, Ala., Aug. 25, 1868; daughter of Jim and Nellie (Moore) Sylvester; public school edn., Mobile, Ala.; took teachers' course in Tuskegee Institute, summer schools; married Oliver Charles Elmore, of Meridian, Miss., Aug. 22, 1883; 6 children: James Sylvester, Oliver, Clemmie, Nellie Lee, Mae Belle, Roxana. Teacher in public schools of Alabama since 1880; was first to teach free-hand drawing and painting in schools of Monroe and Baldwin counties; taught for a secluded number of original white people that had married and intermarried foreigners; supervising industrial teacher in Negro Rural Schools, Baldwin County, since Oct. 1, 1911. Was director Monroe County Institute, 1887-1907; chairman Techers' Reading Circle of Baldwin County. Owns 80 acres farm land. Missionary Baptist. Home: Atmore, Escambia County. Office: Bay Minette, Baldwin County, Ala.

ELMORE, Virginia Anita, supervising industrial teacher; born in Montgomery Co., Ala., Oct. 14, 1888; daughter of Stephen and Lena (Hamilton) Elmore; grad. State Normal School, Montgomery, 1908; summer courses for teachers at Tuskegee Normal and Industrial Institute. Began as teacher in Montgomery County schools, 1908; now supervising industrial teacher Negro Rural Schools of Calhoun County, Ala.; this branch of public instruction is under the State Department of Education; aided by the Anna T. Jeanes Fund the work of 22 supervisors in the state reaches the most remote schools and homes. Baptist. Member Alabama State Teachers' Assn. Club: Young Ladies Art. Home: R. F. D. 2, Box 9, Montgomery. School Address: Anniston, Ala.

EMBRY, Julia A., writer, lecturer; born at Glasgow, Mo., June 12, 1875; daughter of Stockley and Levie (White) Johnson; ed. public schools, Denver, Colo., and Henegar's Business College, Colorado Springs; married Frank E. Embry, of Richmond, Ky., Oct. 24, 1896. Began as newspaper correspondent, Colorado Springs, 1895; contributor to Denver Statesman, The Freeman, Colorado Springs Gazette; organized Langston Literary Society, San Diago, Cal., 1898; an organizer of Tanner Lyceum, Manitou, Colo., and pres., 1899-1906; also a organizer of Embry Mission; recording secretary Negro National Educational Congress 2 years; with the Colorado Springs Eagle, 1910, 1912-13, and first colored woman editor in state. Progressive; in charge party headquarters for colored voters, Colorado Springs, 1912; political speaker during several campaigns in Utah and Colo. African Methodist. Address: 802 N. Walnut St., Colorado Springs, Colo.

EUROPE, James Reese, musician. Leader of National Negro Orchestra; president Tempo Club, musicial organization. Composer: Benefactors, Strength of the Nation, etc. Address: 61 W. 131st St., New York.

F

FARMER, Walter Moran, lawyer; born at Brunswick, Mo., Jan. 16, 1865; son of Asa and Lucretia (Ford) Farmer; preparatory edn. Lincoln Institute, Jefferson City, Mo.; LL.B., Washington Univ., St. Louis, Mo., 1889, and first colored man to graduate from that institution; unmarried. Admitted to Missouri bar, 1889; practiced in St. Louis to 1905; was candidate for assistant prosecuting attorney, 1900; served as special commissioner for Circuit Court; first colored lawyer to argue case before Missouri Supreme Court; attorney in Duncan murder case, which was appealed to U. S. Supreme Court; practiced in Chicago since 1905. Delegate to Republican National Conventions, St. Louis, 1896, Philadelphia, 1900, Chicago, 1904; member speakers bureau of Republican National Committee in charge of work among colored voters, 1908. Baptist. Member Knights of Pythias, True Reformers, United Brothers of Friendship. Home: 4832 Langley Ave. Office: 184 W. Washington St., Chicago, Ill.

FAUSTINA, Gilbert, manufacturer; born at New Orleans, La., Oct. 27, 1897; son of Angeline Faustina; was 9 years old when his mother died; self-educated; married Susie Ritter, of Stockton, Ala., Oct. 25, 1899; 8 children. Began in cigar business in 1902 with capital of $50; now operates factory and has accumulated comfortable fortune, largely invested in real estate; organized (1909) and now supreme knight of the Knights of Peter Claver, a Catholic society for colored people. Office and Factory: Rylands Lane and Basil St., Mobile, Ala.

FELTON,, William C., business man; born at Macon, Ga., June 3, 1869; son of James and Eliza Felton; common school edn.; (Mus.D., Princeton Normal and Industrial Univ., Ind.); married Mattie Terrell, of Aberdeen, Miss., June 7, 1899. Began in grocery business at Macon, 1889; proprietor barber shop, Charleston, Mo., 1895-9; removed to Mt. Vernon, Ind., 1899; since proprietor Blue Front Hotel and Restaurant, owns barber shop connected with hotel; operates skating rink in Felton's Hall; conducts pool room as member firm of Felton & Morris; manufactures Boss Liniment; business manager The Orphan, a periodical; invented improvement on tongs used by oyster men. Was band master Georgia Cadet Band; has played in minstrel bands; now master Butler's Brass Band, Mt. Vernon. Delegate to Masonic Congress, Jamestown, Va., 1904, and 10 times to state conclaves; negotiated purchase of Masonic building in Mt. Vernon and presented with cane by local lodges, worthy master Walden Lodge No. 17.

Republican. Address: Blue Front Hotel, 109 Main St., Mt. Vernon, Ind.

FERGUSON, David Arthur, dentist; born at Portsmouth, O., June 8, 1875; son of William B. and Cornelia Francis (Taylor) Ferguson; ed. public schools, Bowling Green, Ky., to 1889; grad. high school, Portsmouth, 1896; D.D.S., Howard Univ. Dental College, 1899; married Antoinette V. Carter, of Washington, D. C., Nov. 20, 1897; 2 children: Arthur Wilfred, Irma Vivian. Apprentice in dental office of Dr. E. T. Barr, Bowling Green, 1889-92, at wages of $1.50 per month; with Dr. C. P. Dennis, Portsmouth, 1892-6; assistant to demonstrators in dental laboratories of Howard Univ.,· also assistant to 7 dentists in Washington; practiced in Richmond, Va., since 1899; was first colored applicant before Va. state board of dental examiners; sec.-treas. and instructor of anatomy and physiology, Richmond Hospital and Training School for Nurses; director Tidewater Fair Assn., Suffolk, Va.; vice pres. National Medical Assn., 1912-13; pres. Tri-State Dental Assn. of D. C., Md. and Va., 2 terms, 1913-15. Member Civic Improvement League, Citizens Business Club. Address: First and Marshall Sts., Richmond, Va.

FERGUSON, Horace Stephen, restaurateur; born at Lebanon, O., June 19, 1870; son of John C. and Emeline (Brown) Ferguson; grad. grammar school, Lebanon; student normal dept. Wilberforce Univ., 2 years; unmarried. Began in small up-stair restaurant, St. Louis, Mo., Sept. 12, 1904; employed 3 persons and done $5,400 gross business first year; with 6 restaurants and one general store, July to July, 1913-14, gross business amounted to $61,000; employed 52 persons to whom paid wages exceeding $18,000; prop. St. Louis Delicatessen Co., conducting the Quality Cafe, Cozy Corner, Gem Lunchery, Ferguson's Dairy Lunch, Silver Grill; vice-pres. New Era Building & Loan Assn. Republican. Member St. Louis Negro Business Men's League (former treas.). Home: 2803 Pine St. Office: 2321 Market St., St. Louis, Mo.

FERGUSON, Samuel David, bishop; born at Charleston, S. C., Jan. 1, 1842; son of Edward and Roseine Elizabeth Ferguson; emigrated with parents to Liberia, W. Africa, 1848; ed. in schools there; (D.D., Kenyon, 1885; D.C.L., Liberia College, 1893) married Mary L. Montgomery, 1863 (deceased); 2d marriage, Sarah E. Brown, 1879. Appointed teacher, 1862, deacon, 1865, priest, 1868, P. E. Church; elected missionary bishop to Cape Palmas and adjacent regions in W. Africa by the House of Bishops assembled in New York, 1885; is only African ever raised to episcopate of P. E. Church of America. Address: Monrovia, Liberia, West Africa.

FERNANDIS, Sarah ↘Collins, social worker; born at Port de Posit, Md., Mar. 8, 1863; daughter of Caleb Alexander and Mary Jane (Driver) Collins; grad. Hampton Normal and Agricultural Institute, 1882; student New York School of Philanthrophy, summer, 1906; married John A. Fernandis, of Baltimore, Md., June 30, 1902. Teacher under American Missionary Assn. in public schools of Va., Tenn., Ga., Fla., number years; later in Baltimore; organized first social settlement for colored people in Washington, D. C., 1903, in E. Greenwich, R. I., 1908; gen.-sec. of committee organized for social service in Baltimore, 1912; organizer and exec. sec. Woman's Cooperative Civic League of Baltimore, 1913. Methodist. Contributor to The Survey, of New York, special articles on social conditions among colored people. Address: 953 Druid Hill Ave., Baltimore, Md.

FERRIS, William Henry, clergyman, lecturer, writer; born at New Haven, Conn., July 20, 1874; son of David H. and Sarah Ann (Jefferson) Ferris; father was born of free parents in N. Y. state and Vol. in Union Army when 17 years of age; on mother's side Grandfather Jefferson escaped from slavery and afterwards bought wife and two children; A.B., Yale, 1895, A.M., 1899; student Harvard Divinity School, 1897-9; A.M., Harvard, 1900; unmarried. Writer and lecturer since 1895; was teacher in Tallahassee State College, also Florida Baptist College, 1900-1; worked for newspapers, 1902-3; teacher in Kittrell College and Henderson Normal School, N. C., 1903-5, and pastor Christ Congregational Church, 1904-5; in charge colored missions of A. M. E. Zion Church, Lowell and Salem, Mass., and lectured in white churches, 1910-12. Republican. Methodist. Was member Boston Browning Society number years; first colored man received in that literary organization; member Negro Society for Historical Research. Author: Typical Negro Traits, 1908; The African Abroad, 1913. Address: 98 Henry St., New Haven, Conn.

FIELDS, Elijah H., real state; born at Greensboro, Ala., Mar. 19, 1874; son of John H. and Carrie (Taylor) Fields; self-educated; married Zela Herman, of Florence, Ala., Dec. 9, 1908; 2 children: Harris W., Elijah H. Manager Alabama Amusement Co., Sheffield, since 1912; director Alabama Penny Savings Bank, Billup's Mfg. Co.; undertaker; also in real estate business since 1904. Congregationalist. Mason; member Knights of Pythias. Address: Box 271, Sheffield, Ala.

FIELDS, John Charles, clergyman; born at Buford, Ohio; preparatory edn. State Univ., Louisville, Ky.; A.B., Roger Williams Univ., Nashville, Tenn.; B.D., Fisk Univ., 1909; married, June 30, 1903. Missionary Baptist; pastor Pleasant Green Church, Nashville; professor ↗ Roger Williams Univ. President Stone River Sunday School Convention; secretary endownment bureau Roger Williams Univ. Alumni; member National Baptist Publishing Board, Knights of Pythias, United Order of Willing Workers. Home 2030 Jefferson St., Nashville, Tenn.

FISHER, Charles Lewis, clergyman; born in St. Bernard Parish, La., Feb. 16, 1866; son of Alexander and Elizabeth (Love) Fisher; A.B., Leland Univ., New Orleans, La., 1884; B.D., Union Theological Seminary, 1887; (A.M., Leland Univ., 1892, D.D., 1912); married Rosa J. Richardson, of Hammer, Ala., Apr. 20, 1893; children: Gertrude, Mamie Ruth, Annie, Rosa, Cynthia, Charles, Theodore, Mildred, Albert. Ordained Baptist minstry, 1887; student pastor Evanston, Ill., 1 year; teacher at Selma Univ., Ala., 1889-98; pastor 16th Street Church, Birmingham, Ala., 1898-1911, Franklin Street Church, Mobile, Ala., since 1912. Was president 3 years, now part owner Quick Printing Co., Birmingham; edited Baptist Leader 3 years; editor and mgr. Sparks Magazine. Chairman board trustees Selma Univ.; chairman executive committee of trustees Cedar Grove Academy. Republican. Mason; member Knights of Pythias. Author: Social Evils. Home: 256 N. Franklin St., Mobile, Ala.

FISHER, Elijah John, clergyman; born at La Grange, Ga., Aug. 2, 1858; son of Miles and Charlotte (Amos) Fisher; grad. La Grange Seminary, 1879, Atlanta Baptist College, 1890; student in Greek and Hebrew, Univ. of Chicago, 1902-3; (LL.D., Guadalupe College, 1912); married Florida Neely, of La Grange, Sept. 25, 1877; 5 children: S. Mattie, Elijah Jr., James E., Charlotte E., Miles M. Spent early life on father's farm, later in grocery store and drug business, La Grange; teacher in school at Hickory Flat, Ala., 1 year, La Grange Seminary, 6 years. United with Baptist Church, 1863; pastored at La Grange, Ga., Anniston, Ala., Atlanta, Ga., and Nashville, Tenn., before settling in Chicago; built churches at Ragland, Macedonia, Atlanta, Ga.; rebuilt Spruce Street Church edifice, Nashville, Tenn.; completed Olivet Church building, Chicago, Ill., at cost of $46,000. Was moderator Western Union Baptist Assn., 6 years; pres. exec. board Baptist State Convention, Ga., 8 years; pres. Western Baptist Convention, 2 years; General State Baptist Convention, 2 years; vice-pres. National Bapt. Convention, 10 years; dean, 1887-9, pres., 1912-14, Chicago Religious Training Seminary; pastor Olivet Missionary Baptist Church, Chicago, since 1902; chairman Co-operative Board between white and colored Baptists of Chicago, 1914; sec.-treas. Mt. Forest Cemetery Assn.; sec. R. W. Christian Church Furnishing Co.; trustee Bryant's Preparatory School, Spellman Seminary of Atlanta, Ga.; has traveled extensively in Europe. Republican. Member Odd Fellows, Brotherhood Andrew and Peter. Author: The Influence of Baptist Principals and Other Denominations, 1913; A Regenerated Church Membership and Why, 1914; The Purposes of God Through the Church of the World, 1914. Contributor to Illinois Idea, Metropolis Gazette, Western Messenger, and Ga. Baptist papers. Home: 2940 South Park Ave. Church: 27th and Dearborn Sts., Chicago, Ill.

FISHER, Isaac, editor, economist; born at Outpost, La., Jan. 18, 1877; son of Jerry and Sarah Fisher; grad. Tuskegee Normal and Industrial Institute, Ala., 1898; (A.M., Agr. and Mech. College, Normal, Ala., 1910); married Sallie A. McCann, of Birmingham, Ala., Aug., 1901; 1 child: Constance. Began as financial agent in N. E. for Tuskegee Institute; later teacher in Schofield School, Aiken, S. C., also organizer Farmers' Conference for Tuskegee Institute; principal Swayne Public School, Montgomery, Ala., 1 year; pres. Arkansas State Normal School for Negroes, 1902-11; editor The Negro Farmer since Jan. 1914; writer on economic subjects; won more cash prizes in national essay contests than any other Negro. Republican. Member Mosaic Templars. Address: Tuskegee Institute, Ala.

FISHER, Leonard A., physician, surgeon; born at Retro, Tenn., Oct. 8, 1885; son of Alexander A. and Sadie O. (Finley) Fisher; grad. Pearl High School, Nashville, Tenn., 1905; M.D., Meharry Medical College (Walden Univ.), 1909; married Florence M. Slaten, of Columbia, Tenn., Dec. 25, 1911. Practiced in Nashville since July 24, 1909; instructor in histology and embryology at Meharry Medical College; president Rock City Academy of Medicine and Surgery; member Volunteer State Medical Assn. Republican. African Methodist. Mason; member Order Eastern Star, Knights of Pythias. Home: 813 11th Ave. S. Office: 410 1-2 Cedar St., Nashville, Tenn.

FISHER, Peter H., business man; born at Petersburg, Va.; public school edn.; married. Held various important positions with Riker & Hegeman Co., Brooklyn, N. Y., since 1894; one of founders and was first pres. Society of the Sons of Virginia. Baptist. Member Odd Fellows. Home: 579 Herkimer St., Brooklyn, N. Y.

FITZHUGH, Marie Luvernia, blind dramatic soprano, elocutionist; born at St. Louis, Mo., June 15, 1886; daughter of William Grant and Nancy (White) Fitzhugh; ed. Missouri School for the Blind; unmarried. Began as prima donna, 1905; since has conducted musical entertainments in nearly all principal cities in the U. S. and Canada; sings in three different languages, and repertoir embraces songs sung by leading artists; plays the piano, recites pantomine, operates typewriter, knits, sews and does crochet work; is totally blind and in the diversity of her accomplishments is in many respects the equal of Helen Keller; leading artist of The Fitzhugh Concert Co. Baptist. Member Sisters of Mysterious Ten. Address: 541 N. Dearborn St., Indianapolis, Ind.

FLEMING, Thomas Wallace, lawyer, former city councilman; born at Mercer, Pa., May 13, 1874; son of Thomas and Lavina (Green) Fleming; public school edn., Meadville, Pa.; private academic course; grad. Cleveland Law School, 1906 LL.B., Baldwin College, Berea, Ohio; 3 children by first union: Wallace, Russell, Lawrence; 2d marriage, Lethia E. Cousins, of Tazewell, Va., Feb. 21, 1912. Was proprietor Chamber of Commerce Barber Shop, Cleveland, Ohio, 1895-1906; admitted to Ohio bar, 1906; since practiced in Cleveland. Secretary the Men's Auxiliary, and trustee, Home for Aged Colored People; secretary Cleveland Association of Colored Men. Was sergeant-at-arms, 1904, 1912, and alternate delegate from 21st Ohio District, 1908, at Re-

publican National Conventions, Chicago, Ill.; member Cleveland City Council, 1909-11; elected at-large; only colored man ever in the council at Cleveland; served 5 successive terms on Republican State Executive Committee of Ohio. Congregationalist. Member the Elks. Home: 2171 E. 30th St. Office: 2828 Central Ave., Cleveland, Ohio.

FLIPPER,, Joseph Simeon, bishop; born at Atlanta, Ga., Feb. 22, 1859; son of Festue and Isabella (Buckhalter) Flipper; ed. Atlanta Univ., 1869-76; (D.D., Allen Univ., Columbia, S. C., 1893; LL.D., Wilberforce Univ., 1906); married Amanda Slater, of Thomasville, Ga., Feb. 24, 1880. Ordaned A. M. E. ministry, 1882; dean Turner Theological Seminary, Atlanta, 1893-4; pres. Morris Brown College, 1904-8; bishop A. M. E. Church since 1908; presiding bishop 9th Episcopal Dist. Address: 401 Houston St., Atlanta, Ga.

FLOYD, Silas Xavier, teacher; born at Augusta, Ga., Oct. 2, 1869; son of David and Sarah Jane (Nickson) Floyd; A.B., Atlanta Univ., 1891, A.M., 1894; (D.D., Morris Brown College, 1903); married Mrs. Ella James, of Augusta, Ga., May 6, 1901. Principal 3d Ward School, Augusta, 1891-3; asst. prin. Mauge Street School, 1893-6; prin. 1st Ward School, 1903-8, Mauge Street School, since 1908; was editor Augusta Sentinal, 1891-6; dept. editor Voice of Negro, 1904-7; field worker International Sunday School Convention, 1896-9; pastor Tabernacle Church, 1899-1900; Sunday School missionary of American Baptist Publishing Society, 1900-2; vice-president and auditor Ga. Mutual Industrial Life and Health Ins. Co.; vice-pres. American Benefit Assn.; sec. Negro Fair Assn., Standard Mercandise Co., Shiloh Orphanage, Colored Y. M. C. A.; member advisory board Standard Life Ins. Co.; trustee Walker Baptist Institute. Republican. Member American Association Political and Social Science, American Historical Assn. Author: Life of C. T. Walker, D.D., 1902; Gospel of Service and other Sermons, 1902; Floyd's

Flowers, 1905. Address: 1025 12th St,. Augusta, Ga.

FORD, Albert William, city food inspector; born at Kokomo, Ind., Jan. 28, 1879; son of John F. and Isabella (Braboy) Ford; high school edn. Kokomo; grad. State Normal School, Terre Haute, Ind.; student Chicago Law School; married Ada Beatrice Bagby, of Indianapolis, Ind., Nov. 7, 1900; 4 children: Irene V., Albert L., Genevieve E., Rosalynd B. (deceased). Teacher in public schools of Kokomo and Indianapolis, 1897-9; began as tagger, 1899, and meat inspector to 1908, with U. S. Bureau of Animal Industry; meat and food inspector in Health Department, Chicago, 1909; deputy collector in U. S. Internal Revenue Service, 1909-12; food inspector in Department of Health, Chicago, since Apr. 24, 1912; part owner Southern Herb Remedy Co. Trustee Douglass College. Enlisted in Illinois National Guard, Mar. 21, 1910, elected 2d lieut., Co. E. 8th Inf., Dec. 14, 1910, 1st lieut., since July 9, 1913; won War Department medals for marksman, sharpshooter, and expert rifleman; for pistol marksman, and pistol sharpshooter, won gold medal from State of Illinois; the first colored member of National Guard to win gold medal in a state competition. Republican. Cambellite Christian. 33d degree Mason, Knight Templar, Shriner. Home: 3238 Forest Ave. Office: 708 City Hall, Chicago, Ill.

FORD, George William, military cemetery supt.; born at Alexandria, Va., Nov. 23, 1847; son of William W. and Henrietta (Bruce) Ford; ed. public schools of Alexandria and New York; married Hattie E. Bythewood, of Beaufort, S. C., Aug. 29, 1879; 7 children: George W., Dr. Noel B., Hallie C., James I., Cecil B., Elsie J., Vera B. Enlisted in 10th U. S. Cav., Sept. 10, 1867; served through noncommissoined grades; honorably discharged Sept. 10, 1877, with rank of regtl. q.-m.-surgt.; commended in Gen. Orders No. 53, series 1874, Fort Still, Ind. Ty., for acts of good judgement and gallantry in action with hostile Kiowa and Comanche Indians at the Wichita Agency, Aug. 22-23, 1874; served in Ind. Ty., N. Mex., Ariz., Tex., Kan.; commissioned maj. 23rd Kan. Vols., July 15, 1898; served with regt. in Army of Pacification, Cuba, Aug. 1898 to Mar. 1899; mustered out with regt., Apr. 10, 1899; supt. U. S. Military Cemetery, Chattanooga, Tenn., 1878, at Beaufort, S. C., 1878-94, at Ft. Scott, Kan., except during service in Cuba, 1894-1904, at Port Hudson, La., 1904-6; supt. U. S. Military Cemetery, Springfield, Ill., since 1906; only colored person holding similar position. Treasurer and member executive committee National Half-Century Anniversary Celebration and Exposition, Chicago, 1915. Delegate to Republican National Convention, Philadelphia, Pa., 1900; was active in Kansas politics 10 years. Mason; member Odd Fellows, Knights of Pythias, Army and Navy Union, National Indiana War Veterans, United Spanish War Veterans. Club: Literary Research of Springfield, Ill. (president). Address: Riverton, Ill.

FORD, John Elijah, clergyman, teacher, lecturer; born at Owensboro, Ky., Oct. 21, 1862; son of Isom and Anna Eliza (Helm) Ford; grad. high school, Chicago, Ill., 1885; took shorthand course, 1886; student Fisk Univ., Nashville, Tenn., 1886-8, Beloit College, Wis., 1889-91; B.D., Univ. of Chicago, 1895; (D.D., Western College, Macon, Mo., 1906); married Justina L. Warren, of Galesburg, Ill., Dec. 27, 1893. Pastor of Providence Baptist Church, Chicago, 1890-2; ordained, Apr. 19, 1891; pastor Bethesda Church, Chicago, 1893-6, Tabernacle Church, Los Angeles, Cal., 1897-9, Zion Baptist Church, Denver, Col., 1900-6, Bethel Baptist Institutional Church, Jacksonville, Fla., since 1907. Treas. Florida Farm & Home Co.; director Standard Life Ins. Co. Chairman board of trustees Florida Baptist Academy. Republican. Member American Academy Political and Social Science, Southern Sociological Congress, Federal Council of Churches of America, Progressive Order of Men and Women (vice-pres.). Home: 625 W. Union St., Jacksonville, Fla.

FORDE, William, clergyman; born at Barbados, British West Indies; spent nearly 10 years in studies in England; graduated from Pastors' College, London, 1907; unmarried. Ordained, 1907, and since pastored Baptist Church at Port Limon, Costa Rica, Central America; his religious and educational work is widely known among Negroes in U. S. and foreign countries. Founder and president Pan-African Society for Men, also Woman's Onward Movement, each teaching self-respect, manhood, womanhood, and to impart knowledge of one's own work and accomplishments. Home: Apartado 204, Port Limon, Costa Rica, C. A.

FOREMAN, Edgar Seward, lawyer; born at Hartford, Ky., Nov. 23, 1870; son of Jacob Henry and Ann (Taylor) Foreman; A.B., Central Tenn. College, 1898; LL.B., Walden Univ. Law School, 1902; married Esther Sanders, of Columbus, Tenn., Feb. 21, 1904; 2 children: Annie C., Henry J. Teacher in schools of Ky., number years; assistant editor and part owner The Colored Teacher short time; admitted to Tenn. bar, 1902, Ky. bar, 1903; practiced in Hopkinsville, Ky., since 1903; member coal firm of E. S. Foreman Co., since 1909. Secretary Christian County Committee of Progressive party. Methodist. Member Knights of Pythias. Address: Virginia and Sixth Sts., Hopkinsville, Ky.

FORTUNE, Timothy Thomas, editor, publisher; born at Marianna, Fla., Dec. 3, 1856; son of Emanuel and Sarah Jane Allen (Bush) Fortune; self-educated; married Caroline C. Smiley, of Jacksonville, Fla., Feb. 22, 1877. Founded The Globe, New York, 1879; later changed name to The New York Age and was connected with that newspaper to 1914; editor and pub. The Washington Sun, D. C., since Sept. 1, 1914. Address: 1234 You St. N. W., Washington, D. C.

FOSTER, William Othello, druggist; born at Little Rock, Ark., Mar. 13, 1882; son of Isaac Foster; ed. Little Rock High School; student in Greek, Latin, German, Talladega College,

Ala., 1900; Phar. D., Howard Pharm. Dept., 1904; married Mattie L. Boyd, of Prescott, Ark., Nov. 17, 1909; 1 child: Mattie Wilhelmina. In drug business under name of Foster Drug Co., Little Rock, since 1907; began with capital of $300; stock in trade increased to $3,500 in 7 years; Arkansas agent for Stanadrd Life Ins. Co. of Atlanta, Ga. Progressive. Baptist. Mason; member Knights of Pythias, Mosaic Templars. Home: 1912 Cross St. Office: 624 W. 9th St., Little Rock, Arkansas.

FOUNTAIN, William Alfred, clergyman, university president; born at Elberton, Ga., Oct. 29, 1870; son of Richard and Virginia (Harris) Fountain; grad. Allen Univ., Columbia, S. C., 1892 (A.M., 1913); B.D., Central Univ., Indianapolis, Ind., 1898; PhD., 1900; A.B., Morris Brown Univ., Atlanta, Ga., 1901; S.T.B., Turner Theol. Seminary, Morris Brown Univ., 1902; specialized Univ. of Chicago, summer, 1912; married Jessie Williams, of Sumter, S. C., June, 1893; 1 child: William A.; 2d marriage, Julia T. Allen, of Atlanta, Oct. 24, 1899; 3 children: Louise Virginia, Julia Bell, Sue Jett. Licensed to preach A. M. E. Church, Elberton, Elbert Co., Ga., 1892; pastored churches in Athens, Washington, Marrietta, and Allen Temple at Atlanta, Ga., St. Stephen's Church, Wilmington, N. C., Stewart Church, Macon, Ga.; was presiding elder Athens Dist.; president Morris Brown Univ., since 1911; chancellor Morris Brown University System including Payne College, Cuthbert, Ga., and Central Park Normal and Industrial Institute, Savannah. Republican. Mason; member Odd Fellows, Knights of Pythias. Address: Morris Brown University, Atlanta, Ga.

FOUSE, William Henry, supervisor colored school; born at Westerville, Ohio, May 7, 1868; son of Squire and Sarah Fouse; grad. high school, Westerville, 1884; A.B., Otterbein Univ., Ohio, 1893; post-graduate work Ohio State Univ., and Indiana Univ.; studied at Univ. of Cincinnati; special work, 2 summers, Univ. of Chicago; married Lizzie B. Cooke, of

Lexington, Ky., Aug. 10, 1898. Began as teacher in Colored High School, Corydon, Ind., 1893, continuing to 1904; while there taught penmanship in Harrison County Institute, and was clarinet soloist in Corydon Band, both white; principal Lincoln High School, Gallipolis, Ohio, 1904-8; was member Associated Charities in that city; principal William Grant High School, Covington, Ky., 1908-13; supervisor colored schools, Lexington, Ky., since 1913; established the Penny Savings Bank in the colored city city schools at Lexington. Republican. African Methodist. Member National Educational Assn., Kentucky Negro Educational Assn. Mason. Home: 219 N. Upper St. Office: Russell High School, Lexington, Ky.

FRANCIS, Nellie Griswold, club woman, religious and charity worker; born at Nashville, Tenn., Nov. 7, 1874; daughter of Thomas Garrison and Maggie (Seay) Griswold; ed. Knowles Street School, where colored teachers were first employed in Nashville, and public schools, St. Paul; composed essay "The Race Problem," first paper ever read on that subject in Minn.; received special prize for excellence of production; offered scholarship in Univ. of Minn., and Minn. School of Dramatic Art; took course of stenography; married William Trevanne Francis, of St. Paul, Aug. 8, 1893. Began as stenographer with Great Northern Ry. Co., St. Paul, 1891; later with West Pub. Co.; after marriage identified self with clubs, charities, civic and church work; raised $3,300 for pipe organ placed in Pilgrim Baptist Church, half of which was given to her by Andrew Carnegie; supt. Primary Sunday School Dept.; former pres. State Federation of Woman's Clubs; pres. City Federation Woman's Clubs; member executive board Crispus Attucks Old Folks Home, and Y. W. C. A. (colored); member National Congregational Union, Minnesota Congregational Union, Public Health Assn. of Minn., Woman's Welfare League, Suffrage Legislative Convention of Minn., League of Protestant Women (all white); also member Household of Ruth. Clubs: Amateur Art, Social and Literary. Wrote (pamphlet): The Problem of the Negro Home—which she read before National Assn. of Woman's Clubs convention at Wilberforce, O., Aug. 6, 1914. Address: 606 St. Anthony Ave., St. Paul, Minn.

FRANCIS, William Trevanne, lawyer; born at Indianapolis, Ind., Mar. 26, 1870; son of James and Harriett (Taylor) Francis; ed. public schools, Indianapolis, and St. Paul, Minn.; A.B., St. Paul College of Law, 1904; married Nellie Frances Griswold, of Nashville, Tenn., Aug. 8, 1893. Began as stenographer with N. P. Ry., St. Paul, 1893, later clerk in different departments until appointed chief clerk and attorney in law dept., 1904, continuing to 1912; practiced individually since Nov. 1, 1912. Member Republican State Central Com., 1914. Baptist. Member National Association for Advancement of Colored People; appointed member Prisoner's Aid Society by Minn. State Board of Parole, 1914. Mason; member Odd Fellows. Club. Business Men's. Home: 606 St. Anthony Ave. Office: American National Bank Bldg., St. Paul, Minn.

FRANKLIN, Buck Colbert, postmaster, lawyer; born at Homer, Carter Co., Okla., May 6, 1879; son of David Burney and Millie (Colbert) Franklin; attended government and subscription schools, Homer, to 1894; student Dawes Acedemy, Berwyn, Okla., 1896-8, Roger Williams Univ., Nashville, Tenn., 1899-1901, Atlanta Baptist College, Ga., 1901-3; married Mollie Lee Parker, of Brownsville, Tenn., Apr. 1, 1903; 4 children: Mozella D., Buck Colbert, Jr., Annie H., John Hope F. Admitted to the practice of law before the U. S. Land Office, Tiskomingo, Okla., 1903, to Okla. bar, 1907, U. S. Courts, 1908; with another lawyer, S. T. Wiggins, won the "Joe and Dillard Perry land case," and set a precedent which has since been followed in successful Indian litigations. Was assistant U. S. supervisor of schools among the Negroes of the old Chichasaw Nation, Ind.

Ty., 1904; organizer of the colored city school system, Wewoka, Okla., 1905. Editor and pub. The World (weekly newspaper), Ardmore, Okla., 1907-8, The Rentiesville News, Okla., 1913-14; postmaster at Rentiesville since Mar. 9, 1914; member firm of Buck C. Franklin & Co., general merchandise. Trustee Okla. Normal and Industrial Institute, Boley, Okla. Took influential part in making Pauls Valley the seat of Garvin County; opposed the "Jim Crow" law in open letter addressed to the General Assembly of Okla.; secured the selection of Frank J. Stove, white, on the independent ticket as delegate to Okla. Constitutional Convention, 1906. Active in Democratic politics. Member C. M. E. Church; also member Okla. Bar Assn., Postmaster's Assn., Rentiesville Negro Business League, and Odd Fellows. Address: Rentiesville, Okla.

FRANKLIN, Laura C., matron and principal; born at Concord, N. C., Oct., 1858; daughter of Dalia Holmes; ed. Scotia Seminary, Concord; married William Holmes (deceased); 2d marriage, Rev. William H. Franklin, pres. Swift Memorial College, of Rogersville, Tenn., Dec. 24, 1893. Reared under influence of Scotia Seminary and helped in the care of its students; teacher in schools of Concord, 1870-92; became matron, 1892, matron and principal since 1893, with Swift Memorial College; devoted to child welfare work; labored unselfishly and sacrificed much for good of colored race. Address: Swift Memorial College, Rogersville, Tenn.

FRANKLIN, William Henderson, college president; born at Knoxville, Tenn., Apr. 14, 1852; son of Henderson and Elizabeth (Bates) Franklin; A.B., Maryville College, Tenn., 1880, A.M., 1883; S.T.B., Lane Theological Seminary, Cincinnati, O., 1883; (D.D., Maryville College, 1898); married Mrs. Laura C. Emmons, of Concord, N. C., Dec. 24, 1893. Conducted State Teachers Institute, Knoxville, 1881-2; founded Swift Memorial College, Rogersville, Tenn., 1883, and since pres.; gave $1,000 (1912) toward purchasing lot for college building. Presbyterian. Pastor St. Mark's Church, Rogersville, 1883-1914; erected new church on ground secured from the Freedmen's Board of the Presbyterian Church; principal organizer Rogersville Presbytery and Synod of E. Tenn.; gave name and was first moderator of both; again elected moderator of latter by acclamation, 1913; commissioner to General Assembly of Presbyterian Church U. S. A., for Holston Presbytery (white), 1888, 1902. Trustee Maryville College. Republican. Member East Tennessee Colored Teachers' Assn. (pres. 1914). Active in all race matters. Contributor to New York Age, Herald and Presbyter (Cincinnati), the Continent (Chicago), and other papers. Address: Rogersville, Tenn.

FRAZER, Charles Rivers, university dean; born at Auburn, Ala., Aug. 8, 1879; son of Edmund and Estelle (Mitchell) Frazer; A.B., Shaw Univ., Raleigh, N. C., 1900, A.M., 1912; special work in ancient and modern languages, Brown Univ., Providence, R. I., 1900-2; student Univ. of Chicago, summers, 1903-7, A.B., 1907; married Daisy J. Christian, of Richmond, Va., Sept. 2, 1907. Professor of classics and in charge college work, Shaw Univ., 1902-11; dean of the university and professor of classics since 1911. Republican. Missionary Baptist. Mason; member Knights of Pythias. Address: Shaw University, Raleigh, N. C.

FRAZIER, Reuben Eugene, real estate; born at Alexandria, Va., Apr. 23, 1870; son of Govner G. and Mary F.; ed. public schools, Culpeper, Va., to 1882; unmarried. Began as barber, 1890; partner with James W. Brown since 1905; established Frazier & Brown Real Estate Co., 1908; operates employment bureau business as Frazier-Brown & Co. Trustee Ebenezer Baptist Church. Republican; member 20th Ward Committee, 1904-5. Mason. Club: Loendi Social and Literary. Home: 6952 Bennett St. Office: 6231 Penn Ave., Pittsburgh, Pa.

FREEMAN, Elijah, teacher; born at Baltimore, Md., Feb. 12, 1858; son of Elijah and Henrietta (Caldwell) Freeman; ed. public schools, Md. and N. Y.; grad. Storer College, Harper's Ferry, W. Va., 1887, Nichols Latin School, Lewiston, Me., 1892; A.B., Bates College, Lewiston, 1898; unmarried. Began as private teacher, Boston, Mass., 1899; later in Washington, D. C.; teacher in public schools, Woodville, Md., 1903-8, New Market, Md., 6 mos.; prin. public school for colored children, Hagerstown, Md., since 1908. Republican. Free Baptist. Address: Box 487, Hagerstown, Md.

FREEMAN, H. Lawrence, musician, composer; born at Cleveland, Ohio, Oct. 9, 1875; son of Sylvester L. and Agnes (Sims) Freeman; ed. schools of Cleveland, Denver, and Chicago; private music master, Johann Beck; married Charlotta Thomas, of Charleston, S. C., 1899; 1 child living: Valdo. Began musical career in Cleveland, 1889; professor of music for a while at Wilberforce (O.) Univ.; musical director number of years of the late Ernest Hogan "Rufus Rastus Co.," the Pekin Stock Co. (Chicago), and Cole & Johnson's Red Moon Co.; now director Negro Choral Society, and Freeman's School of Music. Composer: The Octoroon, Voodoo, The Martyr, Valdo, Zuluki, and The Prophecy (grand operas); The Lovers of Pompaii (song circle); The Wolf, My Son (cantatas); The Vendetta; The Plantation; An African Kraal; The Tryst, and large number of smaller forms. Member National Teachers' Assn. Episcopalian. Home: 36 W. 136th St. Studio: 124-126 W. 136th St., New York.

FRENCH, Clifton G. A., counsellor-at-law; born at Topeka, Kan.; son of Benjamin Franklin and Mary Luninia (Coney) French; grad. high school, Kansas City, Kan.; student College of City of New York 2 years; B.S., New York Univ.; LL.B., New York Univ. Law School, LL.M., 1912; married, Oct. 28, 1900, Minnie M. Waller, of Kan., daughter of the late John L. Waller, ex-consul to Madagascar, Served 2 terms as deputy recorder of deeds, Wyandotte County (Kansas City), Kan.; private secretary to John

L. Waller in Kansas City; practiced law in New York since graduation; member firm of French & French; was part owner and junior editor the Progressive American (weekly newspaper), 1902-5; has traveled in most parts the U. S. and Canada; lived in Cuba 2 years; visited Porto Rico, South America, and number West Indies Islands. While member Co. C. 23rd Regt. Kan. Vol., served as chief clerk of General Courts-Martial S. O. 43, A. G. O.; now captain proposed Provisional Regt. of Inf., State of New York. Member city, county, senatorial, congressional and judiciary committee of N. Y.; has served twice as chairman of election board. Member Christian Church, the Dunbar Lyceum, and Civic League. Mason. Club: Republican. Home: 19 W. 136th St. Office: 139 W. 135th St., New York.

FRENCH, Minnie Waller, soprano soloist; born at Mt. Vernon, Ohio, ed. in Hobson Normal Institute, at Parsons, Kan.; received teachers certificate and was substitute teacher in Topeka schools; studied in the Zegfield School of Music, Chicago, Ill.; married, Oct. 28, 1900, Clifton C. G. French, formerly of Topeka, Kan., now a lawyer in New York. Has sung at recitals and concerts throughout western part of the United States and Canada; visited France, England, Ireland, Holland, Cape Colony in S. Africa, Port Said in Egypt, Maderia in Canary Islands, Nassau, N. P. (Bahamas), Trinidad, Barbados and number of islands in the West Indies; sang frequenttly before Her Majesty the Queen and His Excellency the Prime Minister of Madagascar, where she lived more than 3 years; also lived in Cuba 2 years; during her concert tour, 1914, sang in London Electric Theatre, Trinidad, and at a recital under the patronage of His Worship, the Mayor of Georgetown, Guiana, S. A.; at New Amsterdam sang for the Olympic Theatre; also gave recital under the patronage of His Worship the Mayor; has written number songs and used them in concerts. Charter member Harlem Congregational

Church. Clubs: Harriet Tubman, and Dunbar Lyceum (New York). Address: 19 W. 136th St., New York.

FULLER, Meta Vaux Warrick, sculptor; born at Philadelphia, Pa., June 9, 1877; daughter of William and Emma (Jones) Warrick; grad. School of Industrial Art, Philadelphia, 1899; studied in Acadimie Collins, and Acadimie Colarossi, Paris, France, 1899-1902, later in Academy of Fine Arts, Philadelphia; married Solomon Carter Fuller, M.D., of Monrovia, Laberia, W. Africa, Feb. 9, 1909; 2 children: Solomon Carter, Jr., William Thomas. Exhibited in Paris Salon, 1903; Jamestown Exposition, Norfolk, Va., 1907; Emancipation Exposition, New York, 1913; annual exhibit Academy of Fine Arts, Philadelphia; private exhibits: Paris, 1901; Woman Painters' and Sculptors, 1902; Phila, delphia, 1903; Framingham, Mass., 1914. Member Alumni Assn. School of Industrial Arts, Philadelphia, Society Arts and Crafts, New York. Episcopalian. Address: 7 Warren Road, S. Framingham, Mass.

FULLER, Solomon Carter, physician; born at Monrovia, Liberia, West Africa, Aug. 11, 1872; son of Solomon C. and Anna (James) Fuller; A.B., Livingstone College, Salisbury, N. C., 1893; M.D., Boston Univ. School of Medicine, 1897; married Meta V. Warrick, of Philadelphia, Pa., Feb. 9, 1909; 2 children: Solomon Carter, Jr., William Thomas. Began practice in Westboro, Mass., 1887; pathologist to Westboro State Hospital, Mass, since 1889. Associate member - American Medico Psychological Assn.; member N. E. Society Psychiatry. Contributor of anatomical and clinical data to periodical literature of mental disease. Address: State Hospital, Westboro. Home: 7 Warren St., So. Framingham, Mass.

FULLER, Thomas O., clergyman, ex-state senator; born at Franklinton, N. C., Oct. 25, 1867; son of Judge Henderson and Mary Eliza (Kearney) Fuller; prep. edn. State Normal School, Franklinton; A.B., Shaw Univ., Raleigh, N. C., 1890, A.M., 1893; (Ph.D., Agri. and Mech. College, Normal, Ala.,

1904; D.D., Shaw Univ., 1908); married, Laura B. Faulkner, of Warrenton, N. C., 1898 (died 1902); 2d marriage, Mrs. Rosa B. Baker, of Memphis, Tenn., 1904; 2 children: Thomas O. Jr., Erskine (deceased). Began as teacher in school at Franklinton, 1893; founded in 1894, and principal to 1896, Girls' Training School; pastor Clayton, Wake Forest and Warrenton to 1900; pastor 1st Baptist Church, Memphis Tenn., since 1900; built new brick edifice and increased value of church property from $4,000 to $20,000; president Howe Institute since 1902; erected 4 new buildings and in 12 years increased value school property from $20,000 to $75,000; director Solvent Savings Bank & Trust Co. Trustee National Training School for Women and Girls, Washington, Colored Old Ladies and Orphans Home, Memphis; assistant sec. National Baptist Convention since 1907; trained many pastors and church workers; assisted number of people to secure own homes. Republican; was member State Senate, N. C., 1898-1900; only colored senator and treated with great courtesy; during his term amendment to state constitution disfranchising Negroes was adopted. Member American Academy Political and Social Science, W. Tenn. Educational Congress, Federated Charities, Memphis Civic League. Author: Twenty Years in Public Life, 1910; special writer for Memphis Commercial Appeal. Address: 476 St. Paul Ave., Memphis, Tenn.

FULTON,, David B., messenger; born in Cumberland Co., N. C., about 1865; son of Benjamin and Lavinia Fulton; married Virginia Moore, of Wilmington, N. C., July 3, 1886. In employe Federal Sugar Refining Co., Yonkers, N. Y., since 1914. Republican. Congregationalist. Charter member and former president Society Sons of N. C., of Brooklyn, N. Y.; secretary Loyal Sons of Africa; librarian Negro Society for Historical Research. Mason. Author: Recollections of a Sleeping Car Porter, 1893; Hanover, or the Persecution of the Lowly, 1902; Eagle Clippings, 1907; A Plea For Social Justice For the Negro Woman, 1914; composer: (song) For You, 1914. Address: 25 Overlook Terrace, Yonkers, N. Y.

FURNISS, Henry Watson, diplomat; born at Brooklyn, N. Y., Feb. 14, 1868; son of William Henry and Mary Elizabeth (Williams) Furniss; public school edn., Brooklyn; M. D., Howard Univ., Washington, D. C., 1891, Ph.D., 1895; post-grad. studies Harvard Medical School, Boston, 1893, New York Post-Graduate School, 1894; married in London, England, Anna Wichmann, Oct. 19, 1904. Began as assistant surgeon Freedmen's Hospital, Washington, 1894, continuing 1 year; practiced in Indianapolis, Ind., 1896-7. Consul at Bahia, Brazil, 1898-1905; E. E. and M. P. to Hayti, Nov. 24, 1905 to Sept. 16, 1913. Member American Medical Assn., American Microscopical Society, American Public Health Assn., Indiana Medical Society, American Society of International Law. 33d degree Mason. Address: 132 W. New York St., Indianapolis, Ind.

FURNISS, Sumner Alexander, physician, surgeon; born at Jackson, Miss., Jan. 30, 1874; son of William Henry and Mary Elizabeth (Williams) Furniss; brother of Henry Watson Furniss; attended public schools of Indianapolis; prep. edn. Lincoln Institute, Jefferson City, Mo.; student Medical College, Indianapolis, and Indiana Univ. School of Medicine; married Lillian Morris, of Louisville, Ky., Oct. 26, 1905. Practiced in Indianapolis since 1894; one of founders and now president Lincoln Hospital, first colored hospital at Indianapolis. State vice-pres. National Medical Assn.; member American Medical Assn., Ind. State Medical Society, Indianapolis Medical Society. Was alternate delegate at-large to Republican National Convention, Chicago, Ill., 1912. African Methodist. 33d degree Mason; member Odd Fellows, Knights of Pythias. Home: 834 North West St. Office: 132 W. New York St., Indianapolis, Ind.

G

GABRIEL, George, interpreter; born at Adis Ababa, Abyssinia, Apr. 20, 1887; son of George and Mary (McKell) Gabriel; ed. in Abyssinia to 1895; Constantinoble, 1903-8; Paris, France, 1908-9; night school, New York, U. S. A., 1914-15; married Theresa Williams, of Austria-Hungary, July 16, 1910; 2 children: George, John. Served the British embassy under Lord Kitchner in India and Egypt, 1896-8; went to Calcutta to learn other languages; interpreter for Sir Nicola Okoma in Constantinoble 5 years; interpreter and guide in New Zealand, Australia, Japan, Argentina, Bulgaria, London, Berlin, Austria, Damascus, Servia, Mecca in Arabia, for W. B. Hurd, and in Africa for Col. Roosevelt; came to America, Dec. 26, 1912; interpreter at Grand Central Terminal, New York, since 1913; speaks and understands 12 languages and 5 dialects. Presented with medals in Bulgaria, Greece, Turkey. Catholic. Address: Grand Central Terminal, 42nd St., New York. Foreign: 62 Post Laoben, Nieder, Austria.

GAINES, Reuben Ira, clergyman; born at Rappahannock, Va., about 1858; son of Ira and Mary (Jackson) Gaines; ed. Kissick's Institute, Brooklyn, and Bible Workers' College, New York; married Anna M. Bates, of Putnam, Conn., Nov. 15, 1898; 4 children: Vera E., Marguerite, Reuben Bates, Joseph Ira. Pastor of Baptist Church in Brooklyn, N. Y.; proprietor of a liniment and remedy manfacturing business under name of R. I. & A. M. B. Gaines Chemical Co. Address: 1588 Pacific St., Brooklyn, N. Y.

GAINES, Wesley John, bishop; born a slave in Wilkes Co., Ga., Oct. 4, 1840; studied at Athens, Ga., under private teacher in theology; married Julia A. Camper, Aug. 30, 1863. Began as minister in M. E. Church, S., 1860; united with A. M. E. Church, 1865; first served as pastor; later presiding elder, and mission secretary; elected bishop, 1888; built Bethel Church, Atlanta; founded Morris Brown College. Trustee Wilberforce Univ., O.; vice-pres. Payne Theol. Seminary, Wilberforce; pres. board of trustees Edward Waters College, Jacksonville, Fla.; pres. financial board A. M. E. Church. Author: African Methodism in the South; The Negro and the White Man, extracts of which appear in Alice Moore Dunbar's book entitled Masterpieces of Negro Eloquence. Address: 360 Houston St., Atlanta, Ga. (Died Jan. 12, 1912.)

GAMBLE, Henry Floyd, physician, surgeon; born at North Garden, Va., Jan. 16, 1862; son of Harman and Willie Ann (Howard) Gamble; A.B., Lincoln (Pa.) Univ., 1888, A.M., later; M.D., Yale, 1891; married Lizzie Gilmer, of Charleston, W. Va., Dec. 6, 1894; 2 children: Katherine, Floyd. Practiced in Charlottsville, Va., 1891-2, Charleston, W. Va., since 1892; surgeon Charleston General Hospital. Was organizer W. Va. State Medical Society; member executive board of National Medical Assn., 1904-8, president, 1911-12. Contributor to Yale Medical Journal, Journal of the National Medical Assn. Baptist. Address: 1401 Washington St., Charleston, W. Va.

GANDY, John Manuel, educator; born at Starkville, Miss., 1870; son of Horace and Mary Ann (Randall) Gandy; prep. edn., Oberlin (O.) College; A.B., Fisk Univ., 1898, A.M., 1901; student Columbia Univ., summer, 1906; non-resident student in philosophy, Ill. Wesleyan Univ., 1903-10; married Carrie S. Brown, of Franklin, Va., 1901; 2 children: Theodore Irving, Marion Elizabeth. Professor of Latin and Greek, Va. Normal and Industrial Institute, Petersburg, 1898-1901, professor of pedogogy, 1901-14, president since 1914; instructor in methods and phychology State Summer School, 1898-1913. Pres. Va. State Teachers' Assn., 2 years; exec. sec. Negro Organization Society; trustee Franklin Normal and Industrial Institute, Dinwiddie Normal and Industrial Institute; organized statewide Health Day in Va. Baptist. Member Order St. Luke, True Reformers.

Club: Social and Literary. Contributor to The Gazette, and The Southern Workman. Address: Virginia Normal and Industrial Institute, Petersburg, Va.

GARLAND, Cornelius N., physician, surgeon; born in Ala.; grad. Livingstone College, Salisbury, N. C.; M.D., Leonard Medical College, Raleigh, N. C., 1901; post-grad. London Univ. Medical College, England, 1902-3; married Maggie Kelsey, of Salisbury, N. C. Practiced in Boston since 1903; founded, 1908, now surgin-chief, Plymouth Hospital and Training School for Nurses, member National Medical Assn., Mass. Medical Society, Boston Society for Medical Improvement, and Boston Business League. Mason; member Knights of Pythias, Knights of Tabor, Elks, Foresters, Good Samaritans. Home: 225 W. Canton St. Office: 15 E. Springfield St., Boston, Mass.

GARRISON, Pleasant Austin, supervising industrial teacher; born at Senatobia, Miss., Apr. 12, 1868; son of Martin Cook and Nancy (Crochet) Garrison; ed. State Normal School, Holly Springs, Miss; Howe Institute, Memphis, Tenn.; Philander Smith College, Little Rock, Ark.; grad. Arkansas Baptist College, Little Rock, 1901; married Malissa May Lee, of Casscoe, Ark., Mar. 9, 1902; 7 children. Began teaching school, Tunica County, Miss., 1893; teacher in public schools of Arkansas Co., Ark., 1896-1906; founded, 1910, principal to 1915, Immanual Industrial Institute, Almyra, Ark.; supervisor of public schools and Jeanes Fund Industrial Teacher in Arkansas Co. Was the founder of the Village of Immanuel, Ark. Baptist. Member Odd Fellows. Address: R. R. No. 1, Almyra, Ark.

GARROTT, Alva Curtis, dentist; born at Marion, Ala., Sept. 18, 1866; son of Curtis and Mary Jane (Pleasant) Garrott; prep. edn. Talladega College, Ala., 1883-6; student Howard Univ. Pharm. Dept., 1890-2 (Pharm.D., 1895); D.D.S., Howard Univ. Dental College, 1899; married Lillie C. de Jarnette, of Montgomery, Ala., Sept. 5, 1893; 3 children: Alva C. Jr., Miriam de Jarnette, Robert W. Began practice in Washington, D. C., 1899; removed to Calif., 1901, since practiced in Los Angeles; first colored dentist in southern Cal.; dir. Peoples Realty Investment Co., Y. M. C. A. Socialist. African Methodist. Member Cal. branch National Medical Assn., Foresters. Home: 1007 W. 5th St., Glendale. Office: 424 S. Broadway, Los Angeles, Cal.

GARY, Daniel Webster, planter; born at Mayersville, Miss., Mar. 4, 1870; son of Adolphus and Mary Ann (Johnson) Gary; B.S., Agri. & Mech. College, Alcorn, Miss., 1895; married Ella M. Aray, of Earlington, Ky., July 29, 1895; 2 children: Daniel McKinley, Carlye. Began as teacher of English, Miss. State School, Rodney, 1898, later professor to 1902; teacher of history, civic and moral science, 1907-10; planter since 1896, owner 250-acre farm. Trustee Campbell College, Jackson, Miss. Alternate delegate from 3d Cong. Dist., Miss., 1896, and delegate to Republican National Conventions, 1900, 4, 8, 12; campaign speaker for Progressive party, N. Y., N. J., Pa., and Ill., 1912. Republican. Mason; member Knights of Pythias, Odd Fellows. Address: Mayersville, Miss.

GAUDET, Frances Joseph, prison reform worker; born in log cabin at Holmesville, Pike Co., Miss., Nov. 25, 1861; daughter of James and Sylvia (Yancey) Thomas; her grandmother was an Indian; father went to the war and never returned; lived with grandparents to age of 8; went to New Orleans with her brother; attended private school and to 4th grade in public schools; was sent to Straight Univ. for while, but did not graduate; first married a man named Joseph; 3 children; 2d marriage, Adolph P. Gaudet, of St. James Parish, La., July 11, 1905. Began work among prisoners in New Orleans, 1894; she held prayer meetings, wrote letters, carried messages, etc., first for colored prisoners and after a time for white as well; she begged clothing and furnished same to discharged prisoners, and performed all sorts of work which gained the encourage-

ment and support of prison officials and city authorities, the governor and Prison Reform Assn.; was first woman, white or colored, to lend moral support and influence to young offenders, and attended the courts before the Juvenile Court was established in New Orleans; president (Frances Willard) Woman's Christian Temperance Union of La., since 1898, and supt. Prison Missionary Work 6 years; was delegate to the International Temperance Convention, Edinburg, Scotland, 1900; founded, 1902, and since manager Colored Industrial Home and School, New Orleans, consisting of 105 acres, 8 buildings, valued at $90,000; has cared for over 700 dependent children. Prohibitionist. African Methodist. Author: He Leadeth Me, 1913, which is a review of her life's work. Address: Gentilly Terrace, New Orleans, La.

GAYLES, George Washington, clergyman, former state senator; born in Wilkerson Co., Miss., June, 1844; son of Perry and Rebecca (Bowe) Gayles; private school edn., East Fork, Bolivar Co., Miss.; (hon. D.D., LL.D.); married Matilda Ross, of S. C., Dec., 1865 (died Apr. 14, 1906); 7 children: Benjamin, Georgia, Wilson, James, Thomas, William, Lettie; 2d marriage, Ada Estelle Sessions, July 31, 1907. Ordained in Baptist ministry at Greenville, Miss., Nov. 4, 1867; since pastored Kindling Altar Missionary Baptist Church of Galesville; also pastor New Morning Star Missionary Baptist Church, Egypt Ridge, since 1868, and Jerusalem Missionary Baptist Church, Lake Bolivar, Miss., since 1869; secretary, 1874-6, president, 1876-95, Missionary Baptist State Convention; during his administration Natchez College was purchased for education of colored children at cost of $5,000; established and now editor Baptist Preachers' Union; was active member among organizers of National Baptist Convention at St. Louis, Mo., 1886; delegate International Baptist Convention, City of Jerusalem, 1904; president Washington County Missionary Baptist Assn. Trustee Natchez College, Mound Bayou Industrial College. Was member 3d district., Board of Police, Bolivar Co., 1869-70; appointed justice of the peace, also supervisor, 5th Dist. in Bolivar Co., Aug., 1870; member Miss. House of Representatives, 1870-3, Senate, 1877-87; delegate Republican National Convention, Chicago, Ill., 1880; was member the "Old Guard" that voted for Ulyssus S. Grant 36 times; holds medal given to commemorate that even. Mason; member Knights of Pythias, Knights and Daughters of Tabor. Home: 505 N. Edison St., Greenville, Miss.

GENTRY, Emery Marcus, teacher; born at Winchester, Ky., Oct. 14, 1880; son of Jacob and Amelia (Barnes) Gentry; ed. public schools in Clark County, and Berea College, Ky.; B.S., Fisk Univ., Nashville, Tenn., 1905; attended Univ. of Mich., summer school; married Mary Frankie Whaley, of Maysville, Ky., June 22, 1910; 2 children: Annamelia, Emery, Jr. Teacher in Clark County, Ky., 1898-1903, at Mays Lick, 1905-8; principal Western High School, Paris, Ky., 1908-10, at 11th Street School, Portsmouth, O., since 1910. Republican. Baptist. Address: 1312 Kinny St., Portsmouth, Ohio.

GEORGE, Albert Bailey, lawyer; born at Washington, D. C., Oct. 23, 1873; son of William M. and Dellaphine George; grad. high school, Washington, 1891, Spencerian Business College, 1892; read law in office of Nicholas P. Mervine, Altoona, Pa., 1894-6; LL.B., Northwestern Univ. Law School, Chicago, Ill., 1897; unmarried. Admitted to Ill. bar, 1897; since practiced in Chicago; attorney in election contest representing Hon. Robert R. Jackson, 1912, who was seated as member Ill. House of Representatives, May 1, 1913. Republican. Presbyterian. Mason; member Knights of Pythias. Home: 5145 Federal St. Office: Ashland Block, 155 N. Clark St., Chicago, Ill.

GIBBS, Ione Elveda, club woman, teacher; born at Burlington, N. J.; daughter of George and Emma (Simmons) Wood; ed. public schools, Burlington; high school, Atlantic City;

normal dept., Kentucky Normal and Theological Institute; A.B., State Univ., Louisville, Ky., 1888; married Jasper Gibbs, of Louisville, 1890; 5 children: Jasper, Jr., Hiram K., Morris M., Mark I., Wendall W. Began educational work in Louisville, 1886; lecturer on woman's work and temperance for number years; was active Sunday School missionary worker in Baptist Church. Served as president Afro-American Woman's Clubs of Minn., 6 years; vice-president National Association of Colored Women, 1912-14; now honorary president State Federation American Association of Woman's Clubs; fraternal delegate to Minnesota State Federation of Woman's Clubs, white, number of times. Christian Scientist. Has held offices in Order of Eastern Star; past officer Court of Calanthe, also True Reformers. Address: 2844 12th Ave. S., Minneapolis, Minn.

GIBBS, Mifflin Wister, ex-consul, former judge, lawyer; born in Philadelphia, Pa., Apr., 1823; common school edn.; read law with an English lawyer in Victoria, B. C.; grad. Oberlin (O.) College, 1870. Served as apprentice in carpentry; later in business for self as contractor and builder; was active in anti-slavery movement and underground railroad; while lecturing on anti-slavery, 1849, gold was discovered in California and he started with the rush, reaching San Francisco in 1850; went into dry goods business with colored man named Peter Lester; later gold was discovered in British Columbia and he removed to Victoria; established first mercantile house there, with one exception, 1858; returned to U. S. and entered Oberlin College. Admitted to Ark. bar, 1870; began practice in Little Rock; elected city judge, 1873, and was first colored man ever held similar office in the U. S.; was register in the U. S. land office, Little Rock, 1877-81, and receiver of public money 8 years. U. S. consul to Tamatave, Madagascar, 1897-1901. Wrote his autobiography under title of "Shadow and Light."

Address: 1518 Chester St., Little Rock, Ark.

GIBSON, Truman Kella, insurance; born at Macon, Ga., Aug. 5, 1882; son of John A. and Annie (Cox) Gibson; A.B., Atlanta (Ga.) Univ., 1905, A.M., 1909; A.B., Harvard, 1908; married Alberta A. Dickerson, of Jersey City, N. J., Oct. 26, 1910; 2 children: Thuman, Jr., Harry H. Gave moving picture exhibitions about 6 months in 1908; newspaper writer at Lynchburg, Va., 1908-9; teacher St. Paul School, Lawrenceville, Va., 1910-14; vice-president and secretary Atlanta Mutual Insurance Assn., since 1914; manager health and accident dept. Standard Life Insurance Co.; secretary Atlanta Loan & Trust Co. Republican. Congregationalist. Mason; member Odd Fellows. Clubs: Monday, The Twelve. Was awarded James Gordon Bennett prize, Harvard, 1907. Home: 54 Walnut St. Office: 202 Auburn Ave., Atlanta, Ga.

GILBERT, Matthew William, clergyman, university pres.; born, Mechanicsville, S. C., July 25, 1862; son of Rev. Mark and Mary (Rembert) Gilbert; A.B., Colgate Univ., Hamilton, N. Y., 1887; B.D., Union Theological Seminary, New York, 1907; (D.D., Guadeloupe College, Seguin, Tex., 1896); married Agnes Boozer, of Columbia, S. C., May 15, 1882; children: Ruth M., William, and Dr. Gilbert. Ordained Baptist ministry, 1882; pastor Nashville, Tenn., 1887-90, Jacksonville, Fla., 1890-2; principal of schools at Live Oak and Jacksonville, 1892-4; pastor Savannah, Ga., 1894-7, Charleston, S. C., 1899-1902; professor in Benedict College, Columbia, S. C., 1902-4; pastor Mt. Olivet Church, New York, 1904-11; pres. Selma Univ., Ala., since 1911. Member Federal Council Churches of Christ in America, and board of managers Baptist City Mission Society, of New York; corresponding secretary American National Baptist Convention; recording sec. Permanent Council Baptists of New York. Trustee National Training School for Women and Girls (Washington), Voorhees Normal School, of Denmark, S. C. Republican. Address: Selma University, Selma, Ala.

GILBERT, Ruth Minnie, teacher; born at Columbia, S. C., Mar. 20, 1886; daughter of Matthew W. (pres. Selma Univ.) and Agnes M. (Boozer) Gilbert; prep. edn. Howard Univ., Washington; A.B., Howard, 1911; took complete course in Gaffey Business College, New York, 1914; unmarried. Began as instructor in English language and literature, Selma Univ., Ala., 1911, now head of the English Dept. Baptist. Address: Selma University, Selma, Ala.

GILES, Francis Fenard, lawyer; born at Raleigh, N. C., Mar. 9, 1860; son of William H. and Charlotte (Jones) Giles; prep. edn. Hampton Normal and Agricultural Institute; A.M., Howard Univ., 1889; studied at Union Theological Seminary, New York, Boston Univ., and Friends School, New Bedford, Mass.; LL.B., New York Law School, 1900; married Laura C. Caldwell, of Kidsville, N. C., July, 1889; 3 childdren: Roscoe C., Francis, Jr., Chauncey D. Licensed to preach A. M. E. Church, 1876; was member New York Conference. Admitted to N. Y. bar, 1901; since practiced in Brooklyn; director Kings County Lawyers' Assn., also 17th Assembly District Club. Progressive. President Society of Sons of North Carolina. Mason. Home: 1603 Pacific St. Office: 13 Willoughby St., Brooklyn, N. Y.

GILES, George, banker; born, St. Georges, Bermuda, 1863; son of Joseph and Mary Giles; common school edn.; came to America, 1883. President Metropolitan Savings Bank, Ocala, Fla., Metropolitan Realty & Investment Co., George Giles & Co. (cotton buyers), R. M. Giles & Co. (general store), Espuncla Cigar Mfg. Co. Address: Ocala, Fla.

GILMER, David J., merchant, ex-soldier; born at Greensboro, N. C., 1874; son of Madison and Caroline (Smith) Gilmer; under-grad. Bennett College, Greensboro; attended Garrison School, U. S. Army, Post of Daroga, Alboy, Philippine Islands;

married Minnie A. Jones, of Greensboro, June 6, 1894. In railway mail service, 1892-4, 1897; was confidential clerk for recorder of deeds, Washington, D. C., 1902-3; prop. Gilmer Grocery, Greensboro, since 1910, and Gilmer Drug Co., established 1912; owner Sanitary Barber Shop since 1912. Served in Spanish-American war from Jan. 23, 1898 to Feb. 4, 1899; was 1st lieut., and promoted to capt. 3d N. C. Vol. Inf.; enlisted in 49th U. S. Inf., and served in Philippine Islands to June 30, 1901, first as lieut. and later as capt.; had honor of raising American flag over town of Sanchez Mira, Lozon, after engagement with insurgents; officially commended for efficiency and bravery by Capt. William D. Edwards, Maj. Ernest Hinds and Gen. Charles C. Hood; again enlisted as 2d lieut. (Scouts) U. S. Army, and promoted to 1st lieut.; served from Mar. 16, 1903 to Jan. 4, 1910; during service filled following detailed positions: quarter-master; recruiting officer; commissary; ordinance officer; range officer; engineer officer; provost marshall; summary judge, and survey officer. Methodist. Mason; member Knights of Pythias. Address: 823 Ashe St., Greensboro, N. C.

GILMER, John Coverdale, editor, former state librarian; born at Charlottesville, Va., Aug. 1, 1875; son of William Scott and Martha (Buckner) Gilmer; ed. public schools, Charleston, W. Va., to 1887; Storer College, Harper's Ferry, W. Va., 1892-3; A.B., Western Univ. of Pa., 1897, A.M., 1900; unmarried. Instructor in W. Va. Colored Institute, 1898-1902; was secretary to S. W. Starks (supreme chancellor Knights of Pythias), 1902-8; editor The Advocate, 1902-8, and publisher, 1908-13; state librarian at Charleston, W. Va., 1908-13. Delegate at-large to Progressive National Convention, Chicago, Ill., 1912. Member American Academy Political and Social Science. Mason; mem. Knights of Pythias. Address: 411 State St., Charleston, W. Va.

GLENN, Joseph William, contractor; born in Henry Co., Ky., Jan. 27, 1879; son of John Franklin and Mary Elithe (Knuckles) Glenn; student Western Univ., Quindaro, Kan., 1903-5; unmarried. Began as employe for mason contractor, Hill City, Kan., 1905, continuing to 1908; since in plastering and cement contracting for self; also conducts farm and raises special grade live stock. Republican. African Methodist. Mason. Address: Hill City, Kan.

GLASS, James Garfield, physician, surgeon; born at Hopkinsville, Ky., Nov. 12, 1884; son of E. W. and Sallie E. (McReynolds) Glass; high school edn., Hopkinsville; grad. Clark Embalming School, Cincinnati, O.; M.D., Meharry Medical College (Walden Univ.), Nashville, Tenn., 1908; clinical work at Univ. of Chicago, 1913; married Ora H. Kennedy, of Henderson, Ky., Nov. 6, 1913. Was in undertaking business with father for some time; practiced medicine in Hopkinsville, 1908-9, and in Henderson since Mar. 17, 1909; medical examiner for several societies; owns fine Residence. Republican. Episcopalian. Member Kentucky State Medical Society, Knights of Pythias, United Brothers of Friendship. Home: 836 Clay St. Office: 905 Clay St., Henderson, Ky.

GLOVER, A. T., banker; born at Wichita, Kan., Dec. 7, 1880; public school edn., Wichita. Began as messenger boy with National Bank of Commerce, Wichita, 1896; after 2 years was advanced to position of bookkeeper; he done all kinds of clerical work and made the regular reports to R. G. Dunn & Co., and Bradstreet's Mercantile Agency; resigned and was with an advertising firm in Louisville, Ky., 1912-13; was placed in charge the Peoples Bank & Trust Co., Muskogee, Okla., 1913. Address: Muskogee, Okla.

GOIN, Edward Franklin, clergyman; born at Florence, Ala., Aug. 27, 1873; son of James J. and Mary Jane (Logwood) Goin; A.B., Fisk Univ., 1898; B.D., Oberlin (O.) College, 1901; A.M., Yale, 1904; married Viola M. Waite, of Oberlin, Aug. 27, 1902; 2 children: Edward Harold, Viola Blanche. Ordained in Congregational ministry, June 12, 1902; since pastor Dixwell Avenue Church at New Haven, Conn.; secretary New Haven Congregational Union; director Organized Charities Association of New Haven; member State Conference of Congregational Churches, New Haven Conference of Congregational Ministers, New Haven West Association of Churches and Ministers. Republican. Mason. Address: 573 Orchard St., New Haven, Conn.

GOIN, Logwood Ulysses, physician, surgeon; born at Florence, Ala., 1874; son of James J. and Mary Jane (Logwood) Goin; brother of Rev. Edward Franklin Goin; A.B., Fisk Univ., Nashville, Tenn., 1896; M.D., Meharry College (Walden Univ.), 1899; twice married; 2d marriage Laura O. Parker, of Washington, D. C., Apr. 10, 1914. Practiced in Birmingham, Ala., since 1899; physician on staff George C. Hall Hospital; director Prudential Savings Bank. Trustee Central Alabama College. Republican. Methodist. Member National Medical Assn., Alabama Medical, Dental and Pharm. Assn., Knights of Pythias, Elks. Home: 1412 7th Ave. Office: 310 N. 18th St., Birmingham, Ala.

GOLER, William Harvey, college president; born at Halifax, Nova Scotia, Jan. 1, 1846; A.B., Lincoln (Pa.) Univ., 1878, S.T.B., 1881 (D.D., 1891); married Emma U. Unthank, of Greensboro, N. C., Apr. 26, 1888. Apprentice to bricklayer, 1861-7; worked as mason and plasterer, Boston, Mass., until 1874. Ordained deacon, 1881, elder, 1884; pastor St. Mathew's Church, Greensboro, 1881-4; began as instructor in Livingstone College, 1884, dean, 1893-4, president of the college since 1894. Address: Livingstone College, Salisbury, N. C.

GOODLOE, Don Speed Smith, principal normal school; born at Lowell, Ky., June 2, 1878; son of Don and Amanda (Reid) Goodloe; student Berea (Ky.) College, 1892-8, Knoxville College, Tenn., 1898-9; A.B., Allegheny College, Meadville, Pa., 1906; grad. Meadville Theological School, 1906; married Fannie Lee

Carey, of Knoxville, June 9, 1899; 3 children: Don B., Wallis A., Reid C. Principal public school at Newport, Tenn., 1899-1900, Greenville College, 1900-1; teacher at Lowell, Ky., 1901-3, Danville, 1906-10,. also in business there; vice-principal Manassas (Va) Industrial School, 1910-11. Toured Europe, 1913, and made study of school systems. Member American Academy of Political and Social Science. Mason; member Knights of Pythias. Home: Bowie, Md. .

GOODRIDGE, Wallace Lloyd, photographer; born at York, Pa., Sept. 4, 1840; son of William and Emily (Wallace) Goodridge; grad. Buxton High School, Ont., Can., 1857; married Margaret H. Jaques, of Baltimore, Md., Aug. 22, 1889. Associated with brother with whom learned photography, York, Pa., 1858-61; removed to Saginaw, Mich., 1862; in business for self under name of Goodridge Bros., since 1863; has largest collection of lumber camp pictures in the world; served practically every family in Saginaw. Republican. Unitarian. Mason. Address: 220 Washington Ave., S. Saginaw, Mich.

GOODWIN, Hilliard Edward, circulation manager, manual training supt.; born at Selma, Ala., Jan. 13, 1883; son of Hilliard Reuben and Mary (Black) Goodwin; attended public schools, San Mateo, and Orange Park Normal School, Fla.; grad. Manual Training School, Orange Park, 1903; B.S., Talladega (Ala.) College, 1906; studied methods of manual training at Bradley Polytechnic Institute; married Helen Whitefield Headen, of Birmingham, Ala., June 26, 1909; 2 children: Hilliard, Jr., Patti May. Supervisor of manual training of Emerson Institute, Mobile, Ala., 1907, at Fisk Univ., Nashville, Tenn., 1908; contractor and builder, St. Augustine, Fla., 1909-11; supervisor manual training in public schools, Mobile, 1911-13; manager of colored circulation for the Mobile Item (evening newspaper, white) since 1913. Congregationalist. Member Knights of Pythias, and Cooperative Progressive League. Home: 215

Gaston St. Office: Mobile Item, 510 Congress St., Mobile, Ala.

GORDON, Wilbur Clarance, physician; born at Ironton, O., May 9, 1879; son of John Calvin and Belle (Finley) Gordon; grad. Kingsbury High School, Ironton, 1898;● M.D., Howard Univ., Washington, D. C., 1904; married Desdemona Valeteen, of Providence, R. I., Nov. 14, 1904. Practiced in Springfield, O., 1904-12; removed to Calif., 1912, since practiced in Los Angeles; was sec., 5 years, pres. 2 years, Ohio Medical Assn.; member National Medical Assn., Southern California Physicians, Dentists and Druggists Assn. (pres.). Baptist. Mason; member Knights of Pythias. Address: 1021 E. Washington St., Los Angeles, Cal.

GRAHAM, Elijah James, Jr., lawyer; born at Albany, Ga., Jan. 5, 1884; son of Elijah J. and Jennie (Brooks) Graham; grad. Cookman Institute, Jacksonville, Fla., 1902; LL.B., Howard Univ. Law School, Washington, D. C., 1910; married Annie L. Spears, of Jacksonville, Sept. 6, 1910; 1 child: Lillian L. Admitted to bar, Washington, 1910, to W. Va. bar, 1911; since practiced in Wheeling; counsel for Defender Pub. Co.; was attorney in case of Steele and others vs. Board of Education, Hancock Co., W. Va., when several children were denied benefit of free school education solely on account of color; by writ of mandamus he compelled the board to furnish and equip a school for colored children; also attorney in number of cases involving segregation of colored citizens. Director Colored Y. M. C. A. Republican. African Methodist. Mason; member Odd Fellows, Elks, Knights of Pythias. Clubs: Coleridge-Taylor, Smart Set Tennis. Home: 1025 Eoff St. Office: 1026 Market St., Wheeling, W. Va.

GRAHAM, Wesley Faul, clergyman; born at Forest, Scott Co., Miss, May 10, 1858; son of Martin Gatewood, and Frances Graham; grad. Branch Normal College, Pine Bluff, Ark, 1881, and Wayland Seminary, Washington, D. C., 1883; (D.D., Guadeloupe College, Seguin, Tex., 1898); married Jose-

pine A. Shields, of Washington, Mar. 12, 1884; 5 children. Ordained in Baptist ministry, 1880; pastor at Pine Bluff, Ark., 1 year, Alexandria, Va., 1883-9, Danville, 1889-92, Richmond, Va., 1892-1911; pastor Holy Trinity Baptist Church, Philadelphia, Pa., since 1911; active in all enterprises connected with National Baptist Convention; paid heavy debt of 4 churches; one of founders and president American Beneficial Ins. Co.; director Mechanics Savings Bank, Richmond, Va. Chairman board of trustees Virginia Theological Seminary and College. Address: 1631 Christian St., Philadelphia, Pa.

GRANT, Samuel Arthur, college professor; born at Savannah, Ga., Aug. 24, 1881; son of Monroe P. and Mary E. (Minis) Grant; prep. edn. Georgia State Industrial College: A.B., Atlanta Univ., 1903; student Columbia Univ., New York, and Univ. of Chicago; married Willie A. Moore, of LaGrange, Ga., Dec. 31, 1913. Began as director of industries at Emerson Institute, Mobile, Ala., 1903; head of normal dept. Ft. Valley High and Industrial School, in Ga., 1905-6; vice-principal State Colored Normal School, Fayetteville, N. C., 1907; professor of English and pedagogy at Georgia State Industrial College, Savannah, since 1908; vice-president Mechanics Bank. Trustee Berean Baptist Academy, also Carnegie Library. Republican. Congregationalist. Member National Association Teachers' in Colored Schools, Georgia State Teachers' Assn., Negro Business and Professional Men's Club, Lincoln Dramatic Club. Mason; member Odd Fellows. Home: 533 E. Park Ave., Savannah, Ga.

GRAVES, Charles Francis, educator; born at Yanceyville, N. C., May 24, 1878; son of William P. and Caroline Mildred (Williamson) Graves; A.B., Shaw Univ., Raleigh, N. C., 1901, A.M., 1906; married Hattie Forester Chavis, of Ahoskie, N. C., June 30, 1904; 3 children: Charles R., Susan M., Hattie M. Began as teacher in public schools, Reidsville, N. C., 1897, continuing 4 years; president Roanoke Collegiate Institute, Elizabeth City, N. C., since 1901; was editor the Roanoke Tribune 3 years; chairman Emancipation Proclamation Assn. of Elizabeth City, and secretary Semi-Centennial Exposition of East North Carolina. Trustee the Theological Division of Shaw Univ.; was presented with gold medal for literary proficiency by Roanoke Collegiate Institute Alumni, 1911. Republican; supported the independent movement as a protest of the little patronage distributed among colored voters, 1898. Member executive committee International Sunday School Convention, and State Baptist Sunday School Convention. Member Knights of Pythias. Wrote (pamphlets): A Plea for Inter-racial Arbitration; The Policy of the Young Negro. Address: Roanoke Collegiate Institute, Elizabeth City, N. C.

GRAY, Amanda V., druggist; born at Linneus, Mo.; daughter of Rice and Maria Brown; public school edn. Atchison, Kan.; grad. Kindergarten Training School, Washington, D. C., 1899; Pharm.D., Howard Univ., 1903; married Dr. Arthur S. Gray, of Lawrence, Kan., Sept. 5, 1893. Taught school in Atchison, Kan.; teacher 3 years in private kindergarten, Washington; pharmacist at Woman's Clinic, 1903-5; partner with husband in drug firm of Gray & Gray since 1905; employs 3 registered pharmacists; ex-president Home for Friendless Girls. Baptist. Member National Medical Assn., ex-member executive board, and former pharmaceutical secretary. Club: Treble Clef. Home: 1833 Vermont Ave. Drug Store: 1200 You St. N. W., Washington, D. C.

GRAY, Arthur Smith, druggist, statistician; born at Lawrence, Kan., Jan. 28, 1869; son of Rev. Gabriel and Caroline (Fox) Gray; attended public schools, Lawrence; student Univ. of Kan., 2 years; LL.B., Howard Univ., Washington, D. C., 1893, Pharm.D., 1910; married Dr. Amanda V. Gray, of Atchison, Kan., Sept. 5, 1893. Began as principal Lincoln School, Lawrence, Kan., 1888; continuing 2 years; in government ser-

vice at Washington since 1890; was stenographer and private secretary to chief in Bureau of Statistics, 1898-1905; statistical writer in Bureau of Foreign and Domestic Commerce since 1905; partner with wife in Fountain Pharmacy; secretary S. Coleridge-Taylor Choral Society. Republican. Baptist. Member National Medical Assn., National Association for Advancement of Colored People, Sigma Pi Phi. Mason. Clubs: Civic, Mu-So-Lit. Home: 1833 Vermont Ave. Office: 1200 You St. N. W., Washington, D. C.

GRAY, Elizabeth Pearl Lewis, teacher; born at Waverly, Va., Dec. 19, 1889; daughter of Robert Henry and Carrie (Anderson) Lewis; grad. high school, 1907, normal, 1909, at Washington; married Hugh M. Gray (M.D.), of Arlington, Va., Jan. 6, 1915. Teacher in public schools, Washington, 1909-15; active member National Association for Advancement of Colored People. Was asst. supt. Sunday School, 19th Street Baptist Church, Washington. Member Prince Hall Chapter, Order Eastern Star, Washington. Address: Box 68, Arlington, Va.

GRAY, Hugh Matthias, physician, surgeon; born at Nauck, Va., Sept. 21, 1889; son of Richard Allen and Lavinia (Lane) Gray; public and high school edn., Washington; student Howard Univ. School of Medicine, 1908-11; M.D., Univ. of Vermont, 1913; married E. Pearl Lewis, of Washington, D. C., Jan. 6, 1915. Practiced in Arlington, Va., since June 20, 1913; president East Arlington Realty Co.; partner with brother in the Lavinia Gray Grocery and Provision Co. Chairman the Arlington Citizens Assn. Delegate to Republican National Convention, Chicago, Ill., 1912; chairman Independnet Negro Voters' Assn. of Alexander Co., Va.; secretary Old Line Republican Club of 8th Cong. Dist., Va. Baptist. Member Vermont State Medical Assn., Young Men's Business Club, Arlington; also member Odd Fellows. Address: Box 68, Alrington, Va.

GREEN, Benjamin Allen Morris, lawyer; first child born in Mound Bayou, Miss., Sept. 30, 1888; son of Benjamin Titus and Eva Pearl (Frances) Green; father was a founder of Negro colony which is now town of Mound Bayou; A.B., Fisk Univ., 1909; LL.B., Harvard, 1914; unmarried. Practiced in Mound Bayou since 1914. Congregationalist. Mason; member Knights of Pythias. Address: Mound Bayou, Miss.

GREEN, Henry Morgan, physician, surgeon; born at Adairsville, Ga., Aug. 26, 1876; son of James W. and Antinette (Shaw) Green; prep. edn. Knoxville (Tenn.) College; student Harvey Medical College, 1896-9; special course in bacteriology, pathology and surgery, Post Graduate Medical College, Chicago, Ill., 1899-1900; M.D., Knoxville Medical College, 1901; post-graduate work at Illinois Medical College, 1906, and Edinburgh, Scotland, Vienna, Austria, 1912, New York Post-Graduate Hospital, 1913; married Emma Louise Maynard, of Knoxville, Oct. 11, 1904. Practiced in Knoxville since 1901; founded East End Infirmary, 1905; surgeon-in-chief of Eliza B. Wallace Memorial Hospital, 1909; assistant surgeon Knoxville, Sevierville & Eastern R. R., since 1909. Was secretary-treas. Knoxville Medical College, 1902-10; president of colored dept. Appilachian Exposition, 1910-11; now president East Tennessee Nurse Training Institute; secretary-treas. Colored Coal Co.; secretary City Real Estate Co. Trustee Roger Williams Univ. Republican; was alderman 2 terms, 1908-12. Baptist. Member National Medical Assn., Volunteer State Medical Society, Tennessee State Medical Assn. (president 1911-12), East Tenn. Medical and Surgical Society (pres. 1912). Mason; member Odd Fellows, Knights of Pythias, Golden Cross of North America. Clubs: Colored Business Men's and Home Makers. Contributor to Journal of National Medical Assn., and other publications. Home: 518 E. Vine St. Office: 108 E. Vine St., Knoxville, Tenn.

GREEN, John E., lieutenant U. S. A.; was detailed as instructor in military science and tactics at Wilberforce (O.) Univ., 1909; 1st lieut. 25th U. S. Inf. Address: War Dept., Washington, D. C.

GREEN, John Paterson ("Daddy of Labor Day"), lawyer; born at Newbern, N. C., Apr. 2, 1845; son of free parents, John R. and Temperance (Durden) Green; father died in 1850; mother and 3 children removed to Cleveland, O., 1857; grad. Central High School, Cleveland, 1869; LL.B., Ohio Union Law College, 1870; (LL.D., Wilberforce Univ., 1890, and Ky. Central College, 1912); 4 children by 1st marriage: William R., Theodore B., lawyers; Jesse B., Clara, now Mrs. Johnson; 2d marriage, Mrs. Lottie E. Mitchell-Richardson, of Oberlin, O., Sept. 5, 1912. Admitted to Ohio bar, 1870; began practice in S. Carolina; was justice of peace, 1873-82, and disposed of over 12,000 cases; member Ohio House of Representatives, 1882-4, again 1888-90, Senate, 1890-2, and only colored man ever elected to that body in Ohio; called "Daddy of Labor Day" because he wrote and introduced the labor day bill which passed the legislature in 1890; presided over the House several times, and over the Senate once which at the time made him de facto lieut.-gov. Visited Europe in 1893; self and family resided in London while children attended schools there, 1894; lectured in various cities of Scotland and traveled in England, Ireland and over the Continent, winter, 1894-5. Was acting supt. of finance, 18 months, and postage stamp agent, Post Office Dept., Washington, 1898-1907; during last year of term manufactured over five billion stamps which were sent out from his dept. to 77,000 postmasters. Family was presented to and blessed by Pope Pius X, during second visit to Europe, 1908; now practicing law at Cleveland. Republican; was author the book circulated anonymously during presidential campaign of James A. Garfield, entitled "Recollections of the Carolina's," 1880. Episcopalian; warden and vestryman of his church. Mason.

Hobby: Reading Greek, Latin, French and English works. Home: 614 E. 107th St. Office: 217 American Trust Bldg., Cleveland, O.

GREEN, Theodore Bliss, lawyer; born at Cleveland, O., Mar. 17, 1877; son of John Paterson and Annie Laura (Walker) Green; his father was only colored man ever elected to Ohio Senate (see sketch); attended public school, Cleveland; student Westbourne Park Academy, London, Eng., 1894-5; LL.B., Howard Univ. School of Law, Washington, 1903; unmarried. Clerk in Post Office Dept., Washington, 1898-1903; practiced law in Cleveland, since Dec., 1903; dir-The G. A. Morgan Heir Refiner Co., Was quarter-master Co. B. 9th Inf., O. N. G. Republican; in a field of 50 candidates, including two other colored men, was nominated for state representative, 1914, but the whole ticket was defeated in the general election. Episcopalian. Member Cuyahoga County Bar Assn., National Association of Colored People, Cleveland Association of Colored Men. Home: 2258 E. 70th St. Office: 507 Superior Bldg., Cleveland, O.

GREENE, Nellie Weaver, teacher domestic science; born at Tuscaloosa, Ala., Nov. 16, 1872; daughter of Lawrence A. and Lucy Elizabeth (Tarrant) Weaver; ed. private school, Tuscaloosa, 7 years; Talladega College 3 years; grad. Fisk Univ., Nashville, Tenn., 1894; attended summer school at Univ. of Chicago, 1911, Kansas State Normal School, 1913; married William Henry Greene, of Beaufort, S. C., Feb. 24, 1907 (deceased); 1 child: William Henry, Jr. Taught schools in Ala., 10 years; principal grammar dept. State Institute for Deaf, Blind and Orphans, Taft, Okla., 5 years; teacher in Muskogee Summer Normal School 4 seasons; now teacher of domestic science Manual Training High School, Muskogee. Methodist. Club: Frances Harper. Home: 1002 S. 5th St., Muskogee, Okla.

GREENER, Richard Theodore, lawyer, ex-consul; born at Philadelphia, Pa., Jan. 30, 1844; son of Richard Wesley Greener; grandson of Jacob G., of Baltimore, Md., who was identified with Lundy and Garrison, 1827-35, and a study opponent of the Colonization Society; prep. edn. Oberlin (O.) College, and Phillips Andover Academy; A.B., Harvard (first colored grad.), 1870; LL.B., Univ. of S. C., 1876; (LL.D., Monrovia College, Liberia, 1882; LL.D., Howard Univ., Washington, 1898). Teacher in Philadelphia and Washington, 1873; professor of metaphysics and logic, Univ. of S. C., 1873-7; while librarian of the university, 1875, rearranged the 27,000 vols. and began new catalogue; was member American Philological Assn., 1875; represented South Carolina in Union League of America, 1875-81. Admitted to S. C. bar, 1876, to bar of D. C., 1877; dean law faculty Howard Univ., 1877-82; law clerk to first comptroller U. S. Treasury, 1880-2; defended the Cadet Whittaker (court of inquiry) at West Point, 1881; demanded and obtained a Court Martial, 1882, establishing a military president—a cadet at U. S. Military Academy is an officer in U. S. Army; admitted to practice in U. S. Supreme Court, 1907; resident of Chicago, Ill., since 1908; not active in the law, but engaged in literary work. Political record dates back to 1872; active in every national campaign to 1896; sec. Congressional Exodus, 1879; member Garfield and Arthur inauguration committee, 1881; principal examiner New York Municipal Civil Service, 1885-90; American consul to Bombey, Jan.-May, 1898; transferred to Vladivostok, Siberian-Russia where served to 1906; represented officially Japanese and British interests in Siberia during Russian-Japanese war; for service to Chinese in Boxer war, 1900, and for aid to Shansi famine sufferers, was decorated with order of Double Dragon by Chinese Government, 1902; only colored man ever so honored. Life trustee American Missionary Assn., also Grant Monument Assn. (sec. 1885-96). Clubs: Society for Exploration of the Amoor (Vladivostok); Narragansett (Dem.), Riverside (Rep.), Reform, and Commonwealth (New York); Iroquois (Dem.), Culture, Anthropological (Chicago). Address: 5237 Ellis Ave., Chicago, Ill.

GREGG, John Andrew, college president; born at Eureka, Kan., Feb. 18, 1877; son of Alexander and Eliza Frances (Allen) Gregg; grad. Eureka High School, 1896, Southern Kansas Academy, 1897; A.B., Kan. State Univ., 1902, only Negro in class of 215 students; married Celia Ann Nelson, of Lawrence, Kan., Aug. 21, 1900. Taught school in Oskaloosa, Kan., 1902-3; A. M. E. Missionary to Cape, Colony, South Africa, 1903-6; was teacher in mission schools and principal Chatsworth Mechanical and Normal Institute, pastor in A. M. E. Church, Leavenworth, Kan., 1906-8, St. Joseph, Mo., 1908-13; president Edward Waters College, Jacksonville, Fla., since Oct. 1, 1913. Served as quarter-master sergt. 23rd Regt. Kan. Vols. in Cuba, during Spanish-American war; mustered out at Ft. Leavenworth, Apr. 10, 1899. Republican. Mason. Address: Edward Waters College, Jacksonville, Fla.

GREGGS, Napoleon Payne, clergyman; born at Cornersville, Tenn., Nov. 17, 1880; son of James L. and Cordelia (McClure) Greggs; attended public schools at Columbia, Tenn.; student Walden Univ., 1892-3, Fisk Univ., 4 years, at Nashville, Tenn.; theological grad. Hoffman Institute, 1902; (D.D., Turner College, Shelbyville, Tenn., 1912); married Bessie T. Vaughn, of McMinnville, Tenn., Oct. 30, 1907; 1 child: Napoleon, Jr. (deceased.) Taught in various schools for number of years; president Steward's Industrial Academy, near Huntsville, Tenn., 1902-3; declined further school offers to enter ministry. Began preaching in small mission near Huntsville, 1903; later pastor at Nashville, Jackson, McMinnville, Tullahoma, and Fayetteville, Tenn.; transferred to California by Bishop H. B. Parks; pastor First A. M. E. Church, Oakland, 1912-13, and at Los Angeles since 1913. Trustee Wilberforce Univ., Turner College (Tenn.). Was known as "Little Silver Tongue

Orator" when a boy, and won gold medal at Coty School, Columbia, Tenn. Republican. Member Southern California Alumni Assn. Mason; past grand captain-general of Grand Commandery, Knights Templar; member Order Eastern Star, Odd Fellows, Knights of Pythias. Home: 1466 Griffith Ave., Los Angeles, California.

GREGORY, James Francis, clergyman, teacher; born at Washington, D. C., Apr. 10, 1876; son of James Monroe and Fannie Emma (Hagan) Gregory; prep. edn. Howard Univ., Washington; A.B., Amherst (Mass.) College, 1898; B.D., Yale Divinity School, New Haven, Conn., 1901; married Ednar Julia Anderson, of Cleveland, O., June 30, 1903; 4 children: Amherst, Julia, LaVerne, Francis, Monroe. Ordained Presbyterian ministry, 1902, and appointed assistant pastor Central Church at Philadelphia; pastor Capitol Street Church, Harrisburg, Pa., 1907-11. Was instructor in English at Manual Training and Industrial School for Colored Youth, Bordentown, N. J., 1901-7, director academic dept., 1902-7, and vice-principal since 1911. Republican. Member American Academy Political and Social Science. Home: 1822 Christian St., Philadelphia, Pa. Office: Manual Training and Industrial School, Bordentown, N. J.

GREGORY, Louis George, lawyer; A.B., Fisk Univ., Nashville, Tenn., 1896; LL.B., Howard Univ., Washington, 1902. In the law division of Treasury Department for some time. Address: 1553 Fourth St. N. W., Washington, D. C.

GREGORY, Montgomery, university professor; born at Washington, D. C., Aug. 31, 1887; son of Prof. James Monroe and Fannie Emma (Hagan) Gregory; prep. edn., Williston Academy, Easthampton, Mass.; A.B., Harvard, 1910; student Columbia Univ., New York, summers, 1912, 13, 14; unmarried. Began as instructor in Howard Univ., Washington, D. C., 1910, assistant professor of English since 1913. Member of winning Debating Teams, Howard vs. Yale, 1909, 10; also member Track Team;

was president Harvard Debating Club, sec. Harvard Political Club, Harvard Council Federated Clubs. Republican. Presbyterian. Member Pi Tau Alpha, Delta Sigma Rho, Sigma Pi Phi. Club: Oracle (of Howard). Author: The Income Tax,1910; compiler: Intercollegiate Debates (article and bibliography on income tax), 1913. Home: Ironsides, Bordentown, N. J. Office: Howard University, Washington, D. C.

GREY, Eula Ross, probation officer; born at Washington, D. C.; daughter of Henry C. and Mary E. (Eddy) Ross; grad. Howard Univ. Teachers' College, 1900; married Ralph B. Grey, of Minneapolis, Minn., Nov. 12, 1908 (deceased); 1 child. Probation officer in Municipal Court at Washington since 1914. Member Prince Hall Chapter, Order of Eastern Star. Episcopalian. Home: 1945 Vermont Ave. N. W., Washington, D. C.

GREY, Idah, teacher; born at Minneapolis, Minn, May, 1889; daughter of William T. and Mary (Goins) Grey; grad. South High School, Minneapolis, 1906, State Normal School, Mankato, Minn., 1908; unmarried. Began teaching at Hugo, Minn., Sept., 1908, continuing 2 years; principal of primary dept. public schools at Forest Lake, Minn., since 1910; also school librarian; among ten teachers is the only colored person and receives second highest salary. Episcopalian. Address: 2819 Chicago Ave., Minneapolis, Minn.

GREY, Odessa Warren, milliner; born at Greenfield, Ohio, Aug. 13, 1883; daughter of Edward A. and Sadie K. (Tyre) Warren; public school edn., Cincinnati, O.; grad. in millinery from training department Public School No. 57, New York, 1908; married Joseph Grey, of Kansas City, Kan., June, 1909. Began business, New York, 1910; widely known under the trade name of "Odessa Millinery"; Gertrude Hoffman, Nora Bayes, Maud Lambert, Sissretta Jones and other professional people are among her patrons. Home: 47 W. 134th St. Parlors: 2221 Seventh Ave., New York.

GRIER, Florencia A. T. Powella, chiropodist; born at Nashville, Tenn., Dec. 15, 1864; daughter of Henry M. and Ellen Hannah Hayes; ed. Mrs. Julia Thomas' private school, Fisk Univ., Walden Univ., Nashville; matriculated for M.D., Hospital College of Medicine, Chicago, Ill., 1913; married Rev. James H. Turner, father of her twin children: James Emmett P., John Braden Turner; married Walter J. Grier, of Chicago, Nov. 29, 1911. Teacher in public schools of Ill., 6 years, also Tenn., Kan., Tex.; edited paper, Cairo, Ill., 1881-3; lectured on industrial training for colored children, 4 years; chartered and founded Tenn. State Normal and Industrial School, 1893, continuing as principal to 1897; editor Columbia Headlight, 1895-7; prin. model dept. Walden Univ., 1897-8; matron in Freedmen's Hospital, Washington, D. C., 1905; began practice of chiropody, Atlantic City, N. J., 1905; edited The Messenger, 1906; removed to Chicago, 1908; prop. Le Grand Foot Parlor; credited as first person to announce medical discovery for complete removal of callous growth on hands and feet by comparative scientific method in article published by Boston Journal, Mass., Aug. 5, 1914. For activity in education for colored people, southern mob prepared to hang her, 1879; account of occurrence appeared in "My Southern Home", book written by Dr. William Wells Brown, 1880; pressed Negro civil rights suit against Louisville, Nashville & Chattanooga R. R., won in Supreme Court, Tenn., securing settlement in 1888. Republican. Kansas was first state that granted franchise to women, 1886; Mrs. Helen M. Gouger, white woman, of Ind., arranged plan for women to form lines and vote at fixed hours thruout state; Mrs. Grier was in command of line of colored women in Leavenworth, and favored with privilege to cast first vote. African Methodist; was church organist and choir instructor 12 years. Address: 1348 N. Clark St., Chicago, Ill.

GRIFFIN, Charles Andrew, insurance regalia mfr.; born at Bellaire,

O., Jan. 24, 1884; son of Rev. James Martin and Sarah Stella (Turner) Griffin; ed. Walnut Hills High School, Cincinnati, O., and Dayton Manual Training School; married Allen Mae Marcus, of Chicago, Ill., Apr. 30, 1913; 1 child: Eudora Alsynthia. Began with the Western Life Indemnity Co., Chicago, about 1902; made practical study in various departments of insurance business; opened number offices in cities in which young men were given charge; instrumental in the appointment of colored physicians as examiners for companies conducted by white people; general agent Clover Leaf Casualty Co.; district agency mgr. Western Life Indemnity Co.; established in 1902, now president, Wilson & Griffin Regalia House, business extending to all parts of the world; prominent with the organization and building the Colored Y. M. C. A.; on board of managers Western Christion Recorder. Trustee Wilberforce Univ.; also Bethel A. M. E. Church, Chicago. Republican; candidate for nomination of alderman from 2d Ward in Spring campaigns, 1914, 1915. Member Chicago Negro Business League, Citizens Political Equality League; also member Odd Fellows, Ancient Order of Foresters, United Brothes Friendship. Club: Annie Walker Conscience. Home: 3721 Prairie Ave. Office: 3518 State St., Chicago, Ill.

GRIFFIN, Mary Campbell Mossell, writer; born at Philadelphia, Pa.; daughter of Dr. Nathan F. and Gertrude E. H. (Bustill) Mossell; ed. F. F. Jones Private School for Girls, Philadelphia; married Dr. J. R. Griffin, Jr., of Richmond, Va., Mar. 14, 1909; 1 child: Francis Raleigh. Taught kindergarten at Darby, Pa., 1907-8; writer for Philadelphia Tribune, Philadelphia Courant, the Washington Sun; president and member advisory board Harriet Tubman Assn.; president Sojourner Truth Suffrage League; chairman suffrage dept. Northeastern Federation of Woman's Clubs; chairman of religious work committee Young Women's Christian Assn., also director; organizer Phyllis Wheatley Literary Society. Episcopalian; member Missionary Society of A. M. E. Church and Ethical Culture Club. Member Woman's League for Good Government, Equal Franchise League, Building Relief Assn. of Frederick Douglass Hospital, also Bustill Family Assn. Author: Afro-American Men and Women Who Count, 1915. Home: 1432 Lombard St., Philadelphia, Pa.

GRIGGS, Allen Ralph, clergyman, editor; born in Hancock Co., Ga., Dec. 15, 1852; son of Elbert and Beazillia Griggs; the slavery system separated him from his mother when 10 years old; set free at Chatfield, Tex., June 19, 1865; worked on farm and in evenings recited lessons to his former master; studied in theological department Virginia Union Univ., Richmond; (D.D., State Univ., Louisville, Ky., 1891); married Emma Hodge, 1870; 3 children: Sutton E., Willie H., Allen R. Jr. Converted and baptized, 1869; ordained Baptist ministry, 1874; district missionary in counties of Henderson, Van Zandt, Kaufman, in Texas; was pastor New Hope Church, Dallas, 10 years; pastored St. Paul Church, Melissa, Mt. Gilead Church, Fort Worth, Tex., 1st Baptist Church, Chattanooga, Tenn.; superintended the organization and building of about 500 Baptist churches in Texas; president National Baptist Convention, State Sunday School Convention, Baptist M. and E. Convention of Tex., each 3 years; was elected general state missionary and supt., as joint representative, Colored State Convention, the Baptist State Convention (white), and American Baptist Home Mission Society of New York; for several years was state foreign mission agent, state educational agent, state organizer Baptist Young People's Union, field sec. National Baptist Convention of Texas, and state supt. Associated Charities; delegate from Texas to World's Baptist Congress, London, Eng., 1905; also attended French National Baptist Convention, Paris, France, 1905; was moderator Northwestern Baptist Assn., about 20 years; now general field missionary secretary National Baptist Educational Board. He founded the Baptist Dallas High School, 1878; when destroyed by fire some years later, led agitation for building the present Colored High School; aided founders of Bishop College, also Hearne Academy, Texas; was pres. Houston Baptist College 3 years. Established the Baptist Journal, first Negro newspaper in state; published the Dallas Leaflet, the Preacher and Teacher, Dallas Appeal, also several booklets, now editor of the Western Star, Houston, Address: 1724 Hall St., Dallas, Tex.

GRIGGS, Sutton E., clergyman; cor. sec. and treas. Educational Board of the National Baptist Convention. Address: 610 Webster St., Nashville, Tenn.

GRIMKE, Archibald Henry, lawyer, former consul to Santa Domingo; born near Charleston, S. C., Aug. 17, 1849; son of Henry and Nancy (Weston) Grimke; brother of Rev. Francis Grimke; A.B., Lincoln (Pa.) Univ., 1870, A.M., 1872; LL.B., Harvard, 1874; married Sarah E. Stanley, of Boston, Mass., Apr. 19, 1879. Editor newspaper called The Hub, Boston, 1883-5; special writer Boston Herald, and Boston Traveler, 1891-2; secretary board of trustee Westboro, (Mass.) Insane Hospital, 1884-94. United States consul to Santo Domingo, Dominican Republic, 1894-8; president American Negro Academy, Washington, D. C., since 1903. Member Authors Club, London, Eng., Authors League of America, American Social Science Assn.; president Frederick Douglass Memorial and Historical Assn. Author: Life of William Lloyd Garrison, 1891; Life of Charles Sumner, 1892; (pamphlets): Rights on the Scaffold, or the Martyrs of 1822; The Negro and the Elective Franchise Symposium; also various others on Anti-Slavery Movement, African Colonization and the advancement of colored people; article on "Why Disfranchisement is Bad" appeared in the Atlantic Monthly, 1904. Address: 1415 Corcoran St., Washington, D. C.

GRIMKE, Francis James, clergyman; born near Charleston, S. C., Nov. 4, 1850; son of Henry and Nancy (Weston) Grimke; brother of Archibald Henry Grimke; A.B., Lincoln (Pa.) Univ., 1870, A.M., later (D.D., 1888); grad. Princeton Theological Seminary, in N. J., 1878. Ordained Presbyterian ministry, 1878; pastor 15th Street Church, Washington, 1878-85, also since 1889; was pastor the years 1885-9 at Jacksonville, Fla. Wrote monographs on the Negro question, and other pamphlets. Address: 1415 Corcoran St., Washington, D. C.

GROSS, Frederick William, college president; born at Marshall, Tex., Jan. 13, 1861; son of Anderson and Minerva (Edmunds) Gross; student Wiley Univ., 1873-8, Fisk Univ., 1879-80; A.B., Bishop College, Marshall, 1885, A.M., 1902; took banking and public finance courses Univ. of Chicago, 1904, 5, 6; married Mary Susie Hill, of Marshall, Sept. 20, 1883; 3 children: Fred W. Jr., Pliny DeWitt, Jessie May. Teacher in various colored schools, 1878-1907; pres. Houston College, since 1907; elected grand secretary United Brothers of Friendship of Tex., 1889, when order was in bankrupt condition; since collected over $800,000, and built a sound institution with assets (1914) in lands, notes and money valued at $260,000; was national grand secretary, 1894-1900. Alternate delegate Republican National Convention, Philadelphia, Pa., 1900, Chicago, 1904; was pres. Baptist Missionary and Educational Convention of Tex., 1895-1905. Address: Houston College, Houston, Tex.

GROVES, Junius George ("Potato King"), grower, shipper; born a slave in Green Co., Ky., Apr. 12, 1859; son of Martin and Mary (Anderson) Groves; self-ed.; read law, agriculture and agricultural science; married Matilda E. Stewart, of Kansas City, Kan., May 9, 1880; 12 children. Through remarkable success and extensive business acquired title of "Potato King"; began as farm laborer at 40 cents a day, Edwardsville, Kan., 1879; rented 9 acres and cleared $125 profit on white and sweet potatoes, 1880; following year rented 20 acres; with 66 acres rented land, 1883, became shipper of potatoes; purchased first 6 acres in 1884; his farm lands in "Groves Center" equalled 503 acres (1914), valued from $250 to $350 an acre. There are 7 houses on the land; has made practice of building new house for each of children that marries; his own residence stands on a beautiful site overlooking a valley and cost $22,000. Began growing various fruits, 1890; set out 7,000 trees in 1896; owns 1,600 acres valuable land in the "wheat belt" of Kan.; owns interest in oil lands in Okla., bank stock, etc.; total wealth exceeds $300,000. Produced 72,154 bushels of white potatoes and shipped 22 additional car load during 1 year; produces as high as 400 bushels Irish potatoes per acre on his Valley farm; makes specialty early and seed potatoes, onions, onion sets, apples, etc.; product is loaded direct to cars of Union Pacific and Rock Island railroads which run thru farm; invented a power potato sorter which screens and assorts car load an hour; prop. J. G. Groves & Son, dealer in general merchandise. Trustee State Industrial Dept. of Western Univ. Republican. Baptist. Mason; member Knights of Tabor, Knights and Ladies of Protection. Address: Edwardsville, Kansas.

GUESS, Henry Augustus, lawyer; born in Hill Co., Tex., Sept. 4, 1869; son of William E. and Bettie (McMullan) Guess; B.S., Paul Quinn College, Waco, Tex., 1894; LL.B., Howard Univ., 1903; married Minnie Jackson, of Guthrie, Okla., June 26, 1901; 4 children: James, Berenice, Wilhelmina, Townsend. Teacher in public schools 9 years; editor, Peoples Protector, Atoka, Okla., Voice of the People, McAlister, 1900-1. Admitted to Okla. bar, June 19, 1903; immediately employed attorney by T. A. Curry Estate, McAlister, continuing to 1910; served short terms as special prosecutor in District Court; practiced in Tulsa, Okla., since 1912; secretary and attorney for Okla. Realty & In-

vestment Co. Was delegate to A. M. E. general conference, Norfolk, Va., 1908. Republican; judge of election, Hartshorne, Okla., 1900. Member Colored National Bar Assn., State Business League, Negro Chamber of Commerce, Tulsa. Mason; member Odd Fellows, Knights of Pythias, Mosaic Templars. Wrote: Critical Survey of Negro Literature in America. Home: 317 Elgin St. Office: 216 E. Archie St., Tulsa, Okla.

GUNNER, Byron, clergyman, lecturer; born at Marion, Ala., July 4, 1857; son of Joseph and Caroline (Jackson) Gunner; ed. in school founded at close of war by American Missionary Assn., and in public schools, Marion; grad. from theological dept. Talladega College, 1880; student Oberlin (O.) College, 1883; married Cicely Savery, of Talladega, Ala., Dec. 28, 1893; 4 children: Mary Frances, Wm. Byron, Cicely Elizabeth, Joseph Townsend. Taught school in Paris, Tex., under American Missionary Assn., 1880-4; while there established and published the People's Informer (weekly newspaper); founded Howe Institute at New Iberia, La., 1884. Ordained to ministry at New Orleans, La., Apr. 5, 1884; pastor St. Paul Congregational Church, New Iberia, 1884-9; organized and pastored 1st Congregational Church, Lexington, Ky., 1890-5; pastor Union Congregational Church, Newport, R. I., 1898-1905, and Brook Chapel (Presbyterian), Hillburn, N. Y., since 1907. President National Independent Equal Rights League. Prohibitionist. Wrote "Let's Cheer the Old Guards", a poem recited in connection with Memorial Day address at Sloatsburg, N. Y., 1911. Address: Hillburn, N. Y.

GUTHRIE, Alfred Omega, principal high school; born at Kerr, Ohio, May 2, 1872; son of William and Nancy (Stewart) Guthrie; grad. Woodward High School, Cincinnati, 1884; married Rebecca Friason, of Cincinnati, 1892; 2 children: Elsie O., Friason U. Principal of Western High School at Owensboro, Ky., since 1896. Republican. Baptist. Mason; member Order Eastern Star, Knights of Pythias,

Court of Calanthe. Address: 1015 E. 6th St., Owensboro, Ky.

H

HALE, John Henry, physician, surgeon; born at Tullahoma, Tenn., June 4, 1879; son of Aaron and Emily Hale; A.B., Walden Univ., Nashville, Tenn., 1903; M.D., Meharry Medical College (Walden Univ.), 1905; married Millie E. Gibson, of Nashville, Dec. 20, 1905; 2 children: Mildred A., John H., Jr. Practiced in Nashville since 1905; physician for Tenn. Colored Institute School, Academy and Industrial School; medical examiner Rock City Academy of Medicine; professor of clinical medicine Meharry Medical College; life member Mayo Clinic; surgeon on staff of George W. Hubbard Hospital; state vice-pres. National Medical Assn.; cor. sec. Volunteer State Medical Society; dir. People's Savings Bank & Trust Co. Trustee Phyllis Wheatley Charity Home; member Nashville Board of Trade, board of management Carnegie Library, Y. M. C. A. African Methodist. Mason; member Odd Fellows, Knights of Pythias. Club: Vingt-et-Cing. Home: 639 Wetmore St. Office: 408 Cedar St., Nashville, Tenn.

HALEY, Victoria Clay, lecturer; born at Macon, Miss., Jan. 1, 1877; daughter of Samuel and Charlotte (Williams) Clay; grad. Sumner High School, St. Louis, Mo., 1895, Sumner Training School, 1897; took course in Ill. Business College, Chicago, 1899; private pupil Perry School of Oratory, St. Louis, 1900; married James L. Haley, of St. Louis, June 15, 1904. Teacher public schools, St. Louis, 1900-4; elected vice-pres. when St. Louis Y. W. C. A. was organized; appointed by Gov. Herbert S. Hadley as member board of commissioners State Industrial School for Incorrigible Negro Girls, two terms, 1909, 12; royal grand matron Order Eastern Star, Mo. jurisdiction, since July 16, 1914; pres. St. Louis Federation Woman's Clubs; 2d rec. sec. National Association of Colored Women; dir-Negro Masonic Hall Assn.; Wayman Free Clinic and Social Settlement Assn.; state supt. Allen Christian Endeavor Leagues of Mo.; supt. St. Paul A. M. E. Sunday School. Contributing editor to St. Louis Afro-American (weekly newspaper); short story writer; suffrage worker; lecturer; elocutionist. Member Calanthians, True Reformers, Heroines, Sojourner Truth (pres.). Clubs: Young Married Ladies Thimble, Historical and Industrial Art; hon. member Des Moines Negro Lyceum (Ia.). Home: 6720 Idaho Ave. Office: 209 N. Jefferson Ave., St. Louis, Mo.

HALL, Elbert Rufus, assistant postmaster in State Capitol; born at Edina, Mo., May 19, 1881; son of William J. and Elizabeth J. Hall; public school and private tuition to 1901; student Northern Illnois Normal School, Dixon, 1901-3; grad., stenography, Dixon Business College, 1904; later studied bookkeeping and law; married Frances M. Walker, of Des Moines, Iowa, Sept. 17, 1908; 1 child: Elbert, Jr. Stenographer for Judge J. W. Watts, Dixon, Ill., 1904, for industrial dept. Tuskegee Normal and Industrial Institute, Ala., 1905; played with Cuban (ex) Giants Baseball Club, New York, 1906; head stenographer for Dr. C. Y. Clement's Medical Institution, Des Moines, 1906-11; appointed letter carrier, 1911, but accepted civil service position as stenographer at Washington, Jan., 1912; assigned to patent office and upon being transferred to position as filing clerk, resigned after 2 weeks' service; assistant postmaster at State Capitol, Des Moines, since 1913. Correspondent for Des Moines Register and Leader since 1908; served as press agent during campaigns for William S. Kenyon, and Albert B. Cummins, and as stenographer for state committees. Won the Inter-State Oratorical contest at Des Moines, 1908; awarded 2d prize at Omaha, Neb., 1909. Republican. Baptist. President and business mgr. Capitol City Band; member Cosmopolitan Literary Society, Des Moines Negro Lyceum Assn. Club: Alpha. Home. 1212 McCormick St. Office: Iowa State Capitol, Des Moines, Iowa.

HALL, George Cleveland, surgeon; born at Ypsilanti, Mich., Feb. 22, 1864; son of John W. and Emeline (Buck) Hall; public school edn., Chicago, Ill.; A.B., Lincoln Univ., Pa., 1886, A.M., 1898; M.D., Bennett Medical College, 1888; post-graduate work Harvey Medical College, Chicago, 1895; married Theodocia J. Brewer, of Council Bluffs, Iowa, Mar. 7, 1894; 1 child: Adrienne Hortense. Practiced in Chicago since 1888; attending surgeon Provident Hospital, Chicago, and Evanston Sanitarium; consulting surgeon at George C. Hall Hospital, Birmingham, Home Infirmary, Decatur, Ala., and Peace Haven Infirmary, Atlanta, Ga.; since 1900 has lectured and held surgical clinics in Tenn., Ky., Ala., Fla., Ga., Miss., Va., Ind., Mo., Kan., and established infirmaries in largest cities of these states. Trustee and treas. Frederick Douglass Center; trustee Provident Hospital, and Grace Presbyterian Church; director American Interchurch College, Nashville, Tenn., and Chicago branch National Association for Advancement of Colored People; chairman board of managers Wabash Ave. Dept. Y. M. C. A., Chicago. Republican. Fellow American Medical Assn.; member National Medical Assn., Illinois State Medical Society, Cook County Surgical Society, Chicago Medical Society, Chicago Gynaecolobical Society, Western Economic Society, Juvenile Court League, Chicago Association of Commerce; member executice com. National Negro Business League. Home and Office: 3408 South Park Ave., Chicago, Ill.

HALSEY, Frederick Douglass, veterinary inspector; born at Neosho, Mo., Jan. 10, 1877; son of Joshua H. and Harriet (Gibson) Halsey; grad. Omaha (Neb.) High School, 1897; D.V.M., Ohio State Univ. College of Veterinary Medicine, 1911; unmarried. Associated with father in Halsey Brick Mfg. Co., 1897-1900; with Swift & Co., Omaha, Neb., St. Joseph, Mo., Ft. Worth, Tex., 1901-7; practiced veterinary medicine, Oklahoma City, Okla., 1911-12; veterinary inspector, National Stock Yards, E. St. Louis, Ill., since 1912. African Methodist. Member Ohio State Veterinary Medical Assn., Ohio State Univ. Alumni Assn., Kappa Chapter, Alpha Phi Alpha. 32d degree Mason; member Odd Fellows. Home: 1200 Kansas Ave., E. St. Louis, Ill. Office: National Stock Yards, Ill.

HAMILTON, Eugene Harrison, clergyman, teacher; born at Greenville, Ala., Apr. 26, 1880; son of Wyatt and Persilla (George) Hamilton; grad. Calhoun School (Ala.), 1899; attended Military School at Calhoun 4 years; B.S., Talladega College, 1907; 7 months course in Y. M. C. A., Buxton, Iowa, 1907-8; married Laurena R. Sams, of Lake Charles, La., June 18, 1911. Secretary, Y. M. C. A., New Orleans, 1908-10; founded, 1910, principal to 1915, Lake Charles High School, private; taught in public and private schools 14 terms; temporary pastor at Woodbury Congregational Church in St. Charles; organized and pastor 1st Congregational Church, Beaumont, Tex. Mason; member Odd Fellows. Address: Beaumont, Tex.

HAMILTON, Sadie Black, probation officer; born at Allegheny (now part of Pittsburgh), Pa., Oct. 20, 1859; daughter of William and Martha (Carroll) Black; attended public schools, Allegheny; grad. Wilberforce (O.) Univ., 1878; married Louis Alexander Hamilton, of Owego, N. Y., Nov. 6, 1878; 6 children. Probation officer in Juvenile Court of Allegheny County since 1909. Episcopalian. Member Frances Harper League. Home: 106 McNaughter St. N. S., Pittsburgh, Pa.

HAMLETT, James Arthur, clergyman, editor; born at Henderson, Tenn., Apr. 10, 1882; ed. Lane College, Jackson, Tenn., Washburn College, Topeka, Kan.; married Lena A. Hercey, of Baldwyn, Miss., Mar., 1904; 4 children: J. Arthur, Jr., Esther B., Annie Mai, William Oliver. Entered Methodist ministry, 1904; pastor at Mason, Tenn., 1904-5, Dresden, 1906-7, Topeka, Kan., 1908-14; established Western Trumpet, 1908; editor Western Index, 1910-14, and Christian Index, Jackson, Tenn., since 1914; elected member executive committee

Federal Council Churches of Christ in America, 1914. Trustee Lane College, also Knights and Ladies of Protection of Kansas. Republican. Mason; member United Brothers of Friendship, Knights of Tabor. Author: Wonder in the World, 1911; Things to Remember, 1912; The Changeless Christ, 1912; Chips From the Workshop, 1913. Home: 227 Middleton St. Office: 109 Shannon St., Jackson, Tenn.

HAMMOND, James Henry, lawyer; descendant of James H. Hammond who served in the British-American war of 1812 under General McDonnough, and on mother's side of Stepney Jones, ship-carpenter of Trinidad; son of James H. and Matilda (Jones) Hammond; born at Baltimore, Md., Dec. 31, 1873; attended public schools, and Reed's Business College, Baltimore; studied law, 1892-4; unmarried. Began in real estate business in Baltimore, 1892; later in social service dept. and teacher in boy's school; treasurer Burgess-Hammond Co., caterers, 1906-11, now vice-president; in real estate business, 1911-13; practiced law since 1913. Sociologist; student of economics and government. Catholic. Member St. James Male Benefit Society. Home: 510 St. Paul St. Office: 215-217 Courtland St., Baltimore, Md.

HARDING, Henry Morgan, real estate; born at Greensboro, N. C., June 23, 1872; son of Surry Harding; public school edn., Greensboro; married Lillian Irene Minor, of Boston, Mass., Sept. 12, 1900. Began in real estate business in office of Henry W. Savage, Boston, 1896, continuing to 1910; one of organizers and member Harding, Cox & Martin Real Estate Syndicate, established, 1910. Republican. Member A. M. E. Zion Church, also Old Fellows. Club: Young Men's Fraternal (Boston). Home: 34 Massachusetts Ave., Cambridge. Office: 121 Kendall St., Boston, Mass.

HARDRICK, John Wesley, artist; born at Indianapolis, Ind., Sept. 21, 1891; son of Shepherd and Georgia E. (West) Hardrick; grad. Manual Training High School, 1910; studied art under Prof. William Forsythe, Otto Stark, Clifford Wheeler; student in John Herron Art School, Indianapolis, 1910-14; married Georgia A. Howard, of Indianapolis, July 20, 1914. Painted the portrait of George L. Knox, editor the Freeman, Indianapolis, which was purchased by Mme. C. J. Walker and presented to the Colored Y. M. C. A.; painted portrait of Rev. Morris Lewis, pastor Bethel A. M. E. Church, now owned by the congregation; his "Peoni Study" was purchased by class of 1914 and presented to School No. 64, Indianapolis; his "Still Life" painting won honorable mention at the Missouri Art Assn., 1913. Methodist. Member Society of Indiana Artists. Home: 323 S. Oakland Ave., Indianapolis, Ind.

HARE, Maud Cuney, concert pianist; born at Galveston, Texas, Feb. 6, 1879; daughter of Norris W., who was prominent in state and national politics, and Adelina (Dowie) Cuney; public high school edn., Galveston; studied music in New England Conservatory of Music, Boston, Mass.; took course in English at Lowell Institute, Harvard Univ.; private pupil of Edmund Ludwig, of the Imperial Russian Institute for Noble Ladies, St. Petersburg (Now Petrograd); also under Edwin Klahre, and Master Liszt; married William Parker Hare, of Boston, Aug. 10, 1904. Teacher in departments of music, piano, theory and harmony in Texas Deaf and Dumb and Blind Institute for Colored Youths at Austin, 1897-8; teacher of piano at Institutional Church, Chicago, Ill., 1900-1 (settlement work); music teacher at State Normal and Industrial College, Prairie View, Tex., 1903-4; teacher and concert pianist in Boston since 1904; her lecture-recitals throughout New England states are under the management of the Eastern-Empire Lyceum Bureau, Boston Mass., and Syracuse, N. Y.; her recitations include: Development of Afro-American Folk-Song; Contribution of the Afro-American to Art and Music; The Romantic Composers; editor of music and art column for the Crisis. Wrote (biography of her father): Norris Wright Cuney, 1913.

Home: 43 Sheridan St., Jamaica Plain, Boston, Mass.

HARRELL, David, tailor; born at Suffolk, Va., 1852; son of David and Nancy (Fisher) Harrell; attended evening school, Boston, Mass.; student Boston Conservatory of Music, 1872; married Lititia B. Windrie, of Halifax, Nova Scotia, June 16, 1875; 4 children: Jessie A. (Douglass), Ira L., Stanley W., Russell W. In tailoring business in Boston since 1872; member Harding, Cox Martin real estate syndicate. Baptist. Home: 63 Windsor St. Office: 20 Brattle Square, Boston, Mass.

HARRIS, Cicero Richardson, bishop; born at Fayetteville, N. C., Aug. 25, 1844; son of Jacob and Charlotte (Dismucks) Harris; public school edn., Chillicothe and Delaware, O.; high school, Cleveland; took correspondence course from Univ. of Chicago; (D.D., Howard Univ., Washington, 1881; A.M., Livingstone College, Salisbury, N. C., 1902); married Maria Elizabeth Guion, of Lincolnton, N. C., Dec. 17, 1879; 6 children: Roberta, Harry, Charles, Viola, Lucile, Mabel. Taught schools at Fayetteville, 1866-72; licensed as exhorter and as preacher, 1872; ordained deacon, Charlotte, N. C., 1873, as elder in Concord, N. C., 1874, and as bishop at Newbern, N. C., 1888, in A. M. E. Zion Church. Was business manager Star of Zion, 1880-4, and general secretary A. M. E. Zion Church, 1882-8; teacher in Livingstone College, 1882-6. Republican. Author: Centennial Catechism, 1896; Historical Catechism, 1898; Chart Primer, 1901. Address: 802 W. Monroe St., Salisbury, North Carolina.

HARRIS, George Wesley, editor, publisher; born at Topeka, Kan., Aug. 1, 1884; son of William and Laura Ellen (Bryant) Harris; attended public and high schools, Topeka; prep. edn. Tufts College, Medford, Mass.; A.B., Harvard, 1907; student Harvard Law School, 1907-8; married Agnes Herbert Kemp, of Brooklyn, June 5, 1912. Correspondent for Boston and New York newspapers at intervals since 1904; former associate editor New York Age; was editor The Amsterdam News, New York, number of years; now editor and pub. The New York News; director National Tram Control & Signal Co. Republican. Methodist. Member National Negro Business League, The Equity Congress. Clubs: College Men's, Citizens. Home: 255 Decatur St., Brooklyn, N. Y. Office: 135 W. 135th St., New York.

HARRIS, Leon R., farmer, teacher; born at Cambridge, O., Oct. 18, 1886; son of William and Catherine (Allbright) Harris; ed. public schools, Cambridge, 4 years; private school in Ky., 3 years; Berea (Ky.) College 1 year; Tuskegee Normal and Industrial Institute, Ala., 3 years; married Gertrude May Bell, of Des Moines, Iowa, Sept. 4, 1904; 1 child: Henrietta G. Worked for McCathy Improvement Co., contractors for public works, at Davenport, Ia., 1904-7; traveled as reader and lecturer, 1907-10; engaged in farming at High Point, N. C., since 1910, and principal Jamestown Colored School since 1912. State lecturer for North Calorina Negro Farmers' Co-operative Unions; among his lectures are: The Rain Sign; The Southern Negro Farmer; Don Myron De Gell; The Steel Driving-Man; Musings—To a Woman—The Narrow Way; The Skinner Skinned; His Home—Darkness; Nancy; Mistaken —Advice. Member Guilford County Colored Teachers' Assn. Progressive. African Methodist. Address: Route 2, High Point, N. C.

HARRISON, John Thomas, editor, publisher; born at Faunsdale, Ala., Oct. 17, 1877; son of John W. and Alice (Truman) Harrison; ed. public schools, Faunsdale; night high school, Cambridge, Mass.; Tuskegee Normal and Industrial Institute, Ala.; unmarried. President the Advocate Company, and editor The Advocate, Cambridge, since 1909; was published daily during the Odd Fellows B. M. C. Convention at Boston, Sept., 1914; made successful fight against the "African Dodger" and stopped the practice at a street fair in Cambridge; director Archer Co-operating & Mercantile Co. Republican. Baptist. Mason; member Knights of Pythias, Elks, Knights of Tabor, United Brothers of Friendship. Address: 798 Main St., Cambridge, Mass.

HARVEY, Edward S., farmer; born in Douglas Co., Kan., Aug. 4, 1870; son of David J. and Rebecca (Brooks) Harvey; A.B., Univ. of Kan., 1894; married Maud Henrie, of Douglas Co., Kan., Oct. 30, 1912; 1 child: Edward David. Began management of 132-acre farm on death of father, 1893; since added 155 acres; by adopting improved methods yield per acre doubled in few years; produces seed wheat and corn sold only after inspection and approval of agricultural college; raises pure bred Percheron horses, Jersey cattle, Poland China hogs; known as feeder, not a breeder. Closely identified with civic affairs; served on school board and was secretary Douglas Co. Farmers' Institute, 1901-13, which had only one other colored member. Took active part in sports while in university; was all-around athlete; won letter (making the team) in baseball, football, track and field; assisted in coaching football team at Univ. of Kan. 2 years after graduating. Republican. Granger. Address: Lawrence, Kan., R. F. D., No. 10.

HATCHETT, James Brier, plumber; born at Norfolk, Va., 1853; son of William C. and Anna Louisa (Farmer) Hatchett; public school edn. Henderson, Ky.; married Martha Smith, of Henderson, 1887; 2 children: James, Ruth. Plumber in employ Henderson Gas Co., since 1883; owns $5,000 residence and other city property. Republican. Missionary Baptist. Home: 328 Alvasta St., Henderson, Ky.

HATHAWAY, Isaac Scott, sculptor, art dealer; born at Lexington, Ky., Apr. 4, 1874; son of Robert Elijah and Rachel (Scott) Hathaway; grad. Chandler Normal School, Lexington, 1891; art student in New England Conservatory of Music, Boston, Mass., 1894-5; studied at Cincinnati Art Academy, Eden Park, 1898-9; married Hettie Ettice Pamplin, of South Boston, Va., Apr. 19, 1911 (deceased); 1

child: Elsmer Pamplin H. Began as teacher in schools of Ky., 1891, continuing during the regular terms to 1896; was demonstrator of anatomy in State College of Ky., Lexington, 2 years, for Dr. J. W. Pryor, for whom he also illustrated a text book; in 1903 he made big model for Marshall Bullitt, who was later solicitor-general of U. S., which was used by him as attorney in the R. C. Whayne insurance case at Louisville, Ky.; made minature model of the old Transylvania Univ., of Lexington, Ky., for Prof. Burris A. Jenkins, and was sent to install it for exhibition at the Louisiana Purchase Exposition, St. Louis, Mo., 1904; made busts of Dr. Booker T. Washington, Frederick Douglass, Bishop Richard Allen, Paul Laurence Dunbar, and others; his life-masks and death-masks number nearly fifty, including those of the late W. C. P. Breckinridge, Gen. Cassius M. Clay, Dr. Booker T. Washington. Dr. W. E. B. DuBois, Prof. Kelly Miller, Paul Laurence Dunbar, Judge M. W. Gibbs, Benjamin Gay, banker, and others; has made casts of the heart, kidneys, spleen and other human organs taken at post-mortems, operations, etc.; in 1914 he assisted in preparing the government exhibit at the U. S. National Museum for the Panama-Pacific Exposition at San Francisco, 1915; the work was under the direction of Dr. Ales Hrdlicka, anthropologist and curator; cut in marble an extra large size relief head of Abraham Lincoln for the National Training School for Women and Girls, Washington, 1915; has taught drawing and modeling to pupils and teachers, white and colored, making models of islands, peninsulas, and water courses. demonstrating how water undercuts the surface at curves of rivers; proprietor the National Afro-Art Co., Washington; has sold work to the Field Museum of National History, Chicago, Ill., Ward's Meseum, Rochester, N. Y., and U. S. Smithsonian Institution, Washington. Served on executive board of the Emancipation Celebration Assn., Lexington, Ky., 5 years. Republican. Member the Christian Church. Home and Studio: 3301 Sherman Ave. N. W., Washington, D. C.

HAWKINS, John Russell, denominational secretary; born at Warrenton, N. C., May 31, 1862; son of Ossian and Christiana (Eaton) Hawkins; ed. high school, Warrenton; Hampton Normal and Agricultural Institute, 1 year; student Colored Y. M. C. A., Boston, Mass., 4 years; grad. Howard Univ. School of Law, Washington, D. C., 1915; married Lillian M. Kennedy, of Sioux Falls, S. Dak., Dec. 28, 1892; 2 children: Esther K., John R. Jr. Began as teacher in public schools, Warren County, N. C., 1878, continuing to 1880; principal of graded schools at Warrenton 2 years; in railway mail service, 1882-4; business manager and instructor, 1887-90, and president, 1890-6, of Kittrell College, N. C.; commissioner of education for A. M. E. Convention, 1896-1912; financial secretary of A. M. E. Church since 1912. Trustee and financial agent Wilberforce Univ. Republican. Mason; member Odd Fellows, Knights of Pythias. Address: 1541 14th St. N. W., Washington, D. C.

HAWKINS, Mason Albert, principal high school; born at Charlottsville, Va., Oct. 21, 1874; son of Albert B. and Edith (Southall) Hawkins; prep. edn. Morgan College, Baltimore, Md.; A.B., Harvard, 1901; A.M., Columbia Univ., New York, 1910; married Margaret Gregory, of Bordentown, N. J., Oct. 14, 1905; 2 children: Gregory, Mason, Jr. Began as teacher of Latin and German in Colored High School, Baltimore, 1901; was head of foreign language dept., 1906, appointed vice-principal, 1909, and principal of the school since 1909. Trustee Provident Hospital. Baptist. Member American Academy Political and Social Science, National Association for Advancement of Colored People. Contributor to Vocational Education, Education, Negro High Schools, and Crisis. Address: 1532 Druid Hill Ave., Baltimore, Md.

HAWKINS, Walter Everette, verse writer; born at Warrenton, N. C., Nov. 17, 1883; son of Ossian and Chris-

tiana (Eaton) Hawkins; ed. public schools, Warrenton; grad. Kittrell College, N. C., 1901; married Lucile Butler, of Wilmington, Del., Sept. 29, 1909; 3 children: Hester Christine, Fannie Walter, Waltrine Geraldine Trotter. Author: Chords and Discords, published by Murray Bros., Washington, D. C., 1909; The Child of the Night; The Black Soldiers; Where Air of Freedom Is; Guardian; Love's Unchangeableness; Too Much Religion, and other of his poems appeared in the African Times and Orient Review, London, Eng., Dec., 1912; in railway mail service since 1912. Member Negro Society for Historical Research. Address: 1411 Morris Road, S. E., Washington, D. C.

HAWKINS, William Ashbie, lawyer; born at Lynchburg, Va., Aug. 2, 1862; son of Rev. Robert and Susan (Cobb) Hawkins; grad. Morgan College, Baltimore, Md., 1881; studied law at Univ. of Md.; LL.B., Howard Univ. School of Law, Washington, D. C., 1892; married Ada M. McMechen, of Wheeling, W. Va., Mar. 14, 1885; 2 children: Aldnia M. (Mrs. John W. Haines), Roberta M. Taught school 11 years; editor at different times, Educational Era, Cambridge Advance, Spokesman, Lancet; admitted to Maryland bar, 1892; since practiced in Baltimore; member firm of Hawkins & McMechen; known as the "Race's Advocate"; appeared in all important litigation in Baltimore related to colored people during years of practice; successful in legal battles against segregation, separate cars, and other discrimination; attorney in many cases in Court of Appeals. Trustee Sharp Street Memorial M. E. Church 14 years; delegate to General Conferences of the church twice. Republican. Member National Independent Political League, National Association for Advancement of Colored People, Gamma Boule, Sigma Pi Phi. 32d degree Mason, Shriner; supreme chancellor Knights of Pythias E. and W. H.; president The Forum. Author (pamphlets): The Negro and the Courts; The Colored Lawyer; His Opportunity and His Duty. Home:

529 Presstman St. Office: 21 E. Saratoga St., Baltimore, Md.

HAYES, Robert Benjamin, college professor; born at Navasota, Tex., May 13, 1876; son of Lucius and Laura (Clayton) Hayes; ed. public schools, Chetopa, Kan., and Guthrie, Okla.; Ph.B., Baker Univ., Baldwin, Kan., 1903, A.M., 1903; special course in science, Univ. of Chicago, summer, 1913; married Hattie P. Melton, of Atlanta, Ga., June 22, 1909. Was first Negro boy ever attended high school in Okla. Ty.; teacher in Logan Co., short time, but quickly realized need of better education; head instructor in department of natural science, Philander Smith College, Little Rock, Ark., since 1903; was prize debater and orator in college; won second prize of faculty oratorical contest, 1902; also member Inter-Soc. and Inter-Collegiate winning teams. Delegate to International Y. M. C. A., Convention, 1907, 10. Progressive. Methodist. Member Odd Fellows. Club: Search Light. Wrote (pamphlet): The Students' Guide to Learning and Morals, 1913. Address: 3700 W. 9th St., Little Rock, Ark.

HAYES, William Preston, clergyman; born in Granville County, N. C., Jan. 18, 1881; son of Rev. William P. and Sarah Frances (Hunt) Hayes; grad. Bennett College, Greensboro, N. C., 1898; B.D., Theological Seminary of Virginia Union Univ., 1907; (D.D., Selma Univ., Ala., 1912); married Carolyn Amee, of Wilmington, N. C., Nov. 16, 1910. Teacher in Boydton (Va.) Institute 3 years, Keystone Institute 1 year; instructor in elocution at Virginia Union Univ., 1907-8. Ordained in Baptist ministry, 1902; pastor, Clarksville, Va., 1902-7, Middlesex, 1908-11, Mt. Olivet Baptist Church, New York, since 1911. Trustee R. I. Academy, Howard Orphanage and Industrial Institute, Music Settlement School for Colored People, Union Rescue Home, Colored Y. M. C. A. Member Odd Fellows, Order of St. Luke. Home: 316 W. 52d St. Study: 159 W. 53d St., New York.

HAYMAN, George Washington, physician, surgeon; born at Sherman, Ark., Aug. 3, 1866; son of Nelson and Sarah Ann Hayman; prep. edn. Wiley Univ., Marshall, Texas; M.D., Meharry Medical College (Walden Univ.), Nashville, Tenn., 1893; (Ph.B., Philander Smith College, Little Rock, Ark., 1899, A.M., 1903); post-graduate work at Chicago Clinical, Cook County Hospital, Alexian Brothers Hospital, St. Augustine Hospital, of Chicago, Ill., 1900; married Lillie L. Ingram, of Little Rock, Feb. 15, 1899; 6 children: George, Pearl, Ruth, Joseph H., Wendell Phillips, Naomi, William A. Taught schools in Ark. and Tex. 10 years; began practice in Lewisville, Ark.; practiced in Little Rock since 1893, also lecturer on hygiene at Philander Smith College; pension examiner in Little Rock Dist., 1900; now medical examiner for Standard Life Insurance Co. One of organizers and former secretary Colored Business League of Ark.; helped organize Colored State Medical Assn., and served as president; appointed member vice commission by Mayor Charles E. Taylor, 1912. Secretary Republican Central Committee of Pulaski County; judge of election in 3d Ward, 1912; was special representative to Arkansas Negro Suffrage League. Methodist. Member National Medical Assn. Mason; past grand chancellor and past medical examiner Grand Lodge, Knights of Pythias of Ark.; member Knights of Tabor, United Brothers of Friendship. Club: Lincoln Emancipation (secretary). Home: 1024 Gaines St. Office: 614 W. 9th St., Little Rock, Ark.

HAYNES, George Edmund, university professor; born at Pine Bluff, Ark., May 11, 1880; prep. edn. Agricultural and Mechanical College, Normal Ala.; A.B., Fisk Univ., Nashville, Tenn., 1903; student Univ. of Chicago, summers, 1906, 1907, and Columbia Univ., New York, 1908-10; grad. New York School of Philanthropy, 1910; Ph.D., Columbia Univ., 1912; one of the few colored men that have earned the degree of Doctor of Philosophy, which is the highest conferred by educational institutions; married Elizabeth Ross, of Mt. Willnig, Ala., Dec. 14,

1910; child: George E. Jr. Began as traveling secretary Colored Men's Dept. International Y. M. C. A., 1905, continuing 3 years; fellow in bureau of social research New York School of Philanthropy, 1908-10; professor of social science Fisk Univ., Nashville, Tenn., since 1910; director National League on Urban Conditions Among Negroes; lecturer on city problems colored people; associate editor A. M. E. Review. Progressive. Congregationalist. Member American Academy Political and Social Science, American Economic Assn., National Geographic Society. Author: The Negro at Work in New York City, 1912. Contributor various articles to the press including: Some Conditions Among Negroes in Cities, The Basis of Race Adjustment, etc. Home: 1611 Harding St. Office: Fisk University, Nashville, Tenn.

HAYS, John W., teacher; born at Chaplin, Ky., Jan. 31, 1884; son of Robert and Eliza (Guthrie) Hays; attended public schools at Chaplin; grad. Normal and Industrial Institute, 1906; student Univ. of Chicago, 1906-8; teacher and pupil at Summer Normal School, Terre Haute, Ind., 2 years; married Sarah Arnold Rankin, of Henderson, Ky., June 29, 1911. Began in employ of Blue Grass Bugle (newspaper), 1909; assistant principal of Douglass High School, Henderson, Ky., since 1909; does institute work through the state; interested in promoting scientific farming among Negroes; lecturer on various subjects. Delegate to Negro National Educational Congress, Oklahoma City, 1914, and has been appointed to number national conventions by governor. Republican. African Zion Methodist. Member Kentucky State Teachers' Assn., Knights of Pythias. Home: 828 Clay St., Henderson, Ky.

HAZEL, Fred C., principal industrial institute; born at Savannah, Ga., July 1, 1884; son of Peter F. and Emma Louisa (Kirk) Hazel; attended Haven Home School, and Georgia State Industrial College, Savannah; grad. Hampton Normal and Agricultural Institute, 1907; married M.

Elizabeth Brown, of Winston-Salem, N. C., Sept. 10, 1913. Proprietor of Hampton Upholstering Co., New York, 1907-11; founded in June, 1912, and since principal Binghamton (N. Y.) Normal, Industrial and Agricultural Institute; incorporated in 1913, and in July, 1914, he deeded the property to the board of trustees. Was pastor's steward in Salem M. E. Church, New York, 1908-11, and organized Salem M. E. Brotherhood as Chapter 851. Republican. Founder and president Binghampton Colored Civic League; member Odd Fellows. Address: Agricultural and Industrial Institute, Binghamton, N. Y.

HEARD, William Henry, bishop; born in Elbert Co., Ga., June 25, 1850; son of George W. and Parthenia (Jones) Heard; ed. South Carolina Univ., 1876-7; Clark Univ., Atlanta, Ga., 1878; Atlanta Univ., 1879; Reformed Episcopal Divinity School, Philadelphia, Pa., 1889; (D.D., Allen Univ., Columbia, S. C., 1891); married Josephine D. Henderson, of Charlotte, S. C., Jan. 22, 1882. Ordained in African Methodist ministry, 1879; elected bishop, 1904; stationed in Africa. Trustee Wilberforce Univ., Payne Theological Seminary. Was member South Carolina House of Representatives, 1876; minister resident and consul-general to Liberia, 1895-9. Mason: member Odd Fellows, True Reformers. Author: The Bright Side of African Life, 1901. Home: 1426 Rockland St., Philadelphia, Pa. Address: Monrovia, Liberia, W. Africa.

HEATHMAN, William Aaron, lawyer; born at Providence, R. I., Sept. 14, 1872; son of William Henry and Susan (Morgan) Heathman; ed. Doyle Avenue Grammar School; Providence English High School; Brown Univ.; Boston Univ. Law School; married Carrie E. Wilson, of Providence, Nov., 1897 (died 1899); 1 child: Joseph William; 2d marriage, Eugenia V. Mitchell, of Jacksonville, Fla., June, 1901. Admitted to Rhode Island bar, 1898, to U. S. Courts, 1901; in practice in Providence. Was selected as historian by Ives Post No. 13, Grand Army of the Republic, 1897; wrote war record of entire membership, living and dead; volume cost $100, and was presented by the late George Henry, wealthy Negro citizen; placed as memorial in archives of State of Rhode Island. Delegate to 100th anniversary Battle of Erie at Put-in-Bay, Ohio, 1913, appointed by Gov Aram J. Pothier; member Lincoln Memorial Commission, appointed, 1914, to erect monument to Abraham Lincoln on State House grounds. Republican; was accountant for State Returning Board, 1902-11. Episcopalian. Member Rhode Island Bar Assn., Providence Chamber of Commerce (only Negro ever elected to membership in that body). 33d degree Mason; officer Supreme Lodge, Knights of Pythias; member Irreproachable Beneficial Assn. of Providence. Club: Republican, of R. I. Home: 169 Lippitt St. Office: 19 College St., Providence, R. I.

HENDERSON, Elias Franklin, clergyman, real estate agent; born in Gallaway County, Mo., Nov. 1, 1848; son of Emanuel and Hester (Sparks) Henderson; may be called self-educated man; was student in Lincoln Institute, Jefferson City, Mo., when 25 years old; married Nellie Catherine Harris, of Calloway County, Mar. 30, 1879; 2 children: Mabel Della, Alma May. Began preaching in Church of the Desciples, Fulton County, Mo., 1876; was chief evangelist under the State Missionary Board of Mo., 1892-8. President the Henderson Realty Co., Los Angeles, Calif., since 1907; also owns poultry and rabbit business. Republican. Mason. Contributor to Los Angeles Eagle. Address: 1543 Central Ave., Los Angeles, California.

HENDERSON, Fred Charles, dancing master; born at Charlotte, N. C., Sept. 6, 1877; son of John and Clarenda (Parks) Henderson; public school edn., Philadelphia, Pa.; studied music under George Yates Kells, Walter Vreerland, J. Shelton Polland; trained in dancing by Profs. Slye, Strickland, and Anderson, Boston; unmarried. Teacher of dancing, Boston, Mass., since 1902; organized Unrivaled Dancing Society, 1895. Republican. Member Pioneer Order Elks. Address: 240 W. Canton, St., Boston, Mass.

HENDERSON, Reuben Andrew, physician, surgeon; born at Bethlehem, Mo., Feb. 11, 1876; son of Thomas and Millie' (Soil) Henderson; grad. high school, Fulton, Mo., 1892; B.S.D., Lincoln Institute, Jefferson City, Mo., 1896; M.D., Meharry Medical College (Walden Univ.), 1904; married Lillian M. Brown, Mar. 31, 1906; 2 children: Langston, Bertram. Teacher in high school, Mexico, Mo., 1896-1900; practiced medicine, Springfield, Mo., 1904-5, Langston, Okla., 1905-11, Pueblo, Colo., since 1911; one of number colored people who are owners of Langston Rural Telephone Co.; sec. Colored Orphanage and Old Folks Home Assn., Pueblo. Republican. Member Disciples Church. Mason; member Knights of Pythias, United Brothers of Friendship, American Woodmen. Home: 1437 Pine St. Office: 226 1-2 S. Union Ave., Pueblo, Colorado.

HENLEY, Anna F. Adams, teacher; born at Chicago, Ill., July 22, 1865; daughter of Andrew J. and Matilda (Graves) Adams; ed. Douglas School, Chicago, 5 years; public school at Sedalia, Mo., 4 years; B.S.D., Lincoln Institute, Jefferson City, Mo., 1888, and grad. domestic science, 1912; married Rev. Henry Henley, of Sadalia, June 14, 1894; 3 children: Ottoway. Virginia and Henry (twins). Began as teacher in public schools at Bonne Terre, Mo., 1888; teacher in Sumner School, Kansas City, Mo., 1890-4, at Ironton, Rolla, Troy, and Louisiana, Mo., period of 4 years, Sedalia, 1908-11; was matron at Lincoln Institute for some time; now teacher in home and economic dept. Douglass High School, Hannibal, Mo. One of founders George R. Smith College. Trustee Sedalia Colored Hospital. Methodist; active in church work, and student in Practical Christianity under Unity Society of Kansas City. Member Missouri Teachers' Assn., Central Missouri Colored Teachers' Assn., Woman's Home Missionary Society, Josephine Silone

Yates Art, Woman's Crochet, and Hannibal Federation Woman's clubs. Home: 240 W. Johnson St., Sedalia, Missouri.

HERNDON, Alonzo Franklin, capitalist; born in Walton Co., Ga., June 26, 1858; son of Sophenie Herndon; common school edn.; married Adriene McNeal; 1 child: Norris B.; 2d marriage, Jessie Gilespie, of Chicago, Ill., May 30, 1912. Began business career in Atlanta, Ga., 1885; now employs about 75 men in 3 barber shops, all modern, one noted as largest sanitary barber shop in the world; founded Atlanta Mutual Insurance Assn., which absorbed 8 other companies, is largest in America owned by Negroes and doing purely industrial insurance business with colored people; president and treasurer Atlanta Mutual Ins. Co., also Atlanta Loan & Trust Co.; secretary Southview Cemetary Assn.; director Atlanta State Savings Bank, Gate City Drug Store, Inc.; owns about 100 rental properties. Trustee Leonard Street Orphan Home, 1st Congregational Church. Republican. Member Odd Fellows. Club: Monday. Home: 1 University Place. Office: 200 Auburn, Ave., Atlanta, Ga.

HICKMAN, John Henry, accountant; born at Claysville, Mo., Mar. 22, 1857; son of Rev. Robert and Minty (Spencer) Hickman; father founded Pilgrim Baptist Church, St. Paul, Minn., first colored church in state; attended public schools, St. Paul; required to study evenings while in employ of L. B. Wait, seed merchant, 1870-3; married Laura Belle Durant, of St. Marys, O., Sept. 24, 1878; 3 children: Maurice A., John H. Jr., Thomas L. Began as "door boy" with dry goods firm of Auerback, Finch & Schaffer, St. Paul, 1874, since continuing with same house which is now known as Finch, Van Slyck & McConville; worked in various depts., now manager Statistical Information Dept.; was also bookkeeper for Adam Felsch,. cigar mgr., evenings, 1888-1905, and Valet Tailoring Co., evenings, for 4 years; twice each year assists in accounting division of four leading department stores of Minneapolis and St. Paul. Republican. Served as president board of trustees, supt. Sunday School, deacon, senior deacon and acting assistant to the pastor, Pilgrim Baptist Church; aided in organizing Memorial Church, 1914. Mason; member St. Lukes, United Brothers of Friendship. Address: 533 Ronda St., St. Paul, Minn.

HICKS, Lucius Sumner, lawyer; born at Plymouth, N. C., Dec. 25, 1881; son of Alexander and Laura Olivia (Guyther) Hicks; prep. edn., Boston Latin School, 1896-1902; student Harvard, 1902-3; LL.B., Boston Univ. Law School, 1908; unmarried. Admitted to Mass. bar, 1909; since practiced in Boston. Pres. St. Mark Musical and Literary Union, 1910-12; organizer and pres. Civic League of Boston, also Citizens Union of 10th Ward. Republican. Episcopalian. Mason. Home: 240 W. Canton St. Office: 702 Winthrop Bldg., 7 Water St., Boston, Mass.

HIGGINS, William Harvey, city councilman, physician; born at Marion, N. C., Dec. 14, 1872; son of Alfred and Clercy (Greenlee) Higgins; ed. public schools of Asheville, Livingstone College, and medical dept. Shaw Univ., S. C.; post-graduate work Long Island College Hospital, New York; married Bertha Grant Thomas, of Jersey City, N. J., Sept. 28, 1898. Practiced medicine in Providence, R. I., since 1903; editorial writer for Providence Advocate; trustee Watchman Industrial School. Member Providence City Council, 2 terms, 1912-14; Republican. Trustee Winter St. A. M. E. Zion Church. Member National Medical Assn., R. I. Medical Assn., Providence Medical Assn. Grand master of R. I. and director endowment dept. Odd Fellows; member Knights of Pythias. Home: 572 Cranston St. Office: 144 Dexter St., Providence, R. I.

HILL, Andrew Henry, clergyman; born at Brentwood, Tenn., June 7, 1870; son of Rev. Alexander and Everline (McGuire) Hill; prep. edn. State Univ. for Negroes, Ark.; A.B., Wilberforce Univ., 1901 (D.D., 1909; A.M.,

Campbell College, Miss, 1913); married Hannah Augusta Dickson, of Springfield, O., Aug. 13, 1904; 3 children: William A., Andrew, Jr., Henry. Licensed to preach in A. M. E. Church, 1889; pastored Marvel, Palmer, Jacksonport, Pine Bluff, Clarendon, Marianna, Ft. Smith, Little Rock, Ark.; while in Wilberforce was pastor, Allen Chapel, Dayton, and Allen Chapel, Springfield, O.; pres. Shorter College, Little Rock, 1904-12; pastor Bethel A. M. E. Church, since 1912. Trustee, Wilberforce Univ., Shorter College. Republican. Mason; member Knights of Pythias, Knights of Tabor, Mosaic Templars. Club: Search Light (literary). Address: 414 W. 9th St., Little Rock, Ark.

HILL, Daniel Webster, institute president, clergyman; born at White Oak Precinct, Dinwiddie Co., Va., Feb., 1865; son of Isaac and Nancy (Bridgeport) Hill; A.B., Va. Normal and Collegiate Institute, 1898; student Yale Divinity School, 1898-9; grad. Newton Theological Seminary, Mass., equivalent to D.D., 1901; post-graduate Union Theological Seminary, New York, 1902; married Stella Geffigen, of Eastern Shore, Va., 1884 (died 1890); 2 children: Elnora, Mary Eliza, both instructors in Clifton Forge N. & I. Institute. Ordained by N. E. Missionary Convention, Bridgeport, Conn., June 15, 1901; organized first colored Baptist Vacation Bible School, Abyssinian Church, summer, 1902; missionary and field secretary Colored Baptist State Convention, New York, Dec, 1902 to July, 1903; financial agent Howard Colored Orphan Asylum, Brooklyn, N. Y., 1903-4; pastor Shiloh Baptist Church, Jamaica, N. Y., 1904-5; founder Mt. Lebanon Church, Brooklyn, 1906, and pastor to 1910; pastor Smith Chapel, Hot Springs, also pres. Clifton Forge Normal and Industrial Institute, Va., since 1910. Address: Clifton Forge, Virginia.

HILL, Ida Alma, supervising industrial teacher; born at Kilbourne, La., Nov. 10, 1889; daughter of Nathan and Almira (Bonner) Hill; ed. at Arkansas Baptist College, Little Rock; attended Branch Normal College, Pine Bluff, Ark., 2 terms; unmarried. Began as public school teacher, Kilbourne, La., 1905; supervising industrial teacher of Negro Rural Schools, Chicot County, Ark., since 1914; she is one of 10 supervisors, or Jeanes Fund Industrial Teachers, under State of Arkansas Department of Education; the work is part of the system of public instruction aided by the Anna T. Jeanes Fund; it reaches the most remote schools and homes in Ark.; she was secretary the Chicot County Teachers' Assn., 1908-11. Missionary Baptist. Address: Box 93, Eudora, Ark.

HILL, J. Leubrie, actor; head of an aggregation of colored professional people under the name of "Darktown Follies"; has written number Lyrics for white theatrical people. Address: New York.

HILL, Johnson Washington, physician, clergyman; born in Dinwiddie Co., Va., 1865; son of Isaac and Nancy (Stepford) Hill; preparatory edn. Va. Normal and Collegiate Institute; S.T.B., Tufts College, 1900 (A.B., 1913); M.D., College of Physicians and Surgeons, Boston, 1908; special student, Harvard, Yale, Brown, Oberlin; married Estelle E. Mason ,of Providence, R. I., Dec. 14, 1898; 5 children: Estelle, Ruth, Gladys, Elenor, Nina. Ordained Baptist ministry, 1895; since pastor St. Stephens Church, Cambridge, Mass.; member National Baptist Convention, and Mass. State Baptist Convention. Practiced medicine in Boston since 1900; registered as physician, 1908; director Metropolitan Mercantile Realty Co., N. Y.; justice of the peace, Boston. Republican. Member National Medical Assn., N. E. Medical Society. 32d degree Mason; member Order of Moses, St. Luke, Good Samaritans. Address: 309 Columbus Ave., Boston, Mass.

HILL, Leslie Pinckney, principal training school; born at Lynchburg, Va., May 14, 1880; son of Samuel Henry and Sarah Elizabeth (Brown) Hill; grad. high school, E. Orange, N. J., 1898; A.B., Harvard, 1903, A.M.,

1904; married Jane Ethel Clark, of Newark, N. J., June 2, 1907; 3 children: Eleanor, Hermlone, Eline. Teacher of English and education at Tuskegee Normal and Industrial Institute, Ala., 1904-7; principal of Manassas Industrial School, Va., 1907-13, and of the Cheyey Training School for Teachers, Cheyney, Pa., since 1913; president board of trustees Manassas Industrial School; secretary-treas. Association of Negro Secondary and Industrial Schools; member board of managers Armstrong Assn., Philadelphia, Pa. Republican. Methodist. Member Phi Beta Kappa. Address: Cheyney, Pa.

HILL, Richard, real estate, former teacher; born at Nashville, Tenn., Oct. 12, 1864; son of James Madison and Rachael (Foxhall) Hill; ed. city schools, Nashville; Gaines High School, Cincinnati, O.; special courses Glens Falls, N. Y., and Chicago, Ill.; married Ruth Eva Burton, of Nashville, Jan. 22, 1885; 6 children: Lillian B. (Mrs. Eugene T. Page), Richard, Jr., William T., Harriett E. (Mrs. Theo. B. Barrett), R. Kathryn, Ruth Ann. Began as teacher in Nashville, 1884; supervisor of music, writing and drawing in city schools 17 years; was first Negro holding supervising position in public schools in southern states; in real estate business since 1901, and first licensed old line life insurance agent among colored people in South; director of Negro Dept., Tennessee Centennial Exposition, 1907; name appears on bronze tablet placed in Centennial Park, Nashville, in commemoration of the centennial event. Secretary board of trustees A. M. E. Church Sunday School Union Publishing House; treasurer Capital Hill Lodge No. 59, A. F. & A. M. Home: 1016 Argyle Ave. Office: 410 1-2 Cedar St., Nashville, Tenn.

HILL, Richard, Jr., lawyer; born at Nashville, Tenn., June 5, 1887; son of Richard and Ruth Eva (Burton) Hill; preparatory and college edn. Fisk Univ.; LL.B., Univ. of Mich., 1911; unmarried. Practiced in Lansing, Mich., 1911-12, Chicago, Ill., since 1912; attorney for number Greek and Italian corporations, banking and business houses; vice-president and attorney for West Side Colored Protective Assn. President Independent Political League; advisory member Illinois Colored Democracy. African Methodist. Member National Geographical Assn., Alpha Phi Alpha. Mason. President Criterian Literary and Musical Club. Home: 1904 W. Lake St. Office: 748 S. Halsted St., Chicago, Ill.

HILL, Robert Leon, physician, surgeon; born at Selma, Ala., Dec. 13, 1872; son of Caleb and Agnes (Peyton) Hill; preparatory edn., Knox Academy, Selma; A.B., Selma Univ., 1892; M.D., Howard Univ. School of Medicine, Washington, D. C., 1897; married Ida A. Hamilton, of Palmyra, Mo., June 24, 1903. Practiced in Boonville, Mo., since 1900; visiting physician and assistant surgeon to St. Joseph Hospital; has served on U. S. pension examining board, Boonville. Republican. Baptist. Secretary Pan-Missouri Medical Assn. Mason; member Odd Fellows, United Brothers of Friendship. Home: 1102 Third St. Office: 503 1-2 Morgan St., Boonville, Mo.

HILL, Tyler Edward, lawyer, publisher; born in Henry Co., Va., Apr. 23, 1883; son of James David and Caroline Virginia (Harris) Hill; ed. public schools, Washington, D. C., Presbyterian Parochial School, Martinsville, Va., and Howard Univ.; married Sallie Stovall, of Bramwell, W. Va., Apr. 23, 1914. Practiced law in Keystone, W. Va., since 1910; legal adv'sor of Keystone Supply Co.; partner of M. T. Whittice in McDowell Times Printing Co., since 1912; associate editor and business mgr. The McDowell Times; his writings on racial subjects, labor and mining conditions attract considerable attention; life threatened on account of articles which resulted in shake-up of police force for treatment of Negroes in Bluefield, 1913; self and partner indicted for mailing matter intending to incite riot; director Fairmont Land Assn. Trustee Kittrell College, N. C., 1903-5. Member McDowell County

Colored Republican Organization; political orator and party leader in southern W. Va. African Methodist. Member exec. com. National Negro Press Assn. Mason; member Odd Fellows, St. Luke's, True Reformers. Club: McDowell Gun. Address: The McDowell Times, Keystone, W. Va.

HILTON, Thomas Harrison, physician; born at Little Rock, Ark., Mar. 31, 1881; son of Thomas H. and Serena (Browne) Hilton; A.B., Fisk Univ., Nashville, Tenn., 1901; M.D., Howard Univ. School of Medicine, Washington, D. C., 1908; unmarried. Practiced in Philadelphia since 1908. Republican. Baptist. Mason; member Odd Fellows, Knights of Pythias. Address:- 1522 Butler St., Philadelphia, Pa.

HILYER, Andrew F., accountant in the Treasury; born at Monroe, Ga., Aug. 14, 1859; son of Alfonso F. and Mary (Johnson) Hilyer; attended public schools, Omaha, Neb.; grad. high school at Minneapolis, Minn., 1878; A.B., Univ. of Minn., 1882; LL.B., Howerd Univ., 1884, LL.M., 1885; took course in higher accountancy at Draughan Business College, Washington, 1907-9; married Mamie E. Nichols, of Washington, July 1, 1886; 2 children: Gale P., Kathleen H. Accountant in the U. S. Treasury since 1882; published Union League Dictionary, 1893-1900; supervised work relative to study of business and social status of colored people in Washington and compiled the report, 1900; was secretary executive committee in charge expenditures of Negro exhibit at Jamestown Exposition, 1907; was one of the first colored writers for standard magazines; invented a hot air register attachment; director Building Association. Trustee Howard University. Member National Negro Business League, National Association for Advancement of Colored People, also a college fraternity. Club: Mu-So-Lit. Address: 2352 5th St. N. W., Washington, D. C.

HOBSON, Carvie Gustavus, pharmacist; born at Mocksville, N. C., Apr. 26, 1888; son of Moses and Elizabeth (Morton) Hobson; attended Slater State Normal School, Winston-Salem, N. C.; studied pharmacy and chemistry at Shaw Univ., Raleigh, N. C., 1912-13; married Virginia Sanders, of Raleigh, June 30, 1914. Passed examination before State Board of Pharmacy and registered under laws of N. J., 1913; in business under name of Leonard Pharmacy Plainfield, since Nov. 20, 1913. President the Negro Business League of Plainfield. Baptist. Home: 535 W. 4th St. Store: 327 Plainfield Ave., Plainfield, N. J.

HODGES, Addiear Lena, writer; born in Shelby County, Tenn., Nov. 23, 1889; daughter of Charles Henry and Mary Ann (Paris) Hodges; public school edn. Published first book, 1915, under title of Once in Christ You Are Never Out. Missionary Baptist. Home: 3653 Calumet Ave., Chicago, Ill.

HOFFMAN, Frances Othenia, supervising industrial teacher; born at Kerrs Creek, Va., Dec. 13, 1890; daughter of John William and Mary Ann (Franklin) Hoffman; grad. Hampton Normal and Agricultural Institute, Va., 1913. One of the 32 supervising industrial teachers under the Board of Education, Va.; in charge the work in schools and homes of Rockbridge County since 1913. Baptice. Home: 30 Fuller St., Lexington, Va.

HOFFMAN, John W., music teacher; deputy sheriff; born at Ossining, N. Y., 1871; grad. Palmer Collegiate and Business Institute, Ossining. Teacher of music for number of years at St. John's School, the Ossining School for Young Ladies, Irving Institute, Dr. Holbrook School, and 12 years in Mount Pleasant Academy; appointed deputy sheriff, 1915. President the Local No. 398, American Federation of Musicians; past commander Camp No. 144, Sons of Veterans; member Westchester County League. Address: Ossining, N. Y.

HOFFMAN, John Wessley, agriculturist, teacher; born in Barbados, B. W. I., Aug. 11, 1870; brought to America, 1882; B.S., Albion (Mich.)

College, 1882; B.S.A., Mich. Agricultural College, 1895; special work in Ontario Agricultural College, Canada, 1895-6; D.Sc., Royal Agricultural College, England, 1905; unmarried. Director of agriculture for the English Government Colony of Southern Nigeria, West Africa, 1902-7; traveled extensively through southern and northern Nigeria provinces of the English Sudan in Africa; speaks the Hausa and Yoruba languages fluently; was the means of introducing cotton growing all through the Niger Territory of Africa; teacher of science and agricultural worker at Tougaloo Univ., Miss., since 1912; organized community work that is producing beneficial results for miles around the university; has practically revolutionized the life of young people through his corn club and social settlement work, and was the means of changing farm life for the better all about Tougaloo; additional to his travels in Africa has visited many parts of Europe and Asia. Fellow Royal Agricultural Society; member French Agricultural Society, Massachusetts Agricultural Society, New York Society Natural History. Home: New Orleans, La. Address, Tougaloo, Miss.

HOLLAND, Arrie Ellsworth, teacher; born at Willis, Texas, Feb. 7, 1876; son of Benjamin and Margaret (Spiller) Holland; high school edn., Willis; B.S., Bishop College, Marshall, Tex., 1901; married Libbie L. Fair of Willis, 1901. Worked on farm to 1896; received teachers' certificate of 1st class that year; taught in rural schools of Walker County, Montgomery, Trinity and Hardin county schools; principal high school, Ennis, Tex., 1910-11; teacher of chemistry and trigonometry at Bishop College, Marshall, since 1912; owner and operator 800-acre farm at Willis. Trustee Marshall City Park. Republican. Missionary Baptist. Member State Teachers' Assn., East Texas Teachers' Assn., Marshall Negro Business League. Mason; member Knights of Pythias, United Brothers of Friendship, American Woodmen, Silver Fleece. Address: Marshall, Texas.

HOLLOWAY, Henry Wesley, editor, publisher; born at Meridian, Miss., Sept. 13, 1868; son of Henderson and Della (Collins) Holloway; attended public schools, Edwards, Miss.; grad. College of Pine Bluff, Ark.; also grad. Sprague's Correspondence School of Law, Detroit, Mich.; took public speaker's course under Greenville Kleiser, and special course in English under Professor Cody, both of Funk & Wagnalls Co., New York; married Alice McNeal, of Helena, Ark., Oct. 30, 1890; 2d marriage, Plymouth Adelaide Tukes, of Helena, Nov. 30, 1902. Editor and owner Interstate Reporter, Helena, Ark., since 1905; prop. Reporter Printing Co.; director Magnolia Cemetary Assn. Trustee Interstate Academy. Republican. Member executive board P. L. M. and D. Baptist Assn. Mason; member Knights of Pythias, Sons and Daughters of Independence Colored Woodmen, National Baptist Benefit Assn. Home: 1329 Franklin St. Office: 525 Ohio St., Helena, Ark.

HOLLOWAY, Isaac H., physician, surgeon; born at Brownsville, Tenn., Mar. 26, 1875; son of Isaac and Lila Holloway; attended LeMoyne Institute, Memphis, Tenn., 1897-1902; student Atlanta (Ga.) Univ.; M.D., College of Physicians and Surgeons (Univ. of Illinois), Chicago, 1911; married Belle C. Anderson, of Memphis, Dec. 28, 1905. Editor Memphis Daily Striker, 1905, one of few daily newspapers ever undertaken by colored people in U. S.; began practice in Chicago, 1911; ambulance surgeon for City of Chicago since June, 1911, civil service appointment; member clinical staff on gynecology Provident Hospital. Baptist. Member National Medical Assn., Illinois Medical Society, Chicago Medical Society, also Physicians, Dentists and Pharmacists Club of Chicago. Member Odd Fellows, Knights of Pythias. Home and Office: 1658 W. Lake St., Chicago, Ill.

HOLLOWAY, John Wesley, clergyman; born in Merriweather Co., Ga., July 28, 1865; son of Houston H. and

Cordelia (Thrash) Holloway; student Atlanta (Ga.) Univ.; A.B., Fisk Univ., Nashville, Tenn., 1894, B.D., 1906; married Henri E. Bransford, of Springfield, Tenn., Sept. 24, 1906; 3 children: Guerney D., Herbert M., Lena May. Taught in rural schools of Ga., 1882-8; was member Fisk Jubilee Singers during tour, 1889; assistant principal Guthrie (Okla.) High School, 1900-4. Ordained Congregational ministry, 1900; pastor in Guthrie 3 years, Newark, N. J., 4 years, Trebes, Ga., since 1909; moderator Georgia State Congregational Convention; associate editor Georgia Congregationalist; evangelist; elocutionist; composer of songs and poems. Republican. Mason; member Odd Fellows, Good Samaritans. Address: Thebes, Ga.

HOLLOWAY, William Harvard, college professor, sociologist, clergyman; born at Raleigh, N. C., 1875; son of William and Annie Holloway; prep. edn. Kittrell (N. C.) College, and Tuskegee Normal and Industrial Institute; B.D., Talladega (Ala.) College; B.D., Yale Divinity School; took special courses in rural social problems at Massachusetts Agricultural College; married Ella L. Hawes, of Macon, Ga., 1913; 1 child: Eunice V. Ordained Congregational ministry, 1900; pastor Thomasville, Ga., 1900-11; director of extension work and professor of practical sociology, Talladega College, since 1911. While at Thomasville, made survey for H. Paul Douglass book of Christian Reconstruction of the South which was published as "A Typical Negro Community"; with his class on sociology at Talladega, makes annual study on convict lease system, Negro wages in mining districts, country Church life, housing of Negroes. and other social conditions, all with view of making the college an important social service institution; organized Annual School of Observation for Talladega County colored teachers, also Talladega County Colored Farmers' Assn.; conductor of the annual pastors' institute and Bible conferences; has directed number co-operative movements among colored people. Address Talladega, Ala.

HOLLY, Alonzo Potter Burgess, homoeopathic physician, surgeon; born at Port au Prince, Haiti, W. I., Sept. 21, 1865; son of Rt. Rev. James Theodore and Sarah (Thompson) Holly; father was first Negro bishop in Protestant Episcopal Church, Haiti, and by invitation during Pan-Anglecan Synod in England, 1878, preached in Westminster Abbey, the only Negro to ever occupy that pulpit; ed. Lycoe Petion, Port au Prince, 1876-9; Harrison College, Barbados, B. W. I., 1879-81; only colored student in Atherstone Grammar School, England, 1881-3 (won athletic champion cup each year, and awarded gold medal, the Alumni Prize for best scholarship, 1883); received certificate for examinations in religious knowledge, Latin, Greek and French, from Cambridge Univ., England, 1883; M.D., New York Homoeopathic Medical College and Flower Hospital, 1888; only Negro in class of 50 students; married Imogene Leandra Morais, of Kingston, Jamaica, Mar. 21, 1885; 7 children: Leila L., Katherine L., James T., Lydia, Eugenie P., Cleomie T., Blanche M. Practiced in Brooklyn, N. Y., 1888-9, Haiti, 1889-99, Nassau, Bahama Islands, 1900-12 (except 1905 in New York), Key West, Fla., 1912-13, Miami, Fla., since 1913, and proprietor Holly Drug Store, Miami; also conducted Bahama Drug Store at Nassau, 1906-12, People's Drug Store at Key West, 1912-13. Was consul for Republic of Haiti in Bahama Islands, 1899-1903; president board of trustees Boynton Normal and Industrial Institute, Nassau, 1905-8; professor of English in high schools in Haiti, and president Board of Health. Was only Negro at banquet following enthronement of Archbishop Benson in England, 1882; there met Prince Edward of Wales, archbishops of Canterbury, York, number bishops of the Church of England, Lord Buxton and other notables; holds exequatur signed by Queen Victoria and Lord Salisbury, dated Mar. 8, 1900. Member National Medical Assn., State

Medical, Dental and Pharm. Assn. of Fla., Dade County Medical Assn. (treas.), Hahnemannian Institute (New York). Mason, Grand Orient of Haiti; member Odd Fellows, Knights of Pythias, Elks, Good Samaritan, Order Eastern Star, Household of Ruth. Author: La Situation Economique de la Republiquo d' Haiti, 1901; Haiti et l' Intervention Etrangere 1902; The Problems of Our Race, Our Duties and Responsibilities, 1903; Applied Hygiene, 1913; The Negro in the Bible, 1915. Home and Office: 519 Third St., Miami, Fla.

HOMES, Dwight Oliver Wendell, vice-principal high school; born at Lewisburg, W. Va., Nov. 15, 1877; son of John A. and Sarah (Bollin) Holmes; attended public schools of Md., N. Y., and Va., 1883-93; A.B., Howard Univ., Washington, D. C., 1901, A.M., 1914; grad Columbia College, N. Y., 1915; married Lucy C. Messer, of Washington, June 24, 1907; 1 child: Dwight, Jr. Instructor in Sumner High School, St. Louis, Mo., 1902; instructor Colored High School, Baltimore, 1902-7, head department of science, 1907, and vice-prin. since 1909. President of General Alumni Assn. of Howard Univ., 1911-14, and Baltimore Schoolmasters' Club, 1914-15. Home: 1418 Druid Hill Ave., Baltimore, Md.

HOLSEY, Lucius Henry, bishop; born near Columbus, Ga., Apr. 25, 1845; son of James and Louisa (Winn) Holsey; attended Baptist College, Augusta, Ga., few months; (D.D., Morris Brown College, 1872, Paine College, 1900); married Harriet Pearce, of Sparta, Ga., Nov. 8, 1863 (died 1909); 6 children: James H., Kate M., Ella D., Charles W., Claude L., Sumner L. Ordained in Colored M. E. ministry, 1869; traveling minister in Ga., 1869-73; consecrated bishop, 1873; traveling bishop throughout southern states since 1873, superintending work of establishing schools and churches. Founded and now trustee Paine College, Augusta; trustee Holsey Industrial Academy, Cordele, Ga., and Helen Cobb Institute for Girls, Barnesville. Was editor Gospel Trumpet 4 years; con-

tributor to Christian Index 40 years. Author: Church Manual, 1892; Church Hymnal, 1892; Racial Problem, 1903; Little Gems (pomes), 1902; Autobiography, Sermons, Essays. Address: 335 Auburn Ave., Atlanta, Ga.

HOMER, Horatio Julius, police sergt.; born at Farmington, Conn., May 24, 1848; public school edn. Served as waiter, steward on steamboats and in dining car service; in last named positions had narrow escapes in number of railroad accidents; appointed messenger in police commissioners headquarters, Boston, Mass., Dec. 24, 1878; police sergt. since 1895. Hobby: Collection of postage stamps. Home: 686 Massachusetts Ave., Boston, Mass.

HOOD, James Walker, bishop; born Kennett Township, Chester County, Pa., May 30, 1831; son of Levi and Harriett (Walker) Hood; attended school only few months in Chester County, and in Delaware, during period, 1841-5; had tutor for Greek, but studied theology without a teacher; (D.D., Lincoln Univ., Pa.; LL.D., Livingstone College, Salisbury, N. C.); married Hannah L. Ralph, of Lancaster, Pa., Sept., 1852; 2d marriage, Sophia J. Nugent, of Washington, D. C., May, 1858; 3d marriage, Mrs. Keziah P. McCoy, of Wilmington, N. C., June 6, 1877. Joined New England Conference A. M. E. Zion Church, 1858; sent to Nova Scotia as missionary, 1860; missionary to freemen within Union army lines in N. C., 1863; ordained bishop, 1872. Wa member North Carolina Constitution Convention, 1868, also superintendent of public instruction in N. C. Republican. Author: The Negro in the Christian Pulpit, 1884; One Hundred Years of the M. E. Zion Church, 1895; The Plan of the Apocalypse, 1900. Address: 445 Ramsey St., Fayetteville, N. C.

HOOD, Solomon Porter, clergyman, teacher, writer; born at Lancaster, Pa., July, 1853; son of Lewis P. and Matilda Catherine (Porter) Hood; attended public schools, Lancaster and New York; A.B., Lincoln (Pa.) Univ., 1873, S.T.B., 1880; attended lectures at Columbia Univ., New York; extension course Univ. of Pa.; post-graduate studies Princeton Theological Seminary. Teacher public schools, Middletown, Pa., 1873-7, in preparatory dept. Lincoln Univ., 1877-80. Ordained Presbyterian ministry, 1877; after few months joined A. M. E. Church; pastor at Oxford, Pa., 1877-80; principal Beaufort (S. C.) Normal and Industrial Academy, 1883-7; missionary to Haiti, 1888-92; pastor Philadelphia, 1893-5, LaMott, Pa., 1896-1900, Reading, 1900-4, Frankford, Philadelphia, 1904-7, Harrisburg, 1907-10, Orange, N. J., 1910-14, Trenton since 1914; literary editor A. M. E. Sunday School Teachers' Quarterly. Was chief organizer and director-general Emancipation Exposition of N. J., 1913. During service at Haiti, acted as under-secretary in American legation; during Haitian revolution, 1890, carried message of peace under the U. S. Flag out of Port au Prince from Legitime to Hypolyte. Republican. Author: Sanchfred Dollars, 1910; What Every African Methodist Should Know, 1913. Address: 311 N. Montgomery St., Trenton, N. J.

HORTON, Judith Carter, librarian, teacher, lecturer; born at Wright City, Mo., May 17, 1866; daughter of Joseph and Ann Carter; A.B., Oberlin (O.) College, 1891; married Daniel Gibbs Horton, of Columbus, Kan., June 23, 1894; 6 children: Joe, Judith, Alice, Mary, Ruth, Louisa. Began as principal high school, Columbus, Kan., 1891; principal high school at Guthrie, Okla., 1892-5; lecturer on racial subjects. Organized the Excelsior Negro Woman's Club of Guthrie, 1906, and under its auspices founded the Excelsior Library, 1908; since served as librarian; the library is now maintained by taxation, and was first ever established in America by a Negro woman; president Library Association. Congregationalist. Member National Association of Colored Women, and was delegate to conventions at Louisville, Ky., 1910, Wilberforce, O., 1914; president Oklahoma Federation of Woman's Clubs; member Oklahoma Negro Teachers' Assn.

Address: Excelsior Library, 321 S. 2d St., Guthrie, Okla.

HOUSTON, Gordon David, university professor; born at Cambridge, Mass., May 6, 1880; son of John Benjamin and Sarah Jane (Wilson) Houston; grad. English High School, Cambridge, Mass., 1898, Latin High School, 1900; A.B., Harvard, 1904; married Dora Mayo Lawrence, of Washington, D. C., Aug. 20, 1907; 2 children: Dorothy Maud, Ethel Augusta. Teacher and head dept. of English, Tuskegee Normal and Industrial Institute, Ala., 1904-7, Colored High School, Baltimore, Md., 1907-10; instructor in English M Street High School, Washington, D. C., 1910-12; professor of English, Howard Univ., since 1912. Is one of seven Negroes that have received special distinction in scholarship at Harvard Univ. Corporal M. V. M., 1898-1901. Baptist. Member Sigma Pi Phi. Clubs: McGregor (Cambridge, Mass.), Mu-So-Lit and School (Washington, D. C.). Contributor to The School Teacher, principal articles being: Every High School Teacher's Place in the English Work, 1910; A Plea for Functional English, 1910. Address: 1920 13th St. N. W., Washington, D. C.

HOWARD, Daniel Edward, eighteenth President of Liberia; born in Monrovia, Liberia, Aug. 1, 1861; attended the Church and State Schools of the Republic; graduate of the College of Liberia. Has filled various positions of trust in both Church and State; was Secretary of State under the seventeenth President of Liberia, The Honorable Arthur Barclay; elected President, and inaugurated January 3, 1912; the term of office was formerly for 2 years; he is the first to serve a 4 year term under the new law. Address: The Honorable Daniel E. Howard, President of Liberia, Monrovia, Liberia, W. Africa.

HOWARD, James H. W., publisher; born at Hamilton, Ont., Mar. 1859; son of Hamilton and Virginia Howard; grad. Buffalo High School, N. Y., 1875, Sinico Academy, 1879; married Ella Dorem, of Westminister, Md., Mar. 29, 1884; 1 child: Layton Leroy.

Publisher of Howard's Negro American Magazine, 1880-5, State Journal, 1885-90, Howard's American Magazine, 1897-1904; member firm of Jas. H. W. Howard & Son, publishers, and editor of The New Era, since 1911; gen newspaper corr., and magazine writer; pres. Mutual Penny Savings Fund; secretary-treas. W. H. Craighead newspaper advertising agency; was member Marshall & Howard fruit and produce firm 18 years; in shirt mfg. business 2 years; promoter of 50th Anniversary of the Emancipation Celebration and Exhibition held in Pa., Sept. 15, to Oct. 1, 1913. Democrat; member City Council, Harrisburg, 1885-8; clerk in office of Secretary of State, 1893-5, in State Treasurer's office, 1906-8. Presbyterian. Member Negro Press Assn., Negro Business League. Mason. Author: Bond and Free, 1889. Home: 306 S. 15th St. Office: 10 S. Court St., Harrisburg, Pa.

HOWARD, John Dalphin, editor, publisher; born at Shelbyville, Ky., May 23, 1869; son of John and Delia Belle (Board) Howard; grad. Scribner High School, New Albany, Ind., 1893; married Anna Marie Everett, of Mt. Sterling, Ky., at Milwaukee, Wis., June 7, 1909. Began as traveling representative for Indianapolis Freeman, 1895, later made advertising manager; was editor and pub. National Domestic Magazine, 1896-8; founded the Indianapolis Ledger, 1912, a newspaper which shows his own personality and ideas. Author: Know Thy Self (a narrative of crime and adventure which was published serially for more than a year in the Indianapolas Freeman); Delma (a short story). Address: 405 Muskingum, St., Indianapolis, Ind.

HOWARD, Perry Wilbur, lawyer; born at Ebenezer, Miss., June 14, 1878; son of Perry and Saran (Malden) Howard; A.B., Rust Univ., Holly Springs, Miss., 1898; student Fisk Univ., Nashville, Tenn., 1899; LL.B., Illinois College of Law, 1906; (LL.D., Cambell College, Jackson, Miss., 1914); married Wilhelmina E. Lucas, of Macon, Miss., Aug. 14, 1907; 2 children. President of Campbell College, 1899-1900; professor of mathematics at Alcorn Agricultural and Mechanical College, Miss., 1900-5; admitted to Miss. bar, 1905; since practiced in Jackson. Trustee Campbell College, Prestiss Industrial College. Progressive; has been delegate to Republican National Convention. Member National Negro Bar Assn. Mason; member Odd Fellows, Knights of Pythias. Home: 502 W. Pearl St. Office: 112 W. Farish St., Jackson, Miss.

HOWARD, Wayne Cox, physician, surgeon; born at Ebenezer, Miss., Dec., 1882; son of Perry and Sallie Howard; preparatory edn. Holly Springs, Miss.; 1896-9; M.D., Meharry Medical College, Walden Univ., Nashville, Tenn., 1906; married Ethel, daughter of Wayne Wellington Cox, of Indianola, Miss.; 1 child: Wayne Cox Howard, Jr. Began practice in Demopolis, Ala., 1906; removed to Bessemer, Ala., 1912; member drug firm of Howard Brothers, 1911-12; proprietor Howard's Drug Store Since 1912. Republican. Baptist. Member National Negro Medical Assn., and Knights of Pythias. Address: Bessemer, Ala.

HOWELL, Smith Allen, clergyman; born in Nansemond County, Va., Dec. 29, 1860; son of James and Edith Howell; ed. Franklinton Christian College, N. C., 1881-5; (D.D., Association College Correspondence School, Baltimore, Md.); married Rosa Artis, of Southampton County, Va., Sept. 7, 1897; 2 children: Susie I., Mary E. Entered the ministry in Nansemond County, 1885; pastor Wesley Grove Christian Church, Newport News, Va., since 1897; president Afro-Christian Convention, Eastern Virginia Christian Conference. Founder and president Sons and Daughters of Peace, Penny Nickel and Dime Savings Bank, the Christian Moral and Industrial Training School, Rescue Home for Erring Women, and Sons and Daughters of Peace; secretary Franklinton Christian College; editor Light of the Race and Christian Herold. Trustee Newport News Training School, Whitaker Memorial Hospital.

Republican. Mason; member Odd Fellows, Order of St. Luke, Good Samaritans. Author (pamphlets): My Ideal Christian Church; My Trip to South America; The Negro in the South, His Condition and the Remedy; The Great Eyeopener to the Doctrine of Entire Holiness and Sanctification. Address: 726 19th St., Newport News, Va.

HOWSE, John Wordsworth, principal public school; born at Murfreesboro, Tenn., 1873; son of John and Elizabeth (Washington) Howse; grad. normal dept., Walden Univ., Nashville, Tenn., 1893; B.S., Fisk Univ., 1879; took course in Wayman Business College, Chicago, Ill.; studied 2 summers at Univ. of Chicago; married Ida Sanders, of Carthage, Tenn., Aug. 18, 1897; 6 children: Alma J., LaCosta, Glady Joy, Olive L., Sander W., Thelma E. Began as principal normal school, Greensburg, La., 1897, contniuing 3 years; prnicipal public school, Tullahoma, Tenn., 1900-10; professor of science, Howard High School, Chattanooga, 2 years; principal Avenue School, So. Chattanooga, since 1913. Methodist. Member Knights of Pythias. Home: 816 E. 5th St., Chattanooga, Tenn.

HOYT, Stewart Ellison ("Mayor"), city clerk collecting dept.; born at Washington, N. C., Jan. 1, 1863; son of John G. and Sarah Ann Hoyt; grad. Roxbury High School, Boston, Mass., 1881; married Martha E. Watkins, of Richmond, Va., Feb. 15, 1888; 1 child: Stewart E. Jr. Began in gents furnishing store, Boston, 1884, continuing to 1894; since employed in various depts., City of Boston, now chief Division of Ancient Records, City Collecting Dept.; commonly called "Mayor" by friends on account long service with city. Member investment board Harding, Cox & Martin Real Estate Syndicate. Organizer and pres. 6 years, Ward 18 Colored Democratic Club. Congregationalist. Mason; G. E. L. K. Grand Lodge of Elks; member Comfort Benevolent Assn. Clubs: Ward 16 Tammany, Coloraine Social (pres.). Contributor to Detroit Plaindealer, New York Age, Amsterdam News, Boston Reliance. Home: 772 Shawmut Ave., Boston, Mass.

HUBERT, Benjamin Franklin, director and agricultural extension lecturer; born at White Plains, Ga., Dec. 25, 1884; son of Zack and Camilla (Hillman) Hubert; attended schools at White Plains; A.B., Morehouse College, 1909; won honors in oratory and debating contests; B.Sc.Agr., Massachusetts Agricultural College, Amherst, 1913; was in charge of agricultural survey made by that college; began post-graduate work at Univ. of Wis., 1913; unmarried. Was director of agriculture at Americus (Ga.) Institute, 1909-10; resigned to enter the college of Amherst; director of agriculture at the State Agricultural and Mechanical College, Orangeburg, S. C., since Aug. 1, 1912; agricultural extension lecturer for the State; travels in all parts giving advice and counsel to the people on rural life problems; his duties as professor of agriculture, the extension service, and special study of colored people in rural districts of the South include much work that is commended by experts in the U. S. Bureau of Education; secretary State A. & M. College Cabinet; field secretary Alumni Association of the college, and director its Athletic Assn.; director S. C. State Colored Fair; editor the Palmetto Farmer since 1914; the extent of his studies is shown in articles on "Rural Life in the South"; wrote "The Farmer's Garden," a bulletin; prepared "Text on General Agriculture." Baptist. Member National Teachers' Assn. in Colored Schools, the City Charity Organization, Knights of Pythias; hon. member S. C. State Federation of Woman's Clubs. Address: State Agricultural and Mechanical College, Orangeburg, S. C.

HUCKABEE, Hattie J., supervising industrial teacher; born at Greensboro, Ala., Aug. 10, 1875; daughter of Homer and Mildred (Watt) Hill; attended district school near farm where she was born, and Tullibody Academy, Greensboro; grad. State Normal School, Montgomery, Ala., 1893; attended Summer Normal

School for Teachers, at Hampton Institute, Va., 1912, 13, 14; married B. E. Huckabee (M.D.) of Greensboro, Nov. 18, 1895. Began as teacher in Tullibody Academy, 1893; was principal Rosedale public school number of years; later principal Fossil's graded school; supervisor of Negro rural schools in Jefferson Co., Ala., since 1912; this branch of public instruction is under State Department of Education; aided by the Anna T. Jeanes Fund the system reaches the most remote schools and homes in the state. Presbyterian. Member Alabama State Teachers' Assn., Jefferson County Teachers' Institute (officer), King's Daughters, City Federation of Clubs, Phillis Wheatley Club, Missionary Club. Home: 920 8th Ave., Birmingham, Ala.

HUCLES, Henry B., business man; born at Richmond, Va., Aug. 31, 1856; son of Samuel S. and Manerva (Boyd) Hucles; ed. Richmond Normal and High School; private instruction under Prof. D. B. Williams; married Ruth Brown, of Charles City, Va., Jan., 1894; 7 children. Teacher public schools 2 years; in mailing division of postoffice at Richmond for number years; agent for Richmond & Danville Electric Ry., 6 years; manager Virginia Beneficial & Insurance Assn., 1889-1914; in mercantile business since 1914. 33d degree Mason. Club: Richmond Athletic. Address: 8 E. Baker St., Richmond, Va.

HUDGINS, Lavinia A. Bess, supervising industrial teacher; born near Hampton, Va., May 22, 1874; daughter of James and Sarah Frances (Elliott) Bess; taught to read, write and cypher by mother; was much further advanced than older children when she entered school at age of 6 years; grad. Hampton Normal and Agricultural Institute, 1893; married Ralph Hudgins, of Mathews County, Va., Dec. 25, 1901. Taught school one term before graduation, and several terms since 1893; appointed supervisor Negro Rural Schools, Mathews Co., Va., 1914; this branch of public instruction is under the State Board of Education; aided by the Anna T. Jeanes Fund it

reaches the most remote schools and homes in the State. Was church organist 6 years, and filled every office in the Sunday School of Zion Methodist Church at Phoebus, Va. Address: Susan, Mathews County, Va.

HUDSON, Oscar, lawyer; born at Clinton, Henry Co., Mo., Jan. 4, 1876; son of Coleman and Martha (Pruitt) Hudson; ed. in schools of Clinton, and City of Mexico, Mexico; married Estelle Rowland, of Rome, Ga., June 6, 1908. Translator of Spanish for troops in U. S. Army in Cuba 7 months, 1898-9; was instructor in Spanish at Colored Y. M. C. A., Los Angeles, California, one term; in real estate business, Los Angeles, 1908-11; practiced law in San Francisco since 1911; appointed Liberian consul for Port of San Francisco, Apr. 22, 1915; secretary Negro Welfare League. Christian Scientist. Progressive. Mason; member Knights of Pythias. Home: 3321 Sacramento St. Office: 372 Monadnock Bldg., San Francisco, California.

HUDSON, Richard B., denominational secretary; born at Uniontown, Ala., Feb. 7, 1866; son of Richard and Mollie (Fleetwood) Hudson; prep. edn. Uniontown District Academy, and Selma Univ., Ala.; A.B., Selma, 1890, A.M., 1898; studied 3 summers, Chautauqua (N. Y.) College of Liberal Arts; married Irene M. Thompson, of Birmingham, Ala., Dec. 26, 1900; 2 children: E. Leola, I. Bernice. Proprietor coal firm of Hudson Bros., 16 years; principal Clark High School, Selma, since 1889; sec. Ala. Baptist State Convention since 1896; sec. National Baptist Convention, also Sunday School Congress of National Baptist Convention, elected 1907; was del. World's Missionary Conference, Edinbaugh, Scotland, 1910; statistical sec. Baptist Sunday School State Convention; assistant cashier Penny Savings Bank; sec. board of trustees Selma Univ.; trustee National Training School for Women and Girls, Washington, D. C. Sec. 10 years, pres. 1 year, Ala. State Teachers' Assn.; pres. Selma Negro Business League. Endowment treas. Masonic Grand

Lodge of Ala. Address: P. O. Box 455, Selma, Ala.

HUMMONS, Henry Lytle, physician; born at Lexington, Ky., Feb. 25, 1873; son of Thomas N. and Mary E. (McPhoetus) Hummons; grad. Knoxville College, Tenn., 1896; M.D., Medical College of Indiana, 1902; post-graduate work Harvard Medical School, Boston, Mass., 1911; married Rose E. Dent, of Springfield, Ohio, Sept. 2, 1903; 3 children: Helen, Henry, Thomas. Practiced in Indianapolis since Jan. 1, 1903; medical inspector of public schools 2 years; director Lincoln Hospital. Republican. Presbyterian (United). Member Tri-State Medical Society of Ind., Ky. and Ohio, Aescupalian Medical Society of Indianapolis. Home: 840 N. California St. Office: 653 N. West St., Indianapolis, Ind.

HUMPHREY, W. Berlin, physician, surgeon; born at Port Gibson, Miss., July 25, 1881; son of Abraham and Martha (Johnson) Humphrey; ed. public schools, Port Gibson, Natchez College, Miss., Walden Univ., Nashville, Tenn.; took course in a business college at Rochester, N. Y.; M.D., Meharry Medical College (Walden Univ.), 1907; married Maude M. Scott, of Holly Springs, Miss., Jan. 2, 1911. Practiced in Fort Smith, Ark., 18 months; removed to Okla., 1909; since practiced in Sapulpa. Pres. Okla. State Medical, Dental and Pharm. Assn., also Sapulpa Negro Business Men's Assn.; was delegate to National Negro Business Men's League, Muskogee, Okla., Aug., 1914. Republican. Baptist. Mason; member Odd Fellows, Knights of Pythias, Knights and Ladies of Harmony of the World. Home: 312 N. Leonard Ave. Office: 233 W. Hobson Ave., Sapulpa, Okla.

HUNT, Robert D., teacher, editor; born at Huntsville, Ala., July 6, 1874; son of Alfred J. and Eliza J. Hunt; public school edn., Huntsville; grad. Agricultural and Mechanical College, Normal, Ala., 1889; unmarried. Editor and publisher of "The Educator," at Huntsville, since 1899; lecturer and demonstrator in pedagogy; was appointed as U. S. guager, District of

Ala., 1903; later promoted to office of deputy collector for the Southern Ala. and Miss. district, with headquarters at Mobile; Republican. Member Knights of Pythias, United Brothers of Friendship, and Mosaic Templars. Address: 323 Church St., Huntsville, Ala.

HUNT, William H., consul; born in Tenn.; appointed U. S. Consul at St. Etienne, France, Nov. 1, 1906, from New York. Address: American Consulate, St. Etienne, France.

HUNTER, John Edaward, surgeon; born in Giles Co., Va., Jan. 1, 1864; son of Augustus and Margaret (Campbell) Hunter; attended rural schools in Va., public schools, Labanon, Ohio; literary edn. Oberlin College; M.D., Western Reserve Univ., Cleveland, O., 1889; post-graduate work Chicago, New York, and Boston; married Mary B. Bush, of Lexington, Ky., Aug. 15, 1891; 4 children: John, Jr., Bush A., Marietta F., Daniel. Practiced in Lexington since Apr. 1, 1889. Republican. Congregationalist. Member National Medical Assn. (ex-pres.), Kentucky State Medical Assn.; also member Knights of Pythias. Home: 441 N. Upper St. Office: 118 N. Broadway, Lexington, Ky.

HUNTON, Addie D. Waites, advisory secretary Y. W. C. A.; born at Norfolk, Va., June 11, 1870; daughter of Jesse and Adaline (Lawton) Waites; grad. public school, Boston, Mass.; only colored person to graduate from Spencerian College of Commerce, Philadelphia, Pa., 1889; studied at Kaiser Wilhelm Univ., Strassburg, Germany, 3 semesters, 1908, 9, 10; speaks Franch and German; married William A. Hunton, of Chatham, Ontario, Can., July 19, 1893; 2 children: Eunice, William Alphaeus, Jr. Began as teacher in public school at Portsmouth, Va.; lady principal State Normal and Agricultural College in Ala., to 1893; secretary and burser Clark Univ., Atlanta, Ga., 1905-6; advisory secretary for work among colored people to National Board, Y. W. C. A., 1907-15; has traveled to most parts the U. S., and extensively in Europe. Member National Association for Advancement of Colored People, National Association Colored Woman's Clubs (national organizer 4 years); also member Brooklyn Y. W. C. A., Brooklyn Woman's Club, Brooklyn Equal Suffrage League. Home: 919 S St. N. W., Washington, D. C. Office: 600 Lexington Ave., New York.

HUNTON, William Alphaeus, senior secretary International Y. M. C. A.; born at Chatham, Ontario, Can., Oct. 31, 1865, in the Hunton home which was an "underground railroad station" where John Brown occasionally held conferences during slavery days; son of Stanton and Mary A. (Johnson) Hunton; A.M., Wilberforce Collegiate Institute, Canada; married Addie D. Waites, of Norfolk, Va., July 19, 1893; 2 children: Eunice, William Alphaeus, Jr. Began as teacher in public schools, Canada; later appointed clerk in Department of Indian Affairs under Canadian government; was first colored secretary in Young Men's Christian Association for work in U. S., 1888; secretary Colored Men's Dept. International Committee of Y. M. C. A. since 1891; delegate to World's Y. M. C. A. Jubilee Convention, London, Eng., 1894, World's Student Conference, Tokio, Japan, 1907; attended Evangelical Conference, Shanghi, China, also made missionary tour in Corea, 1907; delegate to World's Christian Student Conference, Mohonk Lake, N. Y., 1912; has written number pamphlets relative to colored men in Y. M. C. A. work. Methodist. Member American Academy Political and Social Science, Southern Sociological Congress, Sigma Pi Phi (New York Chapter). Club: Brooklyn Citizen. Home: 919 S. St., N. W., Washington, D. C. Office: 1816 12th St., N. W.; New York Office: 124 E. 28th St.

HURST, John, bishop; born at Port au Prince, Haiti, May 10, 1863; son of Thomas and Sylvanie Hurst; attended public school and college (Lycee), Port au Prince; B.D., Wilberforce Univ., Ohio, U. S. A., 1866; married K. Bertha Thompson, of Baltimore, Md., 1890. Began as superintendent of missions, Haiti, and pastor St. Paul's Church, Port au Prince, 1887, continuing to 1889; secretary Haitain Legation, Washington, D. C., 1889-1913; pastor Waters A. M. E. Church, Baltimore, 1894-8; Bethel Church, 1898-1903; Waters Church, again, 1903-8; financial sec. A. M. E. Church, 1908-12; consecrated bishop and appointed to Florida, 1912; also has supervision of the mission fields in the West Indies and South America. Address: 1808 McColloh St., Baltimore, Md.

HYDER, Frank Marion, clergyman, teacher; born at Johnson City, Tenn., Dec. 25, 1868; son of Alfred and Mary Hyder; public school edn. Johnson City; A.B., Lincoln Univ., Pa., 1894; S.T.B., 1897 (D.D., 1911); married Eliza Moton, of Washington, D. C., Dec., 1897. Began as professor civil government and English history, Haines Institute, Augusta, Ga., 1897, continuing 3 years; ordained Presbyterian ministry, 1897; pastor at Augusta to 1903; founded Ninth Street Training School, Bristol, Tenn., 1903, and with assistance of his wife conducted the institution to 1915; now pastor Faith Presbyterian Church, York, Pa.; was selected as lecturer on the Negro problems in New York state by the Board of Missions for Freedmen, 1909; president Ministers' Interdenominational Union, Bristol, Tenn., 12 years; now president Ministers' Interdenominational Union of York. Republican. Home: 634 S. Queen St., York, Pa.

I

INBORDEN, Thomas Sewell, teacher; born in Loudoun Co., Va., 1865; son of Mrs. Harriett Proctor; prep. edn. Oberlin (O.) College, 1883-7; A.B., Fisk Univ., 1891; (A.M., Benedict College, Columbus, S. C., 1903); married Sarah Evans, of Oberlin, 1891; 3 children: Wilson B., Dorothy V., Julian E. Preached in a church at Beaufort, S. C., few months; opened Normal School under American Missionary Assn., Helena, Ark., 1891, continuing as teacher there 3 years; organized Albany Normal School, Ga., and served as principal, 1893-5; principal Joseph Keasbey Brick Agricultural Industrial Institute and Normal School, Enfield (Bricks), N. C., since 1895; member N. C. Teachers' Assn.; was chairman board of awards for Negro Department at Jamestown Exposition, Norfolk, Va., 1907. Congregationalist. Address: Bricks, N. C.

IRVING, Ernest Walker, physician, surgeon; born at Circleville, Ohio, Aug. 9, 1869; son of Richard Henry and Mildred Johnson (Walker) Irving; grad. Circleville High School, 1889; Duckworth Business College, Columbus, O., 1893; M.D., Meharry Medical College (Walden Univ.), Nashville, Tenn., 1897; married Elvina A. Jones, of Memphis, Tenn., Aug. 9, 1899. Principal of Wards Academy (A. M. E.), Natchez, Miss., 1889-90; practiced in Memphis since 1897; member Memphis Board of Health; medical inspector city schools; medical examiner American Association of Accident Underwriters, and Pacific Mutual Ins. Co.; medical examiner and vice-pres. Standard Life Ins. Co.; vice-pres. Solvent Savings Bank & Trust Co.; was treas. Bluff City Laundry, 1900. Republican. Episcopalian. Member Sigma Pi Phi, National Medical Assn., Tri-State Medical Assn., Tennessee State Medical Assn., Bluff City Medical Assn., Negro Board of Trade, Colored Citizens Assn. Home and Office: 598 St. Paul Ave., Memphis, Tenn.

ISAAC, E. W. D., clergyman; born at Marshall, Tex., June 2, 1863; son of Sandy and Mary I.; ed. Marshall Academy and Bishop College; (hon. D.D.). Sec. Baptist Young Peoples Union, National Baptist Convention. Address: 409 Gay St., Nashville, Tenn.

ISH, George William Stanley, physician; A.B., Yale, 1905; M.D., Harvard Medical School, 1909. Practiced in Little Rock since graduation. Address: Little Rock, Ark.

IMES, Elmer Samuel, teacher of science; A.B., Fisk Univ., Nashville, Tenn., 1903, A.M., 1910. Address: Emerson Institute, Mobile, Ala.

J

JACKSON, Algernon Brashear, surgeon; born at Princeton, Ind., May 21, 1878; son of Charles A. and Sarah L. (Brashear) Jackson; grad. Princeton High School; student Indiana Univ.; M.D., Jefferson Medical College, Philadelphia, Pa., 1900; unmarried. Began as assistant surgeon in Philadelphia Polyclinic Hospital (white), 1900, continuing 12 years; superintendent and surgeon-in-chief at Mercy Hospital and School for Nurses; frequent contributor to American and London medical journals; discribed new treatment for acute rheumatism by injections of magnesium-sulphate, which attracted wide attention in the medical world; has written and urged that a foundation be established for practical study of health and social conditions among Negroes. Episcopalian. Member National Medical Assn., Pennsylvania Medical Society, Philadelphia Medical Society; member executive committee National Negro Business League; one of founders Sigma Pi Phi. Mason; member Odd Fellows, Elks. Club: Citizens. Republican. Author: Evolution of Life, 1910. Address: 770 S. 18th St., Philadelphia.

JACKSON, Arthur Smith, educator; born at Waco, Tex., Jan. 1, 1873; son of Smith and Amanda (Brown) Jackson; B.S., Paul Quinn College, 1895; M.S., Wilberforce Univ., 1911; married Maggie Carrie Denham, of Lake City, Fla., June, 1897; 1 child: Louise. Teacher in schools of Tex., 6 years; professor of mathematics, Paul Quinn College, 12 years; commissioner of education of A. M. E. Church since 1912, and trustee all its colleges. Member National Teachers' Assn., National Association of Teachers' in Colored Schools, State Teachers' Assn. of Tex. Mason; member Odd Fellows, Knights of Pythias, United Brothers of Friendship. Address: 823 S. 2d St., Waco, Texas.

JACKSON, Ella Jefferson, commercial teacher; born at Athens, Ga., Nov. 15, 1888; daughter of John Thomas and Araminta (Jefferson) Jackson; grad. Malden High School, Mass., 1909, Malden Commercial School, 1910; unmarried. Teacher in National Religious Training School, Durham, N. C., since 1911. Congregationalist. Home: 22 Granville Ave., Malden, Mass. Address: National Religious Training School, Durham, N. C.

JACKSON, George Washington, high school principal; born in Lee County, Ala., 1856; son of Anderson and Clara (Allen) Jackson; B.S., Fisk Univ., Nashville, Tenn, 1887; married Josie B. Blythe, of Macon, Miss., Dec., 1887; 1 child; 2d marriage, Mrs. Mattie L. Morris, of Helena, Ark., Sept. 8, 1902. Taught school in Ala., 1875-7; removed to Texas, 1877, and was teacher in rural schools number of years; principal high school, Corsicana, since 1882; in point of service is oldest teacher in Texas. Republican. Methodist. Member State Teachers' Assn., former pres.; secretary Negro City Business League. District secretary Grand Lodge No. 25, Odd Fellows. Author (pamphlets): School Room Helps; Helps for Parents and Teachers. Address: Box 185, Corsicana, Texas.

JACKSON, Ida Joyce, teacher, retired; born at Columbus, O., Mar. 28, 1863; daughter of James Wiley and Kate (Roney) Joyce; grad. Central High School, Columbus, 1882; took course in business college; studied sociology and French at Lincoln Institute, Jefferson City, Mo., 1899-1900; married Prof. John Henry Jackson, of Lexington, Ky., July 17, 1889. First assistant under Prof. W. H. Mayo in public schools at Frankfort, Ky., 1885-8; principal in preparatory dept. Kentucky Normal and Industrial Institute, 1888, and professor in normal dept., to 1898. Treasurer National Association of Colored Women since 1910; honorary president Colorado State Federation of Woman's Clubs. Republican; took active part in politics in Colorado; presided at meetings during campaign of Theodore Roosevelt, 1904. Episcopalian; president Woman's Guild of St. Philip's Church, and member Woman's Aux-

iliary. Club: Fortnightly Reading. Address: 548 E. Spring St., Columbus, Ohio.

JACKSON, J. S., financial secretary A. M. E. Zion Church, 402 N. 15th St., Birmingham, Ala.

JACKSON, Mabel Sapho, teacher; born at Athens, Ga., Feb. 9, 1884; daughter of John Thomas and Araminta (Jefferson) Jackson; ed. Knox Institute, Athens, grammar school, Charlotte, N. C., grammar and high school, Malden, Mass.; A.B., Boston Univ., 1909; unmarried. Began as head teacher of academic dept., State Normal School, Elizabeth City, N. C., 1909, teacher of algebra, Latin and penmanship since 1911. Congregationalist. Home: 22 Granville Ave., Malden, Mass. Office: State Normal School, Elizabeth City, N. C.

JACKSON, May Howard, sculptor; born at Philadelphia, Pa., May 12, 1877; daughter of Floarda and Sallie Durham (Miller) Howard; ed. public schools, Philadelphia; grad. J. Liberty Tadd's Art School, and first colored girl to win scholarship to The Academy of Fine Arts, Philadelphia, where she studied for 4 years; married William Tescumsha Sherman Jackson, of Washington, D. C., Mar. 31, 1902. Exhibited in the Veerhoff's Art Galleries, Washington; several of her busts commanded favorable comment from art critics. Address: 1816 16th St. N. W., Washington, D. C.

JACKSON, Oliver Toussiant, farmer, private messenger to Governor; born at Oxford, O., Apr. 6, 1862; son of Hezikiah and Carolina (Shaffer) Jackson; attended public school, Cleveland, O., 2 years; took 3 year Chautauqua course; married Minerva J. Matlock, of St. Joseph, Mo., July 28, 1904. In catering business, Denver, Colo., 1887-90; steward Idaho Springs Club, 1890-2; prop. restaurant, Boulder, 1892-4; farmer since 1894; erected building on farm and conducted Country Club, 15 years; private messenger to Governor John F. Shafroth, 1908-12, to Gov. Ellis M. Ammons, 1912-14; founder Dearfield Townsite and Settlement, comprising

13,500 acres of U. S. Government and Colo. state lands located in Platte River Valley. Trustee People's Union Presbyterian Church, Dearfield. Address: (Dearfield) Masters, Colo.

JACKSON, Robert Cornelius, high school teacher, piano and voice; born at Evansville, Ind., Feb. 11, 1881; son of Newton and Mary (Wilson) Jackson; grad. Clark High School, Evansville, 1900; student, Indiana Univ., 1903, 1911, Indiana State Normal School at Terre Haute, summer terms, 1908, 10, 13, 14, 15; took private instruction on piano; married Carrie Noval Harris, of Hopkinsville, Ky., June 10, 1909; 1 child: Eloise Joy. Began as teacher at King's Mills, Corydon, Ky., 1900; taught school in Vanderburgh County, Ind., 1901-3, Evansville, 1903-7; teacher in grammar school, 1907-13, at Mt. Vernon; assistant principal Booker T. Washington High School, 1913-15, principal since 1915; devotes spare time teaching vocal and instrumental music; member Apollo Quartette; arranges practically all concert programs for schools and churches; proprietor ice cream parlor and cafe called "The Favorite"; conducts playground for colored children with modern equipment; owns property in Evansville, own home, and rooming house. Republican. Member Mt. Vernon Negro Business League, also Boy Scouts. Home: 108 Main St., Mt. Vernon, Ind.

JACKSON, Thomas Taylor, insurance; born at Charlottsville, Va., Jan. 1, 1878; son of Anthony and Linda (Brooks) Jackson; ed. public schools, Newark, N. J. Business College, and school of economics Univ. of Pittsburgh, Pa.; married Lelie. A Jennings, of Roanoke, Va., Sept. 2, 1911. Began in real estate business, Pittsburgh, 1902; resident director Pelican Mutual Life Ins. Co., since 1904; pres. and treas. Thomas T. Jackson Agency; sec. and mgr. Protective Brotherhood. Episcopalian. Mason; member Knights of Pythias, Elks. Club: Loendi Social. Home: 235 Martsolf Ave., West View, North

Side. Office: 806 Wylie Ave., Pittsburgh, Pa.

Jackson, William Tecumseh Sherman, teacher; born in Essex Co., Va., Nov. 18, 1866;; son of Lindsay and Mary Jane (Smith) Jackson; grad. Va. Normal and Collegiate Institute, Petersburg, Va.; A.B., Amherst College (Mass.), 1892, A.M., 1897; first Master of Arts degree conferred on a coloren man by Amherst; S.S.B., Catholic Univ. of America, Brookland, D. C., 1896; married May Howard, of Philadelphia, Pa., Mar. 31, 1902. Teacher of mathematics, M Street High School, Washington, 1892-1906; was lecturer in Howard Univ. School of Law, 1897-8; principal M Street High School, 1906-9; head teacher department of business practice, Colored High School of Washington, since 1912. Congregationalist. Mason. Club: School. Home: 1816 16th St. N. W., Washington, D. C.

JACOBS, Charles Cook, clergyman; born at Camden, S. C., Nov. 16, 1862; A.B., Claflin Univ., Orangeburg, S. C.; A.M., later; (hon. D.D.); married Jennie E. Walker, of Sumter, S. C., Apr. 25, 1895; 6 children. Entered ministry, 1884; field secretary Board of Sunday School for Colored Conferences, M. E. Church, since 1899; was editor Daily Christian Advocate issued during conference of 1908. Trustee Claflin Univ. Republican. Address: 37 Council St., Sumter, S. C.

JACOBS, Robert Edmond, teacher; born at Converse, La., May 22, 1877; son of Solomon and Ellen (Belton) Jacobs; grad. Coleman College, Gibsland, La., 1902; student Univ. of Chicago, 1905; married Mary Lee, of Gibsland, Jan. 28, 1904. Taught school at Hatcher, La., 1897-1901; teacher Coleman College, 1902-3; president and principal Sabine Normal & Industrial Institute, Converse, since Nov. 2, 1903. Progressive. Baptist. Address: Converse, La.

JACOBS, Woody Elmer, principal public school; born at Richmond, Mo., Nov. 3, 1885; son of Rev. John W. and Anna (McGee) Jacobs; attended public schools at Richmond, Kingston and Parksville, Mo., Topeka, Kan.; grad. Lincoln High School, Kansas City, Mo., 1904; student Univ of Kan. School of Medicine, 1904-5; A.B., Univ. of Kan., 1908; atttended summer school, Columbia Uinv., New York, 1912; unmarried. Began as head of normal dept. Mississippi Industrial College at Holly Springs, 1908; principal Bruce School, Kansas City, Kan., 1909-14, also teacher in summer and night schools; principal Lincoln School since 1914; auditor Afro-American Investment & Employment Co.; editor Sunday School column of Christian Index. Republican. African Methodist. President, Kansas City Branch, National Association for Advancement of Colored People. Mason. Author: The Sunday School Teachers' Guide (pamphlet). Address: 2055 N. 3d St., Kansas City, Kansas.

JAMES, Charles H., merchant; born in Ohio, 1863; son of Rev. Francis and Elizabeth (Courtney) James; ed. country schools; married Roxie A. Clark, 1885; 3 children. Teacher in country schools number years; now wholesale produce and fruit merchant doing annual business exceeding $100,000. Progressive. Baptist. Mason; member Knights of Pythias. Address: 23 Summers St., Charleston, W. Va.

JAMESON, Henry Washington, clergyman, lawyer; born at Mexico, Mo., June 15, 1865; son of William and Elizabeth (Miller) Jameson; public school edn., Macon, Mo., 1871-8, Galesburg, Ill., 1878-80; A.B., Knox College, Galesburg, 1888; LL.B., Weslyan Law School, Bloomington, Ill., 1897; studied theology at Morgan Park, Ill.; (LL.D., Central Law School, Louisville, Ky., 1906; D.D., Morris Brown College, Atlanta, Ga., 1907); married Nannie L. Crabbe, of Galva, Ill., June 18, 1887; 2 marriage, Lillian E. Jenkins, of Evansville, Ind., Nov. 19, 1903; 1 child: Henry W. Jr. Admitted to bar at Bloomington, Ill., 1896; was editor and pub. American Pilot, Bloomington. Licensed to preach in A. M. E. Church, 1896; his work has been confined to 4th Episcopal Dist. in the Ill., Iowa, and W. Ky.

conferencés; now pastor Bethel Church, Champaign, Ill.; was delegate from Illinois to World's Sunday School Congress, Washington, D. C., 1910, Zurich, Switzerland, 1913; instructor in Sunday School methods at Young People's Congress, Atlanta, Ga., 1914; his Sunday School work endorsed by 3 Sunday School associations. Trustee Wilberforce Univ. Served in Spanish-American war; commissioned 1st lieut. 8th Ill. Vol. Inf., and later appointed judge-advocate general Courts-Martial, Military Dist. of Mayori, Providence of Santiago, Cuba; was first colored clergyman to serve as chaplain in legislature of Wis.; now chapain Spanish War Veterans, Dept. of Illinois; major U. S. Boy Scouts. Republiacn. Member Kappa Alpha Nu, Masons, Order Eastern Star. Address: 400 E. Park Ave., Champaign, Ill.

JAMISON, Monroe Franklin, bishop; born at Rome, Ga., Nov. 27, 1849; son of George Shorter and Olivia (Shorter) Jamison; never attended school; (hon. D.D.); married Martha A. Flourney, of Leigh, Tex., Feb. 24, 1874. Bishop, Colored M. E. Church, since 1910. Address: Leigh, Tex.

JACKSON, Robert Raymond, publisher, former state legislator; born at Malta, Ill., Sept. 1, 1870; son of William and Sadie (Howard) Jackson; grad. high school, Chicago, 1885; married Annie Green, of Chicago, Ill., May 31, 1888; 2 children: Naomi, George Earl. Began as clerk in Chicago postoffice, 1889, continuing in number departments to asst. supt. Armour Station, 1908; resigned 1909; prop. Fraternal Press, printing and publishing, since 1909; sec. Chicago Giants Base Ball Club; director and auditor African Union Co., mahogany shippers, dealers in African merchandise; dir. Fraternal Globe Bonding Co., Mt. Glenwood Cemetary Assn. Military writer and authority on text books; his criticism of books issued by U. S. A. officers (1905) received favorable comment from War Dept.; in service 25 years; maj. 8th Regt. I. N. G., since 1895; served with regt. in Spanish-American War. Member 48th General Assembly, Ill., (1913-15), from 3rd Senatorial Dist., Chicago; won contest for seat in House over Democratic opponent; apptd. by Governor Edward F. Dunne, member Illinois Commission to arrange Half-Century Anniversary Celebration for Negro Freedom. Republican. African Methodist. Mason; member Odd Fellows, United Brothers of Friendship, Knights of Pythias (maj.-gen. comdg. U.R.), National Association Post Office Clerks, Musicians Union of the World. Club: Appomatox. Home: 435 East 37th St. Office: 3441 State St., Chicago, Ill.

JAYMES, Sully, lawyer; born in Campbell Co., Va., Mar. 30, 1878; son of Hampton and Ella (Anderson) Jaymes; family removed to Everett, Mass., where he attended public school; grad. English High School, Boston; student Boston Univ. Law School, 2 years; LL.B., Univ. of Mich., 1901; married Anna Redmund, of Paris, Ky., Apr. 27, 1905. Admitted to Ohio bar, 1901; practiced in Springfield, O., since 1902; attorney and sec. Independent Chattel & Mortgage Loan Co.; several times appointed by the court to defend in murder cases. Ohio representative of 50th Anniversary of Negro Freedon, Washington. Active in politics since 1904; member exec. com. National Democratic League; one of organizers and was first pres. Colored Independent Political League, Springfield; campaign speaker in Ky., 1914; endorsed by U. S. Senator Pomerene, by Governor Cox and the Democratic State Committee for appointment as recorder of deeds, Washington, 1914. African Methodist; was dir. Central Y. M. C. A., 7 years. Member Knights of Pythias, Elks. Home: 317 E. Euclid Ave. Office: Times Bldg., Springfield, O.

JEFFERSON, James Alvin, physician; born at Columbus, Tex., Oct. 22, 1871; son of Adam Jefferson; student Wiley Univ., Marshall, Tex., 1889-93, Prairie View State Normal and Industrial College, 1894; M.D., Marquette Univ., Medical Dept., Milwaukee, Wis., 1911; married Octavia O. Billups, of Goliad, Tex., Sept. 12, 1894; 3 children: James B., Clementine Anita, Chauncey D. Teacher in public schools of Tex., 7 years; practiced medicine in Des Moines, Ia., since Apr. 1, 1912. President Cosmopolitan Literary Society. Republican. African Methodist. Mason; member Knights of Pythias, Odd Fellows, International Order of Twelve. Club: Des Moines Negro Lyceum. Home: 1322 Day St. Office: 764 9th St., Des Moines, Ia.

JEFFERSON, J. Rupert, principal high school; born at Pomeroy, Ohio, Jan. 27, 1869; grad. Pomeroy Academy, 1888; married Clara Thomas, of Parkersburg, W. Va., June 21, 1898; 2 children: Harry, Miles. Principal colored school at St. Albans, Va., 1888-92, Sumner High School, 1893-1902; recording clerk in office of Secretary of State (W. Va.), 1902-6; principal Sumner High School, Parkersburg, since 1906; was member board of regents Bluefield Colored Institute, 1901-9, governor's appointment. Republican. Methodist. Member Board of Commerce, West Virginia Educational Assn., W. Va., Teachers' Assn. (pres. 1898-9). Member Knights of Pythias; grand worthy counselor Court of Calanthe of W. Va. Address: Box 618, Parkersburg, W. Va.

JEFFERSON, Lottie Adelia, supervising industrial teacher; born at Centralia, Va., Oct. 11, 1885; daughter of John and Bettie (Howlette) Jefferson; attended grammar school S. Richmond, Va.; grad. Va. Normal and Industrial Institute, Petersburg, 1908; studied at Hampton Institute, summer school, 1911, 12; unmarried. Teacher in district schools, Va., 1908-10; supervising industrial teacher in Chesterfield County, under the State Board of Education, Va., since 1910; during winter months teaches sewing, reed, raffia, crocheting, wood work and cooking; has helped school improvement league to raise funds for the extension of school terms, new buildings, repairs, etc.; conducts Girls Canning and Home-makers clubs in homes, summers and fall seasons, and has helped to can many thousand quarts of fruits and vegetables. Baptist. Member State Teachers' Assn. of Va., Negro Organization Society, State B. Y. P. U., State Sunday School Convention, J. R. Giddings and Jollifer Union, Mosaic Templars. Club: Minerva Literary (Richmond). Home: Centralia, Va. Office: Va. Normal and Industrial Institute, Petersburg, Va.

JEFFERSON, Wilson, verse writer; born at Augusta, Ga., July 24, 1879; son of Albert James and Adrienne (Wilson) Jefferson; grad. high school, Augusta, 1896; student Atlanta Univ., 1897-8; married Minnie Owens, of Augusta, Oct. 10, 1910; 2 children: Wilson, Jr., Albert. Postoffice employee, Augusta, since 1903; writer of poems which are accepted and published by New York Independent, Boston Transcript, Christian Register (Boston), Springfield Republican, Mass., and others; "Verses," published 1910, attracted much favorable comment. Baptist. Address: 450 Calhoun St., Augusta, Ga.

JENIFER, John Thomas, clergyman; born at Malborough, Prince Georges Co., Md., Mar. 10, 1835; son of John H. and Catherine (Burgess) Jenifer; attended commercial college, New Bedford, Mass., 2 years; B.D., Wilberforce Univ., 1870, in class of the first theological students from a Negro college with a Negro pres.; married Alice V. Carter, of Cincinnati, O., July 6, 1871; 4 children: Cora, John (deceased), Prof. George D., Bertha B.; 2d marriage, Mrs. Ena Lewis, of Chicago, Nov. 9, 1904. Converted in Baltimore, Md., Apr. 4, 1856; licensed to preach in M. E. Church, New Bedford, Mass., Feb. 5, 1862; ordained deacon, San Francisco, Cal., Apr. 13, 1865, elder at Xenia, O., 1868; elected historian A. M. E. Church at 24th General Conference, Kansas City, Mo., 1914; has traveled 250,000 miles in 42 states of the U. S., and Canada and Central America; preached over 6,000 sermons; served in N. E., Cal., Ohio, Ark., S. Ark., Ia., and Baltimore conferences; brought to the church $250,000 in property and cash; delivered speech at ceremonies during laying base of monument to Richard Allen, first Negro Bishop in America, at Centennial Exposition, Philadelphia, Pa., 1876; built the New Quinn Chapel, Chicago, 1892; pastor Metropolitan Church, Washington, D. C., and preached funeral sermon of Frederick Douglass, 1895; returned to Chicago, and was retired (1909) at own request after 48 years of service for the church. Was member advisory board Auxilliary Congress of African Ethnology at World's Columbian Exposition, Chicago, Ill., 1893, appointed by President Barney, the general mgr.; delivered address of welcome to the Legate Representative of the King of Belgium. Republican. Author: Who was Richard Allen and What Did He Do?; The Broader Mission of the Modern Church; The Light of Isreal and the Light of Africa; The Centennial Retrospect History of the A. M. E. Church; Jenifer's Life and Historical Notes. Address: 3430 Vernon Ave., Chicago, Ill.

JENKINS, Isaac William, newspaper man; born at Beaumont, S. C., Sept. 6, 1875; son of Isaac and Dianna Jenkins; prep. edn. Lincoln Univ., Pa.; grad. Howard Univ., Washington, 1901; B.L., Univ. of Pa.; married Birdie M. Marshburne, of Charleston, S. C., Mar. 14, 1910. Founded Wilkes-Barre (Pa.) Advocate, 1901; established Sumter (S. C.) Weekly Advocate, 1902; editor-in-chief Tampa Intelligencer, Fla., 1903-5; on staff Florida Daily Times-Union, Jacksonville, since 1905; instructor in shorthand and typewriting at Baptist College, 1906-10. Member Republican State Committee. Presbyterian. Mason; member Woodmen. Home: 519 Beaver St. Office: Florida Times-Union, Jacksonville, Fla.

JENKINS, James Frances, poultry farm, market gardner; born at Forsyth, Ga., Aug. 16, 1882; son of James and Mary Jane (Young) Jenkins; A.B., Atlanta Univ., Ga., 1905; took course Bryant and Stratton Business College, Chicago, Ill., 1908; married Eliza Christina DeGroat, of London, Ont., Apr. 30, 1913; 1 child: James

F. Jr. Proprietor poultry farm, The Gore, Ontario, Can., since 1912; added market gardening, 1913; purchased a farm adjoining original property, 1914; has four farm hands and four teams delivering produce to market daily. Baptist. Address: R. R. No. 8, London, Ontario, Canada.

JERNAGIN, William Henry, clergyman; born in Mississippi, Oct. 13, 1869; son of Allen and Julie (Ruff) Jernagin; ed. Meridian College, Alcorn Agricultural and Mechanical College, Jackson (Miss.) College; took course from American Corresponding School of Danville, N. Y.; (D.D., Guadaloupe College, Seguin, Tex.); married Willie A. Stennis, of Miss., 1888; 4 children: Lottie R., Rosebel C., Mattie C., Gertrude E. Ordained Baptist ministry, 1890; pastored number leading churches in Miss.; manaber boarding dept. Alcorn A. & M. College 2 terms; pastor at Oklahoma City, Okla., 1906-12; was leader in Baptist school work and president its educational board; as managing editor of Oklahoma Tribune, led campaign for rights of colored people more than 5 years; pastor Mt. Carmel Church, Washington, D. C., since 1912; purchased edifice in which President Woodrow Wilson worshiped; treasurer Baptist Young People's Union; advisor for the Interdenominational Bible College and Institute for Civic and Social Betterment, which is connected with the Industrial Center in Washington. Trustee Stoddard Baptist Old Folks Home. Alternate delegate to Republican National Convention, St. Louis, Mo., 1896; was president State Constitutional League of Okla., 3 years. Mason; supreme Order of Helpers; member Odd Fellows, Knights of Pythias, Order of Eastern Star. Address: 430 Q St. N. W., Washington, D. C.

JOHNSON, A. N., funeral director, embalmer; born at Marion, Ala., Dec. 22, 1866; ed. Alabama State Normal School, Talladega College, Clark's College of Embalming, Echles College of Embalming, Barnes College of Embalming; married Lillie A. Jones, of Marion, July, 1886; 2 children. President Johnson-Allen Undertaking Co., Mobile, Ala., since 1893; organized firm in Memphis, Tenn., 1902, now under name of Scott, Wilkerson & Scott; proprietor A. N. Johnson Undertaking Co., Nashville, Tenn., since 1906; owner of Lincoln Theatre Building, Johnson Block, and other property. Delegate to Republican National Convention, St. Louis, Mo., 1896, Philadelphia, Pa., 1900, Chicago, Ill., 1904; was member Republican State Committee of Ala., 16 years. Congregationalist. Mason; member Odd Fellows, Knights of Pythias, Knights of Tabor, Mosaic Templars. Address: Nashville, Tenn.

JOHNSON, Edward Austin, corporation lawyer; born at Raleigh, N. C., Nov. 23, 1860; son of Columbus and Eliza A. Johnson; attended Washington School, Raleigh; prep. edn. Atlanta Univ., Ga., LL.B., Shaw Univ. Law School, Raleigh, 1891; studied at Cottage City and Asbury Park Teachers' Training School; married Lena A. Kennedy, of Sioux Falls, S. Dak., Feb. 22, 1894; 1 chhild: Adelaide. Admitted to N. C. bar, 1891, New York bar, 1906, also to practice in U. S. courts; was assistant in office of U. S. district attorney, Raleigh, 9 years; began as instructor, and was later dean of Law Dept. Shaw Univ., for period of 14 years; now practicing in New York; attorney for unmber large corporations; held several receiverships by appointment from judges the U. S. courts. Trustee Teachers' Training School, Durham, N. C. Was alderman at Raleigh 2 terms; chairman North Carolina Congregational Committee 8 years; delegate to 4 Republican National Conventions; member New York County Republican Committee, New York County Bar Assn., New York Peace Society, Harlem Board of Trade, Southern Beneficial League; first compiler of National Negro Business League. Author: School History of Negro Race, a book adopted for use in North Carolina public schools about 1901; Negro Almanac; Light Ahead of the Negro; Negro Soldiers in Spanish-American War; Combined

History of Negro Race and Negro Soldiers in Spanish-American War, 1911. Home: 17 W. 132d St. Office: 154 Nassau St., New York.

JOHNSON, Fenton, newspaper correspondent, verse writer; born at Chicago, Ill., May 7, 1888; son of Elijah H. and Jesse (Taylor) Johnson; ed. Northwestern Univ., also Univ. of Chicago; unmarried. Teacher of English at State Univ., Louisville, Ky., for a time; special writer for Eastern Press Assn.; later acting dramatic editor New York News; contributor to various periodicals. Author: A Little Dreaming, 1913; Visions of the Dusk, 1913 (book of poems). Mrs. Josephine Turck Baker, editor Correct English Magazine was sponsor for first book. Member Authors' League of America; also member Alpha Phi Alpha. Home: 130 W. 134th St., New York.

JOHNSON, Frank H., manufacturer; born at Atchison, Kan., Nov. 6, 1869; son of Pleasant L. and Hettie (Hays) Johnson; public school edn., Kansas; took course in business college; married Anna Ewing, of Nashville, Tenn., Apr. 5, 1913; 1 child: Anita. Proprietor Johnson Carriage Co., Riverside, Calif., among largest dealers in rebuilt vehicles in state. Methodist. Home: 476 E. 12th St. Office: 204-216 10th St., Riverside, Cal.

JOHNSON, Henry Lincoln, lawyer, ex-recorder of deeds; born at Augusta, Ga.; son of Peter and Martha Johnson; A.B., Atlanta Univ.; LL.B., Univ. of Mich.; married Georgia Douglas, of Atlanta, Ga., Sept. 14, 1903. Admitted to Ga. bar and began practice in Jackson; recorder of deeds, Washington, D. C., 1909-13; practiced law in Atlanta since 1913; lecturer on subject of Negroes Political Rights; in great demand during campaigns and central figure in exposing petty politics and discrimination and segregation in government service. Republican. Baptist. Member Odd Fellows. Address: 200 Auburn Ave., Atlanta, Ga.

JOHNSON, John Albert, bishop; born at Oakville, Ont., Can., Oct. 29, 1857; son of John G. and Mary (Mack-

ey) Johnson; married Minnie S. Goosley, of Liverpool, N. S., Jan. 16, 1881. Ordained A. M. E. ministry, 1875; bishop since 1904; stationed in South Africa. Member American Academy Political and Social Science. Home: 1412 N. 18th St., Philadelphia, Pa. Address: 2 Hanover St., Cape Town, S. Africa.

JOHNSON, John J., dentist; born at Culloden, Ga., Sept. 1, 1870; son of Laura Johnson; ed. public schools, Barnesville, Ga.; preparatory course, Knoxville (Tenn.) College, 1886-8, A.B., 1894; D.D.S., Meharry Dental College (Walden Univ.), Nashville, Tenn., 1904; married Lula S. Randals, of Nashville, Tenn., Sept. 27, 1893; 2 children: Gladys, John J. Jr. Practiced in Knoxville since 1904; president Colored Coal Co. Republican. Presbyterian. Home: 1641 Clinton St. Office: 108 E. Vine St., Knoxville, Tenn.

JOHNSON, John Quincy, clergyman; born at Nashville, Tenn., May 30, 1865; son of Andrew and Johnnetta (Lawrence) Johnson; A.B., Fisk Univ., 1890; grad. Hartfort Theological Seminary, 1893; D.D., Morris Brown College, 1898; post course at Princeton Theological Seminary 2 years; married, Feb. 26, 1894, Hallie E. Tanner, daughter of Bishop Benjamin T. Tanner, of Philadelphia, Pa., and sister of H. O. Tanner, artist; she was the first woman to practice medicine in Ala., serving as resident physician Tuskegee Normal and Industrial Institute (died Apr. 26, 1901); 4 children: Sadie, John, Jr., Benjamin T., Henry T.; 2 marriage, Quintella Hall, of Mt. Pleasant, Tenn., October 8, 1901; 1 child: Ruth Quintella. Taught schools in Miss., 15 years; ordained African Methodist ministry, 1893; pastor at Montgomery, Ala., 1895-8, Birmingham, 1898-9, Nashville, Tenn., 1899-1903; presiding elder North Nashville Dist., and of Tennessee Conference since 1903, except while pastor at Shelbyville, 1910-11; private secretary to Bishop J. H. Jones of 9th Episcopal Dist.; newspaper reporter since 1895. Trustee Turner College. Socialist, and Single Taxer. Member

Southern Sociological Congress. Mason. Author: The Negro as a Writer; Sparkling Gems (both published in 20th Century Magazine). Address: 1306 14th Ave. N., Nashville, Tenn.

JOHNSON, J. Rosamond, musician; born at Jacksonville, Fla., 1873; studied at New England Conservatory of Music; developed new and distinct style of Negro music; manager Music School Settlement, New York. Composer: Under the Bamboo Tree; Since You Went Away; The Awakening; Lazy Moon, and the Congo Love Song; has written light operas for Klaw & Erlander, songs for May Irvin, Lillian Russell, and Anna Held. Address: Music School Settlement, 6 W. 131st St., New York.

JOHNSON, Louis R. W., clergyman; born at Staunton, Va., Dec. 11, 1878; son of David P. and Amanda C. (Henderson) Johnson; A.B., Lincoln (Pa.) Univ., 1899, A.M., S.T.B., 1902; married Alberta B. Coles, of Charlottesville, Va., Jan. 4, 1909; 5 children: Louis R. W. Jr., Marguerite W., Roberta M., Alora B., and infant born 1915. Instructor in Greek, Lincoln Univ., 1901-2; professor of Greek and head of Bible dept. at Piedmont Institute, Charlottsville, 1903-7; professor Greek, sciences, and dean theol. dept. Virginia Theological Seminary and College, Lynchburg, 1907-8. Ordained Baptist ministry, 1902; pastor, 1903-7, at Millboro, Whitehall, and Ivy, Va.; pastor Court Street Church, Lynchburg, since 1907; organized Sunday School Congress of Va., Sunday School Institute movement, and Lynchburg Y. M. C. A. Trustee Va. Theological Seminary and College. Author (sermon series): Odd Fellows of the Old Testament. Designed and issued a Hand Chart of the Books and Divisions of the Bible. Home: 618 Taylor St., Lynchburg, Va.

JOHNSON, Maggie Pogue, composer; born at Fincastle, Va.; daughter of Rev. Sampel and Lucy Jane Banister; ed. Virginia Normal and Industrial Institute, Petersburg; married Dr. Walter W. Johnson, of Staunton, Va., Sept. 21, 1904; 1 child: Walter W. Jr. Composer: "I Know That I Love You (words and music), also about 20 other songs; wrote (booklet): "Virginia Dreams". Baptist. President the Covington Literary and Debating Society. Home: 202 Walnut St., Covington, Va.

JOHNSON, Samuel O., teacher; born at Eufaula, Ala., July 4, 1874; son of Benjamin and Annie (Ethridge) Johnson; A. B., State Univ., Louisville, Ky., 1898, A.M., 1905; student Harvard, summer, 1900; married Lillie G. Brannon, of Louisville, July 24, 1912. Taught in district schools of Ala., several years; teacher of methods in public schools, Louisville, 12 years; now teacher of mathematics Central High School; director Walnut Hotel Co. Baptist. Member National Association for Advancement of Colored People. Address: 2015 Magazine St., Louisville, Ky.

JOHNSON, Solomon Charles, editor, publisher; born at Savannah, Ga., Nov. 20, 1869; son of John H. Johnson; grad. West Broad Street School, Savannah, 1883; unmarried. Learned printing trade when a boy; editor and manager The Savannah Tribune since 1899; owns building the plant occupies; president Royall Undertaking Co.; director Wage Earners' Bank, Guaranty Mutual Life & Health Insurance Co., Standard Life Insurance Co.; curator Carnegie Colored Library. Trustee Old Folks Home. Served as private, later commissioned officer under 4 different governor's, in Georgia State Militia; was adjutant of all colored troops of Georgia number years. Secretary Republican State Central Committee since 1912; has served as secretary and chairman executive committee of party in 1st Cong. Dist. of Ga. Congregationalis. Pres., Savannah Branch, National League on Urban Conditions Among Negroes. Mason; grand secretary in Ga., 19 years; one of organizers and grand patron for 12 years, Order of Eastern Star of Ga.; member Odd Fellows, Knights of Pythias. Address: 1009 W. Broad St., Savannah, Ga.

JOHNSON, Walter Alexander, manufacturer; born at Deep Creek near Norfolk, Va., July 10, 1876; son of William and Chestinia (Miller) Johnson; ed. private school at Norfolk, 1884-6; Norfolk Mission College, 1886-8; Franklin Evening School, Boston, Mass., 1896-8; Patrick School of Pharmacy, 1901-2; Gersumky's Dermatology Institute, 1902-3; married Mary Lyle Palmer, of Brookneal, Va., Aug. 5, 1896; 1 child: Walter A., Jr. Began as dermatologist and scalp specialist, Boston, 1899; pres. Johnson Mfg. Co., hair, scalp and face preparations, organized 1911, Johnson's School of Beauty Culture, organized 1911; was secretary Colored Co-operative Pub. Co., 1901-3; pres. Boston Negro Business League, 1913-14. Republican. Baptist. Contributor to The Boston Reliance. Address: 798 Tremont, St., Boston, Mass.

JOHNSON, Walter Werston, physician; born at Staunton, Va., Sept. 3, 1875; son of James A. and Louisa A. (Werston) Johnson; public school edn., Staunton; attended Virginia Normal and Industrial Institute at Petersburg; grad. Virginia Seminary and College, Lynchburg, 1896; M.D., Leonard Medical School, Raleigh, N. C., 1900; married Maggie Y. Pogue, of Fincastle, Va., Sept. 21, 1904; 1 child: Walter W. Jr. Practiced in Covington, Va., since Mar. 1, 1902. Republican. Baptist. Member National Medical Assn., Civic Improvement League, Covington. Mason; great chief of records Independent Order of Red Men; member Odd Fellows, Knights of Pythias, Brothers and Sisters of Love and Charity. Club: Booster. Home and Office: 202 Walnut St., Covington, Va.

JOHNSON, William Bishop, clergyman; born at Toronto, Ont., Can., Dec. 11, 1858; son of John and Matilda Johnson; public school edn., Buffalo, N. Y.; grad. normal school, Toronto, 1878; Wayland Seminary, Washington, D. C., 1879; (D.D., State Univ., Louisville, Ky., 1888; LL.D., Virginia Theological Seminary and College, 1904); married. Ordained in Baptist ministry, 1879; pastor at Frederick, Md., 2 years; general missionary for Md., Va., W. Va., and D. C., under American Baptist Home Missionary Society, 1881; appointed professor of mathematics and science at Wayland Seminary, 1882, continuing 20 years; pastor Second Baptist Church, Washington, since 1883; organized National Baptist Educational Convention, 1891; editor National Baptist Magazine since 1893; corr. editor Christian Review, of Philadelphia; president New England Missionary Baptist Convention, and Washington Evangelical Alliance; secretary-treas. Afro-American School of Correspondence. Trustee Va. Theological Seminary and College, Northern Univ., N. J. Republican; was special agent in securing religious census for U. S. Bureau of the Census, 1906. Mason; member Odd Fellows, Independent Order of St. Luke. Author (pamphlets): Sparks From My Anvil, 1898; Scourging of a Race, 1904; The Story of Negro Baptist, 1907; Arithmetic, Grammar and U. S. History. Home: 445 Fourth St. N. E., Washington, D.C.

JOHNSON, William Decker, clergyman; born at Glasgow, Ga., Nov. 15, 1869; son of Andrew Jackson and Mattie (McCullough) Johnson; ed. Atlanta (Ga.) Univ.; took correspondence course; (D.D., Morris Brown Univ., 1904); married Winifred E. Simon, of Florence, Ga., Dec. 3, 1891; 5 children: William F., Fannie E., Winifred E., Simeon T., Alvin N. Entered A. M. E. ministry, 1887; ordained deacon, 1891, elder, 1893; presiding elder Cuthbert District since 1911; secretary S. W. Georgia Conference. Trustee Johnson Home Industrial College, Morris Brown Univ., Masonic School; secretary Pythian Temple Commission. Republican. Was organizer, now supreme archer, Sublime Order of Archery; director District Grand Lodge No. 8, Odd Fellows; auditor Supreme Council of Benevolence; member Order of Eastern Star, Grand Lodge Knights of Pythias. Author: Precious Jewels, 1896. Home: Archery, Ga. Office: Cuthbert, Ga.

JOHNSTON, J. Thomas, messenger in customs service; born at Richmond, Va., Dec. 5, 1872; son of Cornelius and Nancy Lena (Jones) Johnston; ed. Normal and High School, Richmond, Va.; married Bessie Rosele Brown, of Schroon Lake, N. Y., Apr. 22, 1903; 2 children: Lloyd C., Vivian D. United States custom messenger in New York since 1906. Secretary and trustee Mt. Olivet Baptist Church 12 years. Mason; district grand treasurer Odd Fellows, N. Y., and secretary Theobald Lodge 3890 since 1900; organized, 1902, Arcturns Lodge No. 19, and brigadier-general commanding uniform rank (N. Y.), since 1911, Knights of Pythias. Club: Republican. Home: 26 47th St., Corona, L. I., New York.

JOINER, William A., educator; born at Alton, Ill., July 17, 1869; son of Rev. Edward C. and Frances (Badgett) Joiner; grad. high school, Springfield, Ill., 1886; B.S., Wilberforce Univ., 1888; LL.B., Howard Univ., Washington, D. C., 1892, LL.M., 1893, and graduate in pedagogy, 1898; post-graduate work at Univ. of Chicago summers, 1904-7; has educational credit of Ph.B.; unmarried. Principal public school, Jerseyville, Ill., 1888-91; was clerk in War Dept., Washington, 1891-4; teacher English and Latin in M Street High School, Washington, 1897-1903; director in teachers' training school Howard Univ., 1893-10; supt. normal and industrial departments at Wilberforce Univ., since 1910, also trustee. Presided at meeting when principal speakers included President William H. Taft, Justice John M. Harlem of the U. S. Supreme Court, Ambassador Brice of England, and other notables, at Washington, D. C., Mar. 8, 1910. Methodist. Member W. Va. State Teachers' Assn. Mason. Clubs: Mu-So-Lit, Short Story, Tennis, Washington Wilberforce. Author: Our Douglass. Address: Wilberforce, O.

JONES, Alfred S., hotel prop.; born in Mecklenburg County, Va., June 20, 1861; son of William and Mary Jones; public school edn., Philadelphia, Pa.; married Ella R. Gardner, of Philadelphia, Apr. 14, 1910. In hotel business in Philadelphia since 1883; now proprietor New Roadside Hotel; president Friday Night Banquet Assn.;

treasurer Hotel Brotherhood for 10 years; director Marion Cemetary Co. Was member City Council 1 term; member Citizens Republican Club. Catholic. Member Elks. Address: 514 S. 15th St., Philadelphia, Pa.

JONES, Benjamin Francis, undertaker; born at Petersburg, Va.; ed. public schools, Boston, Mass., and Claverack Academy, New York; married Harriett L. Taylor, of Providence, R. I., June, 1907. Resident of Boston since 1870; established in undertaking business, 1908. Republican. Baptist. Member Negro Business League. Mason; member Odd Fellows, Elks, Knights of Pythias. Address: 639 Shawmut Ave., Boston, Mass.

JONES, Charles Thomas, irrigation operator; born at Ashville, Ala., Sept. 1865; son of William and Annie Jones; common school edn.; married Annetta Garza, of San Antonio, Tex., Feb. 1, 1893; 1 child: Zellie J. Began in restaurant business, Houston, Tex., 1895; later established eating houses along the west coast of Mexico; was owner of quarry and in the building business at Nogales, Ariz., for number of years; retired, 1915; president African Land & Irrigation Co. Republican; was candidate for City Council in spring election, 1914; though there are only 6 colored voters in that white community, he was defeated by only 38 votes. Congregationalist. Home: 206 Walnut St., Nogales, Arizona.

JONES, Edward M., clergyman; born at Marion, Ala., Dec. 14, 1862; son of Sarah Jones; grad. State Normal School, Marion, Ala., 1883; Gammon Theological Seminary, Atlanta, Ga., 1888; (hon. D.D.); married Mittie E. Watthall, of Marion, June, 1889; 5 children: Helen M., Sadae Mae, Susie Agnes, Hattie Price, Wilbur T. Joined Central Alabama Conference, M. E. Church, 1889; pastor 6 years, Montgomery, Huntsville, Birmingham, Ala.; presiding elder 10 years; field secretary Board of Sunday Schools since 1904. Trustee Central Alabama College. Republican. Address: 250 S. Jackson St., Montgomery, Ala.

JONES, Edward Perry, clergyman, insurance, grand mastor Odd Fellows; born in Hinds County, Miss., Feb. 21, 1872; son of George P. and Laverna Jones; attended Alcorn A. & M. College when 8 years old; graduate from city schools, Vicksburg, Miss., 1888; B.S., Natchez College, 1889; (D.D., Rust Univ., 1894); married Harriet Lee Winn, of Greenville, Miss., Nov. 19, 1896; 3 children; Edward P. Jr., McKissack, George P. Ordained in Baptist ministry and pastored for several years; president Union Guaranty Ins. Co. of Miss.; grand master Odd Fellows of Miss. since 1900; grand director Grand United Order of Odd Fellows of America; represented Odd Fellows of U. S. at Burslem (Stoke-on-Trent), England, 1907, and at London and Paris. Trustee Natchez College. Republican; delegate at-large to national convention at Chicago, 1908, 1912; chairman Miss. state convention, 1913. Mason; member Knights of Pythias. Home and Office: 1413 First North St., Vicksburg, Miss.

JONES, Elisha Henry, physician, surgeon; born at Talladega, Ala., Feb. 20, 1883; son of Henry Clay and Jane (Doom) Jones; B.S., Talladega College, 1904; M.D., Univ. of W. Tenn., 1909; married Effie May Murphy, of Montgomery, Ala., July 20, 1910; 2 children: John Belton, Mattie Virginia Ivey. Principal Lauderdale College, Birmingham, Ala., 2 years; teacher of Latin and algebra, Univ. of W. Tenn., while student in Medical Dept.; practiced in Talladega since 1909; connected with New Era Pharmacy, 1909-10, with Highland Drug Co., since 1910. National supreme grand sire Home Benovolent Order; chairman board of directors National Association for Advancement of Colored People; sec. Living Endowment Assn. of Talladega College; chairman Congregational Laymen's Missionary Movement for Ala. Republican. Club: Social Settlement. Address: 124 W. Battle St., Talladega, Ala.

JONES, Eugene Kinckle, social worker; born at Richmond, Va., July 30, 1885; son of Joseph Endom and Rosa Daniel (Kinckle) Jones; prep.

edn. Wayland Academy (Va. Union Univ.); A.B., Va. Union Univ., 1906; A.M., Cornell, 1908; married Blanche Ruby Watson, of Richmond, Mar. 11, 1909; 2 children: Eugene Kinckle, Jr., Adele Rosa. Teacher of sociology and economics, State Univ., Louisville, Ky., 1908-9, Central High School, Louisville, 1909-11; associate director National League on Urban Conditions Among Negroes, New York, since 1911; member committee of management Sojourner Truth House of Delinquent Colored Girls; contributed number of articles on social work to various newspapers and magazines. Progressive. Baptist. Member Alpha Phi Alpha, Southern Beneficial League. Home: 80 Queens Ave., Flushing, N. Y. Office: 110 W. 40th St., New York.

JONES, Gabriel L., special officer, decorator; born in Sumner County, Tenn., Sept. 15, 1858; son of Nimrod and Amanda (Dickerson) Jones; grad. high school, 1882, normal, 1883, at Indianapolis, Ind.; married Allaide Turner, of Summerville, Mich., Aug. 26, 1885; 2 children: Ralph E., Benjamin H. Teacher public schools of Indianapolis, 1883-90; deputy internal collector, 1890-4; clerk in county recorders office, 1894-1901; city policeman, 1901-4; special officer in Federal Building since 1905; proprietor house decorating business. Republican; member Indiana House of Representatives, 1897-8. African Methodist. 32d degree Mason; member Odd Fellows. Address: 1222 W. 25th St., Indianapolis, Indiana.

Jones, Grace Morris Allen, director of industries in country life school; born at Keokuk, Iowa, Jan. 7, 1879; daughter of James Addison and Mary Ellen (Pyles) Morris; public school edn., Burlington, Iowa; took course in Elliot's Business College; studied elocution at Ziegfeld's Chicago Musical College; (A.M., Eckstein-Norton Institute, Cane Springs, Ky., 1910); married, June 29, 1912, Lawrence C. Jones, founder of Piney Woods Life School, Braxton, Miss.; 1 child: Turner Harris. Taught public school in Mo., 3 years; opened Grace M. Allen

Industrial School, Burlington, Iowa, 1908, continuing at head of 5 instructors and 55 students to 1912; was inuntial in the addition of vocational training in schools of Burlington; financial agent for Eckerstein-Norton Institute, 1912-13; director of girls industries at Piney Woods Country Life School since 1913. African Methodist. Address: Braxton, Miss.

JONES, Isham Giggs, teacher, editor, merchant; born at Toomsuba, Miss., Jan. 14, 1887; son of James Isham Gibbs and Sarah Elmira Elizabeth (Knott) Jones; ed. public schools of Lauderdale Co.; grad. high school, Enterprise, Miss.; (A.M., New Hope Academy, 1903); unmarried, Teacher in public schools of Lauderdale County since 1900; proprietor a general merchandise store, established 1909; founded in May, 1909, and since editor the Rising Sun, published every 2 weeks. Trustee New Hope Academy, and Meridian Baptist Seminary; president first New Hope Baptist Sunday School Convention, 1914. Republican. Member Sister's Home and Foreign Mission Society. Mason. Address: Toomsuba, Miss.

JONES, John Emory, dentist; born at Florence, Ala., Aug. 30, 1882; son of John Emory and Janie (Sampson) Jones; grad. Talladega (Ala.) College, 1906; D.D.S., Meharry Medical College (Walden Univ.), Nashville, Tenn., 1912; unmarried. Principal of public school, Shelby, Ala., 2 yrs.; practiced dentistry in Florence since 1912. Treasurer Florence Negro Business League. Congregationalist. Home: 302 S. Cedar St. Office: 118 1-2 Tennessee St., Florence, Ala.

JONES, Joseph Lawrence, merchant; born at Mt. Healthy, Ohio, June 12, 1868; son of Marshhall P. and Sarah E. (Gobson) Jones; grad. Gaines High School, Cincinnati, O., 1886; Sheldon Business College, 1909; married Helena Caffery of Cincinnati, Aug. 18, 1889; 5 children: Myra J. (Mrs. Dr. Henry C. Bryant), J. Lawrence, Helen, Ida, Martha. Teacher public schools Latonia, Ky., 1886-7, Robinson, Tex., 1887-8; principal schools New Richmond, O., 1889-90;

deputy recorder, Hamilton County, O., 1890-5; deputy county clerk, 1895-1904; principal Douglass Night School, Cincinnati, 1897-1904. Organized the Central Regalia Co., 1902, for the manufacture of secret society supplies, and since president; secretary and sales manager African Union Co., dealers in African merchandise and mahogany shippers ($500,000 corpn.); editor Fraternal Monitor. Republican. African Methodist. Member National Negro Press Assn. (vice-pres.) 33d degree Mason; adj.gen. U. R., and vice-supreme chancellor, Knights of Pythias; supreme counsellor Order of Calanthe; member Odd Fellows. Home: 1537 Blair Ave. Office: N. E. Cor. 8th and Plum Sts., Cincinnati, Ohio.

JONES, Joshua H., bishop; born at Swansea, S. C., June 15, 1856; son of Joseph and Sylvia Jones; A.B., Claflin Univ., Orangeburg, S. C., 1885; student Howard Univ.; B.D., Wilberforce Univ., 1887 (D.D., 1893); married Elizabeth Martin (deceased); 2d marriage, Augusta E. Clark, of Wilberforce, O., 1886; 4 children: Joshua, Jr., Gilbert H., Elizabeth, Alexander. Local preacher A. M. E. Church at age of 18; taught in public schools several years; regular pastor at Wheeling, W. Va., 1877, later at Wilberforce, O., Lynn, Mass., Providence, R. I., and Columbus, O.; presiding elder Columbus Dist., 1894-9; pastor at Zanesville, O., 1899; president Wilberforce Univ., 1900-8, and since member executive board; presiding bishop Tenn. and Ala., elected at General Conference, Kansas City, Mo., 1912. Trustee Payne Univ., Selma, Ala., Turner College, Shelbyville, Tenn. Republican. Address: Wilberforce, O.

JONES, Lawrence Clifton, educator; born at St. Joseph, Mo., Nov. 21, 1884; son of John Q. and Lydia (Foster) Jones; attended public schools at St. Joseph; grad. high school, Marshalltown, Iowa, and Iowa Central Business College, 1893; Ph.B., State Univ. of Iowa, 1907; married Grace Morris Allen, of Burlington, Iowa, June 29, 1912; 1 child: Turner Harris. Principal and secretary board

162 WHO'S WHO OF THE COLORED RACE

of trustees The Piney Woods Country
Life School at Braxton, Miss., since
Oct. 1, 1909; he opened this school
under a tree, having neither money
nor aid; has since acquired 478 acres
of land, erecter 12 buildings, employs
11 teachers, and averages about 200
students; extension work reaches
fully 6,000 persons annually; incorporated and is president Piney
Woods Center of Extension Education,
its purpose being the encouragement
of colored people to acquire land and
live in country; editor Pine Torch
since 1910, Backing Up the Farm
(formerly the Successful Negro Farmer), first issued 1911. Republican.
Episcopalian. Club: Lyceum (Des
Moines, Iowa). Author: Survey of
Industrial Art Movement, 1906; Up
Thru Difficulties, 1914. Address: Braxton, Miss.

JONES, Louis Davis, editor; born
at Fort Smith, Ark, Feb. 3, 1873; son
of Lewis and Nancy J. Jones; brought
up on farm; high school edn., Fort
Smith; also studied in night school;
married Cora Irving ("Texas Sweet
Singer"), of Texarkana, Tex., Sept.
10, 1904. Printer by trade; finisher
apprenticeship when 18 years of age;
with a "capital" of 10 cents and oldest brother as sponsor, purchased the
Arkansas Appreciator, 1897; this
newspaper was established by Rev.
L. J. Vanpelt one year before; equipped plant and done own mechanical
work; acquired ownership the Fraternal Union, 1902; consolidated two
papers under name of Appreciator-
Union; removed plant from Fort
Smith to Texarkana, Ark., 1911; book
and job printers. Was U. S. Guard
at Fort Smith, 1906-7. Republican;
active in Ark. politics during administration of President Theodore Roosevelt; delegate to number state conventions. Missionary Baptist; pres.
Baptist Young People's Union, United
Brothers of Friendship. Home: 801
Oak St., Texarkana, Tex. Office: 828
State Line Ave., Texarkana, Ark.

JONES, Robert Elijah, clergyman,
editor; born at Greensboro, N. C.,
Feb. 19, 1872; son of Sidney Dallas
and Mary Jane (Holly) Jones; A.B.,

Bennett College, Greensboro, 1895,
A.M., 1898; (B.D., Gammon Theologi-
cal Seminary, 1905; LL.D., Howard
Univ., 1911); married Valena T. Mac-
Arthur, of Bay St. Louis, Miss., Jan.
2, 1901. Began as local preacher at
Leaksburg, N. C., 1891; ordained M.
E. ministry, 1892, elder, 1896; pastor
Lexington and Thomasville, N. C.,
1892, Lexington, 1893, Reidsville,
1894; asst. mgr. Southwestern Christion Advocate, New Orleans, La., 1897-
1901; field sec. Board of Sunday
Schools, M. E. Church, 1901-4; editor
Southwestern Christian Advocate
since 1904. President Colored Y. M.
C. A., New Orleans; vice-president
and trustee New Orleans Univ.; vice-
pres. of trustees Bennett College;
trustee Gammon Theological Seminary. President Colored Travelers'
Prortective Assn.; 1st vice-pres. National Negro Press Assn.; member
exec. com. National Negro Business
League. "A Few Remarks On Making
a Life" is the title given to extracts
from his Commencement address delivered at Tuskegee Institute, Ala.,
published in Alice Moore Dunbar's
book entitled Masterpieces of Negro
Eloquence. Home: 5207 Constance
St. Office: 631 Baronne St., New
Orleans, Ala.

JONES, Robert Louis, physician,
surgeon; born at Lynchburg, Va.,
June 17, 1875; son of Carter Louis
and Susan Helen (Rayne) Jones; public school edn., Lynchburg; M.D.,
Howard Univ. School of Medicine,
1902; married Ottie M. Brooks, of
Washington, D. C., June 19, 1903; 1
child: Hellen E. Practiced in Charleston, W. Va., since Dec. 1, 1902;
attending physician West Virginia
Collegiate Institute since 1909; state
vice-pres. National Medical Assn.;
secretary W. Va. Medical Society. Republican. Baptist. Mason; member
Odd Fellows, Knights of Pythias.
Home and Office: 507 Dickinson St.,
Charleston, W. Va.

JONES, Rosa Belle, supervising industrial teacher; born at Staunton,
Va., Apr. 23, 1888; daughter of Robert
and Lucy (Jordan) Jones; grad.
Hampton Normal and Agricultural

Institute, Va., 1909; studied in summer school, Hampton, 1912; unmarried. Teacher public schools at Blakes, Mathews Co., Va., 1909-10, public schools Elkton, 1910-12; supervising industrial teacher in charge the work in Rockingham and Shenandoah counties, Va., since 1912; this service is under the State Board of Education and a branch of modern instruction in which the State of Virginia takes much interest; through the aid of the Anna T. Jeanes Fund it reaches into the most remote schools and homes; certain handicraft is taught in the schools, and in the summer months the children are instructed in gardening, canning, etc. at their homes; she is also assistant of the State Board of Charities and Corrections of Va. Baptist. Member County Colored Teachers' Assn., Negro Organization Society of Va.; Home: 124 Winchester Ave., Staunton. Office: Effinger Street Graded School, Harrisonburg, Va.

JONES, Samuel Benjamin, physician; born at Antigua, British West Indies, Apr. 25, 1874; son of James Shepherd and Mary Ann Sophia (Edwards) Jones; ed. grammar school, Antigua, 1889-93; Codrington College, Barbados, 1894; A.B., Durham Univ., England, 1896; A.B., London Univ., 1898, LL.B., intermediate exam., 1900; M.D., Illinois Medical College, 1909; M.D. (honoris causa), Loyola Univ., Chicago, 1911; unmarried. Began as assistant master in grammar school, Antigua, 1896, continuing to 1902; came to America, 1903; teacher of economics and Latin, St. Augustine's School, Raleigh, N. C., 1903; resident physician and director academic dept. Agricultural and Technical College, Greensboro, N. C., since 1910; was chairman hookworm commission of National Medical Assn., 1912. Member Church of England, and Convocation of London University; also member American Academy Political and Social Science, American Sociological Society. Address: Agricultural and Technical College, Greensboro, N. C.

JONES, Sarah Gibson, retired teacher; born at Alexandria, Va., Apr. 13, 1845; daughter of Daniel W. and Mary Jane (Lewis) Gibson; public school edn., Cincinnati, Ohio; studied history, biology, French and German at Univ. of Cincinnati; private instruction under Professors Whitcomb, and Hall; took 4-year course Ohio Teachers' Reading Circle; married M. P. H. Jones, of Cincinnati, June 28, 1865; 3 children: Marshall P., Oliver L., Olive G. Teacher public schools, Cincinnati, 1863-8, Mt. Healthy, Ohio, 1868-70, Columbus, 1872-5, Frederick Douglass School, Cincinnati, 1875-1911; awarded gold medal for service and retired on pension. Served as lady manager Cincinnati Colored Orphans Home for 15 years; secretary board of trustees Crawford Old Men's Home 4 years. Member Union Baptist Church since 1857. Was vice-president State Federation of Colored Woman's Clubs several years, and decked poetess-lareate in 1904; financial secretary Cincinnati Federated Woman's Clubs 7 years. Author (poems): "Lincoln"; "The Present Church"; the first was read in Memorial Hall, Cincinnati, on Lincoln's Birthday, 1909, the second at mortgage burning ceremonies of Union Baptist Church, July 1912. Address: 1537 Blair Ave. (Walnut Hills), Cincinnati, Ohio.

JONES, Theodore Wellington, expressman, retired; born at Hamilton, Canada, Sept. 19, 1853; son of John and Hannah Maria (Tate) Jones; ed. public schools of Hamilton, Can., Lockport, N. Y., Chicago, Ill., and Wheaton (Ill.) College; married Helen C. Lynthecom, of Chicago, Apr., 1881; 3 children: Theodore E., Elizabeth C., Albert W. In the transfer business at 2209 Cottage Grove Ave., Chicago, 40 yrs., under name of T. W. Jones Furniture Transit Co.; retired; sub-treasurer and member executive board, Negro Historical and Industrial Assn., in charge Negro Exposition Celebration the 50th Anniversary of Emancipation, Richmond, Va., 1915; associate editor the Industrial Advocate, official publication of exposition. Was charter member Angelus University, Los Angeles, Calif. Republican; member Board of Commissioners of Cook County, Ill., 1895-6; life member National Negro Business League. Methodist. Mason. Home: 1401 W. Leigh St., Richmond, Va.

JONES, Thomas Adolphus, physician, surgeon; born at Georgetown, British Guiana, May 6, 1873; son of Henry and Jane (Richardson) Jones; attended Kingston Wesleyan School, Georgetown, B. G.; student Howard Univ. School of Medicine, Washington, D. C., 1899-1900; M.D., College of Physicians and Surgeons, Boston, Mass., 1903; M.D., C.M., McGill Univ.,. Montreal, Can., 1915; married Iemina Evelyn, of Demerara, British Guiana, 1899; 6 children: .Tomlin, Evelyn, Charles, Eloise, Gladys, Elbert. Was headmaster Victoria Wesleyan School, British Guiana; came to America, 1899; began practice in New Orleans, La., 1903; professor of pathology and chemistry Flint Medical College, 1903; acting resident physician Sarah Goodrich Hospital, 1904; later removed to Galveston, Tex.; local examining physician for Ancient Order of Pilgrims; director Jones Obstetric School, Gonzales, Tex. Honorary member McGill Medical Society, Montreal, Can., Victoria-Belfield Agricultural Society, and ex-sec. Upper East Coast Teachers' Union, Demarara; president West Indian Assn.; treasurer Galveston Negro Business League. Home and Office: 3424 Avenue M 1-2, Galveston, Texas.

JONES, Thomas Lucius, clergyman, teacher; born at Cincinnati, Ohio, Aug. 24, 1863; son of Littleton and Eliza (Bryant) Jones; public school edn.; (D.D., Selma Univ., Ala., 1911); married Martha A. Foster, of Nashville, Tenn., June 1, 1887. Teacher public schools, Nashville, 1887-99; entered Missionary Baptist ministry, 1887; pastored churches at Huntington, Tenn,, Orange, S. C., and Texas 10 years, and Fla., 2 years; president West Florida Baptist College, 1910-13; head teacher in Voorhees Industrial school since 1913. Republican. Mason. Address: Voorhees Industrial School, Denmark, S. C.

JONES, Wade Anthony, physician; born at Talladega, Ala., Aug. 14, 1874; son of Wade Hampton and Flora Jones; grad. Talladega College, 1896; M.D., Denver (Col.) Homoeopathic Medical College, 1901; married Al berta Vaughn, of St. Louis, Mo., June, 1912. Practiced in Denver since 1901; president Elite Drug Co., Lincoln-Douglass Sanitarium, Colored Ameri can Loan & Realty Co. Progressive. Baptist. Member Colorado Homoe-pathic Medical Society, United Brothers of Friendship, True Reformers. Home: 2205 Marion St. Office: 1027 21 St., Denver, Colorado.

JORDAN, Dock Jackson, educator, lawyer; born at Cuthbert, Ga., 1866; son of Giles D. and Julia (White) Jordan; attended public high school, Cuthbert; B.S., and LL.B., Allen Univ., Columbia, S. C., 1892, M.S., later; married Carrie J. Thomas, of Atlanta, Ga., Dec. 31, 1893; 4 children: Edwin Adolphus, Frederick Douglass, Frances Marie, Julia Alice. Admitted to S. C. Supreme Court bar, 1892, to Ga. bar, 1904; professor in Morris Brown Univ., Atlanta, Ga., 1893-5, 1897-1905; was president Edward Waters College, Jacksonville, Fla., 1895-7; principal city school, Atlanta, 1905-9; president Kittrell (N. C.) College, 1909-12; director Teachers' Training Dept. Agricultural and Technical College, Greensboro, N. C., since 1912. Trustee Morris Brown Univ. Was delegate to General Conference A. M. E. Church, 1896, 1904, 1912; author the law providing for lay representatives in annual conferences, adopted in 1904; delegate to Ecumenical Conference on Methodism, Toronto, Can., 1911. Republican nominee for state legislature from Randolph County, Ga., 1893; delegate to Republican State Convention, 1894, and in 10 minutes speech aided in defeating Tom Watson for nomination as candidate for governor. Mason. Club: Monday (Atlanta). Home: 410 Dudley St. Office: A. & T. College, Greensboro, N. C.

JORDAN, Lewis Garnett, clergyman, foreign missionary secretary; born a slave near Meridian, Miss., about 1852; son of Jack Gaddis and Mariah Carey; after slavery was abolished he adopted a name of his own choice; public school edn., Meridian and Natchez, Miss.; student Roger Williams Univ., Nashville, Tenn.; (D.D., Natchez College, 1880, Guadaloupe College, 1903); married Fanny Armstrong, Dec., 1880 (died 1910); 2d marriage, Mrs. M. J. Marquess, of Helena, Ark., May 29, 1913. Ordained Baptist ministry, 1875; built churches while pastor at Yazoo City, Miss., 1878, San Antonio, Tex., 1883. Waco, 1886, Hearne, Tex., 1888, Philadelphia, Pa., 1893; corresponding sec. Foreign Mission Board of the National Baptist Convention since 1896; for fully 13 years prior to his election to the board little had been accomplished; the mission received scant financial support, no bequests, and was represented by only 7 missionaries; during his administration more than 40 missionaries were sent into its field in South America, the West Indies, the west, south and central parts of Africa; several bequests were received in 1914, latest in importance exceeding $30,000; the board has acquired property in its fields valued at about $47,000. including land, churches, stations, schools, homes; he is editor the Mission Herald; was delegate to World's Baptist Alliance, London, Eng., 1904, World's Missionary Conference, Edinburgh, Scotland, 1910; has visited many parts of the West Indies twice, Africa twice, and S. America once. President Douglass Improvement Co.; trustee State University, Ky., National Training School for Women and Girls, Washington. Prohibitionist. Treas-National Negro Press Assn.; life member Negro Business League. Mason; member Independent Order St. Luke. Author: Up the Ladder in Missions, 1908; Price of Africa, 1911; In Our Stead, 1913. Address: 624 S. 18th St., Philadelphia, Pa.

JORDAN, Scipio A., letter carrier, insurance; born in Montgomery Co., Ark., Jan. 1, 1860; son of Charles and Elizabeth Jordan; public school edn., Little Rock; married Pinkie E. Ven-

able, Jan. 24, 1884. Served as grand menter Knights and Daughters of Tabor more than 16 years; with the Arkansas Union Mutual Benefit Assn., since 1912; letter carrier in Little Rock since 1881. African Methodist. Mason; member Odd Fellows. Address: 1416 Cross St., Little Rock, Arkansas.

JOSENBERGER, Mame Stewart, undertaker; born at Owego, N. Y., Aug. 3, 1868; daughter of Frank and Mary Elizabeth (Turner) Stewart; A.B., Fisk Univ., Nashville, Tenn., 1888; married W. E. Josenberger, of Ft. Smith, Ark., Jan. 3, 1892. Teacher in State Normal School, Holly Springs, Miss., 1888-9, in public school, Ft. Smith, Ark., 1889-1901; on death of husband, Sept. 28, 1909, took charge the undertaking business. Episcopalian. Member National Association for Advancement of Colored People; life member Ft. Smith Business League; member Order Eastern Star, Royal Circle of Friends, Mosaic Templars, Hospital Guild, and Phyllis Club since organized. Home: 703 N. 11th St. Office: 623 N. 9th St., Ft. Smith, Arkansas.

JUST, Ernest Everett, university professor; born at Charleston, S. C., 1884; prep. edn. Kimball Union Academy, Meriden, N. H.; A.B., Dartmouth, 1907. Began doing research work in biology, physiology and zoology, 1909; professor of zoology in College of Arts and Sciences and professor of physiology in School of Medicine, Howard Univ., Washington, D. C., since 1912. Won the first Spingarn medal, a prize worth $100, given to the man or woman of African descent and American citizenship to make the highest achievement in a year in any field of elevated or honorable human endeavor; medal was presented by Gov. Charles S. Whitman at the annual meeting of the National Association for Advancement of Colored People, New York, Feb. 12, 1915. Member Phi Beta Kappa. Home: 1846 Third St., Washington, D. C.

K

KAGWA, Sir Apolo; Prime Minister (Katikiro) of Uganda, East Africa; born 1864; son of Kadumukasa and Nanbi (Nalongo) Kagwa; ed. under the Church Missionary Society, Mengo, Urganda; married Samali Kayaga, of Mengo, 1888; 8 children. Regant to the King of Uganda, 1897-1914; was chief of Singo County, 1888; general in Christian Mahommadan war, 1888-9; Katikiro of Uganda (Prime Minister) since 1889; was principal factor in negotiating treaties with British government signed in Uganda, 1890; represented Uganda in England at coronation of King Edward VII., 1902; loyal friend to England during entire public career; leader in all movements for advancement of his own country; one of the most remarkable men on the east side of Africa. Member Protestant Church of England. Hon. Knight Commander of St. Michael and St. George. Author: (correct titles followed by translations) Basekabaka Bebuganda —History of Kings of Uganda, 2 editions, 1901, 1912; Engero za Baganda —Uganda Folk-lore; Empisa za Baganda—Uganda Customs; Ekitabo kya Nsanene—History of the Grasshopper Clan; Ekitabo kya Bika bya Baganda—History of the Baganda Clans; Ekitabo kyobwami bwa Baganda—History of Old Chieftainships of Uganda; Ekitabo kya Manya ga Basekabaka nebami babwe—List of Kings- of Uganda and their Chief Officers; all except the first were privately printed on his own press. Address: Mengo, Kampala, Uganda, East Africa.

KARNGA, Abayomi Winfred, lawyer, legislator; born at Cape Mount, Liberia, West Africa, Nov. 29, 1882; son of Orange and Sarah (Cook) Karnga; ed. St. John's High School, Cape Mount; A.B., Liberia College, 1903 (A.M., 1911); married Isabella Klade Hodge, of Bigtown, Cape Palmas, Liberia, June 15, 1912. Clerk in general postoffice, 1901, in office of Treasurer-General, 1902; chief clerk of the customs, 1904-5; prin. College Preparatory Edina, 1906-7; sec. in general postoffice, 1907-8; acting postmaster Port of Monrovia, 1909-11; member House of Representatives, Republic of Liberia, 1911-15; editor Liberia Times, Aug., 1913 to Jan. 1914. Admitted as counsellor-at-law and member Supreme Court bar, Jan. 9, 1914; appointed solicitor for City of Monrovia, Jan. 29, 1914; professor of law at Liberia College, since Apr. 1, 1914. Member Protestant Episcopal Church. Author: The Negro Republic of West Africa, 1909; compiler: Index to the Statutes of Liberia, 1909; The Postal Laws of Liberia, 1912; A Guide To Our Civil and Criminal Procedure, 1914. Address: Box 104, West End, Monrovia, Liberia, West Africa.

KEALING, Hightower T., university president; born at Austin, Tex., Apr. 1, 1859; son of Moses and Caroline (Cloud) Kealing; prep. edn. Straight Univ., New Orleans, La.; B.S., Tabor College, Ia., 1881, A.M., 1881; (Ph.D., Morris Brown College; LL.D., Wilberforce Univ.); married Celia Goldie Shaw, of Austin, Dec. 23, 1891; 5 children: Goldie E., Frances F., Caroline I., Cecelia M., Hightower, Jr. President Paul Quinn College, Waco, Tex., number years; asst. prin. Prairie View State Normal and Industrial College, Tex.; prin. high school and supervisor colored schools, Austin; pres. Western Univ., Quindaro, Kan., since 1910. Member all General Conferences of A. M. E. Church, since 1892; delegate and spokesman Ecumenical Conference on Methodism, London ,Eng.; was editor A. M. E. Review, 16 years. Republican. Member American Academy Political and Social Science, International Peace Conference, National Association for Advancement of Colored People, Negro Historical Society, National Educational Assn. Wrote: (pamphlets) History of African Methodism in Texas; Fortune Telling in History; Church Problems; How to Live Longer. Contr. to Century Magazine, Lippincott's, and Journal of Education. Address: Western University, Quindaro, Kan.

KEITH, Hardy Lester, industrial specialist; born at Grantville, Ga., June 18, 1875; son of Jefferson and Adelaide Keith; prep. edn., Atlanta, Uuiv.; A.B., Fisk Univ., 1901; married Cassandra Jenkins, of Newnan, Ga., Aug. 21, 1907; 2d marriage, Emma Lee Reid, of Newnan, July 16, 1911; 3 children: 1st, Marvin J., Urmilla S., 2d, Hardy Lester, Jr. Began educational work in Agricultural and Mechanical College, Normal, Ala., 1902; teacher in Clark Univ., Atlanta, Ga., 1904-7; supervisor Manual Training City Colored Schools, Nashville, Tenn., since 1907; exec. sec. Associated Negro Industrial Workers; chmn. com. of management Colored Y. M. C. A. Republican. Episcopalian. Member Association of School Principals, Middle Tenn. Teachers' Assn. Clubs: Nashville Science, The Twenty-Five (college men). Address: 1109 Eighteenth Ave. N., Nashville, Tenn.

KEMP, William Paul, editor, publisher; born at Plattsmouth, Neb., Mar. 13, 1881; son of Samuel P. and Helen (Helms) Kemp; attended public and high schools; student Univ. of Neb. School of Music; married Mary Della Elder, of Lincoln, Neb., Dec. 24, 1900. Began as editor and pub. Lincoln Leader, Neb., which he established, 1899; was Washington correspondent for Nebraska State Journal, 1900; manager literature dept. Neb. Republican State Central Committee, 1904; published Lincoln Leader again, 1905-7; removed to Detroit, Mich., 1907; issued first number Detroit Leader, Dec., 1907, went out of business Feb. 13, 1908; established the present Detroit Leader, June 26, 1909, and made a success of it; purchased plant of the Owl Printing Co., 1912. Delegate from Mich. to Good Roads Convention, Richmond, Va., 1911. Republican; was first colored clerk in mayor's office, Detroit, apptd., 1909. Episcopalian. Member National Association for Advancement of Colored People, Publishers' Protective Assn., Detroit Assn. of Allied Printers. Mason; member Knights of Pythias, Elks, True Reformers. Clubs: Hexa-gon, Drexel, Pioneer, Union League. Home: 1246 Hastings St. Office: 449 St. Antoine St., Detroit, Mich.

KENNEDY, Paul Horace, clergyman; born near Elizabeth, Hardin County, Ky., Sept. 1, 1848; son of John M. and Caroline Kennedy; ed. Christian Mission, U. S. Army, and Roger Williams Univ.; (D.D., Cadez Normal and Theol. College, 1893); married Mary Jane Roberts, of Logan Co., Ky., Aug. 28, 1870; 3 children: Georgia A., Celilia C., Edwina; 2nd marriage, Virginia Harris, of Henderson, Ky., June 26, 1882; 6 children: Anna V., Mary V., Horace P., Kennedy, Ora H., Lucy B. Missionary Baptist minister since 1888; served as general missionary in Ky., 27 years; conducted New Era Institute 15 years; supt. of Missions and corresponding secretary General Baptist Assn. in Ky.; editor Kentucky Missionary Visitor; pub. Baptist Directory and Year Book; was delegate to World's Missionary Conference, Edinburgh, Scotland. Trustee M. & F. College, Hopkinsville. Served in Co. H. 109th Colored Vol. Inf.; detailed as musician; was instructor for 10 years, organ, piano, violin and band instruments. Delegate to Republican National Convention, St. Louis, Mo., 1896; U. S. Marshall during administration of President William McKinley. Member National Negro Press Assn. Mason; member Odd Fellows, Knights of Pythias. Home: 336 S. Alvasia St., Henderson, Ky.

KENNEY, John Andrew, physician; born in Albemarle County, Va., June 11, 1874; son of John and Caroline (Howard) Kenney; preparatory edn. Hampton Normal and Agricultural Institute; M.D., Shaw Univ., Raleigh, N. C., 1901; married Alice Talbot, of Forest, Va., Dec. 21, 1902 (died 1912); 2d marriage, Freda F. Armstrong, of Boston, Mass., Oct. 29, 1913. Interne at Freedmen's Hospital, Washington, 1901-2; resident physician Tuskegee Normal and Industrial Institute, Ala., since 1902; supt. Nurse Training School and medical director John A. Andrew Memorial Hospital; managing editor Journal of the National Medical Assn. Was secretary the association 8 years and president 1 year; member Alabama State Medical, Dental, Pharm. Assn. Mason. Author (pamphlet): Negro in Medicine, 1912. Address: Tuskegee Institute, Ala.

KENNIEBREW, A. H., physician, surgeon; born at Tuskegee, Ala., May 5, 1875; son of Phillip and Charlotte (Graham) Kenniebrew; grad. Tusgegee Institute, 1892; Central Tenn College, 1894; Meharry Medical College (Walden Univ.), Nashville, Tenn, 1897; post-grad. work, Harvard Medical School, Boston, 1898, Manhattan Eye and Ear Hospital, New York, 1899, Post-Graduate Medical School and Hospital, Chicago, Ill., 1900; widower; 1 child. Assistant surgeon Freedmen's Hospital, Washington, 1897; medical director Tuskegee Institute, 1898-1902; surgeon in charge The Home Sanitarium, Jacksonville, Ill., since 1907; visiting surgeon Our Savior's Hospital, Jacksonville; pres. Jacksonville Civic League; park commissioner City of Jacksonville. Member National Medical Assn., Duval County Medical Society, Tri-State Medical Society of Ill., Mo., and Ia. Republican. Baptist. Mason; member Odd Fellows, Knights of Pythias. Address: 323 W. Morgan St., Jacksonville, Ill.

KINCHEN, Elijah Wesley, clergyman; born at Baldwin, La., Jan. 13, 1874; son of Samuel H. and Marcellett (West) Kinchen; attended Gilbert Academy, Baldwin; grad. Workingmen's School, New York, 1892; Englewood High School, Chicago, Ill., 1893-5; student Fisk Univ., 1895-7; B.D., Gammon Theological Seminary, Atlanta, Ga., 1905; married Bertha W. Alexander, of Bellefontaine, Ohio, Sept. 11, 1901. Ordained deacon at Atlanta, 1905; pastor Mt. Pleasant, Lorain, Columbus, Stubenville, O., to 1900; worked for Pullman Company, 1900-6; pastor Wesley Chapel, M. E. Church, Los Angeles, Cal., since 1906; ordained elder, at Paris, Ky., 1908. Trustee Sojourner Trust Industrial Home, Y. M. C. A. Republican. Mason; member Odd Fellows, Knights of

Pythias. Address: 1473 E. 23d St., Los Angeles, Calif.

KING, William Elisha, publisher; born at Macon, Miss., June 7, 1866; son of Richmond and Margaret King; ed. public schools and private tuition; unmarried. Founded the Fair Play (weekly newspaper) at Meridian, Miss., 1889, the Dallas Express, 1893; later incorporated with capital of $5,000. Was delegate to Republican National Convention, Philadelphia, Pa., 1900. Baptist. Member National Negro Press Assn., Dallas Business League. Mason; member Odd Fellows, Knights of Pythias, Knights of Tabor. Home: 2701 Cochran St. Office: 1607 Jackson St., Dallas, Tex.

KING, William Harold, editor, publisher; born at Gallatin, Sumner Co., Tenn., July 22, 1868; son of Esquire and Martha (Walton) King; grad. Meigs High School, Nashville, Tenn., 1890; awarded State Prize for proficiency in penmanship; married Eliza Foster, of Gallatin; 1 child: Celia Mai; 2 marriage, Lucinda Dean, of Washington, D. C., June 25, 1908. In business for self since 1890; editor and pub. Central Afro-American, weekly newspaper, 1909-14; sold to Argus Pub. Co.; president and general mgr. American Printing & Pub. Co.; prop. the Garden, an open air moving picture theatre with seating capacity of 2,000; founded the Colored Americans' Protective League, and secretary since Feb., 1915; inspector Sidewalk Division of the City of St. Louis; active in various civil movements. Republican. Baptist. Member Knights of Pythias; supreme recorder Peerless Knights. Address: 2138 Market St., St. Louis, Mo.

KINGSLEY, Harold Merrybright, religious educator; born at Mobile, Ala., Mar. 1, 1887; son of William and Mary Susan (Merrybright) Kingsley; grad. Emerson Institute, Mobile, 1904; A.B., Talladega College (Ala.), 1908; B.D., Yale Divinity School, New Haven, Conn., 1911; married Mattie Satyra Jackson, of Anniston, Ala., Dec. 25, 1911; 1 child: Harold K. Ordained in Congregational ministry, 1911; pastor Union Congregational

Church, Newport, R. I., 1911-12, Bethel A. M. E. Church, Bridgeport, Conn., 1912-13; superintendent Congregational Churches in Texas and Okla., since 1913; also teacher of Bible history at Tillotson College, Austin, Tex. Member Alpha Phi Alpha, United Brothers of Friendship. Club: X Y Z (Austin). Address: Tillotson College, Austin, Tex.

KIRKLIN, Henry, truck gardner; born in Boone Co., Mo., June 6, 1858; son of Jacob and Jane Kirklin; self-educated; married Mattie Moss, of Columbia, Mo., May 8, 1880; 2 children: Stella R., Mattie F. Began in employ of J. B. Douglass, nursery and greenhouse business, Boone Co., 1873, continuing 11 years; acquired knowledge of agriculture that led to success; was instructor in Experimental Station of Missouri Horticultural Dept., 1881-4; truck farmer, Columbia, Mo., since 1884; exhibited products at Louisiana Purchase Centennial Exposition, St. Louis, 1904; notable feature of that exhibit included a squash 12 inches in diameter grown in glass globe, and 14 Clyde strawberries which filled quart box; won gold medal, also presented with diploma for best exhibit of vegetable products, Jamestown Exposition, Norfolk, Va., 1907; lecturer for Mo. State Board of Agriculture at county fairs and in Negro schools on practical and scientific agriculture. Trustee Bartlet Agricultural and Industrial School, Dalton, also St. Paul A. M. E. Church, Columbia, Mo. Republican. Mason. Address: 13 W. Switzler St., Columbia, Mo.

KYLES, Linwood W., clergyman, editor; A.B., Lincoln (Pa.) Univ., 1901, S.T.B., 1904. Former editor Home Review at Fayetteville, N. C.; general officer A. M. E. Zion Church and editor the Quarterly Review. Address: 112 S. Bayou St., Mobile, Ala.

L

LaCOUR, Paul Louis, teacher, clergyman; born at New Orleans, La., about 1859; son of Louis Lucien and Henrietta (Thompson) LaCour; A.B.,

Fisk Univ., 1885, B.D., 1893; student Hartford Theological Seminary, Conn., 1 year; married Alice Vassar, of Athens, Ga., 1893; 3 children: Lucile Vivian, Marion Elizabeth, Gretchen Vassar. Teacher in Bowling Green, Ky., 1885; minister at Athens, Ga., 1 1-2 years; principal A. M. E. School, Chapel Hill, N. C., later at Jonesboro, Tenn.; principal and minister, Douglass Academy, Lawndale, N. C., 1907-14; teacher in Talladega College, Ala., since 1914. Republican. Congregationalist. Home: Nashville, Tenn. Address: Talladega, Ala.

LAFARGUE, John Baptist, teacher, editor; born in Avoyelles Parish, La., June, 1864; public school edn.; read law 4 years; married Sarah C. B. Mayo, 1887, daughter of John Mayo a former member Louisiana House of Representatives. Worked in Marksville (La.) Bulletin office 14 years; established first colored people's newspaper in central part of state; former editor National Alliance; now editor and pub. Advance Messenger, Alexandria, La. Founded the Peabody Industrial School, 1884, which is now located at Alexandria; was general mgr. Summer Normal and Teachers' in 1897; organized La. Colored Teachers' Assn.; pres. City Teachers' League. Was commissioner from Avoyelles Parish to Louisiana Colored State Fair, New Orleans, 1886; one of the state representatives at Cotton States Exposition, Atlanta, Ga., 1895, also Tennessee Centennial Exposition, Nashville, 1897; represented Colored Alliance of La., at Arcola, Fla.; chairman local board People's Benevolent Life Ins. Co. President board trustees M. E. Church, Alexandria. Aldermanic candidate at Marksville, 1886, and defeated by 2 votes; also candidate for House of Representatives; usher at Republican National Convention, St. Louis, Mo., 1896. Member National Negro Press Assn., Alexandria Negro Business League. Grand auditor Knights of Canaan; district deputy Knights of Pythias; also Order Eastern Star. Address: Advance-Messenger, Alexandria, La.

LAMBERT, Sterling, real estate; born at Meherrin, Va., May 24, 1870; son of Washington and Louise Lambert; attended public school 18 months; married Emma Williams, of Greenville County, Va., June 26, 1895; 1 child: Russell H. Began in real estate business at Yonkers, N. Y., 1895; now also conducts an employment agency and Yonkers Vacuum Cleaning Co. Trustee Messiah Baptist Church. Republican. Chancellor Commander, Lincoln Lodge, Knights of Pythias. Home: 366 Warburton Ave. Office: 65 N. Broadway, Yonkers, N. Y.

LANDRY, Eldrige Percival, pharmacist; born at New Orleans, La., Feb., 1881; son of Rev. Pierre and Amanda (Grigsby) Landry; prep. edn. New Orleans Univ.; completed course in pharmacy, Flint Medical College; technical course Southern Univ., New Orleans. Pharmacist in U. S. Food and Drug Inspection Laboratory, Savannah, Ga., since 1912. Episcopalian. Address: 623 W. 36th St., Savannah, Ga.

LANDRY. Lord Beaconsfield, physician; born at Donaldsville, La., Mar. 11, 1878; son of Rev. Pierre and Amanda (Grigsby) Landry; A.B., Fisk Univ., 1902; M.D., Meharry Medical College (Walden Univ.), 1908; unmarried. Practiced in Algiers, La., since 1908; teacher of medicine, Flint Medical College, New Orleans. Methodist. Member Odd Fellows , Knights of Pythias. Address: 509 Homer St., Algiers, La.

LANDRY, Pierre, clergyman; born in Parish of Ascension, La., Apr. 16, 1846; son of Roseman and Marcelite (Provost) Landry; ed. in primary and technical school maintained by Bringier family where own children were prepared for higher edn.; private instruction under Rev. W. D. Goodman and Rev. L. G. Atkinson; read law in office of John A. Cheevers and F. B. Earhart, of Donaldsonville, La.; (hon. D.D., 1903); married Amanda Grigsby; 2d marriage, Florence A. Simpkins (both deceased); children: Lord Beaconsfield (M.D.), Oliver W. (M.D.), Eldridge P. (pure food inspector for State of Ga.), Marcelite (wife of Prof. I. M. Terrell), Palmeston (prin. of school), Nellie V. (Mrs. Dr. G. W. Alston), Joseph C., Lewis, Rev. Charles C., Lillian B. (Mrs. Rev. H. H. Dunn), Georgia L.; there are 13 grandchildren occupying prominent positions. Born in Catholic faith; converted to Methodism, 1862; at age of 19, delegate to Miss. Mission Conference held at New Orleans, La., Dec. 25, 1865; first M. E. minister appointed to Donaldsonville; made leader of Class No. 4, and served church in every station; assisted his pastor in establishing a circuit with Landry, Bayou, Goula, Papeonville, Woodlawn, Vioran; delegate to general conference, Brooklyn, N. Y., 1872; ministerial delegate to general conference twice; presiding elder and district supt., 16 years; a founder of New Orleans Univ., now trustee; was trustee Straight Univ., 1875-82; dean and acting pres., Gilbert College, Baldwin, La., 1900-5. In early life was architect and builder; also practiced law and was judge in Donaldsonville. Republican; held office as follows: mayor of Donaldsonville; tax collector, pres. Police Jury; pres. Parish school board, postmaster under Pres. U. S. Grant; justice of peace; member La. House of Representatives 4 years, Senate 6 years; member state constitutional convention, 1879; after the Civil war, when southern states were overrun with radical political leaders, he saw white southern man humiliated and gave his support and influence to number prominent Confederate soldiers for public office and judgeships; has since been regarded faithful representative of colored race, as well as just to white people's interests; one of few colored stockholders in the Exposition of Big Ideas for 1915, New Orleans. Mason; member Knights of Pythias. Home: 5215 Constance St. Office: City Hall Annex, New Orleans, La.

LANE, Isaac, bishop; born at Jackson, Tenn., Mar. 3, 1834; son of Rachel Lane; self-educated; married Francis Ann Boyce, of Madison Co., Tenn., 1853; 2d marriage, Mary E. Smith, of Marshall, Tex., 1895; father of

James Franklin Lane, pres. Lane College. Bishop of Colored M. E. Church since 1873; trustee Connectional Property of the Colored M..E. Church, and Colored M. E. Pub. House; president board of trustee Lane College. Address: Jackson, Tenn.

LANE, James Franklin, college president; born at Jackson, Tenn., Feb. 18, 1878; son of Rt. Rev. Isaac and Frances (Boyce) Lane; preparatory edn. Lane College; A.B., Walden Univ., Nashville, Tenn., 1896, A.M., 1900 (Ph.D., 1912); studied at Harvard, and Univ. of Chicago; married Mary Edna Johnson, of Memphis, Tenn., Sept. 12, 1904. Taught in public schools of Tenn. and Miss.; principal Panola High School, Sardis, Miss., '1897-8; principal grammar school dept., Lane College, Jackson, Tenn., 1899-1900, professor of mathematics 3 years, dean teachers training dept., 1903-4, and president since 1904. Delegate from Colored M. E. Church to Ecumenical Conference on Methodism, London, Eng., 1901. Secretary Madison County Republican Committee; delegate to several state conventions. Member National Geographical Assn., National Association Teachers in Colored Schools, National Negro Protective Society, Negro Business Men's League, Burbanks Society. Mason. Address: Jackson, Tenn.

LANG, Leonard Dwight, teacher; born at Key West, Fla., Sept. 11, 1888; son of Joseph and Julia Lang; ed. public schools, Key West, and St. Joseph's College, Ala.; unmarried. Began as perfect in St. Joseph's College, St. Joseph, Ala., 1908; founded in 1911, now principal the St. Joseph Institute, Opelousas, La.; head of Lang's Home for Colored Boys; organized the Father John Council No. 8, in 1912; now state deputy for Louisiana, and director the National Council, Knights of Peter Claver, an organization for Roman Catholic men. Address: St. Joseph Institute, Opelousas, Louisiana.

LANGFORD, William Milton, clergyman; born at Lexington, Ky., May 15, 1862; son of Green and Eliza (Pulley) Langford; public school edn., Richmond, Ky.; student Berea College; theological course Whittenbery Lutheran School, Springfield, Ohio; M.A.L., Christian College, Oskaloosa, Iowa, correspondence course: (D.D., Livingstone College); married Edna A. White, of Cleveland, Ky., Nov. 9, 1882; 3 children: Eliza, John Wesley, Arena; 2d marriage, Carrie Ellis, of Louisville, Ky. Reared in M. E. Church and joined Lexington Conference, 1887; served charges at Kenney Station, Moorefield, Germantown, and Louisville, Ky., Bellaire, Cleveland, Springfield, and Cincinnati, Ohio, and Jeffersonville, Ind.; withdrew from the M. E. Church, Mar. 22, 1908, and united with the A. M. E. Zion Church, Cincinnati and the Kentucky Conference; transferred by Bishop George Wylie Clinton to the New Jersey Conference; assigned to Trenton and served 3 years; pastor Prince Memorial A. M. E. Zion Temple, Atlantic City, since 1911. Home: 15 N. Ohio Ave., Atlantic City, N. J.

LANIER, Marshall Bell, clergyman, university dean; born at Mocksville, N. C., Mar. 16, 1869; son of Abraham and Mary Jane (Simms) Lanier; grad. Wayland Seminary, 1887; A.B., Lincoln Univ., Pa., 1892; B.D., Western Theological Seminary, Pittsburgh, Pa., 1895; married Maud E. Bryce, of Pittsburgh, June 18, 1901. Began as minister in church at Winston-Salem, N. C., 1887; ordained Baptist ministry, 1895; pastor Grace Church, Pittsburgh, Pa., 15 years; dean Theological dept., State Univ., Louisville, Ky., since 1910; pastor 1st Baptist Church, Irvington, Ky., 1913, Corinthian Church, Frankfort, Ky., since 1913. Trustee Coleman Home for Colored Boys. Republican. Mason. Home: 1704 W. Chestnut St., Louisville, Ky.

LANKFORD, John Anderson, architect, mechanical engineer; born at Potosi, Mo., Dec. 4, 1874; son of Anderson and Nancy (Johnson) Lankford; public school edn., Potosi; student at Lincoln Institute, Jefferson City, Mo., Tuskegee Normal and Industrial Institute, Ala., Architectual College at Scranton, Pa.; B.Sc., Shaw Univ., Raleigh, N. C., 1898; M.Sc.,

Wilberforce Univ., 1902; M.M.Sc., Agricultural and Mechanical College at Normal, Ala.; married, 1901, Charlotte J. Upshaw, granddaughter of Bishop Henry M. Turner, of Atlanta, Ga. In practice since 1897; first Negro to enter the profession in U. S.; was supervising architect for National Negro Fair Assn., Mobile, Ala., directing general at Jamestown Exposition for District of Columbia; supervising architect for A. M. E. Church throughout the world since 1908; designed St. John's, of Norfolk, Va., and St. Phillips $60,000 edifice at Savannah, Ga., John Wesley A. M. E. Zion, Washington, and St. John M. E. at Hillsdale, D. C., also 1st Baptist $40,-000 edifice in Raleigh, N. C.; architect of Palmer Hall, A. & M. College, Normal, Ala., costing $70,000; the the $25,000 office building of Southern Aid Ins. Co., $50,000 flat building for Dr. W. L. Taylor, and $5,000 residence for Dr. D. Webster Davis at Richmond, Va.; stable for undertaking firm of Winslow & Dabney, Washington, Odd Fellows Hall, Hillsdale, D. C., and $125,000 Masonic Temple at Jacksonville, Fla.; practice extends throughout the U. S., with points of contact at Boston, New York, Chicago, St. Louis, Kansas City, Denver, San Francisco, Washington, Atlanta, Savannah, and Jacksonville. Director Y. M. C. A., Jacksonville; president trustee board Army of Rescue and Religion. 33d degree Mason, K. T., Shriner; secretary-treas. Sinking Fund Commission of the Masons in Fla. Address: 1863 Pearce Ave., Jacksonville, Fla.

LATIMER, John Newton Franklin, physician; born at Belton, S. C., Dec. 28, 1877; son of Christopher and May Latimer; prep. edn. Benedict College, Columbia, S. C.; M.D., Meharry Medical College (Walden Univ.), Nashville, Tenn., 1908; married Helen Elizabeth Walker, of Belton, July 19, 1911; 1 child: Walden University Latimer. Practiced in Toccoa, Ga., since Feb. 9, 1909; specializes in chronic diseases, pellagra, dropsy, indigestion, and diseases of women and children. Baptist: Address: Toccoa, Ga.

LATIMER, Lewis Howard, mechanical and electrical engineer, patent solicitor; born at Chelsea, Mass., Sept. 4, 1848; son of George A. and Rebecca (Smith) Latimer; public school edn.; married Mary Wilson Lewis, of Fall River, Mass., Nov. 10, 1873; 2 children: Emma J. (Mrs. Gerald F. Norman), Louis R. Learned mechanical drawing in office of Crosby & Gould, Boston, Mass., and worked on drawing connected with application for Bell Telephone patents this firm made for Alexander Graham Bell; was draughtsman and secretary for Hiram S. Maxim, 1879, the Maxim Gun inventor; manufactured Maxim patent incandescent lamps in London, Eng., 1880-2; electrician with Olmstead Electric Light & Power Co., New York, 1882-3, for Excelsior Electric Co., 1884, continuing as electrical engineer and draughtsman after this concern changed name to General Electric Co., and was finally in the legal department making drawings for court exhibits, also investigating infringements and testifying in trial cases until the department was abolish, 1912; since practicing as mechanical and electrical engineer, and solicitor of patents, New York; as teacher of commercial electricity in night school, New York, was recorded with reward of 98 per cent.; has invented and patented many appliances. Served on gun boat Massasoit in war between the states, under Admiral Porter, and Commander Richard T. Renshaw; later lieut. 4th Bat. Mass. Vol. Militia; adjutant George Huntsman Post No. 60, G. A. R., New York. Unitarian Member New York Electrical Society, Negro Society for Historical Research. Mason (joined Guelpb Lodge, London, Eng.). Club: Citizens (Brooklyn). Author: Incandescent Electrical Lighting, 1892, a practical description of the Edison system. Home: 64 Holly St., Flushing, N. Y. Office: 55 John St., New York.

LAWLESS, Alfred, Jr., clergyman, teacher; born at Tribodaux, La., July 16, 1873; son of Alfred and Serena (Ledet) Lawless; ed. public school,

Lafourche Parish, La.; A.B., Straight Univ., New Orleans, 1902, B.D., 1903; married Harriet O. Dunn, of Tribodaux, May 19, 1892; 3 children: Theodore K., Oscar G., Gertrude E. Began as principal public schools, Tribodaux, 1895, continuing to 1900; principal Pointe Coupee Industrial High School, 1903-4; professor of Greek at Straight Univ., 1910-14; principal Fisk Public School, New Orleans, 1913-14. Was assistant pastor Howard Congregational Church, New Orleans, 1900-3; pastor Beecher Memorial Church, 1904-10, and at Straight Univ., 1910-14; president National Convention of Congregational Workers, 1912-14; superintendent of church work for American Missionary Assn. in Miss. and La., and field agent for Straight and Tougaloo universities since 1914; secretary and editor A. M. A. Alumni League; administrative secretary New Orleans Social Service Commission; pres. 7th Ward Educational League; was member committee of management Booker T. Washington's tour of La. President Progressive Land & Investment Co.; organizer Negro Business League; director Y. M. C. A. Republican. Odd Fellow. Club: Crescent Historical and Literary. Home: 2005 N. Johnson St., New Orleans, La.

LAWRENCE, Osa Alonzo, undertaker, embalmer; born at Oxford, O., Aug. 30, 1878; son of George W. and Adelaide (Williams) Lawrence; grad. Oxford High School, 1895; student Miami Univ., Oxford, O., 2 years, Ohio State Univ., 1 year; B.Sc., Fisk Univ., Nashville, Tenn., 1901; grad. Minnesota College of Embalming (Univ. of Minn.), 1908; married Lillie Reed, of Oxford, June 29, 1904; 2 children: Kathryn, Eleanor. Began as embalmer and funeral director for J. M. Morris Undertaking Co., Minneapolis, Minn., 1909, continuing to 1912; purchased the establishment Apr. 1, 1912; since in business under own name. Baptist. Mason; member Odd Fellows, United Brothers of Friendship. Address: 910 Eighth Ave. S., Minneapolis, Minn.

LAWSON, Jesse, sociologist; born at Nanjemoy, Md., May 8, 1856; son of Jesse and Charlotte (Price) Lawson; A.B., Howard Univ., 1881, LL.B., 1884, A.M., 1885; attended special lectures as a member of the American Academy Political and Social Science at Univ. of Pa., 1901-5; married Rosetta E. Coakley, of Washington, D. C., Dec. 17, 1884; 4 children: Josephine M., James F. (M.D.), Edward H., Wilfred W. Legal examiner at the Bureau of Pensions, Washington, since 1882; was of counsel for John M. Langston in the contested congressional election before the House of Representatives, Washington, 1889. Began as lecturer of sociology in the Lyceum of Second Baptist Church, Washington, 1890; now president and professor of sociology and ethics of the Bible College and Institute for Civic and Social Betterment; founder and president National Sociological Society; member Southern Sociological Congress; was editor The Colored American, 1893-7; national commissioner to Cotton States Exposition, Atlanta, Ga., 1895; member board of the Jamestown Exposition, Norfolk, Va., 1907; pres. National Emancipation Commemorative Society, which was organized in 1909, held its Golden Jubilee in 1912, and celebrates Sept. 22, and Lincoln's Birthday each year. Delegate to Republican National Convention, 1884. Baptist. Author: How to Solve the Race Problem, 1904; (pamphlet): The Ethics of the Labor Problem; The Vacant Chair in Our Educational System. Address: 2011 Vermont Ave. N. W., Washington, D. C.

LAWSON, Raymond Augusta, concert pianist; born at Shelbyville, Kan., Mar. 23, 1875; son of Lewis and Mary (Griffith) Lawson; grad. Fisk Univ., Nashville, Tenn., Music, 1895, A.B., 1896; grad. Hartford (Conn.) School of Music, 1900; studied in Europe with Ossip Gabrilowitsch the noted Russian pianist who married daughter of "Mark Twain"; married Ida Morgan Napier, of Nashville, Tenn., June 25, 1902; 3 children: Warner, Rosalind, Elizabeth. Teacher of piano at Hartford, Conn., since 1896; has given concerts in nearly all prominent cities, and played before Professor Leschetizky the noted teacher of Vienna; soloist in Saint Saens concerts (G. Minor) with Hartford Philharmonic Orchestra, 1911. Republican. Congregationalist. Home: 111 Adelaide St. Office: 926 Main St., Hartford, Conn.

LAWTON, Maria Coles, writer, lecturer; born at Lynchburg, Va., Apr. 30, 1864; daughter of Robert Alexander and Mildred Booker (Cabell) Perkins; ed. Richmond Institute, Va., Lynchburg High School; student Howard Univ., 1882-3; married Rev. William R. Lawton, of St. Louis, Mo., July 13, 1885; 7 children: Ethel, Irene, Eunice, Cuthbert, Frank, Harry, Robert. Teacher public schools, Va., 3 years; public speaker on racial and other topics since 1897; reporter on Brooklyn Daily Standard Union, white, since 1902; contributor to number newspapers; organizer Empire State Federation of Womans' Clubs, and first Colored Neighborhood Club in Greater New York; member Equal Suffrage League, Daughters of Virginia; delegate from N.Y. to National Negro Educational Congress, Oklahoma City, Okla., July 7-10, 1914, appointed by Gov. Martin H. Glynn. Republican. Presbyterian. Clubs: Urban Neighborhood, Womans' Loyal Union, Womans' Club, Queen Ester Circle. Address: 173 Willoughby St., Brooklyn, N. Y.

LAWTON, William Rufus, clergyman; born at Charleston, S. C., May 1, 1860; son of William R. and Elizabeth (Gilliard) Lawton; prep. edn. Lincoln Institute, Jefferson City, Mo.; A.B., Lincoln (Pa.) Univ., 1883, S. T. B., 1886, A.M., 1887 (D.D., 1912); married Maria Coles Perkins, of Lynchburg, Va., July 13, 1885; 7 children: Ethel, Irene, Eunice, Cuthbert, Frank, Harry, Robert. Teacher of mathematics, Lynchburg (Va.) High School, 1886-7; principal Beaufort Normal and Industrial Academy, 1888-9; professor of history, Lincoln Institute, Mo., 1890-2. Ordained by Lynchburg Presbytery, white, 1886; pastor Lynchburg, Va., 1886-8, Brook-

lyn, N. Y., 1892-5, St. James Ch., New York, 1911-14; built new church, Harlem, N. Y., 1915. Was reporter with Brooklyn Daily Standard Union, 10 yrs.; clerk in office district attorney of Kings Co., N. Y., 2 yrs.; recording clerk in marriage license bureau, 6 yrs.; president Colored Republican Organization, Kings Co., 2 yrs.; v.-p. Lincoln Emancipation Assn., 5 yrs.; dir. Union Rescue Home of New York, Clifton Forge Industrial School, Va. Home: 173 Willoughby St., Brooklyn, N. Y.

LEE, Albert R., confidential clerk; born in Somers Township, near Champaign, Ill., June 26, 1874; son of William and Margaret Ann (Mitchell) Lee; grad. high school, Champaign, 1893; student Univ. of Illinois, 1897-8; private tuition for 4 years under professors Univ. of Ill.; grad. Success School of Shorthand, Chicago, 1909; married Marie McCurdy, of Villa Ridge, Ill., Nov. 23, 1898; 3 children: Albert, Maurice, Bernice. Began as messenger in office the president Univ. of Illinois, 1895, assistant clerk, 1907-9, clerk with confidential and secretarial duties to the president since 1909; introduced the president's filing system; assistant editor and compiler Faculty Directory. Colonel and district commander 1st Regt. Illinois U. S. Boy Scouts. Trustee 9 years, secretary since 1905, Bethel A. M. E. Church, Champaign; member Univ. of Ill. Y.M.C.A.; supt Springfield District Sunday School Union; teacher in men's class Sunday School Teachers' Training Class. Treasurer Republican Township Central Committee, 1908. Royal Arch Mason; Shriner, Knight Templar; held nearly all offices in different bodies; representative of Illinois to International Conference of Knights Templar at Pittsburgh, Pa., 1914. Home: 101 N. Walnut St., Campaign. Office: University of Illinois, Urbana, Ill.

LEE, Benjamin Franklin, bishop; born at Bridgeton, N. J., Sept. 18, 1841; A.B., Wilberforce Univ., O., 1872; (hon. D.D.); married Mary E. Ashe, of Mobile, Ala., Dec. 30, 1872. Professor of homiletics, 1873-5, pres.,

1876-84, Wilberforce Univ.; now trustee the Univ., and dir. Payne Theol. Sem.; was editor Christian Recorder, 1884-92; elected bishop A. M. E. Ch., 1892; presiding bishop 4th Dist., including Ky., Ind., Ill., Ia., Wis., Minn., N. Dak., S. Dak. Mem. American Forestry Assn. Author: Wesley the Worker, and Causes of the Success of Methodism. Address: Wilberforce. Ohio.

LEE, Helen Evans Williams, teacher; born at Chelsea, Mass., Nov. 16, 1887; daughter of William and Emily (Stroble) Lee; unmarried; grad., Chelsea High School, 1905; State Normal School, Salem, Mass., 1909. Teacher in State Colored Normal School, Elizabeth City, N. C., since 1910; Professor Newbold, of the N. C. board of education, has several times stated at conventions of white teachers' that "she is best primary teacher ever under his observation." Episcopalian. Member Salem Normal School Alumni Assn., Mass. Home: 77 Norfolk St., Cambridge, Mass. Address: State Colored Normal School, Elizabeth City, N. C.

LEE, John W., clergyman; born in Hartford County, Md., Apr. 22, 1884; student Lincoln (Pa.) Univ., 1894-8 (D.D., 1908). Ordained in Presbyterian ministry, 1898; was first assistant pastor Madison Street Church at Baltimore, Md.; engaged in Sunday School missionary work with headquarters at Annapolis, Md., about 2 years; pastor 1st African Presby. Church, Philadelphia, Pa., since 1900. Was chairman the committee that raised $22,500 building fund for Philadelphia Y. M. C. A.; chairman Freedmen's Educational Committee; member Evangelistic Assn., National Alumni Association of Lincoln Univ. (president). Address: First African Presbyterian Church, Philadelphia, Pa.

LEE, Richard Henry, supervising industrial teacher; born at Marion, Ala., Jan. 9, 1887; son of John Irvin and Bettie H. (Webb) Lee; ed. Marion Baptist Academy to 1899; grad. Lincoln Normal School, 1903; student Talladega College, Ala., 2 yrs.; studied in summer school, Tuskegee Institute, 1911; unmarried. Began as teacher in public schools, Marion, 1906, continuing to 1914; was endorsed by the County Board of Education, and appointed supervisor of Jeanes Fund Industrial Teachers in Perry County, Ala., by the State Board of Education, Oct. 1, 1914; secretary and treas. Douglas Benevolent Protective Assn. Trustee Marion Academy. Secretary Berean Baptist Sunday School since 1909. Republican; census enumerator for U. S., 1910. Member the American Workmen. Address: P. O. Box 352, Marion, Ala.

LEMON, James Garfield, lawyer; teacher; born at Atlanta, Ga.; son of Alexander A. and Mary E. (Maxwell) Lemon; A.B., Atlanta Univ., 1902, A.M., 1904; law student Univ. of Chicago, and took course from Chicago Correspondence School of Law, 1908; married Callie Alicia McKinley, of Atlanta, July 30, 1907; 1 child: James G., Jr. Head teacher in mathematics, Georgia State College since 1905; admitted to Ga. bar, 1913; since practiced in Savannah; attorney for Southwestern Claim & Collection Co.; v.-p. Negro Business and Professional Men's League of Savannah. Member National League of Urban Conditions Among Negroes. Republican. Congregationalist. Member Phi Psi. Address: Georgia State Industrial College, Savannah, Ga.

LESTER, John Angelo, physician, surgeon; born at Lebanon, Tenn., Oct. 29, 1864; son of Austin and Candace (Donnell) Lester; A.B., Fisk Univ., Nashville, Tenn., 1890; M.D., Meharry Medical College (Walden Univ.), 1895; post-graduate work Physicians and Surgeons College, Chicago, Ill.; married Rebecca H. Taylor, of Nashville, May 28, 1902. Began as secretary Y. M. C. A., St. Louis, Mo., 1890; professor of botony, zoology, physics, and assistant professor of agriculture at Alcorn (Miss.) Agricultural and Mechanical College, 1891-3; was house physician in Provident Hospital Chicago, 1895; practiced in Nashville since 1896; professor of physiology, also instructor in electro-therapeutics,

Meharry Medical College; sergt. Hospital Corps No. 6, National Guards of Tenn. Republican. Colored Methodist; president laymen's missionary movement. Member State Medical Society, Rock City Academy of Medical Society, Meharry Alumni Assn., Fisk University Alumni Assn. (secretary). Grand medical register Immaculate Order; national recorder Knights of Friendship. Home: 153 Lafayette St. Office: 408 Cedar St., Nashville, Tenn.

LEWEY, Matthew McFarland, publisher, former legislator; born at Baltimore, Md., Dec. 5, 1844; son of John W. and Elizabeth (McFarland) Lewey; attended private schools, and in 1868 the Presbyterian Mission School, Baltimore; A.B., Lincoln (Pa.) Univ., 1872; studied law Howard Univ., Washington, D. C.; married Bessie K. Chestnut, of Gainesville, Fla., 1883; 2 children: John F., Irene V. Inlisted in 55th Mass. Inf., May, 1863; later assigned as member Color Guard with rank of corporal; with forces during siege of Fort Wagoner, Morris Island, S. C., 1863; at the surrender, forced by naval bombardment, was among first detachment of infantry to enter the fort; engaged in battle of James Island, S. C., July 4, 1863; during bayonet charge in battle of Honey Hill, S. C., Nov. 30, 1864, was shot in right arm, left leg, and right shoulder in succession; honorably discharged at DeCamp General Hospital, David's Inland, N. Y., July, 1865. Went to Florida in 1873 at request of late Josiah T. Walls, former congressman; taught school at Newmansville 3 years; admitted to Fla. bar, 1876; elected mayor of Newmansville, 1876; also appointed postmaster and justice of the peace, continuing to 1878; engaged in raising Sea Island cotton, 1879-81; removed to Gainesville, Fla., and was principal of Union Academy one term. Member Fla. House of Representatives, 1881-3, Gainesville City Council, 2 terms, 1883-7; while in the legislature was instrumental in establishing State Normal School, now the Agricultural and Mechanical College for Negroes, at Tallahassee; as member committee on finance, taxation and education, he took advantage of a bill introduced to establish a State Normal School (white), and finally forced an amendment; after a caucus of the 16 colored members in both houses an agreement was made with others who favored Gainesville for the white school with the result that both schools were established. Founded the Florida Sentinel in Gainesville, 1886; removed plant to Pensacola, 1894, to Jacksonville, 1912; incorporated for $10,000; still owns large interest and is director of the company; sole owner and publisher of The Standard, Jacksonville; president National Negro Press Assn., 2 terms, 1910-12. Was one of organizers, 1900, and member executive committee to 1912, National Negro Business League; organized, 1906, and since president, Florida State Negro Business League. Republican. Presbyterian. Member Odd Fellows. Home: 434 W. Ashley St. Office: Colored Masonic Temple, Jacksonville, Fla.

LEWIS, Edmonia, sculptor; born at New York, 1845; her first exhibition was a bust of Robert Gould Shaw, in Boston, Mass., 1865; she produced "The Death of Cleopatra," which was exhibited at the Centennial Exhibition, Philadelphia, 1876; among her other noted works are "The Marriage of Hiawatha," and "The Freed Woman"; she has resided in Italy since 1865. Home: Rome, Italy.

LEWIS, Eva Jane, teacher; born at Howell, Mich., Feb. 25, 1882; daughter of Mathew Jackson and Martha Pierce (Childers) Lewis; grad. high school, Howell, 1901; A.B., Univ. of Mich., 1910; unmarried. Preceptress and teacher, Sam Houston College, Austin, Tex., 1910-11; head of English dept. State Colored Normal School, Elizabeth City, N. C., since 1912. Methodist. Home: 1009 E. Catherine St., Ann Arbor, Mich. Address: State Colored Normal School, Elizabeth City, N. C.

LEWIS, John Calhoun, principal high school; born at Vine Grove, Ky., Jan. 1, 1857; son of Abraham Lewis;

received early education in boarding school near West Point, Ky.; B.S., Berea (Ky.) College, 1886, M.S., 1896; married Cordelia Scott, of Mt. Sterling, Ky., Dec. 5, 1889; 3 children: Julian H., Clara Vesta, Laura L. Principal of Sumner High School, Cairo, Ill., since 1891, and one of the most widely known colored teachers in America; outside of school work devotes time to his real estate interests. Republican. Baptist. Mason, Knight Templar; member Knights and Daughters of Africa, Cairo Negro Business League. Baptist Building Coterie. Address: 612 12th St., Cairo, Ill.

LEWIS, Leonard William, physician; born at Champaign, Ill., Nov. 17, 1874; son of Charles and Eva (De Rousse) Lewis; grad. high school, Champaign; B.S., Fisk Univ., Nashville, Tenn., 1893; Ph.G., Meharry School of Pharmacy, 1899; married Laura P. Smith, of Lexington, Ky., 1912. Practiced in Chicago since 1899; director Y. W. C. A. for colored girls. Republican. Methodist. Member American Medical Assn., Knights of Pythias. Club: Appomatox. Home: 3737 Prairie Ave. Office: 3601 State St., Chicago, Ill.

LEWIS, Richard Hanna, chemist; born at Chicago, Ill., Apr. 7, 1887; son of Charles C. and Anna (Patterson) Lewis; grad. Wendell Phillips High School, Chicago, later student in Oberlin College, O.; B.S., Univ. of Ill., 1910. Analytical chemist with Allaire & Woodward, Peoria, Ill., 1910-11; appointed as assistant chemist in office of public roads Department of Agriculture, Washington, 1911. Republican. Author (with C. S. S. Reeve) Paper before 1912 Congress of Applied Chem. on Application of Demethye Sulphate Test for detection of small amount of asphalt in tar. Address: 816 12th St., N. W., Washington, D. C.

LEWIS, William Henry, former assistant attorney-general of U. S.; born Nov. 28, 1868, in town of Berkley, now part of Norfolk, Va.; son of Ashley and Josephine (Baker) Lewis; prep. education Virginia Normal and Collegiate Inst., Petersburg; A.B., Amherst College, Mass., 1892; LL.B., Harvard, 1895; married Elizabeth Baker, of Boston, Mass., September, 26, 1896. Began practice in Boston, 1895; member Cambridge City Council three terms, 1899-1901; member Mass. House of Representatives, 1902-3; assistant U. S. attorney for Mass., 1903-6; assistant attorney-general of U. S. for New England states, assigned principally to naturalization and special proceedings, 1907-11; assistant attorney-general of U. S., March 26, 1911, to April 1, 1913; since in private practice in Boston and Cambridge, his success as attorney in important cases has received much notice in public press, but with few exceptions the fact that he is a colored lawyer was omitted. Republican. Member of American Bar Association, American Academy of Political and Social Science. Home: 226 Upland Road, Cambridge, Mass.

LIGHTFOOT, James A. Garfield, lawyer, editor; born at Richmond, Va., Dec. 20, 1882; son of Garland W. and Mary Anna (Newton) Lightfoot; attended public schools, Richmond, and 2 yrs. in Cleveland, O.; prep. edn. St. Paul Normal School, Lawrenceville, Va.; LL.B., Howard Univ., Washington, 1907; later studied under Judge J. J. Crandall, of New Jersey, 2 yrs.; unmarried. Practiced in Atlantic City, N. J., since 1912; associated with I. H. Nutter; firm won more criminal cases than any law firm at Atlantic City bar; out of five murder cases defended, 1911-14, won four; formerly editor and pub. The Atlantic Advocate; pres. real estate firm of J. A. Lightfoot & Co. President N. J. State Republican League; appointed commissioner of deeds for Atlantic City. Episcopalian. Member National Negro Press Assn., Colored Men's Business League (secretary), Tau Delta Sigma (Howard Univ.). Mason; Odd Fellow; past exalted ruler Light House Lodge No. 9, Elks; Club: University (pres.), only similar club chartered to include all university men among colored people. Home:

1803 Arctic Ave. Office: Schwartz-Riddle Bldg., Atlantic City, N. J.

LINDSAY, Anna Laura, music teacher; born at Lexington, Ky.; daughter of Cassius M. Clay and Amanda Theodosia (Green) Lindsay; grad., grammar grade, Chandler Normal School, Lexington, 1893, normal dept. Fish Univ., Nashville, Tenn., 1897, Music, 1898. Teacher of music since 1899, at the Virginia Normal and Industrial Institute, Ettricks, Va.

LINDSAY, Joseph Coppliss, insurance; born at Wadesboro, N. C., Dec. 28, 1868; son of Isaac and Temple (Lyles) Lindsay; ed. public school of Ala.; married Lula B. Lewis, of Anniston, Ala., Feb. 27, 1902; 5 children: Joseph C., Jr., Anna W., Addie A., Richard W., Amelia A. Worked on fathers farm to 1886; hotel employe 4 years; in U. S. government service, 1890-2; grocery business, 1892-9; entered insurance business at Anniston, 1899; manager Savannah district and director Union Mutual Insurance Assn., since 1911. Republican. Baptist. Mason; member Odd Fellows. Club: Golden Circle. Home: 2308 Harden St. Office: 509 W. Broad St., Savannah, Ga.

LIVINGSTONE, Lemuel W., consul; born in and appointed from Florida; U. S. Consul at Cape Haitien, Haiti, since Jan. 14, 1898. Address: Cape Haitien, Haiti.

LOCKE, Alain LeRoy, teacher of philosophy; born at Philadelphia, Pa., Sept. 13, 1886; son of Pliny I. and Mary Jane (Hawkins) Locke; grad. high school, Philadelphia, 1902; A.B., Harvard, 1907; Litt.B., Oxford Univ., 1910, was Rhodes Scholar from Pa.; graduate student Fr. Wilhelm Univ., Berlin, Germany, 1910-11; unmarried. Assistant professor of English and philosophy at Howard Univ., Washington, D. C., since 1911. Was assistant organizer Emancipation Exposition of New Jersey, 1913. Episcopalian. Member African Union Society (London), American Academy Political and Social Science, Negro Society for Historical Research, Negro Historical Society of Philadelphia,

Phi Beta Kappa. Clubs: Harvard (Boston, Berlin and London), United Arts (London). Contributor to Oxford Cosmopolitan, North American Review, The Independent. Home: 579 Stevens St., Camden, N. J. Office: Howard University, Washington, D. C.

LOCKETTE, John Anderson, principal of academy; born in Perry Co., Ala., Nov. 29, 1877; son of John P. and Nancy (Love) Lockette; A.B., Georgia State Industrial College, Savannah, Ga., 1901, A.M., 1907; unmarried. Principal of Tennillee (Ga.) High School, 1903,9, and of Union Academy, Gainesville, Fla., since 1909; was organizer, now president and principal, Gainesville Teachers' Culture Course. Served with Ga. Vol. Mil., 1893-9, from private was advanced to corpl., later to 1st lieut.; captain Co. B. Cadets Bat. of Ga. State College, 1895-1901. Candidate for Georgia House of Representatives, 1902; member executive committee Bryan County Republican Organization, 1902-8. Missionary Baptist; editor Baptist Truth. Member Florida State Teachers' Assn., Alachua County Teachers' Assn. (pres.), Men's Business League. Mason; member Odd Fellows, Knights of Pythias. Address: Gainesville, Fla. Summer Home: Micanopy, Fla.

LONG, Edgar Allen, teacher, clergyman; born at Tuskegee, Ala., Oct. 8, 1871; son of Orange and Lila (Howard) Long; grad. Tuskegee Normal and Industrial Institute, 1895; took business course International Correspondence School, 1900; (Pd.M., Biddle Univ., Charlotte, N. C., 1914); married Anna L. Patterson, of Montgomery, Ala., Dec. 23, 1897; 5 children: Edgar Allen, Jr., Gertrude Irene, Theresa Lila, Andrew Lee, Natalie Mildred. Bookkeeper with Ala. Penny Savings Bank, Birmingham, 1895-6; retains stock in same; business mgr. Ala. Publishing Co., 1896-7; treas., 1897-1906, principal Christiansburg Industrial Institute, Cambria, Va., since July, 1906; member firm of Long & Topseg, booksellers; editor Freedman's Friend; composed and published number poems; pres. Negro Teachers' Assn., 1910-14; organized and chmn. Southwest Va. Negro Conference; chairman board of trustees Asbury M. E. Church, Christiansburg, Va. Republican. Mason. Address: Cambria, Va.

LONG, Frank Cornelius, clergyman, teacher; born at New Orleans, La., Mar. 2, 1860; son of Alexander Dumas and Anna Mae (Hawkins) Long; public school edn., New Orleans; A.B., and first male grad. Leland Univ., 1881, A.M., later; post-grad. courses Univ. of Mich. and Kan. State Normal School; B.D., Union Theological Seminary, Morgan Park, Ill., 1884; grad. Stenographic Inst., Chicago, 1900; married Sarah E. Mumford, of Victoria, Texas, June, 1881; 4 children: Octavia Cornelia, Ethel Elizabeth, Clarence Marcellus, Robert Elliott. Was first colored teacher in Bishop College, Marshall, Texas, serving as instructor of mathematics, 1881-2; principal Langston High School, Hot Springs, Ark., since 1907; this is a first-class Colored High School; its course covers 4 years each in Latin, English, science, history, mathematics; graduates have easily found entrance into freshmen classes of leading American colleges. Republican. Baptist. Member Knights of Pythias, Knights of Honor, United Brothers of Friendship, Mosaic Templars. Home: 132 Silver St., Hot Springs, Ark.

LONG, Samuel Arthur, dentist; born at Franklinton, N. C., Feb. 4, 1879; son of George Robert and Susie Frances (Timberlake) Long; ed. Franklinton Christian College to 1899; high school, Cambridge, Mass., evenings, 1903-4; studied dentistry under Dr. W. Alexander Cox, Cambridge, 1907-11; married Minnie Broadie, of Cambridge, Nov. 14, 1914. With the Pullman Company number years; worked for automobile firm while studying his profession; practiced in Cambridge Dental Parlors since 1911. Member executive board, branch No. 1, of Boston, National Negro Business League, also Advocate Pub. Co., and Commercial Pioneer Institute; director Harding, Cox & Martin Real Estate Syndicate. Baptist. Republi-

can. Member National Medical Assn. Home: 62 Howard St. Office: 586 Massachusetts Ave., Cambridge, Mass.

LONG, Thomas Alexander, university professor; born at Franklinton, N. C.; son of Sanford Lee and Mariah (Levister) Long; A.B., Lincoln Univ., Pa., 1889, A.M., S.T.B., 1892 (Ph.D., 1910); special courses, languages, science and philosophy at Columbia Univ., New York, 1901-2, 1914, and philosophy at Lincoln Univ., 1905-7; studied music in New England Conservatory of Music, Boston , Mass. Principal high school, Danville, Va., 1892-1907; professor in departments of science, language and music at Biddie Univ., Charlotte, N. C., since 1907; taught English in summer school and Chautauqua at Durham, N. C., 1910, 11, 12; owns interest in Progressive Investment Co., Charlotte; director Southern Aid Society, Richmond, Va. Republican. Presbyterian. Member World's Sunday School Assn., and Society for Psychic Research. Author: Across the Continent, 1904. Address: Biddle University, Charlotte, North Carolina.

LOTT, James H., lawyer; born at Orangeburg, S. C.; son of Charlotte Rickenbocker; self-educated; read law in office of Alfred Sample, Paxton, Ill., judge 4th Dist. Appellate Court; married Emma N. Jones, of Indianapolis, Ind., June 18, 1904; 1 child: Lillian. Admitted to Ill. bar, 1884; was first colored attorney to regularly represent railroad in U. S., acting for Wabash R. R. Co., in Ford Co., Ill., 1887-90; engrossing clerk state legislature, 1887, first colored person to hold similar clerkship in Ill.; city attorney Paxton, 1887-9; attorney for plaintiffs in "separate coach case," Anderson et. al., vs. L. & N. R. R., in U. S. Dist. Court, Owensboro, Ky., 1894; practiced in Indianapolis since 1895; grand attorney Knights of Pythias of Ind., since 1908; also attorney for Pythian Savings & Loan Assn. Republican. Home: 808 N. California St. Office: 43 Baldwin Block, Indianapolis, Ind.

LOTTIER, Sarah Peyton, supervising industrial teacher; born at Pulaski, Va., Apr. 11, 1887; daughter of Columbus C. and Elizabeth G. (Smith) Lottier; public school edn., Pulaski; grad. Virginia Normal and Industrial Institute, Ettricks, Va., 1908; received professional teachers certificate; took special course at Christiansburg, Va., 1910; received special instruction in domestic science and manual arts at Hampton Institute, on Saturdays only, 1911. Teacher in public schools of Princess Anne and Pulaski counties, Va., 1909-11; supervisor of Negro Rural Schools in Isle of Wright County since 1911; this branch of public instruction is aided by the Anna T. Jeanes Fund and reaches the most remote parts of the state; as a member Isle of Wright Farmers' Assn., she has done good work for the Home Betterment Clubs of the county; also member Negro Organization Society of Va. Close observer of political movements and favors the Progressive party. Methodist. Member Household of Ruth. Club: Smithfield Art Circle. Home Address: Box 602, Pulaski. Office: Smithfield, Va.

LOVE, George Willard Kirkland, society supplies; born at Kansas City, Mo., Nov. 5, 1880; son of Major W. and Anna Love; grad. Lincoln High School, Kansas City, 1901; married Kitty Wiley, of Kansas City, 1902; 2 children: George W. K. Jr., Marshall B. President and sole owner The Love Regalia Co., Kansas City, Mo., established 1911; secretary Attucks Investment Co.; director Phyllis Wheatly-Provident Hospital Assn.; was clerk in office of city treasurer, 8 years. Member 23d Kan. Vol. Inf.; during Spanish-American War; served as chief clerk, Army Headquarters, San Louis de Cuba; hon. discharged, Mar. 17, 1899. Republican. Baptist. Mason (grand sec. State Grand Lodge); grand patron Order Eastern Star. Club: Ivanhoe. Address: 2418 Flora Ave., Kansas City, Mo.

LOWE, Jacob Israel, clergyman, business manager; born on Harbour Island, Bahama Islands, B. W. I.; son of Matthew and Deborah (Cleare) Lowe; ed. in the Bahama Islands; married Alvene Tynes, of Harbour

Island, Mar. 19, 1866; 6 children. Came to America, 1868; entered the ministry, 1873; returned to the Bahamas and was pastor of A. M. E. Church at Cat Island; came to U. S. the second time, 1875; now general business manager of A. M. E. Book Concern at Philadelphia. Trustee Wilberforce (O.) Univ., and Shorter College, Little Rock, Ark. Republican. Mason. Home: Pine Bluff, Ark. Office: 631 Pine St., Philadelphia, Pa.

LUCAS, Clarence Edward, accountant; born at New Brunswick, N. J., Aug. 13, 1886; son of Charles Thomas and Lavinia A. (Voorhees) Lucas; grad. Commercial High School, Brooklyn, N. Y., 1905; LL.B., Howard Univ., 1912; married Rubie K. Booker, of Brooklyn, July 20, 1910; 2 children: Helen Olivia, Rubie Lavinia. Confidential clerk in private office of George Foster Peabody, and private secretary to L. G. Myers, treas. General Education Board, New York, 1905-8; constructive accountant in charge of all accounts, Howard Univ., Washington, D. C., since 1908; secretary advisory board Howard Univ. Y. M. C. A. Baptist. Hon. member Alpha Phi Alpha (Beta Chapter). Mason. Home: 2406 6th St. N. W. Office: Howard University, Washington, D. C.

LUCAS, William Walter, clergyman; born at Macon, Miss., 1870; son of Mary Lucas; high school edn., Macon; A.B., Clark Univ., Atlanta, Ga., 1888; B.D., Gammon Theological Seminary, Atlanta, 1889 (D.D., 1911); post-graduate course at Boston Univ.; married Ida Estelle Hill, of Winsted, Conn., 1901. Member Mississippi Conference of M. E. Church; delegate to World's Missionary Convention, Edinburgh, Scotland, 1910; was secretary of the Stewart Foundation of Africa, 2 years; principal Meridian Academy, Miss., 2 years; field secretary Board of Foreign Missions of M. E. Church, 3 years; assistant general secretary for Colored Conferences, Epworth League of the M. E. Church, since 1912. Address: Meridian, Miss.

LYNCH, John Roy, army officer, retired; born in Concordia Parish, La.,

Sept. 10, 1847; son of Patrick and Catherine (White) Lynch; self-educated; married Mrs. Cora E. Williamson, of Chicago, Ill., Aug. 12, 1911. Was justice of the peace at Natchez, Miss., 1869; member Mississippi House of Representatives, 1869-72, and speaker last 2 years; member 43d, 44th, and 47th Congress from 6th Dist. (1873-7, 1881-3); was chairman Republican State Committee, 1871-89; member Republican Nat'l Committee, 1884-8; delegate to Republican Nat'l Convention, 1872, 1884, 1892, 1900, and temporary chairman the 1884 convention. Auditor in the Treasury for the Navy Dept., Washington, 1889-93; practiced law in Washington, 1893-8; member firm of Lynch & Terrell; admitted to Miss. bar, 1895, and to Supreme Court of Miss., 1896; paymaster in U. S. Army, 1898-1911; retired with rank of Major. Episcopalian. Mason. Club: Appomatox (honorary member). Author: The Facts of Reconstruction, 1913. Home: 4321 Forestville Ave., Chicago, Ill.

LYNK, Beebe Steven, university professor; born at Mason, Tenn., Oct. 24, 1872; daughter of Henderson and Judiam (Boyd) Steven; grad. Lane College, Jackson, Tenn., 1892; Ph.C., Univ. of W. Tenn., 1903; married Miles V. Lynk, of Memphis, Tenn., Apr. 12, 1893. Professor of pharmacy and chemistry, Univ. of W. Tenn., since 1903. Methodist. Member National Federation of Woman's Clubs, State Federation of Woman's Clubs (treasurer). Author: Advice to Colored Women, 1896. Address: 1190 S. Phillips Place, Memphis, Tenn.

LYNK, Miles Vandahurst, university pres; born at Brownsville, Tenn., June 3, 1871; son of John Henry and Mary Louise Lynk; M.D., Meharry Medical College, Walden Univ., 1891; (M.S., Agricultural and Mechanical College, Normal, Ala., 1901; LL.D., Univ. of W. Tenn., 1901); married Beebe Steven, Apr. 12, 1893. Practiced medicine Jackson, Tenn., 1891-1901; publisher Medical and Surgical Observer, 1892; first medical journal issued by colored man in U. S.; president Univ. of W. Tenn., since 1900.

Republican. Methodist. Member National Medical Assn., National Business League. Author: Afro-American School Speaker and Gems of Literature, 1896; Black Troopers, or Daring Deeds of Negro Soldiers in Spanish-American War. Address: 1190 S. Phillips Place, Memphis, Tenn.

LYON, Ernest, clergyman, teacher, lecturer, diplomat; born, Belize, British Honduras, Oct. 22, 1860; son of Emmanuel and Ann (Bending) Lyon; A.B., New Orleans Univ., U. S. A., 1888, later A.M.; special course Univ. Theological Seminary, New York; (D.D., Wiley Univ., Marshall, Tex.); married Clara F. Bacchus, of Wilmington, Del., June 16, 1893; 2d marriage, Marie Wright, of Baltimore, Md., Mar. 28, 1912; 4 children: Maud Amelia, Annie Belle, Ernest Harrison, Monroe. Entered M. E. Ministry, 1882; pastor La Teche, La., 1883, Mallalieu Church, 1886, Thompson Church, 1889, Simpson Church, 1891, at New Orleans; apptd. Sunday School agent Louisiana Conference, 1894; special agent Freedmen's Aid and Southern Educational Society, 1895; pastor St. Mark's Church, New York, 1896, and member New York City Missionary and Church Extension Society; pastor John Wesley Church, Baltimore, 1901, and professor of church history Morgan College; founded Md. Industrial and Agricultural Institute for education of colored youths. Minister resident and consul-general of U. S. at Monrovia, Liberia, 1903-10; representative Liberia to U. S. since 1910; was member committee for Negro Historical and Industrial Assn., that invited President Woodrow Wilson to deliver address on opening day of 50th anniversary exposition and celebration of emancipation at Fort Lee, Va.; one of 10 persons in an international lecture course arranged by Dept. of Education, Baltimore, to represent the genius, characteristics and contribution of the several races to the civilization of mankind. Auxiliary member Republican National Committee to whom all matters referring to colored vote of East were reported, 1896;

member advisory board apptd. by Republican National Committee, 1900. Home: Laurel, Md. Office: 141 W. Hill St., Baltimore, Md.

LYONS, Maritcha Remond, teacher; born at New York, 1848; daughter of Albro and Mary Joseph (Marshall) Lyons; Negro and Indian descent; ed. St. George's Parochial School, New York, 2 years; grad. Grammar School No. 3, 1863; was first colored graduate from high school, Providence, R. I., 1869; studied languages and music at Brooklyn (N. Y.) Institute, 1870-80. Began teaching in public schools of Brooklyn, 1869; taught in all primary and grammar grades; assistant principal since 1898; responsible for 18 to 23 teachers, and 600 to 900 pupils; speaker at lyceum and woman's meetings; active in philanthropic work. At graduates reunion, Providence High School, name was placed on roll of honor with those whose work was credit to school. Suffragist. Religion: Anglo-Roman. Charter member Brooklyn Teachers' Assn., Brooklyn Teachers' Life Assurance Assn. Clubs: Brooklyn Woman's Charity (hon. member), Woman's Loyal Union (New York and Brooklyn). Home: 195 Elton St., Brooklyn, N. Y.

M

MACBETH, Arthur Laidler, photographic artist; born at Charleston, S. C., Apr. 23, 1864; of African, Dutch and Scotch descent; public and private school edn., and student Avery Normal Institute, Charleston; married Susan Jackson Houston, of Charleston, May 15, 1883 (died 1901); 12 children, 7 living: Hugh E., Chester, Hazel, Gobert, Marguerite (Mrs. Jos. W. Saunders), Kenneth, Lois. Learned photography under German, French and American artists and chemists; began business in Charleston, 1886, since continuing in same line, except 18 months while serving at Jamestown Exposition; removed to Baltimore, Md., 1910; awarded metals and diplomas at South Carolina Fair, 1890, Cotton States Exposition, Atlanta, Ga., 1895, South Carolina Interstate and West Indian Exposition, Charles-

ton, 1902, Jamestown Ter-Centennial Exposition, 1907. Was among the pioneers in moving picture business; exhibited at Charleston, 1899-1906, at Norfolk, Va., 1908-10; has invented "Macbeth's Daylight Projecting Screen," with the purpose of showing stereoptican and moving pictures in daylight. Manager bureau of arts in Negro dept. S. C. Interstate and West Indian Exposition, 1901-2; field agent and director of exhibits in Negro dept. Jamestown Exposition, 1907. Delegate to M. E. Central Conference, Baltimore, 1908; was trustee Centenary Church in Charleston 20 years. Republican. Member Photographers' Association of America (white), National Negro Business League. Mason. Home: 637 Pitcher St. Studio: 1030 Pennsylvania Ave., Baltimore, Md.

MACBETH, Hazel Adrienne, teacher; born at Charleston, S. C., Nov. 22, 1891; daughter of Arthur Laidler and Susan J. (Houston) Macbeth; ed. private and public schools, and Avery Normal Institute, Charleston; grad. Norfolk Mission College, Va., 1910. Began as proof-reader and clerk with the Baltimore Times, 1910, later unitype operator, continuing to 1913; was secretary Phyllis Wheatley Assn., Cleveland, O., 1914; teacher in public school, Baltimore, since 1915. Methodist. Home: 637 Pitcher St., Baltimore, Md.

MACBETH, Hugh Ellwood, lawyer; born at Charleston, S. C., Oct. 14, 1884; son of Arthur Laidler and Susan J. (Houston) Macbeth; private and public school edn., Charleston; grad. Avery Normal Institute, 1902; A.B., Fisk Univ., Nashville, Tenn., 1905; LL.B., Harvard, 1908; married Edwina F. Mayer, of Columbus, Ga., Sept. 7, 1910; 1 child: Emma. Admitted to Maryland bar, 1908; practiced in Baltimore to 1913; founded the Baltimore Times, 1909, and its editor 4 years; member law firm of Tyler & Macbeth, Los Angeles, Calif., 1913; practiced individually since Jan., 1914. Progressive; campaign worker and speaker with and for Theodore Roosevelt in Maryland,

Ohio, New Jersey and New York, during the presidential primary cam-campaign, 1912. Methodist. Mason. Home: 2728 Glassell St. Office: 319 Delta Bldg., Los Angeles, Calif.

MACINTYRE, William Arthur, lawyer; born at Sanfernando, Trinidad, B. W. I., Aug. 21, 1881; son of Arthur George and Amelia Caroline (Brown) Macintyre; came to America, 1902; ed. Government Boys School, Sanfernando, Queen's Royal College, Port of Spain, Trinidad; Tuskegee Normal and Industrial Institute, Ala., 1902-3; A.B., Fisk Univ., 1908; LL.B., Howard, 1911; married Willie Hobbs Page, of Nashville, Tenn., July 27, 1910; 1 child: Almeta Louise. Practiced in Chicago, Ill., since 1912; member law firm of Hill and Macintyre. Episcopalian. Mason; member Foresters. Home: 3564 Vernon Ave. Office: 748 S. Halsted St., Chicago, Ill.

MACKERROW, Horace Gilford, physician, surgeon; born at Halifax, Nova Scotia, Oct. 13, 1879; son of Peter Evander and Mary Elizabeth (Thomas) Mackerrow; ed. Halifax Academy, 1893-7; Delhousie College, Halifax, 1897-8; Montreal Business College, Can., 1899-1900; M.D., Leonard Medical College, Raleigh, N. C., 1904; M.D., C.M., Bishop's Medical College, Montreal, 1905; post-graduate work Western General Hospital, Montreal General Hospital, and Montreal Dispensary, 1904-5; unmarried. Teacher in public schools, Halifax, 1897-9; resident physician Woman's Hospital, Montreal, 1905; practiced in Worcester, Mass., since 1906; passed civil service examination, Oct. 13, 1913, and placed on eligible list for appointment as industrial health inspector. Trustee Home Assn. for Aged Colored People, Worcester; member Harding, Cox & Martin Real Estate Syndicate, Boston; was member exec. com. Citizens No-License League, Worcester, 3 years. Served as batallion sergt.-maj. Halifax Academy Cadet Corps, 1896-7. Progressive delegate to state convention, Boston, 1914. Baptist. Member American Medical Assn., National Association Colored Physicians, Dentists and Pharm., Bay State Medical, Dental and Pharm. Assn., Mass. Medical Society, Worcester District Medical Society. 32d degree Mason; member Odd Fellows, Galileen Fisherman. Club: Hon. member Myles Standish Athletic Assn. Address: 96 Eastern Ave., Worcester, Mass.

MAJORS, Monroe Alphus, physician, surgeon; born at Waco, Tex., Oct. 12, 1864; son of Andrew Jackson and Jane (Barringer) Majors; prep. edn. Tillotson College, Austin, Tex.; S.B., Central Tennessee College, 1886; M.D., Meharry Medical College (Walden Univ.), Nashville, Tenn., 1886; married Georgia Green, of Huntsville, Ala., 1889 (divorced 1904); 2d marriage, Estella C. Bond, of Chicago, Ill., Sept., 1909; 2 children: Grace L., Margaret J. Began practice in Austin, Tex., 1886; removed to Los Angeles, Calif., 1888, and was first Negro physician west of Rocky Mountains, as well as first to pass medical board in Calif.; returned to Texas, and was lecturer in hygiene and sanitation at Paul Quinn College, Waco, 1891-4; superintendent Colored Hospital in Waco, 1899-1901; in practice in Chicago, Ill., since 1901; served with Department of Health, 1908; director Enterprise Institute. Was organizer of first Negro Medical Association in U. S., 1886; president Lone Star Medical Assn., Texas, 1892-6; member National Medical Assn., Negro Historical Society. 32d degree Mason; member Knights of Pythias, United Brothers of Friendship. Author: Noted Negro Women, 1893. Home: 6652 Wabash Ave. Office: 4709 State St., Chicago, Illinois.

MALLORY, Hannah Jane, supervising industrial teacher; grad. normal dept., Talladega (Ala.) College, 1899. Supervisor, Negro Rural Schools, Coosa County, Ala.; this branch of instruction is assisted by the Anna T. Jeanes Fund, and reaches the most remote schools and homes in the state Address: Cottage Grove, Ala.

MALONE, Sarah Francis, rescue home supt.; born at Nashville, Tenn., 1865; daughter of Monroe and Jemina (Askind) Jamison; ed. at Walden

Univ., Nashville; married Bailey Malone, of Greenfield, Tenn., 1880. Founded Florence Crittenton Home for colored at Topeka, Kan., 1905; president and superintendent; the rescue work is same as similar homes (white) throughout the country; appointed officer in welfare work City of Topeka. Baptist. Member Household of Ruth, International Order of Twelve, City Federation Woman's Clubs, Art Club. Author (pamphlet): A Mother's Duty Toward Her Children. Address: 827 Center St., Topeka, Kansas.

MARBLE, Harriett Beecher Stowe, pharmacist; born at Yazoo City, Miss., May 2, 1885; daughter of Solomon and Lear Ann (Molette) Marble; grad. high school, Yazoo City, 1903; Pharm. B., Meharry Medical College (Walden Univ.), Nashville, Tenn., 1906; passed examination and licensed in several states; made best mark of 77 applicants before Miss. State Board of Examiners, 1908; unmarried. In charge drug store for firm of Jeter & Jeter, Oklahoma City, Okla,, 1907-9; with Brown & Fisher Drug Co., Laurel, Miss., 1909-11; hospital pharmacist Tuskegee Normal and Industrial Institute, Ala., 1911-13; in drug business for self, Yazoo City, since 1915. Pharm. sec. National Medical Assn.; member Medical, Dental and Pharm. Assn. Progressive. Catholic. Address: 601 Calhoun St., Yazoo City, Miss.

MARLEY, Joseph Alexander, teacher; born at Danville, Ill., Oct. 28, 1883; son of Henry and Maria (Fields) Marley; grad. Belleville High School, Ill.; student Normal Univ., Ill., 1907-8; Mich. State Normal College, 2 summers; married Clots Johnson, of Woods Station, Ill., June 6, 1914. Teacher public schools, Cahokia, Ill., 1904-5, Rush City School, E. St. Louis, Ill., 1905-7; principal Garfield School, 1908-9, McKinley School, 1909-13, Bond Avenue School since 1913. Republican. Methodist. Member E. St. Louis Teachers' Assn., St. Clair County Teachers' Assn. Address: 1826 Market Ave., E. St. Louis, Illinois.

MARQUESS, John Miller, principal high school; born at Helena, Ark., Feb. 3, 1882; son of John William O. and Maria Jane (Miller) Marquess; grad. Helena Normal School, 1895; A. B., Fisk Univ., Nashville, Tenn., 1902; A. B., Dartmouth College, Hanover, N. H., 1904; married Anna Edna Dickson, of Springfield, Ohio, Aug. 28, 1908; 3 children: Maria Jean, John M. Jr., Anna Elizabeth. Instructor in Latin and mathematics, Shorter College, Argenta, Ark., 1904-6, Kittrell (N. C.) College, 1906-8; principal Sumner High School, Kansas City, Kan., since 1908. African Methodist. Mason; secretary Grand Lodge of Kan., 1914-15; Knight Templar; member Knights of Pythias, United Brothers of Friendship, Royal Circle of Friends, Knights of Tabor. Home: 2010 N. 6th St., Kansas City, Mo.

MARSHALL, Julian Franklin, clergyman; born near Richmond, Va., Apr. 16, 1847; son of Robert and Abberella (Stroud) Marshall; student Straight Univ., and New Orleans Univ., La., brief periods; (D.D., Wiley Univ., Marshall, Tex., 1898); married Alice M. Smith, of New Orleans, La., Jan. 16, 1878; 1 child: Mrs. Littah Marshall Crolley, Chicago, Ill. Licensed to preach, 1877; first postorate, Cheneyville, La., 1877-8; later at New Orleans and Shreveport; was presiding elder 17 years; pastor Newman Memorial M. E. Church, Alexandria, La., since 1913, serving here third time; was elected to General conference, New York, 1888, and Cleveland, 1896. Trustee New Orleans Univ. Republican. Address: Box 408, Alexandria, La.

MARTIN, Charles Douglass, clergyman; born, St. Kitts, British West Indies; son of Joseph and Adriana Martin; attended Church schools, St. Kitts; student Nisky College, and Theological Seminary, St. Thomas; came to America, 1906; studied at Union Theological Seminary, New York; married Ellen Patterson, of Jamaica, B. W. I., 1910. Founded Beth-Tphillah, Fourth Moravian Church, New York, 1908; ordained Presbyter at Nazareth, 1912; only colored minister of the Moravian Church in the country. Member American Academy Political and Social Science, Negro Society for Historical Research (vice.-pres.); has large library of theological works, books on Negro problems, slavery, West Indies, Africa, etc. Home: 124 W. 136th St., New York.

MARTIN, James Arthur, clergyman; born at Stinson, Ga., Sept. 3, 1876; son of Isaac D. and Ann (Bell) Martin; ed. Paine College, Augusta, Ga., 1893-1904; married Eugenia A. Collier, of Barnesville, Ga., July 12, 1908. Traveled as special colporteur to colored people of South for American Bible Society, 1902-6; pastored W. Mitchell St. C. M. E. Church, Atlanta, Ga., Waycross, Americus and Thomasville, 1906-13; pastor in Savannah since 1913; delegate General Conference, St. Louis, Mo., 1914. Trustee Holsey Normal and Industrial Institute, Cordele, Ga. Delegate Republican State Convention, Atlanta, 1900. Member National Geographical Society, Savannah Negro Business League, Odd Fellows, Knights of Pythias. Address: 507 Maple St., Savannah, Ga.

MARTIN, James L., physician and surgeon; born at Jonesville, Va., Nov. 2, 1880; son of Alexander and Armanda (Allen) Martin; ed. public schools, Jonesville; A.B., Swifts Memorial College, Rogersville, Tenn., 1901; M.D., Leonard Medical College, Raleigh, N. C., 1906; unmarried. Practiced in institutions at Philadelphia, Pa., 1907; medical examiner Beneficial Insurance Co., Staunton, Va., since 1907; consulting physician Epps Eldridge Memorial Hospital, Petersburg, since 1911. Republican. Presbyterian. Member National Medical Assn., Tidewater Medical Assn., Elks, Good Samaritans. Address: 501 N. Augusta St., Staunton, Va.

MARTIN, Joseph C., clergyman; born at Trenton, Tenn., 1866; son of Willis and Clara (Penn) Martin; ed. public schools, Trenton; Roger Williams Univ., Nashville; took Bible course at Howe Institute, Memphis, Tenn.; (hon. D.D., Lane College,

Jackson, Tenn., 1907); unmarried. Entered Methodist ministry at Trenton, Tenn., 1890; pastor, Miles Memorial Church, Washington, D. C., 1892-6, Sidney Park Church, Columbus, S. C., 1896-1901, Collins Chapel, Memphis, Tenn., 1901-5; presiding elder of Memphis Dist. Colored M. E. Church, 1905-12; book and financial agent of the church in the publishing house at Jackson, Tenn., since 1912; delegate to Ecumenical Conference on Methodism, London, Eng., 1901; was president the Solvent Savings Bank and Trust Co., Memphis, 1911-12, now 1st vice-pres. Trustee Lane College. Home: Memphis. Office: Publishing House, C. M. E. Church, Jackson, Tenn.

MASON, Henry James, secretary, registrar; born at Hockley, Tex., Nov. 23, 1884; son of Cary Henry and Rhoda (Greeley) Mason; ed. public schools, Hockley; student Wiley Univ.; unmarried. Secretary to president of Wiley Univ., Marshall, Tex., 1903-7; assistant business mgr. Southwestern Christian Advocate, New Orleans, La., 1907-10; secretary to president and registrar at Prairie View State Normal and Industrial College, Tex., since 1910. Episcopalian. Correspondent for Houston Daily Post, Houston Daily Chronicle, Galveston News. Home: Hockley. Office: Prairie View, Texas.

MASON, Madison Charles Butler, clergyman; born at Houma, La., Mar. 27, 1861; son of Alfred and Julia (Ephraim) Mason; A.B., New Orleans Univ., 1888; B.D., Gammon Theological Seminary, Atlanta, Ga., 1891; (D.D., New Orleans Univ., and Wiley Univ., 1902; Ph.D., Alabama State College, 1906); married Mary E. Wright, of Houma, La., Dec. 17, 1879; 4 children: Bessie Noblesse, Winina Agatha, Madison Charles B. Jr., Mamie C. Ordained Methodist ministry, 1883; pastor New Orleans and Atlanta to 1891; field secretary, 1892-5, corresponding secretary, 1896-1912, Freedmen's Aid and Southern Education Society of M. E. Church; corresponding sec. National Association for Advancement of Colored People, 1912-

14; pastor Ebenezer M. E. Church, Jacksonville, Fla.; member Chautauqua Association and prominent among the few colored lecturers at Chautaubua assemblies; director Standard Life Ins. Co. Trustee New Orleans Univ. Mason. Home: 431 W. Ashley St., Jacksonville, Fla.

MASON, Ulysses Grant, physician, surgeon; born at Birmingham, Ala., Nov. 20, 1872; son of Isaac and Mary (de Jarnette) Mason; prep. edn. Huntsville College (now A. & M. College, Normal, Ala.); M.D., Meharry Medical College (Walden Univ.), Nashville, Tenn., 1895; special surgery course Univ. of Edinburgh, Scotland, 1899; married Alice Nelson, of Greensboro, Ala., June 28, 1898; 4 children: Vivian, Ellariz, Ulyssus G., Jr., Alice F. Practiced in Birmingham, Ala., since 1895; assistant city physician nearly 8 years; chairman and surgeon at George C. Hall Hospital; vice-pres. Alabama Penny Savings Bank, 1897-1908; organized Prudential Savings Bank, 1910, and since president. Trustee Central Alabama College, also 16th Street Baptist Church. Delegate at-large to Republican National Conventions, 1908, 12. Member Clinical Congress of Surgeons of North America, National Medical Assn., State Medical, Dental and Pharm. Assn., Jones Valley Medical, Dental and Pharm. Assn. Mason: endowment treasurer Knights of Pythias; member Odd Fellows. Home: 1525 7th Ave. Office: 1717 1-2 Third Ave., Birmingham, Ala.

MATTHEWS, William Baxter, principal high school; born at Powersville, Ga., 1864; grad. Lewis High (now Ballard Normal) School, Macon, Ga.; A.B., Atlanta Univ., 1890; married, Jan. 1, 1895, Josephine Ophelia, daughter of the late Courtney Beale and grand-niece of Bishop Wesley J. Gaines of the A. M. E. Church; 1 child: Florida Louise. Principal, Gate City School, Atlanta, Ga., 1891-1912, and Central High School, Louisville, Ky., since 1912. Trustee Atlanta Univ. Congregationalist; member executive committee International Sunday School Assn. Mason; grand auditor Knights of Pythias, Jurisdiction of Ga.; member Odd Fellows. Address: 1720 W. Chestnut St., Louisville, Ky.

MATTHEWS, William Clarence, special assistant U. S. Attorney; born at Selma, Ala., Jan. 7, 1877; son of William Henry and Elizabeth Matthews; ed. Tuskegee Normal and Industrial Institute, 1897; prep. edn. Phillips Academy, Andover, Miss.; A.B., Harvard, 1905; LL.B., Boston Univ., 1907; married Penelope B. Lloyd, of Haynesville, Ala., July 6, 1907. Admitted to Mass. bar, 1908; since in practice in Boston; special U. S. attorney for Dist. of Mass., 1912-15, assigned principally to immigration land cases and violations of postal laws. Was athletic instructor in high schools, Boston, 1905-11. Served as private with Co. L. 6th Regt. M. V. M. Mason; member Elks, United Brothers of Friendship, Order of St. Luke. Clubs: Varsity, Colraine, Harvard (Boston). Home: 4 Franklin St., Boston, Mass.

MAYERS, Richard, clergyman; born at Barbados, B. W. I., Mar. 6, 1852 (tho the date is in doubt); son of Joseph and Rose F. Mayers; ed. Mt. Tabor public schools; Morovian Mission, Barbados; Rev. Dr. William Henry Engledow's High School, Scarboro, Tobago, B. W. I.; student in pharmacy and medicine, Tobago and Guiana; A.B., Lincoln (Pa.) Univ., 1893, S.T.B., 1893, A.M., 1895; S.T.B., National Univ. of Illinois, 1901; understands French, Latin, Greek, Hebrew, Spanish, Portuguese, Hindustani, and Trinidadian (a broken language); married Marcia Maria Murray, of Pembroke Plantation, Tobago, May 18, 1875; 2d marriage, Mrs. Flora E. Elms, of Maryville, Tenn., Feb. 12, 1902. Began as teacher in Bridgeton, Barbados, at age of 19; farmer and stock raiser, 1869-73; teacher and headmaster at St. Giles and Mt. Tabor, 1873, St. Mary's, 1873-4, Mt. George, 1875-7, Scarboro, 1887-9, British Guiana, 1889-91; came to America in Sept., 1891. Teacher, Gaffney, S. C., 1898-1902; treasurer People's Industrial High School,

Knoxville, 1904, 7; principal Tuggle Institute, Birmingham, Ala., 1905-6. Ordained Presbyterian ministry, 1893; was Sunday School missionary 5 years; pastor Reidville and Wellford, S. C., 1898-1902, Knoxville, Tenn., 1902-4; founded, 1908, and since pastor Gilgal-McKahan Presbyterian Church, Bearden, Tenn.; temperance lecturer; was moderator Synod of East Tennessee, and convened meeting at Knoxville with purpose of ridding city of saloons. Republican. Member Odd Fellows, Knights of Pythias. Wrote "The Journeyman's Daughter," and several songs, essays, etc. Address: 602 Payne St., Knoxville, Tenn.

MAYFIELD, Robert Lee, lawyer; born at Nashville, Tenn., Oct. 10, 1870; son of Nathan and Sarah (Lee) Mayfield; A.B., Fisk Univ., Nashville, 1895; M.D., Howard Univ., Washington, 1899; unmarried. Admitted to Tenn. bar, 1899; since practiced in Nashville; has argued many cases before the Supreme Court, and secured 4 reverse decisions one year. Democrat. Congregationalist. Member Knights of Pythias. Home: 1210 Harding St. Office: 410½ Cedar St., Nashville, Tenn.

MAYS, A. S., clergyman; vice-president Afro-American Presbyterian Council, Rochester, N. Y.

McALLISTER, Clifton Lopez, university professor; born at Aberdeen, Miss., Oct. 29, 1886; son of Rev. Lopez D. and Emmaline McAllister; attended public schools, Aberdeen; Ministeral Institute and Normal School, West Point, Miss.; prep. edn. Roger Williams Univ., Nashville, Tenn.; A.B., Morehouse College, Atlanta, Ga., 1909; unmarried. Teacher in Howe Institute, Memphis, Tenn., 1909-11; mgr. Star Printing Co., 1911-12; pres. Nelson Merry College, Jefferson City, Tenn., 1912-13; professor of history and mathematics Roger Williams Univ., since 1913. Republican. Baptist. National grand sec. International Order of Watchmen. Author: Social Conditions in Atlanta, Ga., 1911; Society in Atlanta, 1912. Home: 385 S. Cynthia Pl.,

Memphis, Tenn. Office: Roger Williams University, Nashville, Tenn.

McCARD, William G., lawyer; born at Rockford, Ill., July 7, 1871; son of James W. and Elizabeth (William) McCard; B.L., Univ. of Wis., 1893; LL.B., Northwestern Univ. School of Law, 1896; married Grace K. Wilkins, Sept. 10, 1903. Admitted to Ill. bar, 1906; began practice in Chicago, later removed to Baltimore, Md. Home: 1940 Druid Hill. Office: 21 E. Saratoga St., Baltimore, Md.

McCLAIN, Thomas Ernest, dentist; born at Nashville, Tenn., Apr. 8, 1876; son of Samuel and Malinda Margurite (Caruthers) McClain; A.B., Roger Williams Univ., Nashville, 1901; D.D.S., Meharry Dental College (Walden Univ.), 1902; married Lafayett Stewart, of Nashville, June 26, 1907; twins: Ernestine, Josephine. Practiced in Denver, Colo., since 1907. Republican. Missionary. Baptist. Mem. True Reformers, Knights of Pythias. Club: Bon Vi Vant. Address: 822 32nd St., Denver, Colo.

McCLELLAN, George Marion, principal public school; born at Belfast, Tenn., Sept. 29, 1860; son of George Fielding and Eliza (Leonard) McClellan; four year preparatory course Fisk Univ., Nashville, Tenn., A.B., 1885, A.M., 1890; B.D., Hartford Theological Seminary (Conn.), 1891; married Maria Augusta Rabb, of Columbus, Miss., Oct. 4, 1888; 2 children: Marion S., Theodore R. Teacher of Latin and English in Central High School, Louisville, Ky., 1899-1911; principal Dunbar Public School since 1911. Republican. Congregationalist. Author: Book of Poems; Old Green Bottom Inn, a short story. Home: 1123 W. Hill St., Louisville, Ky.

McCLELLAN, Maria Rabb, teacher; born at Columbus, Miss.; daughter of Jack and Gillie (Harris) Rabb; attended Union Academy, Columbus; A.B., Fisk Univ., 1895; married George M. McClellan;. Teacher in Garrison School, Kansas City, Mo. Congregationalist. Address: 1022 Virginia Ave., Kansas City, Mo.

McCOWN, Ben, grocer, former councilman; born at Harrodsburg, Mercer Co., Ky., Feb. 14, 1870; son of Ezekiel end Maria (Wilson) McCown; common school edn. In grocery business since 1907; manager Joe E. Bright & Co., undertaking and embalming firm. Republican; was member Harrodsburg City Council, 1913-15. Mason; member Knights of Pythias, United Brothers of Friendship. Address: 352 West Broadway, Harrodsburg, Ky.

McCOY, Joseph L., D.D., clergyman; elected moderator Western Baptist Assn., at 23d annual session held at Riverside, Calif., 1914; pastor Second Baptist Church, Los Angeles, Calif.

McCOY, Lee Marcus, teacher; born at Ruckerville, Miss., May 30, 1882; son of Abraham and Louise (McAllister) McCoy; grad. high school, Little Rock, Ark., 1902; A.B., Rust College, Holly Springs, Miss., 1905, A.M., 1908; married Edña May Hilliard, of Coffeeville, Miss., June 28, 1911; 1 child: Ida Louise. Day laborer with Ferguson Lumber Co., summers, 1902-5, attending college fall and winter months; teacher in public school, 1905-6; professor of mathematics Meredian Academy, Miss., 1906-9, Rust Univ., Holly Springs, 1909-11; principal Lincoln High School, Ft. Smith, Ark., 1911-14; professor or mathematics Philander Smith College, Little Rock, since 1914. Methodist. National secretary Black Men of America. Address: Philander Smith College, Little Rock, Ark.

McCOY, Mary Elenora Delaney, social worker; born in "underground railroad station" at Lawrenceburg, Ind., Jan. 7, 1846; daughter of Jacob C. and Eliza Ann (Montgomery) Delaney; ed. mission schools conducted in homes in Ind., and at Freedman's School, St. Louis, Mo.; married Henry Brownlow, of St. Louis, 1869; 2d, Elijah McCoy, the inventor, of Detroit, Mich., Feb. 25, 1873; 1 child. Was charter member (1895) of 20th Century Club (white), Detroit; called first meeting for organization of Phyllis Wheatley Home for Aged Colored Women, 1897; now vice-pres. Phyllis

Wheatley Assn., and McCoy Home for Children; state organizer and vice-pres. Federated Colored Woman's Clubs of Mich.; vice-pres. Lydian Assn.; member Detroit branch National Assn. for Advancement of Colored People, Willing Workers Society, King's Daughters. African Methodist. Suffragist; flag bearer of famous suffrage parade at Washington, D. C., 1915. Delegate to Half-Century Anniversary Celebration of Negro Freedom, Chicago, Ill., 1915. Home: 180 Rowena St., Detroit, Mich.

McCUNE, Margaret Elizabeth, supervising industrial teacher; born at Cumberland, Ohio, Nov. 6, 1879; daughter of Thomas and Elizabeth Ann (Calman) Pritchett; public school edn., Cumberland and Zanesville, Ohio; grad. Wilberforce Univ., O., 1905; married Charles N. McCune, of Hickory, Miss., Aug. 2, 1908. Began as head teacher in domestic science department at Tuskegee Normal and Industrial Institute, Ala., 1907, continuing to 1908; taught in academic department, Manassas Industrial School, Va.; supervising industrial teacher in Northampton County, Va., since 1909; industrial instruction in Va. is under the State Board of Education; aided by the Anna T. Jeanes Fund it reaches the most remote Negro rural schools and homes in the state. African Methodist. Member Virginia State Teachers' Assn., Northampton Teachers' Assn.; also member Household of Ruth. Address: Tidewater Institute, Chesapeake, Va.

McCurdy, Theodore Edward Alexis, physician; born, British Guiana, S. A., Apr. 27, 1877; son of Josiah E. and Janet (Prince) McCurdy; prep. edn. All Saints English School, British Guiana; came to America, 1900; M.D., Leonard Medical School, Raleigh, N. C., 1904; married Talula M. Shepard, of Durham, N. C., Nov. 27, 1913. Practiced in Springfield, Mass., 1905-6, Boston since 1906; visiting physician, Plymouth Hospital; therapeutist and X-Ray specialist; chairman board directors Harding, Cox & Martin Real Estate Syndicate. Baptist. Member National Medical Assn., Bay State

Medical Assn., Mass. Medical Society. Mason; member Odd Fellows, Elks, Knights of Pythias, Foresters. Clubs: Greater Boston, Round Table. Address: 798 Tremont St., Boston, Mass.

McDONALD, William Madison, bank cashier; born at Johnson Point, Kaufman Co., Texas., June 22, 1866; son of George and Flora (Scott) McDonald; high school edn., Kaufman, Tex.; married Helen Ezell, of Kaufman, June 22, 1896; 1 child: William M. Jr. Began active career as organizer for a colored society, 1885, continuing 3 years; organized the first State Colored Fair, 1886; taught school, 1888-95; was a farmer, 1895-1907; prop. Temple Drug Store, Fort Worth, since 1907; organized and now cashier the Fraternal Bank & Trust Co., Fort Worth, which began business Dec. 31, 1911. Baptist. Delegate to National Republican Convention, Minneapolis, Minn., 1892; temporary chairman at state convention, Texas, 1896; delegate at-large, St. Louis, Mo., 1896, Philadelphia, Pa., 1900, Chicago, Ill., 1904, 08, 12. Mason; grand sec. Grand Lodge of Tex.; since 1899; member Odd Fellows, Knights of Pythias. Office: 401 E. 9th St., Fort Worth, Texas.

McDONALD, J. Frank, clergyman, editor; born near Dover, Lafayette Co., Mo., Sept. 15, 1850; learned to repeat alphabet forward and backward, with eyes shut, but could not pick out a single letter when looking at them; taught to read by a missionary teacher from Iowa; after the war between the states, attended school several terms at Independence, Mo.; student in St. Vincent College, Cape Girardeau, Mo., 2 years; learned Latin, Greek, and an outline of Hebrew; studied law in Kansas City, Mo., 1904; (D.D., Wilberforce Univ.; Ph.D., Paul Quinn College); married L. Louise Sanford, of Macon, Mo., 1878. Escaped from slavery when 12 years old; went to Lexington, Mo., and remained in a Fort 4 months; in Jan., 1863, he joined crowd of fugitive slaves on journey to Kansas; after suffering hunger, frozen feet and general hardships, finally arrived at In-

dependence, Mo.; had made attempt to join Union army at Lexington and later, but was rejected on account of youth, weight and height; finally accepted as body servant by a captain in 2d Colo. Vols., and when President Lincoln made last call for volunteers with a draft he enlisted as a soldier. Was converted during a revival by Rev. T. Wallingford Henderson in Kansas City, Mo., and joined Allen Chapel; returned to Lexington and his studies, and later licensed as a local preacher, teaching in public schools at same time; joined Missouri Conference A. M. E. Church, Sept. 25, 1876; has served as missionary circuit rider, pastor, presiding elder, built churches, paid off debts, etc.; was secretary number years for North Missouri Conference, also Missouri Conference, and delegate to several General Conferences; alternate delegate to Ecumenical Conference on Methodism, London, Eng., 1901; publisher the Church Journal since 1891; general officer of the church and editor the Western Christian Recorder since 1901; has traveled extensively in the U. S. and Canada. 32d degree Mason. Address: 2517 Grove Ave., Kansas City, Mo.

McDOWELL, Cyrus R., clergyman, insurance; born at Bowling Green, Ky., Feb. 4, 1864; son of Cyrus and Lucinda (Strange) McDowell; ed. Bowling Green Academy; (D.D., Western College, Macon, Mo.); married Mary G. Thurman, of Louisville, Ky., Dec. 26, 1883; 3 children. Taught school in Rockfield, Woodburn and Bowling Green, Ky.; established Bowling Green Watchman, 1887; its editor to 1889; one of founders Bowling Green Academy; ordained Baptist ministry, 1890; organized Green River Valley Baptist Assn.; pastor Hartford and Greenville, Ky.; pastor Independence, Mo., 1900; Pilgrim Church, St. Louis, 1900-2, Hannibal Baptist Church, Mo., since 1902; moderator N. Mo. Baptist Assn., 7 years; pres. Home Protective Investment Co., Home Protective Assn; general mgr. Home Protective Pub. Co. Trustee and dir. Western College. Republican. Pres. Hannibal Negro Business League. Mason; member Knights of Tabor, Odd Fellows, United Brothers of Friendship. Address: 210 Center St., Hannibal, Mo.

McGUINN, Warner T., lawyer; born in Goochland Co., Va., Nov. 22, 1863; son of Jarrod and Fanny McGuinn; attended public schools in Richmond, Va., and Baltimore, Md.; A.B., Lincoln (Pa.) Univ., 1884; student Howard Univ. School of Law, Washington, D. C., 1884-5; LL.B., Yale, 1887; for best written oration was awarded the Townsend prize of $100 at Yale; married Anna L. Wallace, of Richmond, Va., Feb. 25, 1892; 1 child: Alma Augusta. Was editor American Citizen, Kansas City, Kan., 2 years; admitted to Kansas bar, 1887; later removed to Baltimore; member law firm of Cummings & McGuinn, 1893-5; in practice individually since 1896; was secretary Baltimore liquor license board, 1896-1900. Director of Baltimore branch National Association for Advancement of Colored People. Republican. Presbyterian. Mason. Home: 1911 Division St. Office: 215 Courtland St., Baltimore, Md.

McKISSACK, E. H., insurance; born at Memphis, Tenn., Nov. 22, 1860; left orphan when 4 years of age; ed. Rust Univ., Holly Springs, Miss.; married Mary Allison Exum, of Yazoo City, Miss., Aug. 24, 1880; 1 child: Dr. A. M. McKissack. Professor at Rust Univ., 1887-1912; secretary of faculty, 1897-1912; treasurer Union Guaranty & Ins. Co., Jackson, Miss., since 1912; sec.-treas. Odd Fellows Benefit Assn.; editor Mississippi Odd Fellow; director Southern Bank, Jackson. Republican. Methodist. Mason; member Order Eastern Star, Odd Fellows, Knights of Pythias, Household of Ruth. Address: Holly Springs, Miss.

McLEAN, Newton Esic, manual training instructor; born at Savannah, Ga., Dec. 4, 1879; son of Rev. John Rufus and Bell (Hardin) McLean; grad. Ballard Normal School, Macon, Ga.; A.B., Talladega (Ala.) College, 1903; took course at Agricultural and Mechanical College, Greensboro, N. C.; correspondence course from Armour Institute of Technology, Chicago, Ill.; married Marie Jennings, of Greensboro, N. C., Feb. 13, 1907. Traveled for American Missionary Assn. of N. Y., erecting school buildings, 1903-8; teacher of manual training in Fessenden (Fla.) Academy 3 years; superintendent of manual training at Dorchester Academy, Arcadia, Ga., since 1911. Congregationalist. Member Knights of Pythias. Address: R. F. D. No. 1, Arcadia, Ga.

McRARY, Robert Baxter, real estate; born at Lexington, N. C.; son of William H. and Jane McRary; A.B., Lincoln (Pa.) Univ., 1885 (LL.D., 1913); student, Berlitz School of Languages, Rome, Italy; married Annie E. Mendenhall, of Greenboro, N. C., 1886. Justice of the peace, Davidson Co., N. C., 6 years; in real estate business since 1894. Trustee Bennett College, Greensboro. Republican. Member board of mgrs. Freedmen's Aid Society of M. E. Church, also general conferences, 1892, 1904, 8, 12; member State Historical and Literary Society. Mason; member Knights of Pythias. Address: Lock Box 504, Lexington, N. C.

MEADDOUGH, Ray James, dentist; born at Fernandina, Fla., Feb. 23, 1869; son of James and Sarah (Thomas) Meaddough; attended schools of Ga. and Fla., as circumstances permitted; D.D.S., Meharry Dental College (Walden Univ.), 1901; married Alice V. Crompton, of Little Rock, Ark., June 17, 1905; 3 children: Miranda, Ray, Joseph. Learned candy making from grandmother and followed business at age of 11-13, selling product to white and colored families, St. Mary's, Ga., later worked in store; night clerk in hotel, Brunswick, Ga., 1882-5; cigar maker in Jacksonville, Key West, Tampa, Fla., and New York, number years; proprietor cigar factory, Fernandina, 1894-5. Practiced dentistry in Little Rock, Ark., since 1901; was pres. Little Rock Lecture Assn., 1909-10; pres. Ark. Negro Dental Assn.; trustee Philander Smith College. One of 6 colored men on reception committee when Theodore Roosevelt visited Little Rock during presidential campaign, 1912. Methodist. Member Business Men's League, Mosaic Templars, Odd Fellows. Clubs: Searchlight, Lincoln Emancipation (pres.). Home: 110 Izarg St. Office. 701 1-2 Main St., Little Rock, Ark.

MEBANE, Albert Leonidas, agriculturalist; born at Greensboro, N. C., June 12, 1880; son of Peter and Esther (Smith) Mebane; public and high school edn., Greensboro; B.Agr., Agricultural and Mechanical College, N. C., 1902; student Massachusetts Agricultural College, 1902-5; postgraduate work A. & M. College, Greensboro (M.S.A., 1910); married Blanche Clover Howard, of Brookville, Md., June 17, 1908; 1 child: Alberta Elaine. Director Eastern Branch agricultural dept. Maryland Agricultural College, at Princess Ann, 1903-6; landscape gardener Tuskegee Normal and Industrial Institute, Ala., 1906-9; director of agricultural Kentucky Normal and Industrial Institute, Frankfort, 1909-11; supt. Agricultural and Technical College farm at Greensboro since 1912. Methodist. Mason. Author (pamphlet): Lessons of Nature. Address: Agricultural and Technical College, Greensboro, N. C.

MELTON, Elijah Stephen, industrial teacher; born at Chattanooga, Tenn.; son of Aaron P. and Mary (Brooks) Melton; grad. Clark Univ., Atlanta, Ga., 1890; unmarried. Principal high school at Hot Springs, Ark., 1891-2; instructor in wood-working department and superintendent of industries, Agricultural and Mechanical College, Normal, Ala., 1892-9; teacher of physics, mechanical drawing, and superintendent of industries and treas. Industrial Dept. Livingstone College, Salisbury, N. C., since 1902; director Salisbury-Spencer Building & Loan Assn. Address: P. O. Box 377, Salisbury, N. C.

MELTON, Julia Ferguson, supervising industrial teacher; born at Charlottsville, Va., Apr. 11, 1888; daughter of James H. and Sarah J. (Farrar) Ferguson; grad. Jefferson

Public School, Charlottsville, 1904, Hampton Normal and Agricultural Institute, Va., 1908; married M. A. Melton (D.D.S.), of Sumter, S. C., Oct. 5, 1913. Began as teacher at Whittier Model School, Hampton, Va., 1908; teacher in public school, Charlottsville, 1908-13; supervising industrial teacher in Christian County, Ky., since 1913; now teacher of domestic science and art in Attuck's High School, Hopkinsville. Methodist. Home: 523 N. Liberty St., Hopkinsville, Ky.

MERCER, Augustus White, physician, surgeon; born at Mt. Pleasant, Jefferson Co., Ohio, Dec. 22, 1867; son of John Hockerty and Sarah Jane (White) Mercer; high school edn., Steubenville, Ohio; grad. Cleveland Homoeopathic Medical College, 1899; M.D., Western Reserve Univ., Cleveland, O., 1901; studied at Post-Graduate Medical School and Hospital, Chicago, Ill., 1913; unmarried. Practiced in Chicago since 1902; president Physicians, Dentists and Pharmacists Club of Chicago, 1912-14. Member National Medical Assn., American Medical Assn. Methodist. Member the Odd Fellows, Knights of Pythias. Home and Office: 1950 Grand Ave., Chicago, Ill.

MERCHANT, Jesse, pharmacist U. S. Department of Agriculture; born at Winchester, Ky., Sept. 15, 1878; son of Alpheus and Georgia A. (Williams) Merchant; high school edn., Lexington, Ky.; Ph.G., Pharmacy College, Louisville, Ky., 1905; unmarried. Began as office boy in law office of J. A. Chiles, Lexington; appointed as pharmacist in U. S. Food Laboratory, Chicago, Ill., 1909; since practiced under direction of Department of Agriculture. Served as civilian postmaster for 10th U. S. Vol. Inf., at Lexington, Ky., and Macon, Ga., during Spanish-American war. Was state secretary Christian Church Convention for Ky., 1898-1906; elected: supt. Interdenominational Sunday School Assn.; vice.-pres. National Association for Advancement of Colored People (Omaha branch), secretary Nebraska State Medical Assn., at Omaha in 1914. Composer: Back to My Old Kentucky Home, dedicated to "Home Coming Week," Louisville, Ky., 1906; has composed number poems; reader of Paul Laurence Dunbar's dialect works. Home: 3763 Wabash Ave., Chicago, Ill.

MERRY, Henry Raymond, teacher; born at Clarksville, Tenn., Feb. 6, 1885; son of Henry Stanley and Mary (Blackman) Merry; A.B., Fisk Univ., Nashville, Tenn., 1907; married Mamie Copeland, cf Nashville, Nov. 24, 1909; 2 children. Teacher in high school, Clarksville, since Sept. 1, 1908; sec.-treas., Trust & Loan Co.; director Golden Hill Cemetary Co. African Methodist. Member Mt. Vernon Lodge No. 1644, Odd Fellows. Address: 157 Kellogg St., Clarksville, Tenn.

MILLER, Clifford Leonard, clergyman; born at Columbia, Tenn., May 23, 1880; son of Rev. James B. and Sarah (Frierson) Miller; A.B., Fisk Univ., Nashville, Tenn., 1904; S.T.B., Andover Seminary, Cambridge, Mass., 1907; student Harvard Graduate School, 1907-8; unmarried. Entered the ministry, 1906; ordained, 1910; pastor Zion Congregational Church, Haverhill, Mass., to 1913, Union Church, Newport, R. I., since 1913; director Fred Douglass Shoe Co. Republican. Member National Association for Advancement of Colored People, Society of Inquiry on Missions, Odd Fellows. Address: 15 Friendship Place, Newport, R. I.

MILLER, Frank O'Hara, physician, surgeon; born at Donalds, S. C., June 17, 1875; son of Cornelius Henry and Ophelia (Calhoun) Miller; ed. Ferguson Academy, S. C. 1896-7; State Agricultural and Mechanical College, Orangeburg, S. C., 1898; grad. Biddle Univ., Charlotte, N. C., 1900; A.B., Princeton (Ind.) Normal and Industrial Univ., 1901 (Ph.D., 1907); M.D., State Univ., Louisville, Ky., 1906; married Elsie M. Upthegrove, of Jamestown, Ohio, Mar. 31, 1909. Practiced in Wichita, Kan., since 1908. Trustee Western Univ., Quindaro, Kan. Republican. Presbyterian. Kansas state vice-president National

Medical Assn.; member Kansas State Medical Assn. 33d degree Mason; brig.-gen. U. R. Knights of Pythias; member Odd Fellows, Knights of Tabor, United Brothers of Friendship. Home: 1035 N. Ohio Ave. Office: 513 N. Main St., Wichita, Kan.

MILLER, George Frazier, clergyman; the emigrant of the Miller family came to America during insurrections of Santo Domingo; descendant on mother's side of Richard Edward DeReef, who in the early part of the 19th century was a prosperous merchant in Charleston, S. C.; son of Alfred A. and Ellen Collins (DeReef) Miller; born at Aiken, S. C., Nov. 28, 1864; A.B., Howard Univ., Washington, 1888, A.M., 1893 (D.D., 1912); grad. General Theological Seminary (Episcopal), New York, 1891; student in philosophy at New York Univ., 1901-2; married Ellen M. Bulkley, of Charleston, S. C., Nov. 2, 1893; 3 children: George F., Jr., Mabel Julia, Alfred Abram III. Rector of St. Augustine's P. E. Church at Brooklyn, N. Y., since 1896. Socialist. Author: Seventh Day Adventists Answered, 1905; Socialism and Its Ethical Basis (pamphlet). Address: 121 N. Oxford St., Brooklyn, N. Y.

MILLER, Kelly, university dean; born at Winnsboro, S. C., July 23, 1863; son of Kelly and Elizabeth Miller; grad. Howard Univ., Washington, 1886, A.M., 1901 (LL.D., 1903); postgraduate work Johns Hopkins Univ., Baltimore, Md., 1887-9; married Annie May Butler, of Baltimore, July 17, 1894; 5 children: Kelly, Jr., Newton, May, Irene, Paul. Entered government service while student in Howard; teacher of mathematics, Washington High School, 1889; professor of mathematics since 1890, also dean of the College of Arts and Sciences since 1907, at Howard Univ.; has lectured widely upon the race problem and other subjects. Progressive. Presbyterian. Member Academy Political and Social Science, American Social Science Assn., American Association for the Advancement of Science, National Educational Assn., Walt Whitman International Fellowship, American Negro Academy. Author: Race Adjustment, 1908; Out of the House of Bondage, 1908. Wrote chapter on "The Education of the Negro," in report of U. S. Bureau of Education, 1901. Contributor to reviews, magazines and newspapers on race problem and relative themes. Address: Howard University, Washington, D. C.

MIMS, Henry L., organizer, piano manufacturer; born at Bryon, Tex., Aug. 13, 1874; son of Alfred and Carrie Mims; grad. high school at Bryan, 1890; married Nannie B. Turner, of Houston, Tex., Dec. 30, 1896; 2 children: Leonard, Alfred. Member firm of Mims & Sons, manufaucturers of pianos, and power organs for churches; clerk in railway mail service since 1893; president National Alliance of Postal Employes since organized, 1913. African Methodist. Member Knights of Pythias. Club: Phalant. Composer: Do You Think of Me; The Judge and the Boy; also other songs. Home: 1716 Rice St., Houston, Texas.

MINTON, Henry McKee, physician; born at Columbia, S. C., Dec. 25, 1871; son of Theophilus J. and M. Virginia (McKee) Minton; grad. Phillips Exeter Academy (N. H.), 1891; Ph.G., Philadelphia College of Pharmacy, 1895; M.D., Jefferson Medical College, 1906; married Edith G. Wormley, of Washington, D. C., Dec. 24, 1902. Proprietor drug store in Philadelphia, 1897-1903; practiced medicine in Philadelphia since 1906; physician to Mercy Hospital; assistant physician Henry Phipps Institute for Study, Prevention and Treatment of Tuberculosis (Univ. of Pa.); treasurer Cherry Building & Loan Assn., Downingtown (Pa.) Industrial School. Trustee Mercy Hospital, S. W. Branch Y. M. C. A.; member advisory board Whittier Center. Baptist. Member American Negro Historical Assn.; also member Sigma Pi Phi, and Odd Fellows. Club: Citizens Republican. Author (pamphlets): Early History of Negroes in Business in Philadelphia, 1913; Causes and Prevention of Tuberculosis, 1915. Home and Office: 1130 S. 18th St., Philadelphia, Pa.

MITCHELL, George Henry, lawyer; born at Washington, D. C., Aug. 27, 1875; son of George William and Elmira (Scott) Mitchell; A.B., Shaw Univ., Raleigh, N. C., 1897, LL.B., 1900; LL.M., New York Univ., 1901; married Maud M. Wood, of Greensboro, N. C., Apr. 3, 1903; 2d marriage, Lucy Case Smith, of Chattanooga, Tenn., Aug. 21, 1912; 2 children: George H. Jr., Edward E. E. Admitted to N. C. bar, 1902, later to U. S. District Court; attorney for Mountain City Mutual Life Ins. Co., Asheville, Union Cooperative & Industrial Assn., Tarboro, Laborers Building & Loan Assn., Pioneer Building & Loan Assn., High Point Industrial Building & Loan Assn., Greensboro; general counselor for Toilers Mutual Life Ins. Co., Tarboro, Piedmont Mutual Life Ins. Co.; counsellor for Grand Lodge, Knights of Pythias, in the investigation of land titles; pres. Greensboro Real Estate Emporium, Afro-American Burial Assn., Colored Business Men's League, State Negro Bar Assn., all of N. C. Trustee Carnegie Library Committee of Greensboro. Republican. Baptist. Home: 135 Dudley St. Office: 108 1-2 S. Davie St., Greensboro, N. C.

MITCHELL, Horace Franklin, university professor; born at Corinth, Miss., Mar. 17, 1864; son of Frank and Mattie (Morrison) Mitchell; private tuition in Miss.; attended public schools, 1872-7, Sumner High School, 1887-9, at St. Louis, Mo.; grad. Le-Moyne Normal Institute, Memphis, Tenn., 1880; student Meharry Medical College, and Fisk Univ., 1881-5; A.B., Fisk Univ., 1907; he reentered this university after a period of 21 years; studied at Univ. of Chicago, summer, 1908; married Mattie Warren, of Memphis, July 11, 1892. Began as principal of Disney Academy, Greenville, Miss, 1892, continuing 3 years; principal of graded and grammar schools, Lake Providence, La., 1895-1907; was supply principal in English Dept., Fisk Univ., 1907; professor of mathemathics at Colored Agricultural and Normal Univ., Langston, Okla., since

1907. Address: Box 123, Langston, Okla.

MITCHELL, John, Jr., banker, publisher; born in Henrico County, Va., July 11, 1863; son of John and Rebecca Mitchell; grad. Richmond Normal and High School, June 14, 1881; unmarried. Founded and now president Mechanics' Savings Bank, Richmond, Va.; proprietor and publisher of the Planet. Republican. Baptist. Fellow Royal Society of Arts (London); member National Geographical Society, American Society for the Advancement of Science, American Bankers Assn. Mason; grand chancellor Grand Lodge, Knights of Pythias; grand worthy chancellor Grand Court, Order of Calanthe; member Odd Fellows. Home: 515 N. 3d St. Office: 311 N. 4th St., Richmond, Va.

MITCHELL, Julius Linoble, lawyer; born in Charleston Co., S. C., Apr. 17, 1867; son of Jackson and Patsy (McKelvey) Mitchell; attended public schools and Avery Institute at Charleston; grad. Hampton Normal and Agricultural Institute, Va.; under instructor D. Augustus Stroker at U. S. Military Academy, West Point; grad. Allen Univ. Law Dept., Columbia, S. C., 1894; married Martha E. Green, of Charleston, S. C., June 12, 1892; 1 child. Admitted to S. C. bar, 1894, U. S. Supreme Court, 1903, Rhode Island bar, 1904, New York bar, 1913; defended John Brownfield charged with murder, Georgetown, S. C., 1899, which case caused the "Georgetown Riot", and terminated in U. S. Supreme Court, 1903; the effect was compelling the jury commissioners of Georgetown County to summon colored men for jury duty; as attorney in 3 cases in Rhode Island, State vs. Russell, State vs. Thompson, State vs. Smith, secured decisions on new points of law which set prescedents for courts in that state; attorney in number important cases since removal to Brooklyn, N. Y.; member number bar associations. Republican. African Methodist. Mason; member Odd Fellows. Club: Citizens (Brooklyn). Address: 375 Fulton St., Brooklyn, N. Y.

MITCHELL, Mayme Katherine, supervising industrial teacher; born at Washington, D. C., Jan . 9, 1892; daughter of Robert L. and Mary Katherine (Orrick) Mitchell; public school edn., Washington; grad. domestic science course, Institute for Colored Youth, Cheyney, Pa., 1910; special work in domestic science Howard Univ., Washington, 1911; unmarried. Began teaching in public schools, Marion, S. C., Oct. 1, 1912; she is one of 22 supervisors in counties of North Carolina under the state supervisor of Elementary Rural Schools; aided by the Anna T. Jeanes Fund this branch of public instruction reaches the most remote schools and homes in the state; the children are taught to mend, sew, cook, can fruit and vegetables, to be self-supporting and economical. Episcopalian. Home: 15 S. Braddock St., Winchester, Va. Address: Box 296, Carthage, North Carolina.

MITCHELL, Robert, clergyman; born in Fulton County, Ky., Mar. 1, 1864; A.B., State Univ., Louisville, Ky.; (D.D., Guadaloupe College, Sequin, Tex.); married Jennie Leach, of Paducah, Ky., Dec. 10, 1885; 1 child: Emma A. Ordained Baptist ministry, 1881; pastor at Paducah, 1881-7, Bowling Green, 1887-96, Lexington, 1896-9, Frankfort, Ky., 1898-1903, Kansas City, Kan., 1903-6, Bowling Green, Ky., since 1906; moderator General Association Baptists of Ky.; auditor National Baptist Convention. Trustee State Univ., Louisville, National Training School for Woman and Girls, Washington. Was president Kentucky State Colored Teachers' Assn., 2 years. Republican. Address: Bowling Green, Ky.

MITCHELL, William Isaac, teacher; born at Columbus, Miss., Dec. 17, 1855; son of Simon and Maria (Barry) Mitchell; student Alcorn Agricultural and Mechanical College, Miss., 1872-4; B.S., Central Miss. College, Kosciusko, 1903; married Susan Whitfield, of Columbus, Miss., Jan. 30,

1878; 5 children: Roxana, Gertrude, Wilda, Juanita, Simon R. Principal, Union Academy, Columbus, since 1876. Trustee Ministerial Institute and College, West Point, Miss. Baptist. Mason; mem. Knights of Pythias; perfect grand master Sacred Order of Perfection. Home: 1608 N. 7th Ave., Columbus, Miss.

MOHAMED, Duce, editor, publisher; born in Egypt; ed. in England. As an outgrowth of the Universal Races Congress which met in London, he founded the African Times and Orient Review, July, 1911; the foreword in the first issue said: "We feel that lack of understanding the African and Oriental has produced non-appreciation, and non-appreciation has unleashed the hydro-headed monster of derision, contempt, and repression. Laudable ambitions have but to be voiced to be appreciated, and that touch of nature which makes the whole world kin has only to be brought into operation to establish that bond of universal brotherhood between White, Yellow, Brown and Black. The man, therefore, who would be well informed as to native aims, capacity and development, will be well advised to study the pages of the African Times and Orient Review, for therein will be found the views of the Colored man, whether African or Oriental." Address: 158 Fleet St. E. C., London, Eng.

MOLLISON, Willie E., lawyer; born at Mayersville, Miss., Sept. 15, 1859; son of Robert and Martha (Gibson) Mollison; ed. Fisk Univ., Nashville, Tenn., and Oberlin (O.) College; (LL.D., Cambell College, Jackson, Miss., 1913); married Ida T. Welborne, of Clinton, Miss., Oct. 5, 1880; 7 children: Willye E., Mabel Z., Annie M., Lydia W., Wilborne A., Irvin C., Walter. Was superintendent of education, Issaquena County, Miss., 1882-3; clerk of Circuit and Chancery Courts, 1883-91; acting district attorney, 1892; now in practice in Vicksburg. Founded and was first president Lincoln Savings Bank of Vicksburg; vice.-pres. Solvant Bank & Trust Co., Memphis, Tenn. Was party nominee

for Secretary of State in Miss., 1889; delegate to each Republican National Convention since 1892; joined Progressive party, 1912. Episcopalian. Member National Geographical Society, American Academy Political and Social Science. Mason; member Odd Fellows, Knights of Pythias. Club: Lincoln. Has written articles for St. Louis Globe-Democrat, and prepared many papers which were read at important meetings. Home: 1216 Fayette St. Office: 1109 Cherry St., Vicksburg, Miss.

MOORE, A. M., physician; born at Whiteville, N. C., Sept. 6, 1863; son of Isreal and Eliza Moore; M.D., Leonard Medical College (Shaw Univ.) Raleigh, N. C., 1888; married Catie S. Dancy, of Tarboro, N. C., Dec. 18, 1889; 2 children. Practiced medicine since 1888; medical director, also secretary-treas. North Carolina Mutual and Provident Assn., since 1899; supt. Lincoln Hospital; director Mechanics' Farmers' Bank, Bull City Drug Co., Violet Park Cemetary. Trustee Shaw Univ., National Religious Training School, Oxford Colored Orphanage. Baptist. Member American Medical Assn., Durham Civic League. Mason. Address: Durham, N. C.

MOORE, Edward, university professor, physician; A.B., Lincoln Univ., Pa., 1879. Professor of Greek and Latin, and secretary of the faculty, Livingstone College, Salisbury, N. C.

MOORE, Fred Randolph, editor, publisher; born in Virginia, June 16, 1857; son of Evelyn Diggs; public school edn., Washington, D. C.; married Ida Lawrence, of Washington, Apr. 9, 1879; 18 children, 6 living. Began as messenger in United States Treasury Department, continuing service under 6 different administrations to 1887; resigned to take charge vaults of Western National Bank, New York; was delivery clerk in New York Clearing House 18 years; deputy internal revenue collector for 2 months; national organizer National Negro Business League, 1904-7; publisher Colored American Magazine 5 years; editor and publisher New York Age since 1907. Republican; appointed as minister to Liberia by President William H. Taft, serving only 1 month. Episcopalian. Member executive committee National League of Urban Conditions Among Negroes; auxiliary member Committee of Fourteen. Home: 14 Douglass St., Brooklyn. Office: 247 W. 46th St., New York.

MOORE, George Sheppard, physician; born at Nashville, Tenn., Sept. 27, 1883; son of Rev. George W. and Ella (Sheppard) Moore; A.B., Fisk Univ., Nashville, Tenn., 1906; M.D., Northwestern Univ. Medical College, Chicago, Ill., 1910; interne Freedmen's Hospital, Washington, D. C., 1910-11; married Julia Alberta Merrill, of Nashville, Oct. 13, 1906; 3 children: George C., Sarah E., Julia A. Practiced in Nashville since June 1, 1911; professor of mental and nervous diseases Meharry Medical College (Walden Univ.). Republican. Congregationalist. Member Tenn. Colored Medical Assn., Rock City Medical Assn., Knights of Pythias. Home: 1034 17th Ave. N. Office: 424 Cedar St., Nashville, Tenn.

MOORE, George Washington, clergyman; born at Nashville, Tenn., Nov. 9, 1854; son of William Moore and Elizabeth Corry, slaves, who were legally married after slavery was abolished; A.B., Fisk Univ., 1881, A.M., 1884; B.D., Oberlin Theological Seminary, O., 1883; (D.D., Howard Univ., 1908); married Ella Sheppard, of Nashville, Dec. 20, 1882; she was of the original Jubilee Singers; 2 children: George S. (M.D.), Clinton Fisk R. Began to exhort in little mission connected with first school he attended; preached in Howard Chapel, Nashville, 1876; ordained Congregational ministry, 1877; while in Oberlin Seminary pastored 1st Congregational Church, Sullivan, O.; in charge 3 churches under Ohio Home Missionary Society, summer, 1882; pastor Lincoln Memorial Church, Washington, D. C., 1883-92; professor of biblical history and literature, Howard Univ., 1887-92; delegate to World's Sunday School Convention, 1889, and delivered address in City Temple, London, Eng.; began as field

missionary with American Missionary Assn., New York, 1892, later appointed supt. in charge southern church work with headquarters at Nashville. Trustee Tillotson College, Fisk Univ. Republican. Address: 926 17th Ave. N., Nashville, Tenn.

MOORE, John Henry, clergyman; born at Huntsville, Ala., Aug. 9, 1876; son of Turner and Savannah (Pettis) Moore; ed. in Rust Univ., Holly Springs, Miss.; (hon. D.D.); married Julia Augusta McCorkel, of Holly Springs, Dec. 23, 1896; 2 children: Henry L., Susie Lorine. Began as brick mason when 16 years old; entered Methodist ministry, 1899; pastored 6 years; presiding elder Meridian Dist., Miss., 1906-9, of Durant District, 1909-14; general secretary of Missions, C. M. E. Church, since May 22, 1914. Trustee Mississippi Industrial College. Mason; vice-pres. Gideon Fraternity of America. Address: Box 153, Holly Springs, Miss.

MOORE, Julia Augusta, former teacher; born at Holy Springs, Miss., July 10, 1878; daughter of Hagan and Ida (Lumpkin) McCorkel; ed. State Normal School, Holly Springs; married Rev. John Henry Moore, of Huntsville, Ala., Dec. 23, 1896; 2 children: Henry L., Susan L. Taught public schools in Marshall Co., Miss., 1887-96; teacher in Mississippi Industrial College, Holly Springs, 1908-11. Member C. M. E. Church. Home: Holly Springs, Miss.

MOORE, Lewis Baxter, college dean; born near Huntsville, Ala., Sept. 1, 1866; son of Henry and Rebecca (Beasley) Moore; A.B., Fisk Univ., Nashville, 1889, A.M., 1893; Ph.D., Univ. of Pa., 1896, and one of the few colored men to earn the Doctor of Philosophy degree in Northern universities; attended summer school at Clark Univ., Worcester, Mass.; studied educational systems in Germany and England; married, Nov. 19, 1895, Sarah E., daughter of Rt. Rev. Benjamin Tucker Tanner, and sister of Henry O. Tanner the noted Negro artist (she died in 1901); 2d marriage, Lavenia E. Waring, of Washington, D. C., June 17, 1902. Began as secretary S. E. Branch Y. M. C. A., Philadelphia, 1889, continuing 6 years; instructor in Howard Univ., Washington, 1895-7, assistant professor, 1897-8, and professor of Latin and pedagogy, 1898-9; professor of philosophy, education, and dean of Teachers' College at Howard since 1899. Ordained in Congregational ministry; was pastor People's Church in Washington, 1903-10. Home: 2460 6th St. N. W. Office: Room 204 Main Hall, Howard University, Washington, D. C.

MOORE, Peter Wredick, principal State Normal School; born in Sampson Co., near Clinton, N. C., 1859; son of Wredick and Elexcy (Thompson) Moore; ed. rural schools in Sampson County and private tuition; A.B., Shaw Univ., Raleigh, N. C., 1887, A.M., later; also attended State Normal School, Newbern, N. C.; married Symera T. Rayner, of Windsor, N. C., 1890; 2 children: Ruth S., Bessie V. Began as assistant principal at State Normal School, Plymouth, N. C., 1887, continuing 4 years; principal of North Carolina State Colored Normal School at Elizabeth City since 1892; teacher of pedagogy and supervisor of teacher-training; has also served as assistant supt. Colored Public Schools; former president and now secretary North Carolina Teachers' Assn.; director County Teachers' Assn.; identified with National Teachers' Assn., for number years. Baptist. Address: State Normal School, Elizabeth City, N. C.

MOORE, Thomas Clay, real estate; born at Nashville, Tenn., Apr. 20, 1882; son of Isaac L. and Frances Lee (Metcalf) Moore; preparatory edn. Roger Williams Univ., Nashville, Tenn.; A.B., Fisk Univ., 1906; student in law dept. Walden Univ., 2 years; married Cleo Florentina Du-Pont, of Key West, Fla., June 25, 1908; 2 children: Ida F., Theresa C. Began in real estate business in Nashville, 1906; sold to Star Realty & Investment Co., 1912, and since director; secretary Acme Real Estate & Loan Co.; manager real estate dept. People's Savings Bank & Trust Co. Trus-

tee Howard Congregational Church; director Nashville Choral Society. Delegate to several county and state Republican conventions; was sergt.-at-arms Progressive National Convention, Chicago, Ill., 1912; state chairman Colored Progressive Organizatoin. Life member National Negro Business League; member Negro Bankers' Assn., Young People's Economical League, Nashville Negro Board of Trade (vice.-pres.). Mason; member Knights of Pythias, United Brothers of Friendship, Mosaic Templars. Home: 2023 Jefferson St. Office: 412 1-2 Cedar St., Nashville, Tenn.

MOORE, William Preston, clerk General Education Board; born, Eastville, Va., Nov. 19, 1873; son of William Preston and Frances (Stevens) Moore; attended public school 9 months; private pupil of John H. Carter, 5 months; practical education acquired thru travel in U. S., So. America, Europe, Asia; married Minnie Pocahontas Bowler, of Crewe, Va., May 18, 1899, (died Mar. 29, 1911), 2d marriage, Lillian Langhorne Lewis, of Ronceverte, W. Va., Aug. 1, 1911; 2 children: Helen Josephine, Evelyn Lewis. Cabin boy in Merchant Marine service, 1886-90; elevator operator, Gladstone Hotel, later the Pomeroy, New York, 1890-1; in U. S. Revenue Marine service, on board cutter Hamilton with headquarters in Philadelphia, Pa., 1891-2; entered U. S. Navy, 1892; served as mess attendant, warrant officer's cook and steward, captain's cook, ship's cook, acting admiral's steward; was on Richmond, Columbia, Vermont, Indiana, Wompatuck, flagship New York, ram Katahdin and in command while ship was in reserve, unusual for a steward; served during blockade off Havana de Cuba, and San Juan, Porto Rico, 1898; was in battle of San Juan, May 12, Santiago de Cuba, July 3, 1898; served thru Spanish-American War, and discharged, Oct. 5, 1899; received medal for good conduct, and one for valiant service in battle; also received prize money for captures by battleship Indiana; chef in Gulick House,

Brooklyn, N. Y., 1900-2. Began as messenger for the General Education Board, New York, 1902; was mailing clerk, 1907-11, general clerk, 1911-15, promoted to general order and mail clerk with said Board, Mar. 1, 1915; in the book giving an account of the activities of the General Education Board, 1902-14, he made all the maps, 31 in number, relating to the investigations, demonstrations, and explanations shown in the book; at his request the words "Negro" and "Negroes" were capitalized, and they are often used in Section VIII, devoted to Negro Education. Was delegate to Fifth Annual National Negro Educational Congress, held at Oklahoma City, Okla., July, 1914, appointed by Gov. Martin H. Glenn; has a large library, and is surrounded with opportunities; he is a well read man. Founded in 1908, now organizer and secretary of the supreme governing board, Benevolent and Philanthropic Order of Roebucks; honorary member Negro Society for Historical Research; charter member the Progressive party, New York. Author: My Cheriton Maid, 1913. Composer: The Song of the Bull Moose, 1912; Bless My Soul! Ain't That Nice?, 1913. Contributor to newspapers and magazines, especially articles on originality in Ethiopian fraternities and societies. Home: 283 Clifton Place, Brooklyn. Office: General Education Board, 61 Broadway, New York.

MOORLAND, Jesse Edward, secretary Y. M. C. A.; born at Coldwater, Ohio, Sept. 10, 1863; son of William E. and Nancy Jane (Moore) Moorland; ed. Northwestern Normal Univ.; (D.D., Howard Univ. School of Theology, Washington, 1905); married Lucy C. Woodson, of Berlin, Ohio, July 25, 1885. Secretary local Young Men's Christian Assn., Washington, 1892-3; pastor, Nashville, Tenn., and Cleveland, O., 1893-8; secretary International Y. M. C. A. since 1898; when Julius Rosenthal, of Chicago, Ill., offered $25,000, conditional, to aid in the construction of Colored Y. M. C. A. buildings, Reverend Moorland took charge the work and helped raise

the required $75,000 for the building fund in 11 different citflies of the U. S.; has written number pamphlets of Y. M. C. A. work. Trustee Howard Univ., and Douglass Home Assn. Republican. Congregationalist.- Member American Negro Academy. 33d degree Mason. Home: 1932 11th St. N. W. Offices: 1816 12th St. N. W., Washington, D. C.; 124 E. 28th St., New York.

MORELAND, John F., secretary Protective Brotherhood of A. M. E. Zion Church, 701 E. 1st St., Charlotte, N. C.

MORGAN, Charles L., physician; born at Oxford, Ala., Aug. 9, 1878; son of George D. and Josie (Draper) Morgan; grad. Dallas High School, Tex., 1897; M.D., Meharry Medical College, (Walden Univ.), Nashville, Tenn., 1909; married L. C. Haynes, of Macon, Ga., July 4, 1910. Began practice at Sparta, Tenn., 1909; president Mecca Sanitarium, Dallas, Tex.; president and treas. Morgan-Busch Sanitarium; medical examiner for American Woodmen. Treasurer Negro Medical, Dental and Pharm. Society. Republican. Methodist (C. M. E.). Member Citizens League, Negro Business Men's League, Odd Fellows, Knights of Pythias, American Woodmen. Club: Young Men's Progressive. Home: 3103 Cochran St. Office: 1027 1-2 Boll Ave., Dallas, Tex.

MORGAN, Clement Garnett, lawyer; A.B., Harvard, 1890, LL.B., 1893. In practice in Boston and Cambridge. Address: 265 Prospect St., Cambridge, Mass.

MORGAN, Garrett Agusta, inventor, manufacturer; born at Paris, Ky., Mar. 4, 1879; son of Sydney A. and Eliza (Reed) Morgan; public school edn., Paris, Ky.; married March Hasek, of Cleveland, Ohio, Sept. 22, 1908; 2 children: J. Pierpont, Garrett James. Went into Cleveland, friendless and pennyless, June 17, 1895; has since learned 3 trades, owns factory and business paying large annual profit, and paid for home; invented woman's hat fastener, round belt fastener, friction drive clutch, and hair straightener, all bearing Morgan name; Morgan's National Safety Hood was his most important invention; it is a smoke and ammonia hemlet—a safety device—used in fire departments, ammonia factories, public buildings, etc., throughout America as a protection against smoke and fumes; it was awarded a gold medal—First Grand Prize—at 2d International Exposition of Safety and Sanitation, New York, 1914; this hood is manufactured by the National Safety Device Co., of which he is general manager; other officers of company are white; for 3 months he urged colored people to subscribe for stock in the company at $10 per share and failed to secure any help; 30 days later some of the stock sold for $100 a share; 2 years later its markèt value exceeded $250, and not a share was for sale; he manufactured skirts 2 years under name of Morgan Skirt Factory; now president G. A. Morgan Hair Refiner Co. Member National Association for Advancement of Colored People; treasurer Cleveland Association of Colored Men; member committee for Home of Aged Colored People; member Phillis Wheatley Assn. Baptist. Mason; Elk. Club: Attucks Republican Home: 5202 Harlem Ave. Factory: 5200 Harlem Ave. Office: 304 Superior Bldg., Cleveland, Ohio.

MORRIS, Edward H., lawyer; born in Kentucky, May 30, 1860; son of Hezekiah and Elizabeth (Hopkins) Morris; ed. St. Ann's School, and St. Patrick's Academy, Chicago, Ill.; married Jessica D. Montgomery, of Chicago, Dec. 16, 1896. Practiced law in Chicago since 1879; was in public eye for number years as defendant attorney for gambling fraternity, and regarded as one of the leading criminal lawyers of Illinois; served as attorney for Town of South Chicago, also as assistant county attorney. Member Illinois House of Representatives, 1890-2, 1902-4. Republican. Baptist. Grand Master Grand United Order of Odd Fellows (U. S.). Home: 3757 Vernon Ave. Office: 219 S. Dearborn St., Chicago, Ill.

MORRIS, Elias Camp, clergyman; born near Spring Place, Murray Co., Ga., May 7, 1855; son of James and Cora C. Morris; ed. public schools of Dalton, Ga., Chattanooga, Tenn., and Stevenson, Ala.; student at Nashville Institute (now Roger Williams Univ.), Tenn., 1874-5; (D.D., State Univ., Louisville, Ky., 1892; Ph.D., Agricultural and Mechanical College, Normal, Ala., 1902); married Fannie E. Austin, of Flackler, Ala., Nov. 27, 1884; 5 children: Elias A., Frederick D., Mattie B., Sadie H., John S. United with Baptist Church at Stephenson, Ala., and licensed to preach, 1874; ordained, 1879; pastor Centennial Baptist Church, Helena, Ark., since June, 1879. Established Baptist Vanguard, 1882; founded, 1884, and since trustee Arkansas Baptist College; president National Baptist Convention since 1894; organized Baptist Home Mission Board, 1899; chairman Arkansas State Mission Board since 1900; assisted to organize General Convention of America, 1903, and is only Negro member executive committee; also assisted to organize Baptist World Alliance (1905) and is only Negro member of the American executive committee; member Peace Conference (English speaking people of the world), and only Negro in that body. Treasurer board of trustees Interstate Academy at Helena; member executive committee Arkansas State Negro Business League; director number business enterprises. Delegate to Republican National Conventions, 1884, 1888, 1904, and alternate delegate at-large, 1908; delegate to every Republican State Convention in Ark., since 1884. Address: Helena,Ark.

MORRIS, James Montgomery, lawyer; born in Louisa County, Va., June 5, 1867; son of Hezekiah and Sarah Ann (Hayden) Morris; grad. Storer College, Harper's Ferry, W. Va., 1888; took elective course Taunton (Mass) High School, 1889; private instruction in classics, 1890-1; LL.B., Howard Univ. School of Law, 1894; married Susie Ella Smith, of Nokesville, Va., July 15, 1895; 2 children: Theresa A., Mabel E. Admitted to Va. bar, 1896, and since practiced in Staunton;

beginning with a total of $21.50 for legal services the first year, his practice gradually grew larger with clients among white and colored; serves as counsel for the general receiver of the Corporatinon Court, City of Staunton, and passes on title as well as value of sacuritites officially received as public funds for investment; general counsel and manager Consolidated Loan & Trust Co.; general counsel for People's Dime Savings Bank, Cole's Co-operative Co. Republican. Mason; member Knights of Pythias. Home: R. F. D. No. 7, Box 147. Office: 30 S. Augusta, St., Staunton, Va.

MORRIS, Samuel Solomon, clergyman; born at Portsmouth, Va., Sept. 2, 1878; son of Samuel and Lucinda Morris; grad. Gammon Theological Seminary, Atlanta, Ga., 1902; A.B., Morris Brown College, 1905; B.D., Turner Theological Seminary, 1907; married Mary H. Lawson, of Danville, Va., Apr. 4, 1912. Licensed to preach, 1899; joined A. M. E. Conference, 1901; pastored West End, Atlanta, Thomasville, Tanners' Creek, Norfolk Co., Va.; state supt. Allen Christian Endeavor League since 1909; pastor 3rd Street Church, Richmond, Va., since 1910; delegate general conference, Kansas City, Mo., 1912; member Missionary Board, 1912-16; pres. Civic League, Richmond. Trustee Kittrell College. Mason; president Grand Fountain, True Reformers; chaplain 2d regt. U. R., Knights of Pythias. Club: Social Study. Address: 18 W. Jackson St., Richmond, Va.

MORRIS, William Richard, lawyer; born in Fleming County, Ky., Feb. 22, 1859; son of Hazekiah Brown and Elizabeth (Hopkins) Morris; brother of Edward H. Morris, of Chicago, Ill.; A.B., Fisk Univ., Nashville, Tenn., 1884, A.M., 1887; married Anna M. LaForce, of Pullman, Ill., July 14, 1896; 1 child: Richard E. Instructor in languages, mathematics and science at Fisk Univ., 1884-9; admitted to Minn. bar, 1889, and since practiced in Minneapolis. Republican. Congregationalist; only color-

ed Sunday School teacher in Plymouth Church. When a member the American Bar Assn., the question of admitting colored lawyers was widely discussed, and he finally dropped out; member Minnesota State Bar Assn., Hennepin County Bar Assn. 33d degree Mason; associate justice Supreme Court, Odd Fellows in America; deputy supreme chancellor, and brig.-gen. U. R. in Minnesota, Knights of Pythias. Home: 3017 Second Ave. S. Office: 1020 Metropolitan Life Bldg., Minneapolis, Minn.

MORRISON, John Oliver, university professor; born at Broad Run, Va., Aug. 16, 1886; son of Alexander and Leana (Armstrong) Morrison; grad. high school, Philipsburg, Pa., 1902; A.B., Howard Univ., Washington, 1908; student, graduate school, Univ. of Chicago, 1912; unmarried. Began as teacher, New Orleans Univ., 1908, professor of English and French since 1910; director of the University Choral Society. Methodist. Member Alpha Phi Alpha. Address: New Orleans University, New Orleans, La.

MORRISON, Marshall Lee, teacher, lawyer; born in Tishomingo Co., Miss., Dec. 9, 1873; son of Tarlton and Barbara Ann (Ransom) Morrison; public school edn., Hopkinsville, Ky.; B.S., Lane College, Jackson, Tenn., 1897; LL.B., Univ. of West Tenn., 1902; married Annie Leland Saunders, of Jackson, Tenn., Sept. 20, 1898; 5 children: Shellie B., Annie Dell, Cordelia E., Marshall Lee, Jr., John W. Began teaching in 1894; principal Bruce High School, Dyersburg, Tenn., since 1912; president Educational Congress of West Tenn. Trustee Lane College. Recording steward Colored M. E. Church; twice member General Conference; was secretary joint board of finance West Tenn. Annual Conference, 1906-8. Mason; member Odd Fellows, Knights of Pythias. Home: 116 Roberts Ave., Dyersburg, Tenn.

MORSELL, Samuel Richard, secretary Y. M. C. A.; born at Baltimore, Md., Mar. 3, 1874; son of John and Eliza Ann (King) Morsell; grad. high school, Baltimore, 1896, Oberlin (O.)

Academy, 1903; A.B., Oberlin College, 1907; B.D., Yale Divinity School, 1910; married Maude L. Wright, of New Haven, Conn., June 28, 1911; 1 child: John Albert. Teacher in public school, Elliott City, Md., 1896-7, Baltimore, 1897-1901; joined M. E. Conference A. M. E. Church, 1908; pastored at Narregansett Pier, R. I., summers, while student in Yale, 1908, 9, 10; secretary Y. M. C. A., Pittsburgh, Pa., since 1910. Mason; member Odd Fellows, Foresters. Home: 20 Junilla St. Office: Colored Y. M. C. A., 1847 Center Ave., Pittsburgh, Pa.

MOSBY, Benjamin Harrison, teacher; born at Brighton, Ill., July 27, 1886; son of Benjamin Lambert and Ellen (Small) Mosby; first colored grad. Carlinville (Ill.) High School, 1904; student Fisk Univ., Nashville, Tenn., 1904-7; A.B., Univ. of Illinois, 1909; unmarried. Began as teacher of civics at Univ. of Illinois, 1908; assistant principal Sumner High School, Cairo, Ill., 1909-10; head teacher department of history, Sumner High School, St. Louis, Mo., since 1911; faculty manager Sumner High School Athletic Assn.; assistant coach of football teams. Was president Athletic Association and captain of the track team at Carlinville High School, 1904; won 100 dash in 10 seconds; was Varsity man in football and baseball at Fisk Univ.; member champion class football team at Univ. of Illinois, 1909; with W. A. Giles, won city double championship in tennis, St. Louis, 1913. Delegate from Illinois to National Negro Educational Congress at St. Louis, 1910. Republican. Methodist. Member American Historical Assn., St. Louis Society of Pedagogy, Elleardsville Civic League, and only colored member committee on instruction of citizenship for St. Louis Civic League. National grand lecturer Ancient United Knights and Daughters of Africa. Address: 4342 W. Belle Place, St. Louis, Mo.

MOSELEY, Beauregard Fritz, lawyer; born at Lincolnton, Lincoln Co., Ga., May 4, 1868; son of Burton and Florida (Williams) Moseley; common school and law edn.; married Carrie H. Hammond, of Terry, Miss., Jan. 2, 1891; 3 children: Burton and Beauregard (deceased); Bertha L. Admitted to Illinois bar, 1896; began with one law book in office at 6303 S. Halsted St., Chicago; now has library of about 5,000 volumes, modern office, and practice equal to $15,000 annually; secretary-treas. Leland Giants Base Ball Amusement Assn.; member managing board Chicago Assembly. President, Non-Partisan Progressive Voters League of Chicago; was committeeman Republican party in 6th Cong. Dist., La., 1888-90; secretary Republican League of Lousiana, 1888-96; presidential elector on Progressive party ticket, 1912. Member Chicago Law Institute. Mason; master's counsel and patriarch in Odd Fellows. Clubs: Appomatox, Half-Century (member managing board). Home: 6248 Sangamon St. Office: 6221 S. Halsted St., Chicago, Ill.

MOSSELL, Gertrude E. H. Bustill, financial agent, special writer; born at Philadelphia, Pa., July 3, 1855; daughter of Charles H. and Emily (Robinson) Bustill; ed. public schools; Institute of Colored Youths; and Robert Vaux Consolidated Schools, Philadelphia; married, July 12, 1880, Dr. Nathan F. Mossell, formerly of Lockport, N. Y., and founder Frederick Douglass Memorial Hospital and Training School, Philadelphia; children: Florence (Mrs. John R. Nicholson), Mary C. (Mrs. Dr. J. H. Griffin, Jr.), and 2 deceased. Was teacher number of years in Camden, N. J., and Philadelphia; collector of the charity fund for Frederick Douglass Memorial Hospital since 1895, and now president its Social Service Auxiliary; prepared plan to raise the $30,000 debt of the hospital building fund; special writer for the Press, Times, and Inquirer, white newspapers of Philadelphia; published post cards called "Emancipation," and "Dear Old Philadelphia"; agent for Afro-American literature; one of founders Bustill Family Assn.; one of organizers National Afro-American Council; member board of managers Young Woman's Christian Assn.; was delegate to National Civic Movement Convention, Kansas City, Mo., 1914, appointed by Gov. John K. Tanner. Presbyterian. Member Harriet Tubman Assn., Sojourner Truth Suffrage League, Northeastern Federation of Woman's Clubs, Philadelphia Civic Club. Author: The Work of the Afro-American Woman; Little Dansie's One Day at Sabbath School. Address: 1432 Lombard St., Philadelphia, Pa.

MOSSELL, Nathan F., physician, surgeon; born at Hamilton, Canada, July 27, 1856; son of Aaron and Eliza (Bowers) Mossell; family removed to Lockport, N. Y., 1865; A.B., Lincoln (Pa) Univ., 1879, A.M., later; M.D., Univ. of Pa., 1882; post-graduate work Polyclinic Hospital, Philadelphia, Pa., Guy's Queens College and St. Thomas Hospital, London, Eng.; married Gertrude E. H. Bustill, of Philadelphia, July 12, 1880; children: Florence (Mrs. John R. Nicholson), Mary C. (Mrs. Dr. J. R. Griffin, Jr.), and 2 deceased. Was associated with the Out-Patient Surgical Department, Univ. of Pa., 1881-2, thru the aid of Dr. D. Hayes Agnew, the noted surgeon who was in charge President James A. Garfield, shot down by an assassin; practiced in Philadelphia since 1882; organized, 1895, and since medical director Frederick Douglass Memorial Hospital and Training School, Philadelphia; erected $100,000 building, which was dedicated Apr. 27, 1909; conducted campaign to clear building of debt before celebration of 20th anniversary of the hospital held Nov. 1, 1915; Andrew Carnegie was liberal contributor; member Board of Visitation, City of Philadelphia, appointed by judges of Common Pleas Court. Member American Hospital Assn., Philadelphia County Medical Society, Philadelphia Academy of Medicine and Allied Sciences, National Medical Assn. (pres., 1908). Author (pamphlet): Hospital Construction, Organization and Management. Address: 1432 Lombard St., Philadelphia, Pa.

MOTON, Robert Russo, commandant at Hampton Institute; born at Rice, Prince Edward County, Va., Aug. 26, 1867; son of Booker Moton; grad. Hampton Normal and Agricultural Institute, 1890, and finished postgraduate work, 1895; read law in office of lawyer in Hampton; married Jennie Doe Booth, of Gloucester, Va., July, 1907; 3 children: Catherine E., Charlotte B., Robert R., Jr. Commandant or executive officer of Hampton Normal and Agricultural Institute since 1890, with rank of major; director Bay Shore Hotel Co., at Buck Roe Beach, Va. President Negro Organization Society; vice-pres. National League on Urban Conditions Among Negroes; secretary executive board of Anna T. Jeanes Fund; director Virginia Manual Labor School at Hanover, and Industrial Home School for Wayward Colored Girls, Peak, Va.; trustee People's Village School, Mt. Meigs, Ala. Baptist. Has addressed social, educational and business associations in many parts of America; his 1912 address at Tuskegee Institute appears in Alice Moore Dunbar's "Masterpieces of Negro Eloquence" under title: Some Elements Necessary to Race Development. Address: Hampton Normal and Agricultural Institute, Hampton, Va.

MUKASA, Ham; County Chief, Mukono, Uganda, B. E. Africa; born, 1870; son of Zakaliya Sensalire and Leya Najazana Mukasa; ed. in the Church Missionary Society in Uganda; married Kana Mawemuko, of Mengo, Uganda, Mar. 26, 1894, daughter of the late Prime Minister of King Mutesa, Uganda; 4 children. Served in the Christian-Mohammadan war, 1888-9; acted as Guardian to H. H. the Kabaka (King) of Uganda during the years of his minority. Country Chief, Mukono, Uganda, since May 29, 1905; one of the most advanced of the 20 chiefs of Uganda. Member Protestant Church of England. Author: Uganda's Katikiro in England (pub. by Hutchinson, London), 1904; it treats of the Prime Minister's visit in England (see sketch of Sir Apolo Kagwa in this volume.) Wrote: A Commentary on St. Matthew Gospel,

1900. Address: "Kwata Empola," Mukono, Uganda.

MURPHY, Carl James, teacher; born at Baltimore, Md., Jan. 17, 1889; son of John Henry and Martha Elizabeth (Howard) Murphy; grad. high school at Baltimore, 1907; A.B., Howard Univ., Washington, 1911; A.M., Harvard, 1913; unmarried. Instructor in German, Howard Univ., since 1913. African Methodist. Member National Association for Advancement of Colored People, Alpha Phi Alpha. Mason. Address: 739 Girard St. N. W., Washington, D. C.

MURPHY, John Henry, editor, pub.; born at Baltimore, Md., Dec. 25, 1840; son of Benjamin and Susan (Coby) Murphy; primary school edn.; married Martha Elizabeth Howard, of Montgomery Co., Md., Jan. 2, 1868; 10 children: George B., John H., Jr., Daniel H., Carl J., Arnold D., Eva S., Lillie B., Harriett E., Martha A., Rose M. Began in feed and produce business, Baltimore, 1878; house decorator for 12 years; established printing plant, 1890, purchased Afro-American (weekly newspaper), 1899, since pres. and general mgr., Afro-American Co., printers and pubs.; editor Afro-American Ledger. Trustee Provident Hospital, Masonic Joint Stock Co., Bethel A. M. E. Church. Served in 30th Regt. U. S. Inf., Mar. 18, 1864 to Dec. 25, 1865. 32d degree Mason. Home: 1320 Druid Hill Ave. Office: 628 N. Eutaw St., Baltimore, Md.

MURRAY, Alexina E. Milton, teacher, verse and song writer; born at Murfreesboro, N. C.; daughter of Rev. Willis and Juliette E. (Weaver) Milton; public school and normal edn., Hertford, N. C.; entered Shaw Univ., Raleigh, N. C., at 15 years of age; student Howard Univ., Washington, 1894-8, and assistant matron; married Prof. Grant S. Murray, Aug. 29, 1900. Was teacher in schools of Hertford, Elizabeth City and others in North Carolina about 20 years; learned dress-making, New Bedford, Mass., and sewed in homes of many of the most wealthy families; teacher in public schools, Metropolis, Ill.,

1900-1; later principal the high school. Has written verse and songs for number years; poem sent to Alice Roosevelt (Mrs. Nicholas Longworth) at time of her marriage commanded letter of thanks, and the incident was published in the public press; wrote the "School Song" for Lincoln Institute, the "State Song" for State Federation of Colored Woman's Clubs, sung by Mo. delegates at national convention, Louisville, Ky., 1910. President for number years, Woman's Charity Club of Jefferson City; supported by the club she organized civic improvement work among colored people, also founded the Milton Hospital and Old Folks Home, 1911; now president board of trustees, supt. and general financial agent; organized Musical Culture Club of Jefferson City, now general mgr.; president the Civic League; state organizer Missouri State Federation Womans' Clubs. Was agent for Fidelity Mutual Ins. Co. of Philadelphia, 1901. Congregationalist. Home: 505 Lafayette St., Jefferson City, Mo.

MURRAY, Daniel, assistant librarian; born at Baltimore, Md. Mar. 3, 1852; son of George and Eliza (Wilson) Murray; ed. public schools and Unitarian Seminary, Baltimore; married Anna Evans, of Oberlin, O., Apr. 2, 1879; 7 children: Daniel, Jr., George H., Nathanial A., Helene, Pinckney, Harold B., Paul Evans. Began in Library of Congress, Washington, D. C., 1871; personal assistant to Ainsworth R. Spofford, librarian, 1874-97; assistant librarian since 1880; in this position acquired valuable knowledge of research work which led to his compilation of "Murray's Encyclopedia of the Colored Race," intended for 6 vols., and representing about 20 years research and labor. Executor and trustee John Savary Estate of $100,000, since 1910; was in real estate business, 1878-93; member National Commission to escort Admiral George Dewey from New York to Washington when presented with $10,000 sword voted by Congress; president Washington Civic Centre; member Washington Board of Trade, Oldest Inhabitants Assn. Home: 934 S St. Office: Library of Congress, Washington, D.C.

MURRAY, Grant Simpson, professor, editor; born in Madison Co., Va.; son of Nehamiah and Caroline (Johnson) Murray; public school edn., Culpeper, Va.; A.B., Howard Univ., Washington, 1898, post-graduate certificate, department of pedagogy, 1900; studied in summer school, Univ. of Wis., 1911; married Alexina E. Milton, of Hertford, N. C., Aug. 29, 1900. Principal public (night) school, Washington, while in pedagogy dept. of Howard Univ.; principal public and high schools, Metropolis, Ill., 1900-1; was agent for Northwestern Life Ins. Co., of Des Moines, Ia., at Metropolis, 1901; began teaching in Lincoln Institute, Jefferson City, Mo., 1901; was professor of chemistry and physics, also at various times instructor in geology, astronomy, physical geography, and other sciences, continuing 12 years; helped organize first summer school for teachers in Missouri, at Lincoln Institute, 3 terms teacher and principal 3 summers; principal Broadway High School, Madison, 1914-15, the first high school commissioned for colored pupils in Indiana. Founder and now editor the Weekly Herald, Jefferson City. President and trustee Milton Hospital Assn. Learned photography, and his pictures of buildings, departments and work of Lincoln Isstitute were exhibited at Louisiana Purchase Exposition, St. Louis, Mo., 1904. Republican. Baptist. Member Missouri State Teachers' Assn. (vice-pres., 1910). Home: 505 Lafayette St., Jefferson City, Mo.

MUSE, Charles Segret, custodian, editor; born at Lawrence, Kan., June 21, 1869; son of George Segret and Matilda Ann (Cunningham) Muse; attended Vermont Street Grammar and the Central schools, Lawrence; grad. high school, Salina, Kan., 1878; student in Univ. of Kan., 1 year; married Lula May Waller, Apr. 4, 1906. Editor the Denver Star, into which have been merged two other newspapers formerly known as the Statesman and the Denver Independent; in charge the property as custodian. Republican. Baptist. Mason; member Odd Fellows, Knights of Pythias, United Brothers of Friendship. Home: 1221 Gaylord St. Office: 1026 19th St., Denver, Col.

MYERS, Joseph Lee, teacher; born at Americus, Ga., Feb. 26, 1889; son of Elbert and Alice (Walker) Myers; grad. public school, Americus, 1902; student Knoxville College, Tenn., 1903; A.B., Biddle Univ., Charlotte, N. C., 1910; special studies at Univ. of Pa.; unmarried. In government service, Washington, D. C., 1910-11; principal public school, Malone, Ga., 1911-14; principal New Canaan High School, Camp Hill, Ala., since 1914; president School Improvement Assn. of the New Canaan school; writer of "Poems for Children," intended for publication in book form. Republican. Methodist. Mason; member American Woodmen. School: Camp Hill, Ala. Permanent Address: 614 Forsythe St., Americus, Ga.

MYERS, Lucille Walker, supervising industrial teacher; born at Americus, Ga., Apr. 25, 1893; daughter of Elbert and Alice (Walker) Myers; ed. grammar school, Americus, to 1908; grad. Masonic Normal and Industrial Schoo., 1912; took manual training and teachers course at Univ. of Pa., Philadelphia, 1913; unmarried. Teacher of mathematics Masonic Normal and Industrial School, Americus, one term, 1913; instructor in manual training and sewing Russell Normal and Industrial School, Hayneville, Ala., 1914; now one of the 22 supervising industrial teachers of Negro Rural Schools in Ala.; this branch of public instruction is under the State Department of Education; aided by the Anna T. Jeanes Fund, the children in remote parts of the state are taught to mend, sew, can fruit and vegetables, to be economical and self supporting. African Methodist. Member Order Eastern Star, American Woodmen. Clubs: Sun Shine, Smart Set, Willing Workers' (treas.). Home: 614 Forsythe St., Americus, Ga.

N

NAIL, John E., real estate. Member firm of Nail & Parker; has charge St. Philip's P. E. Church property, valued over one million dollars, and management of nearly 100 parcels real estate for individual owners; annual collection of rents exceeds $400,000. Address: New York.

NAPIER, James C., former register of the Treasury. Chairman executive committee National Negro Business League; president Negro Board of Trade, Nashville, Tenn.; director National Institute for Negro Christian Workers; trustee Anna T. Jeanes Fund. Address: Nashville, Tenn.

NEAL, Crawford Chambers, clergyman, college pres.; born at Durand, Ga., Sept. 7, 1869; son of James and Jennie (Chambers) Neal; A.B., Paine College, Augusta, Ga.; grad. Gammon Theological Seminary, 1904, Clark Univ., 1910, Atlanta, Ga.; married, Mar. 4, 1888; 1 child. Pastor in Colored M. E. churches of Ga., 10 years; presiding elder 6 years; supt. Sunday Schools of Ga. and Fla., 1 year; pastor in Atlanta, Ga., 1 year; president Texas College, at Tyler, since 1914; president Colored Dept. East Texas Fair Assn. Progressive. Mason. Address: Texas College, Tyler, Texas.

NEILL, James Lincoln, lawyer; born in Tenn.; son of Isaac and Caroline Neill; A.B., Fisk Univ., Nashville, Tenn., 1889; Ph.G., from Pharm. College, 1893, LL.B., School of Law, 1896, at Howard Univ., Washington, D. C.; married Jessie E. King, of Memphis, Tenn., Oct., 1902; 1 child: Elizabeth K. Admitted to bar, 1907, since practiced in Washington. Congregationalist. Member Odd Fellows, Knights of Pythias. Home: 906 Tea St. N. W. Office: 639 F St. N. W., Washington, D. C.

NELSON, Robert John, in state department of mines; born at Reading, Pa., May 20, 1873; son of Levi and Harriett Matilda (Clark) Nelson; grad.. Reading High School, 1892; took course in bookkeeping at Y. M. C. A. Night School; married Mary

Elizabeth Roberts, of Baltimore, Md., June 26, 1902; 3 children: Harriett, Elizabeth, Robert C. Began as clerk for Reading Rolling Mill Co., 1895, continuing to 1902; editor Inter-State Journal, 1902-3; clerk in the Department of Mines, State Capitol Bldg., Harrisburg, Pa., since 1903; pres. The Douglass Publishing Co., publishers of Masterpieces of Negro Eloquence which was edited by Alice Moore Dunbar; also pres. Nelson Supply Co., and The People's Forum. Republican; was chairman National Suffrage Convention, Washington, 1904; in charge the party campaign among colored people of the state outside of Philadelphia, 1912; pres. Afro-American Republican League. Presbyterian. Mason; member Odd Fellows. Chairman exec. com. local branch National Association for Advancement of Colored People. Club: President of Mohicans. Home: 901 Capitol St. Office: Department of Mines, Harrisburg, Pa.

NELSON, William Thomas, physician; born at Maineville, O., May 23, 1875; son of John and Melvina (Scott) Nelson; ed. public schools Cincinnati; A.B., Howard Univ., 1899; M.D., Howard Univ. School of Medicine, 1904; unmarried. Practiced in Cincinnati since Jan. 23, 1905; physician Aged Colored Woman's Home, and Day Nursery; grand medical registrar Knights of Pythias of Ohio, also examining physician Cincinnati lodges; was physician Orphan Asylum, 2 yrs.; vice.-pres. Ohio Branch National Medical Assn.; pres. Howard Alumni Assn. Republican. Baptist. Mason; member Odd Fellows, Knights of Pythias, Good Samaritan's. Address: 415 Smith, St., Cincinnati, O.

NEWMAN, Allen, clergyman; born at Maple, Pa., June 6, 1883; son of Harding and Georgiana (Givens) Newman; grad. Upper Providence High School, Media, Pa., 1901; A.B., Lincoln (Pa.) Univ., 1907, A.M., S.T.B., 1910; unmarried. Ordained in Baptist ministry, 1910; pastor at Media 2 years; called to Utah by Home Mission Society; pastor Calvary Church, Salt Lake City, 1912-15, Colored Baptist Church, San Francisco, Calif., since Jan. 1, 1915; director California Baptist Convention, San Francisco Baptist Church Extension Society; representative of San Francisco colored people at Panama-Pacific International Exposition. Member Odd Fellows. Home: 1299 Hyde St., San Francisco, California.

NEWSOM, Arthur Sumner, real estate; born at Lincoln, Nebr., June 26, 1875; son of Horace Greeley and Agnes (Davis) Newsom; ed. public schools, Hastings, Neb., Akron, Colo., and Omaha Commercial College; married Susie J. Slivers, of Lawrence, Kan., Nov. 22, 1905. Associated with father in real estate and loan firm of H. G. Newson & Son, since 1908; business extends thruout Eastern Colo., with offices at Akron. Republican; was assistant mail clerk under county treasurer William J. Fine, Denver, Colo., 3 years. Methodist. Address: Akron, Colo.

NORTHCROSS, Daisy Hill, physician; born at Montgomery, Ala., Dec. 9, 1881; daughter of William and Francis (Fair) Hill; grad. State Normal School, Montgomery, 1899, Temple College, Philadelphia, Pa., 1904; M.D., Bennett Medical College, Chicago, Ill., 1913; married Dr. David Caneen Northcross, of Montgomery, Aug. 1, 1909; 1 child: Gloria B. Teacher of elocution and vocal music, State Normal, Montgomery, 1904-9; practiced medicine since 1914; specializes in diseases of children; house physician Northcross Sanitarium; owns part interest in People's Drug Co. Methodist. Member Good Sheppards. Home: 6 Sheppard St. Office: 107 Monroe St., Montgomery, Ala.

NORTHCROSS, David Caneen, physican, surgeon; born at Tuscumbia, Ala., Feb. 23, 1876; son of Rev. Wilson E. and Sallie B. (Oats) Northcross; ed. public schools, Tuscumbia, also St. Joseph, Mo.; high school, St. Louis; College of St. Joseph, Mo.; Meharry Medical College (Walden Univ.), Nashville, Tenn.; M.D., College of Physicians and Surgeons, Chicago, 1906; married Daisy L. Hill, of Montgomery, Ala., Aug. 1, 1909; 1

child: Gloria B. Practiced in Montgomery since 1905; surgeon and mgr. The Northcross Sanitarium; pres. People's Drug Co. Republican; registered voter. Baptist. Secretary surgical section National Medical Assn.; member Tri-State Medical, Dental and Pharm. Assn. of Fla., Ga., and Ala., State Medical, Dental and Pharm. Assn. of Ala., Elks, Good Sheppards. Home: 6 Sheppard St. Office: 107 Monroe St., Montgomery, Ala.

NORMAN, Gerald Fitzherbert, teacher; born at Kingston, Jamaica, British West Indies, Mar. 24, 1882; son of William Albury and Margaret (Jones) Norman; brought to America, 1893; ed. Wolmer's School, Jamaica, to 1893; public schools, New York, 1895-7; student College of City of New York, 1898-90, after 2 years absence returned, 1902, B.S., 1905; married E. Jeannette Latimer, of Flushing, N. Y., June 29, 1910; 1 child: Gerald Latimer N. Began as teacher of manual training public schools No. 26 and 32, New York, 1905, permanently in later since 1907; also in vacation schools, summers, since 1906; teacher of English in evening school, No. 67, for foreigners, since 1908; an organizer of Alpha Physical Culture Club, New York, 1904, first athletic organization of character for colored young men in city. Republican. Methodist. Address: 57 Juniper St., Flushing, New York.

NUNN, Charles Sherman, gardener, commission merchant; born at Raleigh, N. C., Nov. 24, 1866; son of James R. and Francis Nunn; attended public school 1 year, Indianapolis, Ind.; married, 1885; widower; 3 children: Arthur, Samuel, Rebecca. Began as truck farmer, Indianapolis, 1887; now owner of 16-acre farm and leases 50 acres for market gardening; president Charles S. Nunn Co., wholesalers and shippers; owner of 8 rental properties in Indianapolis, stock in two banks and one insurance company. Progressive. African Methodist. Mason; member Odd Fellows, National Negro Business League, Colored Business Men's Club of Indianapolis. Address: Haughville R. R. 18, Indianapolis, Ind.

NUTTER, Isaac Henry, lawyer; born at Princess Anne, Md., Aug. 20, 1878; son of William and Emma (Henry) Nutter; LL.B., Howard Univ. School of Law, Washington, D. C., 1901; (hon. LL.D., Wilberforce Univ., 1913); married Alice E. Reed, of Coatesville, Pa., Apr. 26, 1904. Admitted to N. J. bar, 1905; practiced in Atlantic City since June, 1905; was for some time associated with ex-Judge John J. Crandall; court practive averages about 20 civil and criminal cases a month; defended in 30 murder cases, one of which was convicted in 2d degree, 4 sentenced for manslaughter, and 25 acquitted; in the County Court at Mays Landing, N. J., in less than 4 days, Feb. 23-27, 1915, he secured acquittals in 2 cases, and in the middle of the trial of the third client had a "not guilty" of murder plea changed to "guilty" of manslaughter with imprisonment of 1 year; solicitor and general advisor New Jersey State Republican League; solicitor of Atlantic County Republican League; president Nutter Real Estate Co. Methodist. Mason; member Odd Fellows, Knights of Pythias, Elks. Club: University. Home: 1801 Arctic Ave. Office: Schwartz-Riddle Bldg., Atlantic City, N. J.

O

O'Banyoun, Ernest Ganson, baritone soloist; born at Allston, Mass., Jan. 13, 1884; son of Simon F. and Irene (Moffatt) O'Banyoun; grad. Washington High School, Cambridge, Mass., 1897; attended English High School 2 years; pupil under Prof. Fred P. White, piano teacher, and Prof. S. Studley, who was director Boston Ideal Opera Co., 25 years; vocal student under Studley and Prof. Stearnes, Boston; married Ella Stiles Harten, of Yorkville, S. C., Oct. 21, 1908; 3 children: Irene H., Eleanor E., Louise E. Chorister in Union Baptist Church, Cambridge, since 1911; teacher of pianoforte and vocal expression. Representative of The Boston Alliance; secretary board of investments Hard-

ing, Cox & Martin Real Estate Syndicate. Republican. Member Rush A. M. E. Zion Church, Young Men's Brotherhood, Foresters, St. Luke's. Address: 83 Pleasant St., Cambridge, Mass.

OFFICER, Thomas Sterling, physician, surgeon; born in Tenn., June 20, 1876; son of Shaw and Ann Officer; A.B., Walden Univ., Nashville, Tenn., 1902; student Meharry Medical College (Walden Univ.), 2 years; M.D., Jenner Medical College, Chicago, Ill., 1906; married Dr. Olive M. Henderson (D.D.S.), of Chicago, June 7, 1911; one child: Mercedes. Practiced in Chicago since Dec. 20, 1906; examining physician for 15 secret and fraternal orders; president Physicians, Dentists and Pharmacists Club of Chicago. Republican. Methodist; was teacher in Quinn Chapel Sunday School several years. Mason; member Odd Fellows, Knights of Pythias, United Brothers of Friendship. Club: Appomatox. Home: 4217 Wabash Ave. Office: 3243 State St., Chicago, Illinois.

OGLESBY, Mabry Chestly, real estate; born in Chester County, S. C., Jan. 14, 1870; son of Tillman H. and Anna (Jackson) Oglesby; country school edn. to 1883; entered Hampton Normal and Agricultural Institute, 1893, then 24 years old, grad. academic dept., 1897; student Shaw Univ., Raleigh, N. C., 1899-1900; read law 1 year; married, Oct. 17, 1901, Sadie Ethel Shankle, of Concord, N. C., a grad. from Dixie Training School for Nurses. Pullman car porter for 14 years; the purchase of a home on the payment plan at Allston, Mass., was the beginning of his real estate investments which have continued until now controls considerable property. Congregationalist. Address: 32 Seattle St., Allston, Mass.

O'KELLY, Cadd Grant, college president; born at Raleigh, N. C., Feb. 14, 1865; son of John Henry and Anna (Foster) O'Kelly; grad. Johnson High School, Raleigh; A.B., Lincoln Univ., Pa., 1885, S.T.B., 1888, A.M., 1888 (D.D., 1913; Ph.D., Kittrell College, 1903); married Corinne

Gibson, of Norfolk, Va., 1900; 2 children: Annie Foster, Corinne Gibson; 2d marriage, Cora A. Bass, 1906; 1 child: Ruth. Began as teacher, 1888; president Kittrell College, N. C., since 1912; vice-pres. Morris Mattress Co.; director Forsyth Savings & Trust Co. Trustee National Religious Training School, Durham, N. C. Republican. African Methodist. Member True Reformers, Elks. Address: Kittrell, N. C.

OLIVER, George Melville, clergyman; born at Washington, D. C., Dec. 4, 1878; son of George W. and Elizabeth (Brown) Oliver; public school edn., and finished course in theology at Temple Univ., Philadelphia, Pa.; (D.D., Livingstone College, Salisbury, N. C., 1910); married Sadie E. Morris, of Salisbury, Md., June 30, 1901. Licensed to preach in A. M. E. Zion Church, Philadelphia, 1901; since pastored number important churches; now pastor Union Wesley A. M. E. Zion Church at Washington, and secretary the Philadelphia and Baltimore Annual Conference; built St. Paul Church, Salisbury, Md., 1906; rebuilt West Street Church, Carlisle, Pa., 1911, and Union Wesley, Washington, also installed $3,000 pipe organ, 1915; received $1,250 contribution to the organ from Andrew Carnegie. Trustee Dinwiddie (Va.) Agricultural and Industrial School. Republican. Mason. Home: 1309 R St. N. W., Washington, D. C.

O'NEAL, Annie Todd, teacher; born at Frankfort, Ky.; daughter of Robert and Mary (Vaughn) Todd; grad. Clinton Street High School, Frankfort; studied domestic science and arts at Univ. of Chicago, 1909-1910; married Arthur O'Neal, of New Richmond, Ohio, June, 1906; 1 child: Robert T. Teacher of domestic arts in the Kentucky Normal and Industrial Institute, Frankfort, since 1910; an adapt to dressmaking. Baptist. Club: Normal Hill Woman's. Home: 426 Clinton St., Frankfort, Ky.

O'NEAL, Samuel Andrew, physician, clergyman; born at Barnesville, Ga., July 7, 1865; son of Seborn and Tamer (Sullivan) O'Neal; attended public schools at Barnesvillt to 1879; grad., academic course, Central Tennessee College, 1888, later studied theology there; M.D., Meharry Medical College, Nashville, 1889, postgraduate course, 1912; married Carrie Watson, of Nashville, July 2, 1882; 7 children: Charlie Beatrice, Samuel A. Jr., Robert, Warren, Carrie, Mattie, Seaborn. Was farm boy and cotton picker in Ga.; practiced medicine in Henderson, Ky., since 1889; pastor C. M. E. Church; owns farm at Barnesville, Ga., and valuable property at Henderson, stock in Pythian Building, Louisville, and Fraternity Hall, Henderson. Delegate to nearly every Republican state and county convention since 1889. Member National Medical Assn., Medical Association of Ky., Civic Improvement League of Henderson. Mason; regemental sergt. Knights of Friendship of Ky.; charter member, board of endowment, United Brothers of Friendship and Sisters of the Mysterious Ten. past deputy grand master, past national grand chaplin, and medical examiner; grand royal patron Order of Eastern Star of Ky.; member Knights of Tabor. Has prepared his principal work for publication under title of Book of Orations and Lectures. Home: 828 Powell St. Office: 310 Second St., Henderson, Ky.

OUTLAW, John Sutton, physician; born at Windsor, N. C., Sept. 14, 1863; son of James Madison and Sarah (Ryan) Outlaw; apptd. cadet to U. S. Military Academy, West Point, but declined in favor of medical edn.; A.B., Lincoln (Pa.) Univ., 1888; M.D., Howard Univ., Washington, 1891; married Nannie F. Brown, of Washington, June 28, 1899; 2 children. Began practice in Washington, 1891; medical examiner for pension bureau, 1895-1901; removed to Calif., 1901; since practiced in Los Angeles; vice-pres. People's Realty Co., $75,000 corpn. Republican. Presbyterian. Member American Medical Assn., National Medical Assn., Calif. State Medical Assn., Los Angeles County Medical Assn. Mason. Address: 156

Wilson Bldg., 102 S. Spring St., Los Angeles, Cal.

OUSLEY, Benjamin Forsyth, teacher, clergyman; born at Davis Bend, Warren Co., Miss., Oct. 2, 1855; son of Benjamin and Charlotte (Riggins) Ousley, both slaves; attended contraband and missionary schools at Davis Bend during slavery days, and school at Vicksburg, Miss., 1864-5, also 6 months in 1870; A.B., Fisk Univ., Nashville, Tenn., 1881, A.M., 1885; A.M., 1885; B.D., Oberlin (O.) College, 1884; married Henriette Bailey, of Knoxville, Ill., Aug. 14, 1884. Served as missionary in Africa 9 years; now principal of Mound Bayou Normal Institute under the American Missionary Assn. Congregationalist. Republican. Translated into the Sheetswa language "The Story of the Gospel" (Am. Mission Press, S. Africa), 1888; translated "Timhaka Ta ·Evangeli," 1891; this was the Synotical Gospels and the Acts, in the Sheetswa language. Address: Mound Bayou, Miss.

OVERR, Oscar Olen, justice of the peace, real estate; born at Topeka, Kan., May 29, 1876; son of David J. and Eliza (Downey) Overr; public school edn., Topeka; read law in office of G. S. Russell, Tulare County, Calif.; married Mrs. Cora B. Shephard, of Topeka, Oct. 10, 1906. Began as weighmaster, 1900, later assistant general mgr. U. S. Zinc Co., Galena-Joplin zinc and lead dist., Mo., continuing to 1902; in wholesale and retail cigar business, 1902-3; wholesale fruit and vegetable merchant, 1903-6; custodian restricted residence park, Pasadena, Calif., 1906-8; in real estate business since 1908; assisted in the development of Allensworth; pres. Allensworth Realty Co.; executive committee Tulare County Highway Assn.; field secretary proposed Allensworth Polytechnic School. Elected justice of the peace, Allensworth, Nov. 3, 1914. Was 2d lieut. 23d Kan. Vol. Inf.; served in Cuba during Spanish-American war, June 27, 1898, to Apr. 10, 1899. Trustee 1st Baptist Church, Allensworth. Republican; served as judge and inspector of elections various times since 1900. Member Allensworth Board of Trade. Scottish Rite Mason; Shriner. Address: Allensworth, Calif.

OWENS, Pauline Dabney, teacher; born on farm near Mounds, Ill., Oct. 16, 1877; son of Henry and Elmira (Dabney) Owens; ed. Southern Illinois Normal Univ.; unmarried. Teacher in primary school, Mounds, since 1904. Grand register of deeds, Grand Court of Calanthe, jurisdiction of Illinois, since 1910. Republican. Baptist. Club: Woman's. Home: Mounds, Ill.

P

PACE, Harry Herbert, insurance; born at Covington, Ga., Jan. 6, 1884; son of Charles H. and Nannie (Francis) Pace; A.B., Atlanta Univ., 1903; unmarried. Managing editor W. E. B. DuBois first newspaper, The Moon, Memphis, Tenn., 1905-6; professor Latin and Greek, Lincoln Institute, Jefferson City, Mo., 1906-8; cashier Solvent Savings Bank & Trust Co., Memphis, 1908-13; helped organize Standard Life Insurance Co., Atlanta, Ga.; secretary since 1913, now also treas; with W. C. Handy, founded Pace & Handy Music Co., Memphis; organized Colored Citizens Assn., Memphis, for betterment of conditions; secured additional light, better pavements, new schools, colored school examiners, probation officers, and more fair treatment in police courts for colored. Assistant secretary Tenn. State Republican Convention, and only colored delegate at-large to national convention at Chicago, 1912. Episcopalian. Member Atlanta Board of Trade, Sigma Pi Phi. Mason; grand exalted ruler I. B. P. O. Elks; member Odd Fellows; was delegate to B. M. C., Boston, 1914. Club: Athletic and Glee. Author (with W. C. Handy): Girl You Never Have Met; St. Louis Blues; In the Cotton Fields of Dixie, and other songs; has contributed short stories to the Black Cat, Chicago Tribune, New York Independent, The Crisis. Home: 357 W. Fair St. Office: 200 Auburn Ave., Atlanta, Ga.

PAGE, Inman E., university president; born at Warrenton, Va., Dec. 29, 1853; private tuition under George F. T. Cook, of Washington; student Howard Univ., 1868; grad. Brown Univ., Providence, R. I., 1877; (LL.D., Howard Univ.); married Zelia Robshure Ball, of Alexandria, Va., 1878; she was graduated from Wilberforce Univ., 1875; now matron of girls dormitory at Colored Agricultural and Normal Univ., Langston, Okla.; 3 children: Inman, Zeba N., Mary. Taught in Natchez, (Miss.) Seminary, 1877-8; teacher, 1878-89, and president, 1880-98, Lincoln Institute, Jefferson City, Mo.; president Colored Agricultural and Normal Univ., Langston, Okla., since 1898. Member National Association Teachers' in Colored Schools, Oklahoma State Teachers' Assn. Address: Langston University, Langston, Okla.

PAGE, John Lincoln, college president; born at Paulding, Miss., Nov. 1, 1878; son of Alexander and Elmira (Turner) Page; ed. public school, Jasper Co., Miss.; Blue Ridge High School; grad. Meridian Academy, Miss., 1901, B.S., 1903; later studied at Wiley Univ., Marshall, Tex.; married Sallie McDonald, of Jackson, Miss., July 15, 1900; 5 children: John L., King Asa, Elmira, Lincoln, James. Began as teacher in public schools, Miss., 1901, continuing to 1908; principal city schools, McComb, Miss., 1909-12; president Lincoln Normal and Industrial College, Kioto, Miss., since 1912; instructor in summer schools for teachers' at McComb City, Miss., and the Lincoln Normal. Republican. Methodist. Mason; state secretary Grand Charity Bureau of Masonic order; member Odd Fellows, True Reformers. Address: Kioto, Miss.

PAIR, James David, clergyman; born near Raleigh, N. C., Aug. 31, 1873; son of Rev. Harmon and Alie (Lassater) Pair; attended public schools, Wake Co., N. C., 13 years; Shiloah Institute, 1 year; Shaw Univ., college dept., Raleigh, 4 years; Armstrong Business High School, Washington, D. C., evenings, 2 years; grad. Howard Univ. School of Theology,

1911; married Lula N. Thornton, of Warrenton, N. C., Dec. 14, 1899; 6 children: Clarence, James, Hubert, Harmon, Lois, Virginia. Teacher in public schools of Wake Co., 1893-1904; general traveling agent for The Gazette, a state weekly newspaper, Raleigh, 1897; in regular service Post-office Dept., Washington, since 1904; managing editor The Sunday School News Review, quarterly, 1909-11, The National Union, weekly newspaper, 1911; pastor St. John's Baptist Church, Arlington, Va., since 1911. Was sec. Wake County Teachers' Assn., 1896-1904; sec. 1897-9, pres. 1899-1902, of Wake County Sunday School Convention; recording sec. N. C. Baptist State Sunday School Convention, 1898-1905; vice-pres. Sunday School Union, Washington, 1905-7; general sec. Mt. Bethel Baptist Sunday School Convention, 1907-11; pres. Mt. Pleasant-Plains Citizens Assn.; member Northern Va. Baptist Assn., General Baptist Assn. of Washington, Ministers' and Deacons' Union of Northern Va. Republican; served as Township chmn., and register of elections, Wake Co.; also sec. County and Congressional convs., N. C. Mason; member Odd Fellows. Address: G and 53rd Sts. N. E., Washington.

PALMER, Lucian Horatio, real estate, former state legislator; born at Huntsville, Ala., Mar. 12, 1855; son of Rev. John W. and Mary Ann (Mastin) Palmer; father died in 1862; relatives then brought him to Nashville, Tenn., where he attended public school; finished collegiate course at Central Tenn. College (now Walden Univ.), 1876; unmarried. Began active career in Milwaukee, Wis., 1883; was commissioner in charge Wisconsin Negro exhibit at New Orleans Exposition, 1884; appointed clerk in Wis. legislature, 1887; in catering business, 1900-4; supt. Wis. state building at Louisiana Purchase Centennial Exposition, St. Louis, Mo., 1904; in real estate, mortgage loan and insurance business since 1906; administrator for 2 estates. Trustee Wilberforce Univ., Ohio, and St. Mark's A. M. E. Church, Milwaukee.

Republican; member Wis. House of Representatives, 1907-8; district from which elected includes banks, railroad offices, county building, postoffice, etc.; secretary of elections in 4th Ward. Mason; member Odd Fellows. Club: Business Men's. Home: 253 18th St. Office: 14 Grand Ave., Milwaukee, Wis.

PARKER, John Walter, dentist; born at Calvert, Tex., Apr. 19, 1879; son of Sydney and Mattie Parker; B.S., Fisk Univ., 1901; D.D.S., Northwestern Univ., 1905; married Florence E. Davis, of St. Louis, Mo., Apr. 15, 1909; 1 child: Leo D. Practiced in Pine Bluff, Ark., since 1905; secretary Pine Bluff Realty & Mortgage Co.; partner in Moving Picture Theatre; owns 80-acre farm and city property; vice-pres. Business Men's League of Pine Bluff; secretary Ark. Negro Suffrage League, St. John A. M. E. Church. Member Ark. Dental Society. Editor Pine Bluff Weekly Herald. Mason; past chancellor local lodge Knights of Pythias. Home: 1405 Alabama St. Office: 211 1-2 State St., Pine Bluff, Ark.

PARKS, Henry Blanton, bishop; presided over Fifth Episcopal District of A. M. E. Church since the death of Bishop Abram Grant. Home: 3312 Calumet Ave., Chicago, Ill.

PARRISH, Charles Henry, clergyman, social worker; born at Lexington, Ky., Apr. 18, 1859; son of Hiram and Harriet Parrish; A.B., State Univ., Louisville, Ky., 1886, A. M., 1889 (D.D., 1898); married Mary V. Cook, of Bowling Green, Ky., Jan. 26, 1898; 1 child: Charles H. Jr. Ordained Baptist ministry, 1886; since pastor Calvary Church, Louisville; president Foreign Mission Board, National Baptist Convention; chairman executive board Baptist of Ky. Was professor of Greek, State Univ., Ky., 1886; founded the Eckstein-Norton Institute, 1890, and was president 23 years; organized 1908, since pres. Kentucky Home Society for Colored Children; pres. Louisville Negro Business League, Louisville branch the Society for Advancement of Colored People; vice-pres. Central Law School; secretary board of trustees Lincoln Institute, Lincoln Ridge, Ky. Traveled in Holy Land, 1904, in England and Germany, 1905; delegate to Sociological and Educational Congress, 1914; elected moderator Colored Baptist of Ky., Aug., 1914; Louisville representative National Tuberculosis Assn. Fellow Royal Geographical Society (London, Eng.); member American Geographical Society, American Sociological Society, Southern Sociological Congress. Mason; member Odd Fellows, Knights of Pythias, Foresters, Royal Neighbors, Good Samaritans, Mosaic Templars. Author (pamphlets): What We Believe, a hand book for Baptists, 1886; Oriental Lights for the Teacher; Travels in the Holy Land. Address: 847 Sixth St., Louisville, Ky.

PARRISH, William, horse trainer; born at Cincinnati, Ohio, Mar. 1, 1885; son of D. and Ann (Haley) Parrish; ed. public schools at Allisonia, Tenn.; unmarried. Began breaking colts for neighbors at Allisonia when 15 years old; for a while made business of training horses at Bellbuckle, Tenn.; opened first horse training school, Chapel Hill, Tenn., 1898; received course of instruction under Dr. Key, noted colored horse trainer; returned to Bellbuckle, 1907, and opened school where Pet, a horse educated to 150 feats, was trained; conducted training school at Nashville, Tenn., 1907-9, Chicago, Ill., 1910, Watseka, Ill., for 6 months; proprietor Pet's Kind Method Training School, Henderson, Ky., since 1911; while at Chicago gave nightly exhibitions at carnivals under the auspices of West Side churches; has reputation for training horses of most wild disposition in 30 minutes; owns training school equipment and horses of much value; has refused offer of $5,000 for half interest in "Pet," his famous trained horse; special honors conferred by several colleges for his training ability. Republican. Missionary Baptist. Address: 126 Second St., Henderson, Ky.

PATTERSON, Adam Edward, lawyer; born at Walthall, Miss., Dec. 23, 1876; son of Zachary Taylor and Catherine (Archey) Patterson; ed. public schools, Kansas City, Kan.; grad. high school, Pueblo, Colo., 1897; LL.B., Univ. of Kan., 1900; married Nellie Allen, of Chattanooga, Tenn., 1897. Admitted to Illinois bar and began practice at Cairo, 1902; later removed to Okla.; practiced in Muskogee several years; member law firm of Patterson & Wilson, Chicago, Ill., since 1915. Was member board of regents for Oklahoma State Institution to time of abolishment, 1912; appointed by President Woodrow Wilson, 1913, to succeed James C. Napier as register of U. S. Treasury, but withdrew to make possible reelection of senatorial friends; active in politics in Chicago. Democrat. African Methodist. Mason. Club: Appomatox. Home: 3223 S. Park Ave. Office: 3102 S. State St., Chicago, Ill.

PATTERSON, Fred D., manufacture; born at Greenfield, O., 1871; son of C. R. and Josephine Patterson; ed. public schools, Greenfield; A.B., Ohio State Univ.; married Estelline Postell, of Hopkinsville, Ky., 1901; 2 children. General manager firm of C. R. Patterson & Sons, vehicle builders, Greenfield, O., largest plant owned by colored people in U. S. Republican. Member Greenfield Business League. Mason. Address: Greenfield, Ohio.

PATTERSON, Gertrude A., supervising industrial teacher; born at Lynchburg, Va., Aug., 1877; daughter of Thomas and Mary F. Jones; ed. Virginia Theological Seminary and College; summer course Columbia Univ., New York; Institute for Colored Youth, Cheyney, Pa.; Christiansburg and Hampton, Va.; married Prof. U. S. Grant Patterson, of Lynchburg, Apr. 28, 1898; 4 children: Dorothy, Mamie, Ulysses, Jr., Ferdinand. Supervisor in Negro rural schools of Campbell County, Va.; this branch of public instruction is under the State Board of Education; aided by the Anna T. Jeanes Fund the work reaches the most remote schools and homes in Virginia. Baptist. Member endowment advisory board Grand Court of Virginia. Home: 1308 Wise St., Lynchburg, Va.

PATTERSON, Ulysses S. Grant, cornetist, vocalist; born in Franklin County, Va., Jan. 1, 1867; son of Frank and Amelia (Webb) Patterson; ed. public schools in Va.; Tuskegee (Ala.) Normal and Industrial Institute, 1885-6; Virginia Normal and Collegiate Institute, Petersburg, 1891; married Gertrude A. Jones, of Lynchburg, Va., Apr. 28, 1898; 4 children: Dorothy, Mamie, Ulysses, Jr., Ferdinand. Began as band master, Salem, Va., 1884; teacher of band, Charleston, W. Va., 1885, at Tuskegee Normal and Industrial Institute, Ala., 1885-6; teacher in normal dept., 2 years, and band teacher 5 years, at Virginia Normal and Collegiate Institute; opened Spiller Academy and was teacher there, 1892; band master teacher in normal dept., Virginia Theological Seminary and College, 1893-7; traveled with Cleveland Haverly Minstrels, summer, 1896, with A. G. Fields company, 1897-8, Darkest America, as cornetist and vocal director, 1898: musical director, Court Street Baptist Church, and mail carrier, Lynchburg, Va., since 1899. Republican. 32d degree Mason, Shriner; assistant general inspector, uniform rank, and vice-grand chancellor, Knights of Pythias in Va.; past W. C. Grand Court of Va.; supreme scribe Royal Order of Moses. Home: 1308 Wise St., Lynchburg, Va.

PAYNE, Christopher H., consul; born, Sept. 7, 1848, at Red Sulpher Springs, then of Va., now of W. Va.; ed. Richmond Institute; studied theology, and read law. Entered ministry and preached for number years; admitted to bar; was deputy collector internal revenue, 1889-93, internal revenue agent, 1898-9; U. S. consul at St. Thomas, W. I., since May 1, 1903. Address: American Consulate, St. Thomas, West Indies.

PAYNE, George Atlanta, professor; born in Franklin Co., Ga.; son of Rev. William M. and Sarah Jane (Webster) Payne; ed. public schools, Jackson, Tenn.; LL.B., Univ. of W. Tenn., 1903; B.S., Lane College, Jackson, 1907; special work in science, Walden Univ., Nashville, Tenn., in English and French at Univ. of Chicago, summer, 1909; married Jessie Anna Whaley, of Paris, Ky., Mar. 29, 1903. Principal in English dept., Lane College, Jackson, Tenn., 1898-1903; teacher in public school, Jackson, 1903-5; assistant prin. S. Jackson High School, 1905-8; professor of science and vice-pres. Miles Memorial College, Birmingham, Ala., since 1908, acting pres., 1914. Methodist. Member Ala. State Teachers' Assn. Mason. Wrote number poems published in Christian Index. Address: Miles Memorial College, Birmingham, Ala.

PAYNE, George W., engineer, water pipe inspector; born at Union, Boone County, Ky., Oct. 1, 1888; son of Jefferson and Alice (Benson) Payne; public school edn., Mt. Vernon, Ind.; took course in engineering from International Correspondence School; unmarried. Began as wiper and brass cleaner for Mt. Vernon Water, Light & Power Co., when boy about 13 years old; engineer for the company since 1906; city water pipe inspector; has special gift in mechanics; regarded as one of the best engineers and repairers of enginess, etc., in southern Indiana; plays instrument in Butler's Cornet Band (colored). Republican. Catholic. Member Technical and Electrical Engineers' Assn. of America. Mason; member Odd Fellows, Knights of Pythias (uniform rank). Home: 618 Short Sycamore St., Mt. Vernon, Ind.

PAYTON, Philip A. Jr., real estate; born at Westfield, Mass., Feb. 27, 1876; son of Philip A. and Annie M. (Rynes) Payton; ed. high school, Westfield, and Livingstone College, Salisbury, N. C.; married Maggie P. Lee, of Raleigh, N. C., June 28, 1900. Real estate operator in New York since 1900; president and treas. Philip A. Payton, Jr., Co., Revenue Realty Co., Woronoco Corporation. Republican. Mason. Address: 67 W. 134th St., New York.

PEARCE, John Jackson, missionary; grad. normal dept. Fisk Univ., Nashville, Tenn., 1900, B.D., 1901. Missionary A. M. E. Church, Brewerville, Liberia, W. Africa.

PEARSON, Henry, college professor; born at Cokesbury, S. C., Jan. 4, 1864; son of David and Francis Pearson, who were married when slaves; ed. Payne Institute, Cokesbury, 1871, 76, 81; grad. normal dept. Claflin Univ., Orangeburg, S. C., 1884, A.B., Claflin, 1888, A.M., 1892; studied in Chautauqua summer school, 1891, Univ. of Chicago, 1897; married Daisy E. Goodlett, of Spartanburg, S. C., Oct. 3, 1890. Began as instructor Claflin Univ., 1888; prin. Sumter graded school, S. C., 1892-5; professor at Ga. State Industrial College, Savannah, since 1895; now secretary of faculty; president Mechanics Investment Co., a $25,000 corpn. Trustee Haven Academy, Waynesboro, Ga.; trustee and sec. Carnegie Library Assn., Savannah. Methodist. Republican. Member National Association Teachers' in Colored Schools. Contributor under name of "Perse F. Homer" to the Savannah Tribune for several years; number of his peoms have been published in various papers. Address: Georgia State Industrial College, Savannah, Ga.

PEARSON, William Gaston, principal high school; born at Durham, N. C., 1859; son of George W. and Cynthia (Wilkins) Pearson; B.S., Shaw Univ., Raleigh, N. C., 1886, A.M., 1889; grad. Cornell Univ., 1903; married Minnie Sumner, of Charlotte, N. C., June 6, 1893. Began teaching in schools of Durham, 1890; principal City High School, since 1893; pres. Whetted Woodworking Co.; treas. Bull City Drug Co.; dir. Mechanics' and Farmers Bank; member firm of broom mfrs.; in real estate business and owns 22 tenement houses. Trustee National Religious Training School, Lincoln Hospital and School for Nurses, St. Joseph A. M. E. Church. Republican. Mason; managing sec. Rôyal Knights of King David; member Knights of Pythias. Club: Shakesperian Reading. Address: Box 404, Durham, N. C.

PEGUES, Albert Witherspoon, supervisor school for blind; born at Cheraw, S. C., Nov. 15, 1859; prep. edn. Virginia Union Univ., Richmond; A.B.,

Bucknell Univ., Lewisburg, Pa.; married M. Ella Christian, of Richmond, Feb. 18, 1890; 2 children. Principal of Sumner High School at Parkersburg, W. Va., 1 year; was teacher, 1888-1895, and dean theological dept., 1895-1905, at Shaw Univ., Raleigh, N. C.; supervisor North Carolina State School for Blind and Deaf since 1905; president Capital Building & Loan Assn.; secretary Capital Development & Trust Co. President State Baptist Convention; corresponding sec. State Baptist Sunday School Convention; trustee Shaw Univ. Republican. Member American Negro Academy. Author: Our Baptist Ministers and Schools, 1892. Address: State School for Blind, Releigh, N. C.

PENDLETON, Leila Amos, writer, teacher; born at Washington, D. C.; daughter of Joseph Ferdinand and Maria Louise (Bruce) Amos; ed. public, high and normal schools of Washington; married Robert Lewis Pendleton, of Marianna, Fla., Nov. 15, 1893. Teacher in public schools, Washington, 4 years; founded 1898, and for 13 years president, Alpha Charity Club; founded Social Purity League, Washington, 1907, and now president. Episcopalian. Member Order Eastern Star, Heroines of Jericho, Order of the Golden Circle. Author: A Narrative of the Negro, 1812; prepared a work called "An Alphabet for Negro Children," 1915. Home: 1216 You St. N. W., Washington, D. C.

PENDLETON, Robert Lewis, printer, publisher; born at Marianna, Fla., July 19, 1865; son of Robert Lewis and Hastie (Armstead) Pendleton; public school edn., Marianna; married Leila Amos, of Washington, D. C., Nov. 15, 1893. Learned prrinters' trade in Fla.; worked on New York Globe, 1884, People's Advocate, Washington, 1885-6; prop. Pendleton's Quality Printing House since 1886. President Commercial Council; director of Scottish Rite Home Assn., Masonic Hall Building Assn. Republican. Episcopalian. 33d degree Mason; member Odd Fellows. Address: 1216 You St. N. W., Washington, D. C.

PENN, I. G., corresponding secretary Freedmen's Aid Society M. E. Church, 220 W. 4th St., Cincinnati, O.

PENN, James H., counsellor-at-law, master-in-chancery; born at Petersburg, Va., Sept. 26, 1880; son of James A. and Lurania A. (Layton) Penn; ed. Peabody High School, Petersburg; read law in office of William P. Hurley, Passaic, N. J.; married Estella A. Brown, of Westchester Co., N. Y., Nov. 6, 1901. Served as letter carrier at Passaic 8 years; practiced law since 1909, with large clientage among the foreign population; secretary New Jersey Home Extension Co. Republican; candidate for city councilman, 1915. Baptist. Mason; past district grand master Odd Fellows of N. J.; member Citizens Protective Alliance. Clubs: Fourth Ward Social, Polish Citizens, Russian National. Home: 469 Harrison St. Office: Birnbaum Bldg., Passaic, N. J.

PEOPLES, Frank, contractor, builder. Has erected large number houses and sold homes on easy payment plan to colored people in desirable residential districts of city. Office: 236 Boston Block, Minneapolis, Minn.

PERKINS, George Napier, lawyer, editor; born near Franklin, Tenn., Jan. 1, 1841; son of Moses and Millie Perkins; public school edn.; married Maggie A. Dillard, of Ft. Smith, Ark., Jan. 30, 1867. Served 3 years in Union army during war between the states, first as private and later 1st lieut. Admitted to the bar, 1871; since practiced in Ark. and Okla.; was delegate to Arkansas Constitution Convention, 1874; justice of the peace 6 years; member City Council, Little Rock, Ark., 4 years, Guthrie (Okla.) City Council 4 years; editor Oklahoma Guide at Guthrie since 1892. Republican. Missionary Baptist. Member Grand Army of Republic, Commercial Business Men's League. Mason. Address: 522 S. 2d St., Guthrie, Okla.

PETTIFORD, William Reuben, banker; born in S. C., about 1840; parentage unknown; when 21 years of age attended school at Marion, Ala.; later took theological course; (hon.

D.D., Selma Univ., Ala.; LL.D., Shaw Univ., Raleigh, N. C.); married Della Boyd, of Selma, 1880; 3 children. Began missionary work under Baptist Home Mission Board; later was teacher in Selma Univ.; pastor of several churches and built 16th Street Baptist Church edifice, Birmingham, Ala.; was 1st pres. Baptist State Convention; head of settlement work dept. for Tenn. Coal & Iron Co., at different times; pres. Ala. Penny Savings Bank, $100,000 corpn., doing annual business exceeding half million dollars. Pres. National Negro Bankers' Assn.; director National Economic League; trustee Selma Univ. Author: Divinity in Wedlock; The Get-Together Catechism. Address: 310 N. 18th St., Birmingham, Ala.

PERRY, Christopher James, editor, publisher; born at Baltimore, Md., Sept. 15, 1859; son of Christopher and Rebecca (Bowser) Perry; public school edn., Baltimore and Philadelphia; married Cora Harris, of Philadelphia, Pa., May, 1884; 5 children: Bertha F. (Mrs. Paul Prayer), Olivia (Mrs. James Scott), Beatrice, Ethel, Christopher J., Jr. Began as newspaper editor, Nov. 28, 1884; sole owner Philadelphia Tribune. Was clerk in sheriff's office 15 years; member Philadelphia City Council, 6 terms, 1897-1905; Republican. Presbyterian. Club: Citizens Republican. Home: 1319 S. 51st St. Office: 526 S. 16th St., Philadelphia, Pa.

PERRY, John Edward, physician, surgeon; born at Clarksville, Tex., Apr. 27, 1870; son of Anderson and Louise Perry; prep. edn. Bishop College, Marshall, Tex.; M.D., Heharry Medical College (Walden Univ.), Nashville, Tenn., 1895; took course at Post-Graduate Medical School and Hospital, Chicago, Ill., 1897; married Fredericka Douglass Sprague, of Washington, D. C., July 3, 1912; 1 child: Eugene B. Began practice in Mexico, Mo., 1895; later removed to Columbia, Mo., where remained 8 8 years; removed to Kansas City, Mo., 1903, with purpose to aid in establishing a hospital for Negroes; opened Perry Sanitarium, 1910; maintained

same more than 3 years at annual cost of $3,500; charity associations assumed obligations of the sanitarium, Jan. 1, 1914; is assistant surgeon in Kansas City General Hospital; frequently called to assist in surgical operations by prominent white physicians; sec.-treas. S. P. L. Mercantile & Investment Co. Served as 1st lieut. and q.-m., 7th U. S. Vols. Spanish-American war. Republican. Baptist. Member National Medical Assn., Pan-Missouri Medical Assn. (pres.). Mason; member Knights of Pythias, United Brothers of Friendship. Address 1512 E. 18th St., Kansas City, Missouri.

PERRY, Rufus Lewis, proctor in admiralty, amateur artist; born at Brooklyn, N. Y., May 26, 1872; son of Rufus Lewis and Charlotte (Handy) Perry; LL.B., New York Univ., 1892; was first educated for musician; student Greek and Latin, speaks and writes in French; married Lillian S. Buchacher, of Brooklyn, Nov. 18, 1913. Admitted to N. Y. bar, 1892, and began practice in City of New York; removed to Brooklyn, 1894; member firm of Perry & Carmel since 1914; has defended clients in more than 100 murder cases, and is also proctor in admiralty cases; director Hannibal Realty & Improvement Co., Foster Coal, Land & Timber Co. Democrat. Jewish religion (and only one in this volume). Member American Geographical Society, American Society of National Science, Metropolital Museum of Art, Brooklyn Bar Assn., Wilner Verein. Author: Subrogation, 1910; L'Hohmme d'apres la Science et le Talmur, 1912; La Situation Actuele en Haiti, 1913; Positive Authropology, 1914. Home: 405 Cumberland St. Office: 375 Fulton St., Brooklyn, N. Y.

PETTUS, John Wilson, principal high school, supervisor public schools; born at White Haven, Tenn., Nov. 25, 1872; son of Henry and Sina (Wilson) Pettus; A.B., Fisk Univ., Nashville, Tenn., 1903; married Phyllis J. Miller, of Ft. Smith, Ark., June 14, 1905; 3 children: Gladys R., John Wilson, Jr., Velma. Began as instructor in mathematics in high school, Ft. Smith,

1897, continuing to 1906; president Baptist Academy, 1906-7; principal high school, and supervisor of schools, McAlester, Okla., since 1907; conducted country normal school for teachers 6 years. Was editor Arkansas Appreciator, 1898-1900, Fraternal Union (weekly paper), 1900-6; contributor to number daily papers in Ark. and Tenn. Served as secretary Republican State Conventions, Ark., 1902, 04; endorsed by Arkansas Republican Central Committee as consul to Bahia, Brazil, 1905, but not appointed. Baptist. President of Southwestern Association Colored Teachers, and County Reading Circle. Mason; treasurer local lodge Odd Fellows; secretary-treasurer United Brothers of Friendship in Okla.; master of works Knights of Pythias; member Mosaic Templars. Author (pamplet): A Promise Fulfilled, 1899; Vagaries of a Sub (a serial story), 1909-10. Address: 621 Cheroke Ave., McAlester, Okla.

PETTY, Mary Louise, supervising industrial teacher; born at Ronda, N. C., Feb. 12, 1878; daughter of Hugh and Carolina (Guyn) Hickinson; ed. High Point Normal and Industrial School, N. C., 1897-99; Bennett College, Greensboro, N. C., 1900-1; married Arthur C. Petty, of Roaring River, N. C., Aug. 13, 1902. Began teaching public school, 1901; learned photography and followed that line, 1905-14; supervising industrial teacher, Wilkes County, N. C., since 1914; this branch of public instruction is under the Department of Rural Elementary Schools, State of North Carolina, reaching into the most remote schools and homes of the state; certain artcrafts are taught in the schools, and in the summer months instruction in gardening, canning, etc., is given at the homes; she is also supervisor of several Community Betterment Clubs. Methodist. Address: Ronda, N. C.

PEYTON, Randolph Victor, clergyman; born in Caroline County, Va., Aug. 15, 1863; son of Ananias L. and Mary (Sayles) Peyton; prep. edn. Laws Seminary, Washington, D. C.; D.D., Howard Univ. School of Theology, 1899; married Mary J. White, of Caroline Co., Va., July 17, 1878; 1 adopted child: Annetta V. Ordained Baptist ministry, 1880; opened Mt. Hermon Church, Washington, and pastor 5 years; pastor Mt. Horeh Church, 1885-1901, 6th Mt. Zion Church, Richmond, Va., 1902-11, Mt. Jazreel Church, Washington, 1911-13, and 6th Zion, Richmond, since 1913; a organizer and first president Negro Baptist Old Folks Home. Mason; member Knights of Pythias, Good Samaritans. Author: The Way to Salvation, 1908. Address: 809 N. St. James St., Richmond, Va.

PHILLIPS, Charles Evert, dye house proprietor; born at Kansas City, Mo., May 26, 1889; son of Jack and Eliza (Johnson) Phillips; ed. high school, Champaign, Ill., 1904-7; took course in stenography from International Correspondence School; public speaking course from LaSalle Extension Univ., Chicago; married Juanita Overton, of Champaign, 1909; 1 child: Ester May. Head baggage master for C. C. C. & St. L. Ry. (Big Four Route), at Champaign, 1908-10; in cleaning and dying business at Champaign, 1910-11; proprietor Monticello (Ill.) Dying & Cleaning Co., since 1911. Republican. Missionary Baptist. Life member International Technical Society (I. C. S., Scranton, Pa.); president Champaign Negro Business League. Supreme organizer Pilgrim Knights of the World, and adjt.-gen. Military Dept.; member Knights of Pythias. Home: 602 E. High St. Office: 220 W. Washington St., Monticello, Ill.

PHILLIPS, Charles Henry, bishop; born at Milledgeville, Ga., Jan. 17, 1858; son of George Washington and Nancy Phillips; ed. public schools, Milledgeville; student Atlanta Univ., 1874-8; A.B., Walden Univ., Nashville, Tenn., 1880; M.D., Meharry Medical College, Walden Univ., 1882, A.M., 1885; (D.D., Philander-Smith College, Little Rock, Ark., and Wiley Univ., Marshall, Tex., 1890); married Lucy E. Tappan, of Nashville, Dec. 16, 1880 (died, Jan. 4, 1913); 5 children:

Charles H. Jr. (M.D.,), Jasper T. (M.D.), Lady E. L., Lucy S., Charlotta B. Licensed to preach, 1878; elected bishop, 1902; delegate to Ecumenical Conference on Methodism, Washington, D. C., 1891, London, Eng., 1901, Toronto, Can., and only Negro secretary at that conference, 1911; was president Lane College, Jackson, Tenn., 2 years; editor The Christian Index, 8 years. Author: Phillips History of C. M. E. Church, 1898; contributor to several colored Christian papers. Address: 123 14th Ave. N., Nashville, Tenn.

PHILLIPS, Charles Henry, Jr., physician, surgeon; born at Tullahoma, Tenn., May 5, 1882; son of Rt. Rev. Charles Henry and Lucy Ella (Tappan) Phillips; prep. edn. Lane College, Jackson, Tenn.; student Fisk Univ., 1901; B.Pd., Walden Univ., 1904; M.D., Meharry Medical College (Walden), 1908; married Edna Martha French, of Chicago, Ill., Nov. 10, 1909. Began practice in Tyler, Tex., 1908; continuing, among white and colored patients, to 1910; removed to St. Louis, Mo., July, 1910; since gained wide reputation as an internist and diagnostician; specialist in diseases of women, children and chronic diseases of men; orator and principal speaker before many schools and gatherings. Republican; candidate for Congressional nomination from 12th Dist. Mo., 1912; trailed and stumped against Theodore Roosevelt thru state, Sept. 1912; later Mo. Republican choice for register of U. S. Treasury. Member C. M. E. Church. Fellow American Academy Political and Social Science; member National Medical Assn., Tex. Medical Society, Mo. Medical Society. Mason. Clubs: Fortnightly, Anniversary, Dyonysus. Contributor to New York Medical Journal (white), and number colored papers. Home: 4247 Finney Ave. Office: 2607 Lawton, Ave., St. Louis, Missouri.

PHILLIPS, George W. F., teacher, clergyman; born at Milledgeville, Ga., Feb. 10, 1853; son of Rev. Washington and Nancy (Williamson) Phillips; attended A. M. E. School, Milledgeville, and Lewis High School, Macon, Ga.; grad. Atlanta Univ., 1876; (D.D., Texas College); married Lucy B. Wisham, of Americus, Ga., Apr. 8, 1880. Began as teacher in schools of Jones County, Ga., 1870; principal public schools, Americus, 1880-90; member merchandise firm of Phillips & Phillips, 1889-98; entered the ministry, 1896; pastored several churches to 1907; teacher in Holsey Normal and Industrial Academy, Cordele, Ga., since 1907. Member department of education Colored M. E. Church. Republican. Member National Association Teachers in Colored Schools, Georgia Colored Teachers, Assn. Author (pamphlets): Sea Side Homilies, 1900; The Triumph of Merit, 1913. Home (summers): Americus. Address: Cordele, Ga.

PHILLIPS, James Templeman, institute professor; born at Gaines Cross Roads, Va., June 13, 1877; son of James Strother and Susan (Frances) Phillips; A.B., Va. Normal and Collegiate Institute, 1897; A.M., Va. Union Univ., 1910; took special course in sociology, Univ. of Chicago, 1910; home study in pharmacy and law and passed examination in Va.; qualified to practice both professions; married Julia Withers Lottier, of Pulaski, Va., Sept. 12, 1901; 3 children: Jas. T. Jr., Strother L., Hilda D. Teacher in public schools, Va., 1897-8; professor of English and literature, Va. Normal and Industrial Institlte since 1898; student in problems of health and sanitation; first colored man in Va. to make public address on economic value of health to Negroes; has written number of articles for white and colored papers in interest of educational hygiene and social advancement of Negroes, also with reference to improved inter-racial relations; eligible and acceptable as member Authors' League of America. Republican. Baptist. Member exec. com. Negro Organization Society, Va. Negro Teachers' Assn., School Improvement League (pres. 2 years); member Petersburg City Business League. Author: A Quick Review in English Grammar, 1910; A

Quick Review in English Grammar and Elementary Composition, 1913. Address: Virginia Normal and Industrial Institute, Petersburg, Va.

PHILLIPS, Jasper Tappan, physician; born at Jackson, Tenn., May 17, 1884; son of Rt. Rev. Charles H. and Lucy Ellis (Tappan) Phillips; A.B., Fisk Univ., Nashville, Tenn., 1907; M.D., Meharry Medical College (Walden Univ.), 1913; unmarried. Professor of Latin in Texas College at Tyler, 1908-9; interne George W. Hubbard Hospital, 1912-13; practiced in Nashville since 1913; was first colored man in U. S. to serve as monitor over applicants to practice medicine, and assisted Tennessee State Medical Board of Examiners, 1913-14; vice-pres. Rock City Academy of Medicine and Surgery; director People's Savings Bank & Trust Co. Member Colored M. E. Church. Assistant secretary Nashville Negro Board of Trade. Author (words and music): Meharry Song; Y. M. C. A. Rally Song. Home: 123 14th Ave. Office: 1120 Cedar St., Nashville, Tenn.

PICKENS, Minnie G. McAlpine, music teacher; born at York, Ala., Apr. 17, 1880; daughter of Susie Grant; grad. Lincoln School, Meridian, Miss.; A.B., Tougaloo Univ., 1902; married William Pickens, Aug. 10, 1905; 3 children: William, Jr., Hattie Ida, Ruby Annie. Taught in grades at Lincoln Institute and Talladega College; teacher of music at Wiley Univ., since 1914. Congregationalist. Club: Dunbar (Talladega). Address: Wiley University, Marshall, Texas.

PICKENS, William, teacher; born in Anderson County, S. C., Jan. 15, 1881; son of Jacob P. and Fannie (Porter) Pickens; grad. high school, Little Rock, Ark., 1899; A.B., Talladega College, Ala., 1902; A.B., Yale, 1904; A.M., Fisk Univ., Nashville, Tenn., 1908; married Minnie Cooper McAlpine, of Meridian, Miss., Aug. 10, 1905; 3 children: William, Jr., Hattie Ida W., Ruby Annie. Teacher in Talladega College, 1904-14, at Wiley Univ., Marshall, Tex., since Sept.,

1914. Methodist. Republican. Member Nat'l Assn. for Advancement of Colored People, also various educational assns. Mason; member Odd Fellows, Mosaic Templars. Author: Abraham Lincoln, Man and Statesman, 1909; Frederick Douglass and the Spirit of Freedom, 1912; The Heir of Slaves, 1912; A Visit to the Art Centers of the Old World, 1912. Won the Ten Eyck Prize in oratorical contest, Yale Univ., 1903. Address: Wiley University, Marshall, Texas.

PICKETT, Charles Henry, physician, surgeon; born at Richmond, Va., Aug. 28, 1875; son of Charles H. and Mary Magdeline (Jackson) Pickett; prep. edn. Lewis Institute, Chicago, Ill.; M.D., Univ. of Illniois, 1904; married Mabel Lorena Kerr, of Franklin, La., July 7, 1909 (died June 21, 1913). Began practice in Chicago, 1904; removed to St. Mary's Parish, La., 1905; practiced in adjoining towns of Franklyn and Baldwin about 6 years, in Chicago again, 1911-12; wife's health caused return to South and since practiced in Lafayette, La. Mason; member Odd Fellows, Knights of Pythias, and number other organizations and societies. Address: Box 593, Lafayette, La.

PIERSON, Edward Donahue, publisher, teacher; born in Natchitoches Parish, La., Dec. 27, 1872; son of Lewis and Laurine (Antoine) Pierson; grad., Bishop College College, Marshall, Tex., professional course, 1895, B.S., 1904; married Lizzie L. Spears, of Sumter, S. C.; 3 children: Eulalia V., Theodore D., Edward D. Jr. Began as teacher in rural schools, 1892, continuing to 1896; later taught at Big Sandy, Gilmar, and Pittsburg, Texas; now teacher in Colored High School, Houston; treasurer and mgr. Western Star Pub. Co., Houston, since 1907; president Houston Negro Business League. Deacon, Antioch Baptist Church; secretary State Baptist Young People's Union. Republican. Mason; member Knights of Pythias, United Brothers of Friendship. Home: 318 Robin St. Office: 419 1-2 Milam St., Houston, Texas.

PINHEIRO, Don J., dentist; born at Georgetown, Demerara, B. G., Aug. 8, 1870; son of Henry Fitzherbert and Mary (Simon) Pinheiro; attended Catholic primary school, Georgetown; St. Stanislaus grammar school, British Guiana; came to America, 1902; D.D.S., Howard Univ. Dental College, Washington, 1906; unmarried. Compositor in printing office before graduation; practiced dentistry in Boston since 1906; member National Medical Assn., N. E. Medical, Dental and Pharm. Society. Catholic. Member Odd Fellows (Manchester Unity). Address: 694 Shawmut Ave. Boston, Mass.

PINN, James Luther, clergyman; born at Washington, D. C., May 12, 1877; son of James and Lucy J. (Lucas) Pinn; grad. M Street High School, Washington, 1894, continuing studies there to 1895; Washington Normal School, 1896; grad. Howard Univ. School of Theology, 1902; took course in Central Univ., Ind.; married Olia V. Gaskins, of Warrenton, Va., June 15, 1897; 2 children: James R. C., Luther Conrad. Was assistant principal Manassas (Va.) Industrial School, 1896-7; teacher public schools, Washington, 1 year; ordained Baptist ministry, 1901; pastor Bethany Church, Syracuse, N. Y., since 1902; president Afro-American Welfare Assn.(Syracuse); secretary Onondaga County Baptist Social and Missionary Union, also Onondaga County Baptist Assn., composed of 1 colored and 21 white churches; probation officer in Syracuse. Mason; special district grand deputy Odd Fellows, State of N. Y.; grand prelate New York Knights of Pythias; member Order of Eastern Star, Household of Ruth. Author (pamphlet): The Negro's Place in the Divine Economy. Home: 608 E. Washington St., Syracuse, N. Y.

PLUMMER, Henry Vinton, real estate; born at Hyattsville, Prince Georges Co., Md., Dec. 15, 1876; son of Henry V. and Julia Ann (Lomax) Plummer; his father, now deceased, was appointed in 1884 and served number of years as chaplain 9th Regt. U. S. Cav.; grad. Buffalo High School, Wyo., 1889; grad. and valedictorian class of 125, all others white, High School, Omaha, Neb., 1897; student Omaha Medical College (Univ. of Neb., 1897-1900; married Amanda Belle Smith, of Waterford, Va., Apr. 12, 1912. Tax clerk in Douglass County, Neb., 1897-1910, and the first colored clerk employed in the county clerk's office at Omaha; was admitted to the bar and practiced law in Omaha; in real estate business in District of Columbia and Maryland, 1910-15; now secretary Clarke - Williams - Plumner Co., real estate operators. Republican; was candidate for the state legislature at Omaha, 1894, but practically the whole ticket was defeated; was asst. sergt.-at-arms during the Progressive National Convention, Chicago, Ill., 1912; served on Public Comfort Committee at the inauguration of President Woodrow Wilson, Mar. 4, 1913. Episcopalian. Member Odd Fellows, Knights of Pythias. Home: 1443 S St. N. W. Office: 1346 You St. N. W., Washington, D. C.

PLUMMER, Joseph Henry, dentist; born near Memphis, in Haywood Co., Tenn., 1876; son of Fred and Mollie (Johnson) Plummer; attended district schools in Haywood County; Kortrecht High School, Memphis; student Meharry Medical and Dental College (Walden Univ.), Nashville, Tenn., 3 years; D.D.S., Univ. of Illinois, College of Dentistry, Chicago, 1906; married Gertrude Wallace Carter, of Kansas City, Kan., 1903. Was teacher in district schools of Tenn., before entering college; practiced dentistry in Chicago since 1907. Trustee Negro Fellowship League. Member Illinois National Guard 3 years, serving 2-year term in Hospital Corps. Republican. Methodist. Member National Medical Assn., Illinois State Dental Society, Chicago Dental Society, Lincoln Dental Society (trustee). Mason. Home: 3352 Rhodes Ave. Office: 3401 S. State St. Chicago, Ill.

POE, James W., editor; born in Ashe County, N. C., Feb. 18, 1857; son of Jackson and Emeline Poe; ed. public and parochial schools; Biddle

University, N. C.; student Howard Univ. School of Law, 1893-4. Taught in public schools of N. C., 17 years; was newspaper correspondent for some time; clerk in record and pension office War Dept., Washington, 1890-4; now editor The Reformer at Richmond, Va.; director North Carolin Industrial Assn. Member N. C. House of Representatives, 1882-5; Republican. Member A. M. E. Zion Church. Won prize for poem written on death of President James A. Garfield, which was exhibited at North Carolina Industrial Exposition, 1892. Address: 602 N. 2d St., Richmond, Virginia.

POE, Lavinia Marian, accountant; born at Newport News, Va., Aug. 13, 1890; daughter of Archie Royal and Florence M. (Carter) Fleming; grad. Richmond (Va.) High and Normal School, 1908, Smith's Business College, Lynchburg, Va., Sept. 1, 1908; married Abram James Poe, of Fayetteville, N. C., Sept. 20, 1910; 1 child: Florence Alice. Stenographer for Crown Saving Bank, and E. C. Brown, Inc., Newport News, 1908-12; with Star Printing Co., 1913-14; stenographer and bookkeeper for Grand United Order Sons and Daughters of Peace since Feb. 15, 1914; secretary Newport News branch Negro Historical Assn. Baptist. Home: 2410 Jefferson Ave. Office: 548 25th St. Newport News, Va.

POLLARD, Leslie Lawrence, sporting editor; born at Chicago, Ill., Apr. 30, 1886; son of John William Henry and Amanda Ada (Hughes) Pollard; grad. North Division High School, Chicago; student at Dartmouth College, 1908-10; and was member All-American Football Team. Coach for Lincoln (Pa.) University Football Team, 1913-14. Sporting editor New York News, 135 W. 135th St., New York. Home: 1928 Lunt Ave., Chicago, Ill. (Died by asphyxiation in an accident at New York, Apr. 22, 1915.)

PONTON, Mungo Melanchthon, clergyman, college president; born at Halifax, N. C., May 10, 1860; son of Henry and Rachel (Day) Ponton; A.B., Lincoln (Pa.) Univ., 1888; S. T.

B., Boston Univ., 1891; S. T. B., Morris Brown College, Atlanta, Ga., 1899; (D.D., Wilberforce Univ., 1911); married Annie Marie Shober, of Wilmington, N. C., Dec. 16, 1895 (died 1896); 2d marriage, Ida E. Upshaw, of Washington, D. C., July 16, 1900. Founded Turner Theological Seminary (Morris Brown College), 1896, and was dean of same to 1903; supt. John C. Martin Educational Fund, 1903-6, also since 1912; professor philosophy and Bible, Morris Brown College, 1906-7; pres. Cambell College, Jackson, Miss., 1907-12, Lampton College, 1912-14; stockholder Mound Bayou Oil Mill, Miss. Republican; delegate from 5th Dist., O., and seconded nomination of William McKinley for governor, 1892. Africal Methodist. Member American Geographical Society, American Academy Political and Social Science. Mason. Club: Monday (Atlanta). Author: Religion of Religions, 1897; How to Read the Bible, 1902; My Country, My Home, My Mother and My God, 1906. Address: 34 Johnson Ave., Atlanta, Ga.

POPE, Menry, editor, publisher; born near Bentonia, Miss., Mar. 15, 1881; son of H. L. and Patsy (Williams) Pope; ed. Tougaloo Univ., and Natchez College, Miss.; married Annie L. Baffore, of Coila, Miss., Oct. 8, 1911. Learned printers trade in Canton, Miss., where received instruction from a Yale graduate who had served 11 years in the U. S. printing office at Washington; was foreman in office of the Baptist Reporter at Jackson, Miss.; with present partner, H. T. Sims, investigated opportunity for establishing newspaper at Greenwood; learned that 4 papers had failed in town; they brought out an issue of 1,200 copies of The Negro Star, Apr. 24, 1908, and distributed them free; the circulation in 1914 exceeded 1,200, and the business for the calendar year equalled $5,000. Trustee Greenwood Seminary, McKinney Chapel Baptist Church, and New Zion Baptist Church. Mason; member Knights of Pythias, Woodmen, Sons and Daughters of Jacob. Home: 383

Young St. Office: 309 Johnson St., Greenwood, Miss.

PORTER, Henry Moses, lawyer; born at Aiken, S. C., Nov. 9, 1872; son of Daniel and Jane (Cole) Porter; prep. edn. Scofield Normal School, Aiken; A.B., Atlanta (Ga.) Univ., 1892; LL.B., Univ. of Mich., 1895; married Frances L. Burton, of Augusta, Ga., June 28, 1905. Admitted to Mich bar, 1895, Georgia bar, 1896; member firm Lyons & Porter, 1897-8; practiced individually at Augusta to 1908; was attorney in many important cases for colored people, and first Negro lawyer to obtain reversal of decision before State Supreme Court for any colored person convicted in lower courts of Georgia; practiced in Chicago, Ill., since 1908. Republican; was candidate for Congress from 10th Dist. of Ga., 1904. Mason; member Odd Fellows, Knights of Pythias. Home: 3439 Forest Ave. Office: 720 W. 12th St., Chicago, Ill.

PORTER, Henry Phillip, clergyman; born in Rusk County, Tex., Mar. 15, 1879; son of George and Caroline (Mayfield) Porter; ed. public schools of Rusk County to 1883; student Texas College at Tyler 5 years; married Elnora Brooks, of Rusk County, Nov. 24, 1902; 1 child: Bernice. Entered the ministry, 1896; taught schools in Tex., 1898-1903; pastored number Colored M. E. churches; presiding elder since 1904; member General Educational Board in charge all schools of the church; editor Southwestern Christian Index. Trustee Texas College. Mason. Address: Box 426, Nacogdoches, Texas.

PORTER, Henry Ware, secretary Y. M. C. A.; grad. Theological Dept., Talladega (Ala.) College, 1898; general secretary Branch Y. M. C. A., Christian St. near 17th St., Philadelphia, Pa.

PORTER, John Edward, physician; born at Jeffersonville, Ind., Aug. 1, 1857; son of Otho D. and Mary A. (Austin) Porter; A.B., Fisk Univ., Nashville, Tenn., 1880; M.D., Northwestern Univ., Chicago, 1898; married Mattie Anna Myers, of Chicago,

Dec. 26, 1888; 3 children: Wendell M., Alma D., Ruth M. Began practice in St. Paul, Minn., 1898; now in Okmulgee, Okla. Republican. Congregationalist. Member Odd Fellows, Knights of Pythias, Knights and Daughters of Tabor. Home: 115 E. 2d St. Office: 617 E. Main St., Okmulgee, Okla.

PORTER, Otho Dandrith, physician; born in Logan County, Ky., Dec. 16, 1864; son of Robert Henry and Amanda (Poston) Porter; A.B., Fisk Univ., Nashville, Tenn., 1891; M.D., Meharry Medical College (Walden Univ.), 1894; married Carrie Bridges, of Macon, Miss., Apr. 9, 1895. Taught school in Ky., Tenn., and Tex., before graduation; practiced medicine in Bowling Green, Ky., since 1894; was president People's Grocery Co., several years. Missionary Baptist. Member National Medical Assn. and pres., 1900-1; one of organizers Kentucky Medical Society of Negro Physicians and Dentists. Mason; member Odd Fellows, Knights of Pythias, Court of Calanthe. Home: 439 State St. Office: 227 Main St., Bowling Green, Ky.

POSTON, Ephriam, teacher, verse writer; born at Clarksville, Tenn., Oct. 15, 1865; son of Ephriam and Louisa (Rivers) Poston; grad. Roger Williams Univ., Nashville, Tenn., 1886; married Mollie Cox, of Oak Grove, Ky., Dec. 22, 1887; 7 children: Fred Douglass, Ulysses Grant, Robert T. Lincoln, Ephriam, Roberta, Lillian, Theodore Roosevelt. Began as teacher in schools of Ky., at Wickliffe, 1882; professor at Kentucky Normal and Industrial Institute, 1912-14; principal Pembroke High School since 1914; president Christian County Teachers Assn. Baptist. Mason; member Knights of Pythias, United Brothers of Friendship. Clubs: Forum, City Teachers (pres.). Author: Manual on Parliamentary Proceedings, 1905; Pastorial Poems, 1906; Political Satires, series published in Hopkinsville New Era, 1908-12. Home: 643 Hayes St., Hopkinsville, Kentucky.

POSTON, Mollie, supervising industrial teacher; born at Oak Grove,

Christian Co., Ky., Oct. 1, 1872; daughter of Joseph and Hattie (Peay) Cox; ed. Roger Williams Univ., Nashville, Tenn., M. & F. College, and Hopkinsville (Ky.) Industrial School; married Ephriam E. Poston, of Clarksville, Tenn., Dec. 22, 1887; 7 children: Fred Douglass, Ulysses Grant, Robert T. Lincoln, Ephriam, Roberta, Theodore Roosevelt. Teacher in country and city schools of Kentucky, 1886-1912; one of the first of the 5 supervisors of Negro industrial schools in Ky., appointed July 1, 1913. Baptist. Worthy Counselor, Court of Calanthe. Clubs: Forum, City Teachers. Address: 643 Hayes St., Hopkinsville, Ky.

POWELL, Adam Clayton, clergyman; born in Franklin County, Va., May 5, 1865; son of Anthony and Sallie (Dunning) Powell; grad. Virginia Union Univ., 1892; student Yale Divinity School, 1895-6; (D.D., Va. Union Univ., and Virginia Seminary and College, 1904); married Mattie F. Schafer, of Pratt, W. Va., July 30, 1889; 2 children: Blanche F., Adam Clayton, Jr. Ordained in Baptist ministry, 1892; pastor at Philadelphia, Pa., 1892-3, New Haven, Conn., 1893-1908, Abyssinian Church, New York, since 1908 (this church has more property than any other colored Baptist church in America). Trustee Downingtown Industrial and Agricultural College, Virginia Seminary and College, National Training School for Women and Girls, White Rose Industrial School, Young Men's Christian Assn. Republican. Member National League on Urban Conditions Among Negroes. 32d degree Mason; member Odd Fellows, Knights of Pythias. Author (pamphlets): Immanual Baptist Church, Pastor and Members; Some Rights Not Denied the Negro; The Significance of the Hour; A Plea for a Strong Manhood; A Three-Fold Cord. Home: 255 W. 134th St. Study: 242 W. 40th St., New York.

POWELL, William Frank, diplomat, writer; born at Troy, N. Y., June 26, 1845; son of William and Julia (Crawford) Powell; ed. public schools of New York, Brooklyn and Jersey City; student in School of Pharmacy, New York; also student Lincoln Univ., Pa.; grad. N. J. Collegiate Institute, 1865; (LL.D., Lincoln Univ., 1907); married Elizabeth M. Hughes, of Buckingham, N. J.; 2d marriage, Jennie B. Shepard, of Philadelphia, Oct. 20, 1898. Appointed by Presbyterian Board of Home Missions to school for Freedmen at Leesburg, Va., 1868; later opened first state school for freedmen in Alexandria, Va.; principal school at Bordertown, N. J., 1875-81; bookkeeper in U. S. Treasury, Washington, 1881-2; elected district superintendent of schools, Camden, N. J., 1884; introduced manual training in public schools and since in successful operation there; instructor in civic government, ancient and modern history and physicology, Camden High and Training School (white), 1886-94; refused consular appointments, 1881 and 1891; E. E. and M. P. to Haiti, 1897-1905; also American charge d'affaires to Santo Domingo, June 29, 1897 to June 20, 1905; editorial writer with the Philadelphia Tribune since 1909. Served in U. S. Navy short term in 1860. Episcopalian. Member National Educational Assn. of Teachers', Philadelphia Civic League, Camden Business Men's Assn., Literary Society. 33d degree Mason. Club: Camden Democratic. Home: 572 Clinton St., Camden, N. J.

PRENTICE, Bessie E., teacher, business woman; born at Nashville, Tenn., Dec. 23, 1872; ed. public schools at Columbia, Tenn., Roger Williams and Fisk universities at Nashville; married James M. Phentice, of Birmingham, Ala., May 3, 1908; 1 child. Taught in schools of Tenn., Ky., and Iowa for 18 years; removed to California, 1910; partner with husband in dry goods, notions, millinery and clothing business, under name of Prentice New Idea Store, since 1911. African Methodist. Member Pride of the West Circle, California Federation of Woman's Clubs, Mutual Aid Society. Home: 849 Hemlock St. Office: 1324 E. 9th St., Los Angeles, Calif.

PRENTICE, James M., merchant; born in Bibb County, Ala., Mar. 12, 1868; son of Frank and Mary Prentice; common school edn.; married Bessie E. Porter, of Nashville, Tenn., May 3, 1908; 1 child. Worked at blacksmithing and moulding trades in Ala., Ky., Iowa, and Calif., for 29 years; partner with wife in Prentice New Idea Store, at Los Angeles, since 1911. Republican. African Methodist. Home: 849 Hemlock St. Office: 1324 E. 9th St., Los Angeles, California.

PRICE, Charles Richard, dentist; born at Memphis, Tenn., July 21, 1885; son of Joseph Richard and Viney (Demer) Price; grad. high school, Wichita, Kan., 1905; D.D.S., Meharry Dental College (Walden Univ.), Nashville, Tenn., 1913; married Goldie I. Burton, of North Vernon, Ind., Dec. 26, 1912; child: William Charles. Was brought from Memphis to Wichita when 7 years old; mother's illness prevented him attending school from 1905 until entered college in 1909; worked in private family 13 years; practiced dentistry in Wichita since Sept. 15, 1913. Elected director Colored Y. M. C. A., 1909, president since Feb., 1915; vice-pres. John Brown Literary Society; trustee Tabernacle Baptist Church. Republican. Member Knights of Pythias. Home: 915 N. Wichita St. Office: 601 N. Main St., Wichita, Kan.

PRICE, Elida Ann, social worker; born at Chatham, Ont., Canada, Nov. 25, 1859; daughter of Wilson and Jane (Brown) Williams; attended public schools in Chatham; took academic course at New Castle, Pa.; married William W. Price, of Vienna, O.; 7 children. Was charter member (1897) and now corresponding secretary Phillis Wheatley Home Assn.; founded and was first pres. Ruth Mite Missionary Society; organized Busy Bee Literary and Charity Club of Young Women; president Woman's Council; vice-pres. Self-Denial Club; recording secretary Lydian Assn.; past worthy princess, Sisters of Mysterious Ten; assisted in writing constitution of the Scholarship Fund Club; member Golden Rule Circle of King's Daughters; was honorary vice-pres. Lincoln-Douglass Memorial services, Feb. 12, 1915. African Methodist. Home: 818 Beaubien St., Detroit, Mich.

PRICE, Harriet Kilson, teacher, retired; daughter of Alfred and Julia C. (Grandison) Green, both free, who settled in their own home at Cleveland, O., when married, 1853, in which house Harriet was born, Jan. 8, 1868; grad. Central High School, Cleveland Normal School, 1890; married LeRoy J. Price, of Richmond, Va., June 30, 1897. Teacher in public schools of Cleveland 24 years; associated with missionary, charitable, temperance and literary societies more than 30 years; was strong supporter of Woman Suffrage movement. President Thurman Woman Christian Temperance Union; member Mt. Zion Congregational Church Missionary Society, Cleveland Benevolent Assn., Order of Eastern Star. Home: 3324 Cedar Ave., Cleveland, Ohio.

PRICE, William James Monroe, clergyman; born at Nicholsville, Ky., Oct. 8, 1867; son of Napoleon and Josephine (Monroe) Price; public school edn. Nicholsville; (LL.D., McKinley Memorial Univ., Vincennes, Ind., 1913; D.D., State Univ., Louisville, Ky., 1915); married Della M. White, of Lawrenceburg, Ky., Feb. 10, 1902; 1 child: William James Monroe, Jr. Ordained in Baptist ministry at Louisville, 1893; pastor, Lancaster, Ky., 1894, Bloomington, Ind., 1896-7, Sharpsburg, Ky., 1897-9, Ashland, 1900, Lawrenceburg, 1901-4, Maysville, 1904-6, Georgetown, 1906-9; pastor First Baptist Church, Henderson, Ky., since 1909; president State Sunday School Convention. Trustee M. & F. College. Mason; member Odd Fellows, Knights of Pythias, United Brothers of Friendship. Home: 434 Gabe St., Henderson, Ky.

PRILLERMAN, Byrd, institute president; born in Franklin County, Va., Oct. 19, 1859; son of Franklin and Charlotte Prillerman; B.S., Knoxville (Tenn.) College, 1889; A.M., Westminster College, New Wilming-

ton, Pa., 1895; married Mattie E.
Brown, of London, W. Va., July 24,
1893; 4 children: Delbert McCullough,
Henry Lawrence, Ednora Mae, Myrtle Elizabeth. President the West
Virginia Colored Institute, at Institute, since Sept. 23, 1909; owner of
a farm and other property. Trustee
National Training School for Women
and Girls, Washington, D. C. Was
alternate delegate to Republican National Convention, Chicago, Ill., 1904.
Member National Educational Assn.,
since 1891; life member National Association Teachers' in Colored Schools.
Address: Institute, W. Va.

PRINCE, George Washington, physician; born at Clarksdale, Miss.,
Dec. 28,, 1878; son of George W. and
Ann (Lewis) Prince; student Alcorn
(Miss.) Agricultural and Mechanical
College, 1900-4; Meharry Medical College (Walden Univ.), Nashville,
Tenn., 1904-5; M.D., Northwestern
Univ. Medical School, Chicago, 1908;
post-graduate work at Vienna, Austria,
1914-15, and received diploma; unmarried. Teacher in public schools
of Miss., 1895-1900; clerk in postoffice
at Chicago, Ill., 1907-8; in practice
since 1908; was proprietor Relief
Pharmacy, Chicago, 1909-10; part
owned South Side Drug Store, 1910-
11. Republican. Baptist. Member
Physicians, Dentists and Pharmacists Club of Chicago. Address: 3502
State St., Chicago, Ill.

PRIOLEAU, George W., chaplain
United States Army; born at Charleston, S. C., May 15, 1856; son of Rev.
Lewis S. and Susan A. (Smith) Prioleau; ed. Avery Institute at Charleston; B.D., Wilberforce (O.) Univ.,
1884 (D.D., 1895, a degree which was
finally repudiated by the faculty,
1910); married Anna L. Scoville; 2d
marriage, Ethel S. Stafford, of Kansas
City, Kan., Feb. 20, 1905. Teacher
public schools of S. C., 1876-8;
licensed to preach in A. M. E. Church,
1879; pastor at Double Springs Mission, 1 year, Selma, O., 1881-4, Yellow Springs, 1885, Hamilton, 1885-7,
Troy, O., 1887-8; professor of church
history and homiletics at Payne Theo-

logical Seminary, Wilberforce, 1889,
and pastor Trinity Chapel; member
New Orleans Conference, 1890-2, in
charge Springfield District; delegate
to General Conference, 1892; pastor
Xenia, O., 1893-5. First colored man
to serve as chaplain in mixed garrison of U. S. Army; was appointed by
President Grover Cleveland to 9th
Cav., with rank of captain, 1895; was
special recruiting officer during Spanish-American war; served with the
9th Cav. in Philippine Islands 4 years;
with the regt. in Texas, 1911, and on
the border of Mexico in Arizona, 1912-
14; sharpshooter. Republican. Mason; member Odd Fellows. Address:
War Department, Washington, D. C.

PROCTOR, Henry Hugh, clergy-
man; born at Fayetteville, Tenn.,
Dec. 8, 1868; son of Richard and
Hannah Proctor; public school edn.,
Fayetteville; A.B., Fisk Univ., Nashville, Tenn., 1891; B.D., Yale Divinity
School, New Haven, Conn, 1894; (hon.
D.D., Clark Univ., Atlanta, Ga.,
1904); married Adeline Davis, of
Nashville, Aug. 16, 1893; 4 children:
Henry Hugh, Mureil Morgan, Lillian
Steele, Cravath Vaslite. Pastor Congregational Church at Atlanta, Ga.,
since ordained in 1894. Trustee Carrie Steele Orphanage. Club: Monday. Home: 183 Courtland Ave., Atlanta, Ga.

PURNELL, Fillmore Rider, editor;
born at Newport, R. I., Apr. 13, 1868;
son of Joseph and Susan Jane
(Brown) Purnell; public school edn.,
Providence; married Laura J. Harris, of Providence, Mar. 21, 1892; 2
children: Frances, Marion. Organized the Douglass Afro-American
Press Agency, Providence, 1899, sole
owner since 1904; founder of The
Advance, 1906, owner and editor;
pres. Providence Negro Business
League, 7th Ward Colored Real Estate Assn.; dir. Watchman Industrial
School. Republican. Member Irre-
proachable Beneficial Assn. Mason;
member Odd Fellows. Home: 157
Waldo St. Office: 910 Westminister
St., Providence, R. I.

R

RAGLAND, Fountain Gage, clergyman; born at Talladega, Ala., 1856; son of George and Fannie Ragland; grad. Talladega College, 1884; later took special courses; married Addie Stephens, of Montgomery, Ala., Nov. 29, 1876; 6 children. Ordained Congregational ministry, 1884; pastor at Mobile 2 years, Wilmington, N. C., 1896-1902, First Cong'l. Church, Birmingham, Ala., since 1902; part owner Ragland's Pharmacy; was the first president of Mobile Mutual Insurance Co. Republican. Member Ministerial Union, Birmingham, also Knights of Pythias. Address: 1115 8th Ave., Birmingham, Ala.

RAILEY, Howard Hannabal, teacher; born at Charlottsville, Va., Dec. 27, 1867; son of John and Susan (Bowles) Railey; high school edn., Charlottsville; grad. W. Va. Colored Institute, 1896; married F. Donnally Brown, of Institute, W. Va., Nov. 28, 1900. Began as teacher public schools, Nuttallburg, W. Va., 1896; principal Simmons Graded School at Montgomery since 1900. Republican; was member West Virginia House of Representatives, 1905-7. Baptist. Mason; member Knights of Pythias. Address: Montgomery, W. Va.

RANDOLPH, Virginia Estelle, supervising industrial teacher; born at Richmond, Va., June 8, 1875; daughter of Nelson and Sarah Elizabeth (Carter) Randolph; edu. in the Baker Public School, and Richmond Normal School; special work at Virginia Normal and Industrial Institute one year. Was first supervising industrial teacher under the State Board of Education; began in one room building called Mountain Road School, 1897, which is now used as a museum and some of the products of the children in all schools in her district are exhibited there; it is visited by people from many parts of the United State; school board erected new building and changed name to Virginia Randolph School; now supervisor of Negro Schools in Henrico and Alexandria counties; children are taught to make baskets, do pine needle and cone work, mend, sew, cook, gardening, canning, to be economical and self-supporting; the work in the state is now in charge of 32 supervisors; aided by the Anna T. Jeanes Fund, this branch of public instruction reaches the most remote schools and homes in the state; she has helped to establish the system in Alabama, North Carolina and other southern states; was first to observe Arbor Day in colored schools and her first program is preserved in the State Library building at Richmond. Baptist. Home: 813 Moore St., Richmond, Va.

RANKIN, James Warren, clergyman; born near Demopolis, Ala., Nov. 14, 1859; son of James Monroe and Charlotta (Connor) Rankin; public school edn.; honorary D.D., but not a graduate from any college; married Mary A. Hampton, of Forsyth, Ga., May 26, 1880; 3 children. General secretary and treasurer Missionary Dept. A. M. E. Church. Mason; member Knights of Pythias, Odd Fellows, Elks, and other organizations. Home: 275 Taaffe Place, Brooklyn. Office: 61 Bible House, New York.

RANSOM, Freeman Bailey, lawyer; born at Grenada, Miss., July 7, 1884; son of Clem and Louise Ransom; grad. Walden Univ. Law Dept., Nashville, Tenn., 1908; read law at Columbia, Md.; student Columbia Univ., New York; married Nettie L. Cox, of Jackson, Miss., July 31, 1912; 1 child: Frank B. Admitted to Ind. bar, 1910; member firm of Browden & Ransom, Indianapolis, 1910-12; practiced alone since Jan. 1, 1912; attorney for Colored Y. M. C. A., Madam. C. J. Walker Mfg. Co., Dr. E. N. Perkins Cream Float Soap Mfg. Co., Indianapolis branch National Assn. Advancement Colored People; attorney and director Frederick Douglass Life Ins. Co. Republican. African Methodist. Mason; member Knights of Pythias. Home: 828 N. California St. Office: 46 N. Pennsylvania St., Indianapolis, Indiana.

RANSOM, Reverdy Cassius, clergyman, editor; born at Flushing, Ohio,

Jan. 4, 1861; son of George W. and Hattie (Johnson) Ransom, both free; attended public schools, Cambridge, O.; prep. edn. Oberlin College, 1882-3; B.D., Wilberforce Univ., 1886 (D.D., 1897); married Emma S. Conner, of Selma, Ohio, Oct. 25, 1887; 2 children: Harold G., Reverdy C. Jr. Licensed to preach in A. M. E. Church, 1883; ordained elder, 1888; was pastor at Selma, O., 1885-6, Altoona, Pa., 1886-8, Alleghaney, Pa., 1888-90, Springfield, O., 1890-3, Cleveland, O., 1893-6, Chicago, Ill., 1896-1904, New Bedford, Mass., 1904-5, Boston, 1905-7, New York, 1907-12; now editor the A. M. E. Church Review, elected at Kansas City, Mo., 1912. Trustee Wilberforce Univ. Author: School Days at Wilberforce, 1892; published address and orations: Robert G. Ingersoll; William Lloyd Garrison; John Brown; Charles Sumner; Wendell Phillips, and others. Home: 437 W. 35th St., New York. Office: 631 Pine St., Philadelphia, Pa.

RAPHAEL, The Very Reverend Father, priest, apostle, confessor; born at Chapelton, Clarendon, Jamaica, B. W. I.; son of Robert Josias and Mary Ann (Johnson) Morgan; was born 6 months after his father's death and named Robert Josias Morgan; his new baptismal and ecclesiastical name is Raphael; the family name of Morgan has been dropped and should never be used in addressing him; received elementary edn. in native land; left Jamaica when a boy for Colan; later went to British Honduras, back to Jamaica, and to the United States. Began missionary work in Germany; later went to England and from there sent to the Church Missionary Society Grammar School at Freetown, Sierra Leone, W. Africa; studied Greek, Latin and other higher branches of learning; was also second master in a public school at Freetown; took course in the Church Missionary Society College at Fourah Bay in Freetown; appointed a missionary teacher and lay-reader under Rt. Rev. Samuel David Ferguson, bishop of the Protestant Episcopal Church in Liberia; after a num-

ber of years in W. Africa he returned to England and took up course of private studies. From England he came to America and worked among colored people, continuing as lay-reader; was accepted as a Postulant and candidate for Holy Orders in the Protestant Episcopal Church; during canonical period of waiting before ordination returned to England and was a student at Saint Aidan's Theological College, Birkenhead, and finally prosecuted his studies for Holy Orders at King's College, Univ. of London. Returned to America and was ordained to the Protestant Episcopal ministry, in the diocese of Delaware; appointed honorary curate in St. Matthew's, Wilmington; also taught in different public schools in Delaware. For many years he maintained serious doubts concerning the teachings of the whole Anglican Communion; the change that came over him resulted in more than 3 years special study of Anglicanism; he also studied the standards and formularies, and examined the dogmas and doctrinal teachings found in the Roman and Greek Catholic churches; it was his final conviction that the Holy Greek Orthodox Catholic and Apostolic Church is the pillar and ground of the truth; he therefore resigned from the Protestant Episcopal Church and entered upon an extensive tour Abroad; he spent a long time in Russia visiting the convents, monasteries, cloisters and abbeys of the Holy Orthodox Catholic Church; after the foreign tour he studied in America under Greek priests about 3 years. He returned to Europe and received baptism by trine immersion by an archbishop of the Throne of the Holy See of Constantinople, and was confirmed with Holy Chrism in the presence of 3,000 people of the white race; in regular order of succession, at different times, he was ordained sub-deacon, deacon and priest; afterwards at a special service he was duly commissioned Priest-Apostolic from the Ecumenical and Patriarchal Throne of Constantinoble to America and the West Indies. He has resided in Palistine, Syria, Joppa, Greece, Cyprus, Mitylene, Chios, Sicily, Crete, Egypt, Russia, Turkey, Austria, Germany, England, France, Scandanavia, Belgium, Holland, Italy, Switzerland, Bermuda and the United States; he is associated with the Greek Orthodox Catholic Church in Philadelphia, and is the only priest of African descent of that denomination in the world; founder and superior of the Order of the Cross of Golgotha, a religious fraternity. Care should be taken to address all letters to him only as follows: The Very Reverend Father Raphael, Priest-Apostolic, The Greek Orthodox Catholic Church, Poste Restante, Philadelphia, Pa.

RATHEL, Otis Alfonso, commercial teacher; born at Vicksburg, Miss., Sept. 1, 1890; son of Smith Westbrook and Mamie Jane (Black) Rathel; attended public schools at Vicksburg to 1907; grad. Oberlin (O.) Business College, 1911; unmarried. Teller in Lincoln Savings Bank, Vicksburg, 1907-10; private secretary to W. E. Mollison, a lawyer, 1911, to former register of the Treasury, W. T. Vernon, 1912; secretary Campbell College, Jackson, Miss., since 1912. Republican. African Methodist. Member Knights of Pythias. Address: Campbell College, Jackson, Miss.

RAY, Harvey Cincinnatus, agriculturist, farm demonstration agent; born, Bunceton, Mo., Feb. 2, 1889; son of George and Catherine (Davis) Ray; public school edn., Bunceton; grad. Lincoln Institute, Jefferson City, Mo., 1911; post-graduate course Tuskegee Normal and Industrial Institute, Ala., 1913; special work in vocational education and dairying at Kansas State Agricultural College, Manhattan; unmarried. Began as director of agriculture at Langston Univ., Okla., 1912, continuing 3 years; United States farm demonstrator agent in Pulaski County, Ark., since Feb. 1, 1915. African Methodist. Mason. Address: 904 Broadway St., Little Rock, Arkansas.

RAYSOR, Charles Luke, lawyer; born at Honea Path, S. C., May 27, 1882; son of Charles and Emma (Dix-

on) Raysor; ed. public schools at Honea Path to 1900, Brewer Normal School, Greenwood, S. C., 1900-4, Wheaton (Ill.) Academy, 1904-7; student Howard Univ. School of Law, Washington, 1897-8; LL.B., Boston, Univ., 1911; unmarried. Admitted to Mass. bar, 1911; since practiced in Boston. Republican. Baptist. Member the Elks. Home: 32 Seattle St., Allston. Office: 15 Court Square, Boston, Mass.

RAZAFKERIEFO, Paul Andrea, composer, verse writer; born at Washington, D. C., Dec. 16, 1895; son of Henry and Jennie (Waller) Razafkeriefo; father was a Malagasy nobleman, mother eldest daughter of John L. Waller, former U. S. consul to Madagascar. At age of 17 composed first song, "Baltimo," which was sung by member of "The Passing Show of 1913" at Winter Garden, New York. Poems: "Wired, Hired, Fired" (an expression of grief and sorrow that color bars one fitted to position); "Jack Johnson" (touching on defeat with honor). While his work shows a character of its own, the composition is remindful of the late Paul Laurence Dunbar. Address: 70 W. 142 St., New York.

READ, Edward Parker, physician, founder Sanatorium; born at Keysville, Va., 1868; son of Alexander F. and Frances C. Read; attended public school and studied under private tutors; M.D., Baltimore Univ., 1889; received degree Doctor of Refraction, Philadelphia Optical College, 1899; (Ph.D., Princenton (Ind.) Normal and Industrial Univ., 1914); married Martha A. Irving (died, 1907); 2d marriage, Alphonsenia Smith, of Lawnside, N. J., 1910. Began in employ of Dr. Matau's Hospital and College Kingsville, Va.; opened first drug store ever conducted by colored people in Petersburg, Va., 1889; performed operation which gained prominence as physician for women and children; was medical examiner for Consolidated Benefit Assn., Provident Life Assn., Galilean Fishermen, Good Templars, and True Reformers, 1890; founded Assurance and Redemption

Assn., in Va.; opened drug store in Philadelphia, Pa., 1891; manufactured medicines and toilet preparations; established Eclectic Optical Institute and Eureka Sanatorium Assn., Inc., Lawnside N. J. Founded Town of Readville, N. J., 1903; began opening of Readstown, Md., 1905; opened brush and broom factory, Philadelphia, 1907, Baltimore, 1909; has interest in number enterprises. Published (books): How, Where and When to Incorporate, 1895; Geographical Distribution of the Races of Men and Animals, 1896; Buy and Borrow of Ourselves, 1897. Wrote treatise of 50th Anniversary of Negro Freedom 1913; arranged Eureka Perpetual Calendar (Copyright, 1904). Sanatorium: Lawnside, N. J. Office and Drug Store: 1715 South St., Philadelphia, Pa.

READ, George Isaac, teacher; born at Chattanooga, Tenn., Feb. 7, 1886; son of Isaac and Mary (Smith) Read; attended public school, Chattanooga, to 1905; grad. Swift Memorial College, Rogersville, Tenn., 1907; A.B., Lincoln Univ., Pa., 1911; married Rosa Bradley, of Rogersville, Aug. 20, 1913; 1 child: George, Jr., Principal of Smallwood School,, York, Pa., since Aug. 28, 1911. Republican. Presbyterian. Member Knights of Pythias. Won the Bradley gold medal for proficiency in natural science, Lincoln Univ., 1911. Address: 531 S. Queen St., York, Pa.

REED, Harry Gibson, clergyman, editor; born at Beaufort, S. C., 1855; son of Rev. G. and Martha (Ward) Reed; ed. public schools, Beaufort, S. C., and Fla.; married Matilda Wallace, of Beaufort, 1877; 3 children: Walter, Sarah, Julia. Ordained Baptist ministry, 1892, since pastor in Jacksonville, Fla.; editor Jacksonville Sunday School Lesson. Home: 1003 W. Adams St. Office: Adams and Lee Sts., Jacksonville, Fla.

REED, John Hamilton, vice-consulgeneral, educator; native of America; grad. New Orleans Univ., 1891; married; 2 children: Walter, Florence. Began as teacher at Prairie View, Tex.; was professor of mathematics,

Wiley Univ., several years; entered M. E. ministry, secretary Texas Annual Conf., 10 years; transferred to Little Rock Conf., Ark.; pastor Wesley Chapel 4 years; a $30,000 church edifice erected there stands as the best monument of his efforts in the ministry; appointed by board of foreign missions M. E. Church to educational work in the College of West Africa at Monrovia, Liberia, 1905. Vice-consul-general to Liberia since June 15, 1908; appointed by President Daniel E. Howard, of Liberia, as principal of Caroline Donovan Normal and Industrial Institute, Grand Bassa County, Feb., 1914; visited U. S., 1914, to interest organized financial agencies in the institute, also to purchase supplies and equipment for the school. Address: Monrovia, Liberia, W. Africa.

REED, J. Henry, clergyman, editor, publisher; born in Nelson Co., Va., 1868; son of Edward and Ardelia Reed; grad. Peoples' School, Springfield, Mass., 1899; while in the army attended U. S. Post Schools; grad. in topography class, 1893; married Cornelia J. Johnson, of Schuyler, Va., Dec. 25, 1904; 3 children: Johnnie W., Pauline, Philip N. Served in Troup I, 10th U. S. Cav., 1888-96; enlisted as private; promoted to non-commissioned officer, 1890; was expert drill-master 5 years. Baptist minister and publisher church paper, 1898-1908; founded and now president Valley College, Luray, Va.; organized Valley College Glee Club; pres. National Valley Educational Assn.; owner and editor the Colored Churchman. Republican. Author: The Hell Train. Address: P. O. Drawer 377, Luray, Virginia.

REID, Charles Martin, physician; born at Montègo Bay, Jamaica, British West Indies, Apr. 1, 1882; son of William J. and Ann (Finegan) Reid; prep. edn., Port Limon, Costa Rica, Central America; came to America, 1903; M.D., Leonard Medical School (Shaw Univ.), Raleigh, N. C., 1908; M.D., and C.M., McGill Univ., Montreal, Canada, 1911; speaks English, French and Spanish; unmarried.

Practiced medicine in Hare Valley, Va., since Nov. 1, 1912; has won honors and prizes during professional courses in U. S., Canada, and before State Licensing Board of Va. Baptist. Member National Medical Assn. Mason. Address: R. F. D. No. 1, Box 23, Exmore, Va.

REID, Orleanis, teacher; born at Boydton, Va., Oct. 19, 1875; son of James Alfred and Lucy Ellen Reid; ed. public schools, Boydton, to 1887, and E. Richland, Ohio, 3 years; was first colored grad. St. Clairsville High School, Ohio, 1896; grad. Wilberforce Univ., 1899; married Lillian Nix, of Allendale, S. C., 1903; 3 children: Minnie, Edith, Lee. Learned printers' trade, also carpentry; assistant prin., 1899-1912, principal since 1912, New Harden Academy, Allendale. Ruling elder 2d Presbyterian Church, Allendale. Member Odd Fellows, Knights of Pythias, Court of Calanthe. Address: Box 338, Allendale, S. C.

REYNOLDS, James Richard, teacher; born in Rockingham Co., N. C., Feb. 12, 1870; son of Henry Anderson and Julia Ann (Feuill) Reynolds; A.B., Bennett College, Greensboro, N. C., 1895, A.M., 1898; took engineering course American School of Correspondent (Armour Institute), Chicago, Ill.; (Ph.D., Wiley Univ., 1914); married Anna B. Scott, of Staunton, Va., Sept. 20, 1900; 6 children: Arlene, Theresa, Richard, Marion, Margarette, Harry. Teacher in Bennett College, 1895-8; principal Oxford Acad., N. C., 1888-9; teacher public schools, Winston-Salem, 1905; prin. public schools, Reidsville, 1905-9; professor of mathematics Wiley Univ., 1909-11; led group of students who won prize for preparing college algebra key; as electrical engineer constructed lighting plant for Wiley Univ., also installed lighting system in Boley, Okla., largest Negro town in U. S.; secretary and gen.-mgr. Boley Light & Power Co. Methodist. Composer: Hadenopsis (poems), 1891; contributor of articles on High Cost of Living to Southwestern Christian Advocate, also New York Independent. Address, Baldwin, Louisiana.

REYNOLDS, John Douglas, newspaper correspondent; born at Cincinnatti, Ohio., Nov. 14, 1869; son of Ezekiel Pemilton and Caroline Pender (Stewart) Reynolds; public school edn., Sandusky, O.; grad. private school of penmanship, lettering, engrossing, and portraiture; married Parthenia Rollins, of Oxford, O., May, 1886; 1 child. Evelyn. In service of Pullman Company 26 years; staff correspondent with California Eagle since 1913. Republican. Member Church of Christ; also member Odd Fellows, Foresters. Compiler (32-page pamplet): The Scrap Book of Tips on the Race Problem, 1913. Address: 1966 Raymond Ave., Los Angeles, California.

RHEA, Hiawatha W., newspaper man; born at Tuscumbia, Ala., Dec. 30, 1870; son of Jordan and Sallie (Cooper) Rhea; ed. public schools, Tuscumbia; Hyde Park High School, Chicago, Ill.; student Univ. of Chicago, 1890-2; unmarried. Began active career as salesman of drugs, later in other lines; secretary Chicago Lodge No. 43, Elks, 3 years; with American Publishing Co., 1897-8, King Richardson Co., 1899-1901; solicitor for Pan.-American Baking Co., 1902-3, Knickerbocker Club, 1904-5; later with Chicago Conservator Publishing Co., Ill., Chronicle Pub. Co., Robertson Young Bond & Realty Co.; associate editor The Illinois Idea; writer of short stories and poems; compiler of Rhea's Colored Citizens Directory of Chicago and Suburbs, 1908, Rhea's New Citizens Directory of Chicago, 1910. Christian Scientist. Home: 6607 Eberhart Ave. Office: 21 E. 28th St., Chicago, Ill.

RHONE, Daniel Nelson, teacher, real estate agent; born at Opelousas, St. Landry Parish, La., Feb. 27, 1873; son of Marcellus and Celia (Gay) Rhone; grad. Howe Institute, New Iberia, La., 1898; student at Leland Univ., New Orleans, 1899-1902; married Elma Dupree, of Crowley, La., Mar. 6, 1902; 3 children: Felton J., Mildred E.; Elma Viola (died 1910). Principal of Crowley Grammar School since 1903; real estate agent for

Crowley Bank & Trust Co., Bank of Arcadia, and Rayne State Bank; owns home and other property valued at $6,000; manager Mercantile Company; director People's Investment Co., Ltd. Baptist; superintendent Israelite Church Sunday School. Member Arcadia Parish Teachers' Institute; secretary Will of the East Lodge No. 6402, Odd Fellows. Address: Crowley, La.

RICHARDS, William Henry, lawyer, university prof.; born at Athens, Tenn., Jan. 15, 1856, of free parentage. preparatory edn. Warner Institute, Jonesboro, Tenn; LL.B., Howard Univ. Law School, Washington, D. C., 1881, LL.M., 1882; unmarried. Lecturer in law dept. Howard Univ., since 1890; professor the law of evidence, personal property and international law. President Howard Univ. Union Alumni Assn., 1889-1908, Bethel Literary and Historical Assn., 2 terms. Republican; was alderman 2 terms and mayor 1 term, Athens, Tenn. Member American Historical Assn., American Academy Political and Social Science. Home: 525 Florida Ave. N. W. Office: 420 5th St. N. W., Washington, D. C.

RICHARDSON, Arthur St. George, bank cashier, former educator; born at St. Georges, Bermuda, July 5, 1863; son of Samuel Painter and Mary Elizabeth (Algate) Richardson; attended public schools in Bermuda; grad. St. John (N. B.) High School; A.B., Univ. of Brunswick, 1886; married Sarah A. Johnson, of Chatham, Ont., Can., July 19, 1893; 2 children: Arthur St. George, Robert Maxwell. Was president Wilberforce Institute, Chatham, Ont., 1886-7; came to the U. S., 1887; president Morris Brown College, Atlanta, Ga., 1888-98, Edward Waters College, Jacksonville, Fla., 1898-1902; was teller with banking firm of S. H. Hart & Son's, Jacksonville, 1902-5; deputy collector of internal revenue at Jacksonville, 1909-13; assistant cashier in Metropolitan Savings Bank, Ocala, Fla., since 1913; assistant secretary Metropolitan Realty & Investment Co. Republican. African Methodist. Home: 761 W. Church St., Jack-

sonville. Office: Metropolitan Savings Bank, Ocala, Fla.

RICHARDSON, William Howard, concert soloist; born at Liverpool, Nova Scotia, Aug. 23, 1869; son of Joseph Henry and Sarah Ann (Young) Richardson; public school edn., Boston, Mass.; private pupil of George H. Woods, Stephen S. Townsend, and in Arthur J. Hubbard Vocal School; married Minnie A. Williams, of Plymouth, Mass., June 3, 1892; 3 children: Howard I., Percy L., Elba. Baritone soloist Bethany Baptist Church, Boston, 1898-1902, St. Peter's Episcopal Church, Cambridge, Mass., since 1902 (both white); sings modern songs, Negro melodies, and operatic selections at concerts, afternoon teas and recitals; teacher of voice since 1910. Served 9 years in Mass. Vol. Mil. Republican. Episcopalian. Home: 2 Phillips St. Studio: 224 Tremont St., Boston, Mass.

RICHARDSON, William Reuben, clergyman, physician, optician; born at Athens, Ala., Apr. 20, 1866; son of Reuben and Caroline (Lane) Richardson; B.D., State Univ., Louisville, Ky., 1898; M.D., Louisville National Medical College, 1908; Prof.Sc., Institute of Science, Rochester, N. Y.; unmarried. Ordained Baptist ministry, 1890; pastored churches at Brandenburg, Partridge, Greencastle, Prospect and Louisville, Ky.; now pastor 1st Baptist Church at Winchester, Ky.; clerk of state executive board, 1898-1912, and 1st assistant moderator, 1914-16, of the General Association of Kentucky Baptists; agent for National Baptists Foreign Mission Board, U. S. A., for Ky., Tenn., and Ala. Was professor of Hebrew, Greek and theology, State Univ., Ky., 1899-1903; professor of anatomy, Louisville National Medical College, 1909-12; went to Nicaragua, Central America, as commissioner for National Baptists Convention, and appointed as special physician under the Spanish government, and private physician for family of Senor Don Adolpho Campo, governor of Corn Island, Nicaragua. Republican. Mason, Knight Templar;

member Foresters. Home: 2215 Standard Ave., Louisville, Ky.

RICKS, Edgar Ethelred, clergyman; born at Raleigh, N. C., Sept. 15, 1877; son of Harry and Martha whose maiden name was also Ricks; attended St. Augustine School, Raleigh; public school, Washington; grad. Howard Univ. School of Theology, 1901; married Mrs. Lucinda E. Robinson, of Va., June, 1901; 1 child: Helen. Assistant to pastor of 19th St. Baptist Church, Washington, while student in Howard Univ.; ordained Baptist ministry, 1901; pastor St. Philip's Church, 2 years, St. John's Church, 5 years; pastor 1st Baptist Church, Washington, since 1907; his sermon at funeral services of Henry L. Holmes, former commissioner of revenue, Alexander Co., Va., was published in pamphlet form. President Alumni Association School of Theology Howard Univ.; trustee Stoddard Baptist Old Folk's Home, Anti-Saloon League of D. C.; board member Lott Cary Foreign Mission Conv.; member advisory board Alley Improvement Assn.; Odd Fellows Hall Assn.; ex-vice-pres. Christian Endeavor Union. Republican. Member Young Men's Protective League. 32d degree Mason. Address: 1523 Church St. N. W., Washington, D. C.

RIDDICK, Diamond Matthew, real estate; born at Creswell, N. C., Feb. 4, 1873; son of Richard and Emily (Reeves) Riddick; ed. N. C. State Normal School; married Loney A. Overton, of Elizabeth City, N. C., Apr. 1, 1908; 2 children: Alice, Milton. Worked on father's farm to age of 18; farm foreman for M. M. Alexander, 3 years; removed to Boston, Mass., 1894; in real estate business, W. Summerville, Mass., since 1912; chairman investment board Harding, Cox & Martin real estate syndicate. Progressive. Methodist. Mason. Address: 69 A., Elmwood St. W. Somerville, Mass.

RILEY, Franklin Wilbert, clergyman; born in St. Helena Parish, La., 1868; son of Harrison and Margaret Riley; ed. Straight Univ., New Orleans; Livingstone College, Salisbury, N. C.; grad. Talladega College, Ala., 1910; married Ella L. Rempson, of Demopolis, La., Dec., 1902 (died 1909); 1 child: Franklin W. Jr. Converted in Straight Univ., 1886; licensed to preach in A. M. E. Church, 1888; ordained deacon, 1890, elder, 1891; pastored churches in Scranton, Miss., Little Rock, Ark., Talladega; built Pettys Chapel, New Orleans; presiding elder Troy District of Ala., since 1910. Address: Troy, Ala.

RILEY, John Gilmore, principal high school; born at Tallahassee, Fla., Sept. 24, 1857; son of James and Sarah (Wells) Riley; private and public school edn. in Fla.; classical course Oxford Univ., England; married Nellie Vaughn, of Tallahassee, Apr. 4, 1879; 5 children: Dr. James B., Sarah E., Marion, John G., Jr., Emlin. Began as teacher public schools at Tallahassee, 1879; principal since 1893; director Masonic Temple, Jacksonville. Republican. Methodist. 32d degree Mason; grand high priest Royal Arch Masons of Fla. Address: Tallahassee, Fla.

RINGER, Thomas Tazzell, supervising industrial teacher; born in Troup County, Ga., May 5, 1884; son of Rev. Miles L. and Mollie (Philpot) Ringer; attended public schools in Troup County to 1904; prep. edn. Snow Hill Normal and Industrial Institute, Ala., 1904-8; married Cora P. McMillan, of Laurinburg, Scotland Co., N. C., June 22, 1911; 1 child: Belle Christine. Began as head teacher in academic dept. Laurinburg Normal and Industrial Institute, 1908, continuing to 1911; teacher at Franklin, Ga., 1 year; taught one term in Colored Training School, Faison, N. C.; supervising industrial teacher in colored schools of Duplin County since 1913; this branch of public instruction includes artcrafts in the schools, gardening and domestic sciences at the homes; it reaches the most remote schools and homes of the state; he has been instrumental in bringing about many improvements in the schools; organized the Industrial and Improvement League of

Faison. Baptist. Mason. Address: Faison, N. C.

ROBERTS, Carl Glennis, physician; born in Hamilton County, Ind., Dec. 15, 1886; son of John A. and Nancy E. (Simpson) Roberts; grad. Fairmont (Ind.) High School, 1905; student Chicago College of Medicine and Surgery, 1907-11; M.D., Valpariaso Univ., 1911. Practiced in Chicago since 1911; staff physician to German-American Hospital, 1912-13, Lincoln Hospital, 1913-14. Republican. Episcopalian. Member American Medical Assn., Illinois State Medical Assn., Chicago Medical Society, Physicians, Dentists and Pharmacists Clubs of Chicago. Member Knights of Pythias, United Brothers of Friendship, Mosaic Templars, Foresters. Address: 1130 Wells St., Chicago, Ill.

ROBERTS, Frederick Madison, editor, publisher; born at Chillocothe, Ohio, Sept., 1879; high school grad., Los Angeles, 1900; A.B., Colorado College, Colorado Springs, 1906, Barnes School of Mortuary and Sanitary Science, 1910; unmarried. Deputy assessor in El Paso County, Colo., 2 years; was publisher of the "Light" (a weekly newspaper) in Colorado Springs, 1897-1900; established the New Age in Los Angeles, 1914; owns interest in real estate and investment companies; member undertaking firm of A. J. Roberts Sons & Co. Baptist. Mason; member Odd Fellows, Knights of Pythias, Elks, Foresters, United Brothers of Friendship. Home: 1154 S. Los Angeles St. Office: 829 San Pedro St., Los Angeles, Calif.

ROBERTS, James Henry, lawyer; born at Maury City, Tenn., July 20, 1876; son of William and Judia (Spence) Roberts; prep. edn. Roger Williams Univ., Nashville, Tenn.; A.B., Fisk Univ., 1906; student Law Dept. Univ. of Chicago, 1910-12; LL.B., John Marshall Law School, 1913; married Andia M. Hoard, of Okmulgee, Okla., May 31, 1914. Teacher and principal in schools of Tenn., Ark., Mo., and Okla., 15 years; connected with Teachers' Normal Institute of Tenn., 3 years; was secretary Oklahoma State Teachers' Assn., 2 years, Baptist State Educational Board 3 years. Admitted to Okla. bar, 1913; since practiced in Tulsa; member firm of Martin & Roberts. Progressive. Missionary Baptist. Home: 609 N. Elgin Ave. Office: 102 N. Greenwood Ave., Tulsa, Okla.

ROBERTS, Nicholas Franklin, university professor; born at Seaboard, N. C., Oct. 13, 1849; A.B., Shaw Univ., Raleigh, N. C., 1876, A.M., 1879 (D.D., 1885); post-graduate course Univ. of Chicago, 1909; married Mary S. Chavis, of Union, N. C., June 8, 1904; 6 children: John N., Peter F., Mamie, Benjamin A., Amelia L., Richard J. Professor in Shaw Univ., since 1876; member board of mgrs. Missionary Educational Conv. of N. C. Trustee Thompson Institute, Lumberton, N. C.; was member Wake County Board of Education 3 years. Republican; served as alderman, City of Raleigh, 2 years. Baptist. Address: 728 S. Blount St., Raleigh, N. C.

ROBINSON, John Eustace, editor; born at Charlotte C. H., Va., Feb. 24, 1876; son of John and Eliza Robinson; ed. public schools of Va., and New York; unmarried. Began as clerk in a Broadway steamship office, New York, 1897, continuing to 1912; city editor Amsterdam News since June, 1912. Secretary executive committee National Progressive party. Methodist. Mason; member Elks. Home: 244 W. 64th St. Office: 17 W. 135th St., New York.

ROBINSON, Joseph Patterson, clergyman; born at Hernando, Miss.; son of Joe Robinson; ed. Arkansas Baptist College, Little Rock, Ark., (hon. A.M.; D.D., State Univ., Ky.; LL.D., Bible School of Philadelphia); married Amanda T. Talley, of Nashville, Tenn., Feb. 22, 1893. Missionary Baptist. Author (sermons and sermonettes): Catholicism Exposed. Trustee Arkansas Baptist College. Republican. Address: 613 W. 7th St., Little Rock, Ark.

ROBINSON, Lelia Walker, hair culturist; born at Vicksburg, Miss., June 6, 1885; daughter of Mme. C. J. Walker; her mother's maiden name was

Sarah Breedlove, who married Moses McWilliams when 14 years of age and who was a widow at 20; edu. at Knoxville College, Tenn; married John B. Robinson, Oct. 18, 1909. Began in office with her mother at Denver, Col., 1905; a year later that office was closed and they traveled about 2 years; by personally introducing the preparation for growing hair, orders began to be received by mail and an office was opened in Pittsburgh, Pa., 1908; took charge of the business there while mother again traveled and sold the product; now manager the New York office of Madam C. J. Walker Mfg. Co. Address: 108 W. 136th St., New York.

ROCK, William Elijah, editor, publisher; born at Pine Brook, N. J., Jan. 22, 1861; son of Peter and Emma (Schanck) Rock; grandfather came from Africa and settled in N. J., 1700; ed. public schools, Pine Brook; private instruction under Prof. John R. Porter, New York; read law in office of T. W. Throckmonton, Red Bank, N. J., 8 years; married Annie O. Bowles, of Red Bank, Feb. 14, 1894; 3 children: Leroy, Arnold, Rose. Editor and prop. The Echo since 1904; established in Long Branch, N. J., with capital of $50; later removed to Red Bank; plant now valued at more than $3,000, also owner of home clear of debt. Republican. Episcopalian. Member National Negro Press Assn., National Negro Business League, Knights of Pythias. Address: 166 Beach St., Red Bank, New Jersey.

ROGERS, Amsiah, teacher; born in Union Co., Miss., Dec. 27, 1884; son of Whitfield and Sallie (Kelley) Rogers; attended public school Union Co.; grad. Colored High School, New Albany, Miss.; A.B., Rust Univ., Holly Springs, Miss.; married Willie Jones, Feb., 1904 (died 1912); 2 children: Sammie L., and Blanch; 2d marriage, Minnie Allen, of Metropolis, Ill., Apr. 18, 1914. Worked for neighboring farmer to pay way through college; accepted a pig for his wages, which brought forth litters of young; the money from their sale, with further aid of parents and friends, made his education possible. Began as teacher in public schools, Jameson Grove, Miss., 1903; principal New Albany Colored High School. Methodist. Address: New Albany, Miss.

ROMAN, Charles Victor, physician, surgeon; born at Williamsport, Pa., July 4, 1864; son of James William and Anna Walker (McGuinn) Roman; brought up in Canada; prep. edn. Hamilton Collegiate Institute, Ont.; M.D., Meharry Medical College (Walden Univ.), Nashville, Tenn., 1890; post-graduate work Post-Graduate Medical School and College, Chicago, Ill., Royal London Ophthalmic Hospital, and Central London Nose, Throat and Ear Hospital, in England; (A.M., Fisk Univ.; LL.D., Wilberforce Univ.); married Margaret Lee Voorhees, of Columbus, Tenn., 1891. Practiced in Dallas, Texas, to 1904, and Nashville, Tenn., since 1904; was first colored physician to specialize in medicine and surgical practice with the eye, ear, nose and throat south of the Ohio river; professor of eye, ear, nose and throat diseases in Meharry College; editor Journal of the National Medical Assn.; director One Cent Savings Bank. African Methodist. Former president National Medical Assn.; member American Academy Political and Social Science, Southern Sociological Congress; also member Odd Fellows, Knights of Pythias. Author (pamphlets): Eye, Ear, Nose and Throat Formulary, 1909, for use in Meharry Medical College; Racial Solidarity, 1911; Science and Christian Ethics, 1913; Dethronement of a King, 1913; wrote proceedings of Southern Sociological Congress, 1913, 14. Contributor to newspapers and magazines. Home: 130 14th Ave. N. Office: 1303 Church St., Nashville, Tenn.

ROSS, George Gallious, lawyer, newspaper mgr.; born at Leavenworth, Kan., May 18, 1879; son of George Gallious and Vina B. (Johnson) Ross; grad. high school, Las Vegas, N. Mex., 1896, and at Colorado Springs, Col., 1899; LL.B., Howard Univ. School of Law, 1904; married Gertie Nichols, of Denver, Col., Dec. 7, 1910. Practiced in Denver since 1904; secretary, manager and associate editor the Denver Star, which merged the former Statesman and Independent newspapers; secretary Lucky Seven Gold Mining & Milling Co. Trustee Scott M. E. Church, and supt. Sunday School 2 years. Republican. Member Odd Fellows, Knights of Pythias. Home: 2344 Tremont Place. Office: 209 Kittredge Bldg., Denver, Colo.

ROSS, Hubert Washington, dentist; born at New Haven, Conn., Feb. 18, 1874; son of John William and Mary Julia Ross; grad. Hopkins Preparatory School, 1894; student Yale Medical School, 1899-1901; D.M.D. Harvard Dental School, 1904; unmarried. Practiced in Boston, Mass., since 1904; member Harding, Cox & Martin Real Estate Syndicate. Congregationalist. Member National Medical Assn., N. E. Medical, Dental and Pharm. Assn., Mass. Dental Society. Mason; member Elks. Address: 830 Tremont St., Boston, Mass.

ROSS, James Alexander, lawyer, editor; born at Columbus, Ky., Feb. 7, 1867; son of David and Mary (Waters) Ross; father resides in Cairo and is one of the most wealthy colored men in Illinois; ed. in Catholic and public schools, St. Louis, Mo., and Carbondale, Ill.; read law in office of Judge J. C. Nermille 3 years; married Cora B. Paul, of London, Can., Feb. 24, 1897; 3 children: Mary, Michael, Doris. Clerk in law office 2 years; taught schools in southern Illinois and Camden, Ark.; editor and prop. The Reformer, Detroit, Mich., since 1911; publisher Gazetteer and Guide, monthly magaines, Buffalo, N. Y.; associated in practice of law with John O. Herbold, white; in real estate and mortgage loan business; pres. Rossview Park. Was in charge the Negro exhibit at Pan-American Exposition, Buffalo, 1901; confidential clerk to Norman B. Mack, the chmn. N. Y. State Commission Panama-Pacific Exposition, San Francisco, Cal., 1915. Identified with Democratic National Committee since 1900; was

vice-president in charge the National Colored Democratic League Bureau, Chicago, 1912; recommended for the office of recorder of deeds for District of Columbia, 1915; has declined number of political positions, including U. S. consul appmt. to Cape Haitien in 1893. Home: 97 Florida St. Office: 39 E. Chippewa St., Buffalo, N. Y.

ROSSER, Luther E. B., clergyman, relief officer; born at Hogansville, Ga., Feb. 1, 1870; son of Lindsy and Anna (Sewell) Rosser; public school edn., Merriweather Co., Ga.; student at Paine College, Augusta, Ga.; studied law at Howard Univ., Washington, D. C., 2 terms; married Martha Clark, of Tarboro, N. C., Nov. 30, 1895. Entered Methodist ministry, 1889; pastored at Macon, Ga., Greenville, Tex., Washington, D. C., Humboldt, Tenn., Shreveport, La.; delegate to Ecumenical Conference on Methodism, Toronto, Can.; was in government service at Washington, 1907-14; secretary Ministerial Relief Assn. of Colored M. E. Church since 1914. Republican. Mason; member Odd Fellows, Knights of Pythias, Elks. Home: Washington, D. C. Office: Jackson, Tenn.

ROYALL, John Mabery, real estate operator; born in Halifax County, Va., Dec. 16, 1874; son of Pinkney and Lucy Royall; attended public schools at White Oak, Va.; student Virginia Normal and Industrial Institute, Lynchburg, 5 years; took course in Virginia Collegiate Institute, Petersburg; married Pauline Crawford, of Richmond, Va., Jan. 1, 1914. Began with H. J. Heinz Co., in New York, 1902; palace car porter 5 years; in real estate and insurance business, New York, since 1907; owner of several houses and about 100 lots, and agent for owners of large property interests; president Bronz-Brooklyn Corporation, also New York Syndicate; chairman Playground Committee of Harlem. President Negro Business League City of New York, Negro Civic League of New York (political body); vice-president New York County Committee of National Progressive Party; was candidate for Alderman from 21st Assembly District, 1913. One of organizers Lafayette Presbyterian Church, Jersey City, N. J. Member Southern Beneficial League, Clubman's Beneficial League. Mason. Contributor to New York News, Amsterdam News. Address: 21 W. 134th St., New York.

RUSH, Gertrude E. Durden, lecturer, playwright; born at Navasota, Tex., Aug. 5, 1880; daughter of Rev. Frank and Sarah E. (Reinhardt) Durden; ed. high schools, Parsons, Kan., and Quincy, Ill.; took course in Westerman Music Conservatory, Des Moines, Iowa; A.B., Des Moines College, 1914; married James B. Rush, of Des Moines, Dec. 23, 1907. Teacher in government district schools in Okla., 4 years, public schools at Oswego, Kan., 3 years; lecturer since 1911; dramatized Paradise Lost under title of "Satans Revenge". President board of directors Iowa Federation Home for Women and Girls; identified with Associated Charities in interest of poor colored people; organized Woman's Law and Political Study Club, Dramatic Art Club, Colored Woman's Suffrage Club; delegate to National Educational Congress at Denver, Colo., 1912; delegate to Half-Century Exposition of Negro Emancipation at Philadelphia, and member legislative committee to secure appropriation for Iowa Negro Exposition, 1913. Republican. Baptist. Member Order Eastern Star. Author: Sermon on the Mount, 1907; Uncrowned Heroines, 1912; Black Girls Burden, 1913. Composer (songs): If You But Knew; Jesus Loves the Little Children; Christmas Day. Address: 1547 20th St., Des Moines, Iowa.

RUSH, James Buchanan, lawyer, born near Pekin, Montgomery Co., N. C., Apr. 19, 1861; son of George W. and Sylvia Rush; prep. edn. Fayetteville State Normal School, Va.; LL.B., Howard Univ., 1886; married Gertrude E. Durden, of Parsons, Kan., Dec. 23, 1907. Began as editor The Peoples Sentinel, Greensboro, N. C., later teacher in school at Wadesboro and Winston; admitted to Ind. bar, 1892; practiced in Indianapolis, 1892-4, Ft.

Smith, Ark, 1895-8, Des Moines, Ia., since 1898; counsel for North Star Temple Assn., organized to purchase business blocks for enterprises conducted by colored people in Des Moines; vice-president Des Moines Business League. Trustee Corinthian Baptist Church. Delegate to Republican State Conventions; campaign speaker for U. S. Senator Albert B. Cummins, 2 years. Mason. Home: 1547 20th St. Office: 317 Locust St., Des Moines, Ia.

RUSSELL, Alfred Pierpont, Jr., dentist; born at S. Norfolk, Va., Sept. 18, 1881; son of Alfred P. and Joanna (Trotman) Russell; preparatory edn. St. Paul Normal and Industrial School, Lawrenceville, Va.; S.B., Howard Univ., Washington, D. C., 1905; D.M.D., Harvard, 1908; married, Nov. 16, 1910, Mabelle C., daughter of Dr. George Franklin Grant, who was a prominent dentist in Boston, Mass.; 2 children: Lillian A., Inex J. Began practice in Boston, 1908, and became successor to father-in-law upon his death in 1910; conducted clinic on invitation of Massachusetts Dental Society officials at golden anniversary ceremonies held in Boston, May, 1914, with "Some Phases and Results of Cleft-Plate Treatment of Dr. George F. Grant" as the subject. Republican. Episcopalian. President St. Mark Musical and Literary Union; director Security Benefit Assn.; member National Dental Assn., Mass. Dental Society, Wendall Phillips Memorial Assn., Harvard Alumni Assn., Odd Fellows. Home: 706 Columbus Ave. Office: 5 Park Square, Boston, Mass.

RUSSELL, Frank Greenleaf, merchant; born at S. Norfolk, Va., Sept. 5, 1883; son of Alfred P. and Joanna (Trotman) Russell; brother of Dr. Alfred Pierpont Russell; student Howard Univ., Washington, 3 years; grad. Norfolk Mission College, 1910; unmarried. In mercantile business in Norfolk since 1910; director Berkley Citizens Mutual Building & Loan Assn., Hiawatha Beneficial and Social Assn.; journalist and critic for Phyllis Wheatley Literary Society of Berkley; member Aeolian Social and Beneficial Society, Negro Organization Society of Va., Colored Business Assn., Tidewater. Republican. African Methodist; chorister of choirs in St. James Church and active in Sunday School work. Member Knights of Pythias. Home: 30 Third St. Office: 230 St. James St., S. Norfolk, Va.

RUSSELL, Harvey Clarence, teacher; born at Bloomfield, Ky., June 7, 1883; son of George and Maranda (Davenport) Russell; during war between the states his father served in U. S. Vols.; grad. Ky. Normal School, Frankfort, 1905; A.B., Eckstein-Norton College, Ky., 1910; student Univ. of Chicago, summers, 1909, 10; special student in pedagogy Miami Univ., O., 1911; married Harriet V. Tucker, of Louisville, Ky., Aug. 20, 1913; 1 child: Anna H. Principal public school, Bloomfield, 1905-10; head instructor in dept. of pedagogy Ky. Normal School, Frankfort, 1910-14; teacher in Colored Normal School, Louisville, since 1913; instructor in teachers' institute, summers, 1912, 13, 14; editor for Ky. Association of Colored Teachers; vice-pres. People's Pharmacy, Frankfort; part owner of produce business with Howard Russell, Bloomfield. Baptist. Member Odd Fellows; state grand secretary United Brothers of Friendship. Address: 1029 W. Madison St., Louisville, Ky.

RUSSELL, Green Pinckney, educator; born in Logan County, Ky., Dec. 25, 1863; son of Green and Frances Winnie (Goteer) Russell; attended public schools at Russellville, Ky.; B.L., Berea College, 1890; (A.M., Wilberforce Univ., 1913, LL.D., 1913); married Lida E. Wills, of Nashville, Tenn., Aug. 15, 1895; 2 children: Birdie F., Willie P. Teacher district school, Chilesburg, Ky., 1880-90; principal Fourth Street (now Russell) School, Lexington, 1890-6; board of education in Lexington created the office of Supervisor of Negro Schools for him, 1896, in which position he served to 1912; president Kentucky Normal and Industrial Institute at Frankfort since 1912; now ex-officio member board of trustees. Baptist.

Member Kentucky Educational Assn., Association of Principals' of Agricultural and Mechanical Colleges. Mason; member Odd Fellows, Knights of Pythias. Address: Normal Hill, Frankfort, Ky.

S

SALLEY, William Henry, supervising industrial teacher, clergyman; born in Mecklenburg Co., Va., Dec. 22, 1867; son of James and Fanny Salley; attended public school, Mecklenburg County; grad. Thyne Institute, Chase City, Va., 1897; took manual training course at Hampton Normal and Agricultural Institute; married Susan Wilson, of Chase City, Sept. 21, 1898; 4 children: Grace L., Wallicia E., Willie Alberta, Woodrow Halley S. Ordained Baptist ministry, 1897; began teaching public school, 1898; supervising instructor in Rural Colored Schools, Mecklenburg County, since 1909. Trustee Keystone Industrial School. Prohibitionist. Member Virginia Colored Teachers' Assn., Mecklenburg County Teachers' Assn., Negro Organization Society. Address: R. F. D. No. 2, Chase City, Va.

SAMPSON, John Patterson, clergyman; born at Wilmington, N. C., Aug. 13, 1837; son of James Drawhorn and Fannie (Kellogg) Sampson; grad. Comer's College, Boston, Mass., 1856; LL.B., National Law Univ., Washington, 1868; student Western Theological Seminary, Allegheny, Pa., 1868-9; (D.D., Wilberforce Univ., 1888); married Marianna Cole, of Bordentown, N. J., Sept. 10, 1889; 1 child: John P., Jr. Teacher public school at Jamaica, Long Island, N. Y., 1858-60; as editor Colored Citizen in Cincinnati, O., during war between the states, advocated enlistment of colored men in army; clerk in Freedmen's School, Wilmington, N. C., 1865, and later served as assessor; was nominated for congress in 1867; clerk in the Treasury, Washington, 1867-77; took active part in civic affairs during reconstruction period. Admitted to bar at Washington, 1873, and practiced for 5 years; judge in Civil Court, 1876-81. Licensed to preach, 1882; pastor A. M. E.

Church, Bordentown, N. J., 1883-5, Orange, 1885-7, Trenton, 1887-9, and was chaplain N. J. House of Representatives; pastor at Asbury Park, Atlantic City, Princeton, N. J., and Philadelphia, Pa., 1889-93; presiding elder Harrisburg and W. Philadelphia Dists., 1894-1901, and in New England Conference 9 years; pastor Pittsfield, Mass., 1910-11, North Adams, 1911-12, Morristown, N. J., since 1912; was delegate general conferences, 1888, 92, 96, 1900. Organized Ironside Industrial School at Bordentown, N. J., and its first president; president Frederick Douglass Hospital, Philadelphia, 5 years. Republican. Author (pamphlets): Temperment and Phrenology of Mixed Races, 1881; Disappointed Bride, 1883; How to Live One Hundred Years, 1909; Jolly People, 1911. Home: 59 Spring St., Morristown, N. J.

SATTERWHITE, James King, clergyman; born at Satterwhite P. O., Granville Co., N. C., Sept. 7, 1880; son of Harry and Amy Ann (Wilkerson) Satterwhite; grad. St. Augustine's Collegiate Institute, Raleigh, N. C., 1906, Bishop Payne Divinity School, Petersburg, Va., 1909; unmarried. Priest in charge Episcopal Missions, Winston-Salem and Greensboro, N. C., 1909-13; rector St. Ambrose Church, Raleigh, N. C., since 1913. Mason. Address: Box 221, Raleigh, N. C.

SCARBOROUGH, William Sanders, university president; born at Macon, Ga., Feb. 16, 1854; son of Jeremiah and Frances Scarborough; preparatory edn. Atlanta (Ga.) Univ.; A.B., Oberlin College, Ohio, 1875, A.M., 1878; (Ph.D., State Univ. Louisville, Ky.;LL.D., Liberia College, W. Africa; A.M., Morris Brown College, Atlanta, 1908; married Sarah C. Bierce, of Danby, N. Y., Aug. 2, 1881. Professor of Greek, Wilberforse Univ., 1877-91, Hellenistic Greek, Payne Theological Seminary, 1891-5; professor of Greek, head of classical dept., and vice-president, 1895-1908, and president since 1908, Wilberforce Univ. Delegate to Ecumenical Conference on Methodism at London, Eng., 1901; attended Universal Race Congress. Trustee Lincoln Memorial Assn., Ohio, and only colored man on the board. Member Archaeological Institute of America, American Philological Assn., American Academy Political and Social Science, American Social Science Assn., American Negro Academy, American Dialect Society, American Folk-Lore Society, National Geographical Society. Author: First Lessons in Greek, 1881; Theory and Functions of the Thematic Vowel of the Greek Verb; Our Political Status, 1884; Birds of Aristophanes, A Theory of Interpretation, 1886. Address: Wilberforce, Ohio.

SCHOMBURG, Arthur Alfonso, teacher of Spanish; born, San Juan, Porto Rico, Jan. 24, 1874; son of Charles and Mary (Joseph) Schomburg; elementary edn., San Juan; student St. Thomas College, Danish West Indies; grad. Institute de Instruccion, San Juan, P. R.; read law in office of Gen. Roger A. Pryor, 5 years; married Elizabeth Hatcher, of Staunton, Va., June 30, 1895; 2 children: Arthur A., Kingsley; 2d marriage, Elizabeth Marrow Taylor, of Williamsburg, N. C., Mar. 17, 1902; children: Reginald S., Nathaniel T. Served 5 years as sec. Las Dos Antillas Cuban Revolutionary party; came to America, Apr. 17, 1891; member Porto Rico Revolutionary party, New York, 1891-6. Teacher of Spanish in New York since 1896; secretary and treas. Negro Society for Historical Research, Yonkers, N. Y.; co-editor "Murray's Enclopaedia of the Colored Race;" wrote monograph entitled "Placido," 1905. Contributor to African Times and Orient Review (London), The Crisis (New York). Member American Negro Academy, of Washington, D. C.; hon. member Men's Business Club (Yonkers); treas. Loyal Sons of Africa (New York); past master Prince Hall No. 38, F. A. M., and Rising Sun Chapter No. 4, R. A. M.; P. C. D. C. of the Grand Lodge of New York. Home: 63 W. 140th St. Office: Bankers Trust Co., 16 Wall St., N. Y.

SCOTT, Duncan Jackson, merchant; born at Savannah, Ga., Sept. 29, 1880;

son of Duncan S. and Susan M. (Myers) Scott; public school edn., Savannah; A.B., Fisk Univ., Nashville, Tenn., 1904; married Rachel Dolores Pries, of Savannah, Feb. 18, 1914. Merchant in Savannah since 1904; wholesale dealer in ice cream. Trustee Carnegie Colored Library. Episcopalian. Member Savannah Negro Business League. Mason; member Knights of Pythias, United Brotherhood of America. Address: 529 Park Ave., Savannah, Ga.

SCOTT, Edward E. clergyman; born at Gallatin, Miss., May 23, 1866; son of Edward and Mary (Presley) Scott; prep. edn. Tougaloo Univ., Miss., and student in theological dept., 1889-90; grad. Howard Univ. School of Theol., 1892; married Rachel J. Pepper, of Vaughan, Miss., Oct. 31, 1894; 6 children. Apprentice in blacksmithing, wagon-making and carriage trimming while in Tougaloo; in the business for self, Madison, Miss., 1 year; pastor in 3 small Miss. churches, 1892; pastor Congregational Church, Brewton, Ala., 1892-4, Nashville, Tenn., 1894-6, Shelby, Ala., 1896-1904; pastor First Congregational Church, Montgomery, Ala., since 1904; instructor in State Normal School since 1908; was sec. Congregational Assn. of Ala., 10 years, and its moderator in 1908. Prohibitionist; registered voter. Member Capital City Ministers' Union. Wrote: What Has Been the Progress of the Negro, and other articles for the American Missionary. Address: 510 S. Union St., Montgomery, Ala.

SCOTT, Emmett Jay, editor; born at Houston, Tex., Feb. 13, 1873; son of Horace L. and Emma (Kyle) Scott; public school edn., Houston; student Wiley Univ., Marshall, Tex. (A.M., 1905); married Eleonora J. Baker, of Houston, Apr. 14, 1897; 5 children: Emmett, Jr., Evelyn, Clarissa, Lenora, Horace. Began as secretary Tuskegee (Ala.) Normal and Industrial Institute, 1897; now editor the Tuskegee Student; associate publisher Negro Year Book; member advisory board Standard Life Insurance Co.; appointed as member American Commission to Li-

beria, 1909, by President William H. Taft. Was secretary National Negro Business League, and of the International Conference on the Negro at Tuskegee Institute, 1912, 15. Republican. Methodist. Mason; member Mosaic Templars. Address: Tuskegee Institute, Ala.

SCOTT, Isaac Franklin, teacher; born near Lexington, Ky., 1868; son of Isaac and Henrietta (Johnson) Scott; brought up in Macoupin Co., Ill.; attended public school at Shipman, and high school at Alton, 1 year; student Parsons College, Fairfield, Iowa, 3 years; A.B., Fisk Univ., Nashville, Tenn., 1892; married Inez Clement, of Paris, Tex.; 1 child: Clement; 2d marriage, Ruby L. Saddler, of Guthrie, Okla., 1897. Began teaching school at Jerseyville, Ill., 1892; now teacher of science at Raver High School, Guthrie, Okla. Republican. Congregationalist. Mason; member Odd Fellows. Home: 524 E. Grant St., Guthrie, Okla.

SCOTT, Isaiah Benjamin, bishop; born in Woodford Co., Ky., Sept. 30, 1854; son of Benjamin and Polly (Anderson) Scott; student Clark Seminary (now Clark Univ.), Atlanta, Ga., 1874-7; A.B., Central Tennessee College (now Walden Univ.), Nashville, Tenn., 1880, A.M., 1883; studied theology, 1880-1; (D.D., New Orleans Univ., 1893); married Mattie J. Evans, of Franklin, Tenn., May, 1881. Entered Tennessee Conference, M. E. Church, transferred to Texas Conference, and was professor in Prairie View State Normal and Industrial College, 1881; pastor, Houston, Galveston, Austin, and Marshall, Tex., 1882-7; presiding elder, Marshall and Houston districts, 1882-93; president Wiley Univ., Marshall, 1893-6; editor Southwestern Christian Advocate, New Orleans, 1896-1904; elected bishop of Liberia, 1904, and is only colored bishop in M. E. Church. Elected to General Conference, 1888, 92, 96, 1900, 04, by Texas Annual Conference; delegate to Ecumenical Conference on Methodism, Washington, D. C., 1891, London, Eng., 1901, Toronto, Can., 1911. Home:

125 14th Ave. N., Nashville, Tenn. Address: Monrovia, Liberia, W. Africa.

SCOTT, John Jay, banker, undertaker, clergyman; born at Alton, Ill., June 13, 1860; son of Thomas and Sarah Jane (Poe) Scott; prep. edn. Rust Univ., Holly Springs, Miss.; B.S., 1892, graduate theol. dept., 1894, at Fisk Univ., Nashville, Tenn.; studied at Chicago Theological Seminary; married Kate V. De Jarnette, of Montgomery, Ala., Aug. 1, 1898; 3 children: Alma, Robert D., John J., Jr. Ordained Congregational ministry, 1895; pastor at Montgomery, Ala., 1896-7, Knoxville, Tenn., 1899-1900; chaplain at Agricultural and Mechanical College, Normal, Ala., 1900-3; was chaplain with rank of captain in 3d Ala. Vols. during Spanish-American war; member undertaking firm of Scott-Wilkerson & Scott, established 1903; president Fraternal Savings Bank & Trust Co., since 1910. Trustee Sanderlins Academy, at Whites, Tenn., Orphans and Old Folks Home, Memphis. Republican. Mason; member Odd Fellows, Knights of Pythias, Mosaic Templars, Royal Circle, Immaculates. Home: 1240 Race St. Office: 358 Beale St., Memphis, Tenn.

SCOTT, William Alexander, clergyman, fraternal order pres.; born at Port Gibson, Miss., Jan. 2, 1870; son of William and Eloise (Humphrey) Scott; public school edn. in Miss.; A.B., Hiram (O.) College, 1898; (Ph.D., McKinley Memorial Univ., Vincennes, Ind., 1904); married Emmeline Southall, of East Liverpool, O., Apr. 12, 1900. Minister of the Church of Christ since 1898; now pastor Farish Street Christian Church in Jackson, Center Church at Hermanville, and Lorman Church, all in Miss.; president Mississippi Christian Missionary Convention, also Miss. Christian Ministerial Assn.; state evangelist of Mississippi Christian Women Workers Convention; editor Christian Reformer, official publication Church of Christ in Miss.; also editor Calanthe Journal; grand worthy counsellor, and president the endowment board, Excelsior Grand Court of Calanthe of the State

of Miss. Proprietor the Progress Printing House; director Union Guaranty & Ins. Co. Member Jackson Negro Business League. Mason; member Odd Fellows, Knights of Pythias. Author (pamphlet): Evangelization of the Negro Race. Home: 918 N. Farish St. Office: 705 N. Farish St., Jackson, Miss.

SCOTT, William Edoward, artist; born at Indianapolis, Ind., Mar. 11, 1884; son of Edward M. and Caroline (Russell) Scott; graduated Manual Training High School, Indianapolis, 1903; studied in Art Institute of Chicago, 1904; student, Julian Academy, 1912, Colloriesse School, Paris, France, 1913; pupil of Henry Ossawa Tanner, of Trepied-par-Etaples, France. Painter of religious and character pictures; has about 20 mural paintings in schools of Indianapolis, Ind., and Evanston, Ill.; exhibited in Europe, 1910, 11, 12, in Salon, Paris, 1912, 14. Awards: two poster prizes, 1904; Frederick Magnus Brand prizes, Art Institute of Chicago, 1907, 8, 9; scholarship, Toquet, France, 1914; Tanquery prize, Salone de Picardie, Paris, 1914; sold picture to government of Argentine Republic; won honorable mention at the Salon in Paris. Address: 1124 N. Senate Ave., Indianapolis, Ind.

SCRUTCHIN, Charles W., lawyer; born at Richmond, Va., Sept. 11, 1866; son of Charles W. and Barbara (Grafrene) Scrutchin; grad. high school, Spokane, Wash.; student Univ. of Wash., at Seattle, 3 years; married Laura P. Arnold, of Bemidji, Minn., Aug. 27, 1900. Began practice in Chicago, Ill., 1893; practiced in Bemidji since 1898. Republican. Unitarian. Mason; member Odd Fellows. Address: Bemidji, Minn.

SEBASTIAN, S. Powell, physician, surgeon; born at Antiqua, B. W. I., June 10, 1879; son of John and Sarah Elizabeth (Roberts) Sebastian; prep. edn. Mico College, Antiqua; came to America, 1902; M.D., Leonard Medical College, Raleigh, N. C., 1912; unmarried. Principal Wesleyan Methodist School, British West Indies, 1894-6; government school, Antiqua, 1896-1901;

organist and stenographer, Philadelphia, Pa., 1902-3; secretary and professor Agricultural and Mechanical College, Greensboro, N. C., 1903-8; practiced medicine in Greensboro since 1912. Episcopalian. Mason. Home: 227 N. Gilmer St. Office: Sugg's Bldg., Greensboro, N. C.

SELDOM, Benjamin Franklin, social worker; born at Clinton, N. J., Mar. 5, 1884; son of James B. and Frances (Johnson) Seldom; prep. edn. Phillips Exeter Academy, N. H.; student Columbia Univ., New York, 1912-13; married Hortensia Murray, of New Haven, Conn., July 15, 1908. Began as general secretary Young Men's Christian Assn., New Haven, 1906, continuing 2 years; social secretary for the boys in Colored Orphan Asylum, New York, 1910-13; principal grammar school at Freehold, N. J., 1911-12; night supt. City and Suburban Homes Co., New York, since 1913; supt. Walton Boys' Club. Helped organize the pageant conducted by Dr. W. E. B. DuBois at the 50th Anniversary Celebration of Emancipation and Exposition, New York, 1913, and took several parts including that of Frederick Douglass, also the King of the Pageant. Baptist. Home: 244 W. 64th St., New York.

SETTLE, Josiah Thomas, lawyer; former state legislator; born in Cumberland Mountains, Tenn., Sept. 30, 1850; son of Josiah and Nancy (Graves) Settle; prep. edn. Oberlin (O.) College; A.B., Howard Univ., Washington, 1872, LL.B., 1875 (A.M., 1895); married Theresa T. Vogelsang, of Annapolis, Md., May, 1875 (died 1888); 2d marriage, Fannie McCullough, of Memphis, Tenn., Mar., 1890; 2 children: Josiah T., Jr., Francis N. While a student in Washington was elected reading clerk in District Legislature existing at the time; appointed trustee of schools in D. C., 1873; admitted to bar in Washington, 1875, to Mississippi bar, 1875, to U. S. Supreme Court, 1906; practiced in Sardis, Miss., 10 years; was nominated for office of district attorney in 12th Jud. Dist. of Miss.; removed to Memphis, 1885; few months later was appointed assistant attorney-general and served in the Criminal Court 2 years; attorney and director Solvent Savings Bank & Trust Co., Memphis, since 1906. Delivered address at reception of Admiral George Dewey and wife in the Auditorium at Memphis, May 7, 1900. Member Miss. House of Representatives, 1884; was presidential elector at-large for Miss., 1876; delegate to Republican National Convention, Cincinnati, O., 1876, Minneapolis, Minn., 1892, alternate delegate at-large from Tenn., at St. Louis, Mo., 1896, Philadelphia, 1900, Chicago, 1904, 1912. Episcopalian. Member Sigma Pi Phi. Home: 421 S. Orleans St. Office: 184 N. Main St., Memphis, Tenn.

SHACKELFORD, James H., merchant; born in Illinois, 1873; son of Samuel and Mary (Smith) Shackelford; ed. district schools, Corning Academy, and Simpson College, Iowa; married Dora L. Robinson, of Leadville, Colo., 1904. Worked on farm in Iowa to 1903; in missionary work 2 years; dealer in furniture in Los Angeles, Calif., since 1905; president People's Realty Co.; director Masonic Temple Assn. Republican. Methodist. Member Negro Business Men's Assn. Mason; member Odd Fellows. Home: 1158 E. 34th St. Office: 811 Central Ave., Los Angeles, Calif.

SHAFFER, Cornelius Thadeus, bishop; born at Troy, O., Jan. 3, 1847; son of John Shelby and Margaret (Otis) Shaffer; ed. Berea College, Ky., 1867-9; special course, Cadiz, O., 1873, in Hebrew, Brooklyn, N. Y., 1878-9; M.D., Jefferson Medical College, Philadelphia, Pa., 1888; (D.D., Allen Univ., S. C., 1890, Wilberforce Univ., 1905); married Annie Maria Taylor, of Cincinnati, O., Oct. 26, 1870. Served in Ohio Colored Inf. and 100th U. S. Colored Inf., 1864-5. Ordained A. M. E. ministry, 1870; pastored in Ohio, N. Y., Md., Pa.; presiding elder 3 years; sec-treas. Church Extension Board, A. M. E. Church, 1892-1900, bishop since 1900. President Western Univ., Quindara, Kan., 1901-3; state secretary of

N. Y., Good Templars, 1878-9; delegate Ecumenical Conference on Methodism, London, Eng., 1902; held 2 conferences in Africa, 1902. Author: Pastors Visiting Companion and Diary, 1885. Address: 3742 Forest Ave., Chicago, Ill.

SHANNON, William Duncan, clergyman; born at Bridgeton, Barbados, B. W. I., Jan. 1, 1880; son of Robert William and Catherine Anne (Bostick) Shannon; came to U. S., 1905; prep. edn. Barbados and U. S.; attended Montreal Business College, Can.; B.D., Wilberforce Univ., Ohio, 1910; married Osa Ione Watkins, of Richmond, Ind., Nov. 29, 1911. Began as local preacher in James Street Wesleyan Methodist Church, Barbados, at age of 16; pastor of church at Oakville, Ont., Can., 1903, continuing number of years; pastor A. M. E. Church, Evansville, Ind., since 1912. Member Evansville Ministerial Assn. Trustee Wilberforce Univ. Progressive. Mason; member Knights of Pythias. Address: 721 Mulberry St., Evansville, Indiana.

SHAW, George Clayton, president and principal private school; born at Louisburg, N. C., June 19, 1863; son of Matthew and Mary (Thomas) Shaw; A.B., Lincoln (Pa.) Univ., 1886; student Princeton (N. J.) Theological Seminary 1 year; B.D., Auburn (N. Y.) Theological Seminary, 1890; (D.D., Lincoln Univ., 1902); married Mary E. Lewis, of Penn Valley, Pa., May 14, 1890. Founded the Mary Potter Memorial School at Oxford, N. C., 1890, since president and principal; director Biddle Univ., Charlotte, and Scolin Seminary, Concord, N. C.; secretary-treas. Colored Realty Co. Was the organizer of 6 Presbyterian Churches, and built the edifices; twice moderator Cape Fear Presbytery, and the Synod of Catawba once. Member executive committee North Carolina State Teachers' Assn.; was secretary 2 years, and president 2 years. Republican. Address: Oxford, N. C.

SHEEHY, George Alexander, publisher; former customs inspector; born at Great Abaco, Bahama Islands, B. W. I., Dec. 17, 1866; son of George C. and Phyllis R. (Moncur) Sheehy; brought to America, 1872; ed. public schools, Key West, Fla.; night school 1 year; English grades in Clark Univ., Atlanta, Ga.; married Mary E. Colclough, of Gainesville, Fla., June 12, 1893; 4 children: Colclough T., Algernon M., George A., Jr., Florris L. Was inspector of customs at Port of Tampa, Fla., under the administration of President Benjamin Harrison; passed examination for postoffice clerk and mail carrier; instructor in shoemaking at Clark Univ., 1890-1; invoice clerk in Commissary Dept., U. S. Army, at Tampa, during Spanish-American war. Organized the Metropolitan Realty & Investment Co., Ocala, Fla., 1910, secretary and assistant mgr., 18 months; now secretary National Mercantile Realty & Improvement Co., Jacksonville; proprietor Sheehy Society Supply Co.; manager Florida Sentinel Publishing Co.; secretary Florida Negro Business League, Jacksonville Negro Business League. Trustee Odd Fellows Home, Ocala, Fla. Republican. African Methodist. Was grand master Grand Lodge of Odd Fellows, Fla., 1905-7, 1909-11; director S. C. of M. of America, 1911-14. Home: 2120 Davis St. Office: 722 Broad St., Jacksonville, Fla.

SHELTON, James N., undertaker; born at Charlestown, Ind., June 12, 1872; son of Henry H. and Sallie (Smith) Shelton; attended public schools, Indianapolis; student Harvey Medical College, Chicago, Ill.; grad. Chicago School of Embalming, 1900; married Mayme E. Pettiford, of Franklin, Ind., Nov. 28, 1895; 1 child: Z. Marion. Member undertaking firm of Morgan & Shelton, Indianapolis, 1901-5, firm of Shelton & Willis, 1905-14; funeral director and embalmer in own name since 1914; stockholder in Indianapolis Casket Co.; director Sunlite Insurance Co., Smartt Auto & Mfg. Co., Colored Pythian Savings & Loan Co., Colored Pythian Castle Hall Assn. Contributor to Herron Art Institute. Was deputy assessor in Marion County 12 years; assistant door-keeper Republican National Convention, Chicago, Ill., 1904, assistant sergt.-at-arms, 1908, and alternate delegate from Ind., 1912. Baptist. 32d degree Mason; past grand chancellor Knights of Pythias of Ind.; member Odd Fellows, Elks, Household of Ruth, Court of Calanthe. Club: Alexander Dumas. Home: 516 N. California St. Office: 418 Indiana Ave., Indianapolis, Ind.

SHEPARD, James Edward, president religious school, clergyman; born at Raleigh, N. C., Nov. 3, 1875; son of Rev. Augustus and Hattie (Whitted) Shepard; prep. edn. Shaw Univ., 1883-90; Ph.G., Shaw Univ. Pharmacy Dept., 1894; private training in theology; (D.D., Muskingum College, New Concord, Ohio, 1912; A.M., Selma Univ., Ala., 1913); married Mrs. Annie Day Robinson, of Danville, Va., Nov. 5, 1895; 2 children: Majroie A., Annie D. Began as comparer of deeds in recorder's office in District of Columbia, 1899; deputy internal revenue collector, Raleigh, 1900-6; field supt. International Sunday School Assn., 1906-10; treasurer Interdenominational Sunday School Convention, 1909-14; was delegate to World's Sunday School Convention at Rome, Italy, 1907, and only colored speaker; has traveled extensively in Europe, Africa and Asia. Founded the National Religious Training School at Durham, N. C., 1910, and since served as president; director Mechanics' & Farmers' Bank, also North Carolina State Industrial Assn. Trustee Lincoln Hospital. Republican. Baptist. Member N. C. Medical Assn. Mason; member Odd Fellows, Knights of Pythias. One of his lectures appears in Alice Moore Dunbar's book of Masterpieces of Negro Eloquence under title of "Is the Game Worth the Candle"? Address: National Religious Training School, Durham, N. C.

SHEPARD, Pattie Gilliam, matron; born at Oxford, N. C., Feb. 22, 1874; daughter of Alfred and Rebecca (House) Gilliam; ed. Boynton Institute, Va.; Missionary Training School, New York; National Religious Training School, Durham, N. C.; married Rev. Robert Shepard, of Raleigh, N. C., Jan. 22, 1892; 3 children. Began as

supt. State Orphanage, Oxford; general mgr. Baptist Colored Orphans Home, Winston-Salem, N. C.; editor Orphan Home Herald; pres. woman's dept. Home and Foreign Mission Convention; vice-president and state organizer W. C. T. U. Member Federated Colored Woman's Clubs. Missionary Baptist. Address: Colored Orphans Home, Winston-Salem, N. C.

SHEPPARD, William Henry, missionary; born at Waynesboro, Va., Mar. 8, 1865; son of William Henry and Fannie (Martin) Sheppard; ed. Hampton Normal and Agricultural Institute to 1883; grad. Stillman Theological Institute, Tuscaloosa, Ala., 1886; (D.D., Biddle Univ., Charlotte, N. C., 1904); married Lucy Jones Gantt, of Tuscaloosa, Feb. 21, 1894; 2 children: Wilhelmina, Maxamalinge. Missionary of the Southern Presbyterian Church of Congo Belge, Central Africa, 1890-1910; lead first known expedition into forbidden land of King Lukenga; found new tribe called Bakuba; discovered lake in interior of Congo region which in 1910 was named Lake Sheppard by the Belgium government; built over 100 miles of highway, north and south, from American Presbyterian headquarters at Luebo, on Lulua river to King Lukenga's capital, Mushenge; work was conducted by permission and with assistance of the king; built first house of worship in Kassai region, Central Africa, where there are now 12,000 Presbyterians; was successful in expedition when sent against Zappo Zap tribe of raiders (cannibals), 1897; charged with criminal libel concerning Congo atrocities, indicted and arrested by order of King Leopold II, of Belgium, April, 1908, but was exonerated and liberated after 8 months. Fellow Royal Geographical Society (London). Mason. Address: 516 E. Breckinridge St., Louisville, Ky.

SHERMAN, Georgiana H., musician; born at Williamsport, Pa.; attended public school and later took course in music at Dickinson Seminary; course in piano Royal Conservatory of Music, Philadelphia, Pa., 1909; unmarried.

Was with the Southland Sextet, a jubilee company, season, 1913-14; choir dir. Zion Baptist Church, Ardmore, Pa., since 1914. Home: Philadelphia, Pa.

SHERROD, Daniel Webster, physician, surgeon; born at Macon, Miss., Mar. 10, 1867; son of Daniel Webster and Harriett Sherrod; A.B., Fisk Univ., Nashville, Tenn., 1892; M.D., Meharry Medical College (Walden Univ.), 1896; married Bessie Lena Williamson, of Meridian, Miss., Aug. 20, 1913. Practiced in Macon, 1896-1906, and conducted Macon Drug Store last 6 years; in practice in Meridian, Miss., and proprietor Sherrod Drug Co., since 1906; began in debt and has accumulated property exceeding value of $30,000; was secretary U. S. board of examining surgeons for 4 years. Republican. Deacon Missionary Baptist Church. President Mississippi Colored Anti-Tuberculosis League, and Miss. Medical, Dental and Pharm. Assn. Mason; member Odd Fellows, Knights of Pythias. Home: 1202 26th Ave. Office: 401- 1-2 25th Ave., Merilian, Miss.

SHIRLEY, Archie Turner, teacher, retired; born in Va., Jan. 15, 1863; son of Turner and Fannie (Weaver) Shirley; attended public schools of Va.; grad. Storer College, Harpers Ferry, W. Va., 1887; married Martha A. Williams, Dec. 22, 1885; 9 children. Began as teacher of public schools of Va., 1882, continuing to 1909; after 27 years of service retired voluntarily on pension; clerk of Northern Virginia Baptist Assn., since 1893. Trustee Manassas (Va.) Industrial School. Republican. Mason; grand director Odd Fellows in America for 4 years; grand master 2 years, and grand secretary in Va., since 1907, Grand United Order of Odd Fellows. Address: Herndon, Virginia.

SIMMONS, Caesar Felton, postmaster, teacher 33 years; born at Gainesville, Sumter County, Ala., Mar. 23, 1866; son of Caesar and Mariah (Washington) Simmons; attended public school, Starkville, high school, Meridian, Miss.; student Emerson In-

stitute, Mobile, Ala., 4 years; grad. Mississippi State Normal School, at Holly Springs, 1889; studied at Tougaloo Univ., 3 years; married Lula Flewellen, of Brenham, Tex., Dec. 27, 1893; 4 children: Lamas Q. C., Oscar A., Bennie, Willie. Taught schools 6 years in Miss., at Greenwood, Kosciusko, Starkville, Meridian, Scooba, Binnsville, Waynesboro, State Line, Chapel Hill, 2 years at Livingston, Ala., Washington, Tex., 18 years, Chapel Hill; 2 years at Livingston, year; removed to Okla., 1909; teacher in schools at Purcell, Washington, and Rosedale, 5 years; professor of science, zoology, geology, botany, and physiology at Colored Agricultural and Normal Univ., Langston, Okla., 1914-15; postmaster at Boley, Okla., since 1915, appointed for 4-year term by President Woodrow Wilson. Served as local pastor in M. E. Church; superintendent Sunday School in Guthrie (Okla.) district; organized and served as president of several temperance societies; identified with various movements for betterment of race; owns farm at Pursell, Okla. Democrat; was endorsed for position as minister resident and consul-general to Liberia by citizens of Okla., Miss., Ala., and Texas. Member National Association Teachers in Colored Schools, Texas State Teachers' Assn., Oklahoma State Teachers' Assn., Men's Christian Assn. Mason; member Knights of Pythias. Author (poem): A Song of Faith and Hope. Wrote (autobiography): Striving or Climbing Up, With Hope in God, 1915. Address: Boley, Okla.

SIMMS, William David, clergyman; born at Columbus, Miss., May 15, 1860; son of James W. and Phebe (Winston) Simms; attended public school at Columbus; student, Penn's Theological Seminary, Oskaloosa, Iowa, 1886-7; Baptist College, Wichita, Kan., 1887-8; (D.D., Princeton (Ind.) Normal and Industrial Univ., 1906); married Fannie Grace Sloan, of Arkadelphia, Ark., Jan. 19, 1880; 3 children: James W., Cordelia, Josephine; 2d marriage, Louisa Trice, of Newburg, Ind., Oct.

6, 1906. Worked on father's farm in Miss. to 1874; was deputy U. S. marshall, 1876-82; in mercantile business at Oskaloosa, Ia., 12 years. Ordained in Baptist ministry, 1886; had charges in Iowa, Mich., Ill., Ind., Ky., and Va.; now pastor at Newburg, Ind.; general missionary for state of Ind. Trustee Macon (Ga.) Baptist College. Owns 80-acre tract near Bowling Green, Ky., 9 lots and other property in Newburg. Was editor Fort Smith (Ark.) Post, 1889-92. Republican. Address: Newburg, Ind.

SIMONS, Robert Edward, contractor, builder; born at Charleston, S. C., July 15, 1865; son of Kating B. and Dorintha (Smalls) Simons; ed. Morris State Normal School, Charleston; married Harriet Fell, of Charleston, Aug. 27, 1890. Began as builder in Charleston; now builder and contractor, New York; was contractor for Rev. Dr. William H. Brooks in the erection of $75,000 parish house of St. Mark's M. E. Church; first building of its kind erected by exclusively colored craftsmen; firm of Tandy & Foster, also colored, were the architects. Mason; member Odd Fellows, Elks. Methodist. Home: 232 E. 85th St. Office: 72 E. 82nd St., New York.

SIMS, Felix Rice, clergyman; born at Silver Run, Ala., Mar. 1, 1863; son of David and Evaline (Jenkins) Sims; grad. Normal Dept., 1886, B.D., Theol. Dept., 1889, at Talladega (Ala.) College; (D.D., Morris Brown Univ., Atlanta, Ga., 1905); married Emma E. Griffin, of Selma, Ala., Sept. 16, 1884; 5 children: David H., Miriam B., George T., Pauline J., Yancy L. Entered Methodist ministry at Talladega, Ala., 1889; was presiding elder in Macon (Ga.) District for some time; now pastor Big Bethel A. M. E. Church, Atlanta, Ga. Trustee Wilberforce Univ., Morris Brown Univ. Served as postmaster at Thebes, Ga., 1894-9; was assistant custodian Postoffice and U. S. Court building, Savannah, Ga., 1904. Republican. Member Odd Fellows, Knights of Pythias. Home: 4 Gartrel St. Study: Bethel A. M. E. Church, Atlanta, Ga.

SIMS, George Henry, clergyman; born at Cumberland Court House, Va., Apr. 8, 1871; son of R. T. and Millie Sims; attended public schools, Cumberland C. H., 7 years; private training from tutor of the Missionary Alliance Training College; (D.D., Guadaloupe College, Seguin, Tex., June 1, 1905); married Louise D. Russell, of Cumberland, C. H., Nov. 2, 1909; 2 children: Edith Thelma, George H., Jr. Ordained Baptist ministry, 1895; was pastor at Nyack, N. Y., 4 months; pastor Union Baptist Church, New York, since 1898; erected 2 edifices, the first which is now used as mother's day nursery and kindergarten cost $13,500, the second costing $52,000; president N. Y. Colored Baptist State Convention since Nov., 1913; member board of managers New England Baptist Missionary Convention. Trustee Lynchburg School, Va., Was member the Commission in charge Emancipation Proclamation Celebration, New York, appointed by Gov. William Sulzer, May 16, 1913. Member New York Republican County Committee. Home: 210 W. 63rd St. Study: Union Baptist Church, 204 W. 63rd St., N. Y.

SIMS, Hollie Turner, editor, pub.; born at Madison Station, Miss., Feb. 6, 1884; son of Rev. Dr. R. T. and Mary (Crabb) Sims; ed. State Baptist College, Miss.; married Virginia M. Burt, of Kosciusko, Miss., Mar. 16, 1908; 1 child: Helene. Learned printer's trade in Canton, Miss.; was foreman Mississippi Baptist, Canton, 9 years, the Baptist Reporter, Jackson, Miss., for short time; with Henry Pope established The Negro Star, Greenwood, Miss., Apr. 24, 1908; it occurred that 4 papers had failed at Greenwood and they began with free distribution; now has paid circulation of 1,200 and gross business exceeding $5,000 annually. Trustee Greenwood Seminary, McKinney Chapel Baptist Church, and New Zion Baptist Church. Mason; member Knights of Pythias, Woodmens' Union, Sons and Daughters of Jacob. Home: 443 Young St. Office: 309 Johnston St., Greenwood, Mississippi.

SIMS, Otis Astor, physician; born in Upson County, Ga., Sept. 4, 1874; son of Jesse and Millie Ann Frances (Justice) Sims; attended public schools at Liberty Hill, Milner and Barnesville, Ga.; grad. Knoxville College, Tenn., 1898; M.D., Knoxville Medical College, 1909; married Katie Green, of Dalton, Ga., Aug. 27, 1903; 5 children: Jesse Byron, Henry Green, Otis Warren, Wilbur Euville, and an infant. Practiced in Dalton since 1906. Republican. Presbyterian. Member Georgia State Medical Assn.; also member Knights of Pythias, Elks. Home: 48 Depot St. Office: 13 1-2 Hamilton St., Dalton, Ga.

SINGLETON, Richard Henry, clergyman; born at Hilton Head, S. C., Sept. 11, 1865; son of Richard and Celia (Kettles) Singleton; prep. edn., Giles Academy, Hilton Head, and Morris Brown College, Atlanta, Ga.; grad. Turner Theological Seminary, 1901, D.D., 1904; married Mrs. Josephine Hymes, of Darien, Ga., Apr. 18, 1889. Licensed to preach in A. M. E. Church, 1892; built Payne Chapel, Brunswick, Ga., and was pastor 5 years; pastor Gaines Chapel, Waycross, 1897-9, St. Philip Monumental Church, Savannah, 1899-1904, rebuilt edifice; presiding elder, Valdosta Dist., Ga., 1904-8, W. Savannah Dist., 1908-9; pastor St. Philip Church, Savannah, since 1909; was delegate General Conferences, 1904, 8, 12; honored with number votes as bishop to W. Africa, 1908. Director Union Development Co.; founded Central Park Nor. and Indus. Inst., Savannah; life trustee, Morris Brown College, Wilberforce Univ.; pres. Evangelical Ministers' Union, Savannah. Mason; member Odd Fellows, Knights of Pythias, American Woodmen. Address: 507 Charles St., Savannah, Ga.

SLATER, George Washington, Jr., clergyman, lecturer; born at Richmond, Ray Co., Mo., Sept. 22, 1872; son of George W. and Sarah Ann (Venerable) Slater; grad. high school, Aurora, Neb., 1890; attended South Division High School and Polytechnic Busintss College, Chicago; prep. edn., Wesleyan Univ., Bloomington, Ill.; student Penn College, Oskaloosa, Ia., Payne Theological Seminary (Wilberforce Univ.); married Lethe Jones, of Chicago, Mar. 16, 1893 (deceased); 2d, Missouri Dozier, of Clinton, Ia., Apr. 1, 1911; children: Fred W., Florence L., Helen, Ann, Richard P., Annabelle, Alexander A., Pearl; George W. and Sigournia (deceased). Licensed to preach in A. M. E. Church, 1894; was pastor in Chicago 7 years; pastor of Trinity Church, Wilberforce, O., also holding position as university pastor at Wilberforce Univ., 1905-6; served at different times as supply teacher at Wilberforce Univ., of the president's classes in psychology, moral philosophy, and political economy; special secretary for the colored race and member general executive committee the Christian Socialist Fellowship of America. Mason. Home: 309 Third St., Clinton, Iowa.

SLAUGHTER, Henry Proctor, editor; born at Louisville, Ky., Sept. 17, 1871; son of Charles Henry and Sarah Jane (Smith) Slaughter; grad. Central High School, Louisville, 1891; LL.B., Howard Univ. School of Law, Washington, D. C., 1900, LL.M., 1901; married Ella M. Russell, of Jonesboro, Tenn., Apr. 27, 1904 (died Nov. 2, 1914). Served full indentured apprentice term in the printing trade; was foreman for Champion Pub. Co., Louisville, 1893; foreman with the Intelligence Pub. Co., and associate editor Lexington (Ky.) Standard, 1894; foreman at A. M. E. Zion Church Pub. Co., Charlotte, N. C., 1895-6; compositor in U. S. government printing office, Washington, 1896-1910, proof-reader, monotypist, linotype operator and machinist; editor the Odd Fellows Journal since Nov. 10, 1910; director Odd Fellows Hall Assn. (Washington), People's Savings Bank at Staunton, Va.; private library contains over 2000 bound voumes on Africa, slavery and the colored people. Episcopalian. Secretary the Kentucky Republican Club in Washington; served as committeeman at inauguration of Presidents William McKinley, Theodore

Roosevelt, William H. Taft, Woodrow Wilson. Member National Association for Advancement of Colored People, Columbia Typographical Union, No. 101, Washington, D. C. 32d degree Mason; member all branches Grand United Order of Odd Fellows. Clubs: Pen and Pencil (ex-president). Home: 2236 13th St. N. W. Office: 1344 You St. N. W., Washington, D. C.

SLAUGHTER, Howard S., funeral director, embalmer; born at Urbana, Ohio, Oct. 19, 1890; son of Hugh Campbell and Clara O. (Wills) Slaughter; public school edn., Urbana; grad. Cleveland Training School for Embalmers, Jan. 17, 1914; married Ruby A. Yates, of Cleveland, Ohio, June 3, 1913; 1 child: Howard S., Jr. Began with undertaking firm of J. W. Wills & Sons, Cleveland, 1911; licensed by Ohio State Board of Embalming Examiners, Feb. 26, 1914; since member firm of Slaughter Bros., funeral directors and embalmers. Member National Funeral Directors and Embalmers Assn. Address: 3923 Central Ave., Cleveland, Ohio.

SLAUGHTER, Leslie A., funeral director, embalmer; born at Urbana, Ohio, Oct. 13, 1892; son of Hugh Campbell and Clara O. (Wills) Slaughter; ed. public schools, Urbana; high school, Springfield, O.; grad. Cleveland Training School for Embalmers, 1914; unmarried. Began as assistant to his instructor, J. Walter Wills, Cleveland, 1913; licensed by Ohio State Board of Embalming Examiners, June 1, 1914; secretary-treas. Slaughter Bros., since Jan. 1, 1915. Member National Funeral Directors and Embalmers Assn. African Methodist. Address: 3923 Central Ave., Cleveland, Ohio.

SMALL, Thomas Frederick, publisher; born at Philadelphia, Pa., Nov. 15, 1880; son of Thomas C. and Georgana (Elgin) Small; grad. High School No. 10, Philadelphia; A.B., Catholic Institute, private, 1896; married Ellnoro Tate, of Savannah, Ga., Aug. 10, 1904; 2 children: Effie G., Thomas C. Established first Negro Programme Pub. Co., Philadelphia, 1896; later director Middle Atlantic Realty Co.; published Newport and Boston Union, first Negro paper in Newport, R. I.; president T. Frederick Small Co., New York, pub. Small's Illustrated Monthly, established 1905, Small's Negro Trade Journal, established 1906; manager Small's National Advertising Agency. Vice-pres. County Gen. Com. of 17th Assembly Dist. for United Colored Democracy. Catholic. Member National Negro Press Assn., Business Men's League of New York, Odd Fellows, Elks. Club: The Clubmen's Social. Home: 46 W. 99th St. Office: 12 W. 135th St., New York.

SMITH, Amanda, evangelist; born a slave in Md., 1837; learned to read by cutting large letters out of newspapers and making them into words with assistance of her mother; her father was paid for extra work and saved enough to purchase the freedom of self and family, then removed to Pennsylvania. She became a Christian in early life and has since devoted much of her time to church work; in the years following 1870, she attended camp-meetings in Ohio and Illinois and first attracted attention at these gatherings; finally her evangelistic labors extended to Africa, India, England and Scotland; founded the Amanda Smith Orphan's Home for Colored Children, Harvey, Ill.; later associate national supt. Woman's Christian Temperance Union, her work being among colored people. Wrote her autobiography entitled "Amanda Smith's Own Story." Address: Amanda Smith Orphan's Home, Harvey, Ill. (Died Mar. 1, 1915, at age of 78 years.)

SMITH, Brown Sylvester, lawyer; born in Washington County, Ark., Aug., 1863; son of Alfred and Charlotte Smith; grad. high school, Springfield, Ill., 1883; Univ. of Mich. Law School, 1886; married Laura B. Porter, of Greenfield, Iowa, Sept. 4, 1890. Admitted to bar and began practice in Kansas City, Kan., 1886; was first assistant county attorney, Wyandotte County, 1899-1907; now in practice in Minneapolis, Minn. Republican; was presidential elector in Kan., 1892, and member City Council in Kansas City, 1892-6. Mason. Home: 3358 Oakland Ave. Office: 802 Sykes Block, Minneapolis, Minn.

SMITH, Charles Spencer, bishop; born at Colborne, Canada, Mar. 16, 1852; son of Nehemiah Henry and Catherine Smith; common school edn. in Canada; M.D., Meharry Medical College (Walden Univ.), Nashville, Tenn., 1880; (D.D., Victoria College, Toronto, Can., 1911; D.D., 1911, LL.D., 1913, by Wilberforce Univ.); married Katie Josephine Black, of Nashville, Tenn., 1875 (died 1885); 2d marriage, Christine Shoecraft, of Muncie, Ind., Dec. 31, 1888; children: Susie E., Charles S., Jr. Ordained to ministry A. M. E. Church, 1871; founded Sunday School Union of A. M. E. Church, 1882, and served as secretary-treas. to 1890; visited various parts in Africa, 1894; elected bishop at General Conference in Columbus, Ohio, 1900; presiding bishop for his church in Texas. Was member Alabama House of Reprtsentatives, 1874-6. Author: Glimpses of Africa, West and Southwest Coast, 1895. Address: 35 Alexandrine Ave. E., Detroit, Mich.

SMITH, Charles Sumner, editor and publisher the Twin City Star; member executive committee National Negro Press Assn. Address: 305 S. 5th St., Minneapolis, Minn.

SMITH, Charles William Thomas, physician, surgeon; born in Pembroke Parish, Bermuda, Feb. 12, 1847; son of Edward Joseph and Caroline (Jennings-Williams) Smith; ed. Joseph H. Thomas' School, Parish of Pembroke, and Augustus Swan School; M.D., Howard Univ., Washington, D. C., 1872; married Francis E. Jackson, of Parish of Pembroke, Jan., 1873; 4 children: Matilda, Charles, Edward, George. First native colored physician to practice in Bermuda; had large practice among white and colored people at St. Georges; received first appointment by special recommendation of the governor, 1873; was surgeon for Parish Asylum in St. Georges 15 years; now senior regis-

tered medical practitioner and public vaccinator; founded Trott's School for colored children, private; member 2d Division of the Devonshire College. Was nominated for member of the Honorable the House of Assembly, from Parish of Pembroke, 1906, and defeated by only 12 votes in 1911. Formerly member British Medical Assn. (London); grand register of Ireland the Free and Accepted Masons; member Grand United Order of Odd Fellows of America. Address: P. O. Box 32, Hamilton, Bermuda.

SMITH, Emory Byington, clergyman; born at Raleigh, N. C., June 12, 1886; son of George C. and Elizabeth (Outlaw) Smith; prep. edn. Hampton Normal and Agricultural Institute, Va., and New York Evening High School for Men; A.B., Howard Univ., Washington; B.D., Howard Univ. School of Theol., 1914; B.D., Yale School of Religion, 1915; unmarried. Ordained Congregational ministry, 1914; pastor Lincoln Memorial Congregational Temple, Washington, since Dec. 20, 1914. Member Alpha Phi Alpha. Home: 2435 Georgia Ave., Washington, D. C.

SMITH, Ernest Ollington, teacher, library pres.; born at Shelby, Ala., July 4, 1880; son of Dudley James and Gabella (Glasscock) Smith; ed. public schools, Tuscaloosa and Birmingham, Ala.; A.B., Fisk Univ., 1903; married Nina Francis Erwin, of Nashville, Tenn., June 14, 1906; 3 children. Began as teacher in Shadygrove, Tenn., 1899; principal public school, Houston, Tex.; president Colored Carnegie Library since 1907; was instrumental in securing this library for Houston; secretary-treas. real estate and loan firm of Roberts & Smith, organized, 1912; director Social Service Federation. Republican. Congregationalist. Member Longshoremen and Cotton-jammers Assn. (sec.). Address: 1214 O'Neil St., Houston, Tex.

SMITH, Ezekiel Ezra, principal normal school, former counsul-general to Liberia; born at Mt. Olive, N. C., May 23, 1852; son of Alexander and Catherine (Wallace) Smith; grad. high school, Goldsboro, N. C., 1872; A.B., Shaw Univ., Raleigh, N. C., 1878, A.M., 1881 (Ph.D., 1892); married Willie A. Burnett, of Greensboro, 1889; 2d marriage, Nannie L. Goode, of Goldsboro, 1908. Editor North Carolina Enterprise, 1881-6; secretary Baptist State Convention, 1881-8; principal State Colored Normal School at Fayetteville, 1883-8; U. S. minister resident and consul-general to Liberia, 1888-91; principal State Colored Normal School, 1895-8, and since 1899; president Farmers' & Mechanics' Building & Loan Assn., Cape Fear Investment Co. Was commissioned major 4th Bat. N. C. State Guard, 1881; regimental adjutant in Spanish-American war. Missionary Baptist; has served more than 30 years as secretary Baptist State Convention. Mason; member Knights of Pythias. Address: Fayetteville, N. C.

SMITH, George D., dentist; born in South Carolina; grad. State Normal School, Salisbury, N. C., 1901; Livingstone College, 1903; D.D.S., Meharry Dental College (Walden Univ.), Nashville, Tenn., 1907. Began practice in Bristol, Tenn., 1907; later removed to Columbus, Ohio; now practicing in Louisville, Ky. Office: 1003 1-2 W. Chestnut St., Louisville, Ky.

SMITH, Harry C., editor, former legislator; born at Clarksburg, W. Va., Jan. 28, 1863; son of John R. and Sarah Smith; grad. high school, Cleveland, Ohio, 1882; unmarried. Editor and publisher the Cleveland Gazette since 1883. Was deputy state oil inspector in Ohio during both terms of Gov. Joseph B. Foraker, 1886-90; member Ohio House of Representatives, 1894-6, 1896-8, 1900-2; nominated for 4th term, 1905, but defeated in general election with entire Republican ticket; introduced and was factor in passage of the Ohio civil rights law, 1894; also introduced Ohio anti-lynching law; his success in the legislature bespeaks the co-operation of fellow members, and possibly no American of African descent was ever treated with more courtesy by any law-making

body. Home: 2322 E. 30th St. Office: Blackstone Building, Cleveland, Ohio.

SMITH, Isabella Gwynn, supervising industrial teacher; born at James Store, Gloucester Co., Va., Sept. 1, 1867; daughter of Jeremiah and Maria Susan (Lumkin) Gregory; edn. at Hampton Normal and Agricultural Institute, Va.; married Frank Smith, Jr., of Gloucester Co., May 17, 1911. Teacher in public schools of Va. for 25 years; supervising industrial teacher, Gloucester County, since Oct. 1, 1911; this branch of modern instruction in Virginia is under the supervision of the State Board of Education; it reaches the most remote homes and schools of colored people through the aid of the Anna R. Jeanes Fund. Baptist. Home: James Store, Gloucester County, Va.

SMITH, James Franklin, physician; born at Lafayette, Ala., Feb. 17, 1882; son of Wade Carlyle and Mattie Smith; A.B., Talladega (Ala.) College, 1905; student Armour Institute of Technology, Chicago, Ill., 1906; M.D., Meharry Medical College (Walden Univ.), Nashville, Tenn., 1912; unmarried. Was director of mechanics in the Emerson Institute, Mobile, Ala., 1 year, at Haines Institute, Augusta, Ga., 2 years; practiced medicine in Madison, Ga., since May 12, 1912. Congregationalist. Member Odd Fellows. Address: Madison, Ga.

SMITH, James Leonard, printer, lawyer; born in Ga., Aug. 11, 1864; son of Major and Caroline (Medows) Smith; ed. Knoxville College, Tenn., 1885-6; Clark Univ., Atlanta, Ga., 1886-90; LL.B., Howard Univ. School of Law, 1909; married Rosa B. Simmons, of Roanoke, Va., Nov., 1897. Teacher public schools, S. Pittsburg, Tenn., 1886-91; established The Knoxville Gleaner, 1891, continuing as editor to 1897; conducted campaign of education, editorially in Gleaner, with result that colored teacher was appointed in Knoxville College, and Insane Asylum opened and operated by colored people, supported by the State; purchased Cleaner Co. plant, 1912; since in job printing business under name of

Comet Printing Co. Admitted to bar, Washington, D. C., 1910, Tenn. bar, 1915. Methodist; trustee E. Vine Ave. Church. Member Knights of Pythias. Address: 131 1-2 W. Vine Ave., Knoxville, Tenn.

SMITH, Lucius, principal high school; born in Putnam Co., Ga., May 4, 1883; son of Samuel and Millie Smith; public school edn., Putnam County; high school, Madison, Ga.; A.B., Shaw Univ., Raleigh, N. C., 1911; married C. Eleanor Brown, of Macon, Ga., Dec. 30, 1914. Began as teacher in public school, Morgan Co., Ga., 1898; merchant tailor, Madison, Ga., 1900-4; entered Shaw Univ., 1905; principal and supt. Temperance Normal and Collegiate Institute, Claremont, Va., 1912; with Standard Life Insurance Co., Atlanta, Ga., 1913; principal Eddy High School, Milledgeville, Ga., since 1914. Methodist. Member Texas State Teachers' Assn., Georgia State Teachers' Assn. Mason. Home: 207 Carter St., Atlanta. Address: 813 Wilkerson St., Milledgeville, Ga.

SMITH, Robert Floyd, banker; born at Charleston, S. C., Jan. 8, 1861; son of Francis Arthur and Mary Hamilton (Talbot) Smith; ed. public schools, Charleston; Avery Normal Institute; South Carolina Univ.; Atlanta (Ga.), Univ.; married Francis I. Isaacs, of Oakland, Tex., Nov. 15, 1900; 2 children. President the Farmers' Improvement Bank of Waco since 1910; manufacturer of overalls since 1914; director Laborers' Cooperative Mercantile Co. Was member Texas House of Representatives 2 terms; also served as United States Marshall. Methodist. Member American Academy Political and Social Science. Home: 817 N. 4th St. Office: 114 Bridge St., Waco, Texas.

SMITH, Theodore Parker, teacher, penman, accountant; born near Fenton, Mo., 1860; son of Jacob Galloway and Mary (Vanderver) Smith; grad. grammar school, St. Louis, Mo.; prep. edn. Lincoln Institute, Jefferson City, Mo.; A.B., Lincoln (Pa.) Univ., 1888, and student in theological dept., 2

years; special courses, Chaffee's Phonographic Institute, Oswego, N. Y., Dixon (Ill.) Pen Art School, Bryant & Stratton Commercial School, Boston, Mass.; married Clara R. Alexander, of Lynchburg, Va., Dec. 22, 1898; 1 child: Myra L. Taught school at Stymetz and Labado, Mo., when young man; opened Richmond (Va.) Commercial School, 1892, Virginia Seminary Business College at Lynchburg, 1893; president Smith's Business College, Lynchburg, since 1895; dean of commercial dept. National Religious Training School, Durham, N. C., since 1912; accountant for True Reformers Bank at Richmond; newspaper correspondent and writer of short stories; invented a cabinet reading card. Republican. Baptist. Mason. Address: National Religious Training School, Durham, N. C., or Smith's Business College, Lynchburg, Va.

SMITH, William Alexander, druggist; born at Laurinburg, N. C., Mar. 7, 1882; son of James and Julia Smith; prep. edn. Albion Academy, Franklinton, N. C., 1901-4; Ph.G., Shaw Univ., Raleigh, N. C., 1909; unmarried. Began as pharmacist, Durham, N. C., 1909; later employed at Greensboro, N. C., New York, and passed board of registration in pharmacy, Mass., 1912; with H. C. Blue established Bay State Pharmacy, Boston, Nov. 1, 1913; only drug store owned and operated by colored men in Mass.; is also only colored member Mass. State Pharmacy Assn.; member N. E. Medical Dental and Pharm. Soc. Republican. Methodist. Member Mass. Lodge No. 8612, Odd Fellows. Address: 840 Tremont St., Boston, Mass.

SMITH, William M., supervisor in postoffice; born at Cincinnati, O., Oct. 30, 1862; son of Isaac and Pauline (Jackson) Smith; ed. public and high schools, Cincinnati; married Katie L. Mason, of Minneapolis, Minn., Feb. 16, 1889. Began as clerk in postoffice, Minneapolis, 1890, continuing in different depts. to 1908, when promoted to position of supervisor. Socialist. Episcopalian. Charter member Pride of Minnesota, Knights of Pythias. Address: 2441 Fifth Ave. S., Minneapolis, Minn.

SMITHERMAN, Andrew Jackson, editor, publisher; born at Childersburg, Ala., Dec. 27, 1883; son of James and Elizabeth (Phillips) Smitherman; ed. public schools, Birmingham and Bessmer, Ala., high school, Centerville, La.; married Ollie B. Murphy, of Sevier Co., Ark., June 29, 1910; 2 children: Andrew T., Carol M. Began in newspaper business as mgr. The Muskogee Cimiter, Okla., 1908, continuing to 1910; published The Muskogee Star, 1911; foreman of employes Okla. State Legislature, 1912; same year removed his paper to Tulsa, Okla., since publisher under name of The Tulsa Star, and is sole owner; as leading Negro paper in state is influential opponent of "Grandfather Clause" and other forms of race prejudice. Was vice-pres. Western Negro Press Assn., 1910-11, president since 1911. Democrat. Catholic. Member Knights of Pythias, Odd Fellows, Knights and Ladies of Honor. Home: 402 N. Elgin St. Office: 501 N. Greenwood St., Tulsa, Okla.

SNYDER, Charles William, physician; born at Hartford, Conn., Jan. 16, 1870; son of Charles Henry and Sophia (Hensley) Snyder; public school edn., Hartford; A.B., Fisk Univ., Nashville, Tenn., 1896; M.D., Yale, 1900; married Birdie Maria Wills, of Nashville, Tenn., Dec. 31, 1903. Began practice in Cambridge, Mass., 1900; removed to New Albany, Ind., 1903. Republican. Congregationalist. Odd Fellow. Home and Office: 514 State St., New Albany, Indiana.

SOMERVILLE, C. C., clergyman; born in Warren Co., N. C., Mar. 16, 1859; son of Richard and Mary (Trip) Somerville; prep. edn., State Normal School, Salisbury, N. C.; A.B., Shaw Univ., Raleigh, 1899; (D.D., Livingstone College); married Addie L. Brown, of Salisbury, 1886; 8 children. Ordained Baptist ministry, Statesville, N. C., 1886; was principal in schools at Salisbury and Reidsville; president Rowan Normal and Industrial Institute, Reidsville, 1900-5; pastor Eben-

ezer Church, Portsmouth, Va.; member executive board Lott Cary Foreign Mission; director Y. M. C. A.; trustee Corey Memorial Institute. Republican. Member Va. State Teachers' Assn. Mason; member Black Men of America. Author: My Brothers, 1886; The Farmer's Boy, 1906; Uncrowned Queen, 1913; Sharps and Flats. Address: 812 Columbia St., Portsmouth, Virginia.

SPARROW, William S., tailor; born at Newbern, N. C., Oct. 23, 1875; son of William and Frances Sparrow; public school edn.; grad. Boston School of Cutting; married Carolyn Stanford, of Boston, Mass., Dec. 31, 1910. Custom tailor and haberdasher. Methodist. Mason; member Elks, Odd Fellows, Sons of North Carolina. Club: Greater Boston. Home: 50 Windsor St. Office: 639 Tremont St., Boston, Mass.

SPAULDING, Charles Clinton, insurance; born at Clarkton, N. C., Aug. 1, 1874; son of Benjamin and Margaret (Moore) Spaulding; high school edn., Durham, N. C.; married Fannie Jones, of Washington, D. C., Sept. 26, 1900; 3 children: Margaret L., Charles C., Jr., John A. Was first agent employed by North Carolina Mutual & Provident Assn., 1899; appointed manager of the company, 1900, now vice-president and general manager; director Mechanics' & Farmers' Bank. Trustee Lincoln Hospital; connected with City Juvenile Court. Missionary Baptist. Member Durham Negro Business League. Mason. Home: 1006 Fayetteville St. Office: 214 Farrish St., Durham, N. C.

SPENCER, Sarah Elizabeth, hair culturist; born at Norfolk, Va., June, 1887; daughter of Richard and Ellen (Phillips) Smith; common school edn.; attended Norfolk Mission College, 1902; graduate in hairdressing from Mme. M. E. Joyce's School, York, Pa., 1912; married. Began treatment of the scalp in Atlantic City, N. J., 1913; secured formula for preparation to aid growth of hair which she manufacturs under name of Apex Hair Pomade; employs force of 50 selling agents;

president Apex Hair Co. Baptist. Address: 1723 Arctic Ave., Atlantic City, New Jersey.

SPIGNER, W. H., photographer; born at Prattsville, Ala., July 2, 1866; son of W. H. and Catherine (Pratt) Spigner; public school edn.; married Cynthia A. Johnson, of Atchison, Kan., Dec. 3, 1889. Proprietor Spigner's Northern Studio, Los Angeles, since 1911. Republican. African Methodist. Member Odd Fellows, Knights of Pythias. Home: 273 S. Union Ave. Office: 849 San Pedro St., Los Angeles, Calif.

SPRADLING, Will Wallace, real estate; born at Louisville, Ky., Apr. 7, 1866; son of Washington and Henrietta (Richardson) Spradling; public school edn.; married Mary E. Wilson, of Lyons Station, Ky., Mar. 1, 1905. In real estate business, Louisville, since 1887; owner more real estate in city than any other colored person; vice-president Louisville Cemetery Assn.; director Falls City Realty Co. Trustee Jacob St. Tabernacle; was first treas. Ky. Home Society for Colored Children. Republican; was financial secretary largest Colored Republican League ever organized in city; delegate to convention that nominated James F. Grinstead, Republican mayor, 1907; member city and county committee in interest of Colored Voters. Methodist. Mason. Club: Progressive. Address: 501 Roselane St., Louisville, Ky.

SPRATLIN, Paul Edward, physician; born at Wetumpka, Ala., Oct. 9, 1861; son of Calloway and Jennie (Woodruff) Spratlin; A.B., Atlanta (Ga.) Univ., 1881, A.M., later; M.D., Denver Medical College (Denver Univ.), Colo., 1892; married Martha L. Joseph, of New Orleans, La., Apr. 4, 1895; 4 children: Maceo, Valaurez, Estreldo, Devonia. Taught school in Ga., Tenn., and Tex., 1881-9; practiced medicine in Denver since 1892; chief medical inspector City of Denver, 1895-9; secretary-treas. Douglass Undertaking Co., Congo Mining, Milling & T. Co.; secretary Golden Chest Mining, Milling & T. Co. Trustee Lincoln-Douglass Consumptive Sanitarium, National Preachers' Home of A. M. E. Church at Colorado Springs. Progressive. Member Colorado Commercial Alliance. Mason; member Odd Fellows, United Brothers of Friendship. Home: 2230 Clarkson St. Office: 32 Good Block, Denver, Colo.

SPRINGS, Andrew Wilton, physician, surgeon; born at Charlotte, N. C., May 22, 1869; son of Thomas and Mary Ann (Burwell) Springs; public school edn., Durham, N. C.; B.S., Fisk Univ., Nashville, Tenn., 1901; M.D., National Medical Univ., Chicago, Ill., 1906; grad. Illinois Mine Rescue and First Aid Commission Station, Benton, Ill., 1914; studied helmet work at American Mine Safety Assn., Pittsburgh, Pa., 1914; married Birdie E. McLain (M.D.), of Chicago, Sept. 18, 1907; 2 children: Pearl E. (deceased), Fannie Ann. Began practice in Chicago, 1907; physician and surgeon to Madison Coal Corporation at Dewmaine, Ill., since 1912; physician in charge the Corporation Hospital; medical lecturer to First Aid Assn.; instructor to Dewmaine Self Culture Club; first physician, white or colored, to pass examination in helmet work as prescribed by Illinois Mine Rescue Commission; director Dewmaine public schools. Served as sergeant and member Hospital Corps in Illinois National Guard, 1906-8. Republican. Episcopalian. Fellow American Medical Society; member Illinois State Medical Society, Williamson County Medical Society, Egyptian Medical Society; member committee on first aid methods American Mine Safety Assn. Mason; member Odd Fellows, Knights of Pythias. Address: Dewmaine, Ill.

SPRINGS, Birdie E. McLain, physician, hospital superintendent; born at Carthagene, O., Dec. 4, 1886; daughter of Thomas and Amanda (Moss) McLain; grad. high school, Chicago, Ill., 1901; M.D., Bennett Medical College, 1912; grad. Illinois Mine Rescue Commission Station, Benton, Ill., 1914, Chautauqua School of Nursing, 1914; married Dr. Andrew Wilton Springs, of Chicago, Sept. 18, 1907; 2 children:

Pearl E. (deceased), Fannie Ann. Practiced since 1912; superintendent Madison Coal Corporation Hospital, Dewmaine, Ill.; instructor to Junior First Aid Corps; instructor in physiology and hygiene in Dewmaine Self Culture Club. Republican. African Methodist. Service member American Mine Safety Assn.; deputy, jurisdiction of Illinois, International Order of Twelve; past royal queen Tabernacle No. 103, Daughters of the Tabernacle; member Court of Calanthe. Address: Dewmaine, Ill.

STANTON, William Henry, lawyer; born at Pittsburgh, Pa., Apr. 9, 1874; son of Henry and Margaret (Crowe) Stanton; grad. Central High School, 1891; read law in office of Charles F. McKenna, former judge U. S. District Court; married Mary E. Brown, of Pittsburgh, Oct. 2, 1901; 3 children: Janice, Wendell, Louise. Admitted to Pa. bar, 1895; since practiced in Pittsburgh; defended 28 men and women charged with murder; only one convicted in first degree; secured reversal by Supreme Court where one first degree verdict had been rendered; first time in 19 years a local court had been reversed under such circumstances; secured acquittal in homicide case when jury broke time record of Allegheny County, deliberating 52 hours and 20 minutes; was counsel for colored man involved in celebrated Hartje divorce case; first lawyer in Western Pa., white or colored, appointed by court to defend a pauper charged with murder and to be paid by county for service; received maximum fee permitted under the law; defendant's atty. in first case tried in newly created County Court; attorney and secretary Douglass Loan & Investment Co.; attorney Home for Aged and Infirm Colored Women, also for Davis Temporary Home for Colored Children and Day Nursery; grand attorney Elks; ex-grand attorney Knights of Pythias. Mason; member Odd Fellows, True Reformers, Cosmopolitan Civic League. Republican. African Methodist. Club: Leondi (ex-

pres.). Home: 5512 Claybourne St. Office: 518 4th Ave., Pittsburgh, Pa.

STARKS, James Rockelle, clergyman, editor; born at Keatchie, La., June 16, 1873; son of Adolphus and Jane (Brantley) Starks; theological edn., Stillman Institute, Tuscaloosa, Ala.; married Mrs. Fannie C. Lane, of Jackson, Tenn., Dec. 1, 1913. Pastor in Colored M. E. churches since 1898; editor the official publication of the church, The Western Index, since May, 1914; member Methodist Ministers' Alliance. Republican. Member Knights of Pythias, Knights of Tabor. Home: 309 Crump St., Fort Worth, Texas.

STEPHENS, Charlotte E., teacher; born at Little Rock, Ark., May 9, 1854; daughter of William Wallace and Carolyn (Sherman) Andrews; during slavery days her father was allowed advantages of acquiring an education and became minister, as well as teacher of first freedmen's school opened in Ark.; here she received her early education; later attended denominational schools in Mo., and one term in first public school for colored children in Little Rock, 1869; student Oberlin (O.) College, 1870-3; married John H. Stephens, of Washington, Ark., Feb. 21, 1877; 6 children: William A., John H., Jr., Bessie, Frank S., Elbert L., Carolyn R. Teacher public schools, Little Rock, since 1869; in point of service is one of the oldest teachers in America. Methodist. Member National Assn. Teachers' in Colored Schools, State Colored Teachers' Assn., Woman's Home Missionary Society, Woman's Christian Temperance Union, United Sisters No. 1, of Little Rock. Address: 916 Broadway, Little Rock, Ark.

STERRS, Willis Edward, physician, surgeon; born at Montgomery, Ala., Oct. 18, 1868; son of Charles and Harriett Sterrs; attended Swayne School, Montgomery, to 1880; grad. Lincoln Univ., Marion, Ala., 1885; M.D., Univ. of Mich., Ann Arbor, 1888; married Eva A. Young, of Detroit, Mich., Dec. 26, 1888. Began practice in Montgomery, 1888, continuing to 1890; since practiced in Decatur, Ala.; was professor of bacteriology, Meharry Medical College (Walden Univ.), Nashville, Tenn., 1891; proprietor Magnolia Drug Store, Decatur, since 1891; pension surgeon for U. S., 1892-1914; conducted Cottage Houe Infirmary and Nurse Training School since 1908. Chairman board trustees North Alabama Baptist Academy, at Courtland, Republican. Member National Medical Assn. (was sec. 4 years); president 9 years, Alabama Medical Assn. Mason; member Knights of Pythias. Home: 701 W. Vine St. Office: 310 Bank St,, Decatur, Ala.

STEVENS, Andrew Frazier, Jr., investment securities, insurance; born at Philadelphia, Pa., Mar. 24, 1868; son of Andrew F. and Isabel Le Conte (Cole) Stevens; educated in Philadelphia at Robert Vaux, U. S. Grant Grammar, Swarthmore Preparatory schools, and Univ. of Pa.; unmarried. Member brokerage firm of Brown & Stevens, insurance, bonds, mortgages and other securities; member Philadelphia Fire & Underwriters' Assn.; president Home Extension & Insurance Assn., Fred Dauglass Hospital; director Home for Aged and Infirm Colored People, and Historical Society of Pa. Trustee Downingtown Industrial and Agricultural College. Was captain National Guard of Pa., 1892, major, 1898. Delegate to Republican National Convention, Chicago, Ill., 1912; chairman Republican State Committee, 1912, 1914. Accounting warden St. James P. E. Church. Member Delta Eta Sigma (U. of Pa.). Club: Citizens' Republican, 1st vice-pres., and chairman board of managers. Home: 1345 Lombard St. Office: 17th and Bainbridge Sts., Philadelphia, Pa.

STEVENS, Henry Clay, physician; born in Virginia, 1870; son of Richard P. and Malvina (Jones) Stevens; prep. edn. Bennett College, Greensboro, N. C.; M.D., Howard Univ., Washington, D. C., 1891; post-graduate work Philadelphia Polyclinic; married Mary A. Hayes, of New York, 1899. Practiced in Wilmington, Del., since 1891; member firm of Elbert & Stevens, proprie-

tors of the Franch Street Pharmacy. Republican. Methodist. Member Elks. Address: 711 W. 10th St., Wilmington, Delaware.

STEWARD, Theophilus Gould, university professor; born at Gouldtown (Bridgeton) N. J., Apr. 17, 1843; son of James and Rebecca (Gould) Steward; grad. W. Philadelphia Divinity School, 1880; student Univ. of Mont., 1898; married Elizabeth Gadschen, of Charleston, S. C., Jan. 1, 1866; 8 children: James, Charles, Frank, Stephen, Benjamin, Theophilus, Gustavus, Walter. Chaplain in U. S. Army, 1891-1907, retired; professor of history, Wilberforce Univ., since 1907. Republican. Methodist. Member American Historical Society, American Forestry Society. Author: Memories of Rebecca Steward; Genesis Reread, 1884; Charleston Love Story, 1899; Colored Regulars, 1904; (with William Steward) Gouldtown, 1913. Address: Wilberforce, Ohio.

STEWART, Charles, newspaper correspondent; born at Frankfort, Ky., May 28, 1869; son of Henry and Harriet (Lucas) Stewart; public school edn., Frankfort, grad. State Univ., Louisville, Ky., 1885; took course in Athenaeum Business College, Chicago, Ill., 1886; (A.M., Agricultural and Mechanical College, Normal, Ala.; D.D., Campbell College, Jackson, Miss.); married Elvie L. Washington, of Galveston, Tex., June 6, 1901; 1 child: Charles, Jr. General newspaper correspondent since 1887, and press agent for National Baptist Convention since 1896; president and manager Stewart's General Press Bureau at Chicago. Republican. Member National Negro Press Assn. Mason; member Odd Fellows, Knights of Pythias, United Brothers of Friendship. Address: 5922 Aberdeen St., Chicago, Ill.

STEWART, Ferdinand Augustus, surgeon, university professor; born at Mobile, Ala., Aug. 6, 1862; son of Henderson and Louisa (Jones) Stewart; grad. Emerson Institute, Mobile, 1880; A.B., Fisk Univ., Nashville, Tenn., 1885, A.M., 1890; M.D., Harvard Univ. Medical School, 1888; married Annie

May Compton, of Nashville, Jan. 25, 1899; 2 children: Ferdinand A., Jr., Annie L. Practiced in Nashville since 1888; physician and surgeon to Fisk Univ., since 1889; professor of pathology, 1889-1908, of surgery since 1908, at Meharry Medical College (Walden Univ.); member finance committee of People's Savings Bank & Trust Co.; chairman executive committee Nashville Negro Board of Trade. Republican. Member National Medical Assn., Tennessee State Medical Assn. (president). Home: 215 8th Ave. N. Office: 323 8th Ave. N., Nashville, Tenn.

STEWART, Forrest Ewart, undertaker, real estate agent; born in Gonzales County, Tex., Dec. 14, 1879; son of Monroe and Evelene (Johnson) Stewart; public school edn., Gonzales County; read law 2 years; married Alice Brown, of Waelder, Tex., Feb. 2, 1902; one child: Carl Ewart. Messenger for mayor of San Antonio, Tex., 1893-4, 5; began as mailing clerk and collector with real estate firm of John Adriance & Sons, Galveston, 1905, continuing to 1912; undertaker and embalmer, also real estate business connected, since Jan. 1, 1912; manager of firm of White & Stewart, dealers in monuments. Former clerk and vestryman Protestant Episcopal Church. Republican. President Anti-Lynching League; secretary Galveston Negro Business Men's League. Mason; member Knights of Pythias, Knights of Tabor, United Brothers of Friendship, Pilgrims. Home: 2617 Avenue M. Office: 2216 Church St., Galveston, Texas.

STEWART, George Pheldon, editor, publisher; born at Vincennes, Ind., Mar. 13, 1874; son of William H. and Josephine (Placeau) Stewart; grad. Vincennes High School, 1891; married Frances Caldwell, of Indianapolis, Sept. 28, 1898; 4 children: Joyce C., Marcus C., Fredonia H., Clarence P. Founded in 1896, and since editor and publisher The Indianapolis Recorder; is owner only printing office operated by colored people in Indianapolis; employs 10 people regularly; secretary and treas. Rankins Mfg. Co. Republi-

can. African Methodist. Home: 1138 Fayette St. Office: Pythian Temple Bldg., 240 W. Walnut St., Indianapolis, Indiana.

STEWART, George Washington, bishop; born at Lynchburg, Va., Feb. 3, 1859; son of John and Charlotte (Caldwell) Stewart; grad. Walden Univ., Nashville, Tenn., 1889; later from Gammon Theological Seminary, Atlanta, Ga.; (D.D., Texas College, Tyler, 1908); married Jessie Lee Smyly, of Pleasant Hill, Ala., Apr. 29, 1890; 6 children: George W., Jr., Luther, Sara, Ruth, Frankye, Smyly. Licensed to preach, 1880; pastored 12 years; presiding elder, 1894-1904; was delegate to Ecumenical Conference on Methodism, England, 1901; gen. sec. Young People's Society of Colored M. E. Church, 1903-10; editor Epworth Courier, 1903-10; elected bishop, May 16, 1910. Mason; member Good Shepard, Mosaic Templars. Address: Miles Memorial College, Birmingham, Alabama.

STEWART, Logan Henry, real estate; born in Union Co., Ky., July 22, 1879; son of Wesley and Victoria (Rapier) Stewart; grad. Evansville High School, Ind., 1899, Evansville Commercial High School, 1900; LL.B., Lincoln-Jefferson Univ., Hammond, 1913; married Sallie L. Wyatt, of Evansville, Ind., Nov. 30, 1911. Began as newsboy and found color no bar to successful career; in real estate business, Evansville, since 1900; opened Stewart sub-division, 1904, sold lots for $10 a front foot which rapidly advance in value to $20 and $30; opened new tract, 1914, near Oak Hill factory dist.; owner of quarter block stores and shops in business dist., known as Stewart place; also in building business, and manufacturer of concrete building stone. Evansville Negro population paid taxes on property valued less than $10,000 in 1900; contributed directly and indirectly to Negro investments and increasing this valuation to more than $200,000; personally assisted many now prosperous colored business men of Evansville. Republican. Methodist; aided to establish local branch Y. M. C. A. Pres. Negro Business League, Evansviille, 8 years. Home: 700 Lincoln Ave. Office: 3 N. Evans Ave., Evansville, Ind.

STEWART, William Richard, lawyer, former legislator; born at New Castle, Pa., Oct. 29, 1864; son of Lemuel A. and Mary (Richard) Stewart; grad. Raven High School, Youngstown, Ohio, 1880; LL.B., Cincinnati Law School, 1888; married, May 6, 1890, Consuelo Clark, M.D., the daughter of Prof. Peter H. Clark, of St. Louis, Mo.; (she died Apr. 17, 1909). Admitted to Ohio bar, 1888; since practiced in Youngstown; also admitted to practice in the Supreme Court of U. S.; principal attorney in number cases related to the rights of aliens under our treaties with foreign governments; has acted as attorney for the Royal Italian consul, the Imperial Russian Consulate, the Imperial and Royal consul of Austria-Hungary; represented prevalent party in Supreme Court of Ohio when "Bulk Sales" law was declared unconstitutional; has won cases against the Pennsylvania, Erie, Lake Shore and Michigan Southern, Baltimore & Ohio, Pittsburgh & Lake Erie, Mahoning Valley, and other railroads; also against the American Steel Foundries, American Sheet & Tin Plate Co., Youngstown Sheet & Tube Co., Brier Hill Steel Co., Youngstown Consolidated Gas & Electric Co., and secured judgments in a great many cases of importance; obtained largest judgment during May term, 1914, U. S. District Court at Cleveland against the Carnegie Steel Co.; has largest law library in Youngstown. Republican; was member Ohio House of Representatives, 2 terms, 1896-1900. Member Ohio State Bar Assn., Mahoning County Bar Assn., Youngstown Law Library Assn., Youngstown Public Library Assn., Youngstown Chamber of Commerce. Club: Republican. Home: 522 North Ave. Office: Diamond Block, Youngstown, Ohio.

STOKES, Eunice Eugenia Marie, supervising industrial teacher; born, Hayes Store, Gloucester, Va., Nov. 30, 1889; daughter of John and Martha Jane (Smith) Stokes; grad. Virginia Normal and Industrial Institute, Petersburg, Jan. 15, 1909; unmarried. Began as teacher in schools of King and Queen Co., Va., 1909, continuing 2 years; teacher in Henrico County, 1911-12, Westmoreland, 1913, James City, Va., 1914; supervising industrial teacher of colored schools in Westmoreland Co., Va., since 1914; she is one of the 32 supervisors under the State Board of Education; it is a branch of public instruction that reaches the most remote schools and homes in the state. Baptist. Member Virginia State Colored Teachers' Assn. Home: Hayes Store, Gloucester Co. Address: Hague Post Office, Westmoreland Co., Va.

STOUT, Rufus Sea, denominational secretary, lawyer, traction manager; born in Rust County, Tex., Sept. 15, 1868; son of James and Ellen (Campbell) Stout; grad. Longview (Tex.) High School, 1880; (LL.B., specially conferred; hon. D.D., Texas College); married Richie O. Kelley, of Houston, Tex., Dec. 26, 1893; 3 children: Ellen N., Rufus S., Charles O. Admitted to practice of law in Supreme Courts of Tex., La., Calif.; general manager Haygood Light & Traction Co., Washington, Ark.; stockholder Mound Bayon Oil Mill & Mfg. Co., Miss., Farmers' & Citizens' Savings Bank, Palestine, Tex., Fraternal Savings Bank & Trust Co., Memphis, Tenn., Magnolia Ice Cream Co., Pine Bluff, Ark.; general secretary Extension Dept. Colored M. E. Church; delegate to five general conferences of the church; organizer and president board of directors Colored Y. M. C. A., Pine Bluff. Trustee Haygood Seminary, Washington, Ark., and Central Industrial School, Pine Bluff. Was chaplain with rank of captain of Texas Colored Vol.; served one term as deputy U. S. Marshall in Eastern Dist., Tex. Democrat. Mason; member Odd Fellows, Knights of Pythias, Knights of Tabor, United Brothers of Friendship, Mosaic Templars, Royal Circle. Home: 519 E. 13th Ave., Pine Bluff, Ark.

STOVALL, L., physician, surgeon; born at Atlanta, Ga., Dec. 16, 1887; son of Jerry and Mary (Scott) Stovall; grad. Union High School, Hollywood, Cal., 1906; studied medicine in Univ. of Southern Ca., 2 years; M.D., Univ. of Cal., 1912; unmarried. Practiced in Los Angeles since 1912; visiting surgeon Selwyn Emmett Graves Dispensary, Univ. of Cal.; attending physician Municipal Child Welfare Station, 1914; grand medical examiner U. B. F. of Cal.; physician for Foresters, Odd Fellows, Knights of Pythias; president Georgia State Society; cor. sec. Negro State Societies of Southern Calif. Republican. Methodist. Member American Medical Assn., Calif. State Medical Assn., Los Angeles County Medical Assn., Southern Cal. Physicians, Dental and Pharm. Assn. Address: 1300 Fleming St., Los Angeles, Cal.

STOWERS, Walter Haslip, lawyer; born at Owensboro, Ky., Feb. 7, 1859; son of Jesse and Hester Stowers; grad. Detroit High School, Mich., 1879, Mahews Business Univ., 1881; LL.B., Detroit College of Law, 1895; married Susie F. Wallace, of Oberlin, O., Feb. 26, 1886; 2 children: Marjorie R., Walter J. Began as associate editor and pub. Detroit Plain Dealer, 1881, continuing to 1893; admitted to Mich. bar, 1895; since practiced in Detroit; member law firm of Barnes & Stowers; attorney for White Sewing Machine Co., Acme Repair & Tire Co., Almo Amusement Co., Zelah Amusement Co., Villa Amusement Co.; financially interested in the Almo, Zelah, Villa, and Grand Circus Amusement and Acme companies. Trustee Phyllis Wheatley Home for Aged Colored Women. Republican; was clerk of assessors 4 years, deputy sheriff 4 years, deputy county clerk 12 years, assistant chief clerk more than 3 years. Presbyterian. Member Detroit Bar Assn. Mason. Author (with William H. Anderson, Detroit): Appointed, 1888. Home: 306 Meldrum Ave. Office: Chamber of Commerce Bldg., Detroit, Mich.

STRICKLAND, George Wilson, physician, surgeon; born at Claxton, Ga., Apr. 1, 1875; son of Morgan and Visa (Brewton)Strickland; A.B., Fisk Univ., Nashville, Tenn., 1901; M.D., Illinois Medical College, 1905; M.D., College of Physicians and Surgeons (Univ. of Illinois), 1908; unmarried. Practiced in Newport, Ark., and was president Standard Drug Store, 1905-7; in practice in Pittsburgh, Pa., since 1908; president Lincoln Drug Co. Republican. Congregationalist. Member American Medical Assn., Allegheny County Medical Society. Mason; member Odd Fellows, Knights of Pythias, Elks. Address: 6266 Frankstown Ave., Pittsburgh, Pa.

SUGGS, Daniel Cato, college professor and vice-president; son of George W. and Esther Suggs; prep. edn. St. Augustine's Normal School at Raleigh, N. C.,; A.B., Lincoln (Pa.) Univ., 1884; studied at Cornell, Harvard, and Univ. of Chicago; (hon. A.M., Ph.D.); married Mamie A. Nocho, of Greensboro, N. C., Sept. 29, 1902; 3 children: Christine, Daniel Cato, Jr., Beatrice. Principal of school at Kington, N. C., 1884-6, Asheville, 1886-8; professor of mathematics and physical science, Livingstone College, Salisbury, N. C., 1888-91; director department of natural scence and vice-pres. Georgia State Industrial College, Savannah, since 1891; president Mutual Fire Insurance Co., Dixie Mercantile Co.; vice-president and treas. Union Savings Bank; wealth equals $100,000. Member A. M. E. Zion Church, Odd Fellows, Knights of Pythias. Home: 401 E. Market St., Greensboro, N. C. Office: Georgia State Industrial College, Savannah, Ga.

SWAIN, Benjamin Wilson, clergyman; born at Southport, N. C., Sept. 23, 1866; son of George R. and Sarah (Wescott) Swain; public school and private tuition, Southport; studied theology under Rev. Drs. D. H. Tuttle, B. F. Saunders, J. A. Williamson; (D.D., Livingstone College, Salisbury, N. C., 1906); widower: 3 children: Lloyd W., George L., Earle A. W. Entered Methodist ministry at Southport, Apr. 13, 1889; pastored A. M. E. Zion churches at Bath, Johnstown and

Jamestown, N. Y., Berkley, Va., Paterson, N. J., Worcester, Mass., Hartford, Conn.; now pastor A. M. E. Zion Church, Boston; secretary Barber Memorial Home for Aged Ministers; recording secretary New England Annual Conference; chairman board of Varick Christian Endeavor. Mason. Home: 702 Columbus Ave., Boston, Mass.

SWEENEY, William Allison, writer, orator; born at Superior, Washtenaw Co., Mich., July 27, 1851; son of William Jacob and Aurilla (Day) Sweeney; ed. public school, Ann Arbor, Mich., and district schools Ingham Co.; married Rene Clark, of Battle Creek, Oct. 5, 1872; 2d marriage, Roberta Lomax Erskine, of Cincinnati, O., Apr. 9, 1879 (died 1903); 2 children by first union: Max Ashly (died 1877), Alice S. (Mrs. Harry Winborn, of Battle Creek, Mich.). Began active career as newspaper writer, 1879; contributor to The People and The Herald (white), Indianapolis, Ind., and various metropolitan papers, 1880-3; first Negro to serve on U. S. jury in W. Va., 1885; editor and publisher The People, Wheeling, W. Va., 1885-6, The National People, Detroit, Mich., 1886-7; editor and mgr. The Freeman, Indianapolis, 1890-8, Chicago Conservator, Ill., 1904-5; editor and part owner Chicago Leader, 1905-6; writer and public speaker on racial and other subjects since 1906. Was affiliated with Liberal Republican party and campaign speaker for Horace Greeley, 1872; employed by non-partisan committee of One Hundred, Philadelphia, Pa., in the municipal campaign, 1882, to canvass the city in its first uprising against "boss rule"; supported Benjamain Harrison during presidential campaigns, 1888, 1892; canvassed state of Ind. for William McKinley, 1896; leader of successful Negro Republican revolt, Marion Co., Ind., when Harry S. New, member Republican National Committee, and so-called "bosses" were charged with treating Negro voters unfair, 1897; chairman Independent Colored Republican Voter's League, 5 years; custodian Tom-

linson Hall, bureau the Department of Public Works, 4 years; canvassed in interest of William H. Taft during campaign, 1908, assigned as speaker in Lincoln and Omaha., Nebr., Minneapolis and St. Paul, Minn.; supported regular Republican nominee in presidential campaign, 1912, speaking in southern and western Ill., also portions of Mo. Author: The Other Fellows Burden, 1913 (inspired by Rudyard Kipling's, The White Man's Burden). Poems: Lincoln; A Certain American Beauty at the President's Levee; No Chance for the Negro?; Baby; A Name Among the Princely Few. Address: 3250 Vernon Ave., Chicago, Ill.

T

TALBERT, Henry Payne, assistant secretary Wilberforce Univ.; born at Albany, N. Y., Mar. 13, 1884; son of Rev. Horace and Sarah Franklin (Black) Talbert; ed, Wilberforce and Howard universities; married Dora A. Russell, of Xenia, Ohio, June 9, 1909; 4 children: Ellen F., Florance E., Henry P., Jr., Dora A. Assistant to the secretary of Wilberforce Univ., O., since 1908; director of public schools of Wilberforce; member real estate firm of Talbert Bros., Xenia. Republican. African Methodist. Member Green County Improvement Assn. Mason; member Elks. Address: R. R. No. 5, Xenia, Ohio.

TALBERT, Horace, clergyman, university secretary; born at Louisville, Ky., 1859; son of William and Jane Ellen (Dory) Talbert; grad. Wilberforce Univ., 1877; (hon. A.M., D.D., by several institutions); married Sarah Franklin Black, of Washington, D. C., 1879; 14 children: Annie A., Dumas S., Eugene H., Homer A., Horace, Jr., Henry P., Vergil P., Wendell P., Ruby M., William E., Elizabeth R., Benjamin B., Helen J., Ulysses G. Pastored A. M. E. churches 20 years; professor of languages at Wilberforce Univ., 2 years; in charge New York Conference High School, 3 years; editor and manager the African Watchman, 3 years; secretary and financial officer of Wilberforce Univ., since 1897; part owner mail order house of Talbert Specialty Co. Trustee Green County Township Schools. Republican. Mason; member Odd Fellows, Knights of Pythias. Author: The Sons of Allen, 1904. Address: R. R. No. 5, Xenia, O.

TALBERT, Mary Burnett, teacher, lecturer; born at Oberlin, O., Sept. 17, 1865; daughter of Cornelius J. and Caroline (Nichols) Burnett; S.P.B., Oberlin College, 1894; married William H. H. Talbert, of Buffalo, N. Y., Sept. 8, 1891; 1 child: Sarah May. Chairman executive board National Assn. of Colored Women; president Empire State Federation of Woman's Clubs, Christian Culture Congress, and Phyllis Wheatley Club of Buffalo. Was teacher in high school at Little Rock, Ark., 6 years; lecturer on racial subjects. Baptist. Member Order of Eastern Star, Household of Ruth. Contributor to several magazines. Address: 521 Michigan St., Buffalo, N. Y.

TALBERT, William Herbert Hilton, organization pres.; born at Red Bluff, Cal., Jan. 27, 1866; son of Robert and Anna Maria (Harris) Talbert; public school edn., Buffalo, N. Y.; married Mary M. Burnett, of Oberlin, O., Sept. 8, 1891; 1 child: Sarah May. Pres. Buffalo Colored Republican League, since 1911; clerk in office of city treas.; has been in real estate business since 1889. Baptist. Home: 521 Michigan St. Office: 79 Clinton St., Buffalo, N. Y.

TALLEY, Thomas Washington, university professor; born at Shelbyville, Tenn.; son of Charles Washington and Lucinda (Williams) Talley; A.B., Fisk Univ., Nashville, Tenn., 1890, A.M., 1892; Sc.D., Walden Univ., Nashville, 1899; married Ellen E. Roberts, of Jacksonville, Fla., Aug. 28, 1900; 2 children: Sonoma C., Thomasina W. Instructor in science Alcorn (Miss.) Agricultural and Mechanical College, 1899-1900; professor of sciences and vice-pres. State Agricultural and Mechanical College, Tallahassee, Fla., 1900-2; instructor in analytical and applied chemistry in Tuskegee Normal and Industrial Institute, Ala., 1902-3;

professor of chemistry and biology at Fisk Univ., since 1903. Member Society of Arts, and Society of Chemical Industry (London, Eng.), American Chemical Society. Address: 908 17th Ave. N., Nashville, Tenn.

TANNER, Benjamin Tucker, bishop; born at Pittsburgh, Pa., Dec. 25, 1835; son of Hugh and Isabel Tanner; ed. Avery College, Allegheny, Pa., and Western Theological Seminary; (A.M., Avery, 1870; D.D., LL.D., Wilberforce Univ.); married Sarah Elizabeth Miller, Aug. 19, 1858; father of number children, including Henry O. Tanner, artist. United with A. M. E. Church and ordained in Pittsburgh; elected bishop, 1888; was editor Christian Recorder 16 years; founder, and editor 4 years, A. M. E. Church Review. Member American Negro Academy. Author: The Origin of the Negro; Is the Negro Cursed?; Apology for African Methodism; Outlines of African Methodist Episcopal Church History; The Dispensations of the History of the Church; The Negro in Holy Writ; A Hint to Ministers, Especially of the African Methodist Episcopal Church; The Color of Solomon—What? Was delegate to Ecumenical Conference on Methodism, London, Eng., 1901, and read paper at that time on "The Elements of Pulpit Effectiveness." Home: 2908 Diamond St., Philadelphia, Pa.

TANNER, Henry Ossawa, artist; born at Pittsburgh, Pa., June 21, 1859; son of Rt. Rev. Benjamin T. and Sarah Elizabeth (Miller) Tanner; married in London, Eng., Jessie Macauley, of San Francisco, Cal., Dec. 14, 1899. Studied in Pennsylvania Academy of Fine Arts under Thomas Eakins; pupil in Paris of Jean Paul Laurens and Benjamin Constant. Painter of religious subjects; honorable mention in Salon, Paris, 1896; awards: 3d class medal, 1897; 2d class medal, 1897; won Walter Lippincott prize at Philadelphia, Pa., and Harris prize, Chicago, Ill., 1900; 2d medal at Paris Exposition, 1900; 2d medal, Pan-American Exposition, Buffalo, N. Y., 1901; 2d medal, Louisiana Purchase Exposition, St. Louis, Mo., 1904. Represented with paintings in the Luxembough, the Wilstach Collection, Carnegie Institute at Pittsburgh, Pennsylvania Academy of Fine Arts, and Art Institute of Chicago; sold the famous painting, "Rising of Lazarus," to Luxembourg galleries. Associate National Academician; member Paris Society of American Painters, Societe International de Peinture et Sculpture, American Art Assn., Paris. Studio: 70 bis, Rue Notre Dame –des Champs, Paris. Home: Trepied-par Etaples, France.

TARLETON, William Albert, physician, surgeon; born at Savannah, Ga., 1880; prep. edn., Georgia State College, Savannah; grad. Howard Univ. School of Medicine, Washington, D. C. Was interne at Mercy Hospital and George H. Hubbard Hospital, Nashville, Tenn.; assistant to Dr. Daniel Williams, of Chicago, Ill., for a time; practiced in Los Angeles, Cal., since Dec. 21, 1914; in 1915 he installed the French Dearsondal Violet Ray Treatment and X-Ray Machine. Office: 412 Germain Bldg., Los Angeles, Cal.

TAYLOR, Edmund Bernard, caterer; born at Baltimore, Md., Dec. 11, 1877; son of Richard and Louisa V. (Stark) Taylor; grad. high school, Baltimore, 1897; unmarried. Began as dishwasher in club house, and advanced to steward; later steward 3 clubs at same time; purchased catering business of the late Louis Butler, 1905; in 8 years value increased from $5,000 to about $40,000; incorporated under name of E. B. Taylor with capital stock of $60,000; principal owner and president of company; has served 8,000 people daily during conventions, and banquets of 3,500; served members of Royal families number times; exports terrapin to England and Germany; introduced number fancy foods and drinks. Was first vocational teacher in Colored High School, Baltimore; promoter of Home Shoe Co.; one of founders The Lancet (newspaper); owns 360-acre farm in Charles County, Md. Was chairman Citizens' Committee to raise $120,000 for Morgan College; also chairman of committee that rebuilt Provident Hospital;

vice-president Home for Friendless Colored Children; director Baltimore Branch, National Assn. for Advancement of Colored People; governor of Baltimore Assembly (social organization). Republican. 33d degree Mason; member Knights of Pythias, Elks. Home: 305 W. Biddle St. Office: 886 Linden Ave., Baltimore, Md.

TAYLOR, Junius LaFayette, clergyman; born in Virginia, Nov. 6. 1871; son of James M. and Francis (Vaughan) Taylor; prep. edn. St. Paul Normal and Industrial School, Lawrenceville, Va.; grad. Bishop Payne Divinity School, Petersburg, Va.; (D.D., Livingstone College, N. C., 1908); married Lucy W. Putney, of Petersburg, June 21, 1905; 4 children: Carl A., Lillian L., Francis V., Junius LaF., Jr. Ordained Episcopal ministry, 1904; pastor Mother Church at St. Stephen's Church, Va., and other mission stations, to 1910; as pastor St. Cyprian's Parish, Newbern, N. C., 1910-13, erected brick edifice at cost of 15,000, beautiful in architecture and largest Episcopal church in the south; pastor St. Stephen's, Savannah, Ga., since Oct. 1, 1913, regarded as the leading Colored Episcopal Church in southern states. Member National League on Urban Conditions Among Negroes, Savannah Negro Business League. Mason. Club: Men's. Address: 313 E. Harris St., Savannah, Ga.

TAYLOR, W. Walter, designer, millinery; born at Newbern, N. C., June 12, 1868; son of Lewis Henry and Fannie (Bryant) Taylor; public school edn., Cambridge, Mass.; married Laura E. Hunter, of Boston, June 20, 1900; 4 children; Frances, Emily, W. Walter, Jr., Lewis Henry. Apprentice in millinery business with C. C. Gregg, Boylston St., Boston, 1888-90; with W. B. Crocker since Jan. 1, 1890, first in Boston, later took charge the New York store; traveled extensively for the house; representative of colored people in art of designing millinery. Republican. Member New York Civic League. Mason. Clubs: Riverside Motor, Diamond Whist. Home: 552

Lenox Ave. Office: 375 Fifth Ave., New York.

TERRELL, Alexander Bismarck, physician; born at Ft. Worth, Tex., Dec. 18, 1885; son of Isaiah M. and Marcelite (Landry) Terrell; grandson of Rev. Pierre Landry, of New Orleans, La.; ed. public schools, Ft. Worth; B.S., Univ. of Chicago, 1907; M.D., Harvard Medical College, 1910; unmarried. Practiced in Ft. Worth since Oct., 1910. Republican. Baptist. Member Odd Fellows, Knights and Daughters of Tabor. Home: 616 Jennings Ave. Office: 108 1-2 E. 9th St., Ft. Worth, Texas.

TERRELL, Isaiah Milligan, principal high school; born at Anderson, Tex., Jan. 4, 1859; A.B., Straight Univ., New Orleans, La., 1881, A.M., 1900; married Marcelite Landry, of Donaldsonville, La., Feb. 7, 1883; 2 children: Isaiah M., Jr., Alexander Bismarck. Taught school in Texas since 1882; now principal high school at Ft. Worth, and supervisor of colored schools. Republican. Baptist. Member Odd Fellows. Address: 616 Jennngs Ave., Ft. Worth, Texas.

TERRELL, Marcelite Landry, teacher; born at Donaldsonville, La., June 20, 1866; daughter of Rev. Pierre and Amanda (Grisby) Landry; ed. Straight Univ., New Orleans, La., and Ginn & Co. Summer School of Music; married Isaiah M. Terrell, of Anderson, Tex., Feb. 7, 1883; 2 children: Isaiah M., Alexander Bismarck. Supervisor of music in public school, Ft. Worth, Tex. Baptist. Member Household of Ruth. Address: 616 Jennings Ave., Ft. Worth, Texas.

TERRELL, Robert Herberton, municipal judge; born in Orange County, Va., Nov. 25, 1857; son of Harrison and Louisa (Coleman) Terrell; attended public schools in Washington, D. C.; prep. edn. Lawrence Academy, Groton, Mass.; A.B., Harvard, 1884; LL.B., Howard Univ., 1889, LL.M., 1893, A.M., 1900; (LL.D., Livingstone College, Salisbury, N. C., 1913); married Mary Church, of Memphis, Tenn., Oct. 28, 1891; children: Mary Phyllis (and 3 deceased). Began as teacher,

1884, later principal Colored High School at Washington to 1889; was chief of a division in the Treasury, 1889-93; admitted to D. C. bar, 1893; associated with John M. Lynch 5 years under firm name of Lynch & Terrell; civil magistrate, 1902-9, and judge in Municipal Court, D. C., since 1909; appointed by Presidents Theodore Roosevelt, William H. Taft, Woodrow Wilson; the Senate confirmed the 1914 appointment after a more or less sensational struggle. Republican. Congregationalist. Member Sigma Pi Phi. Mason; past grand master his lodge 4 terms; member Odd Fellows. Home: 1826 13th St. N. W. Office: Municipal Court, Washington, D. C.

TERRELL, Wendell Phillips, teacher of mechanics; born at Ft. Worth, Tex., Mar. 1, 1884; son of Isaiah M. and Marcelite (Landry) Terrell; grandson of Rev. Pierre Landry, of New Orleans; grad. high school, Ft. Worth, 1901; Kansas State Agricultural College, 1904; S.B., Massachusetts Institute of Technology, 1906; unmarried. Superintendent of mechanics and mechanical engineer at Prairie Piew (Tex.) State Normal and Industrial College. Baptist. Member American Society of Engineers. Mason. Address: Prairie View, Texas.

TERRELL, William H., real estate; born at Hopkinsville, Ky., June 4, 1876; son of Samuel S. and Martha (Smooth) Terrell; grammar school edn., Louisville; student State Univ., Ky.; took course in Bryant & Stratton Business College, Chicago, Ill.; unmarried. Began as agent for Mass. Accident Co.; was member real estate firm of Murry & Terrell number years; with W. B. Anderson since 1910, under name of Anderson & Terrell; president A-T Varnish Remover Co., a corporation. President Standard Literary Society. Baptist. Member South Side Voters' League. Mason; member Foresters. Club: Matoka Class. Home: 3763 Wabash Ave. Office: 3512 State St., Chicago, Ill.

TERRY, Clifford Edward, physician, surgeon; born at Columbus, Ga., July 27, 1885; son of William E. and Celestia Terry; grad. public school, Columbus, 1901; A.B., Lincoln (Pa.) Univ., 1908; M.D., New York Homoeopathic Medical College and Flower Hospital, 1912; unmarried. Began practice in Plainfield, N. J., 1912; later removed to Columbus, Ga.; member firm with 2 brothers, People's Drug Store. Presbyterian. Member American Institute of Homoeopathy, National Medical Assn., North Jersey Medical Assn. Club: Bachelor-Benedict (president), New York. Home: 308 N. 3d St., Plainfield, N. J. Office: 20 10th St., Columbus, Ga.

TERRY, Watt, real estate; identified with all movements in his state for advancement of colored people; large tax payer in home city. Address: Main St., Brockton, Mass.

THOMAS, Charles Lee, dentist; born at Weston, W. Va., July 24, 1881; son of Leroy and Flora (Lee) Thomas; grad. High School, Zanesville, Ohio, 1902; student Ohio Wesleyan Univ., 1903-5; D.D.S., Ohio Medical College, Columbus, 1908; unmarried. In practice in St. Louis, Mo., since Nov. 1, 1909. African Methodist. Member St. Louis Dental Society, Mound City Medical Assn. Mason. Club: Bass Clef. Home and Office: 2607 Lawton Ave., St. Louis, Mo.

THOMAS, Elise Oliver Minton, playground director; born at Charleston, S. C., Mar. 16, 1880; daughter of Warren Gustavus and Modestine Sophia (Fields) Minton; grad. Avery Normal Institute, S. C., 1898; A.B., Fisk Univ., 1903; married Dr. George Washington Thomas, Jr., of Smithfield, Va., June 21, 1911. Began as teacher in St. Paul's Normal and Industrial School, Lawrenceville, Va., 1903, later St. Athanasius School, Brunswick, Ga.; in charge social work Stillman House Settlement, New York, 4 years; director Walt's Playground, Chester, Pa., 2 years. Episcopalian. Address: 1422 W. 3d St., Chester, Pa.

THOMAS, George Jefferson, teacher; born in Dooly Co., Ga., Aug. 10, 1878; son of George Franklin and Moaning (Everett) Thomas; prep. edn., Talladega College, Ala., 1904;

B.S., Knoxville College, Tenn., 1908; B.Ped., Atlanta Normal, 1914; married Winnie C. Whitaker, of Rockford, Ala., June 28, 1911; 2 children: Partia H., Winnie C. Principal Autauga Institute, Prattville, Ala., 1906-7, high school, Wooldridge, Tenn, 1908-11; principal Evergreen Academy, Ashburn, Ga., since 1911; president Geo. F. Thomas Sons, Hawkinsville, Ga., 1912-14; president Turner County Institute for Colored Teachers. Delegate from Knoxville College to 36th annual convention International Y. M. C. A., 1907. Chairman executive committee Republican County Committee of Pulaski County, Ga., 1912; delegate to Republican State Convention, Atlanta, also District Convention, Americus, 1912. Missionary Baptist. Member Knights of Pythias; chancellor commander Stringer Lodge No. 25, Hawkinsville. Address: P. O. Box 32, Ashburn, Ga.

THOMAS, George Washington, Jr., physician; born at Smithfield, Isle of Wright Co., Va., June 2, 1875; son of George W. and Adeline (Boykin) Thomas; ed. public schools, Smithfield; grad. Va. Normal and Collegiate Institute, Petersburg, 1893; Pharm.D., Howard Univ. Pharm. College, 1903; M.D., Howard, 1908; married Elise Oliver Minton, of Charleston, S. C., June 21, 1911. Teacher in public schools of Va., 6 years; drug clerk, Philadelphia, Pa., 1 year; practiced in Chester, Pa., since 1909. Republican. African Methodist. Member Philadelphia Academy of Medicine and Allied Sciences, Physicians' Assn., of Chester; also member Odd Fellows, Elks, Knights of Pythias. Club: Professional (Phila.). Address: 1422 W. 3d St., Chester, Pa.

THOMAS, James C., undertaker, embalmer; born at Galveston, Tex., Dec. 25, 1863; common school edn. to age of 8 years; grad. Philadelphia Training School for Embalmers (now Eckels College of Embalming), 1897; married Ella A. Rollins, of Richmond, Va.; 7 children: James C., Jr., Ella, Lillie, Madge, Corinne, Evelyn, Ruth. Undertaker and embalmer in New

York since 1897; has demonstrated art of scientific embalming in New York colleges number times. Trustee Bethel A. M. E. Church. Progressive. Member National Funeral Directors' Assn., New York State Undertakers' Assn., Colored Business League of New York, Equity Congress. Mason; member Odd Fellows. Address: 89 W. 134th St., New York.

THOMAS, Mary Etta, supervising industrial teacher; born at Snow Hill, Ala., Mar. 7, 1873; daughter of John and Fannie Elizabeth (Johnson) Thomas; public school edn., Snow Hill; grad. Tuskegee Normal and Industrial Institute, Ala., 1897; took course in the School of Education at Univ. of Chicago; unmarried. Began as teacher in Tuskegee Institute, 1898; teacher at Snow Hill Institute, 1898-1904, and in rural schools of Calhoun, Chilton, Autauga, and Lowndes Counties, Ala., to 1914; supervising industrial teacher in Negro Rural Schools, Monroe County, Ala., since Oct., 1914; she is one of the 22 supervisors under the state supervisor; with the aid of the Anna T. Jeanes Fund this branch of modern public instruction reaches the most remote schools and homes of the state. African Methodist. Home: Snow Hill, Ala.

THOMAS, Thomas M., clergyman; born at Orangeburg, S. C., Nov. 2, 1867; son of John W. and Frances (Barr) Thomas; prep. edn., Claflin Univ., Orangeburg; A.B., Lincoln (Pa.) Univ., 1895, A.M., S.T.B., 1898; married Mary B. Nugent, of Chester, Pa., Oct. 10, 1906; 1 child. Ordained in Presbyterian ministry, June, 1898; since pastor at Chester; president Afro-American Presbyterian Council; principal Chester Industrial School; conducts only job printing plant owned by Negro in Delaware Co., Pa. Republican. Home: 1706 W. 2d St. Office: 1817 W. 3d St., Chester, Pa.

THOMAS, Victor Philip, merchandise sampler in custom house, writer; born in Ascension Parish, La., Feb. 14, 1863; son of Alcide and Mathilde (Brierre) Thomas; public school and private tuition in Ascension Parish; student curriculum New Orleans Univ., Leland Univ., Straight Univ.; secured teachers' certificate of first grade; married Mary Emsley, of Ascension Parish, May 25, 1885; 12 children. Was principal Donaldsonville (La.) Academy, 12 years; deputy collector of internal revenue, Louisiana Dist., 1893; editor and pub. Business Herald, Donaldsonville, 1898-1903; newspaper correspondent; has written in defense of Negroes rights to white newspapers many years; book reviewer and translator of French writings; merchandise sampler in U. S. appraiser's office, Customs House, New Orleans, since 1903. Appointed delegate to Farmers' Conference by mayor of New Orleans, and by Gov. Luther E. Hall to National Half-Century Anniversary Celebration of Negro Freedom, Chicago, Ill., 1915. Republican; served party as secretary and as chairman Parish Committee, also secretary 3d Cong. Dist. Committee; delegate to several state and district conventions. Catholic. Owns a home and 2 acres near Donaldsonville. Residence: 1811 Terpsichore St. Office: U. S. Appraiser's Dept., Customs House, New Orleans, La.

THOMPSON, Eloise Bibb, writer; born at New Orleans, La., June 29, 1878; daughter of Charles H. and Catherine Adele Bibb; father was inspector of U. S. Customs about 40 years; grad. New Orleans Univ., 1895; student Oberlin College, Ohio, 1901-2; grad. Teachers' College, Howard Univ., 1908; special study in New York School of Philanthrophy; married Noah D. Thompson, of Chicago, Ill., Aug. 4, 1911. Head resident Social Settlement House, Howard Univ., Washington, D. C., 1908-11; writer for Los Angeles Tribune, Cal., since 1914. Catholic. Author: Poems, 1895. Address: 1711 E. 55th St., Los Angeles, California.

THOMPSON, John Lay, lawyer, editor; born in Decatur County, Iowa, May 28, 1869; son of Andy and Catherine (Shepard) Thompson; ed. public schools; grad. Iowa Business College, 1894; LL.B., Drake Univ., Des Moines,

Iowa, 1898; married Maud O. Watkins, of Albany, Mo., Aug. 15, 1901; 2 children: Enola Vera, John N. Admitted to Iowa bar and U. S. District Court, 1898; since practiced in Des Moines; was file clerk Iowa State Senate, 1899-1901, elected from Grand River in Decatur County to the 3 sessions over white competitors, yet there was no other colored family in the county; was deputy county treasurer 1 term; clerk in Iowa Hospital Dept., 1900-6; editor and publisher Iowa State Bystander; president North Star Masonic Temple Assn.; treasurer and trustee Union Congregational Church. Delegate to Republican State Convention from Decatur County, 1900; delegate to state and county conventions from Polk County number of years. Member Des Moines Negro Business League; grand master M. W. United Grand Lodge A. F. & A. M. for Iowa and jurisdiction. Won 1st prize (gold medal) in oratorical contest against 8 colleges in Iowa at Drake Univ., 1897; the oration was published in pamphlet form. Home: 1306 W. 20th St. Office: 201 W. 7th St., Des Moines, Iowa.

THOMPSON, Noah D., real estate; born at Baltimore, Md., June 9, 1874; son of William P. and Sarah (Woods) Thompson; public school edn., Baltimore; took course in Greggs Business College, Chicago, Ill.; married Lillian B. Murphy, of Baltimore, Nov. 6, 1901 (died 1905); 2d marriage, Eloise A. Bibb, of New Orleans, La., Aug. 4, 1911; 1 child, Noah Murphy. Began as general solicitor for U. S. Express Co., Chicago, 1909; circulation manager and assistant to the treasurer at Tuskegee Normal and Industrial Institute, Ala., 1910-11; operated real estate and loan business as The Noah D. Thompson Realty Co., Los Angeles, Cal., since 1911; associate editor the Liberator. Was offered appointment as sergt.-at-arms to American Commission of Paris Exposition, 1900; member advisory council National Half-Century Anniversary of Negro Freedom, Chicago, 1915. Catholic. Member Los Angeles Chamber of Commerce. Home: 1711 E. 55th St. Office: Long Beach Ave. and 55th St., Los Angeles, Cal.

THOMPSON, Richard W., writer, clerk Treasury Dept.; born at Brandenburg, Meade Co., Ky., Dec. 20, 1865; son of Rev. Powhatan S. and Jane L. Thompson; public school edn., Indianapolis, Ind.; married Grace Lucas, of Indianapolis, Nov. 5, 1901; 1 child: Vivian Lucile. Learned printers' trade in office of Bagly & Co. (Indianapolis Leader), 1881; later city editor Indianapolis World; contributed special matter to Indianapolis Daily Sentinel, and a weekly—The People, both white; managing editor, Indianapolis Freemen, 1888-92, Washington Colored American (D. C.), 1894-1903; founded, 1903, since manager Thompson's National News Bureau; organized first meeting of National Negro Press Assn., at Louisville, Ky., 1909; was president, 1909-13, and reported its conventions annually; served as special newspaper representative during number state tours of Dr. Booker T. Washington; writer on social, industrial, political and other current topics. Was first colored page in Indiana legislature, 1880-1; letter carrier in Indianapolis, 1888-93; clerk in government service at Washington since 1894; served in U. S. Printing Office, Bureau of the Census, War Dept., and others; now clerk in Treasury Dept. Special agent for Tuskegee Normal and Industrial Institute. Republican. Episcopalian. Was president Second Baptist Church Lyceum, Washington, 1900-13. Clubs: Mu-So-Lit (corr. sec.); Pen and Pencil (charter member). Home: 1223 S St. N. W., Washington, D. C.

THORNE, Philip M., lawyer; born at Charleston, S. C., July 19, 1885; son of Philip M. and Susan E. (Massey) Thorne; grad. Avery Normal Institute, Charleston, 1902; Boys High School, Brooklyn, N. Y., 1906; LL.B., Yale, 1909; unmarried. Began as clerk with law firm of Thompson & Ballantine, New York, 1909; in office of Robert S. Patterson, 1910-13; admitted to N. Y. bar, 1913, and since in practice in New York. Progressive. Member Alpha Phi Alpha. Mason; Knight Templar, Shriner; member Odd Fellows, Foresters. Clubs: St. Philip's Guild, Smart Set Athletic. Home: 85 Pulaski St., Brooklyn. Office: 51 Chambers St., New York.

THURSTON, Roger Graves, ex-soldier; born at Louise, Va., Apr. 28, 1880; son of Samuel Thurston; ed. public schools, Louise; grad. W. Va. Colored Normal and Industrial Institute, 1911; married Carrie L. Jones, of Mt. Hope, W. Va., June 15, 1911; 2 children: Roger J., Samuel M. Served in 25th Inf. U. S. A., Cuba and Philippine Islands, 1898-1902, in 9th Cav., 1902-5, Q. M. Corps, Ft. Myer, Va., 2 yrs.; blacksmith, Ft. Myer, since 1912. Mason. Home: Rosslyn, Va. (P. O. Box 93). Office: Ft. Myer, Va.

THURSTON, Thomas Wellington, Jr., silk manufacturer, clergyman; born at Moorefield, W. Va., Apr. 9, 1866; son of Thomas W. and Betty (Jones) Thurston; grad. Romney High School, W. Va.; studied theology under Rev. Dr. J. A. Gayley, of Princeton Univ., N. J.; (hon. D.D., Lotta Univ., Raleigh, N. C.); married Julia Lacey, of Washington, D. C., 1890; 7 children: Virginia, Pauline, Ruth, Marie, Derrick, Douglas, Dwight. Ordained Baptist ministry, 1894; pastor St. John Temple Church, Washington, D. C.; principal Barnwell Normal and Farm Life School for Colored Youth, Fort Barnwell, N. C.; editorial writer for Free-will Baptist Advocate. Began as silk manufacturer, 1895; established the Five Points Silk Mills that year at Columbia, Pa.; built the Mammoth Silk Mills, Fayetteville, N. C., 1900, the Twins Silk Mills, Kinston, N. C., 1906; now manager W. H. Ashley Silk Co.; employs average of about 600 operatives; only American silk manufacturer of African descent. Republican. Mason; member Odd Fellows. Address; Kinston, N. C.

THWEATT, Hiram Harold, principal high school; born at Tuskegee, Ala., June 11, 1864; son of Raymond F. and Lucinda (Wright) Thweatt; ed. Tuskegee Normal and Industrial Institute; received private instruction in French, German, Latin; real estate correspondence course from National Co-operative Realty School, Washington, D. C.; married Jancie Hunter, of Apelika, Ala., Dec. 29, 1901 (died 1910); 2d marriage, Itaska B. Giddens, of Paris, Tex., Apr. 26, 1913; 3 children: Lillian C., Desmemona O., McKinley H. Worked at carpenters trade, 1870-84; assistant principal school in Lafayette, Ala., 1885-6; teacher of carpentry and assistant principal Clay Street Industrial School, Thomasville, Ga., 1890-2; taught at Sunny Hill, Fla., 1892; principal Brewton (Ala.) Academy, 1892-3, Christiansburg Institute, Cambria, Va., 1893-6, Clay Street Industrial School, Thomasville, 1896-1901, Clay Street High School since 1901. Republican. Choir leader and active in all work with St. Thomas A. M. E. Church, Thomasville, and supt. Sunday Schools in various places more than 15 years. Was president Thomas County Institute, 1896-1903, Georgia State Teachers' Assn., 1904-6; vice-president National Negro Teachers' Assn. of Ga., 1905-6; while census clerk in Washington, 1910, was president Census Social Club, in which 36 states were represented. Member National Educational Assn., National Negro Business League; also member Knights of Pythias, Court of Calanthe, Sons and Daughters of Emancipation Society (founder). Clubs: Sunshine, Tennis, Eureka Whist; honorary member Worthy Women. Author: What the Newspapers Say of Negro Soldiers in the Spanish-American War (2 vols.), 1899, 1906. Address: 232 W. Calhoun St., or Box 243, Thomasville, Ga.

TILDON, Frederick Douglas, clergyman; born at Michaelsville, Harford Co., Md., Feb. 21, 1867; son of Benjamin W. and Cecelia L. (Dallam) Tildon; public school edn., Harford County to 1886; A.B., Lincoln Univ., Pa., 1890, S.T.B., April, A.M., June, 1893; married Ella Butler, of Baltimore, Md., July 10, 1894; 9 children: Rugus A., H. Clifford, John Calvin,

Bessie May, Grace, Paul D., Earle Le-Roy, Ralph B., Olga Louise (Grace and Earle deceased). Ordained Presbyterian ministry, 1893; pastor at Hillburn, N. Y., 1893-6, Bethel Chapel, Plainfield, N. J., since 1896; was commissioner to General Assembly, 1910; member Plainfield Council the Boy Scouts of America, 1913. Republican. Home: 825 Richmond St., Plainfield, N. J.

TINSLEY, Henry Clay, physician, surgeon; born at London, Ky., July 5, 1869; son of Preston and Caroline (Severe) Tinsley; B.L., Berea (Ky.) College, 1900; M.D., Meharry Medical College (Walden Univ.), Nashville, Tenn., 1903; married Lottie W. Woodford, of Indianapolis, Ind., June 25, 1901. Worked on farm and in mines, taught school, and was clerk at various summer resorts; traveling agent for Berea College, 1899-1900; assistant teacher in Meharry Medical College, 1902; practised medicine and surgery in Georgetown since 1903; medical director Knights of Pythias, Odd Fellows, United Brothers of Friendship; vice-president Georgetown Mercantile Stock Co. Republican. Member Church in Christ. President Kentucky State Medical Assn. Address: 139 N. Hamilton St., Georgetown, Ky.

TOBIAS, Channing Higgie, secretary international committee Y. M. C. A.; born at Augusta, Ga., Feb. 1, 1882; son of Fair J. and Clara Belle (Robinson) Tobias; A.B., Paine College, Augusta, 1902; B.D., Drew Theological Seminary, Madison, N. J., 1905; student Univ. of Pa., summer, 1908; attended Students Conference of Eastern Colleges, Northfield, Mass., summers, 1912, 13; married Mary Pritchard, of Milledgeville, Ga., Nov. 10, 1908; 2 children: Belle C., Mary P. Began as teacher of Biblical literature in Paine College, Augusta, 1905, continuing to 1911; secretary international committee Young Men's Christian Associations since 1911, also teacher of colored secretaries in Chesapeake Summer School, at Arundel-on-the-Bay, Md.; assisted in conducting Negro Students Confer-

ence, Kings Mountain, N. C., 1912, 13. Was delegate to International Convention Y. M. C. A., Washington, D. C., 1907, Cincinnati, Ohio, 1913, to World's Student Christian Federation Conference, Lake Mohonk, N. Y., June 2-8, 1913; executive secretary Negro Christian Student Convention, Atlanta, Ga., 1914; member executive committee Federal Council of Churches of America. Colored Methodist. Home: 1450 Grinnett St., Augusta, Ga. Office: 1816 12th St. N. W., Washington, D. C.

TOLIVER, William Robert, clergyman, editor; born at Giddings, Lee Co., Texas, Apr. 16, 1880; son of Rev. Isaac and Mary (Bonford) Toliver; attended public school, Rockdale, Tex.; prep. edn., Hearne Academy, Tex.; grad. Bishop College, Marshall, Tex., 1900; married Della Quinn, of Fort Smith, Ark., Dec., 1900; 1 child: Wm. Robert, Jr. Ordained Baptist ministry, 1900; pastor 2d Bapt. Ch., Helena, Ark., to 1904, Providence Ch., Greensboro, N. C., 1904-7, Union Ch., Augusta, Ga., 1907-9; dean of theol. dept. Walker Baptist College, Augusta, 1907-9; pastor 1st Bapt. Ch., Corsicana, Tex., 1909-10, Boley, Okla., 1910-12; also editor Boley Progress, 1910-12; pastor Bethel Ch., Calvert, Tex., 1912-14; now general field sec. National Baptist Publishing Board; editor National Baptist Union Review; prop. Toliver Pub. Co., Nashville, Tenn. Republican. Mason; member Knights of Pythias. Wrote: Life and Sermons of Rev. Isaac Toliver, published 1915. Home: 1145 21st St. N. W., Washington, D. C. Office: 523 Second Ave. N., Nashville, Tenn.

TOMPKINS, George Ricks, mechanical engineer; born at Rochester, N. Y., Oct. 23, 1881; son of George C. and Emma Burns (Ricks) Tompkins; grad. high school, Buffalo, N. Y., 1900; M.E., Cornell Univ., Ithaca, N. Y. 1907; married Carolyn R. Moore, of Phelps, N. Y., Oct. 20, 1907; 2 children: Harry R., George R., Jr. Assistant foreman in the Pierce-Arrow automobile house of George N. Pierce Co., 1900-1; machinist in Buffalo Division of Erie Railroad, 1903-7, and engineer of road tests, 1907-8; director of mechanical department Agricultural and Mechanical College, Greensboro, N. C., 1908-10; mechanical engineer Wilberforce, Ohio, since 1910. Republican. Episcopalian. Mason. Clubs: Fortnightly (Buffalo), Pastime Tennis (Wilberforce). Address: Wilberforce, Ohio.

TORRENCE, William G., physician, surgeon; born in South Carolina, Nov. 16, 1880; son of Henry G. and Viollette (Brown) Torrence; married Elna F. Williams, of Raleigh, N. C., Aug. 1, 1909. Resident physician and general mgr. The Torrence Hospital, Asheville, N. C. Baptist. Member Odd Fellows, Knights of Pythias. Address: 95 Hill St., Asheville, N. C.

TOWNS, George Alexander, university professor; born at Albany, Ga., Mar. 5, 1870; son of Luke and Mary (Coates) Towns; A.B., Atlanta Univ., 1894, A.M., 1900; A.B., Harvard, 1900; took course in philosophy and education at Graduate School of Arts and Sciences, Harvard Univ.; married Nellie H. McNair, of Atlanta, Ga., Sept. 17, 1902; 3 children. Professor of pedagogy in Atlanta University since 1900. Member the Citizens League. Club: Monday. Address: 2 University Place, Atlanta, Ga.

TOWNSEND, Arthur Melvin, university president; born at Winchester, Tenn., Oct. 26, 1875; son of Doc Anderson and Emma Alice (Singleton) Townsend; public school edn., Winchester; A.B., Roger Williams Univ., Nashville, Tenn., 1898; M.D., Meharry Medical College (Walden Univ.), 1902; married Lilla Ann Hadley, of Nashville, June 11, 1902; 1 child: Arthur M., Jr. Practiced medicine in Nashville, and professor of pathology in Meharry Medical College, 1902-13; president Roger Williams Univ., since 1913; director People's Savings Bank & Trust Co., Star Realty & Investment Co., and Negro Board of Trade. Member National Medical Assn., Rock City Academy of Medicine and Surgery. Mason; member Odd Fellows; grand keeper records and seal Knights of Pythias of Tenn. Club: Vinx-Cing.

Contributor to Journal of the National Medical Assn. Address: Roger Williams University, Nashville, Tenn.

TOWNSEND, Willa A., teacher of music, elocution, English; born at Nashville, Tenn., Apr. 22, 1880; daughter of S. P. and Alice (Morris) Hadley; grad. Pearl High School, Nashville, 1899; studied music in Fisk Univ.; student Roger Williams Univ., 1913-14; married, June 11, 1902, Dr. Arthur M. Townsend, of Winchester, Tenn., now president Roger Williams Univ.; 1 child: Arthur M., Jr. Began as teacher public school, Nashville, 1899, continuing to 1902; was editor "Miladi" column of Nashville Globe several years, also "George Eliot" column in Nashville Clarion; principal English dept. Roger Williams Univ., since 1913; is also a teacher of music and elocution; trained the National Baptist Young People's Union Congress Quartette for service at Savannah, Ga., 1913, and the Male Quartette that toured Tennessee for the benefit of Roger Williams Univ.; organist in Spruce Street Church; gospel singer, also has dramatic ability; closely identified with George W. Hubbard Hospital. Club: Phillis Wheatley. Address: Roger Williams University, Nashville, Tenn.

TOWNSEND, William Bolden, lawyer; born at Huntsville, Ala.; son of Wesley and Margaret (Richardson) Townsend; preparatory edn., State Normal School, Leavenworth, Kan.; LL.B., Univ. of Kan. School of Law, 1891. Admitted to Kansas bar, 1891; practiced in Leavenworth, 1891-1901, Pueblo, Colo., 1901-9, Denver since 1909; grand attorney for Colo. jurisdiction Knights of Pythias. Republican. Office: 313 Kittredge, Bldg., Denver, Colorado.

TRAYLOR, Thomas Regis, tailor, former editor; born in Troup Co., Ga., Apr. 12, 1886; son of Martha Cooke Traylor; educated at Tuskegee Normal and Industrial Institute; attended the children's house, 1899-1900, and the institute 2 terms, 1900-1, 1906-7; married Pinnie Pearl Willis of West Point, Ga., Dec. 8, 1914. Began in tailoring business, West Point, 1904, continuing to time reentered Tuskegee Institute, 1906; returned to West Point in 1907, and since prop. Twin City Tailoring Business; conducted a 5 and 10 cent store, 1909-12; was editor and publisher "The Trailer" 9 months, 1911-12; discontinued on account of financial difficulties; now in mail order business under name of Southern Distributing House. Progressive. Baptist. Address: West Point, Ga.

TRIGPEN, Timothy S., editor; born at Heidelburg, Miss., Oct. 13, 1878; son of Jake and Lottie (Nixon) Trigpen; grad. Meridian Academy, 1902; married Ellen Jones, of Demopolis, Ala., Sept. 8, 1902; 4 children. Editor and publisher Weekly Times at Hattiesburg, Miss., since 1903; assistant cashier People's Bank, 1906-7; founded Industrial Toilers of America. Republican; delegate to National Convention, Chicago, Ill., 1908. Methodist. Member Odd Fellows, Knights of Pythias. Address: 427 Mobile St., Hattiesburg, Miss.

TROTTER, William Monroe, editor, publisher; born in Springfield Township, O., Apr. 7, 1872; son of James M. and Virginia (Isaacs) Trotter; (father served in war between the states as 2d Lieutenant 58th Mass. Vol. Inf.; recorder of deeds, Washington, D. C., 1885-7; author: Music and Some Highly Musical People); grad. Hyde Park High School, Mass., 1890; A.B., Harvard, 1895; A.M., 1896; married Geraldine L. Pindell, of Boston, June 27, 1899. Editor and pub. The Guardian, Boston, since established in 1901; president New England Suffrage League; corresponding sec. National Independent Equal Rights League. His activity in important matters affecting colored people has attracted much attention throughout the country; the indifference of Republican party to oppression of colored people in southern states aroused his sensitive nature; his editorials condemned act of President Theodore Roosevelt for discharge of the battalion of colored soldiers at Brownsville, Tex.; during campaign of 1908 he opposed William H. Taft for his participation in same affair; supported Woodrow Wilson during campaign of 1912; was spokesman for Equal Rights League when a delegation presented an anti-segregation petition to President Wilson, Nov. 6, 1913; also spokesman for delegation that made second protest in Washington, Nov. 12, 1914; it was then set forth that public humiliation and degradation resulted from segregation of colored people in service of the government; his speech in rebuttal caused the President to notify the deputation that if it came again to the White House it would have to select another spokesman; the incident was given wide publicity; it should be said, however, that the segregation policy objected to was quite generally condemned at the time by northern newspapers, as well as by a certain southern university. Member Phi Beta Kappa (Harvard). Address: 49 Cornhill, Boston, Mass.

TUGGLE, Carrie A., institute president; born at Eufaula, Ala., May 28, 1859; daughter of Warren and Charity (Crofford) Griggs; public school edn., Eufaula; married J. L. Tuggle, of Columbus, Ga., Nov. 17, 1877; widow; 9 children. Founded in 1903 and since president Tuggle Institute, Birmingham, Ala. Founder and grand worthy mother Rising Sons and Daughters of Protection; grand worthy counsellor Order of Calantha in State of Ala.; these societies aid in the support of the institute. African Methodist. Address: Box 472, Birmingham, Ala.

TURNER, Charles Henry, neurologist, comparative psychologist; born at Cincinnati, O., Feb. 3, 1867; son of Thomas and Adeline (Campbell) Turner; B.S., Univ. of Cincinnati, 1891, M.S., 1892; Ph.D., Univ. of Chicago, 1907; one of the few colored men who have received the Doctor of Philosophy degree; married Leontine Troy, of Cincinnati, 1888 (died 1894); 2d marriage, Lillian Porter, of Augusta, Ga., Nov. 19, 1908; 3 children: Mae, Henry O., Darwin Romanes. Teacher in public schools, Evansville, Ind., 1888-89;

sub-teacher, Cincinnati, 1889; assistant in biology Univ. of Cincinnati, 1890-2; professor of biology Clark Univ., Atlanta, Ga., 1892-1905; principal College Hill School, Cleveland, Tenn., 1906; professor of biology and chemistry Haines Normal and Industrial School, Augusta, Ga., 1907-8; instructor in biology Sumner High School, St. Louis, Mo., since 1908. Scientific investigator and writer of research papers treating of varieties, laws, form and arrangement of invertebrates and of invertebrate animal behavior; his many contributions to technical magazines include: Morphology of the Avian Brain; Ecological Notes on the Cladocera and Copepoda of Augusta; Morphology of the Nervous System of the Genus Cypris; the Mushroom Bodies of the Crawfish; the Homing of Ants; the Homing of the Burrowing Bees; Experiments on Color Vision of the Honey Bee; the Reactions of the Mason Wasp; Behavior of the Common Roach, also others treating of the behavior of higher vertebrates. Director Colored Branch, St. Louis Y. M. C. A., Wayman Free Clinic and Social Settlement Assn.,Elleardsville Civic League. Presbyterian. Member Entomological Society of America, Academy of Science of Ill., Academy of Science of St. Louis, Sigma Chi, Sigma Pi Phi and Knights of Pythias. Author: (with C. L. Herrick) Entomostraca if Minnesota, 1895. Address: 4540 Garfield Ave., St. Louis, Mo.

TURNER, Henry McNeal, bishop; born Newberry Court House, N. C., Feb. 1, 1834; son of Hardy and Sarah (Greer) Turner; married Eliza Ann Peacher, of Columbus, S. C., Aug. 31, 1856; 2d marriage, Mrs. Martha DeWitt, of Bristol, Pa., Aug., 1893; 3d, Mrs. Harriet A. Wayman, of Baltimore, Md., Aug. 16, 1900; 4th, Laura Pearle Lemon, of Atlanta, Ga., Dec. 3, 1907; learned to read and write without aid; young lawyers assisted him with studies while office boy with a law firm at Abbyville Court House; studied geography, arithmetic, history, astronomy, hygiene and anatomy.

Licensed to preach in M. E. Church S., 1858, and joined Missouri Conference; became itinerant minister; transferred to Baltimore Conference by Bishop D. A. Payne, D.D.; during 4 years there studied Greek, Hebrew and divinity at Trinity College; (LL.D., Univ. of Pa., 1872; D.D., Wilberforce Univ., 1873; D.L.C.); pastor Israel Church, Washington, D. C., 1863. Commissioned chaplain U. S. Colored Troops by President Abraham Lincoln; mustered out in Sept., 1865; commissioned chaplain in regular army by President Andrew Johnson, and detailed as officer at Freedman's Bureau in Ga.; resigned to resume ministry. Organized colored school about 1867; elected member Georgia Legislature, 1868, reelected 1870; appointed postmaster at Macon, Ga., later inspector of customs, then as U. S. secret detective. Elected manager of publications A. M. E. Church by General Conference at Philadelphia, 1876; consecrated bishop, 1880; historigrapher for the church and chief editor The Theological Institute for many years. Organized 4 Annual Conferences in Africa, 1 in Sierra Leone, 1 in Liberia, 1 in Praetoria, Transvaal, 1 in Queenstown, S. Africa; was among the principal agitators for return of Negroes to Africa. Author: Methodist Polity; Hymn Book of A. M. E. Church; a catechism, a number of sermons and lectures. Address: 30 Yonge St., Atlanta, Ga. (Died in Windsor, Ont., Can., May 8, 1915).

TURNER, James Arthur, teacher; born Atlanta, Ga., Mar. 29, 1882; son of James Arthur and Mary (Brewer) Turner; B.S., Clark Univ., Atlanta, 1906, A.M., 1909; special course at Massachusetts Agricultural College, 1906-8; grad. summer course, Cornell Univ., 1911; unmarried. Began teaching in Clark Univ., Atlanta, 1908; teacher of biology at Colored High School, Baltimore, Md., since 1913. Baptist. Mason. Club: School Masters. Home: 539 Presstman St., Baltimore, Md.

TURNER, John P., physician; born at Raleigh, N. C., Nov. 1, 1866; son of

Jesse E. and Jennie (Edwards) Turner; prep. edn. College of the City of New York; M.D., Shaw Univ., Raleigh; married Marion C. Harris, of Washington, Apr. 15, 1909; 1 child. Practiced in Philadelphia since 1906; appointed medical inspector public schools, 1912; only colored physician among the 60 inspectors; medical director Keystone Aid Insurance Co.; assistant surgeon Douglass Hospital; director Armstrong Assn. African Methodist. Member American Medical Assn., National Medical Assn., Pa. State Medical Society, Philadelphia Academy Medicine and Allied Sciences; member Supreme Lodge, Knights of Pythias. Club: Professional. Author: The Physician and the Church. Address: 1302 S. 10th St., Philadelphia, Pa.

TURNER, Laura Lemon, religious worker; born at McDonough, Ga., Aug. 4, 1880; daughter of George and Louise (Fields) Lemon; prep. edn. Clark Univ., Atlanta, Ga.; grad. Morris Brown Univ., 1895 (A.M., 1903; A.M., Agricultural and Mechanical College, Normal, Ala., 1903; Ph.D., Campbell College, Jackson, Miss., 1911); married, Dec. 3, 1907, Rt. Rev. Henry McNeal Turner, bishop of the A. M. E. Church, Atlanta, Ga. (died 1915). President Woman's Home and Foreign Missionary Society of A. M. E. Church since 1908; founded Woman's Missionary Recorder, Atlanta, 1908, which was adopted as official publication by the General Conference at Kansas City., Mo., 1912, and she was elected editor. Member Atlanta Parent Teachers' Assn., Atlanta Ministers' Wives Alliance, Order of Eastern Star. Club: Atlanta Woman's. Home: 30 Yonge St., Atlanta, Ga. Official Address: 206 Public Square, Nashville, Tenn.

TURNER, Thomas Wyatt, university professor; born at Hughesville, Md., Nov. 16, 1877; son of Eli and Linnie (Gross) Turner; A.B., Howard Univ., Washington, D. C., 1901, A.M., 1905; matriculated for Ph.D., Catholic Univ. of America, 1901; took special course in biology Johns Hopkins Univ., Baltimore, Univ. of Rochester, N. Y.,

Biological Laboratory at Cold Spring Harbor, Long Island, N. Y.; graduate work in botony Columbia Univ., New York; married Laura Elaine Miller, of Hampton, Va., Dec. 28, 1907. Began as teacher in Tuskegee Normal and Industrial Institute, Ala., 1901; teacher of biology Colored High School, Baltimore, Md., 1902-10, Summer High School, St. Louis, Mo., 1910-11, Baltimore, 1911-13; professor of the teaching of the biological sciences in Howard Univ., since 1913. Was director Provident Hospital, Baltimore, 1910-11, and Provident Hospital, St. Louis, 1 year. Member number of charitable and educational organizations. Catholic. Contributor to Southern Workman, and other papers, advocating the teaching of biology in schools. Address: 1850 3rd St. N. W., Washington, D. C.

TURNER, Valdo, physician, surgeon; born at Dixon Spring, Tenn., Dec. 10, 1866; son of Pleasant and Caroline (Cardwell) Turner; grad. Literary School, Knoxville, Tenn., 1890; M.D., Meharry Medical College, Walden Univ., Nashville, Tenn., 1894; post-graduate course at Univ. of Minn., 1913; attended Mayo Clinic, 5 years; married Lillian A. Anderson, of Springfield, O., June 6, 1895. Practiced at Shelbyville, Tenn., 1894-7, in St. Paul, Minn., since 1898; about 75 per cent of practice is among white people; has affable access to all hospitals. Republican. Baptist. Member National Medical Assn.; chairman executive board National Association for Advancement of Colored People. Mason; member Odd Fellows, Knights of Pythias. Home: 386 N. St. Albans St. Office: 27 E. 7th St., St. Paul, Minn.

TWINE, William Henry, lawyer, editor; born at Richmond, Ky., Dec. 10, 1862; son of William H. and Amanda (Barnett) Twine; married Mittie A. Richardson, of Groesbeck, Tex., Mar. 12, 1888; 6 children: William H., Jr., David R., Edgar H., Pliny S., Chauncey D., Thomas J.; grad. Blackburn's High School, Xenia, O., 1881; read law while teaching school in Texas; first colored man ever took examination as lawyer in Limestone Co. Admitted to Texas bar, 1888; practiced in Groesbeck, 3 years; removed to Guthrie, Okla., 1891, to Indian Territory, 1897; since practiced in all courts of Oklahoma; in defence of George Curley, 1897, gained record as first colored lawyer to carry capital case from U. S. Court, Northern Dist., Indian Territory., to Supreme Court of U. S.; attorney for Southern Real Estate Co., Hoffman, Okla.; editor Muskogee Cimeter since 1897; was first Negro paper in Indian Territory; its activity induced great numbers of colored people to locate in vicinity of Muskogee; it always stood for peace among black, white, and red men and may be partly credited with conditions in that section; no person was ever lynched in Muskogee Co.; secretary-treas. Grand Masons Burial Assn., Okla. Republican; was a leader of "the boys in the trenches" who fought with knives and revolvers for the "stand-patter's" against the "lillie white" faction of the Republican party of Okla., in the "Battle of Lannings Hall," one of the historical events connected with the selection of delegates to the Constitutional Convention, related to the time Oklahoma was admitted as a state, Nov. 16, 1907. Methodist. Mason; member Knights of Pythias, Odd Fellows, United Brothers of Friendship. Home: 706 S. 5th St. Office: 211 S 2d St., Muskogee, Okla.

TYLER, Ralph W., newspaper man, former auditor for the navy; born at Columbus, O.; public school edn., Columbus. Began as writer on staff of the Columbus Evening Dispatch about 1884, continuing 17 years, also assistant to the manager and confidential secretary to the publisher; with the Ohio State Journal 3 years; only colored person regularly employed on staff of white daily papers in Ohio; now writer for both white and Negro publications. Auditor for the U. S. Navy, 1905-13; appointed by President Theodore Roosevelt, unsolicited, reappointed by President William H. Taft. Address: Columbus, Ohio.

TYLER, Willis Oliver, lawyer; born at Bloomington, Ind., July 19, 1880; son of Isiah and Mary Ann (McCaw) Tyler; A.B., Ind. Univ., 1902; LL.B., Harvard, 1908; unmarried. Admitted to Illinois bar, 1908; practiced in Chicago, 1 year; admitted to California bar, 1911; since practiced in Los Angeles; member firm of Tyler & Macbeth; director R. C. Owens Investment Co. Served as corporal, Co. B. Ind. Colored Vol. Inf., Spanish-American war, July, 1898-Jan., 1899. Republican. African Methodist. Home: 1542 E. Addams St. Office: 312 Germain Bldg., Los Angeles, Cal.

TYREE, Evans, bishop; born in DeKalb Co., Tenn., Aug. 19, 1854; son of Harry and Winnie Tyree; educated in theology and medicine; (D.D., Livingstone College, Salisbury, N. C., 1897); married Ellen Thompkins, of Smith Co., Tenn., Jan. 12, 1871. Joined A. M. E. Church, 1866; licensed to exhort, 1869; ordained deacon, 1874, elder, 1876; elected bishop May 23, 1900. Address: 15 N. Hill St., Nashville, Tenn.

TYRELL, Bernard, college professor, clergyman; born in Albemarle Co., Va., Mar. 15, 1859; son of Joseph and Caroline (Coleman) Tyrell; prep. edn. Storer College, Harper's Ferry, W. Va.; A.B., Hillsdale (Mich.) College, 1888, A.M., 1893; B.D., Yale Divinity School, New Haven, Conn., 1893; (D.D., Guadaloupe College, Seguin, Tex., 1901); married Elizabeth Wilkerson, of Lynchburg, Va., Sept. 12, 1894; 2 children: Wilkie, Beulah. Teacher in schools of Virginia and W. Va., 1879-82, Storer College, 1888-9, and traveling financial agent in New England and Western states for Storer College. Ordained Baptist ministry at New Haven, Conn., May 18, 1893; pastor Holcombe Rock Church, Va., 1894-5, Diamond Hill Church since 1895; dean of theological dept. Virginia Theological Seminary and College, 1893-1903, and since 1911, now professor of Greek, Hebrew, theology and homiletics; vice-president Virginia Baptist Convention since 1899; was president National Baptist Convention,

1905-11, and served on Baptist Young People's Mission, Foreign Missions, National Benefit Educational, and National Theological Seminary boards. Republican. Member Order of St. Luke. Address: 1307 12th St., Lynchburg, Va.

U

UNCLES, Rev. Charles Randolph, S.S.J., priest; born at Baltimore, Md.; collegiate studies at St. Hyacinth, Canada; philosophy and theology at St. Joseph's Seminary, and St. Mary's Seminary, Baltimore. Ordained by His Eminence James Cardinal Gibbons; was first colored man ordained to Catholic priesthood in U. S.; professor in the Epiphany Apostolic College, Walbrook, Baltimore, Md.

UNDERWOOD, Edward Ellsworth, physician; born at Mt. Pleasant, O., June 7, 1864; son of Rev. Johnson and Harriett (Clanton) Underwood; grad. Mt. Pleasant High School, 1881; M.D., Western Reserve Univ., Cleveland, O., 1891; married Sarah J. Walker, of Frankfort, Ky., July 3, 1895; 2 children: Ellsworth W., Robert M. Teacher public schools, Emerson, O., 8 years; pastor A. M. E. Church, 6 years; editor Blue Grass Bugle, Frankfort, Ky., 10 years; practiced medicine in Frankfort since 1891; assistant city physician, 1897; secretary board of pension examining surgeons, 1900-14; established People's Pharmacy, 1911, its president to 1912, since secretary of company; educational editor Lexington Weekly News. President Franklin County Agricultural and Industrial Assn.; secretary Anti-Tuberculosis League; was secretary Anti-Separate Coach State Executive Committee, 1891; commissioner to Cotton States Exposition, Atlanta, Ga., 1895, Tennessee Centennial Exposition, Nashville, 1897; first colored trustee of Ky. State Normal School, appointed by Gov. William O. Bradley, 1898, Gov. Augustus E. Willson, 1907, 1910. First colored member Jefferson County Republican Committee, 1887-8; member Franklin County Committee and delegate to every Republican State Convention since 1892; delegate-at-large National Convention at Chicago, 1904; was organizer and president State League of Republican Colored Clubs; candidate for register of the treasury, 1909. African Methodist. Member National Medical Assn., National Association of Pension Examining Surgeons, Kentucky State Medical Society, Frankfort Negro Business League. Mason; supreme keeper records and seal Knights of Pythias; member Odd Fellows, Mosaic Templars, United Brothers of Friendship, Union Benevolent Society. Author: History of Colored Churches, 1898. Home: 310 Mero St. Office: Washington and Clinton Sts., Frankfort, Ky.

V

VALENTINE, William Robert, teacher, supervisor; born in Loudoun Co., Va., Oct. 7, 1879; son of Stephen and Rosa (Pierson) Valentine; grad. high school, Montclair, N. J., 1899; A.B., Harvard, 1904; attended Columbia Univ., N. Y., summer session, 1905; married Grace Booth, of New Haven, Conn., Aug. 10, 1907; 2 children: William R., Jr., Dorothy. Supervising principal public school No. 26, Indianapolis, Ind., 1904-15; an article in the June issue, 1914, of the Popular Educator described his experiment of using the school building and plant for social settlement work and community regeneration; the experiment is founded upon faith in the possibilities of the public school as an active, constructive and aggressive agency for the uplift of the people; his work has received recognition and hearty approval of some of our leading educators; principal Bordentown (N. J.) Industrial School since 1915. Progressive. Member Knights of Pythias. Clubs: Principals'; Browning. Home: 833 N. California St., Indianapolis, Ind. Address: Bordentown Industrial School, Bordentown, N. J.

VALLE, Lincoln Charles, editor, collector for St. Monica's Catholic Church; born at St. Louis, Mo., Apr. 30, 1863; public school edn.; took civil engineering course from International

Correspondence Schools; married Mrs. Yoular Glaspy, of Aurora, Ill., Nov. 27, 1905. Began as representative of newspaper in St. Louis, 1880, continuing 4 years; during latter part of 1884, was traveling representative for the Catholic Tribune (colored weekly) of Cincinnati, Ohio; collector for St. Monica's Church (colored) at Chicago since 1884, appointed by Archbishop Patrick Feehan; was one of organizers first Colored Catholic Congress held in U. S., and assisted in preliminary work to build several churches and schools; editor Chicago Conservator, 1896-8; now editor the Catholic Truth; in charge Catholic Bureau and church work connected with National Half-Century Anniversary of Negro Freedom and The Lincoln Jubilee, Chicago, 1915. Member 8th Inf. Illinois National Guard 10 years; served with regiment in Spanish-American war, and commissioned to commissary with rank of captain, June 28, 1902. Republican; served as deputy assessor, tax collector, and inspector for Sanitary District of Chicago. Member American Federation of Catholic Societies, Catholic Order of Foresters, Camp No. 11, United Spanish War Veterans, Dept. of Ill. Home: 3607 Forest Ave. Office: 21 E. 28th St., Chicago, Ill.

VANCE, J. Madison, lawyer; graduate Straight Univ. Law Dept., New Orleans, 1886. Address: New Orleans, Louisiana.

VAN DYKE, Edward Burton, chief clerk Odd Fellows; born at Philadelphia, Pa., May 29, 1860; son of Edward and Emeline (Burton) Van Dyke; grad. Richard Vaux Grammar School, 1880; entered high school, Philadelphia; took course in German under Prof. Shafer; married Katie Jeffrey, of New Haven, Conn., June, 1884; 4 children: Olivia, Christine, Edward J., Lillian. Began in early life as mailing clerk with iron firm of William R. Hart & Co., Philadelphia, continuing for some time; passed examination for clerkship in postoffice; assistant grand secretary since 1893, chief clerk sub-committee of management of headquarters, Grand United Order of Odd Fellows, and secretary Fraternal Lodge No. 893; director G. U. O. Odd Fellows Hall Assn.; secretary Mt. Lebanon Lodge No. 9, F. & A. M.; treasurer Masonic Hall Assn. Member the 36th Ward Republican Executive Committee. Episcopalian; member Vestry of St. Simon the Cyrenian Church. Home: 2219 Reed St. Office: 1201 Spruce St., Philadelphia, Pa.

VASS, Samuel N., bible lecturer; born at Raleigh, N. C., May 22, 1866; son of Maj. W. W. and Annie Victoria (Mitchell) Vass; A.B., Shaw Univ., Raleigh, 1882, A.M., 1885, D.D., 1888; (D.D., Livingstone College, 1901); married Mary Eliza Haywood, of Raleigh, June, 1885; 2 children: Maud Lillian (Mrs. N. F. Bass), Dr. R. S. Began as teacher public schools, Raleigh, at age of 14, continuing to 1885; professor collegiate branches Shaw Univ., 1885-93; Sunday School missionary for Va., Md., and D. C., 1893; supt. Negro work throughout U. S., for American Baptist Publication Society, Philadelphia, since 1893; wide reputation as bible lecturer. Republican. Member American Academy Political and Social Sciences. Author: Consecration, 1898; The Progress of the Negro Race, 1904; The Divine Message of Ham, 1907. Home: 300 E. South St. Office: 136½ S. Wilmington, St., Raleigh, N. C.

VERNON, William Tecumseh, ex-register of the treasury, college president; born at Lebanon, Mo., July 11, 1871; son of Adam and Margaret (Hooker) Vernon; secured degree Bachelor of Diadactics, and A.M., Lincoln Institute, Mo.; (hon. D.D., LL.D., Wilberforce Univ.); married Emily Jane Embry, of Philadelphia, Pa., Aug. 18, 1901. Taught in public schools of Missouri until called to take charge at Western University, Quindaro, Kan., 1896; at that time the school had only one building and about a dozen students; now one of the leading Negro institutions in U. S.; its growth was due to the untiring efforts and success of Dr. Vernon, who secured a quarter million dollars for the school; he continued as president to 1906; was register of the U. S. Treasury, Washington, 1906-10; while in that position traveled all over the country delivering lectures and addresses; resigned lucrative government position to work among colored people in the South; ordained minister in A. M. E. Church; now president Campbell College, Jackson, Miss.; under his administration conditions have greatly improved and it is now among the leading institutions for Christian education. Mason; member Odd Fellows. Republican. Address: Campbell College, Jackson, Mississippi.

VINCENT, Andrew Brown, clergyman, editor; born in Caswell County, N. C., 1858; son of Nellie Vincent; A.B., Shaw Univ., Raleigh, N. C., 1885, A.M., later (D.D., 1912); attended State Normal School, Westfield, and Summer Bible School, Northfield, Mass.; married Cora P. Exum, of Wayne Co., N. C., 1884; 7 children. Began as teacher in Shaw Univ., 1884, continuing 9 years; in missionary, educational and Sunday School work since 1893; served as conductor of Bible and Ministers' institutes, general missionary among Baptists of N. C., and pastor in number of places; former president State Teachers' Assn.; now member board of managers and historian Baptist State Sunday School Convention; editor and publisher the Searchlight since 1910; also in real estate and home building business. Mason. Home: 713 S. Blount St., Raleigh, N. C.

VINCENT, Mary Berta, supervising industrial teacher; born at Mebane, N. C., May 24, 1880; daughter of Pleasant and Mary Catherine (Mebane) Graves; attended public schools, Mebane, to 1896; grad. from grammar dept., Scotia Seminary for Girls, 1903; married Thomas Vincent, of Mebane, Sept. 30, 1913; 1 child: Thomas Graves V. Teacher in graded school, Oxford, N. C., 7 years, and at Mebane 2 years; supervising industrial teacher of Negro Rural Schools in Alamance County, N. C., since Oct. 1, 1913, under the State Department of Public In-

struction; the work is aided by the Anna T. Jeanes Fund, and reaches the most remote colored schools and homes throughout the state. Presbyterian. Address: Box 155, Mebane, North Carolina.

W

WADE, Claude Melnotte, physician; born at Huntsville, Ala., 1863; attended Rust Institute, Huntsville; preparatory edn. Atlanta Univ., Ga.; finished course in dental dept. Meharry Medical College, Nashville, Tenn., 1888; M.D., Louisville (Ky.) Medical College, 1891. Began practice in Ky.; after few years removed to Ark., and since practiced in Hot Springs; as a member Supreme Lodge Knights of Pythias, influenced that body to purchase a bath house and sanitarium in Hot Springs; member number of other organizations. Address: 501½ Malvern Ave., Hot Springs, Ark.

WALDRON, John Milton, clergyman; born at Lynchburg, Va., May 19, 1863; son of Isaac and Susan Gilmore (Barrett) Waldron; preparatory edn. Richmond Institute; A.B., Lincoln (Pa.) Univ., 1886; grad. Newton Theological Institute, Mass., 1889; married Martha N. Matthews, of Albany, N. Y., Apr. 18, 1892. Lestured among white people on race problem in over 300 churches and Y. M. C. A.'s, northern and western states, 1889-90, again 1901-3; pastor Berean Baptist Church, Washington, D. C., 1890-2; editor Young Men's Friend, magazine, 1890, Alley Mission Herald, 1890-2, The Defender, 1893-4, Florida Evangelist, 1896-1901, Florida Standard, 1904-6; pastor Shiloh Bapt. Ch., Washington, since 1906. Established The Afro-American Industrial & Benefit Assn. and was pres., 1899-1905; one of founders National Association for Advancement of Colored People; pres. Alley Improvelent Assn., National Gospel Workers Aid Assn.; vice-pres. National Temperance Society and Publishing House; trustee Anti-Saloon League of D. C.; officer Baptist Ministers' Union; member Evangelical Ministers' Alliance of Washington and vicinity. Was member inaugural committee which inducted Woodrow Wilson into office as President of the U. S. Socialist. Address: 1334 V St. N. W., Washington, D. C.

WALKER, Mme, C. J., manufacturer, hair culturist; born at Delta, La., Dec. 23, 1867; daughter of Owen and Minerva Breedlove; orphan at age 6 yrs., married at 14, widow when 20 years of age; 1 child: Ledia (Mrs. John B. Robinson); educated in night school at St. Louis, Mo. Began to introduce hair growing preparation, 1905; remained in Denver, Colo., 1 year, then traveled 2 years; located in Pittsburgh, Pa., 1908, but left business in charge of daughter and continued selling product on the road; finally settled at Indianapolis, Ind., 1910; now president Mme. C. J. Walker Mfg. Co.; has large laboratory, employs about 2,000 agents, annual business exceeds $50,000, owns $10,000 home; regarded leading colored business woman in U. S.; gave $1,000 to Y. M. C. A. building fund, Indianapolis, and has contributed to other worthy causes. African Methodist. Member Indianapolis Negro Business League, Household of Ruth, Court of Calanthe, Elizabeth Council, Woman's Council. Address: 640 N. West St., Indianapolis, Ind.

WALKER, Harry L., merchant; born at Lexington, Va., July 4, 1875; common school edn.; married Eliza Bannister, of Lexington, 1894; 4 children. Began as cattle driver when 11 years of age at 50 cents per week; later became meat cutter for first employer, continuing with same market during several changes of ownership and wages were gradually increased until he was receiving $100 a month; in meat business for self since 1908; built first slaughter house in Lexington; owns home site of 13 acres; value of real estate holdings exceeds $20,000. Deacon in First Baptist Church. Address: Lexington, Va.

WALKER, Nathaniel Daniel, physician; born at Selma, Ala., Jan. 3,

1886; son of Benjaman Franklin and Sophonia Arimenta (Thompson) Walker; attended Knox Academy, Selma, to 1902; A.B., Talladega College, 1909; M.D., Shaw Univ., Raleigh, N. C., 1913; married Ethyl Tyler McAlpine, of Selma, Dec. 10, 1914; 1 child: Helen E. Practiced in western No. Carolina since 1913. Missionary Baptist. Address: Box 746, Hendersonville, N. C.

WALKER, Thomas Hamilton Beb, clergyman, novelist; born at Tallahassee, Fla., July 15, 1873; son of May F. D. and Elizabeth (Christy) Walker; attended public schools at Tallahassee; student Cookman Institute, Jacksonville, Fla., 4 yrs.; grad. Gammon Theological Seminary, Atlanta, Ga., 1903; (D.D., College of West Africa, Monrovia, Liberia, 1907); married Luanna Jenkins, of Hawthorn, Fla., Dec. 20, 1894; children: May F. D., Nathaniel R. B., Thomas H. B., Muzzaffa, Lucius Eden, William Simon, Georgia Elizabeth Susie (4 others deceased). Worked as clerk when 7 years of age, as horticulturist while attending public sch., carpenter and book agent during preparatory course; taught school 2 yrs.; entered Methodist ministry at age of 16; pastored largest churches of his conference; erected Institutional Church edifice at Tampa, Fla., at cost of $17-000; served as editor of Seven Stars Banner, the Quarterly Review, and the Church and Society World—a 64-page magazine; secretary Reform School for Boys. Founded in 1897, and supreme chief St. Joseph Aid Society; has 1189 lodges and 59,500 members throughout southern states; was former owner the site of Montana City to Ybor, Fla., but sold the property to white real estate firm of Sexton & Harris; owns costly brick residence and prominent place among visitors to Jacksonville; has large rental property. Author: The Man Without Blemish, 1902; Egyptology, 1906; Bebbly the Victorious Preacher, 1910; Aunt Dysie's Vision of Hell, 1910; The Revelation of Epic, 1912; The Biographies of Presidents of Liberia, 1915; The School History of Liberia and several novels are nearly ready for press, 1915. Republican. 32d Mason. Home: 1150 Darwin St., Jacksonville, Fla.

WALLACE, Thomas Walker, clergyman, editor; born at Shelby, Ala., Mar. 24, 1879; son of William Leroy and Onie (McCloud) Wallace; grad., literary and industrial courses, Tuskegee Normal and Industrial Institute, 1895; A.B., Livingstone College, Salisbury, N. C., 1900 (A.M., 1912); summer courses in chemistry and physics at Columbia Univ., New York; married Lauretta J. Lawson, of Louisville, Ky., May 3, 1902; 6 children: Wm. James Lord, Thomas Walker, Jr., Wales McCloud, Emmeline Onie, John A. Leroy, Lauretta Julia. Began as teacher in Livingstone College, 1896, instructor in printing 4 years, teacher in grammar school dept., 1900-3, in normal dept., 1903-6, professor of natural sciences since 1906; also pastored churches since 1906; elected editor Western Star of Zion by General Conference A. M. E. Zion Church at Charlotte, N. C., 1912. Trustee Walters Institute, Warren, Ark. Republican. Mason; member Odd Fellows, Knights of Pythias, Elks. Home: 1902 Bond Ave. Office: 13 S Rock Road, E. St. Louis, Ill.

WALLER, Alexander Arthur, real estate; born in Terrell County, Ga., June 1, 1872; son of Alexander and Louvinia (Brown) Waller; educated Howard School, Chattanooga, Tenn.; took correspondence course in real estate; married Mrs. Carrie S. Braxton, of Denver, Colo., Apr. 4, 1904. Secretary to the manager Colored American Loan & Realty Co., Denver, since 1907; secretary Elite Drug Co.; treasurer Denver Star Publishing Co. Assistant supt. Zion Baptist Sunday School, and supt. Home Dept.; clerk of the church and director Zion choir. Corresponding secretary Great Western Assn. Republican. Club: Azalia Hackley Choral. Home: 2606 Gilpin St. Office: 1027 21st St., Denver, Colo.

WALLER, Calvin Hoffman, college professor; born at Macon, Ga., May 5, 1880; son of Frank H. and Julia (Hubbard) Waller; ed. Tuskegee Normal and Industrial Institute, Ala., 4 years; Mt. Hermon (Mass.) School 2 years: degree L.I., Colored Normal, Industrial and Mechanical College, Orangeburg, S. C., 1898; B.C., Pennsylvania State College, 1905; married Annie M. Walton, of Augusta, Ga., June 21, 1908; 1 child: Walton C. Professor of agriculture at Prairie View (Tex.) State Normal and Industrial College since 1907; director College Bank & Trust Co. Republican. Presbyterian. Member Alpha Beta. Mason. Club: Gun. Address: State Normal and Industrial College, Prairie View, Texas.

WALLIS. Nathaniel Thomas, dentist; born at Camden, Ark., July 20, 1885; son of Charles B. and Mary C. (Townsend) Wallis; grad. Camden High School, 1899; prep. edn. Fisk Univ., Nashville, Tenn., 1900-2; D.D.S., Meharry Dental College (Walden Univ.), 1907; married Bertha L. Simms, of Fort Worth, Tex., June 16, 1909; 2 children: Charles Oscar, Cloter Natella. Practiced in Ft. Worth since 1907. African Methodist. Member National Medical Assn., Lone Star Medical Dental and Pharm. Assn. Mason; member Odd Fellows, Knights of Pythias, United Brothers of Friendship. Home: 951 White St. Office: 911½ Jones St., Fort Worth, Texas.

WALTERS, Alexander, bishop; born at Bardstown, Ky., Aug. 1, 1858; son of Henry and Harriett Walters; public school edn., and studied theology under private tutors; (D.D., Livingstone College, Salisbury, N. C., 1891); married Katie Knox, of Indianapolis, Ind., Aug. 28, 1877; 2d marriage, Lelia Brown, 1903. Licensed to preach in A. M. E. Zion Church, 1877; pastored in Ky., Calif., Tenn., New York; elected bishop 1892; delegate to General Conference, 1884, 88, 92, to Ecumenical Conference on Methodism, Washington, 1891, London, Eng., 1901, Toronto, Can., 1911; president Afro-American Council 7 terms; trustee National Christian Endeavor Society, 1893-1914. Address: 208 W. 134th St., New York.

WALTON, James Tart, physician, surgeon; real estate; born at Bryan,

Tex., 1875; son of John and Arabella (Marshcook) Walton; prep. edn. State Normal School, Tex.; M.D., Meharry Medical College (Walden U.), Nashville, Tenn., 1896; received gold medal for proficiency in obstetrics; unmarried. Practiced in San Antonio, Tex., since 1896; specialist in children's diseases; owner and mgr. Walton Realty & Construction Co.; owner Walton Villa Development Co.; built over 400 houses for colored people on easy payment plan; largest taxpayer among colored people in city and only colored person in state that owns subdivision; vice-pres. Alamo Loan & Trust Co., sec. Inquirer Printing Co.; treas. Palace Drug Co. Trustee Colored People's Hospital. Republican. Methodist. Member Lone Star Medical, Dental and Pharm. Assn., San Antonio Colored Medical Society. Member Odd Fellows, Knights of Pythias, American Woodmen, United Brothers of Friendship. Home: 1220 E. Crockett St. Office: 503 E. Commerce St., San Antonio, Texas.

WALTON, Lester A., editor, theatrical manager; born at St. Louis, Mo., about 1881; son of Benjamin A. and Allie Walton; public school edn.; married Gladys Moore, daughter of Fred R. Moore, publisher of the New York Age; 2 csildren. Began as reporter on a daily paper, St. Louis, continuing 6 yrs.; managing and dramatic editor of the New York Age since 1907; with C. W. Monganstern, leased the Lafayette Theatre in May, 1914. Address: The New York Age, 247 W. 46th St., or Lafayette Theatre, 7th Ave. between 131st and 132d Sts., New York.

WARFIELD, William A., physician, surgeon; born at Hyattstown, Montgomery Co., Md., Nov. 17, 1866; son of William R. and Rachel (Lyles) Warfield; grad. Morgan College, Baltimore, Md., 1890; M.D., Howard Univ. School of Medicine, Washington, D. C., 1894; married Violet B. Thompson, of Baltimore, Oct. 31, 1891; 2 children: William, Violet. Practiced in Freedmen's Hospital, Washington, since graduation; in-

terne, 1894-5, 2d assistant surgeon, 1895-6, 1st assistant, 1897-1901, surgeon-in-chief since 1901; professor of abdominal surgery at Howard Univ.; member Board of Children's Guardians in District of Columbia. Republican. Methodist. Member American Hospital Assn., National Medical Assn., Medico-Chirurgical Society of D.C. Mason. Home: 1901 11th St. N. W. Office: Freedmen's Hospital, Washington, D. C.

WARNER, Andrew Jackson, bishop; born at Washington, Macon Co., Ky., Mar. 4, 1850; son of Reuben and Emily (Payne) Warner; finished high school course, Cincinnati, Ohio, 1867; theological education under private tutors; (D.D., Livingstone College, Salisbury, N. C., 1893; A.M., Atkinson College, 1906); married Annie Weddington, of Charlotte, N. C., July 6, 1910; 1 child. Entered Methodist ministry at Greenville, Ky., 1877; elected bishop A. M. E. Zion Church at General Conference in Philadelphia. Pa., 1908; now presiding in 8th Episcopalian District; vice-president Royal Fraternal Ins. Co. Trustee Livingstone College; director Reform School at Charlotte, N. C. Was drummer boy and rose to rank of sergt. Co. C. 27th Regt. U. S. Colored Troops. Candidate for Congress from 1st Dist., Ala., 1890; delegate at-large to Republican National Convention, St. Louis, Mo., and presidential elector, 1896; nominee for governor of Ala., 1898. Mason. Home 220 E. Boundary St., Charlotte, N. C.

WARREN, Francis Herbert, lawyer; born at Sarnia, Ont., Sept. 3, 1864; son of Joseph and Sarah (Judson) Warren; ed. public schools, Saginaw, Mich.; Bryant & Stratton's Business College, Chicago, Ill.; LL.B., Detroit College of Law, 1903; married Margaret Edgar, of Egbert, Ont., Can., Dec. 8, 1898. Began active career as plastering contractor with father, 1880; later barber, proprietor restaurant, and in laundry business; admitted to Mich. bar, 1903; since practiced in Detroit; attorney for Detroit branch National Association for Advancement of Colored People;

secretary Wolst-Rees Silver Mining Co.; president Mich. Life & Accident Assn.; was newspaper correspondent at Mackinac Island, 1890-1900; has written many articles on single tax, economic and racial subjects; opposed police discrimination against colored persons; successfully opposed legislation in Michigan against inter-marriage of white and colored. Member exec. com. National Independent Political League; was clerk in Wayne County Treasurer's office, Detroit, 1903-5. Episcopalian. Mason; member Knights of Pythias, Elks. Home: 26 Grant Ct. Office: 325 Broadway Market Bldg., Detroit, Mich.

WARREN, Laura Elizabeth, hair culturist; born at Knoxville, Tenn., Dec. 20, 1866; daughter of Rhyle and Susan Annie (Russell) Warren; public schools edn., Knoxville. Began as hairdresser in Pittsburgh, Pa., 1909; later removed to Cleveland, Ohio, where she has made success with preparation known as Warren's Hair Grower. Methodist. Home: 2740 Central Ave. Parlors: 3927 Central Ave., Cleveland, Ohio.

WARREN, Rhoda Adalia, supervising industrial teacher; born at Wateree, S. C., 1891; daughter of Simon and Caroline (Randolph) Warren; attended Benedict College, Columbia, S. C., to 1903; finished course at Schofield School, Aiken, S. C., 1905, and Tuskegee Normal and Industrial Institute, Ala., 1912; unmarried. Supervising industial teacher of colored schools in Wilson County, N. C., since Oct. 1, 1912; this branch of public instruction is under the State Department of Rural Elementary Schools; certain artcrafts are taught in the schools, and in the summer months instruction is given at the homes in gardening, canning, etc.; aided by the Anna T. Jeanes Fund the system reaches to the most remote schools and homes in the state. Missionary Baptist. Member the Tent Society. Address: Wilson, N. C.

WASHINGTON, Benjamin, instructor in physics; born at Washington, D. C., 1873; son of John M. and Annie

E. (Gordon) Washington; grad. high school, 1895; normal school, 1896; Pd.B., Howard Univ., Washington, 1902; summer courses at Hampton, 1899, 1914, Harvard, 1906, Armour Institute of Technology, 1910; married Mary E. Grimshaw, of Washington, Nov. 25, 1908; 1 child: Evelyn Elizabeth. Began as model practice teacher, 1896; now instructor in physics at Armstrong Manual Training School, Washington. Secretary board of trustees 19th Street Baptist Church; secretary board of managers Y. M. C. A. Member National Assn. for Advancement of Colored People, Young Men's Protective League. Mason. Home: 936 S St. N. W., Washington, D. C.

WASHINGTON, Booker Taliaferro, educator; born at Halesford, Franklin Co., Va., 1858 or 1859; parentage unknown; grad. Hampton Normal and Agricultural Institute, Va., 1876; student Wayland Seminary, Washington, D. C., 1878-9; (A.M., Harvard, 1896; LL.D., Dartmouth, 1901); married Maggie J. Murray, of Aberdeen, Miss., Oct. 12, 1893; 3 children: Portia, Booker, Jr., Ernest Davidson. Teacher in Hampton Institute, 1875, 1876-7; principal Tuskegee Normal and Industrial Institute, Ala., since 1880; was elected by state authorities; organized and make Tuskegee an educational center of international importance; is one of the noted educators of present age; factor in interracial understanding and co-operation; one of leaders in movement for world peace. Trustee Howard Univ., Washington, Fisk Univ., Nashville, Tenn.; chairman board of directors Anna T. Jeanes Foundation. Baptist. Member International Committee of New Educational Movement, American Academy Political and Social Science, National Peace Congress, American Peace Society, National Geographical Society, National Municipal League, The Civic Forum, Committee of Twelve. Author: The Future of the American Negro, 1899; Sowing and Reaping, 1900; Up From Slavery, 1901; Character Building, 1902; The Story of My Life and Work, 1903;

Working With the Hands, 1904; Tuskegee and Its People, 1905; Putting the Most Into Life, 1905; Frederick Douglass, 1907; The Story of the Negro, 1909; My Larger Education, 1911; the Man Farthest Down, 1912. Address: Tuskegee Institute, Ala.

WASHINGTON, Margaret J. Murray, superintendent in girls institute at Tuskegee; born at Macon, Ga., Mar. 9, 1865; daughter of James and Lucy Murray; prep. edn., Macon; A.B., Fisk Univ., Nashville, Tenn., 1889; married, Oct. 12, 1893, Dr. Booker T. Washington, the organizer and head of Tuskegee Institute; 3 children: Portia, Booker, Jr., Ernest D. Was dean of women, 1889-1902, and since 1899 has served as director of girls industries at Tuskegee Normal and Industrial Institute; president since 1897, Tuskegee Woman's Club, composed of women from the normal and college departments; chairman advisory board Boys Reformatory at Meigs, Ala., since 1912; was appointed by Gov. Emmet O'Neal; president National Assn. of Woman's Clubs; connected with prison work, the Alms House, Mother's Club, Open Air Sunday School, and all uplift movements. Congregationalist. Address: Tuskegee Institute, Ala.

WATKINS, Samuel Asbury Thompson, lawyer; born at Memphis, Tenn., Jan. 25, 1869; son of Lawson B. and Ada (Caldwell) Watkins; grad. Le-Moyne Institute, Memphis, 1888; read law in office of T. F. Cassels, assistant attorney-general of Tenn.; married Mittie M. Robinson, of Memphis, Mar. 1, 1891; 1 child: Caldwell. Admitted to Tenn. bar, 1891; member law firm of Cassels & Watkins 2 years; admitted to Illinois bar, 1893; since practiced in Chicago; assistant prosecuting attorney City of Chicago, 1898-1907; appointed assistant corporation counsel, 1911; supreme attorney Knights of Pythias of N. America, S. America, Europe, Asia, Africa and Australia; when K. of P. of Georgia, white, secured court order restraining the colored K. of P. from using the organization name and emblem, he carried case to United States Supreme Court and won; Chief Justice Edward Douglass White handed down decision, June 10, 1912, which determined the right to use of name and emblem and practically settled the status of colored fraternal organizations; has also won several cases which settled important questions of benefit to the City of Chicago. Democrat. Episcopalian. Club: Appomatox. Home: 3332 Calumet Ave. O ce: 36 W. Randolph St., Chicago, Ill.

WATSON, Eugene Alexander, newspaper correspondent; born at Pawtucket, R. I., Feb. 21, 1870; son of Charles and Lucy Adelaide (Curless) Watson; high school edn., Pawtucket; unmarried. Postoffice clerk, Pawtucket, 1886-7; city editor New England Torchlight, 1890-1900; secretary American Protective League, 1900-5; Providence Business League, 1911-12; correspondent Douglass Press Agency since 1912, also Journal and Bulletin, News, Tribune and other Providence, Boston and New York newspapers; managing editor The Advance, Providence; organist and saxaphone soloist. Republican. Episcopalian. Member R. I. Citizens Historical Assn. Mason. Home: 157 Waldo St. Office: 910 Westminister St., Providence, R. I.

WATSON, Hattie Rutherford, music teacher; born at Rome, Ga., Nov. 23, 1884; daughter of Samuel W. and Mary Ann (Lemon) Rutherford; ed. public schools, Rome, to 1892; A.B., Spellman Seminary, Atlanta, Ga., 1907, later studied music there; married John Brown Watson, of Tyler, Tex., Sept. 25, 1907. Music teacher in Atlanta since 1907; president Parent Neighborhood Union; member Gate City Free Kindergarten Assn. Address: 140 N. Henry St., Atlanta, Ga.

WATSON, James Samuel, lawyer; born at Jamaica, British West Indies, May 29, 1882; son of James M. and Elizabeth J. Watson; came to America, 1905; ed. Cathedral High School of Jamaica, Harlem Evening High School, N. Y., and College of City of New York; LL.B., New York Law School, 1913; unmarried. Began on editorial staff Musical Magazine, New

York, 1907, continuing to 1908; junior clerk, 1908-10, senior clerk, 1910-13, and acting managing attorney since 1914, with law firm of House, Grossman & Vorhaus; was admitted to New York bar and U. S. Courts, 1914; has won many cases of importance. Republican. Episcopalian. Member New York Law School Alumni Assn. Clubs: Political Science, Alpha Physical Culture (dir.). Home: 234 W. 53d St. Office: 115 Broadway, New York.

WATSON, John Brown, secretary Y. M. C. A.; born in Smith County, Tex., Dec. 28, 1872; son of Frank and Christial (Gary) Watson; prep. edn. Bishop Academy, Marshall, Tex.; student Colgate Univ., Hamilton, N. Y., 1900-1; Ph.B., Brown Univ., Providence, R. I., 1904; married Hattie R. Rutherford, of Atlanta, Ga., Sept. 25, 1907. Teacher in Morehouse College, Atlanta, Ga., 1904-8; secretary International Committee Y. M. C. A., with headquarters in New York, since 1908; his chosen life work is principally for the advancement of colored boys, but is also devoted to the general betterment of conditions for the race. Baptist. Member Odd Fellows. Home: 140 Henry St., Atlanta, Ga.

WEAVER, Bessie May, florist; born at Wathena, Kan., Apr. 12, 1882; daughter of Joe and Mary (Jackson) Henderson; ed. Lincoln School, Atchison, Kan.; married Fortune J. Weaver, of Council Grove, Kan., Sept. 15, 1901; 1 child: Comoleta O. Manager of Weaver Floral Co., established 1911; only colored person in florist business in Kansas City, Mo., and successfully competing with white people; connected with Afro-American Employment & Realty Co. Baptist. Member Kansas City Colored Business League, Woman's League, Relief Workers. Queen of Sheba Temple, Court and Chapter, Court Calanthe; member Household of Ruth. Club: Phillis Wheatly Art. Home: 2635 Euclid St. Office: 1510 E. 18th St., Kansas City, Mo.

WEAVER, Fortune J., real estate; born at Council Grove, Kan., May 8, 1874; son of Fortune Weaver; public school edn., Council Grove; married Bessie May Henderson, of Atchison, Kan., Sept. 15, 1901; 2 children: Fortune, Jr., Comoleta O. Real estate operator in Kansas City., Mo., since 1904; from a small beginning, without capital, has gradually increased to extent that 22 people were in his employ, 1914; sold homes to more than 200 colored people in desirable sections of city; president and manager, Afro-American Investment & Employment Co., Acme Contracting Co.; president Weaver Floral Co.; secretary and manager Jackson County Negro Fair Assn. Organized in 1909 and since president Negro Business League of Greater Kansas City; chairman finance committee Kansas City branch of National Assn. for Advancement of Colored People. Baptist. Mason; member Odd Fellows, Knights of Pythias. Home: 2635 Euclid Ave. Office: 911 MaGee St., Kansas City, Missouri.

WEAVER, Frank Harvey, pharmacist; born at Baltimore, Md., July 16, 1889; son of John Roland and Mary Virginia (Jackson) Weaver; ed. high school, Baltimore; Phar.D., Howard Univ., Washington, D. C., 1910; married Ella Bailey, of Pittsburgh, Pa., June 2, 1915. Registered as druggist in Maryland and Pennsylvania, 1910, Ohio, 1912; was clerk in Liberty Pharmacy, Pittsburgh, 1 year; manager 1 year, proprietor since 1912, The Peoples Drug Store at Cleveland. Republican; judge and register of elections. Congregationalist. Member Cleveland Assn. of Colored Men, Alpha Phi Alpha. Mason. Clubs: Patritian, Howard University of Cleveland (secretary). Home: 3412 Central Ave. Store: 3315 Central Ave. S. E., Cleveland, Ohio.

WEBB, James Morris, evangelist; born at Nashville, Tenn., May 1, 1874; son of George Washington and Mary Ann (Bostis) Webb; edn. in public schools, Nashville, and Austin Seminary; married Nannie F. Tait, of Nashville, Sept. 29, 1897; 2 children: Frankie Nannie, Mary Ann. Traveling evangelist and lecturer on racial subjects; the lecture entitled "The

Black Man's Part in the Bible" is cause for much newspaper comment; has published 2 issues each of "Jesus Was Born Out of the Black Tribe" (1904, 1914), "The Black Man the Father of Civilization" (1910, 1914). Address: 3545 Prairie Ave., Chicago, Illinois.

WEIR, William R., musician; born at Albany, N. Y.; son of Rev. George Weir; public school and musical edn. Teacher of piano. Address: 575 Central Ave., St. Paul, Minn.

WELCH, Thomas Lee, physician; born at Houma, La., Sept. 25, 1882; son of Thomas L. and Sarah (Carter) Welch; ed. Houma Academy, 1894-8; M.D., Flint Medical College (New Orleans Univ.), 1907; married Susie A. Dumas, of Houma, Dec. 24, 1908; 2 children: Clyde Sarah; Timothy (died infant). Began practice at Crowley, La., 1907; removed to New Iberia, 1911; president and secretary Welch-Pemilton Drug Store; president New Iberia Negro Business League; was president local entertainment committee, Apr. 13-16, at reception of Dr. Booker T. Washington on tour through state. Baptist. Member Louisiana Medical, Dental and Pharm. Assn. (sec. 1911-12); secretary Southwestern Parish Medical Council. Member Odd Fellows, Knights of Pythias, Household of Ruth, Wise Men Council. Home: 119 Field St. Office: 321 W. Main St., New Iberia, La.

WESLEY, Allen Alexander, physician, surgeon; born at Dublin, Ind., Sept., 1856; son of Edward E. and Elizabeth Ann (Davis) Wesley; ed. public schools, Cincinnati; Bryant & Stratton Business College, Chicago; A.B., Fisk Univ., Nashville, Tenn., 1884; studied medicine under Dr. William Mussey, Cincinnati, and R. N. Isham, Chicago; M.D., Northwestern Univ. Medical School, 1887; unmarried. Teacher of mathematics and Latin in Fisk Univ., 1878-83; practiced in Chicago since 1887; clinical assistant to Dr. Walter Hay, mental and nervous diseases, 1885-9, to Prof. R. N. Isham, surgery, 1886-8, at Chicago Medical College; one of founders

Provident Hospital, Chicago; was gynecologist at the hospital, 1891, surgeon-in-charge, 1894, vice-president since 1900, now lecturer on surgical emergencies Provident Nurse Training School; district physician for Cook County. Was major-surgeon 8th Inf. Vols., 1898, and served with regiment in Spanish-American war; major and surgeon 8th Inf. Illinois National Guard since 1902. Republican. Congregationalist. Member American Medical Assn., Illinois State Medical Society, Chicago Medical Society. Mason; grand chancellor Knights of Pythias of Illinois. Author (pamphlet): The Spanish-American War as Seen by the Military Surgeon, 1900. Home: 3149 Prairie Ave. Office: 3102 State St., Chicago, Ill.

WEST, Abel E., physician; born at Nandua, Accomac Co., Va., Apr. 11, 1876; son of Jane West; prep. edn., Va. Normal and Industrial Institute, Petersburg; M.D., Shaw Univ., Raleigh, N. C., 1908; unmarried. Practiced in Reading, Pa., 1909-11, in Nandua, Va., since Jan. 15, 1911; medical examiner Downing's Fraternal Endowment; director Brickhouse Banking Co. Progressive. Baptist. Member National Medical Assn. Mason. Address: Nandua, Va.

WEST, Fred Columbus, teacher, former city councilman; born in Van Buren Co., Mich., Feb. 15, 1870; son of Hopkins and Jane (Castile) West; attended graded schools in Mich.; grad. High School, Arkansas City, Kan.; LL.B., Univ. of Kansas, 1893; married Minnie Rowena Johnson, of Lawrence, Kan., Apr. 4, 1894; 2 children: Gordon, Herman. Began as principal of schools in Lawrence, 1893, continuing 15 years; principal at Leavenworth, 1908-12, and of the L'Ouverture School, Wichita, since 1912. Republican; was member city council 6 years, of which served as chairman 4 years on police and license committee, and of committee on sewers 2 years, at Lawrence. African Methodist. Life member Inter-State Literary Assn. of Kansas and the West (former president). Mason. Club:

John Brown Literary. Home: 1109 Ohio Ave., Wichita, Kan.

WESTBROOK, Joseph Henry Parson, physician, surgeon; born at Hernando, Miss., Feb. 20, 1878; son of Dr. Joseph and Mollie (Walla) Westbrook; ed. Miss. State Normal School; Rust Univ., Holly Springs; Fisk Univ., Nashville, Tenn.; M.D., Meharry Medical College (Walden Univ.), Nashville, 1905; post-graduate work Denver Homoeopathic Medical College, Denver, Colo., 1906; married Laura A. Trimble, of Nashville, Dec. 25, 1904. Practiced in Denver since 1905; tuberculosis specialist; secretary Devonia Gold Mining & Milling Co.; organized Elite Drug Co.; was first president and manager Denver Independent Publishing Co.; stockholder Afro-American Mercantile Co., Mound Bayou, Miss. Episcopalian. Member Denver Medical Society. Mason; grand chancellor 4 years, Knights of Pythias, and supreme representative to conventions at Kansas City, Mo., 1909, Indianapolis, Ind., 1911, Baltimore, Md., 1913; member Elks, United Brothers of Friendship. Home: 1029 21st St. Office: 31 Good Block, Denver, Colo.

WHEATLAND, Marcus Fitzherbert, physician; born at Bridgetown, Barnadoes, B. W. I., Feb. 17, 1868; son of John and Helen (Stoute) Wheatland; prep. edn., Barbadoes; M.D., Howard Univ., Washington, D. C., 1895, A.M., 1906; married Irone De Mortie, of Boston, Mass., June 22, 1896. Practiced in Providence, R. I., since 1898; examining physician R. I. State Sanatarium. Member American Electro-Therapeutic Assn., American Medical Assn., National Medical Assn., American Anthropological Society, American Association for Advancement of Science., R. I., Medical Society, Newport Medical Society, Newport Assn. for Relief and Prevention of Tuberculosis, Newport Charity Organization Society. Address: 84 John St., Newport, R. I.

WHEATON, J. Frank, lawyer, former legislator; born at Hagerstown, Md., May 8, 1866; son of Jacob F. and Emily Berthanie (Green) Wheaton; public school edn., Hagerstown; grad. Storer College, Harper's Ferry, W. Va., 1882, Dixon (Ill.) Business College, 1888; studied law at Howard Univ., Washington, D. C.; LL.B., Univ. of Minn., 1894; was class orator; married Ella A. Chambers, of Hagerstown, June 6, 1889; 2 children: Layton J., Frank P. Began practice of law at Hagerstown, Md., 1893; was clerk of Municipal Court, Minneapolis, Minn., 1895-9; later admitted to New York bar; member firm of Wheaton & Curtis; has won many murder cases; successful pleader in jury trials; founded the Equity Congress in New York, 1910. Was delegate to Republican National Convention, Chicago, 1888, St. Louis, Mo., 1896, Philadelphia, 1900; member Minnesota House of Representatives, 1898-1900. Catholic. Member Bar Assn. City of New York; also member Elks of World; grand exalted ruler, 1910-12, elected at Washington convention. Home: 21 W. 135th St. Office: Temple Court Bldg., 5 Beekman St., New York.

WHITBY, Abraham Baxter, dentist; born at Goliad, Tex., Jan. 8, 1868; son of Carter and Frances Whitby; attended public schools and institute at Goliad; prep. edn. Clark Univ., Atlanta, Ga.; student Illinois Medical College; grad. Illinois Dental School; married Beatrice Smith, of Nashville, Tenn., Dec. 23, 1902; 4 children: Francis C., Malcolm S., Leo, Abraham, Jr. Began as professor of chemistry and physics George R. Smith College, Sedalia, Mo., 1897, continuing to 1902; instructor Colored Agricultural and Normal Univ., Langston, Okla., 1902-7; practiced dentistry in Oklahoma City since 1907. Trustee Methodist State College, Muskogee, Okla. Republican. Member Medical, Dental and Pharm. Asso. of Oklahoma (president 1913-14). Mason; member Odd Fellows, United Brothers of Friendship. Home: 620 E. 2d St. Office: 209 E. 1st St., Oklahoma City, Okla.

WHITE, Clarence Cameron, violin soloist, teacher; born at Clarkesville, Tenn., Aug. 10, 1879; son of James

Wm. and Jennie C. (Scott) White; student in Howard Univ., Oberlin Conservatory of Music, O., and under private tutors, Cleveland, O., New Haven, Conn.; private pupil of M. Zacharewitsch, and S. Coleridge-Taylor, London, Eng., 1908-10; married Beatrice Warrick, of Washington, D. C., Apr. 24, 1905; 2 children: William, (Clarence, Jr., died Jan. 30, 1913). In government service, Washington, D. C., 1900-1; teacher of music in public schools 1906-7; 1st violinist String Players Club, London, 1908-10; violin soloist and teacher, Boston, Mass., since 1912; conductor Victorian Concert Orchestra since 1913; lecturer on opera for Chaminade Music Club, season 1913-14; has composed one comic opera and number selections for piano, violin and voice, also compiled technical book on violin study. Republican. Congregationalist. Honorary member Alpha Society, Newport, R. I. Address: 802 Tremont St., Boston, Mass.

WHITE, George Henry, lawyer, former congressman; born at Rosindale, N. C., Dec. 18, 1852; son of Wiley F. and Mary White; grad. Howard Univ., Washington, D. C., 1877; (LL.D., Livingstone College, and Mechanical College, Normal, Ala.); widower. Principal of State Normal and other schools of N. C., several years; admitted to North Carolina bar, 1879, later to Court of D. C., and U. S. Supreme Court; solicitor and prosecuting attorney in 2d Judicial Dist. of N. C., 1886-94. Was member N. C. House of Representatives, 1881, Senate, 1885; nominated for Congress, 1894, but withdrew that time in interest of party harmony; member of Congress from 2d N. C. Dist., 1897-1901; has practiced law in Philadelphia since 1905; secretary-treasurer George H. White Land & Improvement Co. Trustee Howard Univ. Address: 1508 Lombard St., Philadelphia, Pa.

WHITE, Thomas Henry, clergyman; born at Walkerton, King and Queen Co., Va., Oct. 8, 1869; son of Rev. General and Mary (Green) White; ed. public schools, Henrico Co., Va.; Y.

M. C. A. School, Richmond; B.D., Va. Theological Seminary and College, Lynchburg, 1897; (D.D., 1907); married Martha A. Harper, of Richmond, Va., June 20, 1900; 3 children: Jennellett, Ruth Harper, Naomi Altha. Elected assistant pastor 1st Baptist Ch., Richmond, 1897; ordained, 1898; professor of mathematics and church policy in Va. Theological Seminary and College, 1898-1900, also pastor Mt. Carmel Church; pastor, Harrisonburg, Va., 1900-2, 1st Baptist Church, Clifton Forge since 1902; corresponding sec. Va. Baptist State Convention; representative from Va., Home Mission Board of National Baptist Convention; twice commissioned by governor of Va. as representative at National Educational Conventions. Trustee Va. Theological Seminary and College, National Training School for Women and Girls (Washington). Life member Va. Bapt. State Conv., Nat. Bapt. Conv. Mason; grand prelate Knights of Pythias of Va. Home: 5 Prospect Walk, Clifton Forge, Va.

WHITLEY, George Washington, real estate; born in Mo., Mar. 26, 1865; son of James and Orenday (Ellis) Whitley; attended public school 9 months; married Maggie Jane Trusty, of W. Liberty, Ia., April 12, 1905; 1 child by adoption: Charles W. In real estate business, Los Angeles, Cal., since 1909; founded the Mutual Organization League of California, 1909, an educational labor organization including all crafts, regardless of race, color, creed or sex. Socialist; candidate for City Council, 1911; member People's Charter Conference, 1913, and offered amendment for proportional representation in Council, which was defeated, Mar. 24, 1913. African Methodist; member A. M. E. Benevolent Society, Foresters. Club: Union Labor Political. Home: 3660 Halldale Ave. Office: 105 E. 1st St., Los Angeles, Cal.

WIDGEON, John William, curator, naturalist, clergyman; born in Northampton Co., Va., July 28, 1850; son of William and Susan (Kellum) Widgeon; common school education; (M.Sc., Clayton-Williams Academy,

Baltimore, 1912); married Lucy Stevens, of St. Mary's Co., Md., Aug. 6, 1883; 3 children: Eva, Elsie, John, Jr. (Edward, adopted). Began as janitor, 1875, at the Maryland Academy of Sciences; acquired practical knowledge of photography, chemistry, geology, archaeology, and natural science; curator at the Academy many years; elected life member, 1915, the only colored man ever so honored by similar society in U. S.; only naturalist among colored people in America; has mounted many specimens collected by self in Jamaica, B. W. I.; he gathered part of the early collection of geological exhibits in Johns Hopkins Univ.; was lecturer number years at Clayton-Williams Institute; ordained in Baptist ministry; pastor of church near Baltimore. Home: Fairview, Md. Office: 105 W. Franklin St., Baltimore.

WILEY, Josephus Lee, president of academy; born in Tenn., 1873; A.B., Fisk Univ., Nashville, 1895. Admitted to Tennessee bar, 1896, and practiced law for short time; president Fessenden (Fla.) Academy since 1898; presented 100 acres of land to the agricultural department of the academy which (1915) had a total of 300 acres valued at $75,000; vice-president Metropolitan Savings Bank, Metropolitan Realty & Investment Co., Ocala, Fla. Congregationalist. Member American Academy Political and Social Science. Contributor to American Missionary Magazine, New York Age, Florida Times-Union, The Freeman. Address: Ocala, Fla.

WILKINSON, Garnet Crummel, teacher; born at Summerville, S. C., Jan. 10, 1879; son of James William and Grace Ann (Allston) Wilkinson; grad. M Street High School, Washington, D. C., 1898; A.B., Oberlin (O.) College, 1902; LL.B., Howard Univ. School of Law, 1909; married Blanche Elizabeth Colder, June 21, 1905. Began as teacher M Street High School, Washington, 1902, continuing to 1912; principal Armstrong Manual Training High School since 1912. Republican. Methodist. Member college frat. The

Boule. Mason. Club: Mu-So-Lit. Home: 406 You St., Washington, D. C.

WILKINSON, Robert Shaw, college president; born at Charleston, S. C., Feb. 18, 1865; son of Charles H. and Lavinia Wilkinson; preparatory edn. Avery Institute, Charleston; was cadet U. S. Military Academy, West Point, 1884, but resigned on account of health; A.B., Oberlin (O.) College, 1891, A.M., 1894; Ph.D., State Univ., Louisville, Ky., 1896; studied electrical engineering Columbia College, New York, 1902-3; married Marion Raven Birnie, of Charleston, June 29, 1897; 4 children: Helen Raven, Robert Shaw, Frost Birnie, Lula Love. Began teaching school at Louisville, Ky., 1897; connected with State Agricultural and Mechanical College, Orangeburg, S. C., since 1906; elected president, March 29, 1911. Episcopalian. Member Association of American Agricultural Colleges. Mason; member Knights of Pythias. Address: State A. & M. College, Orangeburg, South Carolina.

WILLIAMS, Augustus Lewis, lawyer; born in Greenwood Co., S. C., July 16, 1873; son of Wesley and Julia (Coleman) Williams; student Benedict College, Columbia, S. C., 1889-90; finished course in Atheneum Business College, Chicago, Ill., 1892; A.B., Illinois College of Law, 1905; unmarried. In employ City of Chicago during administration of Mayor George B. Swift, 1895-7; deputy in office of county treasurer, 1900-9; practiced law in Chicago since 1906; attorney and director Allen Derrigible Air Ship Co.; owner of valuable improved real estate in Hyde Park district, Chicago, and vacant lots in different parts of Cook County, also Lakewood, Mich.; agent for other Hyde Park owners. Active in Republican politics; takes prominent part in all matters relating to colored people in his district. Baptist. 32d Mason; past chancellor Cicero Lodge, Knights of Pythias. Clubs: Sixth Ward Republican, Appomatox. Home: 5548 Harper Ave. Office: 184 W. Washington St., Chicago, Ill.

WILLIAMS, A. Wilberforce, physician, surgeon; born at Monroe, La., Jan. 31, 1865; son of Baptiste and Flora Williams; grad. Normal School, Jefferson City, Mo., Northwestern Univ. Medical School, 1894, Sheldon Business College, Chicago, 1907; married Mary Elizabeth Tibbs, of Danville, Ky., June 25, 1902. Practiced in Chicago since 1894; staff physician at Provident Hospital since 1897; attending physician to Provident Hospital Dispensary, also Municipal Tuberculosis Dispensary; specializes in internal medicine treatment of tuberculosis and heart disease; editor Health Column in the Chicago Defender; contributed article on "Tuberculosis and the Negro" for Mississippi Conference on Tuberculosis which appeared in the Journal of Outdoor Life, Feb. 1915. Republican. Episcopalian. Member National Assn. for Study and Prevention of Tuberculosis, Mississippi Valley Conference on Tuberculosis, Robert Koch Society for Study and Prevention of Tuberculosis; treasurer National Medical Assn., 7 years, now state vice-president; member American Medical Assn., Illinois State Medical Society, Chicago Medical Society, Men's League of Sunday Evening Club, Frederick Douglass Center; also member Odd Fellows, Knights of Pythias. Clubs: Appomatox, Social Service. Home: 3408 Vernon Ave. Office: 3255 S. State St., Chicago, Ill.

WILLIAMS, Bert., actor; born in New Providence, Nassau, British Bahama Islands; brought to New York when 2 years old; father was a papier-mache maker with patrons among theatre people, and in this way the son became attached to the stage; family removed to Cal., where he received his education; grad. high school, Riverside; later went to San Francisco with intent to take course in civil engring., but abandoned his purpose. Began professional career as member a little mountebank minstrel company, showing lumber and mining camps of Cal.; later became noted as member Williams & Walker Co., which gained wide fame; later star of The Follies Co., a well known vaudeville organization of white people which makes annual tour of principal American cities; regarded as one of the leading comedians in America. Address: Frogs Club, New York.

WILLIAMS, Charles Grant, teacher, farmer; born at Frankford, Mo., Nov. 2, 1863; son of Thomas and Mary Williams; public school edn., Hannibal, Mo.; married Josie E. Rollins, of Hannibal, May 22, 1885; 1 child: Estelle. Began teaching in Mo., 1884; principal Ashley, 1 yr., Palmyra 4 yrs., Fulton 7 yrs., Boonville since 1895; owns and operates 320 acre farm; editor and supt. U. B. F. Searchlight, Sedalia. Trustee Bartlett Agricultural and Industrial School, Dalton, Mo. Republican. African Methodist. Mason; sec. United Brothers of Friendship; member Knights of Pythias. Address: Boonville, Mo. Farm Address: Frankford, Mo.

WILLIAMS, Daniel Hale, physician, surgeon; born at Hollidaysburg, Pa., Jan. 18, 1858; son of Daniel and Sarah (Price) Williams; attended public school, Hollidaysburg, and Stanton School, Annapolis, Md., the home of his mother; after death of father removed to Rockford, Ill., later to Janesville, Wis., where he graduated from high school, also Hare's Classical Academy; medical student, 1884, in office of Surg.-Gen. Henry Palmer, of Janesville, who served on staff of General U. S. Grant in the war between the states, and was one of the most distinguished surgeons in Ill. and Wis.; M.D., Northwestern Univ. Medical School, Chicago, 1883; (LL.D., Wilberforce Univ., 1909); married Alice D. Johnson, of Washington, 1898. Began practice of medicine in Chicago, 1883; took up active surgical work in connection with South Side Dispensary, 1884; appointed assistant physician Protestant Orphan Asylum, on retirement of Dr. H. P. Hatfield, 1885; was demonstrator of anatomy, Northwestern Univ. Med. Sch. 4 yrs.; member Illinois State Board of Health, 1887-91; because Chicago hospitals and nurse training schools refused colored men as internes and colored women as pupil nurses he interested others in his plans to have an institution where color would be no bar; as a result the Provident Hospital was founded in 1891, with the first Training School for Colored Nurses in the U. S.; remained as attending surgeon to 1912, resigned; performed first successful operation on the human heart in 1893; apptd. surgeon-in-chief Freedmen's Hospital, Washington, during President Grover Cleveland's administration, 1893, continuing until he resigned, 1898; reorganized that hospital, established Training School for Colored Nurses, and put the institution on modern basis; returned to practice in Chicago, 1898; professor of clinical surgery at Meharry Medical College, Nashville, Tenn., since 1900; makes annual visits and holds clinic for benefit of large number of students; was attending surgeon Cook County Hospital, 1903-9; associate on staff of St. Luke's Hospital, Chicago. Fellow of the American College of Surgeons since Nov. 13, 1913. Home: 445 E. 42nd St. Office: 3129 Indiana Ave., Chicago.

WILLIAMS, David Benjamin, real estate; born at Washington, D. C., May 3, 1890; son of David George and Fannie (Smith) Williams; grad. public school, Washington; took special course in Bryant & Bratton Commercial College, Boston, Mass.; student Howard Univ. School of Law; married Lelia E. Fitzgerald, of Atlantic City, N. J., Sept. 1, 1914. Treasurer and manager the rent department of Clarke-Williams-Plummer Co., real estate operators. Served in the Public School Militia, Washington, 3 years. Episcopalian. Home: 933 S St. N. W. Office: 1346 You St. N. W., Washington, D. C.

WILLIAMS, George Grant, editor; born at Peekskill, N. Y., Apr. 3, 1868; son of John and Anna Eliza (Green) Williams; public school edn., Peekskill; married Theresa A. de Courlander, of S. Bethlehem, Pa., June 1, 1911. City editor and mgr. The Philadelphia Tribune since 1903; proprietor G. Grant Williams Advertising Agency; promotor and manager of concerts, recitals and musical entertainments. Trustee Masonic Hall. Republican. Episcopalian. Mason; member Odd Fellows; past exalted ruler O. V. Catto Lodge, No. 20, Elks. Clubs: Citizens Republican, Hotel Brotherhood. Home: 1355 S. Markoe St. Office: 526 S. 16th St., philadelphia, Pa.

WILLIAMS, James S., undertaker; born in Franklin Parish, La., Apr. 21, 1871; son of Bud C. and Eliza Williams; could not write name until 14 years old; worked 18 months as bootblack while attending New Orleans Univ.; married Carrie B. Thomas, of Shreveport, La., Jan. 24, 1900; 5 children. Began business career as barber in Rayville, La.; later in livery stable business 5 years; failed at first venture as undertaker in Shreveport; also failed as grocer; with greater determination opened undertaking establishment second time in Shreveport and succeeded; has livery stable and real estate business. Member number societies; vice-pres. Undertakers' Assn. of U. S.; member National Negro Business League, State Negro Business League (president). Address: 1122 Texas Ave., Shreveport, La.

WILLIAMS, R. Reche, physician, surgeon; born near Williston, Marion Co., Fla., Feb. 25, 1881; son of John and Mary E. (Tiner) Williams; ed. schools of Marion County to 1897; grad. Cookman Institute, Jacksonville, Fla., 1902; M.D., Meharry Medical College (Walden Univ.), Nashville, Tenn., 1907; married Clotelle Chappelle, daughter of Rt. Rev. William D. Chappelle, of Columbia, S. C., Jan. 7, 1914. Worked as Pullman porter in Chicago and New York, summers, while studying medicine; began practice in Fernandina, Fla., 1907; operated drug store there to Sept., 1911; practiced in Ocala, Fla., since 1912; assistant surgeon uniform rank Knights of Pythias; grand medical director Odd Fellows of Fla., elected May 6, 1915; manager Metropolitan Drug Store; director Metropolitan Savings Bank. Trustee A. M. E. Ch.; delegate to general conference of the church, 1916. Republican. Member National Medical Assn., Tri-State Medical, Dental and Pharm. Assn. of Fla., Ga., Ala., also Florida Medical, Dental and Pharm. Assn. (ex-president). Home: 658 W. Broadway. Office: Metropolitan Block, Ocala, Fla.

WILLIAMS, Robert Simeon, bishop; born at Caddo, La., Oct. 27, 1858; son of William J. and Edith Williams, slaves; ed. public schools, Caddo; finished normal course Wiley Univ., Marshall, Tex., 1886; student Howard Univ., Washington, D. C., 2 yrs.; married Willie A. Nockolls, of Washington, Oct. 21, 1891; 6 children: Catherine, Artoria, Roberta, Burtelle, Edith, Georgine; also 2 adopted boys: Frank Pierce Gardner, Nathaniel Hills. Converted in Colored M. E. Church when 16 years old; soon after was refused license to preach on account of age; persistance resulted in license to exhort, then local preacher, and later to full work in ministry; first pastorate at Longview, Tex., also published the Christian Work; worked on farm 2 summers and taught school to meet expenses in college. Pastor of Israel Metropolitan Church, Washington, D. C., 1886-8, Sidney Park Ch., Columbia, S. C., 1888-92, Trinity Ch., Augusta, Ga., 1892-4; elected bishop at General Conference C. M. E. Church, Memphis, Tenn., 1894; now presiding in 2d Episcopal Dist., including D. C., Md., N. J., Pa., N. C., S. C.; was secretary College of Bishops numbers yrs., now treasurer its Emergency Fund; attended every general conference since 1886; delegate to Ecumenical Conference on Methodism, Washington, 1891, London, Eng., 1901; while in London preached from pulpit long occupied by John Wesley. President board trustees Miles Memorial College; vice-pres. trustee board of Paine Univ. Republican. Mason; member Odd Fellows, Mosaic Templars. Home: 912 15th St., Augusta, Ga.

WILLIAMS, Samuel Laing, lawyer; born at Savannah, Ga., 1863; son of S. Laing and Nancy Williams; A.B., Univ. of Mich., 1884; LL.M., Columbia Univ. (now George Washington) Law

School, Washington, D. C., 1888; married Fannie Barrier, of Brockport, N. Y., 1885. Admitted to Illinois bar, 1885; since practiced in Chicago; assistant United States attorney for Northern District of Illinois several years; has served as examiner of pensions, Washington, and appraiser of inheritance taxes in Chicago. Republican. Unitarian. Home: 4203 St. Lawrence Ave. Office: 3439 S. State St., Chicago, Ill.

WILLIAMS, Thomas Calvin, industrial school treasurer and business mgr.; born at Rock Hill, S. C., Nov. 15, 1875; son of Rufus and Susan (Barber) Williams; ed. schools of York County, S. C., to 1890; Brainerd Institute, Chester, S. C., 2 years; preparatory edn. Shaw Univ., Raleigh, N. C., and 2 years in Cambridge (Mass.) Latin High School; A.B., Harvard, 1904; married Urie Elaine Grasty, of Winston, Va., June 16, 1912; 1 child: Evelyn May. Began as teacher in Dinwiddie (Va.) Agricultural and Industrial School, 1904; treasurer and business manager Manassas (Va.) Industrial School since 1908. Baptist. Address: Manassas Industrial School, Manassas, Va.

WILLIAMS, William Frank, clerk to governor; born at St. Paul, Minn., Oct. 24, 1878; son of George and Barbara Williams; grad. high school, St. Paul; unmarried. Began as messenger, 1899, for John Lind then governor of Minn., and who was President Woodrow Wilson's special and confidential representative to investigate conditions in Mexico, 1914-15; assistant in physical dept. St. Paul Y. M. C. A., 1901-5; messenger and clerk under Gov. John A. Johnson, 1905-9, and Gov. A. O. Eberhart since 1909; prepared plans and specifications for files established in the governor's office, iron stairs and balcony being the features; baseball player and all-round athlete. Republican. Catholic. Home: 264 W. Central Ave. Office: Capitol Building, St. Paul, Minn.

WILLIAMSON, Charles Frederick, principal high school; born at Madison, Ind., Jan. 18, 1880; son of Charles

W. and Sarah Elizabeth Williamson; grad. Broadway High School, Madison, 1897; prep. edn. Indiana State Normal School; A.B., Ind. Univ., 1907; married Mabel Leona Wright, of Xenia, O., Aug., 1910; 2 children: Lillian L., Earl A. Served as page boy, Ind. House of Representatives during 60th General Assembly, 1897; began teaching at Madison, 1898; principal Scribner High School, New Albany, Ind., since 1909. Republican. Baptist. Mason; member Odd Fellows. Home: 515 Pearl St., New Albany, Ind.

WILLIAMSON, Henry Albro, chiropodist; born at Plainfield, N. J., Oct. 25, 1875; son of William Edward and Mary Pauline (Lyons) Williamson; ed. public schools San Francisco and Brooklyn; married Laura J. Moulton, of Brooklyn, N. Y., Apr. 10, 1901. With Clark & Company, paper manufacturers, 1895-1909; clerk in government service for while; chiropodist in Brooklyn since 1910. Has held various offices in Masonic bodies since 1904; appointed grand historian, 1909, secretary, 1911-14, elected senior grand warden, 1915, Grand Lodge of N. Y.; compiled history of that lodge covering period, 1812-1912; wrote number "Freemasonry and Negroes" articles which were published in "Freemason," London, Eng., and "Tyler-Keystone," Ann Arbor, Mich.; entire series prepared for pamphlet form; wrote open letter on subject of "The Position of the Black Race in Masonry" to grand master United Grand Orient of Lusitania, Lisbon, Portugal, which was widely published; in touch with white Masons in London, Eng., Australia, Switzerland, and U. S. Member Majestic Lodge No. 7, Knights of Pythias (New York); past patron Queen Esther Chapter No. 9, Order of Eastern Star; past royal patron Viola Court No. 2, Order of Amaranth (both Brooklyn). Republican. Episcopalian. Club: Crooklyn Citizens. Address: 294 Putnam Ave., Brooklyn, N. Y.

WILLIS, Lucas B., undertaken; born at Frankfort, Ky., Nov. 3, 1874; son of Samuel and Apperline (Reynolds) Willis; attended public school to 1888; grad. Mass. College of Embalming, Boston, 1898; post-grad. work at Renouard Training School for Embalming; married Cora L. Christy, of Indianapolis, Ind., May 9, 1903. Began undertaking business with Thomas K. Robb, Frankfort, 1897; removed to Indianapolis, 1900; associated with C. M. C. Willis to 1904; member undertaking firm of Shelton & Willis, 1904-10; in business for self since 1910. Republican. African Methodist. Mason; member Odd Fellows, Knights of Pythias, Court of Calanthe. Club: Lotus (president). Address: 413 W. Michigan St., Indianapolis, Ind.

WILLIS, William Andrew, dentist; born at Baton Rogue, La., June 19, 1875; son of George and Parthenia (Morgan) Willis; attended public schools, New Orleans, La.; D.D.S., Meharry Dental College (Walden Univ.), Nashville, Tenn., 1910; married Odelia E. Smizer, of Galveston, Tex., Sept. 7, 1912. Practiced in Galveston since Dec., 1910. African Methodist. Member Texas Medical, Dental and Pharm. Assn. Mason. Club: Iroquois (New Orleans). Home: 1814 Avenue N ½. Office: 426½ 25th St., Galveston, Texas.

WILSON, Christopher Columbus, printer, former president U. S. Civil Service Board; born in Iberville Parish, La., Feb. 20, 1859; son of Jefferson and Elizabeth (Cox) Wilson; attended public sch., New Orleans, also night school in Straight Univ.; took special course for 5 yrs., and received certificate of proficiency in grammar and English from International Correspondence Schools of Scranton, Pa.; married Alice Finnie, of New Orleans, La., July 20, 1880; 2 children: Christopher C., Jr., Corina; 2d marriage, Malvine Elizabeth Dixon, of New Orleans, Dec. 16, 1891; 1 child: Harrison C. Began in printing business, New Orleans, 1896; editor and publisher the Southern Age, 1906-12; now prop. Southern Age Printing Office; read estate operator; was secretary, later president for 2 yrs., Louisiana Emmigration Land and Improvement Co. Ltd. Member Republican State Committee, 1892-1900; during same period was pres. Rep. Parish Committee; president United States Civil Service Board, for the mint and essay service, New Orleans, 1900; appointed by John R. Proctor, president Civil Service Commission; so far as we learn, no other colored man was ever so commissioned; was storekeeper U. S. Mint, New Orleans, 1899-1910. Has commercial Agency rating, $10,000 to $15,000. Address: 7718 Maple St., New Orleans, La.

WILSON, Elisha Arlington, clergyman; born at Garland City, Ark., Oct. 22, 1876; son of Bryant and Katherine (Miller) Wilson; high school course, Texarkana, Tex.; prep. edn. Bishop College, Marshall, Tex.; M.A.L., Christian Univ., Canton, Mo., 1899, took Bible course and Sacred literature; Ph.B., Kansas City Univ., Kan., 1904, the first colored graduate earning degree Bachelor of Philosophy at Kansas City Univ.; (D.D., Eckstein-Norton Univ., Cane Springs, Ky., 1907); married Leurlean Snadon, of Kansas City, Mo., July 12, 1899. Began traveling at early age as the "Boy Preacher"; pastor Metropolitan Baptist Church, Kansas City, Kan., 1897-1913, and First Bapt. Ch., Muskogee, Okla., since 1913; was pres. Kansas Bapt. Convention, 1902-13; now corresponding secretary the Oklahoma, recording secretary the Western, and assistant secretary the National Baptist Convention. Trustee Topeka Normal and Industrial Institue, and Old Folks Home of Lawrence, Kan. Republican. Member Negro Business League, Muskogee. 32d degree Mason; national grand recorder United Brothers of Friendship; member Odd Felolws, Knights of Tabor, Sons of Joseph. Author (pamphlets): The Burning Message for the Young Men; Marching Orders; The Heavenly Vision; Armageddon; A Call to Duty; The King's Business; High Ground; Service Not Honor; All At It; Our Faces to the Future. Home: 312 N. 5th St., Muskogee, Okla.

WILSON, Eliza, social worker; born at Richmond, Va., May 16, 1845; daughter of William H. and Elizabeth (Taylor) Clayton; normal school edn.; received private instruction and took course in Gray's Hairdressing Sch., Chicago, Ill., 1865; married Nathan Wilson, of Buffalo, N. Y., 1868; 2 children. President and trustee Phillis Wheatley Home, Detroit, Mich.; in hair dressing business and mfr. hair goods. Episcopalian. Pres. Needlework Guild of America; mem. Household of Ruth, Willing Workers, Kings Daughters. Home: 204 E. Elizabeth St., Detroit, Mich.

WILSON, Hyland Emilio Slatre, music conservatory dean, concert organist, pianist, lecturer; born at Syracuse, N. Y., Dec. 8, 1879; son of Edward H. and Sarah Elizabeth (Slatre) Wilson; attended public schools, Syracuse and New York, also Brooklyn High Sch.; A.M., Mus. Doc., Univ. State of New York, 1907; married Thomasina Wilder Williamson, Brooklyn, N. Y., June 22, 1904; 5 children. His work as an organist in Brooklyn reached the ears of John Alexander Dowie in 1903; the founder of both the Christian-Catholic Apostolic Church and Zion City sent for him, offering the organistship of the choir at Zion City which at that time had 710 singers; accepted the offer and has served as organist at Shiloh Tabernacle, Zion City, Ill., since Feb. 3, 1904; the choir now has 500 members, and the organ is one of the largest and most noted instruments in the world. President the Kenosha Grand Conservatory of Music, which is affiliated to the University of the State of New York, also Chicago Musical College, the two musical institutions having an exchange of teachers; the Kenosha Conservatory occupies entire second floor of the Kenosha Y. M. C. A. building, has its own recital hall, equipped with Grand pianos; the faculty consists of 27 instructors, several being members of the Chicago Symphony Orchestra and others of world wide reputation; in early part of 1915, he engaged Ettore Tita Ruffo, one of the greatest voice teachers from Europe; he founded the Zion Conservatory of Music and Art, now dean and director of same; also director Zion City Philharmonic Orchestra; associate member board of directors Chicago Musical College; dean and examiner Grand Conservatory of Music of New York State Univ., for states of Illinois and Wisconsin; examiner London College of Music, England; is president Slatre-Wilson Co., dealers in pianos, organs and music. Member National Association of Organists, National Song Society of America; also member Christian-Catholic Apostolic Church. Republican. Possibly no other sketch in this book points out more clearly the fact that a colored person, working along purely business lines and proving his worth, will command business, respect, and recognition in what may be called white communities; there are no colored people in Kenosha and Zion City; in both schools (to 1915) they had over 400 students of which only 7 were colored; he has had only one colored teacher; the departments include: Piano; Violin; Vocal, Theory, Harmony and Composition; Band Instruments; Embroideries; painting, drawing and Cartooning; Department of Expression. Home: 2806 Bethel Boul., Zion City, Ill. Office: Kenosha Grand Conservatory of Music, Kenosha, Wis.

WILSON, John Allen, principal high school; born at Mathews, Ala., Feb. 14, 1877; son of Zimmerman and Laura Jane (Gray) Wilson; grad. Agricultural and Mechanical College, Normal, Ala., 1907; student State Normal School at Montgomery 1 summer, also at Tuskegee Normal and Industrial Institute; unmarried. Teacher of mathematics, and assigned to special research work, Agricultural and Mechanical College at Normal, 1904-7; teacher public school, Brighton, Ala., 1907-9; principal high school, Decatur, Ala., since 1909. Baptist. Member Alabama State Teachers' Assn., Morgan County Colored Teachers' Assn. (president), Alpha Literary Society (also pres.). Home: Mathews. Office: Decatur, Ala.

WILSON, Leroy Oliver, state librarian; born at Pomeroy, O., Aug. 25, 1871; son of John and Eliza (Stewart) Wilson; graduate academic department of Union School, Pomeroy, 1889; unmarried. Teacher at Pleasant Ridge, O., 1889-91; and schools at Weston, W. Va., 1898-1914; president since 1909, Pythian Mutual Investment Association; accepted the office when debt nearly forced the association to dissolve, and gradually improved conditions until it is practically out of debt (1914) and owns property valued at $75,000; state librarian of W. Va., since Aug. 1, 1914; when appointed to this position white newspapers of Weston spoke of him in the highest terms. Republican; active in politics since 1895; was director colored bureau Republican State Headquarters during campaigns of 1912-14, first colored man ever stationed at that bureau; member State Central Committee, 1912-16. Wesleyan Methodist. Grand chancellor Knights of Pythias. Author (pamphlet): A Few Thoughts on This and That, 1909. Home: Weston. Office: State Library, Charleston, W. Va.

WILSON, William H., physician; born at Murray, Ky., Nov. 9, 1879; son of Lina Beauraguard; public school edn., Murray; State Normal School at Frankfort, Ky., 1898-1900; grad. Berea (Ky.) College, 1903; student Univ. of Chicago 2 years; M.D., Univ. of Ill. College of Medicine, 1910; married Ora E. Johnson, of Independence, Kan., June 30, 1910 (died Apr. 28, 1914). Teacher in public schools of Ky., 12 years; pharmacist at Lakeside Hospital, Chicago, Ill., 1910-11; practiced medicine, Clayton, Ky., 1911-13, Henderson since 1913; examiner for number local lodges; owns 3 houses and other city property. Republican. Baptist. Member Kentucky State Medical Assn. Mason; member Knights of Pythias, Knights of Tabor. Office: 2d and Main Sts., Henderson, Kentucky.

WINGO, Estelle Bradley, supervising industrial teacher; born at Amelia Court House, Va., Feb. 22, 1878; daughter of William C. and Emma (Boisseau) Bradley; attended public schools at Russell Grove, Amelia C. H., and Pittsburgh, Pa.; grad. Ingleside Academy, Burkesville, Va., 1897; married Andrew B. Wingo, of Amelia C. H., June 19, 1901; 2 children: John W., Donald C. Began as teacher. in public schools of Va., 1897, continuing 15 yrs.; supervisor of Negro Rural schools, Amelia County, Va., since Sept. 1, 1913; she is one of 32 supervising industrial teachers in this branch of modern public instruction under the Va. State Board of Education; with the aid of the Anna T. Jeanes Fund the system reaches the most remote schools and homes in the state. Presbyterian. Address: Amelia Court House, Va.

WINN, A. G., clergyman; born in Texas; grad. Prairie View State Normal and Industrial College, Prairie View, Tex. Licensed to preach in A. M. E. Church, 1902; pastor at Hearne 3 yrs., and member Texas Conference 8 yrs.; transferred to Northern Texas Conf.; pastor at Terrell since 1910. Address: Terrell, Texas.

WINSTON, Louise Elenor, supervising industrial teacher; born at Williamsport, Pa., Oct. 21, 1889; daughter of William Letcher and Lelia Rosabelle (Parsons) Winston; grad. Virginia Normal and Industrial Institute, Petersburg, May 14, 1909. Began as instructor in domestic science and manual training in rural schools, 1912; supervising industrial teacher in Sussex County, Va., since Oct. 15, 1914; one of the 32 supervisors under the State Board of Education; aided by the Anna T. Jeanes Fund, this branch of public instruction reaches the most remote schools and homes in Virginia. Baptist. Member Va. State Teachers' Assn., Negro Organization Society of Va. Home: Clifton Forge. Office: Waverly, Va.

WINTERS, Henry H., teacher; born at Rippon, W. Va., 1860; son of John and Susanna (Russ) Winters; ed. Storer College, Harper's Ferry, W. Va., and Pennsylvania State College; married Lizzie C. Lincoln, of Wadesville, Va., Feb. 22, 1892; 4 children: Eva E., Florida A., Henry H., Lincoln H. Taught in schools of W. Va., 21 years; teacher of agriculture at Storer College since 1903. Free Bap-

tist. Republican. Mason; member ber True Reformers. Address Storer College, Harper's Ferry, W. Va.

WOOD, John Wesley, clergyman, missionary secretary; born in Talbot Co., Ga., May 10, 1865; parents, Isom and Amanda Burks, died in his infancy; was first taken by family named Cleveland, later by his grandfather, Levi Woods, which explains his name; did not know the alphabet when 16 years old; attended night school in Troup Co., 1885-6; student in Lagrange Academy, Ga., 1887-9; (hon. D.D., Livingstone College, Salisbury, N. C., 1907); married Jannie Edmond, of Humboldt, Tenn., Nov. 8, 1891; 5 children: Jessie S., Ethel R., Inex A., Lillian B., Charleszine R. Entered Methodist ministry, 1885; ordained deacon A. M. E. Zion Church, 1889, elder, 1891; was president Edenton High and Industrial School 3 years, and pastor of church at Edenton, N. C.; also pastor at Norfolk, Va., Indianapolis, Ind., Mobile, Ala.; has traveled in many parts of Europe; visited Africa in interest of Foreign Missions; made study of customs and habits of number West Gold Coast tribes; missionary secretary A. M. E. Zion Church since 1912; editor the Missionary Seer. Home: 1046 Traub Ave., Indianapolis, Ind. Office: 420 S. 11th St., Philadelphia, Pa.

WOODBEY, George Washington, clergyman, lecturer; born in Johnson Co., Tenn., Oct. 5, 1854; son of Charles and Rachel (Wagner) Woodbey; self-educated, except 2 terms in common school; married Annie R. Goodin, of Kansas, Nov. 13, 1873 (died 1891); 5 children; 2d, Mary E. Hart, of New York, Nov. 14, 1908. Ordained Baptist ministry, Emporia, Kan., 1874; later pastored in number western cities; lecturer on socialism, theological, literary, scientific, and historical subjects, since 1889. Was active in Republican party of Missouri, 1876, and in Kansas, 1880; removed to Neb., 1883; candidate for lieut-governor on Prohibitionist ticket, 1890, and for Congress in 1st Dist., Neb., 1894; elected member the Prohibitionist National Committee, 1896, but left party with the "bolters" that year; joined Populist party, 1897; supported the fusion ticket and William Jennings Bryan, presidential candidate, 1900; during that campaign heard Eugene V. Debs and joined the Socialist party after election; removed to Calif., 1902; delegate to Socialist National Convention, 1904, 08, 12; elected member state executive board of Socialist party in Calif.; was candidate for state treasurer, 1914. Member the Western Baptist Assn. Author: What to Do and How to Do It, 1904; The Bible and Socialism, 1904; The Distribution of Wealth, 1910. Home: No. 12 29th St., San Diego. Office: 831 S. San Pedro St., Los Angeles, Calif.

WOODHOUSE, Henry Francis, clergyman, editor, publisher; born at Norfolk, Va., Jan. 24, 1847; son of Rev. Dr. Amercus and Mariah (Wilson) Woodhouse; public school edn., Norfolk; high school, Hampton, Va.; married Mairna Wood, Aug. 18, 1883 (died 1885; 2d, Charlotte Jane Butt, of Elizabeth City, N. C., Sept. 8, 1895; 1 child: John A. Editor the Signs of the Times, Elizabeth City, since founded in 1902; general mgr. Woodhouse Pub. Co.; mgr. 5 and 10 Cent Store; mfr. Woodhouse Nickle Water Filters; national supreme grand pres. Eastern Workmen. Republican. Baptist; in ministry number years. Served 3 years as drummer, Co. G., 36th U. S. Colored Inf., in war between the states; was wounded in battle at Deep Bottom, Va. Mason; member Odd Fellows. Address: R. F. D. No. 6, Box 30, Elizabeth City, N. C.

WOODS, Robert Clisson, college president; born at Stewartsville, Va., Nov. 17, 1882; son of Edward William and Bettie (Burnett) Woods; A.B., Virginia Theological Seminary and College, 1906, B.D., 1906 (D.D., 1911; A.M., Clayton-Williams Univ., Baltimore, Md., 1911); married Octavia Hunter of Franklin, Va., June 6, 1907; 4 children: Octavia M., Reginald C., Maurice F., Alcia. President of Clayton-Williams Theological Seminary (now Clayton-Williams Univ.), Balti-

more, 1906-8; ordained Baptist ministry, 1908; pastor at Staunton, Va., 1908-11; corresponding secretary Virginia Baptist Convention, 1909-12; president Virginia Theological Seminary and College since 1911; member from Va. on Educational board of National Baptist Convention since 1913. Republican. Member American Academy Political and Social Science, Odd Fellows, Red Men, True Reformers. Author (3 editions in pamphlet form): Why I Am a Baptist. Contributor to number publications. Address: Va. Theol. Sem. and College, Lynchburg, Virginia.

WOODS, Samuel Ellsworth, real estate; born at Pruce River, Canada, May 7, 1871; son of Alick T. and Charlotte (Woolfork) Woods; attended district schools of Wayne Co., Mich., 1881-4; studied in night school, Washington, D. C., 1899-1903; private instruction under Mrs. Cody Parker, Washington; married Lillian M. Lee, of Cleveland, O., Aug. 13, 1910; 2 children: Edith Violia, Samuel Ellsworth, Jr. Began as assistant messenger in patent office at Washington, 1899, continuing to 1902; skilled laborer in bureau of internal revenue Treasury Dept., 1902-3; carpenter for board of education, Cleveland, 1904-5; cement work contractor, 1905-7; attendant in House of Representatives, Washington 1907-8, deputy sheriff Cuyahoga Co., O., 1908-11; in real estate and mortgage loan business, Cleveland, since 1911; manager Central Business Exchange; secretary board of directors Brooks Investment Co.; director G. A. Morgan Hair Refining Co.; lessee and manager Clayton Hall used by 11 colored fraternal societies. Served as artificer in Co. D. 9th Bat., Ohio Natl. Guard, 2 years. Republican; nominated H. T. Eubanks for state representative, and Thomas W. Fleming for City Council. African Methodist. Member Cleveland Assn. of Colored Men, Men's Auxiliary to Home for Aged Colored People, Knights of Pythias. Home: 2192 E. 43d St. Office: 2828 Central Ave., Cleveland, O.

WOODS, William Daniel, fraternal order officer, clergyman; born in Va., Mar. 10, 1867; son of T. Annie Woods; B.D., Virginia Theological Seminary and College, Lynchburg, 1900; (D.D., W. Va. Seminary and College, 1911); married Julia A. Johnson, Dec. 27, 1901; 5 children: Willie, Gregory, Lucile, Julia, Aleas. Ordained Baptist ministry, 1900; since pastor in number of churches; founded in 1905, and now great incohonee Grand Council, Independent Order of Red Men and Daughters of Pocahontas; during first 10 years the order paid $75,000 in sick benefits; he owns Roanoke property valued at about $50,000; vice-president Virginia Baptist State Educational Convention; secretary Valley Baptist Assn. Trustee Virginia Theological Seminary and College. Address: 224 Rutherford Ave. N. E., Roanoke, Va.

WOODSON, Carter Goodwin, teacher; born at New Canton, Va., Dec. 19, 1875; son of James and Ann Eliza (Riddle) Woodson; grad. Douglass High School, Huntington, W. Va., 1896; Litt.B., Berea (Ky.) College, 1903; traveled in Europe and Asia, and studied in Univ. of Paris, France, 1907; A.B., Univ. of Chicago, 1908, A.M., later; Ph.D., Harvard, 1912; self and W E. B. DuBois are the only colored men that have thus far received the degree of Doctor of Philosophy from Harvard Univ.; unmarried. Began as principal Douglass High School, Huntington, 1900, continuing 3 years; supervisor of schools Philippine Islands, 1903-6; instructor in M. Street High School, Washington, since 1909. Baptist. Member American Historical Assn., American Negro Academy. Club: Mu-So-Lit. Author: Educating the Negro Before 1860 (Putnam's Sons, New York), 1915; Disruption of Virginia, 1915. Address: 2223 12th St. N. W., Washington, D. C.

WORK, Frederick Jerome, music teacher; born at Nashville, Tenn.; son of John W. and Samuella (Boyd) Work; A.B., Fisk Univ., Nashville, 1902, grad. in music, 1904; studied piano under J. M. Orth, harmony and composition under H. Clough-Leighter, Boston, Mass., 1906; made special study of Negro Folk-Song number years; married Nannie Isabel Sumner, of Nashville, Feb. 4, 1909; 1 child: Nona I. Began musical career as member Fisk Jubilee Co., 1900; director Fisk Quartette, 1903-4; teacher of music, Clark Univ., Atlanta, Ga., 1904-5, Talladega (Ala.) College, 1905-9, high school, Dallas, Tex., 1909-10, Lincoln High School, Kansas City, Mo., since 1910; musical editor and treas. Work Bros. & Hart Co.; edited Folk-Songs of American Negro (2 vols.). Baptist. Mason. Home: 1526 16th Ave. N., Nashville, Tenn. Office: Lincoln High School, Kansas City, Mo.

WORK, John Wesley, university professor; born at Nashville, Tenn., Aug. 6, 1873; son of John Wesley and Samuella (Boyd) Work; A.B., Fisk Univ., 1895, A.M., 1898; post-graduate work, Harvard, 1896-7, Univ. of Chicago, 1908; married Agnes Morris Haynes, of Staunton, Va., Apr. 26, 1899; 6 children: (Charlotte, deceased), John Wesley, Jr., Agnes S., Merrill C., Helen E., Julian C. Principal public schools, Tullahoma, Tenn., 1895; instructor, 1898, professor of Latin, 1903, professor of history and Latin since 1904, at Fisk Univ., Nashville; president Work Bros. & Hart, music pub. Republican. Baptist. Member Classical Assn. of Middle West and South. Club: Vingt et Cing. Address: 1607 Harding St., Nashville, Tenn.

WORK, Monroe Nathan, sociologist, statistician; born in Iredell Co., N. C., Aug. 15, 1866; son of Alexander and Eliza (Hobbs) Work; grad. high school, Arkansas City, Kan., 1892, Chicago Theological Seminary (English course), 1898; Ph.D., Univ. of Chicago, 1902, A.M., 1903; specialized in sociology; married Florence Evelyn Hendrichson, of Savannah, Ga., Dec. 27, 1904. In charge the division of records and research at Tuskegee Normal and Industrial Institute, Ala., since 1908; editor the Negro Year Book which was first issued in 1912; it is an annual encyclopedia of the

Negro and commands reviews in metropolitan newspapers all over the country; it records current events, historical and sociological facts, is a directory of persons and a bibliographical guide to the literature of the subjects discussed; its value is inestimable; published by The Negro Year Book Co., Tuskegee Institute, Ala. Republican. African Methodist. Member American Sociological Society, Southern Sociological Congress, National Council the National Economic League. Author: Industrial Work of Tuskegee Graduates and Former Students. Address: Tuskegee Institute, Ala.

WORMLEY, Roscoe Conklin, dentist; born at Washington, D. C., July 22, 1882; son of Garrett Smith and Amelia E. (Brent) Wormley; grad. M Street High School, Washington, 1902; D.D.S., Howard Univ. School of Medicine, 1905; married Beatrice F. Nalle, of Washington, July 10, 1907; 2 children: Sumner Minton, Roscoe Conklin, Jr. Passed examining board, Dis-of Columbia, 1905, and state board for registration and examination in Dentistry of N. J., 1906; practiced in Plainfield 3 years; accepted appointment and was demonstrator in dental dept. Howard Univ., Washington, 1909-12; passed civil service examination for appointment as dental inspector in public schools of Washington, 1912; practiced in Plainfield since his return to N. J., Oct. 15, 1913. Served in Washington High School Battalion, as corporal, 1900, 3d sergt., 1901, 1st lieut. and adjutant, 1902. Republican. Presbyterian. Member Robert Freeman Dental Assn. (Washington), North Jersey Medical Society. Address: 308 E. 3rd St., Plainfield, N. J.

WRIGHT, Eugene Ignatius, dentist; born at Lititz, Jamaica, B. W. I., Jan. 25, 1872; son of Alexander W. and Frances (Lyons) Wright; prep. edn. Fairfield Training College in Jamaica; came to U. S., 1899; D.D.S., Howard Univ. Dental College, Washington, D. C., 1903; married Ray Louise Swaley, of Spur Tree, Manchester, Jamaica, Feb. 2, 1910; 2 children. Eugene, Jr.,

Vivian E. Began as principal retirement school of 1st class, 1895; principal Brinkly School, 1895-6, Port Royal School, 1896-9, at Kingston, Jamaica; practiced dentistry in Boston, Mass., since 1905; member Harding, Cox & Martin real estate syndicate. Moravian religion. Member Jamaica Union of Teachers, 1896, and was vice-president North St. Elizabeth Teachers' Assn.; member National Medical Assn., New England Medical, Dental and Pharm. Assn. (president); also member Odd Fellows, Brothers and Sisters of Love and Charity. Home: 71 Windsor St. Office: 681 Shawmut Ave., Boston, Mass.

WRIGHT, Edwina MaBelle, teacher; born at Augusta, Ga., July, 1891; daughter of Richard Robert and Lydia Elizabeth (Howard) Wright; sister of Richard Robert Wright, Jr.; grad. Georgia State Industrial College, Savannah, Ga., 1907; Atlanta Univ., 1908; Pratt Institute, 1913; unmarried. Began as teacher in Branch Normal College, Pine Bluff, Ark.; now teacher of domestic art in Virginia Normal and Industrial Institute, Petersburg, Va. African Methodist. Home: Sarah, Ga. Address: Virginia Normal and Industrial Institute, Petersburg, Va.

WRIGHT, Herbert Richard, consul; born in Iowa; LL.B., Univ. of Iowa, 1901; U. S. Consul at Puerto Cabello since Jan. 13, 1909. Address: American Consulate, Puerto Cabello, Venezuela.

WHIGHT, Richard Robert, college president; born at Dalton, Ga., May 16, 1855; son of Richard Waddell and Harriett (Lynch) Wright; A.B., Atlanta (Ga.) Univ., 1876, A.M., 1879; student at Harvard, 1896; LL.D., Wilberforce Univ., 1899); married Lydia Elizabeth Howard, of Columbus, Ga., June 7, 1877; 9 children: Richard R., Jr., Julia O., Elsie W. (Thompson), Lillian M., Edmund (deceased), Edwina M., Whittier H., Harriett B. (Stowe), Emanuel C. Principal of high school at Cuthbert, Ga., 1876-8, Ware High School, Augusta, 1880-91; president Georgia State Industrial College, Savannah, since 1891, and instructor in mental and moral science and English language; president Georgia State Agricultural and Industrial Fair Assn., since 1900, also Savannah Negro Civic League since 1912. Served as additional paymaster, with rank of major, in Ga. State Vols., 1898. Delegate to all Republican National Conventions, 1880 to 1900, also at Chicago, 1908; was offered appointment as E. E. and M. P. to Liberia by President William McKinley, but declined. Member American Historical Assn., National Educational Assn., National Colored Teachers' Assn., National Association Teachers' in Colored Schools (pres. 1908). Mason. Author: Historical Sketch of Negro in Education in Georgia, 1886; The Negroes Contribution to Civilization in America, 1900; The Negro as an Inventor; The Negro as a Discoverer. Contributor to American Industries magazine, Political and Social Science Magazine, the Independent and other papers. Address: Georgia State Industrial College, Savannah, Ga.

WRIGHT, Richard Robert, Jr., editor; born at Cuthbert, Ga., Apr. 16, 1878; son of Richard Robert and Lydia Elizabeth (Howard) Wright; A.B., Georgia State Industrial College, Savannah, 1898; B.D., Univ. of Chicago, 1901, A.M., 1904 (Ph.D., 1911); student Univ. of Berlin, 1903, Univ. of Leipsic, 1904, in Germany; research fellow in sociology Univ. of Pa. 1905-7; married Charlotte Crogman, of Atlanta, Ga., Sept. 8, 1909; 3 children: Charlotte R., Richard R., III., Alberta. Manager of Georgia State College Journal, 1896-8; paymaster's clerk U. S. A., Dept. of the Gulf, in Spanish-American war, 1898. Was professor of Hebrew and Hellenistic Greek at Wilberforce (O.) Univ., 1901-3; president 8th Ward Settlement Building & Loan Assn., Philadelphia, Pa., since 1906; field secretary for Armstrong Assn. of Philadelphia, 1908-9; secretary People's Savings Bank, 1908-11; manager A. M. E. Book Concern, 1909-12; editor Christian Recorder (A. M. E. Church journal), since 1909. Was

director of exhibits for Emancipation Proclamation Exposition of Pa., 1913. Trustee Wilberforce Univ., Payne Theological Seminary, Spring Street Social Settlement, National Assn. for Advancement of Colored Women, National Assn. for Advancement of Colored People (Phila. branch), Abolition Society; member American Academy Political and Social Science, American Negro Historical Society, American Negro Academy; life member National Assn. Teachers' in Colored Schools. Republican. Mason. Author: Teachings of Jesus, 2 vols., 1903, 1912; Negro in Xenia, Ohio, 1904; The Negro Problem, 1911; Home Owning Among Negroes in Pennsylvania, 1911; The Negro in Pennsylvania (social study), 1912; Fifty Years of Negro Progress, 1913; Negro in Industry in Philadelphia and Pittsburgh, 1913. Compiler of Philadelphia Colored Directory. Home: 5111 Chestnut St. Office: 631 Pine St., Philadelphia, Pa.

WYATT, Josephine Ernestine Hughes, dramatic reader; born at Fulton, Ky., Dec. 25, 1884; daughter of William Henry and Martha (McFall) Hughes; married Dr. C. W. Wyatt, of Dyersburg, Tenn., Nov. 25, 1903. Grad. high school, Fulton, 1900; student Cumnock School of Oratory, Northwestern Univ., Evanston, Ill., 1906; private study under white teachers; lyceum work with Independent Lyceum Bureau, New York, Menely Chautauqua Bureau, Chicago, Ill.; traveled in Chautauqua work for white race, also short term for colored; dramatic reader and interpreter of Dunbar's works since 1900; regarded as elocutionist of much ability. Missionary Baptist. President Pearless Literary and Social Club. Address: Box 68, Fulton, Ky.

Y

YERBY, Cecilia Kennedy, school library supervisor; born at Clarksville, Tenn., May 26, 1874; daughter of Paul Horace and Mary Jane (Roberts) Kennedy; grad. Roger Williams Univ., Nashville, Tenn., 1896; studied literature, history and French, Ecolé Pigier,

Paris, France 3½ years; took private lessons in French history, 1908-11; married Dr. William J. Yerby, 1897, who is U. S. Consul to Sierre Leone, West Africa; 2 children: Cecilia, Clementine. Teacher in public schools, Henderson, Ky., 1893, 5, 6; teacher in Howe Institute, Memphis, Tenn., 1897-9; supervisor colored school dept. Cossett Library, Memphis, since 1913. Baptist. Home: 816 Mississippi Boulevard. Office: 493 St. Paul Ave., Memphis, Tenn.

YERBY, William James, consul; born in Arkansas, Sept. 22, 1869; A.B., Roger Williams Univ., Nashville, Tenn.; M.D., Meharry Medical College (Walden Univ.), Nashville; married Cecilia Kennedy, of Henderson, Ky., June 30, 1897; 2 children: Cecilia, Clementine. Began practice of medicine in Memphis, Tenn., immediately after graduation. U. S. consul at Sierra Leone, West Africa, since 1906; appointed by President Theodore Roosevelt. Republican. Home: 816 Mississippi Blvd., Memphis, Tenn. Address: American Consulate, Freetown, Sierra Leone, West Africa.

YOUNG, Charles, major U. S. Cav.; third Negro graduate United States Military Academy, West Point, N. Y. Major 9th U. S. Cav.; was instructor in military science and tactics, also in French and trigonometry, at Wilberforce Univ., for some time; later appointed on special duty to Liberia. Address: Ninth U. S. Cav., War Department, Washington, D. C.

YOUNG, George, bookseller; born in Halifax Co., Va., Oct. 16, 1869; son of Beverly C. and Ellen (Carington) Young; self-educated; unmarried. Proprietor of Young's Book Exchange, New York; makes specialty of works on race problems and by colored authors. Member Ethical Culture Society of New York, also St. Mark's (M. E. Church) Lyceum. Republican. Member National Assn. for Advancement of Colored People, National League on Urban Condition Among Negroes. Home: 328 W. 53d St. Office: 135 W. 135th St., New York.

YOUNG, Isaac Wilhelm, mayor,

physician, editor; born at Glencoe, La., Jan. 2, 1874; son of John and Elizabeth (Bell) Young; ed. high school, Gilbert Industrial College (Baldwin, La.), New Orleans Univ.; M.D., Flint Medical College, 1900; married Adelia E. Ambler, of Alexandria, La., Sept. 19, 1900; 2 children: Leo N., Bridgeford. Began practice in Alexandria, La., 1900; removed to Okla., 1911; mayor of Boley, 1915-17; managing editor Boley Progress. Republican. Methodist. President Tri-State Medical Assn., Mo., Kan., Okla.; former president Louisiana and Oklahoma Medical Assn. Mason (secretary M. B. A. of Okla.); member Odd Fellows, Knights of Pythias. Club: Boley Commercial (ex-sec.). Address: Boley, Okla.

YOUNG, Joseph A., Jr., editor, publisher; born at Natchez, Miss., Dec. 14, 1886; son of Joseph A. and Annie B. (Brenham) Young; high school edn., Natchez; studies in Natchez College; unmarried. Began business career as retail grocer, Natchez, 1899; later clerk in shoe store; owner and editor the Weekly Reporter, Natchez, since 1909; job printer. Republican. Baptist. Mason: member Knights of Pythias. Sons and Daughters of Rebecca. Clubs: Busy Mission Workers, Campus Beautifiers of Natchez College. Home: 697 E. Union St., Natchez, Miss.

YOUNG, Joseph Franklin, city councilman, real estate; born at Harrodsburg, Mercer Co., Ky., Sept. 6, 1871; son of Thomas C. and Harriet (Walker) Young; district school edn., Mercer Co.; married Florance A. Utley, of Harrodsburg, Dec. 27, 1905; 2 children: Florance A., Maria Josephine. In the furniture business, also handling stoves, clothing and other merchandise; also identified with real estate transactions. Active in politics since 18 years of age; member Harrodsburg City Council 7 terms, 1901-15; was district committeeman, 1900-8; state auditor's messenger, 1908-11; Republican. African Methodist. President Union Benevolent Society No. 1; permanent sec. Blue Grass Lodge No. 1674, Odd Fellows; chancellor condr. and deputy dist. grand chancellor Mercer Lodgs No. 71, Knights of Pythias; was an organizer and president for 3 years, Mercer County Colored Fair Assn. Home: 402 College St. Office: 252 Childs St., Harrodsburg, Ky.

YOUNG, Nathan Benjamin, college president; born at Newbern, Ala., Sept. 15, 1862; son of Frank and Susan (Smith) Young; grad. Talladega College, Ala., 1884; A.B., Oberlin (O.) College, 1888, A.M., 1891; married Emma Mae Garrett, of Selma, Ala., Dec. 30, 1892; 2d marriage, Margaret Bulkley, of Orangeburg, S. C., Nov. 15, 1904; 5 children. Principal of public schools, Shelby, Ala., 1888-9, city school, Birmingham, Ala., 1889-92; head teacher at Tuskegee Normal and Industrial Institute, 1892-7; teacher of pedagogy Georgia State College, Savannah, 1897-1901; president Florida Agricultural and Mechanical College, Tallahassee, since 1901; president National Assn. of Teachers' in Colored Schools; director Standard Life Ins. Co. Trustee Talladega College. Republican. Congregationalist. Member National Education Assn., American Geographical Society, American Economic Assn., American Academy Political and Social Science. Address: Florida Agri. & Mech. College, Tallahassee, Fla.